WOMEN AND ARCHITECTURAL HISTORY

In this book, prominent architectural historians, who happen to be women, reflect on their practice and the intervention this has made in the discipline. Of particular concern are the ways in which feminine subjectivities have been embodied in the discourses of architectural history. Each of the chapters examines the author's own position and the disruptive presence of women as both subject and object in the historiography of a specific field of enquiry. The aim is not to replace male lives with female lives, or to write women into the masculinist narratives of architectural history. Instead, this book aims to broaden the discourses of architectural history to explore how the potentially 'unnatural rule' of women subverts canonical norms through the empowerment of otherness rather than a process of perceived emasculation.

The essays examine the historiographic and socio/cultural implications of the role of women in the narratives and writing of architectural history with particular reference to Western traditions of scholarship on the period 1600–1950. Rather than subscribing to a single position, individual voices critically engage with past and present canonical histories disclosing assumptions, biases, and absences in the architectural historiography of the West. This book is a crucial reflection upon historiographical practice, exploring potential openings that may contribute further transformation of the theory and methods of architectural history.

Dana Arnold is Professor of Architecture at the Manchester School of Architecture. Her work focuses on histories and historiographies of architecture and urbanism in relation to social and cultural theory. She is the author of *The Georgian Country House: Architecture, Landscape and Society* (1998); *Re-presenting the Metropolis* (2000); *Reading Architectural History* (2002); *Rural Urbanism: London Landscapes in the Early Nineteenth Century* (2006); *The Spaces of the Hospital: Spatiality and Urban Change in London 1680–1820* (2013); and *Architecture and Ekphrasis: Space, Time and the Embodied Description of the Past* (2020). Her most recent book *British Architecture: A very short introduction*, was published in 2024.

WOMEN AND ARCHITECTURAL HISTORY

The Monstrous Regiment Then and Now

Edited by
Dana Arnold

Routledge
Taylor & Francis Group
LONDON AND NEW YORK

Designed cover image: © The Yorck Project / Wikimedia Commons

First published 2025
by Routledge
4 Park Square, Milton Park, Abingdon, Oxon OX14 4RN

and by Routledge
605 Third Avenue, New York, NY 10158

Routledge is an imprint of the Taylor & Francis Group, an informa business

Chapter 9 is part of a project that has received funding from the European Research Council (ERC) under the European Union's Horizon 2020 research and innovation programme (grant agreement no. 101019419).

British Library Cataloguing-in-Publication Data
A catalogue record for this book is available from the British Library

Library of Congress Cataloging-in-Publication Data
Names: Arnold, Dana, editor.
Title: Women and architectural history : the monstrous regiment then and now /
edited by Dana Arnold.
Description: Abingdon, Oxon : Routledge, 2024. |
Includes bibliographical references and index.
Identifiers: LCCN 2024001259 (print) | LCCN 2024001260 (ebook) |
ISBN 9781032124568 (hardback) | ISBN 9781032124582 (paperback) |
ISBN 9781003224662 (ebook)
Subjects: LCSH: Architecture—Historiography. | Architecture and women. |
Influence (Literary, artistic, etc.)
Classification: LCC NA190 .W66 2024 (print) |
LCC NA190 (ebook) | DDC 720.82—dc23/eng/20240508
LC record available at https://lccn.loc.gov/2024001259
LC ebook record available at https://lccn.loc.gov/2024001260

ISBN: 9781032124568 (hbk)
ISBN: 9781032124582 (pbk)
ISBN: 9781003224662 (ebk)

DOI: 10.4324/9781003224662

Typeset in Times New Roman
by codeMantra

CONTENTS

FIGURES

CONTRIBUTORS

Annmarie Adams is an architectural historian and holds the Stevenson Chair at McGill University, Montreal. She is jointly appointed in the Peter Guo-hua Fu School of Architecture and the Department of Social Studies of Medicine. Her research focuses on the cultural landscapes of homes and hospitals. Her 1996 book, *Architecture in the Family Way: Women, Houses, and Doctors, 1870–1900*, won the Jason A. Hannah Medal from the Royal Society of Canada as an outstanding contribution to the history of medicine. *Designing Women: Gender and the Architectural Profession*, co-authored with sociologist Peta Tancred in 2000, provides an interdisciplinary study of Canada's women architects. In 2008, Adams published *Medicine by Design: The Architect and the Modern Hospital, 1893–1943*, which looks inside healthcare planning. She is currently writing a book on the life of physician and museum curator Maude Abbott.

Adams is a leader in architectural and medical education, having served as Chair of the Canadian Council of University Schools of Architecture and, currently, as President of the Canadian Society for the History of Medicine. She is a fellow of the Royal Architectural Institute of Canada, the Canadian Academy of Health Sciences, and the Society of Architectural Historians.

Dana Arnold is Professor of Architecture at the Manchester School of Architecture. Her work focuses on histories and historiographies of architecture and urbanism in relation to social and cultural theory. She is the author of *The Georgian Country House: Architecture, Landscape and Society* (1998); *Re-presenting the Metropolis* (2000); *Reading Architectural History* (2002); *Rural Urbanism: London Landscapes in the Early Nineteenth Century* (2006); *The Spaces of the Hospital: Spatiality and Urban Change in London 1680–1820* (2013); and *Architecture and Ekphrasis: Space, Time and the Embodied Description of the Past* (2020). Her many edited and co-edited volumes include *Architecture as Experience* (2004); *Rethinking Architectural Historiography* (2006); *Biographies and Space* (2008); *Interdisciplinary Encounters* (2014); and *Paris-Londres* (2016).

Arnold has held research fellowships at the Getty Research Institute, Yale University, and the University of Cambridge. She was a guest professor at the International Research Centre for Chinese Cultural Heritage Conservation, Faculty of Architecture, Tianjin University (2009–2019) and Honorary Professor at the Architecture Faculty, Middle East Technical University, Ankara

(2007–2015). Her latest book, *British Architecture: A Very Short Introduction* (2024), is a significant re-working of the subject offering new insights into the fluid relationship between architecture and culture.

Swati Chattopadhyay is Professor in the Department of History of Art and Architecture at the University of California, Santa Barbara. She specializes in modern architecture and urbanism, and the cultural landscape of the British empire. A founding editor of PLATFORM, she is the author of *Representing Calcutta: Modernity, Nationalism, and the Colonial Uncanny* (2005); *Unlearning the City: Infrastructure in a New Optical Field* (2012); and *Small Spaces: Recasting the Architecture of Empire* (2023). Among her current book projects is *Nature's Infrastructure: The British Empire and the Making of the Gangetic Plains, 1760–1880*, funded by the Guggenheim Foundation.

Joan Coutu is a professor of Art History and Visual Culture at the University of Waterloo in Canada. Her research concentrates on the built environment of the eighteenth-century British Empire as well as the legacies of that empire in early twentieth-century Canada. Her work focuses on monuments, buildings, sculpture, and city planning, and their relationship with politics, temporality, and identity. She has published extensively, including two books, *Persuasion and Propaganda: Monuments and the Eighteenth-century British Empire* (2006) and *Then and Now: Collecting and Classicism in Eighteenth-century England* (2015), and a co-edited volume of essays, *Politics and the English Country House, 1688–1800* (2023). She is currently co-editing a volume of essays titled *Utopia and Hubris: Classicism in Canada, c. 1900–1939*.

Elizabeth Darling is an architectural historian who researches, consults, curates, and publishes in the field of architecture and gender, as well as being a specialist in the history of British architectural modernism. Her books include *Women and the Making of Built Space in England* (2006); *Re-forming Britain, Narratives of Modernity before Reconstruction* (2007); *Wells Coates* (2012); and *Suffragette City* (2020). She has also published extensively in journals including *Gender and History*, the *Journal of British Studies*, and *Architectural History*. From 2014 to 2017, with Lynne Walker, she was Consultant to the project AA XX 100, which commemorated the centenary of women's admission to London's Architectural Association School of Architecture, and which resulted in an exhibition, book, and international conference. In 2022-23, she conceived and led the 'Surfacing Stories' project with the RIBA + V&A Architecture Gallery, which offered a series of reinterpretations of exhibits through an intersectional lens. She is Chair of the Society of Architectural Historians of Great Britain, having previously convened its Women Architectural Historians Network. She is currently writing a book that explores the material and spatial culture of broadcasting in 1920s and 1930s Britain.

Alice T. Friedman is the Grace Slack McNeil professor emerita of Art at Wellesley College and former director of the Architecture Program there. Her forthcoming book, a study of visual culture and queer bohemia, is titled *All That Glamour and Loneliness: Max Ewing's Queer New York, 1923–1934*. She is the author of three other books, including *House and Household in Elizabethan England* (1989); *Women and the Making of the Modern House* (1998); and *American Glamour and the Evolution of Modern Architecture* (2010), as well as numerous articles on architecture, gender, and social history.

Kathleen James-Chakraborty is Professor of Art History at University College Dublin. She has previously taught at the University of California Berkeley and was the Vincent Scully visiting professor of Architectural History at Yale. Her books include *Architecture since 1400* (2014) and *Modernism as Memory: Building Identity the Federal Republic of Germany* (2018) as well as the edited collections *India in Art in Ireland* (Routledge, 2016) and (co-edited with Sabine Kriebel) *Bauhaus Effects in Art, Architecture, and Design* (Routledge, 2022). She is the recipient of the 2018 Gold Medal in the Humanities from the Royal Irish Academy. In 2021–2022, she was an Ailsa Mellon Bruce senior fellow at the Center for Advanced Studies in the Visual Arts at the National Gallery of Art in Washington, D.C. She currently holds an Advanced Grant from the European Research Council.

Elizabeth McKellar is Professor Emerita in Architectural History at the Open University, having previously held posts at Birkbeck College, London and the Victoria and Albert Museum, where she was Head of Higher Education. She specializes in British architecture and culture and urbanism, particularly that of London. She is the author of many books and articles, including *The Birth of Modern London: The Development and Design of the City 1660–1720* (1999); *Articulating British Classicism: New Approaches in Eighteenth-Century Architecture* (2004); *Neo-Georgian Architecture 1880–1970: A Reappraisal* (2016); and *Landscapes of London: The City, the Country and the Suburbs 1660–1840* (2013). She held a Leverhulme Research Fellowship in 2011–12 to research the latter book, which was the winner of the Society of Architectural Historians (US) Elisabeth Blair Macdougall Award 2017. She has previously been a member of the Editorial Board of *The London Journal*, The London Record Society, and a member of Historic England's London Advisory Committee. She is currently the president of the Society of Architectural Historians of Great Britain and is writing a cultural biography of Sir John Summerson, for which she was awarded a Paul Mellon Senior Fellowship in 2018–19 and a Leverhulme Emeritus Fellowship for 2021–24.

Jane Pavitt is Head of Research and Learning for the Zaha Hadid Foundation, and a curator, writer, and historian of architecture and design. Previous roles include Dean of Humanities at the Royal College of Art, and Professor of Architectural and Design History and Head of Research and Impact at Kingston University. As Principal Research Fellow at the V&A and University of Brighton, she curated and co-curated several major international exhibitions of twentieth-century design and culture including *Cold War Modern: Art and Design 1945–70* (2008, with David Crowley) and *Postmodernism: Style and Subversion* (2011, with Glenn Adamson). She also curated *Superstructures: The New Architecture 1960–1990* (2018, with Abraham Thomas), an examination of the architecture of High Tech, at the Sainsbury Centre for Visual Arts in Norwich. She is the lead curator for the forthcoming international retrospective exhibition on Zaha Hadid, which will originate in London in 2025. She is also Visiting Professor at Kingston University.

Nancy Stieber is an architectural historian who studies the interactions between the built environment and people. She received her Ph.D. from MIT's Program in the History, Theory, and Criticism of Architecture and taught architectural history at the University of Massachusetts Boston from 1983 to 2016. Her book *Housing Design and Society in Amsterdam: Reconfiguring Urban Order and Identity, 1900–1920* received the Spiro Kostof Award in 1999. She is currently working on a book titled *The Metaphorical City: Representations of Fin-de-Siècle Amsterdam.*

Recipient of numerous grants and fellowships, she was Editor of the *Journal of the Society of Architectural Historians* from 2002 to 2006. In 2013, she was inducted as a fellow of the Society of Architectural historians for lifetime achievement and is an honorary member of the European Architectural History Network, an organization which she helped found.

Nora Wendl is currently Associate Professor of Architecture at the University of New Mexico, where she teaches both architectural design and theory. Since 2021, she has been Executive Editor of the *Journal of Architectural Education.* Her exhibition work on feminist and experimental historiographic practices has been supported by the Graham Foundation, Santa Fe Art Institute, and the National Trust for Historic Preservation. Her essays have been published and translated widely in *Arquine, Revista Arquitectura*, the *Journal of Architectural Education, Architecture and Culture, Thresholds*, and *Offramp,* among others. In 2022, her book manuscript *The Edith Project* – an autotheoretical approach to writing architectural history – was a finalist for the Graywolf Nonfiction Prize. Wendl holds B.Arch. and M.Arch. degrees from Iowa State University, where she was also a Pearl Hogrefe fellow in Creative Writing.

Mary N. Woods is Professor Emerita of Architectural History and Urbanism at Cornell University, where she was the first woman to receive tenure in the Cornell architecture department. She was also the inaugural Michael A. McCarthy chair of Architectural Theory there. Her publications include such seminal books as *From Craft to Profession* (1999); *Beyond the Architect's Eye* (2009); and *Women Architects in India* (2016). Woods has held fellowships from the Canadian Centre for Architecture; the Clarence Stein Institute; the Fulbright Program; the American Institute of Indian Studies; and the American Council of Learned Societies. With filmmaker Vani Subramanian she completed *Cinema Pe Cinema: The Movies. The Theatres. And Us*, a documentary about India's single screens, in 2024. Woods is currently working on an exhibit about Mumbai's architecture of the night with photographer Chirodeep Chaudhuri and book on postindustrial landscapes in the US and India with Nipun Prabhakar and Annie Schentag. Ever since first traveling to India in 1998, she is a wannabe Mumbaikar.

ACKNOWLEDGEMENTS

There are many people to thank for their contribution to this book. My Monstrous Regiment must come first on the list. I am extremely grateful for the ways in which they responded to the challenges presented in the prospectus for this book. I note in particularly but not exclusively, their generosity of spirit in sharing their personal experiences and the sense of collegial, collective endeavour in the roundtable and the one-to-one conversations that went on between authors during the preparation of their essays. The richness and depth this brings to the volume is more than I could have wished for. I am also indebted to Nancy Stieber for taking on the role of respondent and providing such valuable insights. Our editors at Routledge, Fran Ford and Hannah Studd, have been enormously supportive of this volume, and their engagement with the roundtable was welcomed by all. I would also like to thank the anonymous reviewers of the original proposal for their unanimous enthusiasm for the project. Clare Barry has been exemplary in her editorial assistance in the preparation of this volume, including the logistics of the roundtable discussion. My final thank you goes to Nigel King for his support and enthusiasm for this volume, which has preoccupied me for some time.

Dana Arnold
London, 2023

Introduction

1

ASSEMBLING THE MONSTROUS REGIMENT

Dana Arnold

In this book, prominent architectural historians, who happen to be women, reflect on their practice and the intervention this has made in the discipline. Of particular concern are the ways in which feminine subjectivities have been embodied in the discourses of architectural history. Each of the chapters examines the author's own position and the disruptive presence of women as both subject and object in the historiography of a specific field of enquiry. Collectively, the essays examine the historiographic and socio/cultural implications of the role of women in the narratives and writing of architectural history with particular reference to Western traditions of scholarship focussing on the period 1600–1950. Rather than subscribing to a single position, individual voices critically engage with past and present canonical histories, disclosing assumptions, biases, and absences in the architectural historiography of the West. The common strand is the porosity of the discipline and how women can renegotiate its foundational boundaries to encompass a broad field of methodological and theoretical plurality. In this way, *Women and Architectural History* complements contemporary practices of decolonising Western canons whilst at the same time it remains a discrete, distinctive, and timely project that focuses on feminine subjectivities. This book is, then, a crucial reflection on historiographical practice and process, exploring potential openings that may contribute further transformation of the disciplines and theories of architectural history and its historiography. So much for 'Women and Architectural History' what about the 'Monstrous Regiment'?

In 1558 John Knox published *The First Blast of the Trumpet Against the Monstruous Regiment of Women*. The phrase 'monstruous regiment' means 'unnatural rule', and the target of Knox's misogynistic attack is gynarchy which he argues goes against the laws of God and nature.[1] He declares that female rule challenges the God-given authority of men over women who lack the masculine capacities necessary to govern. He pronounces that women are incompetent to rule, being weak, foolish, and cruel by nature. Knox compares female rulers to Amazons, half-mythical warrior women from the new world who were portrayed as a subversive threat to social order. My aim in this book is to see how women have subverted and disrupted the 'order' of architectural history. The aim is not to replace male lives with female lives, or to write women into the masculinist narratives of architectural history. Instead, *Women and Architectural History* aims to broaden the discourses of architectural history and explore how the potentially

DOI: 10.4324/9781003224662-2

'monstruous regiment' of women subverts canonical norms through the empowerment of otherness rather than a process of perceived emasculation.

From the outset, I was clear that *Women and Architectural History* should not be a monograph written by many hands with contributors adhering to a tight editorial brief. Instead, the core purpose of the volume is to challenge the homogeneity of architectural historical discourse. As such, I could not (or indeed should not) have written this book myself.[2] My challenge was to initiate a project that encouraged latitude and diversity yet achieve some kind of coherence. Authors were invited to contribute discursive essays that consider the interventions their own feminine practices have made in the conceptual frameworks and narrative structures of histories of architecture and the subsequent impact on our perception and understanding of the architecture of the past. I was expectant of narratives that reveal the authentic voices of female subjects that an editor could not solicit through assigning a contributor a pre-existing slot in a carefully structured volume. My role in this introductory chapter is to relay the richness and diversity of the essays, tease out meanings, examine points of convergence and difference, and present these reflections on historical practice and process in the most effective way whilst preserving their distinctiveness.

The invitation to contribute to this book included a series of provocations in relation to the architectural history and historiography of the West focusing on c.1600–1950. The provocations were listed in no particular order of priority, and were not intended as a sequence or as the running order for the book. The contributors were encouraged to engage (or not) with any or all of these themes as they felt appropriate.

My first provocation was around the notions of spatial position and temporality which are intrinsic to architectural history and its historiography. Authors were invited to disrupt the traditional, linear progression of past, present, and future and to explore the paradigm of feminine temporality as a foundational concept for causal relationships that unfold and become perceptible over time. This might be achieved by identifying strategies for operationalising the time dimension and time-related variables in empirical research. In this way, the notion of historicity in architecture as the historical actuality, authenticity, and factuality of people and events can be called into question. Instead, feminine subjectivities can reveal a plurality of meaning, histories, and interpretations of the architecture of the past. This led to my second theme of spatial experience where authors were asked to investigate the perception and appropriation of places by and for women across intervals of time and culture. The particular concern here was to explore ways in which empirical research can be refracted through a feminine lens leaving it re-animated but not overwhelmed. I was expectant of essays that demonstrated the juxtaposition of the continuity of an architectural space and alternative historical perspectives, in which recognisable features are shown in different lights. These new ways of thinking might yield surprising results, inverting the common idea of a historic space or place as having an enduring, immutable meaning. The third provocation raised the question of (auto)biography and space. I was particularly interested in the ways in which biographical methods of historical investigation can bring out the authentic voice of subjects, revealing personal meanings and strategies in architecture and the spaces it contains and creates, as well as providing a means to analyse relations between the personal and the social. I was keen for contributors to write about both actual and imagined space, and consider how women as subjects and objects can be used as a means of explaining sets of social, cultural, and spatial relationships. This accent on female agency was intended to highlight the increasing fluidity and interaction between theory, methods, and history. And this segues into the final provocation that focussed on social and cultural flows. Here, the nature and perception of feminine social and cultural flows were mapped against different kinds of architectural environments – including the urban, domestic, and institutional to investigate how architecture and its textual narratives have been produced, disseminated, consumed, and how they work to create identities. By focussing on women, we can see the tensions and interactions between the ideas of place and displacement, and centre and periphery inherent in cultural flows and how social flows are evidence of personal intentionality to interact with the built environment. Architecture becomes a matrix of social and cultural flows that are the emblematic expression of different kinds of female identities.

Unsurprisingly, I received a stunning array of abstracts that were bound to deliver much more than my provocations could have foreseen. A central theme of this volume is process – the process of thinking, writing, experiencing, and theorising space, time, and architectural history that is by, for, and about women. I was interested in capturing the 'gap' between the initial author abstract and the final essay to explore what is lost and what is retained during the process of writing. The contributors, some of whom knew each other well whilst others had never met, were invited to a roundtable where we shared our work and outlined the challenges and surprises in writing our essays. The initial abstracts I had received were circulated to everyone in advance. Inevitably, not everyone could attend but there were also exchanges and dialogues between contributors before and after the roundtable that enriched the discourse. Our editors also listened in.

The Roundtable

Collaboration was a key aspect of the round table. It became clear that everyone had travelled a considerable distance from their original ideas as expressed in the abstracts that had been circulated beforehand. Our discussion was a collegial sharing of our processes as architectural historians and experiences of being women in the academy. The premise of the book had triggered new ways of thinking about how autobiography and architectural history can become intertwined. And these reflections presented interesting counterpoints. Whilst there was common ground between those who had undertaken doctoral study in the same department at the same institution, there was also a view that architectural history was a nomadic discipline existing on the edges of art history, architecture, and history. Perhaps unsurprisingly, the liminality of women as subjects, objects, and authors of architectural history was a persistent theme in our discussion. What follows is a digest of the initial abstracts and interventions made at the roundtable as my authors reflected on their essays and more broadly on their practice as architectural historians. With the exception of Nancy Stieber, our respondent, we moved round the virtual table alphabetically by last name. This was merely a heuristic technique employed to solve the problem of the running order. And for once, I did not have to go first. Annmarie Adams remarked as she introduced 'Maud & Me' 'I think it's the tyranny of alphabetical order, which my whole life has been shaped by'. The heuristic device of the running order and Annmarie's title raised an issue common to many of the contributors – do we call our subjects by their first names or their last names? Clearly, this matters as first-name terms can imply familiarity but does it also risk diminishing the subject. When writing about a male architect, it would be unusual to use his first name. We came to no definitive conclusion and you will see different approaches in the essays which in the interests of heterogeneity I have not 'edited' out. But I will leave you, the reader, to reflect on this. The 'Monstrous Regiment' spoke in the first person and I have retained this authentic voice. As you will see, writing in the first person as opposed to the authorial sleight of hand of apparently 'neutral' prose is something that I pick up on in my own essay 'Refracting feminine subjectivities through space, time, and architectural history'. But to be clear, what follows is not a transcript; instead, it is a digest to convey the conversation that took place at the roundtable. Alongside reporting and some tidying, my editorial intervention also includes re-ordering the authors' abstracts and presentations to follow the sequence of the chapters in this book. These are grouped around the initial themes identified in my provocations (auto)biography, social and cultural flows, spatial position and temporality, and spatial experience, which have been expanded and enhanced by the contributors' responses to them. But as will become apparent very quickly, the essays intersect and complement each other in so many enriching ways. Deciding on the groupings and running order was an exceptional and very engaging 'quality problem' for me as editor.

(Auto)Biographies

My opening chapter 'Refracting Feminine Subjectivities Through Space, Time, and Architectural History' explores my interest in the ways in which feminine subjectivities have disrupted the canonical discourses of architectural history. In much of my work, I employ the tropes of time and space to investigate the perception and appropriation of architecture by and for women. These lines of enquiry enable me to juxtapose the continuity of architectural space with alternative historical perspectives. My essay reflects in part on my practice as an architectural historian and demonstrates the ways in which feminine subjectivities reveal a plurality of meaning, histories, and interpretations of the architecture of the past. More broadly, my essay lays out one of the fundamental concerns of this volume; to investigate the ways in which empirical research can be refracted through a feminine lens leaving it re-animated but not overwhelmed. Architecture is often thought of as being designed and used by humankind – what is really meant here is mankind. The female user of space is subsumed or invisible. But, like our race and our social class, gender works to define who we are. There is no such thing as gender neutral space whether it be architectural space, time, or indeed the spaces of the printed page.

I found Christine de Pizan's *The Book of the City of Ladies* (1405) an unexpected but erudite frame for my own reflections and for the intellectual premise and experimental editorial practice I have investigated in this volume.[3] Of particular note is Pizan's use of architectural space to both retell and challenge social and cultural norms. Her narrative meshes the biographies of women from across time with the construction of the spaces of the city to present a proto-feminist fable. Moreover, the way in which she projects her chosen women through architecture, time, and the virtual spaces of the page is a provocative narrative technique. I remain intrigued by how she places these women within her allegorical city and uses them to augment its architecture and the status of women. Indeed, the reputation, status, and agency of women are built alongside the city itself within the spaces of the page. Pizan raises questions concerning gender, (auto)biography, language, space, and time all of which have informed my own interests as an architectural historian. She became my guide as I reflected on my practice and how I defined my own area of study. My starting point is that my gender must inflect on my work. How can it be otherwise? But where do I begin to analyse and narrate this? I experience space as a woman but how do I know this is different from a man? Is my experience of space intrinsic to my being or was I programmed? Looking back, I can see the ways in which I was programmed about how to think about myself in relation to space. And this leads me to question who is writing/shaping and what is being written and shaped. Would a (auto)biography be different in a different spatial location?

In thinking about an ontology or system of the built environment in this way it is necessary to try to think about theories of both subjects and objects (and here I include auto/biography) and their ties particularly in this case feminine biographies and space. And it is helpful to think about criteria for distinguishing various types of subjects and objects for instance: concrete and abstract, existent and non-existent, real and ideal, independent and dependent and their ties in other words: relations, dependences, and predication. In addition, the notion of time is important as the (auto)biographical trace transforms itself and is transformed by time. In 2008, I wrote an essay '(Auto)biographies and Space', in a volume I also co-edited.[4] I used an (auto)biographical anecdote to explore the entanglement between subjects, objects, their ties and their relationship to both space and time. I cite the anecdote here as it remains a predicate for my essay and indeed one of the key themes in this volume. It also intertwines with Annmarie Adams' essay which follows my own in the sequence of this book.

Strange Bedfellows

I have been fortunate enough to hold visiting fellowships at Yale University, The Getty Research Institute and the University of Cambridge, where accommodation was generously provided. This continual turnaround of living space for the ongoing procession of international scholars made me think about how many members of the academic community had slept in the same bed. My apartment at Yale had been the residence of Henri Focillon, and I was reliably informed that he had died in the very bed in which I, and many other art historians, had subsequently slept. The wardrobes and cupboards contained some of his books that had never been removed, all containing his neat signature in the inside cover declaring both ownership and a (auto)biographical trace.

My puzzlement at this space-time phenomenon grew during my tenure at the Getty Research Institute. Here academics from across the world shared the same bed, so to speak (and in real time sat in the jacuzzi together – a very different kind of close encounter). Although all traces of the previous occupant were expunged from the apartments, remnants were sometimes to be found in the assigned mailbox. But most strangely an odd ritual had evolved of putting the unwanted contents of a soon to be vacated apartment, presumably too good to throw away – half full bottles of olive oil, cleaning products, coffee or even hairdryers, on a table in the communal lounge for the remaining scholars to take as they wished. These relics, the material remains of occupation and existence, manifested to me not only choices made about what was worth keeping, but also about the nature of the legacy one left behind, as this pile of former belongings became a strange kind of epitaph. Although deracinated from the actual space of occupation, the biographical trace evoked by these objects was no less forceful. These two events prompted me to think about architecture, or rather the space it encloses, and the meanings and identities that can be conferred on objects within that space. The space and the objects do not change but our understanding of them does, and this can be influenced by social and cultural circumstances. Moreover, the fragments of material culture and of material identities – Focillon's books or half used bottles of lavatory cleaner made me think of a kind of archaeology in both the literal and Foucauldian sense.

It took my fellowship at Cambridge for me to fully realize how these events from my own biography could help me to think about the *performative* qualities of the built environment.[5] The preceding visiting fellow and previous occupant of my set (apartment) in King's College had been Edward Said. Yes, same bed, and indeed same bath, but we've already been

> there … but in the bottom of the wardrobe was a pair of socks – not brightly plaid argylls in case you are interested, just plain grey ribbed wool. These became objects of fascination for me – were they Said's, and perhaps more importantly were they clean? The meaning and importance of this abandoned or forgotten item of clothing ranged from cultural relic to evidence of bad housekeeping. Were they Said's? Or did he look at them thinking they belonged to the occupant before him? The spatial location of everyday objects together with a narrative that could place them at a certain point in time made these socks potentially culturally significant in providing biographical traces of Said. Indeed, during his stay in King's, Said wrote a new preface to the edition of *Orientalism* published in 2003. Had this been drafted at the desk where I worked, and was he wearing these very socks to keep his feet warm.
>
> In this opening section of my discussion of biographies and space I want to give a final word to the socks, or at least the anxieties that still rest within me in about them. Even though I trained as an art historian, I did not take a picture. And I left them untouched, in situ undisturbed. But did whoever occupied the set in King's after me think they were my socks? And, would anyone really believe that I would wear grey ribbed woollen socks?

At one level my personal and perhaps initially frivolous sounding anecdotes exemplify questions about being, and highlight the most basic problems in ontology: finding a subject, a relationship, and an object to talk about evoking questions such as 'what am I?' and 'what is describing this to me?' But these narratives also show how my biography intersects with those of others through specific spatial locations and ruptured temporal continuities. And here we begin to see the role time can play in this interaction. The spatial location of objects and subjects imposes a kind of performativity on them, as they enact or represent different biographical traces. Using Christine de Pizan's *City of Ladies* as my frame, my essay in this volume refracts my (auto)biographical reflections and feminine subjectivities through space and time.

The entanglement that I identified in my chapter continues as a theme in Annmarie Adams' contribution, which she articulated as being a kind of auto-ethnography where she was 'spilling out my story'. She spoke in the first person and, as noted above, I retain it in order to maintain her authentic voice: I'm a sixty-two-year-old architectural historian. I am writing a spatial biography of a relatively famous female physician, Maude Abbott, who died in 1940 at the age of seventy-one. Abbott is very famous in Canada – she's kind of like the Julia Morgan of medicine - there are prizes named for her and streets, and lots of regret that she wasn't treated well during her lifetime. There are many books about her, but they all say the same thing. I'm trying to do something very different. It's what I call a spatial biography and I've been working on it for almost ten years, and it's about 80% finished. A major inspiration for the book was Dana's essay in her collection, *Biography and Space* and her story of finding what may have been Edward Said's grey socks, and a wardrobe in her apartment – it really stuck with me. And so, the chapter I'm writing for this book, for Dana's book, may be something like the conclusion to my [Maude] Abbott book, and I'm working on the two together. I guess it's an auto-ethnography, because I explore how I got to this strange urge to write a biography of a woman doctor, how distant that is from architectural history and how my work is entangled so much in my own life, the kind of thing you usually get in the acknowledgements. For example, in a section I explain how I was writing about childbirth and architecture and having babies myself, I mean, things that I don't usually reveal.

I engage the history of architecture and its tools in the Abbott project by telling a life story through ten spaces Abbott occupied, rather than the barriers she faced. Almost like an archaeologist, I dig deeply at particular events and locations, looking for evidence of Abbott's biographical traces. This methodology which emphasises social and physical settings accomplishes a couple of things. It de-stabilises the accounts of her life shaped by others, especially male doctor-biographers, who have tended to see her life as a series of hardships.[6] It also, I think, gives a more authentic account of Abbott's experiences. I see the sites I have chosen as a series of multi-dimensional snapshots that showcase relations between the personal and the social, the private and the public Maude Abbott.

It is, as they say, 'a stretch' from traditional architectural history. There are no architects in my story and very few famous buildings.[7] Abbott wasn't even interested in architecture, as far as I can tell. In this essay, I tease out how I have arrived at the project through my own biographical arc, especially second-wave feminism, 1980s American architectural education, and where I now live. Trained to conceal my personal feelings about my subjects, I have only recently come to embrace the entangled relationship of subject and author, work and life. In the early 1990s, I wrote a dissertation on British women, houses, and health, that became the book *Architecture in the Family Way*. I argued that women learned about health and illness through domestic architecture. The work was almost solely based on prescriptive sources, a fact which has haunted me during the subsequent 30 plus years. A second transformative (for me) publication was an essay on a post-war suburban house in California, 'The Eichler Home: Intention and Experience in Postwar Suburbia' also first written when I was a graduate student at the University of California at Berkeley.[8] In that paper, I argued that the modern house prescribed a particular lifestyle for women and children, but that real traces showed that the family lived quite differently. It was about a different context and time period, but in retrospect I see the questions from the dissertation somewhat addressed in the Eichler paper. Modern architecture projected particular expectations that women resisted. All that to say that the current Abbott project brings together these questions of prescription, evidence, and agency that for me remain open. An additional factor is that almost every day, (pre- and post-COVID), I traverse the Montreal spaces that Abbott occupied and I teach in classrooms that kept her out. Her beloved medical specimens are now a museum, which I love to visit. I twice gave birth in a hospital she knew well. I sometimes eat lunch at a club she frequented. I walk on the streets she walked. My own life unfolds in the sources I study.

My chapter for this book starts with the Abbott book, but then it looks backwards and covers a lot of ground. I've divided it into four sections: reading, teaching, learning, and living and what has changed through the process of writing it. I think the thing is that I thought it would be easy to write and it I found it kind of hard. And I mean, it's easy because it's my story, so I don't have to do any research, I just have to tell the story, but the entanglements are so complex, that it's difficult to decide what to include. For example, I thought I'd write much more about what it was like to study at Berkeley in the 1980s with Dolores Hayden and Gwendolyn Wright, and their ghosts all around us in Wurster Hall and that kind of impact that had on me. I haven't really done that much on that. But the keen observation of a PhD student who was also my TA for the past two years, and who's very interested in literature and autobiography, has shown me that I already narrate my own story when I teach. I frequently use my own photographs and often explain how my position on this or that building has changed since I took the photo so now, I'm writing about that too.

Swati Chattopadhyay's essay 'Looking Back: Small Spaces as Countermapping Architectural History' juxtaposes two memoirs to explore how the relation between land, garden, and architecture was understood by their women authors. They were not architects and might seem to have little in common, be each brought a distinctive narrative strategy to their understanding of the land in terms of 'small spaces'. This juxtaposition is aimed at exploring how social positioning and narrative framing enable the creation of architectural and landscape pasts. Again, I will leave this passage in the first person to retain Swati's authentic voice:

I think there's something in common with Annmarie, which is that I'm also thinking about autobiographies and the 'autos' of biography, but they're not my own. I find myself looking at a lot of biographies and autobiographies when I do my research. The book I just finished has an entire section on memoirs, so what I would like to do is pick out some of those threads and think about what I call 'small spaces'. And 'small spaces' are not simply about actual small dimensional spaces, it's also about short durations and things like that. When Dana invited us to this roundtable, I looked at the abstract I had sent. I said I'd talk about memoirs. They are Harriet Jacobs' *Incidents in the Life of a Slave Girl* (1861), which was published with the subtitle *Written by Herself* because nobody believed a black woman could write like that.[9] And then a Bengali text by Rani Chanda *My Mother's Father's House*, which was written in the early 1970s and published in 1977 but it's really about the second decade of the twentieth century.[10] What I find useful in these works, what I find in common is that they do talk about spaces that have no history in architectural history. These are things like the garret, or, actually even the veranda – in Bengali it's a particular kind of veranda – an open veranda and it typically refers to rural earthern construction households, and that has a certain sense of the household-ness in it. So, partly it is about trying to speak about those spaces for which we do not have an outdated history but also to think about why is it that these are so prominent in women's memoirs? And why – and this is the self-reflective part – why I find them so useful in telling architectural histories, what is it about the smallness of those that's essential. I go back to my first days of taking classes with Jim Deetz, and reading his *In Small Things Forgotten* (1977), which had a deep impression on me. It is really the small things that people remember particularly. These are women who are writing much later in their lives looking back at their younger selves, and the trials and tribulations and they really settled on small incidents, which actually have big repercussions. But they are really articulated in a very fine language. Although my jumping off point is Jim Deetz perhaps, theoretically, I can lean on anthropologist Kathleen Stewart's idea of 'slow looking'.[11] Slow looking doesn't mean what you know as an art historian, one might be interested in doing is looking at details or close observation. But for Stewart it is not about the viewers' volition and intent, it is about something that occurs from within the viewer, without the viewer anticipating. As Stewart remarks 'slow looking slows down the quick jump to representational thinking and evaluative critique'. In other words, it picks out connections that are not dominant or bold, or those that defy the language of representation, and might pass under the radar of authority.

Spatial Position and Temporality

My provocation around spatial position and temporality developed into an exploration of women and the archive. Mary Woods could not join the roundtable but her chapter in this volume 'Going against the Grain: Women Architects Rereading and Reimagining the Archive and Monograph' is an evocative exploration of the issues at stake, as well as Mary's own reflections on her practice as an architectural historian. Mary notes that women have trained and worked in architecture in the global north and global south since the late nineteenth and early twentieth centuries. Nevertheless, they are still notable for their absence rather than their presence in the catalogues of architectural archives. At best women account for only slightly more than 1% in such collections as Avery Archives and Drawings at Columbia University. They have long been the archives' keepers and guardians rather than subjects whose papers and other artifacts are preserved in the collections. Such an exclusion is, as art historian Griselda Pollock has noted, especially 'un-modern and un-historical' because such a large part of modern history is about women becoming more visible and prominent in the public realm. To contest such absences, architectural historian Samia Henni argues we must 'learn to read the archives against the grain', alert to the objects therein as carriers of histories concealed as well as revealed. Mary then speaks directly in her abstract: I explore how a handful of women architects in the US and India have gone beyond Henni's admonition to read archival objects against the grain. Although these women have reread the archives' materials, they have also remade the very idea of archives. Asserting their agency, they have reimagined archives in forms, spaces, and materials markedly different from those of state and institutional collections of architecture. These women have foregrounded the intimate, subjective, collaborative, and representative, subverting the canonical and hagiographical ends archives typically serve. Contributing work to some of their 'against the grain' archives, I also question and reflect on my own practices and the discourses of architectural history from the inside out.

Elizabeth Darling continues the discussion of women and the archive in her essay 'In Plain Sight: Women in and Around the Archive' Like many of the contributors to this volume, Elizabeth found it both a novel and stimulating process to be so personal because it feels as though it has been important not to be personal as a historian. Her chapter reflects on how her personal experience of embarking on doctoral research in architectural history through the lens of one individual led to the subversion of the canonical, monographical approach. Many of Elizabeth's remarks address concerns raised across the chapters in this volume. She began, I've become very interested in how coming from a feminist perspective – not sure about the word feminine – is about looking properly or seeing fully or seeing what is often not seen. My focus is the housing consultant Elizabeth Denby (1894–1965) who was involved in the making of architecture in various ways. This was a way of stepping outside the idea of the architect as a professionally trained individual, which when I was training as an art historian was how I was led to understood how architecture was made. My chapter has been about kind of tracing that process and thinking of architecture as a kind of continuous process and something which starts but doesn't necessarily stop once the building is completed. It is also about thinking whether there is a kind of locational politics around architectural history and whether it might be different depending on where you're writing or where you're teaching or where you were trained. And similarly, whether there are differences in being interested in feminism, femaleness, or femininity, and if architecture differs depending on what century you're talking about, and what century you teach, and the nature of your evidence. These queries arise from my PhD research as I was writing about a person who didn't have any papers. I had to write around her and contextualise her in different ways, which led me to this idea of architecture as process. I mean if when you're writing about earlier periods or when you don't have perhaps a plethora of sources, it makes you do your history in different ways. So those were interesting things to revisit and go over. I also think about some of the experiences I have had in the last two or three years in talking, and being asked to talk about women and architecture in a very practice-based context where there seems to be a kind of obsession with reclamation. I am not trying not to be negative because I think lots of amazing and ground shifting work has been done. But I am curious about the sort of tensions there are between different understandings of the feminist architectural history project. For me, it is a hugely disruptive, productive process which gets us to think beyond the architect in many ways. Yet there is a desire at a more 'popular' (for want of a better word) level to focus on individuals. I wonder whether there is a way resolving or reconciling this paradox.

The tensions between the disruptive processes of feminist architectural history and the focus on reclaiming women and on the individual lives of women architects and their practice present a different set of conundrums in the case of the Zaha Hadid Foundation. Jane Pavitt addresses these in her essay 'Making the Zaha Hadid Foundation'. Jane's essay explores the opportunities and challenges involved in establishing a foundation devoted to a female architect – Dame Zaha Hadid (1950–2016), an Iraqi woman architect who settled in the United Kingdom in the 1970s. Unlike many other women architects, the process of retrieval was not necessary for Hadid (or do I call her Zaha?). At the point of her untimely death, Zaha Hadid was the world's most prominent female architect. She was the first woman to be awarded the Pritzker Prize (2004) and the Royal Gold Medal (2015) and was twice-winner of the Stirling Prize for architecture (2010, 2011). In 2013, Hadid established a Foundation in her name. Its mission is to preserve her legacy, archive, and collections, and to pursue research, educational, and curatorial activities in support of this. The Foundation was launched in early 2022. Jane's initial abstract for this book was written just after she had taken up her role as Head of Research and Learning at the Zaha Hadid Foundation, consequently it was quite speculative. The roundtable captured how both the Foundation as an entity and Jane's own thinking had developed. Jane's own words outline the intertwining of (auto)biography and archive in the context of the only foundation dedicated to a sole woman architect.

I suppose what's happened in the process of kind of getting about halfway through writing the essay is that there is an interesting and productive tension. I'm both a feminist historian reading Hadid's archives and I'm setting up a number of research projects. But I'm also on the management board with some of the responsibility for setting up the operations of the organisation and for drafting the strategy and the mission statement of the Foundation. I might reflect on the interaction between these two roles towards the end of the essay. What has emerged really is a kind of tripartite essay, the first part is going to focus on the setting up of a foundation in the name of a solo woman architect who was also an émigré Iraqi, and I'll give you a quote from Zaha herself, 'I'm a woman. I'm an Arab. I'm an architect. Biology and geography define the first two, the third has taken forty years of hard work'. Our archive is about forty years of work. Given the lack of non-profit organisations devoted to solo woman architects or designers, and we may be the only foundation really set up on these terms in the world. There are a number of foundations devoted to married partnerships in architecture and design, but nevertheless, this solo career is very unusual. The questions we face include what models might we draw on and in what ways do we frame her gender and ethnicity in relation to her practice and how do we function as a foundation. We might look to other established foundations such as the Norman Foster Foundation or the Renzo Piano Foundation as examples of the 'norm' of dealing with a celebrity or 'starchitect'. But the question of celebrity looms very large for Hadid. The intersection of her personal life and professional work is a constant question for us in sorting out and unboxing the collection. We own her extensive fashion collection of one and a half thousand pieces in her wardrobe, her personal ephemera and the contents of her flats and so forth. We are thinking hard about a suitable curatorial approach to the collections of a women architect whose personal style and private life were the subject of such scrutiny. It is an unusual situation and I can guarantee having visited the

Norman Foster Foundation, I'm pretty sure that there's no collection of turtleneck sweaters at the back of the archive room.

The second part of my essay looks at the media and scholarly analysis of Zaha in her lifetime. Throughout her career, her media portrayal was heavily coloured by intrusive and negative questioning of her gender and her Arab heritage. She was consistently asked about do you have a boyfriend? Why aren't you married? Why haven't you had children? Do you have space for a private life? Why don't you have a kitchen? These questions imply a rejection of being 'feminine' in her quest for a successful career, and it was a subject of huge irritation and pain to her and Zaha often said, I don't like to be discussed in these contexts. My second section considers the scholarly and professional discussion of women in architecture, which continually uses Hadid as the exception that proves the rule. I think of as 'even and despite', many writings on the position of contemporary women in architecture may not focus on her but then start a paragraph with 'even Zaha Hadid experienced' or 'despite Zaha Hadid' and so forth. Consequently, she acquires a kind of outsider status within the canon of great architects, a rare beast to triumph over adversity and join the pantheon of men. How should the foundation negotiate this quite cliched presentation? Gender and ethnicity will be front and centre to our research interests and to the mission of the foundation in terms of contemporary architecture, and the paradox here is that Zaha would have resisted this to a certain extent in her lifetime. In the third section of my essay, I'm trying to extend the issues of gender and race to look at several building projects. And it's the bit I'm kind of struggling with, I suppose, using this intersectional lens, but I'll just give a couple of examples and they're more really to give you a taste of what we might be dealing with. There is a rare and early project which had gender as its brief, a competition design for the International Building Exhibition in Berlin in '87, which was a feminist response to the all-male commissioning bodies of the IBA. Secondly, the Cardiff Opera House, her most prestigious competition win. It was eventually cancelled due to a vitriolic campaign against her, which was heavily inflected with racism and sexism and she called this out in a justifiably angry response.

Social and Cultural Flows

This provocation sought to explore the nature and perception of feminine social and cultural flows and how they were mapped against different kinds of architectural environments – including the urban, domestic, and institutional. The aim was to investigate how architecture and its textual narratives have been produced, disseminated, consumed, and how they work to create identities. I was also interested in the flow of ideas between and influences on women architectural historians. By focussing on women, we can see the tensions and interactions between the ideas of place and displacement, and centre and periphery inherent in cultural flows and how social flows are evidence of personal intentionality to interact with the built environment. Architecture becomes a matrix of social and cultural flows that are the emblematic expression of different kinds of female identities relating to class, race, and nationhood.

When I invited Alice Friedman to contribute to this volume, her positive response included the idea of writing a collaborative piece with Nora Wendl, as she wanted to explore the lasting value or the influence of what we do. Nora had been working with Scott Mehaffey, the Director of the Farnsworth House in Plano, Illinois on an exhibition to re-focus the narrative about the house and its history. The aim was to pay closer attention to the role of Dr Edith Farnsworth – a gifted nephrologist, medical researcher, musician, and poet – who was the client, and giving less time to the well-known, hero-worshipping stories about the architect, Mies van der Rohe. The onsite exhibition, *Edith Farnsworth, Reconsidered* returned its first occupant to her weekend home through furnishings, books, and other personal details. It was intended to open in March 2020, but was delayed by the pandemic. Consequently, Alice and Nora decided to record a short, online dialogue, focusing on their research and their efforts as scholars to 'shift the paradigm' toward a view that allowed for collaboration, creativity, and stories told by multiple voices.

Their dialogue informs their essay in this book 'Feminist Architectural History 2.0' which focuses on their own work about the Farnsworth House and also addresses the evolution of feminist architectural history over the course of the last half century. Alongside the many areas of congruence in their work, a shift in thinking became apparent through differences in their voices and approaches, research methodologies and treatment of evidence, and the emergence of new ways of seeing and speaking about buildings. Here's Alice talking about her own work.

I've have had a lifetime of being called a rank formalist by historians and cultural historians, as being obsessed with the fetishising of the building, and then being considered by the formalists as just a horrible feminist historian that didn't think enough about the building. I've always enjoyed being at that sort of tipping point where everyone's annoyed for one reason or another. That said, I was really interested in, for lack of a better word, the lasting value or the influence of what we do. I started that process by thinking about influences, or scholars, or writers that had created the conditions for a different kind of mental or intellectual headset and why it was that I felt it was important to work on women clients. Alongside this I was developing the idea of the constellation of actors around any given project in order to not forget about the bankers, architects, builders and craftspeople, and all those that participate in making the building. I began by thinking about why did the question present itself? To answer this, I looked at women clients and the issue of gender through an analysis of a Wollaton Hall and Hardwick Hall in the Elizabethan period. Reflecting on this reminded me of the importance of finding archives of letters or documents that help us understand gender identities and roles. In addition, I remembered the impact of the work of women such as Joan Kelly-Gadol's essay 'Did Women have a Renaissance?'[12] This was earth shattering to me because no one had ever said there's a gender difference in this category we call the Renaissance. Recently I have been revisiting categories like gender, which at the time I was writing *Women and the Making of the Modern House*, or my studies on Wollaton and Hardwick were so clear.[13] There were women and there were men, and now that seems to be very old fashioned as queer studies is one of the great advances of the recent years. My current project is a book called *Poker Faces*. I've turned *Women and the Making the Modern House* on its head to some extent. The book is about houses that don't look modern at all, but are sort of camouflage because they're for queer clients and the interiors or programmes or interior circulation is very unconventional.

Nora then added: I remember reading *Women and the Making of the Modern House* when I began my graduate work and was very inspired by it. The exhibition at the Farnsworth House *Edith Farnsworth, Reconsidered,* refurnishes the house with reproductions of the furnishings Farnsworth chose instead of the furniture that Mies van der Rohe built or designed for houses and pavilions in Europe and the 1920s, which is usually on display. The Farnsworth archives were an important source for my research and these were available because Alice had actually convinced the nephew of Dr Farnsworth to gift all of her papers to the Newberry library. I didn't realise when I started this research that I was in a way finishing another person's sentences. But I have also developed what I call in my piece of the chapter an auto-theoretical relationship to

Dr Farnsworth's work and her life history, which is both as the client but also as a woman and also as a sort of poet and translator of poetry. I engage with contemporary artists who are functioning in a way that I think architectural historians might do so in the future. Brian Sheridan and Ryan Kelly, are two artists who have used the archives of modern houses to study the clients and other actors' career histories and then re-enact these performatively, both choreographically and through scripts. This expanded archive merges with the lives of the performers and you see a sort of blending of the personal, the autobiographical, as well as the historical that you cannot distinguish in the performance itself.

Kathleen James-Chakraborty followed on from Alice and Nora and her response to their intervention was one of those unexpected moments of serendipity. And I have retained this sequence in the roundtable in the order of the book. Kathleen's opening remark continued the exploration of the impact of what we do as architectural historians:

> nobody's been a greater influence on my career since 1984 than Alice Friedman, so I'm lucky to have known her even before I went to grad school and to have had her advising me whenever I needed it along the way.

Kathleen went on to outline the process involved in writing her own chapter in this volume 'Expanding Agency: Ethel Power, *House Beautiful*, and the Writing of the History of American architecture'. I started out writing an essay about Ethel Power, who was the editor of *House Beautiful* from 1923–34, focusing on the balance between the way in the 1920s she wrote to empower women as consumers of a fairly traditional approach to design. She went on to engage Henry Russell Hitchcock and Philip Johnson as well as Ise Gropius and Dorothy Todd to write for the magazine, which informed a much larger public than saw the Museum of Modern Art exhibition about the *International Style in Europe* (1931). But when I began to read *House Beautiful* online through the *Internet Archive*, I was in my mother's living room in northern New Hampshire, which had been decorated and furnished in the 1920s and 30s by my step great-grandmother, a woman I never knew, who was born exactly the same year as Power and who decorated that room with American furnishings, mostly from the second quarter of the nineteenth century, that very much fit Powers' own ideas about design. As a historian of modern architecture, and also as a woman who grow up absolutely surrounded by this type of décor, at one level I don't have much sympathy for it. But on the other hand, one of the things I like most about my step great-grandmother were her friends including Frances Perkins, who very often rented the house and also visited as a guest and sat in the same chairs and worked at the same desk as I did when perusing *House Beautiful* online. So there's a tension there. And the more I thought about it, I thought about the ways in which my grandmothers in particular my step grandmother all furnished houses in this way, although two of them were pioneering patrons of the International Style in the 1930s on the East Coast. One of them was a pioneering epilepsy researcher who looked at the electroencephalograph; one was a farmer who churned butter and knew how to look at a cow's udder and birth a calf, which she did the morning of my father's funeral, from which I have always derived great sustenance. One was a military historian and one was a spy. They got around and so the extent to which I had trouble was when I really thought about how the furnishings that surround me as I'm writing this essay, are largely ones I've inherited from them. I haven't let go of the furnishings because they mattered so much to them, even though they're not my style. They're not worth anything anymore, but twenty years ago they were – I could have sold them and bought something that is more my style. I am also trying to grapple with these layers of inherited privilege, without which I'm sure I wouldn't have been able to become an architectural historian.

But it was a man, Vincent Scully, who when I was a student, first pushed me to examine periodicals NOT written for architects as an important source for understanding American architectural culture. It took me forty years, however, to move beyond using newspapers to supplement the stories I and my colleagues easily found in well-indexed professional architectural journals and turn my attention to the shelter press, that is to journals that target female consumers of architecture and design. Why so long? Did I presume that middle-class women were not as worthy subjects as the male makers upon whom I focused for much of my career as an architectural historian? Certainly, I was less interested in the taste of my grandmothers and their sisters and its impact upon my mother than in modernist alternatives to their familiar approaches to the decoration of their homes. Yet once I scanned the pages of *House Beautiful* in the years it was edited by Ethel Power, and the contributions she made to its pages immediately afterwards, it became clear that I had greatly underestimated the impact of women in shaping taste in the United States in the 1920s and 30s. This included, but was by no means limited to their impact upon the reception of modern European architecture, and to their creation of networks that supported women's professional careers as architects, interior decorators, and landscape architects, and the personal choices of those involved in same-sex relationships.

Spatial Experience

The theme of spatial experience aimed to investigate the perception and appropriation of places by and for women across intervals of time and culture. The essays by Elizabeth McKellar and Joan Coutu responded to this theme while foregrounding the liminal nature of architectural history both as a discipline and within institutions. The nomadic nature of architectural history is addressed in other essays both implicitly and explicitly. And its varied number of disciplinary 'homes', for example within history, heritage, art history, architecture or indeed professional practice impact on how we might operate as architectural historians, who happen to be women. But the final two chapters bring the marginality or edge condition of the discipline and its women subjects, objects, and authors to the fore. Elizabeth could not join us at the roundtable, but her abstract 'Beyond the Walls: Traversing the Boundaries of Architectural History' written in the first person was circulated and discussed.

In this essay I will attempt to trace my journey as an architectural historian over the past thirty-five years or so. In so doing I will reflect not just on my writings but also on my institutional and professional history that has shaped my path as a woman through architectural history. The greater part of my research has been focused on urban history, particularly that of early modern London, and this will form the main subject of the essay. However, for the past fifteen years or so I have also been researching late nineteenth- and early twentieth-century British architecture culminating in my present project – writing a cultural biography of Sir John Summerson, which unites my periods of expertise. In both these eras I have largely focused on 'history from below' investigating topics such as: housing; building practice; the architectural and urban experiences of the middle classes; forgotten figures in architectural history; and the city's undiscovered aspects and peripheries. I will discuss how I am currently combining my research into the social and cultural dynamics of architecture with biographical studies. Besides my work on Summerson, I will discuss a recent forthcoming essay on Annabel Dott, a hitherto unknown woman builder of the early twentieth century. My work has generally been produced from the margins of the discipline both historiographically and institutionally. I have tried to use my peripheral position as a strength drawing on a wide range of subject areas and sources to take architectural history beyond its usual methodological bases and preoccupations, particularly in creating a landscape approach to urban history. This essay will attempt to show how the inherently inter-disciplinary nature of architectural history can be used creatively to form new narratives and areas of investigation.

Joan Coutu expanded this discussion when she outlined her contribution to the volume 'Looking Softly at Architectural History: Eroding the Hegemony of Formalism'. Here, 'soft' concepts such identity, home, domesticity, nostalgia, nuance, and tradition are central to people's lives and condition the spaces we build and how we interact with them. They are also familiar tropes now regularly used in Western universities to study the history of architecture and built environments more generally.[14] They have displaced formalism – the aesthetics of form and style without consideration of the use or social implications of architecture – as the primary, and what was often the only, mode of analysis. In contrast to most other humanities-oriented disciplines which were grounded in comparable formalist methodologies in the mid-twentieth century, the shift away from formalism in architectural history came late, and, when it did come, it happened quickly.

Joan explained: I address the imbrication of feminine and settler perspectives within the study of the architecture of the British Empire. This is consistent with my areas of research - built environments in the emerging empire in the eighteenth century and those in Canada in the early twentieth century - and is informed by my lived experience as a French-Scottish Canadian academic who is based in Canada. Joan noted the influence of Annmarie Adams and Kathleen James-Chakraborty on her thinking about how she tackled the 'troubling' of the centre-periphery imperial model through two intertwined approaches. One is a locative approach that considers geographic and topographic place: what did it mean to build particular buildings in particular locations? The second is a phenomenological approach that considers the physical, or imagined, experience of being in one of these places. These include English country estates situated far from London, planters' houses and parish churches in the British West Indies, and institutional and tourist spaces in early twentieth-century Canada. Both approaches explore the impact on various people who were, and continue to be, caught up in the imperial enterprise.

Afterword

Nancy Stieber responded to the presentations at the roundtable observing that given the themes of my provocations, she fully expected a rejection by everyone of linear history, canonical history, and the history of great buildings. She was not disappointed and went on to identify some further themes that had emerged in the discussion. The first was a rejection of narratives about the 'great building'. Instead, we might look at the built environment which is not necessarily just architecture with the capital 'A'. The focus on everyday life and the awareness of the spaces that we occupy, as just living human beings, leads to a different kind of historical investigation. Coupled with this is that traditionally women have been involved in the making of everyday life and the spaces where we act it out. The second theme, an emphasis on the experiential, expands on the first one. This included the autobiographical reflections by contributors in their progress and processes as architectural historians. In addition, experience can include the specific questioning of how people interact with their environment and how a subject's life might be understood through the environment and through episodes that involved a particular space.

An unexpected revelation for Nancy was the way in which all the contributors were engaged in coming up with new or revised narrative models for writing history about the built environment and the importance of this for the notion of the archive. She noted two perceptions of archival material that had become apparent in our discussion. First is the use we make of the archive as historians through our own curiosity and our own explorations of it. Second is the further life of that product of our own narrative inquiry as we turn it into something that is visible, understandable, and serviceable to a broader public. Nancy concluded by returning to my starting point for this volume – the emphasis on collaboration and teamwork and how this comes out of women's own experience remarking that, and I quote her, 'It takes a team to make architecture, to make buildings, and this makes us even more aware that heroic (male) architect model is simply absurd.'

The roundtable discussion certainly signalled the rich and diverse range of voices and methods to be found in the essays that follow. This heterogeneity of the approaches underscores that for us feminine subjectivities is not just another word for women, rather the term disrupts this essentialised concept. It was also clear that, in contrast to the period post-1950, female subjectivities in regard to the writing and historiography of Western architecture 1600-1950 remain underexplored. We also noted that some of our insights were informed by feminist studies and other identity-based interventions in the humanities, and these are explored variously in the individual chapters. If there were any kind of concluding remarks, they would cohere around the hope that this volume will open up further lines of enquiry that unsettle the architectural historiography of other geographies and epochs, and bring different voices to the fore. I would like to add a final afterword as editor. Most importantly, it is the collaborative and collective endeavour of the contributors that has produced such a powerful exploration of Women and Architectural History through their reflections on being the Monstrous Regiment then and now.

Notes

1 'Monstruous' is from the Latin mōnstruōsus which means 'unnatural' and 'regiment' is also from the Latin regimentum or regimen meaning 'rule' or 'government'. The title is frequently found with the spelling slightly modernised, for example 'monstrous regiment' and this should not be confused with 'regiment' as in a military unit. 'Monstruous Regiment' has been re-used as a title on a number of occasions some of which adhere to the correct translation of unnatural rule. Notably Winifred Ashton writing as Clemence Danes called her first novel *Regiment of Women* (1917), which is a veiled story about a lesbian relationship. The phrase has also become an ironic feminist cliché as seen in the British theatre troupe, the Monstrous Regiment Theatre Company founded in 1975.

2 My own track record of editorial practice has been innovative and exploratory, as seen for instance in *Reading Architectural History* (New York and Oxford: Routledge, 2002) where I juxtaposed new essays with canonical historical texts and theoretical writings, and more recently in *Interdisciplinary Encounters: Hidden and Visible Explorations of the Work of Adrian Rifkin* (New York and London: I. B. Tauris, 2015) where I explore the interface of text and image, author and artist within the confines of the printed page. Here, my editorial approach becomes integral to the nature of the field of enquiry by working to encourage heterogeneity and difference.

3 Christine de Pizan, *The Book of the City of Ladies*, 1405, trans. Rosalind Grant-Brown (London: Penguin, 2000).

4 Dana Arnold, '(Auto)biographies and Space,' in *Biographies and Space: Placing the Subject in Art and Architecture*, eds. Dana Arnold and Joanna Sofaer (New York and Oxford: Routledge, 2008), 6–16.

5 I acknowledge the important work of Judith Butler on performance theory and notions of performativity. See for instance J. Butler, *Gender Trouble: Feminism and the Subversion of Identity* (London and New York: Routledge, 1990) and *Bodies that Matter, on the Discursive Limits of 'Sex'* (London and New York: Routledge, 1993).

6 See Annmarie Adams, 'Encountering Maude Abbott,' *Feminist Encounters: A Journal of Critical Studies in Culture and Politics* 2, no. 2 (2018): 21. https://doi.org/10.20897/femenc/3889.

7 Annmarie Adams, *Architecture in the Family Way: Doctors, Houses, and Women, 1870–1900* (Montreal: McGill-Queen's University Press, 1996).

8 Annmarie Adams, 'The Eichler Home: Intention and Experience in Postwar Suburbia,' in *Gender, Class, and Shelter: Perspectives in Vernacular Architecture* V, eds. Elizabeth Colins Cromley and Carter L. Hudgins (Knoxville: University of Tennessee Press, 1995), 164–78.

9 Harriet Jacobs, *Incidents in the Life of a Slave Girl Written by Herself* (1861) with an introduction and notes by Nell Irvin Painter (Harmondsworth: Penguin, 2000).

10 Rani Chanda, *Amar Ma'r Baper Bari* (Kolkata: Viswabharati, 1977).

11 Kathleen Stewart, *Ordinary Affects* (Durham: Duke University Press, 2007).

12 Joan Kelly-Gadol, *Becoming Visible: Women in European History* (1st ed.) (Boston: Houghton Mifflin, 1977). Ch 'Did Women Have a Renaissance'? 137–64.

13 Alice T. Friedman, *Women and the Making of the Modern House* (1st ed.) (New Haven: Yale, 1998); *House and Household in Elizabethan England: Wollaton Hall and the Willoughby Family* (Chicago: University of Chicago Press, 1989); 'Architecture, Authority, and the Female Gaze: Planning and Representation in the Early Modern Country House', *Assemblage* 18 (Aug., 1992): 40–61.

14 Joan Coutu noted that she was using the term 'Western' as short-hand for European, Eurocentric, and the European imperial diaspora.

PART I

(Auto)Biographies

2

REFRACTING FEMININE SUBJECTIVITIES THROUGH SPACE, TIME, AND ARCHITECTURAL HISTORY

Dana Arnold

I am interested in how feminine subjectivities have disrupted the canonical discourses of architectural history. My particular concern is to explore the ways in which empirical research can be refracted through a feminine lens, leaving it re-animated but not overwhelmed. In much of my work, I employ the tropes of time and space to investigate the perception and appropriation of architecture by and for women. These lines of enquiry enable me to juxtapose the continuity of architectural space with alternative historical perspectives. This essay reflects in part on my practice as an architectural historian and demonstrates the ways in which feminine subjectivities reveal a plurality of meaning, histories, and interpretations of the architecture of the past. Architecture is often thought of as being designed and used by humankind – what is really meant here is mankind. The female user of space is subsumed or invisible. But, like our race and our social class, gender works to define who we are. There is no such thing as gender neutral space whether it be architectural space, time, or indeed the spaces of the printed page. Where do I begin?

It Was Ever Thus

My questions and concerns are not new, nor are they confined to the discourses of architectural history.

> This thought inspired such a great sense of disgust and sadness in me that I began to despise myself and the whole of my sex as an aberration in nature.[1]

These words appear in the opening section of Christine de Pizan's *The Book of the City of Ladies* (1405), (*Le Livre de la Cité des Dames)*.[2] (Figure 2.1) Her sense of self disgust is in response to reading *The Lamentations of Matheolus*, (*Liber lamentationum Matheoluli)*.[3] This highly misogynistic and misogamistic work argues against marriage as women make men's lives miserable. Christine was also responding to the popular poem *The Romance of the Rose* (c. 1275), which similarly portrayed the sexes as incompatible.[4] Misogyny, misogamy, and popular writing are not unusual companions.[5] But they were (and are) rarely challenged. Understandably,

DOI: 10.4324/9781003224662-4

FIGURE 2.1 'The Three Virtues appear in Christine's study as she stands at her desk and Christine and Reason begin to build the wall of the city,' Master of the City of Ladies (fl. from 1400 until 1415), *Le Livre de la Cité des dames*.

scholarly attention has focused on Christine's rebuttal of these views and her defence of women and marriage, which she does within a Christian frame.[6]

My interest is in Christine's choice of method and narrative technique to oppose the prevailing negative view of women. To do this, she creates an allegorical city which she builds to house a wide array of famous women, both mythological and historical, as well as Biblical. Christine narrates the women's biographies and her own autobiography through the construction of the virtual spaces of the city. The book begins with Christine, who writes in the first person, describing her reaction on reading Matheolus' diatribe, after which three female Virtues: Reason, Rectitude, and Justice arrive to aid Christine construct the City of Ladies. Importantly, Christine includes the dialogue she has with each of them, as a consequence we hear both their and Christine's voices in the text. The Virtues help Christine build the walls, foundations, and houses of the city, as well as select the women who will reside in it. Each of the women chosen by the Virtues to live in the city acts as a positive example for other women to follow. They are also examples of the beneficial influence women have had on society.[7]

The narrative meshes the biographies of women from across time with the construction of the spaces of the city. The book is divided into three parts and the choice of women in each section is distinctive. In Part I, Lady Reason chooses women from classical antiquity and mythology to demonstrate that women are not evil or useless creatures but instead have a significant place within society. She also helps Christine build the external walls of the city and answers her questions about the antagonism of men towards women. The act of construction and the selection of female figures assist Christine in preparing the metaphorical ground on which the city will be built. Lady Reason takes Christine to the Field of Letters and instructs her thus:

> Take the spade of your intelligence and dig deep to make a trench all around where you see the line I have traced I will help to carry away the hods of earth on my shoulders.[8]

These 'hods of earth' define the parameters of the allegorical city and act as a metaphor for Christine's belief that women must be wicked as she thought it unlikely that

> [...] so many learned men, who seemed to be endowed with such great intelligence and insight into all things, could possibly have lied on so many different occasions.[9]

Lady Reason would carry away this erroneous belief, as well as Christine's preference 'to give more weight to what others said than to my own judgement and experience'.[10]

She instructs both Christine and the reader on how to free themselves from their own self-consciousness and feelings of physical and intellectual inadequacy. The male, deleterious view of women can be countered by all the remarkable female endeavours and achievements of the inhabitants of the City of Ladies. The foundations for a new form of feminine identity are laid. It is Lady Rectitude who guides Christine in Part II to 'construct the houses and buildings inside the walls of the City of Ladies'. She directs her not to hesitate in mixing 'the mortar well in [her] inkpot and set to on the masonry work with great strokes of [her] pen'.[11] Lady Rectitude has prepared stones from ladies of great renown from both the Old and New Testaments, and from classical antiquity to build the new 'Realm of Femininia'. Once completed the city is populated with more women who counter the male myth that wives behave badly in marriage. Part III describes how, aided by Lady Justice, Christine adds the finishing touches to the city. This time only female saints and martyrs from the New Testament are selected and the Virgin Mary becomes the queen who will rule the city. Finally, Christine states the 'city has been founded and built to accommodate all deserving women' ... 'of the past but also the present and the future'.[12]

As an architectural historian, it is Christine's use of architectural space to both retell and challenge social and cultural norms that has stayed with me. Moreover, the way she refracts her chosen women through architecture, time, and the virtual spaces of the page is a provocative narrative technique. I remain intrigued by how she places these women within her allegorical city and uses them to augment its architecture and the status of women. Indeed, the reputation, status, and agency of women are built alongside the city itself within the spaces of the page. What, then, could I learn from this narrative technique?

Taking Up My Pen

In her *Letter to the God of Loves* (1399) (*L'Épistre au Dieu d'amours*), Christine asserted that it was perhaps only when a female writer took up her pen that a truly unequivocal case for women would be put forward.[13] And she certainly achieves this in *The Book of the City of Ladies* which intertwines autobiography, biography, and the historical record into an allegory that focuses on the status of women. This disrupts traditional, masculinist, linear histories and historiographies through the continuity between past and present. Moreover, Christine inserts herself into the text through her use of the self-reflexive I. The book begins with an autobiographical account of Christine reading and this sits alongside the factual and fictional biographies of her women. In this way she inhabits the spaces of her book alongside her women. Christine's definition of the word 'lady/ies' as women of noble spirit instead of noble birth has provoked critique from some feminist scholars who would prefer the use of 'woman/women'. But arguably, Christine's is the more inclusive category and stands in distinction to the tendency in some feminist writing to focus on white, Western, middle-class women – a point to which I will return. *The Book of the City of Ladies* raises questions concerning gender, (auto)biography, language, space, and time all of which have informed my own interests as an architectural historian. Perhaps Christine can be my guide as I take up *my pen* to reflect on my practice and how I defined my area of study and removed my own 'hods of earth'.

My starting point is that my gender must inflect on my work. How can it be otherwise? But where do I begin to analyse and narrate this? I experience space as a woman but how do I know this is different from a man? Is my experience of space intrinsic to my being or was I programmed? Looking back, I can see the ways in which I was programmed about how to think about myself in relation to space. My all-girls school taught me how to get out of a sports car without showing my underwear (keep your knees together, which might as well have been the school motto) and I learned how to enter and exit the defined space of a room. Less frivolously, I studied ballet but not PE which was considered unladylike, at least I was not obliged to 'throw like a girl'.[14] All of this made it clear to me that girls' bodies were different and, if I were to believe the popular press and magazines aimed at women and teenagers in the late sixties and seventies, our bodies were also the subjects and objects of scrutiny. The Slumber Party Barbie doll with her weighing scales (set permanently at 110lbs) and her books entitled *How to Diet* and *Don't Eat* arrived on the scene shortly after I did in 1965. Not much had changed by the time I went to university in the early 1980s.

As an undergraduate reading art history, I learned about great male artists, women inhabited and were confined by the spaces of the canvas. They were the subjects and objects of the artist's gaze. Linda Nochlin's seminal article *Why Are There no Great Women Artists* had appeared in 1971.[15] A decade later Griselda Pollock and Rozsika Parker's ground-breaking *Old Mistresses: Women, Art and Ideology* was published.[16] Nevertheless, the emphasis in my degree was on the male genius, as witnessed through formal analysis and a Hegelian notion of (Western) progress, and the syllabus remained untroubled by these feminist scholars. But I was particularly troubled by the orthodoxy that architecture was the creation of great male architects who apparently produced buildings single-handedly. Women were nowhere to be found in these narratives, either as makers or patrons, or as inhabitants or users of the spaces these men designed. But I knew they were there. The question in my mind was how could I find them?

Part I: Parameters and Foundations

> [...] take the spade of [her] intelligence and dig deep to make a trench all around [the city] ... [and Reason will] help to carry away the hods of earth on [her] shoulders.

Deciding which 'hods of earth' should be carried away in order to define the parameters around my interest in finding the feminine presence in architectural history was not without its complexities. Certainly, the invisibility of women in the canon of architectural history might well lead us to conclude that women have no history, and consequently no agency. If this is the case surely we are trapped in the present. A feminist history could emancipate women from their anonymity in these texts and write them into the histories of architecture. But I was concerned that inserting women in canonical histories would mean I was making women fit into the established masculinist narrative structures. Adding women's involvement with architecture to a history that is predicated on the contribution of individual men would surely be a process of subsumption. Equally, constructing an alternative history of known women practitioner/patrons would risk replacing one hegemony with another. Critiques of feminist histories have pinpointed the tendency of assuming a single undifferentiated category of woman which can represent all women from the past and present regardless of their age, ethnicity and sexual orientation. Moreover, I was worried that I might project my views back on women in the past. It is not always evident that they saw themselves as oppressed unless we look at that past through the lens of the present. My dilemma was clear – should I as a historian privilege my own interpretation of another's life in itself a hallmark of masculinist ideology or should I compromise my commitment to challenging oppression even if the historical subject does not identify it as such? My aim remains not to replace male lives with other lives, or to write women into the masculinist narratives of architecture and its history. Instead, I continue to seek to broaden the discourses of architectural history to explore how to subvert canonical norms through the empowerment of otherness rather than a process of subsumption or indeed perceived emasculation. In this way, the diversity of the female subject can be maintained and celebrated. Early on, I was taken with Joan W. Scott's belief that new historical investigation/feminist analysis should 'disrupt the notion of fixity, to discover the nature of the debate or repression that leads to the appearance of timeless permanence in binary gender representation'[17] The challenge was how to disrupt these binaries, especially as the established narrative and linguistic structures of academic discourse are predicated on masculinist norms.

Writing Nicely, or the Historian's Sleight of Hand

The predominance of the white male as the subject and object of architectural history has shaped its canonical formulae. We see this in the emphasis on chronology and sequence, and on authorship and a kind of Roarkist genius. In order to develop alternative narrative strategies, it is important to think about how we write architectural history. Here I mean the invisible cultural norms and predicates that exist within the language used in its discourses. The tendency to accept whatever 'is' as natural in academic discourse is aided by the linguistic acknowledgement of women as different. We tend, for example, to use 'she' instead of the assumed neutral 'one', in reality the white Western male position accepted as natural, or the hidden 'he' as the subject of all scholarly predicates.[18] This acquiescence impacts on histories where the authentic voice of the author is subsumed and the male viewpoint is unconsciously and unquestioningly taken as 'the' viewpoint of the historian. The use of the third-person or the passive voice is fatally flawed and may well be intellectual fatal, as it means that history fails to take account of the implicit value system where we find an overlap between subject and object in historical investigation. Early on, I adopted the use of the first person when writing scholarly prose. This was not writing 'nicely' but I wanted a direct relationship with the subjects and objects of my writing, and ultimately with my reader. Self-reflexivity provided me with a methodological tool and a rhetorical device with which to do this.[19] It seemed to me essential to re-examine the narratives, concepts, chronologies, and boundaries of architectural history in order to reveal the authorial sleight of hand and displace the white Western male subject. This would make architectural history a site of potential conflicts where I might seek to understand the disunity of the experience and agency of the subjects and objects of study rather than recreate a (fictional) notion of reality. Surely this would disrupt the 'binaries of gender representation'?

The most pressing challenge was the language I should use to write about women and architecture. I remain intrigued by the affect when a feminising adjective is used in conjunction with an abstract or concrete noun such as space, time or architect. The connotations of women's spaces or female architect reinforce the gender binary assumptions of these nouns – where the supposition is that space or an architect is male and a woman's space or a female architect is a modification that requires note. This remains a fundamental issue and let me give you an example. Here is Frank Gehry talking about Zaha Hadid shortly after her death in 2016. Hadid did not want to be considered a female architect instead of just an architect and Gehry's referred to her as 'one of the guys'. He added

> [That's] sexist in its own way I suppose. ... I don't mean it that way. She was undaunted by all the stuff that would be against a woman coming into a field at that level. She didn't pay attention to it ... She was very confident.[20]

I do not wish to single out Gehry, but to my mind his remarks both identify and reinforce the binary gender assumptions inherent in the term architect. At what point does an architect become 'daunted' rather than 'undaunted', 'attentive' rather than 'inattentive', 'unconfident' rather than 'confident'. Certainly, Gehry is not alone in distinguishing the values seen to be positive assets as being inherent in the word 'architect' with all is masculine associations. Conversely, why does the modification of the word by the adjective 'woman' diminish the idea of the architect? But if we follow Hadid's and Gehry's viewpoint and write women into the masculinist narratives of architecture, we risk reinforcing gender binaries and miss an opportunity to expand our understanding of the word architect.

These discourses of difference between the sexes are pervasive. Understanding how sexism and patriarchy continue to be replicated enables us to understand how what is artificial can nonetheless be nearly ubiquitous. The idealised appeal of these outdated yet enduring values can be seen as the survival of practices of alienation. An analysis of the narrative structures of architectural history reveals how the historian's sleight of hand ensures the persistence of such processes. It became clear to me that the affect of the apparently 'natural' narration of 'inert' historical linear, chronological data or empirical information, as what happened had to happen the way it did, is one of the principal methodological problems that spring from canonical masculinist architectural history. There appears to be no other logical course of history other than the one presented in these alienating narrative structures that are written 'nicely' and conform to academic norms. Feminism had begun to address these issues, but there were snags in trying to replace one set of linguistic conventions with another. I continue to admire Donna Haraway's ironic critique of the contradictions in socialist feminism typified in her observation:

> Feminisms and Marxisms have run aground on Western epistemological imperatives to construct a revolutionary subject from the perspective of a hierarchy of oppressions and/or a latent position of moral superiority, innocence, and greater closeness to nature. With no available original dream of a common language or original symbiosis promising protection from hostile 'masculine' separation. [21]

My search became for those methods that allow me to re-textualise architectural history, whilst not proposing a new vision or replacing one hegemony with another.

The Field of Letters

I was aware that any call for change cannot and should not reconfigure the historical writing that has mapped out the terrain of the discipline. This canonical body of work is, in any event, an intrinsic part of architectural history and its historiography. All that said, an awareness of the implications of the master narratives of the discipline is essential and enables us to begin to re-think architectural history, as well as how we formulate new histories and start to move away from the need for progression and closure. Architectural history is not a monolith, and we must appreciate its complexity and diversity, as well as the different sets of values that operate within its various cultural frames. But my area of specialisation – British architecture in the long eighteenth century had been defined by monolithic studies that privileged the male author genius, and the classical style. This is evident in the work of Sir John Summerson, Sir Howard Colvin, and Sir Nikolaus Pevsner, to name a few of the male historians who had charted my course through this period in British architecture. How then could I construct my own map of the subject to allow me to cross the same terrain using a different set of co-ordinates to reach different destinations. I wanted to engage and challenge canonical architectural history but leave it coherent yet interrogated, unpacked yet intact. Architecture remained my focus and theory became my tool for exploring its history and historiography. I did not worry about the hybridity of this approach. Cultural theory was an instrument in and not the core of my enquiry. Nor I did not align myself to the feminist camp, which in any case had left pre-twentieth century architectural history mostly undisturbed.[22] And my first monograph *Re-presenting the Metropolis: Architecture, urban experience and social life in London 1800–1840* (2000) meant I had quickly become a lost cause as far the architectural history establishment was concerned.[23] (Subsequently, I have never been 'found'.) But the absence of fixity and the fluidity that resulted from the resonance between theory and archive enabled me to create new readings of architecture that address the question of what do our constructions of histories of architecture tell us about ourselves? Crucially, these readings remain in flux.

In 2002, I published *Reading Architectural History* – a series of discursive essays on the historiographic and socio/cultural implications of British architectural history with particular reference to the long eighteenth century.[24] The chapters covered biographical and social histories, as well as visual surveys and guidebooks to examine the narrative structures of histories of architecture and their impact on the perception and understanding of the architecture of the past. Each essay was followed by an extract from a canonical history juxtaposed with a piece of theoretical writing. The book was not intended to be a negative one that picked holes in the primary narratives of architectural history without offering alternatives. The intention was more to raise questions and prompt awareness of the consequences of our narrative practices. In so doing, my aim was to reveal that these writings are richer than we have perhaps recognised and that architectural production in this period can be interrogated in the same way as that from more recent past – and it can be read in a variety of ways. Although the volume focused on British architecture, it seemed to meet a broader need to rethink architectural history and its historiography. As a result of a Fellowship at the Getty Research Institute as part of the Biography theme year, a Fellowship at CRASSH, University of Cambridge, and a British Academy funded collaborative project *Ambivalent Geographies*, I co-edited two volumes *Rethinking Architectural Historiography* (2006) and *Biographies and Space: Placing the Subject in Art and Architecture* (2008) that aimed to define the parameters for further enquiry.[25] These studies renegotiated the disciplinary and geographical boundaries of architectural history and explored the relationship between biography and space and how specific subjects are used as a means of explaining sets of social, cultural, and spatial relationships. Both works engage with past and present histories, disclosing assumptions, biases, and absences in architectural historiography. Together these three volumes explored how discourse shapes our experience of architecture and the built environment as a visual object and as an agent in the formation of social identity. Importantly for me, the many volumes I have edited and co-edited underscore the richness of collective endeavour. The curation of the knowledge and expertise of individuals within the boundaries of a specific theme remains a privilege, not least in regards to this book.

The foundations had been dug, the walls of my imaginary city built, and the hods of earth were slowly being carried away. My interest in the locating the feminine presence in the built space and the spaces of the page focused on the architecture of the long eighteenth century. The challenge remained how I should 'construct the houses and buildings inside the walls of the City of Ladies' to ensure they are undiminished women's spaces and not spaces that contain women.[26]

Part 2 Houses and Buildings

> '[mixing] the mortar well in [my] inkpot and set to on the masonry work with great strokes of [my] pen'[27]

I have written a great deal about the physical and virtual spaces women inhabit.[28] My lines of enquiry have focused on how we experience the built environment, especially cities, and more recently on how we negotiate architectural prints and drawings through the lens of gender. I have never attempted to be comprehensive or replace one hegemony with another, nor has my viewpoint been heteronormative. Instead, I explore architecture and the space and time it encloses in ways that are absent from canonical histories in order to enhance or broaden our purview rather than eclipse or replace perceived norms. My building blocks remain the resonance between theory and archive.

Looking back (and forward) I still wonder about the effect/affect of knowing a specific room was used by women or was designed by/was for a woman has on our understanding of it. Perhaps more pertinently, does designating a space as domestic with all the implied feminine associations downgrade it? After all, everyday life is not the stuff of grand narratives predicated on the (male) author genius architect or patron. If we think about the Georgian country house or townhouse as (family) homes. Should we then think about them differently. Perhaps the space is or becomes 'the enclosed space that is a modality of femininity' where '[t]he woman lives her space as confined and closed around her, at least in part as projecting some small area in which she can exist as a free subject'.[29] Or perhaps that is what the space is not – instead it keeps the woman in her 'place'. The idea of the family can be used as a means of promoting this male hegemony. And its architectural expression in the family 'home' is a good example. For instance, the phrase 'A man's home is his castle'[30] harks back to the mastery of feudal times evoking an image of an inherited home and birthright into the idea of the present-day mortgaged property. Subversion of this male 'domain' through alternative sexuality or the privileging of the female sex would undermine this ideology. Furthermore, phrases such as 'housewife' or indeed its French equivalent 'La femme au foyer', translated literally as 'the woman in the hearth', put women firmly in their place in both the language and architectural/cultural geography of 'home'.[31]

FIGURE 2.2 Unisex toilets sign. This image is from a collection commissioned by the United States Department of Transportation and designed by AIGA. 2007.

These contradictory positions hinge on whether the feminine trace can be signified by space or can space be signified by feminine presence, whether named or anonymous. Leading on from this, does the ambiguity about the relationship between space and gender become another instance of binary opposition. If so, it is our culturally determined viewpoint that makes a space represent masculinity or femininity. I found Jacques Lacan's analysis of the toilet signs 'Ladies' and 'Gentlemen', helpful in pinpointing these binaries.[32] (Figure 2.2) The signs do not refer to the toilet (the signifier) but to the chain of associated signifiers assigned by history, culture, and social mores separately and reciprocally to the sexual differentiation implied in them.[33] The gender linguistics and the linguistic predicates of architectural history would suggest this to be the case. And we have already seen this in relation to the word 'architect'.

Spaces that Contain Women

The intersection and interaction of textual and physical space can be explained further if we think about women's space and spatial experience. Iris Marion Young identifies space as an agent of confinement that restricts women's bodily movements and pushes them to absent themselves from space to become invisible occupying no space whatsoever, 'a space surrounds them in imagination which we are not free to move beyond; the space available to our movement is a constricted space'.[34] At one level the female body is an object for which the gaze imposes and confirms certain patterns of comportment. Restricted movements in a real or imagined space that are 'ladylike' assert 'woman' as subject by avoiding the objectification of the gaze. Female bodily movements do not fill the spaces inhabited by a woman and for Young this represents the tension between a woman's immanence and transcendence, her role as subject and object.[35] I would contest that these conflicting attitudes towards the female body are germane to the construction of architectural space and the creation of the illusion of space.

The spaces that contain(ed) women in the long eighteenth century were often cloaked in the apparent respectability of the classical style. In canonical architectural history classicism is a distinct territory with its own set of boundaries that can promote the idea that the past is a nice place – and this worries me. We see a stream of history that flows from antiquity to the present day with a reliance on the named author genius that continues to promote and maintain the sovereign white male subject and impose hierarchies of quality of design. This point of view might at first appear to jar against the comfortable image of the genteel, 'gentlemanly' custom of engaging with classical culture. And this is where I, as a subject and object, have difficulties. I am not a white, Western, male subject, yet the classical architecture of the long eighteenth century interests me. Moreover, I do not want the past to be a nice place at the expense of suppressing the voice of others or at best pushing them to the margins of the discourse. Nor, as I noted above, do I want to turn my back on a substantial chunk of British architectural history and its historiography. But where could I find my women and how should I house them?

Through my work on country houses, cities, and hospitals it was possible to move beyond social histories of architecture and explore how the discourses around women reveal their experience of space and how in turn space becomes an agent in the formation of social identity. The burgeoning print culture as witnessed in novels and the wealth of representations of urban and rural scenes in topographical prints and drawings has proved to be a rich archival source for identifying and narrating other histories of space and spatial experience. For example, the rise of the epistolary novel such as Samuel Richardson's *Pamela or Virtue Rewarded* (1740) and *Clarissa* (1747–48) have female narrators and we are able to read the thoughts of the principal character through their letters. Cheaper printing techniques meant these works and images of key scenes from them reached a broad public.[36] Similarly, William Hogarth produced numerous picture cycles of modern moral subjects, including the *Harlot's Progress* (1731) which also sold as prints alongside his visual documentary subjects such as *Gin Lane* (1751).[37] Much of the action in Hogarth, Highmore, and Richardson's narratives features women and takes place in domestic interiors; it is enclosed by the space of the room. In this way, the perception of the spaces of the room ran in parallel to the perception of the thoughts of the various women characters, who have agency. More broadly, Rudolph Ackermann's *The Microcosm of London* (1808–10), and journal *The Repository of Arts, Literature, Commerce, Manufactures, Fashions, and Politics*, (1809–28) are just two instances of the response to the urban development of London in the early nineteenth century. This rich archival seam is complemented by a plethora of guidebooks and commentaries instructing the reader how to view and experience the city. Notably, these verbal and visual sources also showed us that women operated in these urban spaces and importantly, we encounter women of all social classes.

I was aware that I risked re-locating women away from the evidence base of normative histories. Moreover, the personal meanings and strategies of these women were enacted in spaces that in canonical histories are defined by men. Most obviously, country houses were generally designed by men for men, typically in some kind of all'antica style. That women, through a socially advantageous marriage, often supplied the wealth required for such grand projects is not dwelled upon in canonical histories. There were women who maintained their own households and controlled their own wealth, although they were dowagers or unmarried. However, they were usually to be found in the townhouses of the Georgian city whose design conformed to a kind of set of abstract classical proportions. Perhaps there was another way of thinking about classical architecture, or perhaps there was not? Recently, I have become particularly interested in prints and drawings of antique architecture, as well as architectural treatises.[38] These are a mainstay of canonical architectural history, as they meet the needs of narratives that focus on style, and the architect/patron nexus. At first glance, apart from supplying illustrations of and narratives about the origins of the caryatids or the Ionic order, it is hard to locate a feminine trace. It seemed as if classical architecture was indeed indexical of the predominant notion that the white male subject/object is what the past is all about. I will show you what I mean in these challenging examples.

Trapped in Space

The well-known example of *The Vitruvian Man* demonstrates how patriarchy is inherent in classically-designed architectural space.[39] (Figure 2.3) It is an illustration of a passage from Vitruvius' *De architectura (The Ten Books on Architecture)*, where Vitruvius describes how a man in two superimposed positions with his arms and legs apart can be inscribed in a circle and square. This establishes the so-called 'canon of proportions' as predicated on the male body.

> For if a man be placed flat on his back, with his hands and feet extended … [his] body yields a circular outline, so too a square figure may be found from it.[40]

The 'canon of proportions' dominated both the recording of the architecture of antiquity and its reprise in the classically-inspired design of the long eighteenth century.

In some ways, this is the visual equivalent of the cultural norms and predicates that govern how architectural history is written 'nicely' I discussed earlier on in this essay. Here the natural and neutral hidden 'he' is not in the language, but in the proportions that govern design. I want to push this point a little further with a provocation and see what happens when we replace the *Vitruvian Man* with the *Vitruvian Woman.* (Figure 2.4) Most obviously, the canon of proportions that we have seen dominates the theories and practices, representations and reconstructions of antique architecture would be rather different, if based on the female body. But the image of a woman with her arms and legs apart and inscribed in a circle and square would not perhaps in the first instance imply that woman is the measure of all things. Instead, our pre-conditioned sensibilities might initially be challenged. Indeed, this can be explained further if we think about women's space and spatial experience – or spatial bodily existence – as both an object constituted by space as well as being a spatially constituted subject. Central to this is the feminine body, which is positioned in space by a set of patriarchal co-ordinates that impose modes of performativity that constitute an 'unnatural' notion of woman. Simply put: the *Vitruvian Woman* connotes subjugation and sexual readiness, rather than supplying the governing proportions for classical architecture.

My provocation can be pushed a little further if we think about the *costruzione legittima* – a horizontal grid comprising orthogonal and transverse lines. The grid becomes as a visual metaphor how the female body can be positioned in space by a set of patriarchal co-ordinates which impose modes of performativity that constitute our notion of woman.[41] This geometric technique of creating the illusion of depth and volume is based on the masculine body. The spacing of the lines of the *costruzione legittima* is governed by one braccio (roughly one third of a man's height).[42] These individual braccio divisions are joined to the perspective focus to give the orthogonals, thus creating a kind of V shape. The overall effect is a grid

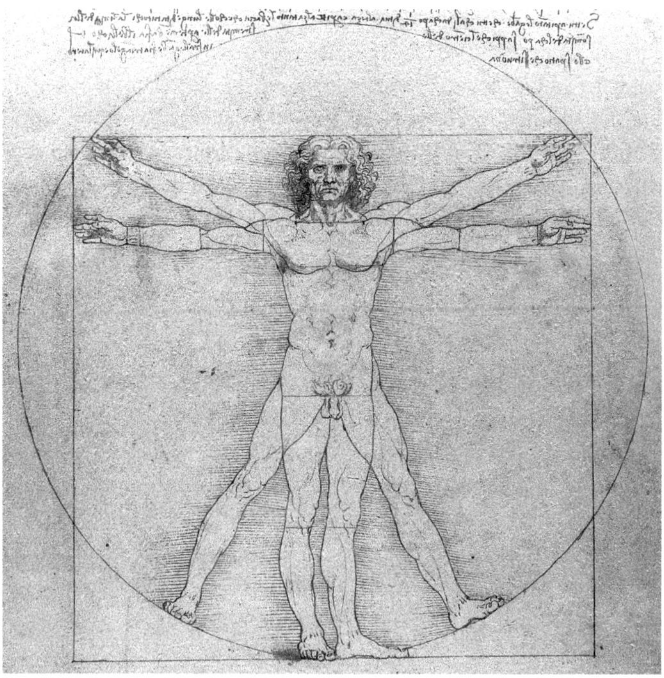

FIGURE 2.3 The Vitruvian Man, Leonardo da Vinci, c.1492.

comprising squares each of which is based on the measurement of the male body. Albrecht Dürer illustrated this method in his *The Painter's Manual*, the first edition of which appeared in 1525[43]. (Figure 2.5) We see him demonstrating how to draw a nude, reclining female body using a grid based on male proportions. Looking at this image, it is hard to think of a better visual metaphor for both the female body contained in and feminine experience of masculine space.

Classical architecture is promoted by words, and drawn in lines that become linear histories. Was there a way of locating women in the visual images of the classical style in order to tell other histories that 'disrupt the notion of fixity, to discover the nature of the debate or repression that leads to the appearance of timeless permanence in binary gender representation'[44]

Cherchez la Femme

In my recent book *Architecture and Ekphrasis: Space, time and the embodied description of the past* (2020) I wanted to locate the feminine trace across the space and time of the printed and drawn page. I began with Hogarth's *The Analysis of Beauty* (1753) in which he feminises the line and identifies the waving line as the 'line of beauty' and the serpentine line as the 'line of grace'.[45] This feminised line has agency as it has the ability to lead the eye, and I was following it through the 'wanton kind of chase' Hogarth describes.[46] My query became how this agency, when combined with the mnemonic and descriptive qualities of the line identified by Hogarth, could challenge, or at least present an alternative truth, to linear, verbal histories.[47] Hogarth's idea of the motion of the chase made me think about Gilles Deleuze and the way in which he

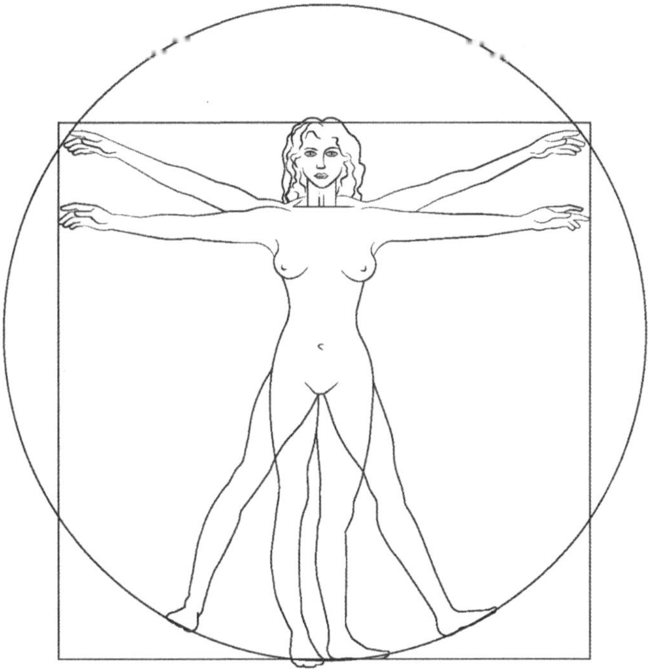

FIGURE 2.4 Vitruvian Woman, (© Clare Barry).

FIGURE 2.5 Draughtsman Making a Perspective Drawing of a Reclining Woman, Albrecht Dürer, c.1525.

privileges the geographies of movement over history. Deleuze's 'line of flight' produces a transport or lift which can be interpreted as 'a sort of delirium'. . . . 'There is something demoniacal or demonic in a line of flight. [. . .] What demons do is jump across intervals, and from one interval to another'.[48] We can, then, begin to unpick the linear and chronological viewpoints that are a hallmark of masculinist historical thinking. As a consequence, it is possible to see how graphic images of the architecture of the past can be independent of the progressive chronologies that dominate normative histories. In this way a line can form visible and invisible pathways and these fluid processes work to locate memory and recollection and ultimately time through their shifting, crossing, and repeating. For Deleuze, the line both frees us from linear histories whilst operating as a process of historicisation. As we have seen, the line forms the basis of textual and visual histories. But the eye engages with history in a different way when looking at it rather than reading it – it is not sequential left-to-right movement, instead it is a more random 'wanton kind of chase' of history. And this line is feminine.

The practice of printmaking reinforces the agency and feminisation of the line. Although not normally, formally apprenticed, women played an active role in the production of prints.[49] These women were not part of the elite and usually worked in the family home, so changing the nature of domestic space. At this time, engravings were the most common kind of prints produced using the intaglio method.[50] Here the image is cut into the surface of a metal plate. When the plate is inked, the ink is pushed into the incised lines. The plate is then passed through a press with a sheet of dampened paper which pulls the ink out of the lines and transfers them to the paper producing a reversed image of that incised on the plate.[51] The force of pressure applied by the press, which was powered by the exertion of the printmaker, results in an outline of the metal plate itself being impressed into the paper. This is known as the plate-mark. Prints in the age before machine-powered presses were, then, produced by the efforts of the body, which could be male or female.[52] The relationship between the burin (a small, V-shaped chisel used to cut the lines into the plate), the plate itself, and the movement of the engraver complicates the relationship between print and printmaker. The process of engraving is fundamentally that of two linear movements, one straight and the other circular. The engraver produces straight lines by moving the burin diagonally across the plate, usually from right to left placing the plate in front of him or herself.[53] In this way, the movement of the engraver is embodied in the creation of the line. By contrast, curved lines are more complex requiring the combined movement of the burin and the plate. The latter is placed on a cushion filled with sand and rotated against the burin. Instead of the draftsman's hand moving across the surface, here the surface moves across the draftsman's hand so reversing the relationship between draftsman and surface we have just seen in the creation of straight lines.[54] In this way, the production of the serpentine, feminised line disembodies the efforts of the engraver and gives agency to the line itself. Prints and drawings become an archive in their own right, which can be freed from masculinist categorisation and taxonomies.

Part 3 The Finishing Touches

> 'the finishing touches [....] the arrival of both the queen and her retinue [to] the City of Ladies housing 'the whole of womankind[55]

There is no queen in my City of Ladies – it is a democracy. My search for feminine subjectivities across space, time, and architectural history has not been about locating a new elite. Architecture involves all of its users and consumers and architectural history concerns both the authors and active recipients of its various narratives. The complexity of meaning and interpretation embedded in architectural space should prompt us to move away from those rigid frameworks that establish structures within the social history of architecture as a way of explaining the built environment of the past. As we have seen, the epistemological systems, especially as applied to architecture in the long eighteenth century, relate strongly to the dominant social groups. Until recently, the tendency has been almost exclusively to view architecture as evidence of the white male hegemony rather than accepting this as the history of only one of a range of social groups who interacted in and with the built environment. We cannot ignore or erase this elite group from history; however, we can question and interrogate established hegemonies rather than accept them as the normative history. Indeed, we can, and in fact must, seek out and tell other histories. As I noted earlier on in this essay, the absence of fixity and the fluidity in my readings of architecture that resulted from the resonance between theory and archive enabled me to create new readings of architecture that address the question of what do our constructions of histories of architecture tell us about ourselves? Importantly, these readings remain in flux. I am happy to confirm this is still the case; there are no finishing touches only unfinished business.

When I Say 'gender' You Think Women

I first used this provocation in 2002.[56] And it is true that most gender history has been written from a woman-centred perspective. But, more recently alongside feminist writing, we have seen important moves to explore gender as non-binary. These shifts have further disrupted the canonical, gender-specific cultural definitions of behaviours and social practices that are considered appropriate. Recently, gender debates have become important elements in the re-thinking of power relationships within architecture that extend beyond sexuality to issues of race and authorship. In this essay I have already examined the relationship between gender and architecture through a dissembling of the term architect with its monolithic, masculinist, white assumptions. I concentrated on women as the subject object relationship overlaps through my role as author, historian, and woman. Moreover, a consideration of the relationship between (female) gender and architecture has prompted me to rethink or at least challenge/question a great deal of the canon of British architectural history. Is it possible to destabilise the fixed concept of the heroic model of the male architect further? We have seen how the addition of adjectives such as 'female' can be seen to diminish abstract and concrete nouns such as space, time, and architect. I became curious to explore what happens if we add BAME/POC/, 'queer', or collective/collaborative to these nouns. These words together with 'female' might promote difference and revise rather than moderate the meaning of the word architect. In other words, is there another way of subverting canonical norms through the empowerment of difference?

I have just finished writing *British Architecture: A very short introduction*.[57] It is probably one of the first revisionist surveys of British architecture in the wake of the Me Too and Black Lives Matter movements. I was interested to explore how intersectionality could disrupt the accepted narratives of British architecture with their underlying class and gender assumptions. Most importantly, I wanted to make British architectural history more diverse and inclusive in both its purview and readership. One immediate question was should I omit architecture that had been a mainstay of the grand masculinist narratives of architectural history? Take, for example the Georgian country house, which I discussed earlier on in relation to women. But it was also a site of oppression for many. It was often funded through the profits from the slave trade and slavery, colonialisation, and the exploitation of local communities. The challenge was how to reconfigure architecture and its histories over a broad sweep of time to make these narratives more inclusive whilst recognising their meaning and value can shift over time and mean different things to different publics.

Stuart Hall commenting on the Black experience remarked how the dominant white Western discourses had 'the power to make us see and experience *ourselves* as "Other".'[58] I needed to entice the reader to look through the 'other' end of the telescope at the dominant discourses to view them from without rather than within. Without this empathy, attempts at inter/cultural analysis or revisionist histories will result in superficial 'understanding' without any move toward real change. As a result, the colonised subject will simply be re-inscribed within the boundaries of colonial discourse. What I am getting at here is the porosity between edges of these narratives shows there is no single history, just a series of culturally determined accounts. Different communities may value different things and again these may change over time. If we expand our purview beyond the established tropes of style, chronological sequence, and the primacy of the usually white male architect, we can understand architecture in a much wider inclusive context. We can also disrupt further the standard narratives of architectural history by acknowledging architectural practice as collaborative or collective choreography, and by understanding the absurdity of the heroic male model. Moreover, this concept reveals the fluidity and changeability of architectural history and its historiography as the acts of reading and writing histories are always culturally determined. As we move towards the edges, we can discover how we might further re-think architectural history and expand its purview and make its parameters porous.

It was ever thus redux

Throughout this essay I have indicated that my search for feminine subjectivities in architectural history has had a broad outlook. Clearly, at the outset I was influenced by second wave feminism, but recently I have endeavoured to have a more inclusive purview. Intersectionality has been an important influence for my work and has also informed my collaborations with colleagues in the Near and Middle East, and China. Arguably, the Girlboss and Bimbo feminists have undermined intersectionality and with it the genuine feminist project. I am certainly observing the same social, racial, and gender injustices as I have been witnessing since the 1980s, if not before. In this essay Christine de Pizan has been my guide in reflecting on my practice as an architectural historian. Her *City of Ladies* is an admirable piece of feminist fiction that crosses over into the real world. It is sometimes easy to forget she was writing in the early fifteenth century. It is difficult to pinpoint what popular culture might have been at that time. But is an odd paradox that as I am writing this essay in the summer of 2023, Pizan's fable *City of Ladies* has a stronger note of radical feminism than the hyperfeminized *Barbieland* that has returned to dominate present-day popular culture. I can't help but wonder if the real irony of the sparkles on the pink costumes is that they are in fact shards from the glass ceilings that I, my 'Monstrous Regiment', and many other women have punched through, rather than a fourth-wave feminist statement of girlpower? Has, then, nothing changed, and has the feminist project stalled completely?

Looking back (and forward) at my practice and processes as an architectural historian, at the sexism and (un)conscious bias, at the social programming, and the never quite fitting in, I have often thought of the dictum 'Sure he [Fred Astaire] was great, but don't forget that Ginger Rogers did everything he did, backwards… and in high heels'.[59] But I wonder if in reality building a City of Women remains 'more like wrestling than dancing', then at least a sparkly costume becomes optional.[60]

Notes

1 Christine de Pizan, *The Book of the City of Ladies*, 1405, trans. Rosalind Grant-Brown (London: Penguin, 2000), I am quoting from an abridged version published in 2005, see Part I, ch. 1, p. 3.
2 Christine de Pizan's (c.1364–1430) was born in Italy but her father became astrologer to Charles V, and she spent her childhood at the French court. She was widowed after ten years of marriage, aged twenty-five, and took up writing in order to support herself and her three young children.
3 *Liber lamentationum Matheoluli* (c.1295). It had been translated into French by Jean Le Fèvre in 1390.
4 Guillame de Lorris and Jean de Meun, *The Romance of the Rose*, trans. Charles Dahlberg (Hanover: UP of New England, 1983). The text was written in two stages by Guillaume de Lorris 1230 and Jean de Meun's c.1275. This text is somewhat contradictory. It claims that the inevitable antagonism inherent in marriage could be avoided through courtly love, however love outside of marriage would lead to physical and moral degradation. See also Kevin Brownlee, 'Discourses of the Self: Christine de Pizan and *The Romance of the Rose*', *Romanic Review*, 79 (1988), pp. 199–221.
5 Rosalind Brown-Grant, 'Christine de Pizan as a Defender of Women', in *Christine de Pizan: A Casebook*, ed. Barbara K. Altmann and Deborah L. McGrady (New York and London: Routledge, 2002), pp. 81–100.
6 See Ibid., and Glenda Mcleod and Katharina Wilson, 'A Clerk in Name Only-a Clerk in All But Name: The Misogamous Tradition and La Cité des dames,' in *The City of Scholars: New Approaches to Christine de Pizan*, eds. Margarete Zimmermann and Dina De Rentiis (Berlin and New York: De Gruyter, 1994), pp. 67–76.
7 For a detailed analysis of the whole text see Maureen Quilligan, *The Allegory of Female Authority: Christine de Pizan's Cité Des Dames* (Ithaca and New York: Cornell University Press, 1991).
8 Christine de Pizan op.cit., as note 1, Part I, ch. 8, p. 7.
9 Christine de Pizan op.cit., as note 1, Part I, ch. 1, p. 3.
10 Ibid.
11 Christine de Pizan op.cit., as note 1, Part II, ch. 1, p. 48.
12 Christine de Pizan op.cit., as note 1, Part III, ch. 19, p. 118.
13 Christine de Pizan, *Epistre au Dieu d'amours* in *Poems of Cupid, God of Love: Christine de Pizan's Epistre au Dieu d'amours and Dit de la Rose, Thomas Hoccleve's Letter of Cupid. With George Sewell's The Proclamation of Cupid*, trans. and eds. Thelma S. Fenster and Mary Carpenter Erler (Leiden: E. J. Brill, 1990), pp. 54–55, 11.417–18.
14 Iris Marion Young, 'Throwing Like a Girl: A Phenomenology of Feminine Body Comportment, Motility and Spatiality', *Human Studies*, 3 (1980), pp. 137–56.
15 Linda Nochlin, 'Why Are There No Great Women Artists?', in *Woman in Sexist Society: Studies in Power and Powerlessness*, eds. Vivian Gornick and Barbara K. Moran (New York: Basic Books, 1971), pp. 1–39.
16 Griselda Pollock and Rozsika Parker, *Old Mistresses*: *Women, Art and Ideology* (London: Routledge & Kegan, 1981).
17 Joan W. Scott, 'Gender: A Useful Category of Historical Analysis', *The American Historical Review*, 91, no. 5 (Dec., 1986), pp. 1053–1075.
18 See Kathleen Canning, 'Feminist History after the Linguistic Turn: Historicising Discourse and Experience', *Signs: Journal of Women in Culture and Society*, 19, no. 2 (1994), pp. 368–404.
19 I note with some irony that when writing in French I also use the first person. Despite the work of, inter alia, Pierre Bourdieu, Bruno Latour, Roland Barthes, and Jacques Derrida many of my French colleagues remain resistant to my use of the self-reflexivity as a methodological tool and rhetorical device.
20 Frank Gehry, 'Frank Gehry Remembers Zaha Hadid, Who "Found Her Niche and Went With It"' interview with Sarah Begley, *Time*, 31 March 2016 (shortly after Hadid's death). https://time.com/4278610/frank-gehry-remembers-zaha-hadid-who-found-her-niche-and-went-with-it/.
21 Donna Haraway, 'A Cyborg Manifesto: Science, Technology and Socialist Feminism in the Late Twentieth Century,' in *Simians, Cyborgs and Women: The Reinvention of Nature* (New York: Routledge, 1991), p. 176. (Originally published as 'Manifesto for Cyborgs: Science, Technology, and Socialist Feminism in the 1980s'. *Socialist Review*, 80 (1985), pp. 65–108.).
22 A notable exception is Alice T. Friedman, *House and Household in Elizabethan England: Wollaton Hall and the Willoughby Family* (Chicago: University of Chicago Press, 1988) and her seminal article

'Architecture, Authority, and the Female Gaze: Planning and Representation in the Early Modern Country House', *Assemblage*, 18 (Aug., 1992), pp. 40–61.
23 Dana Arnold, *Re-presenting the Metropolis: Architecture, Urban Experience and Social Life in London 1800-1840* (Aldershot: Ashgate, 2000, and pbk London and New York: Routledge, 2018).
24 Dana Arnold, *Reading Architectural History* (London and New York: Routledge, 2002).
25 Dana Arnold and Joanna Sofaer (eds.), *Biographies and Space: Placing the Subject in Art and Architecture* (London and New York: Routledge, 2008); Dana Arnold, Elvan Ergut and Belgin Ozkaya (eds.), *Rethinking Architectural Historiography* (London and New York: Routledge, 2006).
26 Christine de Pizan op.cit., as note 1, Part II, ch. 1, p. 48.
27 Ibid.
28 Dana Arnold, *Architecture and Ekphrasis: Space, Time and the Embodied Description of the Past* (Manchester: Manchester University Press, 2020); D. Arnold, *The Spaces of the Hospital: Spatiality and Urban Change in London 1680–1820* (London and New York: Routledge, 2013); *Rural Urbanism: London Landscapes in the Early Nineteenth Century* (Manchester: Manchester University Press, 2006); *Re-presenting the Metropolis: Architecture, Urban Experience and Social Life in London 1800–1840* (Aldershot: Ashgate, 2000, pbk 2018); *The Georgian Country House: Architecture Landscape and Society* (Stroud: Sutton Publishing, 1998 and pbk 2003), (third edition Cheltenham: The History Press, 2014).
29 Iris Marion Young, 'Throwing Like a Girl: A Phenomenology of Feminine Body Comportment, Motility and Spatiality', *Human Studies*, 3 (1980), p. 154.
30 See Eve Sedgwick, *Between Men English Literature and Homosocial Desire* (New York: Columbia University Press, 1985), pp. 1–15 esp.
31 I discuss the idea of 'home' more fully in Dana Arnold, '(Auto)biographies and Space', in *Biographies and Space: Placing the Subject in Art and Architecture*, eds. Dana Arnold and Joanna Sofaer (London and New York: Routledge, 2008), pp. 6–16 and Dana Arnold, *British Architecture: A Very Short Introduction* (Oxford: Oxford University Press, 2024), ch. 3 esp.
32 Dana Arnold, '(Auto)biographies and Space', in *Biographies and Space: Placing the Subject in Art and Architecture*, eds. Dana Arnold and Joanna Sofaer (London and New York: Routledge, 2008), p. 10.
33 Jacques Lacan, *Ecrits, A Selection*, trans. Alan Sheridan (New York: Norton, 1977), pp. 150–52.
34 Iris Marion Young, 'Throwing Like a Girl: A Phenomenology of Feminine Body Comportment, Motility and Spatiality', *Human Studies*, 3 (1980), pp. 137–56, p. 143.
35 See Young loc.cit. Here Young is making reference to Simone de Beauvoir's concept of immanence and transcendence. See Simone de Beauvoir, *The Second Sex* (New York: Vintage Books, 1974).
36 For example, Joseph Highmore illustrated *Pamela* in twelve paintings produced one scene from *Clarissa* 1745–47 which were circulated as prints. On this point see Thomas Keymer and Peter Sabor, *'Pamela' in the Marketplace: Literary Controversy and Print Culture in Eighteenth-Century Britain and Ireland* (Cambridge: Cambridge University Press, 2005), p. 222.
37 There is a broad literature on William Hogarth's picture cycles see for instance Ronald Paulson, *Hogarth's Graphic Works*, 3rd edn (London: The Print Room, 1989) and *Hogarth*, 3 vols (New Brunswick: Rutgers University Press, 1991–93).
38 See, for instance, Dana Arnold, *Architecture and Ekphrasis: Space, Time and the Embodied Description of the Past* (Manchester: Manchester University Press, 2020)
39 Also known as *Le proporzioni del corpo umano secondo Vitruvio* (The proportions of the human body according to Vitruvius), is a pen and ink drawing by Leonardo da Vinci from around 1490.
40 Vitruvius, *The Ten Books on Architecture*, trans. Morris Hickey Morgan (New York: Dover, 1960), Book III, chapter I, paragraph 2–3, pp. 72–73.
41 Cecil Grayson, 'L.B. Alberti's "Costruzione Legittima"', *Italian Studies*, 19, no. 1 (1964), pp. 14–27 explores the differences between the Italian and Latin versions of the text and issues of translation. See also a response to Grayson by Samuel Y. Edgerton Jr., 'Alberti's Perspective: A New Discovery and a New Evaluation', *The Art Bulletin*, 48, no. 3–4 (1966), pp. 367–78.
42 A braccio is a Florentine unit of measurement equal to one third of the height of a man, (taken to be approximately 23 inches or 58.4 cm).
43 Albrecht Dürer, *The Painter's Manual: A Manual of Measurement of Lines, Areas, and Solids by Means of Compass and Ruler Assembled by Albrecht Dürer for the Use of All Lovers of Art with Appropriate Illustrations Arranged to be Printed in the Year MDXXV*, 2nd edn [1538], trans. Walter L. Strauss (New York: Abaris, 1977).

44 Joan W. Scott, 'Gender: A Useful Category of Historical Analysis', *The American Historical Review*, 91, no. 5 (Dec., 1986), pp. 1053–75.

45 William Hogarth, *The Analysis of Beauty* (London. Printed by John Reeves for the Author, 1753) chapter VII, Of Lines, p. 38.

46 Ibid., chapter V, 'Of Intricacy', p. 25.

47 Ibid., chapter VII, 'Of Lines', p. 37; William Hogarth, *The Analysis of Beauty: With the Rejected Passages from the Manuscript Drafts and Autobiographical Notes*, ed. Joseph Burke (Oxford: Clarendon Press, 1955), p. 206 and p. 231.

48 Gilles Deleuze and Claire Parnet, *Dialogues* (Paris: Flammarion, 1977) and trans. Hugh Tomlinson and Barbara Habberjarn (London: Athlone, 1987), p. 40.

49 Lia Markey, 'The Female Printmaker and the Culture of the Reproductive Print Workshop', in *Paper Museums: The Reproductive Print in Europe, 1500–1800*, eds. Rebecca Zorach and Elizabeth Rodini (Chicago: David and Alfred Smart Museum of Art, University of Chicago, 2005), pp. 51–73.

50 Antony Griffiths, *The Print before Photography: An Introduction to European Printmaking, 1550–1820* (London: The British Museum Press, 2016), p. 21 and Tim Clayton, *The English Print 1688–1802* (New Haven and London: Yale University Press, 1997).

51 Engravers could use a mirror to transfer the image to the plate. On this point see Griffiths, loc.cit.

52 The physical processes of printing are described in detail in Carl Goldstein, *Print Culture in Early Modern France: Abraham Bosse and the Purposes of Print* (Cambridge: Cambridge University Press, 2012), p. 22 esp.

53 Lia Markey, op.cit., as note 49.

54 Griffiths, loc.cit. See also William M. Ivins, Jr., *Prints and Visual Communication* (Cambridge, Massachusetts: MIT, 1969).

55 Christine de Pizan op.cit., as note 1, Part III, ch. 1, p. 107.

56 Dana Arnold, *Reading Architectural History* (London and New York: Routledge, 2002), ch. 6, 'Reading Architectural Herstories: The Discourses of Gender', pp. 199–211.

57 Dana Arnold, *British Architecture: A Very Short Introduction* (Oxford: Oxford University Press, 2024).

58 S. Hall, 'Cultural Identity and Diaspora', in *Colonial Discourse and Postcolonial Theory*, eds. P. Williams and L. Chrisman (London and New York: Routledge, 1994), pp. 392–403, p. 394.

59 This appeared in 1982 in a comic strip *Fred and Ernest* by Robert Thaves.

60 *The Meditations of Marcus Aurelius*, Book VII, paragraph 61, trans. Jeremy Collier, revised by Alice Zimmern (London: George Routledge, 1894), p. 117.

3

MAUDE & ME[1]

Annmarie Adams

I'm a sixty-four-year-old woman living in Montreal, Canada. For more than thirty years, I've taught architectural history at the School of Architecture at McGill University. For four years, I served as its first woman Director, as well as the first to have a Ph.D. Since 2016, I've had a half-appointment in the Department of Social Studies of Medicine, where I get to teach medical students about architecture. At the moment, I am writing a spatial biography of a relatively famous woman physician, Maude Abbott, who died in 1940. Abbott is known for her work on congenital cardiac disease and also as a trailblazer in the world of medical museums. In my purposefully feminist book project, I engage the history of architecture and its tools by telling Abbott's life story through ten spaces she occupied. The existing Abbott biographies, by contrast, are all about the barriers she faced as a woman physician. This is a grand narrative familiar to many of us who have worked on women architects. For example, biographers note that Abbott had no admitting privileges in a hospital, so she had to manage a museum (Figure 3.1). A very famous male doctor, William Osler, praised her work, so it got published, they say. One particularly irksome thing about the existing biographies is that the authors frequently refer to Abbott by her first name, or even the diminutive 'Maudie', while male physicians are called by their surnames and sometimes even Dr. So-and-so. I am attempting to provide a fresh perspective: to produce a new narrative of a female subject by focusing on space and granting her some agency (and respect).

The range of ten spaces I survey is wide in terms of scale. The list includes several whole buildings, a museum interior, a birthday party, a scrapbook, and even a letter. It is, as they say (and I sometimes worry), 'a stretch' from traditional architectural history. There are no architects in my story and very few famous buildings. Abbott wasn't even interested in architecture, as far as I can tell. For most of her life, she occupied the rural village house where she and her sister Alice had grown up with their grandmother, Frances Mary Smith Abbott (sometimes referred to as Mrs. William Abbott), 100 kilometres from where she worked. She sometimes rented apartments here and there, in Montreal but also in Philadelphia, where she lived and worked for two years in the early 1920s. An avid diarist, she rarely mentioned her homes, workplaces, or any other buildings. She mostly notes who she saw on any given day; sometimes the weather; sometimes what she ate or her health; always whether she got a 'hair wave'. When she

DOI: 10.4324/9781003224662-5

FIGURE 3.1 Maude Abbott Medical Museum, McGill University, Montreal. Photograph by Annmarie Adams.

travelled, though, mostly in Europe, Abbott would sometimes refer to famous places she visited. On May 13, 1932, for example, she visited the Parthenon in Athens: 'spent a heavenly two hours climbing about & over it & seeing those wonderful pillars & arches'. That's as architectural as she gets.

The challenge in writing about Abbott is not a dearth of archives. Rather it's that the same old things are repeated in every publication. I believe this is because she wrote a thirty-six-page (handwritten) autobiographical essay in 1928 that was subsequently published in 1959. That's what everybody used. In the ensuing decades, a series of books and articles came out almost exclusively written by physician-historians which basically 'contextualize' Abbott's own narrative. One such book was published a year after she died. The author admitted on the first page: 'her own autobiographical sketch . . . has also been of great aid'.[2] Very few of these authors did original archival research and if so, they relied almost exclusively on material in Montreal collections.

While my focuses are spaces, I am also interested in her social world, so I devised a method I call 'friendship archaeology' to get at her relations with other doctors (including some who wrote about her) and to architectural and urban space. It is archaeological in the sense that I dig deeply at particular events and locations, looking for evidence of Abbott's biographical traces. According to the *Oxford English Dictionary*, 'traces' are 'vestiges or marks remaining and indicating the former presence, existence, or action of something; *singular* a vestige, an indication'. I'm testing what architecture can *indicate* about a life story. This approach accomplishes a couple of things. It destabilizes the accounts of how her life was mostly shaped by others.[3] It also, I think, provides a more authentic account of Abbott's career.

In addition to 'friendship archaeology', I engage feminist, user-based approaches to architecture to analyse specific settings. This means assessing the design of places Abbott occupied from her perspective (as an individual, a doctor, a museum expert, a woman). The purpose-built design of the medical museum she managed, for example, indicates its importance at the university in 1909. The renovated home of William and Grace Osler in Oxford, 'The Open Arms', indicates a powerful culture of medical 'hospitality' to which she contributed. Abbott recuperated there in the spring of 1911. When the spaces are less strictly 'architectural', my approach is informed by methods in material culture studies. I trace the spatial trajectory of one famous museum specimen, for example, from an autopsy and its ever-changing place in the ever-changing museum, to its popularity on social media today. Several sections of the book look at images of Abbott by famous and less famous artists, noting their provenance but also their sporadic invisibility. The book wraps up with an exploration of the understudied Abbott's work as an editor and historian.

A consequence of my methodology, then, is the opportunity to read medical, social, and personal (in other words, non-architectural) archives from an architectural perspective, to illuminate the experience of space. For example, I've mapped the location of Abbott's correspondents; I've located everyday spaces (like hotel rooms and restaurants) she occupied. Even phantom buildings are of interest, for example, I have stood in the now-empty lot where her Philadelphia abode once stood. I have a list of every 'place' mentioned in the diaries, whether or not they are extant, plus those commonly linked to the people she meets. The experience of research helps me to understand Abbott's experience. The resulting narrative is much more episodic than the standard accounts of her life and work, which tend to focus on her medical accomplishments and the hardships she faced. The division of her life into ten, too, is inspired by the way she organized the medical museum as decimal-based knowledge system.

At a recent roundtable event where the authors of this volume shared our in-process observations, editor Dana Arnold reminded us:

> "Rereading Women" aims to broaden the discourses of architectural history to explore how the potentially "unnatural rule" of women subverts canonical norms through the empowerment of otherness rather than a process of perceived emasculation. . . The common strand is the porosity of the discipline and how women can renegotiate its foundational boundaries to encompass a broad field of methodological and theoretical plurality.[4]

This simultaneous porosity and expansion are exactly what I want to achieve for architectural history in the Abbott book. As an architectural historian, I want to subvert the canonical norms by *biographizing* it; and at the same time, I am attempting to *architecturalize* a biography, to read a life through three-dimensional spaces.

Biography is new to me. Most days I feel like I have no clue what I'm doing. I'm even less familiar with autoethnography, which is a mode that foregrounds a writer's subjectivity.[5] I'm thus somewhat comforted by feminist sociologist Elizabeth Ettorre's insistence that: 'autoethnographers look back and forth "through an ethnographic wide-angle lens, focusing outward on cultural aspects of personal experience; then inward, exposing a vulnerable self"'.[6] In this essay, I try to tease out how I have arrived at the Abbott project and others through my own biographical arc, through reading, learning, teaching and living (in Montreal). Trained as both an architect and an architectural historian, I have always suppressed my own relationship to my subjects.[7] What happens when we let go of that urge to be neutral and distant from a subject? That is why it's called Maude & Me. There I am, vulnerable me, even in the title.

Reading

My particular concept of spatial biography is very much inspired by Dana Arnold's proposition in the introduction of the co-edited (with Joanna Sofaer Derevenski) 2008 collection, *Biographies and Space*, where she says that women's biography and space are in dynamic interplay. In the book, Arnold recounts powerful anecdotes of how the personal effects, books, and even half-gone cleaning supplies of other researchers prompted her to explore the performative qualities of the built environments she herself occupied and to wonder 'conversely what kinds of performative identities can be imposed on bodies by the spaces that enclose them'.[8] The story that really stuck with me was how Arnold had found a pair of clean grey socks in the wardrobe of her King's College apartment, which had previously been occupied by cultural critic Edward Said, and how that made her think about the space differently. The socks were a powerful, material reminder of how spaces are haunted by material traces:

> The spatial location of everyday objects together with a narrative that could place them at a certain point in time made these socks potentially culturally significant in providing a biographical trace of Said. Indeed, during his stay at King's, Said wrote a new preface to the edition of Orientalism published in 2003. Had this been drafted at the desk where I worked, and was he wearing these very socks to keep his feet warm?[9]

Arnold's proposition for new work on biography and space was clearly gendered. What really excited me about it was how she engaged her own occupation of space to get at the questions, blurring biography and autobiography. We all know that despite women's long and close connection to material artefacts, we are relatively under-represented in archives, museums, and libraries. An archive which I often use at my university, for example, has only two collections from women, while they boast hundreds from men. Another archive in which I worked as a student was similar, though their women's collections were of super famous women. The glaring absence of information on women architects and their buildings is well known among architectural historians; the information on women users of buildings is even more difficult to find. Taking up Arnold's challenge to look at spaces as biographical traces including the autobiographical occupation of the researcher thus adds a powerful and under-used primary source to the short list of how we can get at women's life stories, far beyond women architects (and doctors). Of all women. All of us.

Long before I read Arnold, three other works had already profoundly inspired me. The author of one has strong personal ties and led me to the other. Abigail Van Slyck's book review of four books on women architects, written in the now-defunct *Design Book Review* (DBR) in 1992, got me started. Abby is a close personal friend and was a few years ahead of me in graduate school in the 1980s. Each of the four books she reviewed focused on one famous woman architect: Theodate Pope Riddle, Mary Colter, Eleanor Raymond, and Julia Morgan. In her thoughtful assessment, Van Slyck called for a new type of biography that could embrace women architects' actual experiences, rather than trying to fit them in a masculinist arc. She also invoked Carolyn Heilbrun's 1988 *Writing a Woman's Life*, where Heilbrun had insisted that traditional biography doesn't work as a framework for most women's lives. Abby's compelling review sent me directly to Heilbrun and made me rethink much of my own work on women architects, which was ongoing in the early 1990s. It especially made me avoid biographical approaches to the subject, despite pressure from publishers, colleagues, and many woman architects. Before 1992 I had only known of Heilbrun through her feminist mystery novels written under the *nom de plume*, Amanda Cross. I later learned about how Heilbrun's identity as Cross allowed her to track the sexism and ageism she witnessed in the English department at Columbia University, which interestingly implicated Edward Said.[10] In all honesty I think I was very affected at that time, too, by having joined a school of architecture with no other women professors, a situation which persisted until 2012 (that is for twenty-two years I was the sole woman). In the early years, this inspired me to seek out women colleagues in other departments, especially in the Faculty of Arts, where feminist research methods were already well entrenched.[11] This was not as extreme an example as Heilbrun's parallel track as Amanda Cross, but in any case it was a way for me to build a 'second life' in terms of research production.

Back to the future. More officially, the Abbott book project has also been inspired by three recent 'biographical' and relatively non-academic books. *The Real Jane Austen: A Life in Small Things* (2013) by Paula Byrne; Martha Ackermann, *These Fevered Days: Ten Pivotal Moments in the Making of Emily Dickinson* (2020); and *Square Haunting* (2020), by Francesca Wade. What these three authors taught me is the power of the zoom. Byrne's book on Austen zooms into the British author's work through ten seemingly everyday artefacts, with next to no links among the things themselves or sections of the book. Ackermann writes in the introduction about the power of teaching courses on Dickinson in the house itself. Perhaps the most spatial of the three, Wade's book looks at a single place in London, Mecklenburgh Square, whose edges were sequentially occupied by five women authors. She shows how women of different generations have inhabited urban and domestic spaces in a kind of layered way, and how the same space might mean something completely different to another person. Most importantly, Wade links women's autonomy, in this case as authors, to the occupation of space and also writes about her own engagement with the square today.

Ackermann's book is the most episodic of the three with a focus on time. She 'peoples the poet's world'[12] through ten transformative days. The book is arranged around times or moments, rather than on things like Byrne or spaces like Wade (or spaces like mine). Nonetheless, architecture figures largely in Ackermann's account, especially the Dickinson's own house in Amherst, Massachusetts. All three books produce alternative, experiential narratives that complement existing accounts. They are popular, widely read biographies, rather than books written for academic libraries. Most significantly, especially by focusing on things and spaces, I think, they humanize and perhaps feminize their subjects, in each case liberating them from the traditional, masculinist arc of biography and sometimes acknowledging the subjectivity of the authors.

Just as these authors have produced alternative biographies for life stories we thought we knew, my intention is likewise to counter the existing historiography of my subject. The handful of existing biographies of Abbott are textbook illustrations of a genre [books on women doctors/scientists] that needs feminist critique.[13] Echoing Heilbrun's insights, nearly all of them try to fit Abbott's unconventional life and career into this traditional, biographical arc inspired by men's life stories. Birth, childhood, education, career, success, and death. In order to achieve the fit, past biographers have focused on Abbott's struggle, on what she couldn't do, rather than on her accomplishments. She was raised by her maternal grandmother, whose surname she took, because her mother died and her father fled Canada, after being accused of murder. She attended Bishop's Medical School, not McGill University where she had studied Arts, because she had been rejected on account of her gender. She never married and took care of her unwell sister, Alice, until her death in 1934.[14] Her extraordinary medical achievements were only appreciated later – McGill gave her the MDCM degree *honoris causa* in 1910. These are all recurring themes in even the shortest biographical entries on Abbott's life. University historian Stanley Frost engaged an apt architectural metaphor in emphasizing the barriers she faced, calling her rejection from medical school and other difficulties, 'closed doors'.[15]

Is a biography of open doors useful or interesting? Yes.

Learning

I married social historian Peter Gossage in 1995, whose work on the history of family and home continues to inspire my work. When we became parents in the summer of 1996, I had already researched childbirth and its relation to home. Abby calls it my 'womb-room' work. In the early 1990s, I had written a dissertation on British women, houses, and health, that a few years later became the book *Architecture in the Family Way*.[16] In the thesis and the book I argued that middle-class women in the late nineteenth century learned about health and illness through domestic architecture. I wrote the fourth chapter first, about childbirth at home, which provided the title for the book, and something of a template for other sections. The work was almost solely based on prescriptive sources, a fact which has haunted me during the subsequent decades. The texts I used for evidence, for example, told women how to be ideal mothers or how to fix plumbing, with no proof whatsoever that they did so (Figure 3.2). It also showcased buildings designed by doctors. As I was finishing up, I got to curate the dissertation research as a small exhibition at the Canadian Centre for Architecture, Corpus Sanum in Domo Sano, which I think really pressed me to strengthen the arguments with material evidence.[17] Needless to say, I also learned how to curate an architectural exhibition.

For both my professional education as an architect and subsequent Ph.D. in architectural history, I studied at the University of California at Berkeley. It was 1982 and I was attracted to the idea of Berkeley's so-called Option III program, which accepted students into a professional Master's program who had studied other subjects as undergraduates, since I had studied art history. I finished my M.Arch. in 1985 and was lucky enough to win a travel award, the so-called John K. Branner Fellowship, which allowed me to travel for nine months with two of my classmates, Melissa Harris and Cathy Schwabe, and experience a wide range of buildings from Leningrad to Barcelona.[18] During our Branner year, we made a point of drawing everything we saw; plus I took thousands of Kodachrome slides that became the basis of my teaching slide collection. Before departing on the transformative trip, however, I had learned about the value of experiencing architecture in person from studio instructors like Joe Esherick, Richard Peters, and Marc Treib. Horst Rittel and Christopher Alexander were there too, revolutionizing architectural theory. When I returned from the year away, I entered the Ph.D. program under the

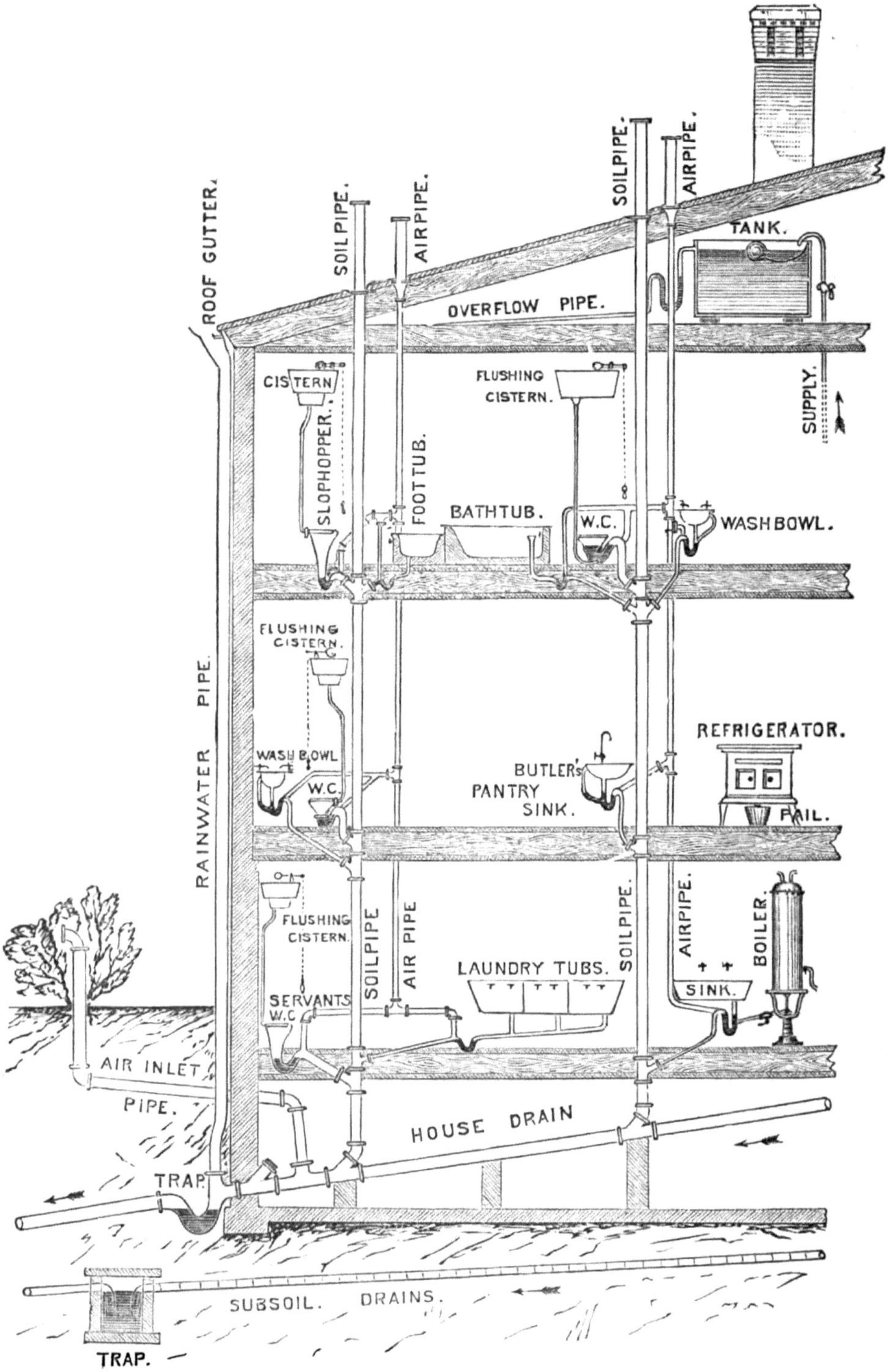

FIGURE 3.2 "A properly plumbed house – Woman's sphere" from H.M. Plunkett, *Women, Plumbers, and Doctors: Or, Household Sanitation*, New York: D. Appleton, 1893, 112.

supervision of architectural historian Dell Upton, a young Americanist and a pioneer in the field of the study of everyday places. Other Berkeley historians also had a profound impact on me in the Ph.D. program, including the late Paul Groth, who like Upton studied cultural landscapes; art historian Margaretta Lovell, who sees art and architecture as visual history; and feminist Mary Ryan in the history department, who let me (and Abby) sit in on her classes. The lectures of architectural historian Spiro Kostof captivated us all and made teaching world architectural history look easy. The other students in the Ph.D. program taught me more than they know and many of us have stayed close. It was a good time to be at Berkeley.

Even though she was long gone from the concrete corridors of Wurster Hall, I was also inspired by the work of Gwendolyn Wright, who had graduated in 1978, eight years before I even started my Ph.D. Wright had worked on American women and houses. But decisions about my research focus were also subject to other, uncontrollable influences. In 1989, when I travelled to London to undertake the archival work for my Ph.D. dissertation, my project had no medical or health angle whatsoever. What I planned to do was a sort of British version of Wright's *Moralism and the Model Home*, the book eventually published in 1980 from her earlier thesis. My original dissertation proposal even had a similarly 'moral' tone. It was entitled 'The Angel in the House' invoking Coventry Patmore's 1854 poem.

Like many Ph.D. projects, however, it changed focus in the process. Much to my surprise (and horror), the Royal Institute of British Architects (RIBA) Library was unexpectedly closed for renovations when I arrived to do my fieldwork in the summer of 1989. It seems unfathomable today, but this was before the internet age so we were far less aware of changing circumstances when we planned travel. Faced with a closed library, the promise of a tenure-track job at McGill University that would start in six months, and supported by funding from the Social Sciences and Humanities Research Council (SSHRC) for my time away, postponing the archival work was simply not an option. Somebody (I wish I could remember who) suggested that I go to the nearby Wellcome Institute for the History of Medicine [WIHM] instead, because its extraordinary library included a wide range of books on houses. I distinctly remember being told these books about houses were 'funny', by which I don't think they meant humorous. Because many of those funny books, and the researchers I subsequently met at the Wellcome, were entrenched in the history of medicine, the health angle of my work started to grow and eventually became the central theme of the dissertation. I mention this because it illustrates how circumstances (and one might even argue spatial circumstances) beyond our control can completely change a research trajectory. I often think of how the closure of the RIBA Library, which at first glance might have been a problem or barrier, actually enhanced my dissertation and my subsequent degree to a great extent.

In addition to my dissertation, a second transformative publication, also first written when I was a graduate student at the University of California at Berkeley, was an essay on a post-war suburban house in California designed by the real estate developer Joseph Eichler. I wrote the paper as a lecture for a course I was TA-ing in the History of Art department (the instructor was Lovell) on the history of American homes. Having taken the course myself as a student, I was hyper aware of the high standards set by previous Teaching Assistants, especially with regard to the expectation that we would present original material. In the lecture (and its subsequent publication in *Perspectives in Vernacular Architecture*),[19] I argued that the modern suburban house prescribed a particular lifestyle for women and children, but that real traces showed that the family lived quite differently. In a nutshell, I demonstrated how the house registered women's resistance to modernism. My extraordinary access to the house and its occupants was key to my methodology (this privilege would prove crucial to later work on hospitals, notoriously difficult to access). The daughter in the family who owned the Eichler house was the sister-in-law of one of my Masters classmates. She is Gail Clarkson in the publication, but her real name is Gail Bateson. She had grown up in the house and her parents still lived there in the early 1980s, when I prepared the original lecture. The Eichler paper was about a different context and time period (American and post-World War II) than my dissertation (British and late nineteenth century), but in retrospect they addressed similar questions via different methodologies.

In the many years between my time as a Berkeley student and my current book project on Abbott – what Arnold might call a 'ruptured temporal continuity'[20] – I have written dozens of papers on houses, mostly through themes of cultural landscapes, gender expectations, and/or medical theories. The subjects and time periods vary but they all deal with these same questions of prescription, evidence, and agency. Like the early work on the Eichler house, focusing on one building or one family, even if the house type is ubiquitous, has often allowed me to really concentrate on how individuals interacted with their space at a minute scale. I could find their traces. In every instance I insisted on spending significant time in each house. Sometimes the nature of my access to the house became part of the story. Sometimes I felt ill-equipped to assess a house, so I co-authored with experts in other fields, such as social history, women's history, and even medical specialists, such as paediatrics or tuberculosis.

Teaching

The entanglement of my life and my work and its relation to (feminist) architectural history is at the core of the first-year architectural history course I teach at McGill, currently called ARCH 251: Architecture Since 1960. I have taught this course in one form or another since 1990, yet it has only recently dawned on me that I was born the year the course begins. The course thus covers the architecture that I've witnessed, so to speak. In the introductory lecture, which I try to improve every year, I model how we can study five decades of history through a long list of themes. I always start by showing Thomas Cole's 1840 painting, 'The Architect's Dream', and discuss how the past has been variously explained by key textbook authors such as Banister Fletcher, Sigfried Giedion, and Spiro Kostof, to name a few. For me, Cole's painting is the ideal illustration of how history is a construction, with its magnificent green curtain framing a set of curated and canonical buildings, as in a theatre. I showcase my own interest in ordinary buildings, gender, race, social class, and even medicine through a series of slide pairs. I think even in that first hour of the class students come to understand how my Berkeley education, with its emphasis on the social history of architecture, rather than the work of 'genius' architects, shapes my worldview and by implication the course they are about to take.

After the introductory lecture, we explore the Chicago World's Fair and Chicago skyscrapers (even though they are so much earlier, another temporal rupture), but then jump immediately to the Eichler house, but in this second lecture I juxtapose it with Philip Johnson's glass house (of course inspired by Alice Friedman's work on how it housed Johnson's gay identity).[21] By the time we get to Brutalism, I can't resist showing Wurster Hall, the UC Berkeley architecture building, alongside Boston City Hall, Yale Art and Architecture, and a host of North American university libraries. Every lecture illustrates how some histories are hidden, with an imperative to recover them. Also in every lecture I insist on using my own photographs, to reinforce the subjectivity of architectural photography. I learned this from Dell Upton, who additionally also measured and drew the buildings he studied. Using my own photos, and identifying them as such, gives

FIGURE 3.3 Photograph from ARCH 711 at the CCA. Photograph by Annmarie Adams.

students a double historical layer, the historical context of the architecture we are studying plus the historical/life context in which I took the photos. Sometimes a photograph reveals what I initially thought about a building (or how it once looked) and others might illustrate how it looks now. Nearly every photo includes people and communicate to students the importance of visiting real buildings, not just studying them in classrooms, books, and online. Many of the photos I use in the course are scans of Kodachrome slides I took during my Branner year of travelling in 1985–86. The long-time Teaching Assistant for ARCH 251, Cigdem Talu, says that

> the fact that each lecture has a very specific and well-composed argument is not only because you've been teaching that class for a long time and honed the arguments, but because those arguments are completely embedded in and enforced by your own lived experience.

Needless to say, I always invite Teaching Assistants to give a lecture.

In Fall 2019, I got to teach a seminar to incoming and second-year Ph.D. students – we call the course ARCH 711 – and I chose the theme of *Architecture as Biography*. In order to emphasize the role of primary sources in research, and to test some of the ideas floating around my head from Arnold and others at that time, I arranged to hold the course in the magnificent library of the Canadian Centre for Architecture (Figure 3.3). Each week we'd read secondary sources on biography and try and link them to a tableful of extraordinary models, photographs, and/or drawings that the archivists would display just for us. Unsurprisingly, Arnold's was the first reading I assigned, but we also consumed other favourite authors, especially those who had linked domestic architecture to social values, such as Katarina Bonnevier, Alice Friedman, Diana Fuss, Jane Rendall, Despina Stratigakos, Dell Upton, and others. During the semester I was also working on a famous Art Deco house and its garden, trying to understand it as a feminist landscape, so thc whole package – provocative syllabus, extraordinary setting, primary sources, open-minded students –allowed me to advance my thinking on biography.[22]

One thing we quickly learned in ARCH 711 was that other fields are way ahead of architectural history on feminizing or even modernizing biography. Literary critics long ago noted how feminist biographers often use alternative sources such as photography and material culture to compensate for the dearth of traditional textual sources as bearers of women's history and make creative use of fragments in constructing life stories. Traces and fragments. Since spatial traces often come from disparate places, they are by nature fragmentary. Spatial fragments are ubiquitous and are located outside these mainstream, institutional collections. As such they offer additional viewpoints, which may be illegible or contrary to the data from written or curated

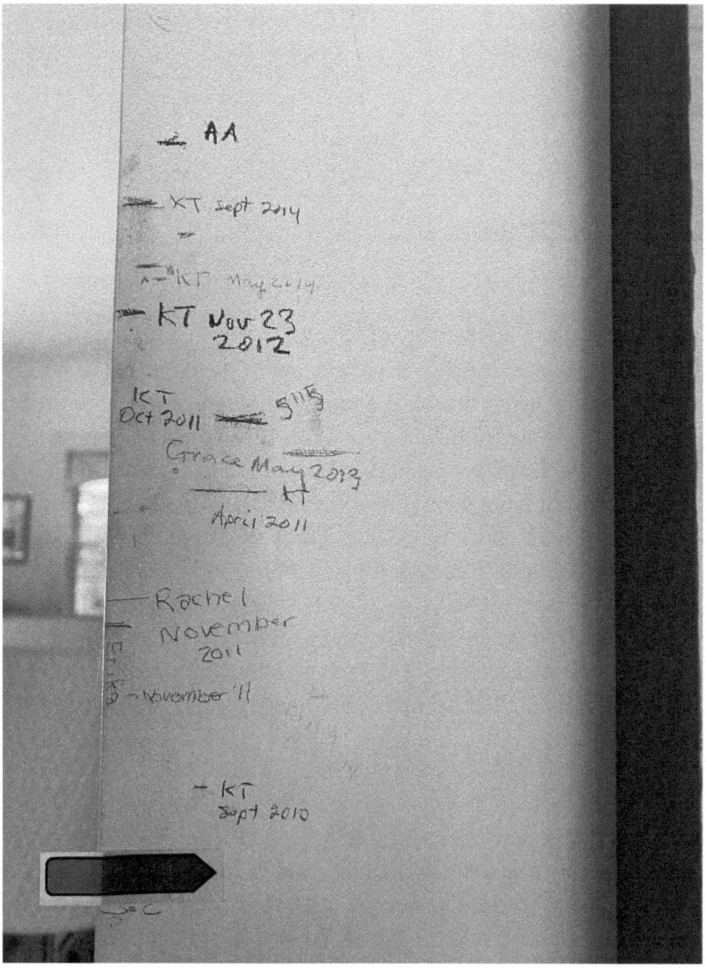

FIGURE 3.4 Knowlton kitchen. Photograph by Annmarie Adams.

sources. Sometimes I think about biographical traces in my own homes, such as the column of pencil marks on the kitchen wall where we've documented the changing heights of our growing children (Figure 3.4). Apparently when people sell houses, they sometimes insist on taking such growth charts with them, making them fragments I suppose. Elizabeth Ettorre says: '[autoethnography] locates research experience in the changing ebb of emotional life'.[23] I felt like I was getting somewhere.

Living

Almost every day, I traverse the Montreal spaces that Maude Abbott knew. I teach in university classrooms that kept her out. As one of McGill's earliest women students, her whereabouts were highly restricted. A splendid amphitheatre in the university's natural history museum, The Redpath Museum, has preserved carved graffiti (Figure 3.5) from early students, possibly including women who were known as Donaldas. This unusual nickname comes from Donald Smith, later known as Lord Strathcona, who gave the university money on the condition that it would provide women students with the same quality education as men. Strathcona also founded Royal Victoria College (RVC) for women, a significant purpose-built residence designed by American architect Bruce Price. In 1978, as a first-year undergraduate student at McGill, I lived at RVC, knowing nothing of Donaldas let alone Maude Abbott.

Abbott's beloved medical specimens are now a museum, which I often visit and have helped to refurbish. Today the Maude Abbott Medical Museum is back in the Strathcona Medical Building, but for decades it was in closets, and corridors, and wherever pathologist Rick Fraser could find room for it. Even during Abbott's lifetime, the museum moved often. Before Abbott was named curator in 1899, it was in McGill's original medical building, called Old Medical and destroyed by fire in 1907. Its next iteration was in the Strathcona Medical Building, its current home, named for the same man who opened the doors for women students at the university. In 1924, it moved to a purpose-built space in the new Pathology Institute, designed by architects Percy Nobbs and George Hyde. About this same time, however, Abbott moved to Philadelphia for two years and pathologist Horst Oertel began to nudge her out of the position as curator. I've studied both these buildings from multiple perspectives. Just this past winter I got to teach ARCH 251 in the Strathcona Building, just as we were inching back from COVID restrictions. It felt uncanny.

The McGill Faculty Club has a complicated history with regards to Abbott and women in general. German sugar tycoon Baron Alfred Baumgarten built it in 1886 with special features, such as a ballroom, to showcase his daughters. Now two traces point to Abbott's legacy: an upstairs room is now named for her and a lovely pencil sketch (Figure 3.6) is displayed in the second-floor corridor. These are rather recent points of progress. Even when I was a young professor, the women's washroom at the club said 'Wives' and was far from the main floor, where most of us met. Now the Faculty Club boasts Maude Abbott as its first woman member. Other business clubs near the university did not accept women members until the 1980s, although Abbott seems to have dined at some as a visitor in the 1930s. As a single, professional woman with long hours and a long commute home, Abbott frequently ate out. She mentions eating in the Faculty Club, and also reveals it as a site for meetings, for 'tea', and for playing bridge. Here is a typical Abbott diary entry (Figure 3.7) from 5 June 1939, which mentions the Faculty Club: 'Monday. Dr Rosencrantz arrived from a place near Boston at Mt Royal Hotel. Took her to Osler Library. Lunch with her & WWF at Faculty Club Tea with Harriet. Left for St A at 4.20

FIGURE 3.5 Redpath Museum auditorium carvings. Photograph by Cigdem Talu.

FIGURE 3.6 Framed sketch of Maude Abbott at the Faculty Club, McGill University, Montreal. Photograph by Annmarie Adams.

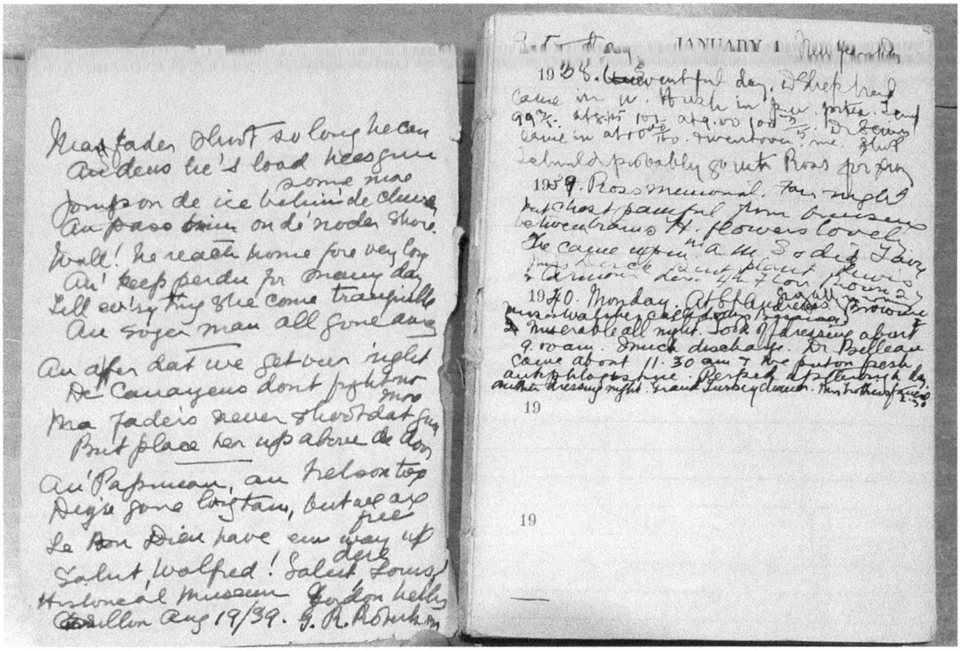

FIGURE 3.7 Diary Page, McGill University Archives, MG1070 Maude Abbott Fonds, Five Year Diary 1938–1940.

standard'. WWF is doctor-librarian William Willoughby Francis and St A is St Andrew's East (now called Saint-André-d'Argenteuil) Quebec. Remarkably, I've never been there.

My final example of a place where Abbott and I overlap is a building that has consumed me for the last three decades. The Royal Victoria Hospital (RVH), an example of the popular nineteenth-century pavilion-plan typology, allegedly kept Abbott out as an admitting physician, yet hundreds of her museum specimens came from there and she herself was treated as a patient at the hospital. The RVH is located just above and between two locations of Abbott's museums, the Strathcona Medical Building and the Pathology Institute, but it predates both by a few decades. The main pavilion was designed by British hospital specialist architect Henry Saxon Snell in 1893.

I started studying the RVH almost exactly a century later, once my dissertation was finished, as a way to test the methodologies I had developed in the thesis at a larger scale. I started out by writing a simple paper on how nurses occupied the massive, pavilion plan building, which was first published in 1994.[24] Little did I know what was ahead. About this same time, five hospitals in Montreal merged and a plan was proposed to abandon all the hospitals and build a new one, named the McGill University Health Centre (MUHC), on a polluted former railway site, some distance from the university. On November 16, 1998, I gave a public lecture to the university's main heritage association where I critiqued this plan, from the perspective of architectural history. The response from those in charge of the project was immediate and ferocious. The head of the movement to merge the hospitals demanded a copy of my notes, which I refused to share. The daily newspaper, the *Montreal Gazette*, wanted to print the lecture in full. Pregnant with our second child and newly tenured, I was hardly in a position to take on the medical establishment,

FIGURE 3.8 Empty ward, Royal Victoria Hospital, Montreal. Photograph by Annmarie Adams.

but somehow I stood firm. I wrote dozens of letters to the editor. I gave interviews. I appeared on live radio arguing against high-level university administrators. Much of what the doctors said about architecture was ludicrous, but in the end the project was approved and the RVH was abandoned in 2015. It has sat empty for seven years. More interesting, perhaps, is that I ended up writing a book about the building and getting an academic chair from the CIHR to study hospitals. Today the empty RVH (Figure 3.8) is still my go-to building for anything I want to further understand about twentieth-century hospital design and I am on the four-person committee of experts for the Quebec government to help decide its fate.

Abbott's relationship to the RVH is similarly political. She rarely mentions it in her diaries, although many of her professional colleagues and friends would have worked there. As noted, Abbott was also an RVH patient in 1939, following an accident whereby she was 'crushed between two railway cars'.[25] Much to my delight, she even records what room she occupied. Here is her diary entry for New Year's Day, 1939: 'Ross memorial. Fair night but chest painful from bruising between trams. H. Flowers lovely. …4th floor Room 27'.

The Ross Memorial Pavilion was also where Maude Abbott's sister Alice had died on 9 October 1934. Here is what she says in her diary:

> Tuesday. My darling Allie died at 10 minutes to 9 at the R.V.H. Ross. I got there half an hour before and held her close but she gave us sigh [sic]– only grew quieter and went very quietly. . . . She looked so beautiful beyond words. Mrs Lamb helping. Flowers came from [Miss] F.

The Ross Memorial Pavilion at the Royal Victoria Hospital is Canada's first private patients' pavilion and a building I now know well. Its architecture and that of its close neighbour, the so-called Women's Pavilion, were designed by the same architectural firm: Stevens & Lee. These buildings form the core of my book, *Medicine by Design,* published in 2008. During my political battles over the future of the Royal Vic, I gave birth there twice, in 1996 and 1999. Beyond becoming a mother, these were extraordinary experiences, especially to recover in the Women's Pavilion, a building I had so closely studied. The reviews of *Architecture in the Family Way* came out while I was in the hospital with our first child. You can't make this stuff up!

Here is the *coup de grâce*. Zoom ahead exactly twenty years and in 2016 I accepted an invitation to become Chair of McGill's Department of Social Studies of Medicine, a unit I had long admired. My new corner office, as it turned out, would be in the guest room of the JKL Ross house, a stunning neo-classical pavilion designed in 1909 for the family who had endowed the Ross Memorial Pavilion at the Royal Victoria. The architects? The Maxwell brothers, the same firm that designed the Hersey Pavilion, the nurses' residence that first brought me to study the RVH. Although I had no doubts whatsoever about taking the job, the location of the office clinched the deal. The Ross family had lost their fortune on lavish spending, philanthropy, and race horses, which was now my gain.

Conclusion

My life and my research are entangled. In this essay, I have outlined how my current work on the Abbott project is shaped by my own biographical arc, through reading, learning, teaching, and living. Readings by Dana Arnold, Carolyn Heilbrun, Abigail Van Slyck, and a host of new books frame my current research; my own Ph.D. dissertation and the teachers who supported it continue to shape my approach to the field, including close friends and some I've never met. Certain papers, too, have stayed with me for many years, and continue to fuel the questions I ask. Teaching both architecture and medical students has offered opportunities (often subconsciously) to expound on the material, including the use of my own photographs and experience as factors. Finally, traversing the same spaces as my subject/s, decades or even a century later, has been crucial to my process. My conclusion is that the research unfolds in the places I occupy and that this occupation matters. Acknowledging and embracing such overlaps feels liberating, after decades of suppressing a relationship to my subjects.

Notes

1 Thanks to Cigdem Talu for assistance and inspiration.
2 H.E. MacDermot, *Maude Abbott: A Memoir* (Toronto: Macmillan, 1941), v.
3 Annmarie Adams, "Encountering Maude Abbott," *Feminist Encounters: A Journal of Critical Studies in Culture and Politics* 2, nos. 2, 21 (2018), 15.

4 Dana Arnold, Nancy Stieber, and Clare Barry, "Rereading Women and Architecture Roundtable: Introduction and Response," Email, 2022.
5 My main guide has been Elizabeth Ettorre, "Introduction: Autoethnography as Feminist Method," in *Autoethnography as Feminist Method: Sensitising the Feminist 'I'* (London: Routledge, 2017), 1–23.
6 Ettorre, "Introduction," 3.
7 An exception is a recent essay inspired by *The Princess Bride*. See Annmarie Adams, "Feeling Penfield," in *Feeling Dis-ease: Experiencing Medicine and Illness in Modern History*, eds. Rob Boddice and Bettina Hitzer (London: Bloomsbury Academic, 2022), 255–72.
8 Dana Arnold, "(Auto)biographies and Space," in *Biographies and Space: Placing the Subject in Art and Architecture,* eds. Dana Arnold and Joanna Sofaer (London: Routledge, 2008), 8.
9 Arnold, "(Auto)biographies and Space," 7–8.
10 Marlowe Benn, "Crime in a Tenured Position: The Feminist Mysteries of Carolyn Heilbrun," *Crime Reads* (17 June 2020), https://crimereads.com/crime-in-a-tenured-position-the-feminist-mysteries-of-carolyn-heilbrun/#.
11 I wrote a bit about this in *Parlour*: https://parlour.org.au/opinion-analysis/remembering-peta-tancred/ (last accessed 30 September 2022).
12 Megan Marshall, 'Reviving Emily Dickinson in 10 Episodes,' *New York Times*, 25 February 2020. https://www.nytimes.com/2020/02/25/books/review/these-fevered-days-martha-ackmann.html (last accessed 30 September 2022).
13 The biographical articles and books considered here include E. Abbott, *All Heart*. Unpublished paper. Osler Library of the History of Medicine (McGill University, 1997); Barbara Brookes, "An Illness in the Family: Dr. Maude Abbott and Her Sister, Alice Abbott," *Canadian Bulletin of Medical History/ Bulletin canadien d'histoire de la médecine* 28, no. 1 (2011); Stanley Frost, "The Abbotts of McGill," *McGill Journal of Education* 13, no. 3 (1978); Margaret Gillett, "The Lonely Heart: Maude E. Abbott, 1869–1940," in *Lone Voyagers: Academic Women in Coeducational Universities*, 1870–1937, ed. G. J. Clifford (New York: The Feminist Press, 1989) and Gillett, Margaret, "The Heart of the Matter," in *Despite the Odds: Essays on Canadian Women and Science*, ed. M. Gosztonyi Ainley (Montreal: Véhicule Press, 1990); MacDermot, *Maude Abbott*; Claire Rothman, *The Heart Specialist* (Toronto: Cormorant, 2009); Douglas Waugh, *Maudie of McGill: Dr Maude Abbott and the Foundations of Heart Surgery* (Toronto: Dundurn Press, 1992); as well as Abbott's own autobiographical notes from 1928.
14 Brookes, "An Illness in the Family," 173.
15 Frost, "Abbotts of McGill," 266.
16 Annmarie Adams, *Architecture in the Family Way: Doctors, Houses, and Women, 1870–1900* (Montreal: McGill-Queen's University Press, 1996).
17 Annmarie Adams, "Corpus sanum in domo sano," *CCA*, 2020. https://www.cca.qc.ca/en/articles/issues/23/take-care/40168/corpus-sanum-in-domo-sano (last accessed 30 September 2022).
18 Annmarie Adams, Melissa Harris, and Cathy Schwabe, "Travels with Annmarie, Melissa and Cathy," *The Fifth Column* 10, nos. 2/3 (1998), 38–51.
19 Annmarie Adams, "The Eichler Home: Intention and Experience in Postwar Suburbia," in *Gender, Class, and Shelter: Perspectives in Vernacular Architecture V*, eds. Elizabeth Collins Cromley and Carter L. Hudgins (Knoxville: University of Tennessee Press, 1995), 164–78.
20 Arnold, *Biographies and Space*, 8.
21 Alice T. Friedman, *Women and the Making of the Modern House: A Social and Architectural History* (New York: Abrams, 1998), 126–59.
22 This project on the Cormier house garden resulted in Annmarie Adams and Cynthia Hammond, "Marking Time in the Art Deco Garden: A Landscape History of Montreal's Cormier House," https://www.youtube.com/watch?v=MxaclZ6yZ5A (last accessed 30 September 2022).
23 Elizabeth Ettorre, *Autoethnography as Feminist Method: Sensitising the Feminist "I"* (London: Routledge, 2017), 3.
24 Annmarie Adams, "Rooms of Their Own: The Nurses' Residences at Montréal's Royal Victoria Hospital," *Material History Review* 40 (Fall 1994), 29–41.
25 MacDermot, *Maude Abbott,* 233.

4

LOOKING BACK

Small Spaces as Countermapping Architectural History

Swati Chattopadhyay

"We *could have given them a different story*."[1]

Reminiscing

Asked to write an autobiography in his 40s, Rabindranath Tagore (1861–1941) began the first of his memoirs, *Jiban-smriti* (1912), contemplating the nature of reminiscence.[2] When he found the time to "look back" upon his childhood, the past appeared as image-impressions:

> I do not know who paints the pictures on the canvas of memory. Whoever does so, his task is to paint pictures. He does not sit brush in hand to reproduce whatever that happens in front of him. He deletes much and keeps much else in accordance with his own taste. He reduces big events to small episodes and enlarges those that are small. He hesitates not a bit to alter the sequence of events.[3]

In the figure of an invisible painter-agent who selectively retains impressions, Rabindranath invoked the idea of scalar manipulation, only partially as a function of the author's volition. As his own work would prove, a memoir allows one to settle on the small things of everyday life that traditional history writing resists and thus consigns to the realm of either literary fiction or ethnography.[4] Although he remarked that "there is nothing in these memories that deserves to be rendered eternally memorable," Rabindranath was not simply being modest. Attentive to durational limits, it was a mode of releasing the picture-memories from the burden of standing as evidence, of revealing more than they possibly could tell.[5] It also freed him from adhering to the norms of Bengali male autobiographical writing. He could lean on a feminine strain—indulge in the painfully personal, the affect of prosaic domesticity, and the utterly ordinary details of familial relations, without embarrassment or accusations of emotive excess. As material for a biography, he described these impressions trivial—"incomplete and unnecessary."[6] As literary material, he hoped, his recollections would have some merit.

DOI: 10.4324/9781003224662-6

Rabindranath's notion of history was far from naive or reductive. In the heyday of scientific history, he argued for the need to popularize history by injecting it with the magic of good storytelling.[7] Rabindranath's claim that this is not the stuff of history is thus not an academic distinction, but an insistence that imagination (*kalpana*) be given a free rein in reflecting upon one's experience. His memoirs thus may be seen as a way of expressing how he came to acquire this habit of imagination.[8]

As Lorna Martens has argued, before Freudian psychoanalysis took hold of memory theory, particularly the fragmentary and episodic memories of childhood, memoirs held great promise as literary narrative and ways of knowing the past, particularly acts of placemaking. Speaking specifically of childhood memoirs and the importance of things and places in them, Martens writes:

> personal things and places afford solace to those who are disempowered, as children often feel themselves to be. . . . One's places and things afford an imaginative self-extension; they are a hedge against diminution and loss. Memory itself can be seen to fulfill the same function.[9]

Memoirs harbor the possibility of recovering not simply other pasts but other senses of duration and temporality.

Rabindranath's memoirs are exceptionally attuned to small things and spaces and the promise of other temporalities they harbor. Growing up in a household in which children's lives were severely circumscribed within the realm of servants and consigned to marginal spaces, his reminiscence offers approaches with which to apprehend the lives of those who are marginalized in historical accounts. Nevertheless, as a male author celebrated in his own milieu, he did not carry the burden of speaking as a marginalized person about the past and of small things forgotten. In contrast, women writers of the modern era, irrespective of their geographical location, had to craft strategies for asserting the narrative integrity of their memoirs. The burden of writing as a marginalized woman of color was double-fold.[10] In this essay I summon two such autobiographical narratives—Harriet Jacobs's *Incidents in the Life of a Slave Girl* (1861) and Rani Chanda's *Amar Ma'r Baper Bari* (My Mother's Father's House, 1977) to consider the role of small spaces in recollections of the past. Separated by over a century and arising from entirely different contexts and concerns, these memoirs convey exceptional opportunities to consider how certain narrative strategies might usefully introduce countermapping in architectural histories. To countermap is to articulate a set of geographical relations that runs counter to the hegemonic understanding of space.[11]

That I invoke Rabindranath at the outset is a function of my task as a contributor to this volume and also because I am fascinated with memoirs as the stuff of historical writing. As contributors we have been asked to reflect upon our relation to architectural history. For me this task must be attentive to its own temporal imagination—of how a research project figures temporality. If "looking back" is the essential preoccupation of historical writing, we might profit from carefully considering what it means to look back, how it differs given one's subject position, and how we might benefit from considering literary narratives of the past as ways of seeing space from the vantage of the marginalized. The first part of this task—how *I* came to acquire the imagination of architectural history—is relatively easy and can suffer abbreviation, with the hope that it will provide a segue to the remaining essay which constitutes a discussion on the two above-mentioned memoirs.

Small Spaces

I am an architectural historian by accident. As an architect interested in the social formation of the built environment and its historical underpinnings, I began to envision myself as an architectural historian only after arriving at Berkeley to do my doctoral studies. The first semester I chanced upon James Deetz's classic *In Small Things Forgotten: The Archeology of Early American Life* (1977). Jim Deetz (1930–2000) and Burton Benedict (1923–2010) at Berkeley gave me the liberty to take seriously what I had always found fascinating and endearing: everyday objects and places. Two visiting faculty in that first year—Anthony D. King (1931–2022) and Jamie Horwitz with their capacious imagination—made it possible to think through those aspects of our lives and histories that were rarely seen as fit subjects for architectural investigation: from verandahs in colonial houses to shelves in grocery stores. Simultaneously studying the historiography of British colonialism with Thomas Metcalf, I got productively side-tracked with the work of the Subaltern Studies group that was reshaping the parameters of South Asian history. It was also in that first year I read Marcel Proust's *Remembrance of Things Past*—a text that Spiro Kostof (1936–1991) had assigned for the architectural history methods course. While I did not take that class, I was grateful for that introduction. The second year I became acquainted with Dell Upton's approach to everyday landscapes as architectural history; his article "Architectural History or Landscape History?" (1991) published that year was a gamechanger for me.

These early academic impressions remain the touchstones in my thinking about architecture and history. Bringing together these disparate strands of disciplinary endeavors, however, has required locating among them the points of resonance and deciphering a method to make these sensible to the realm of practices that intrigue me: the world of small spaces. These are spaces that do not fall within traditional architectural history and its focus on big events and major historical players. These are lived spaces we don't notice: service spaces, storage spaces, spaces in the basement and attic, spaces such as root cellars, garrets, backstairs, verandahs, courtyards, and terraces—which even when they are large are merely treated as backdrops rather than spaces that deserve analytic focus. They are treated as supplementary to the principal spaces in a building. As adjunct spaces they do not press for attention. Small spaces remain peripheral to our vision. Not surprisingly these are also the spaces where women, servants and the enslaved lived and worked. This is where we find the labor infrastructure that supports everyday life, past and present.[12]

When I started studying colonial buildings in India three decades ago, I realized that adjunct spaces such as verandahs worked as de facto work spaces for servants, and the spatial relation between inside and outside in these buildings admitted a porosity that made it very difficult to adhere to lines of class and race as a measure of the distance between masters and servants.[13] I extensively used journals and memoirs of European women trying to gauge their sense of (dis) comfort in terms of their servants and caretakers. While these documents provide useful nuggets of information about the spatial organization of these buildings, I was drawn to their characterization of social relations—of how apparently insignificant things like distributing dusters among servants or ordering a meal was made into a larger story about health, taste, discipline, racial difference and ultimately about ruling empire. By the same token, such memoirs reveal the fragility of the colonizer's command over space, overwhelmed by their dependence on the labor of the colonized. Here we find the traces of how the disempowered marshaled their scant resources to manipulate space to withstand authority, sometimes challenge it and at other times to make it work toward their own ends. These archival traces help us to imagine ways of viewing and experiencing the landscape that reside outside the dominant spatial script.

In my conceptualization, small spaces are not limited by size, but are a function of their relative social significance and may well extend to those spaces that are dimensionally large but considered beyond civilized occupation: jungles, swamps, and marshes, and spaces deemed unproductive and waste. These spaces associated with and consigned to the historically marginalized, I contend, challenge our preconceptions of authority, agency and social significance. What connects the dimensionally small spaces with the peripheral but extensive spaces such as swamps is how their temporal orders are understood. Defined by unanticipated expansion and contraction of time, such small spaces attenuate time; they are experienced in terms of waiting, watching, servicing time. Their temporal characteristics offer opportunities for producing spatial descriptions that are counter to the dominant script of viewing architecture and landscape.

Escape

Consider Harriet Jacobs's (1813–97) autobiographical work, *Incidents in the Life of a Slave Girl* (1861). As a young enslaved woman trying to flee the sexual predation of a white enslaver, she narrates the many spaces through which she negotiated her escape from the town of Edenton, North Carolina, northward, to Philadelphia, New York, and Boston. When she realized that escape from bondage was the only means of survival for her and her two infant children, she plotted plans of escape with the help of friends, both enslaved and free, white and Black.

Harriet describes her escape as a movement from one hiding space to another: in storage spaces as well as the dangerous space of the swamp. The spaces she describes are peripheral by definition. The first is a storeroom for "things that are out of use" above the sleeping apartments of a slaveowner's house where the mistress of the household had concealed her.[14] From there she is hurried into a hidey hole under the kitchen floor by Betty the cook: the storeroom being close to the principal apartments of the house had become too risky. In the kitchen under the floor planks, she had room just enough to bring her hands to her face to keep the dust out of her eyes when Betty walked from the fireplace to the dresser "twenty times in an hour."[15] From that house she had to disguise herself as a sailor and take a boat. The clothes were meant to conceal in plain daylight—as if she had never exited her confinement. While waiting on the river for a passage north, she was obliged to hide in Snaky Swamp. Also known as the Great Dismal Swamp, the location of Harriet's escape was on the edges of Albemarle Sound. To reach a hiding spot her friend Peter who escorted her had to cut a path through high bamboo stalks and impenetrable briars. Before they could reach a safe space, they were swarmed with mosquitoes and snakes:

> As the light increased, I saw snake after snake crawling round us. I had been accustomed to the sight of snakes all my life, but these were larger than any I had ever seen. . . . As evening approached, the number of snakes increased so much that we were continually obliged to thrash them with sticks to keep them from crawling over us. The bamboos were so high and so thick that it was impossible to see beyond a very short distance.
>
> Just before it became dark we procured a seat nearer to the entrance of the swamp, being fearful of losing our way back to the boat. It was not long before we heard the paddle of oars, and the low whistle, which had been agreed upon as a signal. We made haste to enter the boat, and were rowed back to the vessel. I passed a wretched night; for the heat of the swamp, the mosquitos, and the constant terror of snakes, had brought on a burning fever. I had just

> dropped asleep, when they came and told me it was time to go back to that horrid swamp. I could scarcely summon courage to rise. But even those large, venomous snakes were less dreadful to my imagination than the white men in that community called civilized.[16]

The impenetrability of the swamp *was* the protection. The captain of the boat in which Harriet would ultimately escape described it as "a slave territory that defies all laws."[17] Here sight did not reach far, edges of a space that help orient were not perceptible, and no preexisting path suggested the way. The standing water and sinkholes made movement difficult to say the least. Its vastness was not panoramic and amenable to surveying and surveillance; it isolated those who ventured into that terrain. And yet it was an improvement on life under slavery.[18]

Harriet did not stay in the swamp for long. From there she had to return to her grandmother's house and be concealed in a garret nine by seven feet in dimension. The highest part of its sloping roof was three feet. The space was entirely dark and bereft of openings. Her uncle Philip, a carpenter, created a concealed trap door which communicated with the storeroom so that she could enter the garret: "The air was stifling; the darkness total."[19] She stayed in that garret for almost seven years, occasionally descending to the storeroom so that she did not completely lose the use of her limbs.

One day Harriet made an accidental discovery. She found a gimlet that her uncle had left sticking in the roof. She drilled a hole one-inch wide so she could observe the goings-on in the street outside.[20] A whiff of air entered the interior. In summer the space was unbearably hot, during rains the thin layer of shingles leaked and she got drenched, the winter chill was numbing.[21] Only that inch-wide aperture was her opening to the world. When there is no space to call one's own, no enclosure that the law would heed, this was a spatial discovery.

Countermapping

Harriet Jacobs wrote *Incidents* between 1853 and 1858, and when it was published in 1861 her own name was withheld. Published under a pseudonym, Linda Brent, the title had to impress on the reader that it was indeed written by a formerly enslaved author: *LINDA: Incidents in the Life of a Slave Girl, seven years concealed in Slavery, Written by Herself.* She was after all a fugitive under the Fugitive Slave Act of 1850, who had to flee from one house to another even after her escape to the North, lest slave-hunters found her. Even when she could assert herself as free, the freedom to speak was circumscribed by her position as an African American. As Nell Irvin Painter notes in her introduction to the 2000 edition of *Incidents*, apart from recording the physical harm that owners and their agents inflicted upon the enslaved, Harriet conveyed the "soul-murdering psychological violations" inflicted upon them. Harriet's narrative was a strident protest against white politicians and journalists who declared that slavery was "a great moral, social, and political blessing; a blessing to the master, and a blessing to the slave!"[22] She reserved her most solemn denunciation for those who cast slavery as attachment and affection.

Recalling the death and funeral of her aunt Nancy, and that her mistress wanted Nancy to be buried in the white-only burial ground, Harriet remarked that perhaps the mistress "thought it would be a beautiful illustration of the attachment existing between slaveholder and slave, if the body of her old worn-out servant was buried at her feet."[23] Nancy was never allowed to sleep anywhere except on the floor outside her mistress's door, "so that she might be within call."[24] Nancy's family refused to give over her body for the mistress's satisfaction. She was buried in the "old graveyard of the slaves," in a defiant stand to keep the African American family together.

Scattered for generations, without any recourse to self-determination or protection from the law, this African American family's effort to create sites of meaning and connection was not only precarious, but was misrepresented by whites. Noting the willful misreading of social dynamics of slavery Harriet wrote how Aunt Nancy's funeral, which her mistress attended, might have been represented by authors oblivious to the enslaved's predicament:

> Northern travellers, passing through the place, might have described this tribute of respect to the humble dead as a beautiful feature in the "patriarchal institution;" a touching proof of the attachment between slaveholders and their servants; . . . *We* could have told them a different story (emphasis in the original). We could have given them a chapter of wrongs and sufferings, that would have touched their hearts, if they had any hearts to feel for the colored people. We could have told them how the poor old slave-mother had toiled, year after year, to earn eight hundred dollars to buy her son Phillip's right to his own earnings; and how that same Phillip paid the expenses of the funeral, which they regarded as doing so much credit to the master. We could also have told them of a poor, blighted young creature, shut up in a living grave for years, to avoid the tortures that would be inflicted on her, if she ventured to come out and look on the face of her departed friend.[25]

Harriet's narrative not only contradicts arguments put forth by slave-holders and their supporters but is also a profound spatial critique that would indict the views of those who purport to write about landscapes. Take Frederick Law Olmstead's narrative of his journey in the slave states.[26] He claimed to write about the landscape of slavery with authority and objectivity, being "influenced by no partisan bias."[27] And yet, the white slaveholder's view of the land and its economy were assumed as the baseline for his formulation of a landscape narrative. Seen from horseback or a railway carriage, as a privileged traveler, the land unfolded as landscape, revealing its resources, beauty, and economic worth. The enslaved appeared in his writing at best as caricatures and objects of pity, reconciled in various degrees to a life of bondage and to being "driven."

Rebecca Ginsburg in her discussion of the "slave landscape" writes about the distinction between the hidden "system of paths, places, and rhythms that a community of enslaved people created as an alternative, often as a refuge, to the landscape systems of planters and other whites," that depended on "display and vistas" to proclaim its power.[28] The enslaved exploited whatever opportunities their environment afforded and used subversive yet seemingly compliant practices as is often "a necessity for those without political and economic power." She describes the landscape of the enslaved as a way of knowing the land as well as white people:

> By participating in a shared, hidden landscape, enslaved people formed bonds of support, trust, and resistance to white control. In the process, they became aware of what many white people never were—namely, the extent of the sphere of black activity that co-existed with planter-enslavers and their allies but was beyond their control. . . . Slaves believed they knew what master did not—that there was more than one way of seeing, ordering, and traveling on the land in the antebellum South.[29]

This simple point: that there is more than one way of seeing the land and traversing it, has escaped much of architectural history writing. I thus take Harriet Jacob's narrative also as an indictment of our disciplinary practices that pose the voice of colonial authority and white privilege as the objective point of view as the only point of view. In the social history of architecture, seldom do we see the narrator's specific point of view articulated. Stories of buildings, cities and landscapes are spoken from an Archimedean vantage, a practice that wittingly and unwittingly marginalizes those who are left out of the imagination of architecture and history.

In Harriet's recalling, we see two methods of conveying the experience of the land. The world of the white masters and their litany of prohibitions that set limits to movement, education, family life, earnings, and spiritual well-being. From the enslaved's point of view, this was a life of threats, curfews, passes, shackles, slave auction blocks, whipping posts, and runaway posters that dictated how, when and where they could move. These were not just designated sites: any space by the sheer dint of the enslaver's authority could become a site of torture, be it a kitchen, a street, a yard or a field. As Harriet points out about the vicious attacks that transpired after Nat Turner's Rebellion: white mobs could enter the houses of unfree and free African American residents and vandalize at will.[30]

Harriet speaks of these instances as fragmenting space, but also draws attention to those spaces that elude the white masters' and travelers' gaze and the fragile modes through which the land is construed as meaningful from the enslaved's point of view. Let's think of this as creating a countermap: In this countermapping, the garret, hidey hole, and swamp show up as elements of a shared landscape. They are connected by not only obscure pathways, but through expansion and contraction of time that define the spaces of the marginalized. A countermap is both a spatial and a temporal register of the experience of the marginalized. For Harriet, on the one hand, her running in the pitch-dark night, slashing through bamboo and bramble in an anxious desire to secure a safe perch in the swamp, registers time as compressed to an existential limit. Her confinement in a constricted space, on the other hand, brings about a delirious sense of time:

> Countless were the nights that I sat late at the little loophole scarcely large enough to give me a glimpse of one twinkling star. There, I heard the patrols and slave-hunters conferring together about the capture of runaways, well knowing how rejoiced they would be to catch me.
>
> Season after season, year after year, I peeped at my children's faces, and heard their sweet voices, with a heart yearning all the while to say, "Your mother is here." Sometimes it appeared to me as if ages had rolled away since I entered upon that gloomy, monotonous existence. At times, I was stupefied and listless; at other times I became very impatient to know when these dark years would end, and I should again be allowed to feel the sunshine, and breathe the pure air.[31]

Harriet's experience of time is interlaced with her changing affective states of fear, sadness, despair, hope, and resolve. The space of seclusion is defined not just by its physical parameters of smallness but of a fluctuating, erratic sense of time. The two are related, however. The materiality of the space is experienced at the intersections of the spatial and temporal. The spatial circumscription and temporal anguish cast an impress on her body. The ever-present fear of being captured by slave hunters extracts a price: "for my body still suffers from the effects of that long imprisonment, to say nothing of my soul."[32] Spatial experience seizes the body and remains as embodied memory. Thus, the truth value of *Incidents* that was important to Harriet ultimately could only be evidenced in her bodily performance, as traces of a countermap that remained imprinted on her body.

Stories about architecture from the perspective of the marginalized produce countermaps not only by describing different topographies, but more importantly because they signal alternate temporal imaginations that are resistant to prevailing methods of cartography or architectural representation.[33] As spaces that are typically not designed with care, the garret or verandahs as service spaces that I have alluded to earlier are often architecturally undistinguished. They thus do not give themselves readily to architectural reading through conventional analysis, let alone convey the experience of the marginalized. The physical traces of those spaces might even be missing—as ephemeral spaces, or spaces that have been demolished, or remain inaccessible. Yet the character of such a space could remain as memory traces and articulated as an embodied sense of space. Memoirs bring to the surface such embodied experience and alert us to this form of spatial reading.

Slow Looking

Countermapping relies on scalar alterity. Because memoirs allow expansion and contraction of time and space—making big things small and small things big as Rabindranath notes in his memoir—they often change the scalar relation that is imposed by authority, and thus provide narrative access to such spaces and agentic moments that would have otherwise remained invisible. The move to scalar alterity—accessing the Other through scalar manipulation—is enabled by what Kathleen Stewart calls "slow looking," paying attention to the ordinary everyday events and watch for their potentiality to emerge.[34] We see this technique of altering temporality in Rani Chanda's (1912–97) recollection of her mother's father's house in the rural backwaters of eastern Bengal.[35]

Writer, painter, dancer, Rani Chanda's memoir *Amar Ma'r Bap'er Bari* is written as a tribute to her mother (and Rabindranath) as a form of looking back at her own childhood days. Rani's original inspiration to write about this small village came from her mentor, Rabindranath Tagore. A young Rani spoke of her mother's village with such enthusiasm that Rabindranath asked her to write down these remembrances. Express the good in village life like a picture; leave out its unpleasant aspects, he said: "since you won't get back the village life; write, write it down."[36]

But she didn't. "What is there to write about?" she had thought. The stories, sparkling with childhood memories though pleasant in conversation, seemed commonplace, unimportant, ill-suited to a life in ink and print. Only after her mother's death did she realize why Rabindranath might have urged her to commit the memories to paper: writing brought comfort. Rani began with short pieces. Only later did she put together these scattered recollections into a narrative.

The home was Rani's mother's father's house in Gangadharpur (alternatively Sridharpur) village in the erstwhile Bikrampur pargana in eastern Bengal,[37] now Bangladesh: a small village, "enveloped in shade, filled with water and greens."[38] Rani's story is a narrative of returns to the rural home: on holiday visits from Dhaka, and later for a permanent stay, until they moved to Calcutta. The spatial centerpiece of Rani's narrative is the *daowa* or raised porch of the house where her mother did her daily chores while she conversed with neighbors. A space that is architecturally undistinguished becomes in Rani's narrative a pivotal setting. It is recalled through convergences of people and conversation, and an aesthetic that centers on domestic labor.

In the morning, Rani's mother would sit in the *daowa* of the southern apartment and cut vegetables:

> She has always fancied this task. The manner in which she cuts the vegetables, rinses them in water and arranges them in portions on the wooden platters—it looks as if *naivedya* (ritual offering of food) has been laid out in front of the goddess. . . .
>
> Her skill in cutting vegetables is something to learn—something to see. The julienned bottle gourd arranged in a pile looks like a heap of jasmines . . . .
>
> Ma cuts vegetables—so many people from the village and the neighborhood drop by. The *daowa* fills up. They speak and Ma listens . . . So many stories of happiness and sorrow. . . stories of the past and the future.[39]

Her mother's household labor transforms the modest and otherwise unremarkable *daowa* into a venue and a site for stories; stories of a dynamic landscape patterned by arrivals and departures, droughts and floods, festive times and tastes. Here the white flesh of bottle gourd is rendered light and airy by an expert hand, becoming food fit to be dedicated to gods. The performance of an ordinary chore shines in its skilled brilliance—it becomes an event worth experiencing, and worth recounting.[40]

The present tense in Rani's text conveys immediacy and the expectation of continuity and return. The refrain—"she cuts vegetables"—reiterates the long duration of domestic labor and offers the rhythm of daily routine against which all interactions and events gain significance. Her (re)turn to present tense is an invitation to witness the aesthetic episode, as if it had never ended—it continues into the present.

Duration is essential to materiality. Many of the building materials used in the house—mud and bamboo—require frequent maintenance. The seasonal storms challenge the structural integrity of the thin walls and roofs, and rains erode the earthen plinth. The bamboo walls have to be repaired, the courtyard and *daowa* have to be resurfaced, and the plinth mended before and after the rainy season. The earthen *daowa* has to be plastered every day.

The main compartment of Rani's grandparents' house had a tin roof. While a light tin roof requires less maintenance than thatch, and is an improvement of sorts—more modern, it is susceptible to "lift" in stormy weather and can be lethal if carried by a gale. Storms are distinguished in this region by their timing and force. In early summer, before the mango pits had hardened, the norwester or *kal-baishakhi* ominously shows up in the late afternoon without warning, and the storm—*toofan*—season begins. It is an anxious time. *Kalbaishaki* is an occasional storm; *toofan* is a routine afternoon occurrence in this region.

Daily routines change during the storm season. Dinner is finished early, while there is still some light in the sky. Everyone gets inside the southern sleeping apartment, the strongest structure in the premises. The storm makes the walls shudder, the roof groans under stress; the sound of trees collapsing in the storm adds to the tense atmosphere of early evening. The storm passes and the morning sun shines on the courtyard filled with fallen leaves and branches. By afternoon the courtyard is again made spotlessly clean. Then they wait for the next storm.

During one such storm, while the children huddled under the bed, Rani's uncles stood ready with axes in case they needed to cut the roof ties that tethered the roof to the sturdy columns. This was to prevent the entire structure being carried off by the force of the wind. Then came the sound of big raindrops on the roof. And relief. Once the rain starts, the *toofan* calms down.[41]

Duration is fundamental in another sense. As if in keeping with the riverine landscape, the built spaces ebb and flow with time and with the seasons: "the white-earth courtyard shines all day and night like a brimming tank shimmering with light in the breeze."[42] This aquatic imagery is in keeping with the region's topography—a land crisscrossed by wide rivers and innumerable small streams that braid the land and give sustenance to the humans and other-than-human creatures who live in this *jal'er desh*, water-country. The social rituals of the village are intimately tied to the seasons and its riverine geography.

Some spaces are brought close together at certain moments and dispersed at other times. The connectivity revolves around shared religious and domestic rituals in this neighborhood of Hindu households. In the evening the sound of conch-shells from every house creates a collective space. Rani's mother's *ashor*, convivial gathering, in the southern *daowa* is full from morning till evening, and the activities on that *daowa* and the adjoining courtyard shape the spatial and social links. Rani's aunts flit through the courtyard all day fetching things from one room to another. In the afternoon, the laughter and chatter of the children gathering in the schoolroom fills the courtyard. Rani's eldest aunt was the teacher in this village elementary school. Whether her mother is cutting vegetables, knitting lace, reading, carving stone molds for sweets and mango pulp, or distributing homeopathic medicine among the villagers, the comings and goings create nodes of activity and conversation amid the constancy of domestic chores. These spatial nodes are intersections of multiple temporalities: seasonal and cyclic time of harvesting crops—rice and jute, the homogenous time of print culture, modern medicine and labor in a colonial-capitalist regime, and the ritual time of household gods and community.[43]

Narrative Paths

The paths that connect the destinations in Rani's story of a rural community are neither fixed nor available in the same manner throughout the year. In a village with a poor road infrastructure, movement defines paths, rather than paths movement. The clustering of residences based on religious and caste affiliations are overlaid with durational factors to create spatial knots comprising the village. The clusters change as boundaries between land and water shift with the seasons. We see the paths and spatial clusters finding definition through Rani's childhood recollection of the seasons and her access: where she could go, what she could see and hear.

Like the storms, flood is an annual occurrence. The path of the floodwater is predictable as it moves from the canal to the large ponds, sinking the village paths and then moves into the courtyard of the house: "five fingers, ankle deep, knee deep—up to the waist and then the gurgling stops. . . . All around the calm water stands still." Rani's grandmother hauls the kids onto the *daowa*. Her uncles settle on the bed with their books and papers. Her mother sits down to stitch a *kantha*, while her aunts return to their domestic chores.[44]

Much preparation has already taken place in anticipation of the rainy season. The earthen foundation of the *daowa* has been strengthened. A temporary bamboo bridge has been suspended across the courtyard to facilitate movement among the apartments. A canoe made from plantain trunk is used to convey goods between the rooms. Moving between households now requires boats.[45] As the "white water" settles just short of the raised *daowa*, defining a new edge between land and water, the *daowa* becomes fishing platform and a dock of sorts.[46]

The rains turn the rural landscape into one continuous stretch of water. Houses are built on high grounds because the land remains flooded three to four months a year. The water levels increase and recede according to an expected sequence. With the downpour the paths between households—low-lying foot tracks during the dry season—become small canals.[47] The seasonal floods facilitate movement. The region did not have roads to speak of, and therefore travel by boat was easier than travel on foot.

The immersed land opens up fresh vistas and opportunities. Once the muddy waters have stilled, the mud sinks to the bottom—now the children can play in the clarified water. And Rani can accompany her uncle to the *shapla* woods that defines the edge of the *beel* to gather a boatload of these edible pink water lilies.

The water recedes the same way it arrives. Dramatically. The water in the courtyard is gone in four days. Now the hardships begin. A thick layer of mud everywhere; the stench of foliage rotting in the sun; the proliferation of mosquitoes, snakes and frogs; and then there is illness.[48] One day their neighbor notices the rice fields in the distance moving. He sounds the alarm. Prolonged inundation has loosened the rice saplings from the ground. The receding water is taking away with it this upper layer of rice field. There is no time to consider whose field it is. Bamboo stalks are rapidly cut and hauled onto boats: the rice fields have to be fenced-in because the force of one such rushing field will unmoor adjoining fields. The stalks will end up who knows where in this mobile land. Stabilized, the crop remains in the field. In the days to come the plants will grip the earth, the stalks will stand erect, and the green shoots will smile in the sun.

Mobility, migration, loss and permanence gather a particular constellation of meanings in this seasonal world making. Flood here is not an exceptional natural calamity.[49] It is a routine seasonal occurrence that forces a changed pattern of living. It produces a different rhythm of daily life and is accommodated through temporary infrastructure, by raising the levels of courtyards and plinths, and by learning to notice the turns and flows of water. The movement of water moves the land, creates new ones and destroys existing ones. Building with materials that cannot move with the wind and water, and can be easily patched up and renewed is folly.

Making Place

Although the stories constitute several visits, the beginning and end of the Rani's book captures the temporal and experiential limits of her acquaintance with the world of this small village. It is the temporal distance and its placement flanked by the two large cities—Dhaka and Calcutta—that make the ordinary spaces of a rural landowning family appear luminescent with longing. If Rani's story commemorates both Rabindranath and her mother, her narrative is built on loss in more ways than one.

Unlike her mother, Rani did not have a "father's house" to return to. Her father had died when she was a child. The house that he had built on the banks of the Padma River in his ancestral village, imagining it to be a retirement home, had long been swallowed by the river. Along with the house, the entire village had disappeared. Her mother's natal house, which in the tradition of patrilineal Bengali families would not be considered her mother's "permanent" home filled that absence. That loss made it possible to create a matrilineal tradition of belonging: "In my connection with the soil of this village," she wrote, "is my link to the soil of all villages."[50]

By the time Rani was penning her memoirs there was a well-established genre of Bengali writing that took the Bengal village as its chief site of exploration. And study of village life from the standpoint of folklore had been advocated and conducted for three quarters of a century. The Bengal village, as the quintessential site of Bengali nationalist imagination in its opposition to the colonial city, had become both the site of reform—modernizing agriculture, education and health facilities—and simultaneously a fertile locale of landscape imagination expressed in poetry and paintings. Rani Chanda's story of her mother's father's house skirts the moralizing tendencies of the bulk of the nationalist writings on the village to carve out a path that can comfortably settle on the prosaic details of rural life. Seen through a joyous aesthetic, the wretched aspects of village life are registered and incorporated in the storytelling. The references to misery in the village community are woven into the bliss so intricately that the negative spaces cannot be pried away from the positive spaces of the village landscape with any resolve.

Rani's recollection is predicated on never returning again. This home was already a distant site of memory; the house might be there, and even some of the people, but that time had passed. The story of this village was already of a village past. When Rani looked back to think of her mother, she saw the village home. As if to express her mother's character she needed the physical settings that comprised her mother's father's home and the extended village community. It was in that village milieu she found her mother fulfilled and appreciated. She belonged there: the only daughter among eight sons, her father's house was Rani's mother's "throne." She was consulted in all matters by her mother and brothers. She was effectively the eldest among the siblings because the only brother older to her had left home never to return. It is clear that this beloved daughter and sister maintained her position in the family by applying herself and assuming the responsibility of the person in charge of the household. She was, however, filling the space of a son who never returned. This position as the head of the family was always provisional. She too could never return.

Rani did not remember her mother before she was widowed. This is to say she never saw her mother dressed in colorful clothes, with vermillion in the parting of her hair, wearing jewelry appropriate for a Bengali married woman. The possibility of framing her mother within such a convention of beauty was unavailable to her. But there was a small patch of memory that stayed. It was the luminous image of her mother having returned from her *mouni-snan*—silent shower. That day no words were to be uttered before the morning bath. Her mother had just returned from the pond after an early-morning dip. Rani could recall the patch of her exposed right shoulder, and next to it a bit of the wide "biscuit-patterned" necklace:

> Her fair complexion and the gold of the necklace mingled, I recall clearly. The color of her skin has faded with the suffering of life, in the sun and rain. But when she comes and stands in the courtyard after her *mouni-snan*, the first rays of the sun fall on her body, that image of her shoulder seen in childhood still comes to my eyes.[51]

Where speech stops, sight attains acuity. It produces a singular instance of time-space that stays with her and it is that sense of embodied space that her text reaches to recover.

The patches of memory that constitute Rani's narrative forcefully speak to some fundamental issues of home, belonging and land imagination constructed in the colonial milieu. Rani's narrative appears as a set of digressions that seems to shift their loci and refuse a narrative resolution or the kind of moral efficacy demanded by nationalist narratives. In some ways this has to do with the disappearance of the home of the past, literally and figuratively. It is the absence of her father's house that prompts her to create a diverse set of narrative tracks as acts of placemaking. Thus, her nostalgic return is not geared toward locating a lost site of permanence. Her narrative fabricates space by attending to the ephemeral—to a land that moves, flood water that shapes living space, alert to small disturbances in the fabric of everyday life—producing an imagination of materiality that subtends the nationalist desire for a pure site of cultural origin. In that way it does not conform to what Susan Stewart calls the "social disease of nostalgia."[52]

Different Stories

Harriet's and Rani's narratives might appear to have little in common. Harriet's work was an indictment of and testimonial against slaveholding. In order to do so, she showed her readers how to see the landscape with critical empathy. She wanted them to follow her through her trials and bear witness to her suffering. That required heeding the architecture of spaces that the readers would otherwise neither notice nor inhabit. Harriet's claim—"*We* could have given them a different story"—was a profound gesture of refusing the dominant script. Rani's task in comparison was easy—she wrote for her own consolation; for a reminiscence oriented toward the public, however, she needed to craft a spatial vocabulary that could attend to the aesthetics of the backwaters without being unmindful of its shortcomings. The works share a few features. They are both quietly confident that they have other stories to tell. Though literary works, they stake claims to history—of narrating the ordinary fabric of their communities as once lived. They are both works of countermapping—launching a spatial script of the land they knew, contravening the dominant perspective. And to do so, they chose remarkable vantages for telling their stories: the garret for Harriet and the *daowa* for Rani. By shifting vantage—by dislocating the reader—they could rescript the land. Architectural historians might profit from these strategies of storytelling.

Architectural history as a mode of looking back is not just about a story of spaces; it has its own narrative spatiality that determines which sites and connections become visible and sensible, and which ones remain beyond grasp. The ordinary, undistinguished spaces inhabited by the marginalized come through in memoirs as small spaces which, even when ephemeral, short-lived or non-extant, remain as memory traces and patchworks. They are recalled and constituted as embodied spaces to create countermaps. The language of materiality that animates such countermapping urges us to rethink relations of power, and gives us narrative openings in to lifeworlds beyond the dominant historiography of the field.

Notes

1 Harriet Jacobs, *Incidents in the Life of a Slave Girl Written by Herself* (1861) with an introduction and notes by Nell Irvin Painter (Harmondsworth: Penguin, 2000), 164.
2 Rabindranath started writing poetry at a very young age and flourished as a poet, novelist, essayist, playwright, composer, and in the latter part of his life as a painter. He received the Nobel Prize in Literature in 1913 and founded a school-turned-university, Viswabharati, at Santiniketan, Bengal. The other memoir was written late in his life: *Chelebela* (Boyhood Days, 1940).
3 Rabindranath, "Jibansmriti," *Rabindra Rachanabali*, vol. 9 (Calcutta: Viswabharati, 1994), 411.
4 The works of Rainer Maria Rilke (*Die Aufzeichnungen des Malte Laurids Brigge*, 1910) and Marcel Proust (*À la recherche du temps perdu,* 1913–27), that have made major contributions to the literature and theory of memory were published as literary fictions.
5 Rabindranath, "Jibansmriti," 411.
6 Rabindranath, "Jibansmriti," 412.
7 For Rabindranath's views on history see Dipesh Chakrabarty, *The Calling of History: Jadunath Sarkar and His Empire of Truth* (Chicago: University of Chicago Press, 2015).
8 In this connection see Dipesh Chakrabarty's explanation of the idea of imagination in Rabindranath's poetry: "Nation and Imagination," *Provincializing Europe* (Princeton: Princeton University Press, 2000).
9 Lorna Martens, *The Promise of Memory: Childhood Recollection and its Objects in Literary Modernism* (Cambridge: Harvard University Press, 2011), 47.
10 For a discussion of Bengali autobiographies by women as narrative mode, see Partha Chatterjee, *The Nation and its Fragments* (Princeton: Princeton University Press, 1993); and Rimli Bhattacharya, *Binodini Dasi's "My Story and My Life as an Actress"* (New Delhi: Kali for Women, 1998).

11 For an explanation of countermapping see, Leila M. Harris and Helen D. Hazen, "Power of Maps: (Counter) Mapping for Conservation," *ACME: An International E-Journal for Critical Geographies* 4, no. 1 (2006): 99–130.
12 For a more elaborate treatment of this idea see Swati Chattopadhyay, *Small Spaces: Recasting the Architecture of Empire* (London: Bloomsbury Academic Press, 2023).
13 This was first published as "Blurring Boundaries: The Limits of White Town in Colonial Calcutta," *Journal of the Society of Architectural Historians* 59, no. 2 (June 2000): 154–79.
14 Jacobs, *Incidents*, 112.
15 Jacobs, *Incidents*, 116.
16 Jacobs, *Incidents*, 126.
17 Jacobs, *Incidents*, 177.
18 For a historical archeology of the Dismal Swamp see Daniel Sayers, *Desolate Place for a Defiant People: The Archeology of Maroons, Indigenous Americans, and Enslaved Laborers in the Great Dismal Swamp* (Gainesville: University of Florida Press, 2014).
19 Jacobs, *Incidents*, 128.
20 Jacobs, *Incidents*, 129.
21 Jacobs, *Incidents*, 130–31, 135.
22 Jacobs, *Incidents*, 136.
23 Jacobs, *Incidents*, 163.
24 Jacobs, *Incidents*, 160.
25 Jacobs, *Incidents*, 164.
26 Frederick Law Olmstead, *Journey in the Seaboard Slave States* (New York: Dix & Edwards, 1856).
27 Olmstead, *Journey,* Preface to the 1856 edition.
28 Rebecca Ginsburg, "Freedom and the Slave Landscape," *Landscape Journal* 26, no. 1 (2007): 1.
29 Ginsburg, "Freedom and the Slave Landscape," 41–42.
30 Jacobs, *Incidents,* 70–75.
31 Jacobs, *Incidents*, 166.
32 Jacobs, *Incidents*, 166.
33 For a useful method of thinking about countermapping beyond the visual, see R. Shareah Taleghani, "On Forms of Life: Countermapping and Emotional Geographies," in *Readings in Syrian Prison Literature: The Poetics of Human Rights* (New York: Syracuse University Press, 2021), 91–124.
34 Kathleen Stewart, *Ordinary Affects* (Durham: Duke University Press, 2007).
35 Rani Chanda, *Amar Ma'r Baper Bari* (Kolkata: Viswabharati, 1977), 39. Much of the discussion of Rani Chanda's book that follows is derived from my monograph *Small Spaces* that contains a longer discussion of the work.
36 Chanda, *Amar Ma'r Baper Bari*, Preface.
37 Pargana is an administrative unit, a subdivision.
38 Chanda, *Amar Ma'r Baper Bari*, 1.
39 Chanda, *Amar Ma'r Baper Bari*, 6–7. Other sources such as Mukul Dey's reminiscence notes the name of the village as Sridharpur.
40 In a discussion of the politics of women's domestic labor and its aestheticization in colonial Bengal, see Utsa Ray, *Culinary Culture in Colonial India: A Cosmopolitan Platter and the Middle Class* (Cambridge: Cambridge University Press, 2015), 130–33. Reading Rani Chanda's description as simply ideology misses something important about the mode of narration and why small spaces such as kitchens needed an aesthetic code.
41 Chanda, *Amar Ma'r Baper Bari*, 104.
42 Chanda, *Amar Ma'r Baper Bari*, 66.
43 Rani's family was well-connected to contemporary literary and art worlds in Calcutta, Santiniketan, Tokyo, London and beyond. Rani's father Kulachandra Dey was an officer in the colonial government, a poet and a close friend of Rabindranath. Rani's memoir of this rural world is bracketed by the death of her father in 1917 and the career of her eldest brother, the artist Mukul Dey, whose return from London in 1927 concludes her narrative. By the time Mukul Dey left for London in 1920, his paintings had already been published in *Prabasi, Bharati* and *Modern Review*.
44 Chanda, *Amar Ma'r Baper Bari*, 39–41.
45 Chanda, *Amar Ma'r Baper Bari,* 106–7.
46 Chanda, *Amar Ma'r Baper Bari*, 115–16.
47 Chanda, *Amar Ma'r Baper Bari,* 9.

48 The dreaded diseases were malaria and cholera. The incidence of malaria had increased rapidly with the construction of the railways in eastern Bengal that impeded natural draining and led to water stagnation.

49 A growing body of works has attempted to understand the complexity of floods in colonial Bengal and how one might effectively understand floods as process. See for example, Christopher V. Hill, "Water and Power: Riparian Legislation and Agrarian Control in Colonial Bengal," *Environmental History Review* 14, no. 4 (1990): 1–20; Iftekhar Iqbal, *The Bengal Delta: Ecology, State and Social Change, 1840–1943* (New York: Palgrave Macmillan, 2010); K. Kuntala Lahiri-Dutt and Gopa Samanta, *Dancing with the River: People and Life on the Chars of South Asia* (New Haven, CT: Yale University Press, 2013); Nitin Sinha, "Fluvial Landscapes and the State: Property and the Gangetic Diaras in Colonial India, 1790s–1890s," *Environment and History* 20 (2014): 209–37.

50 Chanda, *Amar Ma'r Baper Bari*, 61.

51 Chanda, *Amar Ma'r Baper Bari*, 140.

52 Susan Stewart, *On Longing: Narratives of the Miniature, the Gigantic, the Souvenir, the Collection* (Durham: Duke University Press, 1993), 23.

PART II

Spatial Position and Temporality

5

AGAINST THE GRAIN

Women Architects Rereading and Reimagining the Archive and Monograph

Mary N. Woods

Archive Nostalgia

Several decades ago, Jacques Derrida observed that the word archive is related to the Greek word *arche* meaning both commencement and commandment.[1] This etymology has a personal resonance for me. The archive is where I began my journey as a scholar; and it is, I was taught, the basis for historical research and meaning. As a woman of a certain age, I am nostalgic about my first experiences as a graduate student in the Avery Library architectural archives at Columbia University. They were my refuge, a quiet and contemplative space removed from the rivalries and intrigues of graduate student life unfolding elsewhere. Their rituals were familiar and comforting to a white woman raised in the South during the 1950s and 1960s: speaking in hushed tones, writing in pencil, and even wearing white gloves.[2] Today when we are so carefully vetted and surveilled to prevent theft or vandalism in the archives, my explorations there some fifty years ago seem especially carefree and innocent.

Drawn to American art and architecture, I was an outlier in Columbia's art history department. When I was a doctoral student, the powerhouse areas were Renaissance and Baroque art and architecture and French Impressionist and Post-Impressionist painting. Then there was only one Americanist on the Columbia art history faculty. Most of the faculty and my fellow graduate students considered American works to be pallid imitations of European masterpieces created by provincials. But I found other scholars of American art and architecture, which then meant only the United States, elsewhere. At Barnard College Barbara Novak studied American art, especially landscape painting, through ideas and constructs of nature and culture. James Marston Fitch taught in the school of architecture where he co-founded the first historic preservation program in the United States. His classes analyzed American building through the historical and environmental forces that shaped it. Also in the architecture school were Jacqueline Leavitt and M. Christine Boyer, urban planner and urban historian respectively; they offered one of the first courses on gender, planning, and architecture there. They also taught me about agency, activism, and community in the built environment. These professors challenged me to look beyond monographical studies of artists and architects.

DOI: 10.4324/9781003224662-8

Trying to follow their example, I studied American architecture's trajectory from craft to profession through those the canon erased and enshrined. How photographers, especially women, shape our perceptions and expectations of the built environment was another subject of my work. Past and present women architects in Mumbai and Delhi taught me to see other ways of being an architect born out of choice and necessity. Committed to craft, activism, conservation, and community, these women showed me architects can aspire to much more than simply designing iconic buildings.[3]

Many years ago, my colleague Jorge Rigau made me appreciate working in the margins. Based in Puerto Rico, Rigau is an architect, historian, educator, and preservationist of the Caribbean. He astutely observed that from the periphery one can see the center with greater clarity and criticality.[4] The women profiled in what follows confront the challenges of marginalization in institutional archives and architectural monographs. And in doing so they have reinvented and reimagined these collections and publications.

Love and Death in the Archives

At his death in 1988 the personal archive of Luis Barragán, the renowned Mexican modern architect, remained in his house and studio. However, his professional archive was bequeathed to an architectural partner whose widow later sold it to Rolf Fehlbaum, owner of the Vitra furniture company, in 1995. Fehlbaum acquired the drawings, photographs, slides, transparencies, and copyright to these materials as well as Barragán's name. Purchased for a reported three million dollars, the archive was rumored to be a gift to art historian Federica Zanco, then his fiancée and soon his wife. Removed from Mexico City to a space underneath Vitra's headquarters, the Barragán archive remained inaccessible to the public for almost three decades.[5] When performance artist Jill Magid heard the story of Fehlbaum, Zanco, and the Barragán archive in 2012 she created a project, "The Proposal," to continue her probing of institutions. Using their own protocols and regulations, Magid tries to seduce, subvert, and humanize these organizations.

Securing the Barragán family's permission, the artist had a diamond made by compressing the architect's ashes. Her plan was to "propose" to Zanco, offering her the diamond made from Barragán's remains. In exchange Zanco would repatriate the archive to Mexico making it accessible to the public there. "I've always called the archive her [Zanco's] lover", Magid explained, "to marry one man, she negotiated owning another man, whom she's devoted her life to. It's a weird love triangle, and I'm the other woman." Pursuing Zanco through letters, phone calls, exhibitions, and one face-to-face meeting, Magid never received a direct reply to her proposal. The archive was transferred to the Vitra Design Museum in 2022 where selected materials are on exhibit, and researchers' requests to consult it are reviewed on a "case-by-case basis" according to the museum website. "The Proposal" recalls Derrida's association of the archive with both Eros, the pleasure principle, and Thanatos, the death drive. Magid's proposal was about the desire to possess and control the past in order to overcome destruction and shape the future.[6]

"The Proposal" is disturbing as well as fascinating. It is a struggle between two women over the architectural remains of a celebrated male architect. As such, it underlines that women have usually been the archives' keepers and guardians instead of their subjects.[7] Since antiquity official archives have preserved records and documents related to state actors, overwhelmingly white and male, and the institutions they led. Women's growing claims to agency and public space, historian Griselda Pollock argued, are one of the principal features of modern life and modernism. Their absence from the archives, she maintained, makes histories created from these collections un-modern and un-historical.[8]

Antoinette Burton and other enterprising historians, however, have found other materials and other ways to tell women's stories. Burton discovered that some Indian women created and preserved artifacts, oral histories, and memoirs in their homes during the colonial era. She used these materials for counternarratives to histories drawn from state archives that erased women.[9] Burton's discovery of these materials is not surprising according to historian Linda Colley. Women often assumed, she wrote, the "archival and memorializing role within their families. Their restricted lives have given them time to bear witness, and perhaps a desire, in this indirect way, to impose a stamp and form on past events." [10] However, only women of a certain class and education had the time, space, and leisure "to dwell in the archive," as Burton puts it, of their own making. Remembering her immigrant parents, novelist Gish Jen reminds us how class, race, and culture impact who dwells in the archive:

> There was not a lot of time for storytelling. I don't remember one minute of my childhood being dedicated to anything but getting through the day. My parents were not of an autobiographical cast of mind—in the world that you and I inhabit, it's very important to self-narrate so that others can know you. But for them, there was a privileging of the unspoken—if something is important, you definitely don't talk about it.[11]

Architectural Monographs

Publications by builders, architects, and theoreticians have a long history. Still used today the *Vastu Shastra* codified ancient Hindu and Buddhist principles governing design and construction for builders, designers, priests, and patrons in South Asia.[12] Ancient Greek and Roman architects and builders wrote treatises and handbooks of which Vitruvius's *Ten Books on Architecture* (27 BCE) is the only surviving example. Italian Renaissance designers like Andrea Palladio resurrected and reinterpreted Vitruvius's treatise for their own purposes. Recognizing the treatise's promotional potential, Palladio discussed and extensively illustrated his own work in *The Four Books of Architecture* (1570).[13] His volumes gave rise to the modern-day architectural monograph, a heavily illustrated text focusing on a single designer's body of work. Monographs can be polemical as well as documentary like Le Corbusier's *Oeuvre Complète* (1929–70) created in close collaboration with him over four decades.

Although long-lived as a publishing genre, architectural monographs usually have limited audiences unless they are designed as lavish picture books too. Typically illustrated with airbrushed photographs devoid of any human life, monographs are, the late architect James S. Polshek once told me, the "soft porn of architecture." A so-called open monograph, produced by a living architect, can be reflective and/or simply promotional. A closed monograph, recounting a deceased architect's life and work, is all too often hagiographic. Despite the digital revolution and expense of publishing heavily illustrated books, the architectural monograph somehow endures.[14] There is at last some gender parity in architectural monographs. Women architects like the late Minnette De Silva and Brinda Somaya have published monographs equal in size and heft to those of prominent male architects (Figure 5.1).

Nevertheless, De Silva and Somaya reread the monograph against its traditional grain. Along with Chitra Vishwanath they, I argue in what follows, reimagine the archive and monograph, to tell very different stories about their work and lives.

FIGURE 5.1 Architectural Monographs in the Stacks, Mui Ho Fine Arts Library, Cornell University, December 20, 2019 (© Mary N. Woods, photographer)

Scrapbook and Reminiscence as Archive: *Minnette De Silva: The Life and Work of an Asian Woman Architect*

Minnette De Silva (1918–98) was born to a prominent family in what was then the British colony of Ceylon. Her parents were leaders in the independence movement. De Silva's mother also crusaded for women's suffrage and championed the island's arts and crafts. Although intensely proud of her country, De Silva was also a citizen of the world. Educated at Sir J. J. School (probably Asia's first architecture program) in Bombay, she credited Minocher J. P. Mistri, who had studied at the Architectural Association (AA), with introducing her "to the world of avant-garde modern architectural thinking." He was the brother of Perin Mistri, the first woman architecture graduate of Sir J. J. and India's first woman architect. In 1945 De Silva become one of the founders and editors of *MARG*, a journal of modern and traditional art and architecture based in Bombay.[15]

Continuing her studies at the AA, she participated in the CIAM where she met Le Corbusier who became her longtime friend. In the late 1940s, she returned to what was now an independent

Sri Lanka. Instead of the capital Colombo she established her practice in Kandy, her family's home, in the central highlands. Transforming her parents' small sitting room into a studio, De Silva began designing in what she called "a modern tradition." Inspired by Sri Lankan art, crafts, and vernacular buildings, she set about to create an architecture for the new nation. [16]

"One of the most interesting discoveries about India," De Silva wrote in her monograph (published posthumously in 1998) "was the outstanding quality of Indian women." She admired women like Sarojini Naidu and Kamaladevi Chattopadhyay who were leaders of the Indian independence movement and champions of its arts and crafts. [17] Along with her mother Agnes, they imbued De Silva with a deep appreciation for women's shaping of culture and history. Instead of waiting for a scholar or archivist to discover her work, De Silva took matters into her own hands. During her last years she began writing a monograph. Planned as two volumes, the first book, she wrote, was "mostly [a] facsimile of my archives which covers a long period of time: 90, 80, 70, 60 years & up to date." The second volume, which De Silva did not live to publish, was reputedly to be an analysis and synthesis of her life and work. She was another South Asian woman whose family home, as Burton observed, "can and should be seen not simply as a dwelling-place for women's memory but as one of the foundations of history—history conceived of, that is, as a narrative, a practice, and site of desire."[18]

The title of De Silva's monograph, *The Life and Work of an Asian Woman Architect*, emphasized her gender and place in the world. Unlike many women architects who object to being described by their gender, De Silva took great pride in being Sri Lanka's first female architect.[19] The front and back of the dust jacket reproduce a photograph of the Kandyan Art Association, a project especially close to De Silva's heart. One of her few public buildings it is an exhibition and performance space overlooking the lake in Kandy. However, the reader looks in vain for any discussion of the building in her text. It was commissioned decades after De Silva abruptly ended the first volume of her monograph with the trauma of her mother's death in 1961. While the photograph of the Kandy arts center shows an uninhabited building, the image De Silva chose for the endpapers is of a painter with his brush. He looks to have just whitewashed the podium wall shown behind him. Making visible the usually invisible craft and labor in this photograph, De Silva seems to reference the very process of making her book that the reader has just opened.

De Silva used her bold cursive script for the monograph's cover, title page, and dedication, alluding to the personal tone of her text. "Many, many moons ago," she wrote in the prologue, "I decided to write a kind of autobiography of the unique experiences of being an Asian woman architect, illuminated by photographs of actual events and memorabilia of importance." In the acknowledgments that followed, she singled out her first clients (often family friends) "who braved established opinion and had faith in my pioneering projects, withstanding ridicule for trusting an unknown woman architect with impossible ideas." She then thanked her friend and client Susil Siriwardene (Pieris) and especially architect Ashley De Vos for their advice and support of the publication. She also took "great satisfaction and pleasure," that her book was designed and published wholly in Sri Lanka.[20]

Her narrative was remarkably candid, often painfully so, and unlike any found in architectural monographs of my experience. Alternating between the third and first person, De Silva wrote:

> With her varied background and the example in her family of unusual and socially relevant accomplishment, Minnette De Silva has been well placed to make an original and valuable contribution to the architecture of present day Sri Lanka. This she did but not without struggle.

> The experience of digging up the past has been so devastatingly traumatic. Memories of wrong directions and mistakes, and of lost opportunities . . . . in my working personal life: and to remain an integrated person the cost seems to have been incalculable.[21]

De Silva described her monograph as an "unorthodox concept of a scrapbook approach with its stream of consciousness writing." She scrupulously followed the definition of scrapbooks as

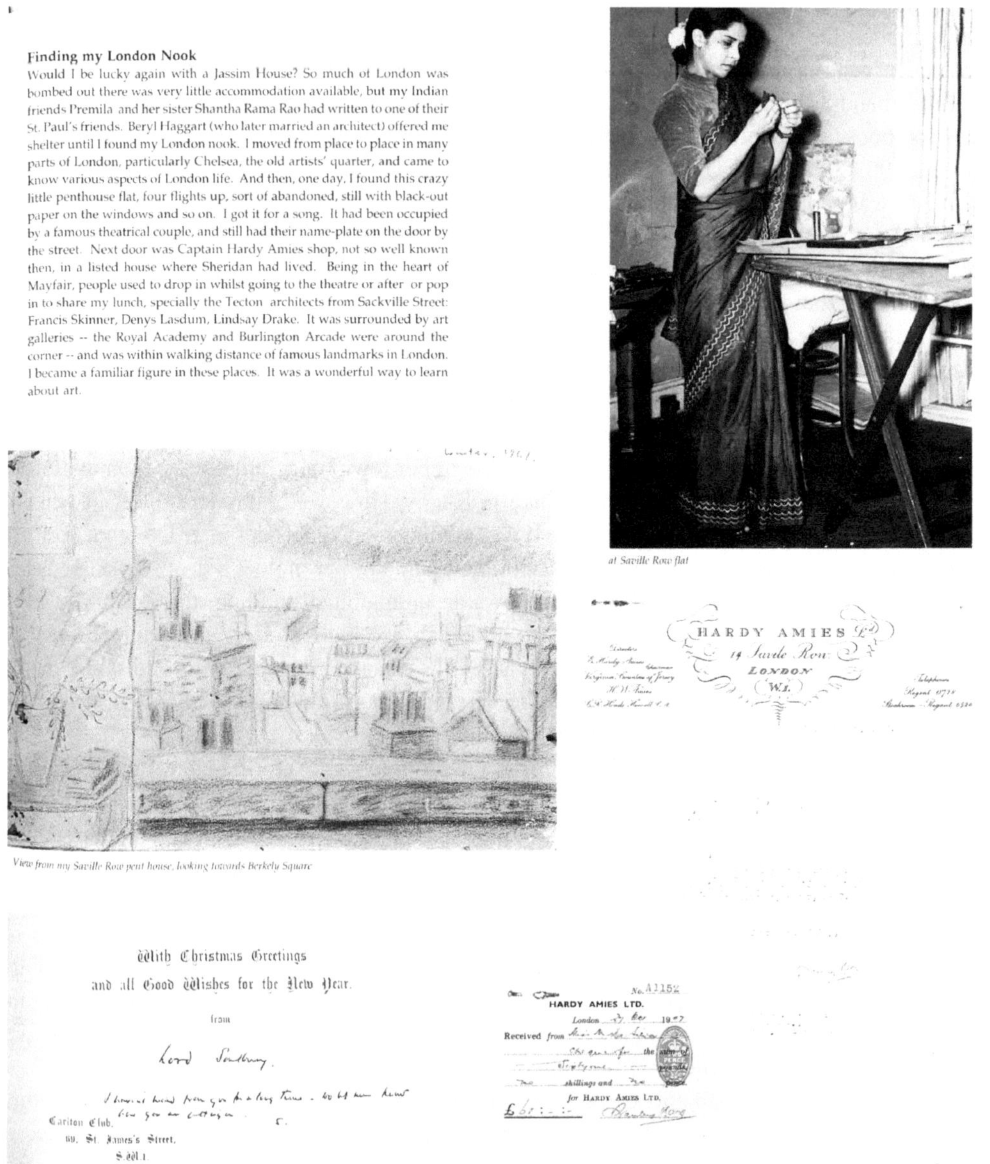

FIGURE 5.2 "Finding My London Nook", *Minnette De Silva, The Life & Work of an Asian Woman Architect*, editors: Minnette De Silva; Ashley De Vos; and Susil Sirivardana, Smart Media Productions, Colombo, p. 83 (© Minnette De Silva Private Ltd.)

personal and family keepsakes compiled from scraps like clippings, mementos, and calendars.[22] The rarefied social, cultural, and professional circles she moved in are evident from the memorabilia she reproduces in the monograph. She combines a sketch of the view from her Saville Row penthouse with her rent receipt and holiday greetings from an English lord in the page devoted to her London years at the AA (Figure 5.2).

Along with photographs of her family, friends, and travels, De Silva reproduces many pictures of herself. Clad in exquisite saris, she is shown working at her drafting table, attending

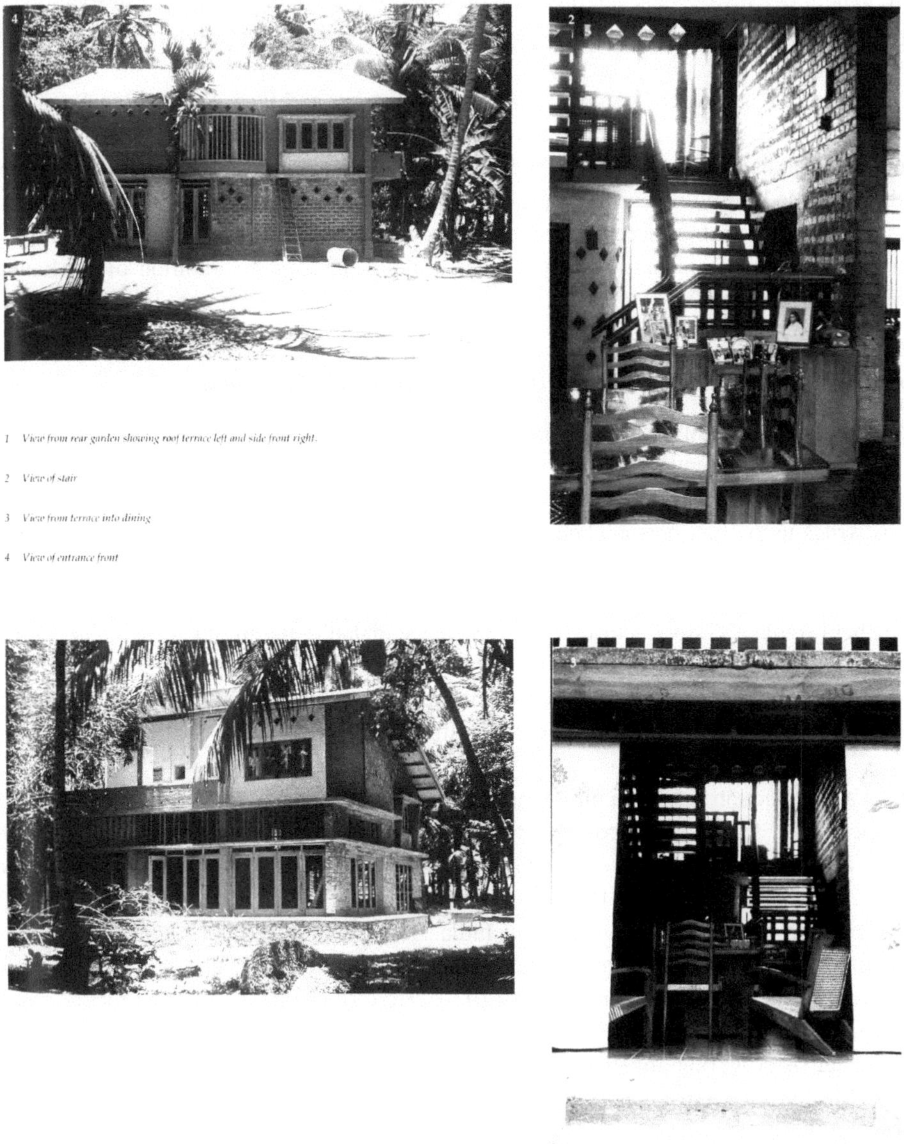

FIGURE 5.3 "C.H.Fernando House, Wellawatte, 1954", *Minnette De Silva, The Life & Work of an Asian Woman Architect*, editors: Minnette De Silva; Ashley De Vos; and Susil Sirivardana, Smart Media Productions, Colombo, p. 199 (© Minnette De Silva Private Ltd.)

a CIAM conference, climbing a ladder on a building site, and standing next to her completed buildings. The monograph's large format and superb reproductions ensure even the smallest details of the archival materials are legible. Its graphics and composition make it a design object too. Like De Silva's architecture, her monograph is an artfully constructed collage of disparate elements (Figure 5.3).

Reminiscences about school holidays and sari prices, for example, appear beside a photograph of the kitchen pantry De Silva designed for her mother. The late Anuradha Mathur, landscape architect and professor, worked on the Kandy art building as a student. She then returned to help De Silva choose architectural drawings for the book. Mathur's observation that De Silva's work was about how "one lived architecture in everything" captures the essence of the monograph too.[23]

De Silva was all too prescient about the need to publish her archives. As historian Anooradha Iyer Siddiqi noted, De Silva's personal archives and office papers disappeared when her home and studio were apparently plundered as she was dying in a Kandy hospital.[24] Minnette de Silva refused to be erased. Curating her own past, she published her archives and reminiscences, both personal and professional, between the covers of her monograph. Besides her extant buildings, it is the principal source for any account of her life and the modern tradition of Sri Lankan architecture she pioneered.

Monograph as Curated Archive: *Brinda Somaya: Works & Continuities*

Two decades after De Silva's death Brinda Somaya published a monograph documenting twenty-four projects in depth from the nearly 200 she and her office had completed by 2018. Somaya's publication is a carefully curated archive narrating and analyzing her practice. She, like De Silva, writes in the first person about her personal as well as professional life. Her daughter Nandini Somaya Sampat, architect and editor of the monograph, describes the monograph as:

> telling her [Somaya's] story, narrative, and journey and that of the studio, growing in parallel. Each project tells its own story, unique, and each one has its own narrative. The journey of the architect is a personal and intuitive experience. An experience juxtaposed with that of the nation, India. The monograph is about story telling.[25]

In Sampat's introduction there is a photograph of her mother surrounded by husband, children, and grandchildren. In the accompanying text she narrates the family history of her mother. Somaya's father and mother, an electrical engineer and zoologist respectively, were Indian patriots who steeped her and her sister Ranjini in Indian history, culture, and tradition. They taught their daughters to help build an independent India. Somaya followed her sister into Sir J. J.'s architecture program. After earning a graduate degree in liberal studies at Smith College in the US, Somaya returned to Bombay in the early 1970s. Here she began to build a practice from a garden shed behind her house.

She and her sister worked together as Somaya and Kalappa, their respective married names, for a few years until Ranjini's husband was transferred abroad. Yet Somaya has always kept her sister's name on the practice to acknowledge Ranjini was her only architectural mentor. The support of her parents and husband, whom she had known since childhood, helped her persevere on her own in a male-dominated profession. [26] Sampat joined her mother in 2007, making Somaya and Kalappa once again a family practice and a rare mother-daughter partnership.

The emphasis on the personal and family, as in De Silva's publication, is unusual in an architect's monograph. But it is timely given the current debate over life-work balance in the profession. Taught to revere architecture as only an art and calling instead of labor too, activist Peggy Deamer argued, architects are preconditioned to accept meagre pay and punishingly long hours. OMA's posting of a job opening with the stipulation "No 9-5 mentality" provoked such outrage on social media the firm had to hastily walk it back. Burned out by the pandemic, some architectural workers in New York have called out the life-work imbalance in their efforts to unionize, albeit with little success.[27] As Sampat writes in the monograph, role models like Somaya are especially important now: "To have the chance to observe a successful woman at her profession is an experience any individual is fortunate to witness. But I have seen a successful woman work, love, and live. This is my fortune. Greater still, she is my mother."[28]

I know the Somaya monograph well having contributed to its planning, interviews, and essays.[29] Part of the challenge with a monograph covering so many decades was to find, restore, and even recreate drawings, photographs and other materials documenting the practice. In addition to the extended discussion of selected projects there are vitae, bibliography, and a chronology of built and unbuilt work. There is also a list of credits identifying office colleagues and outside consultants.[30] It testifies to Somaya's expanded field of practice encompassing conservation, planning, research, and community projects as well as architecture.

There are also stories here usually left untold in most architectural monographs. Telling is the photograph of Somaya with her woman project architect and the women headloaders (unskilled construction workers who carry debris and materials on their heads) for the Goa Institute of Management. All the women wear hardhats with those of the headloaders specially designed for their work. Somaya has long made her contractors provide proper safety equipment for all workers. And she insisted, as she has before, the contractor build a school for the workers' children near the Goa construction site. The Chauhan family, biscuit and confectionary manufacturers, is also discussed and pictured. The Chauhans gave Somaya her first real job, a small office and extension to a warehouse for wheat, in 1976. "In those days who would give a young woman an industrial project," Somaya mused, except a family-run corporate in Mumbai known as the Indian city where women can best thrive. In the decades since then the Chauhans have returned to Somaya for homes, offices, and factories across India.[31]

Voices from inside and outside architecture contributed essays or participated in dialogues with Somaya: such collaborators as Tod Williams and Billie Tsien; historians like myself; colleagues like the late architect Kamu Iyer; art historian Saryu Doshi; and economist and journalist Arun Shourie (Figure 5.4).

Both the essays and dialogues situate Somaya and her practice within a broader context of the arts, society, history, and the profession. Moreover, architect Ruturaj Parikh, who curated the monograph, noted the projects chosen for extensive discussion all raise issues outside architecture:

> [they are] a thin slice through varying scales and typologies that frame the core concerns of Brinda Somaya's practice. It exemplifies their perpetual effort to have an impact that is larger than delivering on the programme or creating meaningful pieces of design. This diagonal cut through time and typology is a reflection on the struggle of a practice that resists being pushed to the periphery of the society it serves. The works presented in this monograph

BS We should fight?

AS You know, write.

BS Write for our own applause!

AS As professionals, we need to acquire more self-confidence and look not for admiration but for appreciation from our own small community. There will be in time a general debasement of standards and values, and this would be a way of preserving the oasis.

BS Do you think the oasis will spread? It could.

AS Yes, at least it will survive. Sometimes in a period of drought, all you can do is to keep some saplings alive for when the rain comes, so we can sow.

BS I am an optimist. I always believe that if we nurture the seeds, they will grow. But I do believe we live in significant times and that we must rise up to it.

Brinda Somaya in conversation with Arun Shourie at Lavasa.

Recorded on 27th January, 2016. Moderated by Ruturaj Parikh

On India · 31

FIGURE 5.4 "On India, Arun Shourie and Brinda Somaya," *Brinda Somaya: Works & Continuities – An Architectural Monograph*, Curator: Ruturaj Parikh, Editor: Nandini Somaya Sampat, Mapin Publishing in association with The Hecar Foundation, 2018, p. 31 (© Somaya and Kalappa Consultants)

> attempts [sic] to structure a discourse on the value of being in the mainstream while also concerning oneself with the greater agenda.[32]

Like De Silva Somaya reproduces drawings and photographs documenting buildings from inception to completion. Unusually, however, she had several buildings re-photographed to show their afterlives over time.[33] A photograph of the Jubilee Church in Navi Mumbai shows

FIGURE 5.5 Somaya and Kalappa, Jubilee Church, Church of North India, Navi Mumbai, 2000–2001, *Brinda Somaya: Works & Continuities – An Architectural Monograph*, Curator: Ruturaj Parikh, Editor: Nandini Somaya Sampat, Mapin Publishing in association with The Hecar Foundation, 2018, p. 232 (© Somaya and Kalappa Consultants)

how the congregation altered the original design with a blue roofing sheet erected over the terrace. It was a quick and inexpensive solution the church needed for its growing number of worshipers (Figure 5.5).

Prominently reproducing a photograph of the church and modification to its terrace across two pages, Somaya wrote with rare empathy about the congregation's alteration to her design:

> In situations like this, one must come to terms with the contradictions in which our buildings exist in a country like India. With its demanding programmes, watertight budgets, heat, dust, and rain, people take ownership of the buildings and intervene in ways that are not always in alignment with the original design or intent. Sometimes the changes are insensitive, but sometimes they discover an opportunity that I would not have thought of while designing. This is perhaps why many architects in India never re-photograph their buildings once they are in use. In an ideal world, an architect wishes to be involved with additions and alterations in the building well after the project is completed. But to me, the fact that the building is used well beyond its capacity is rewarding in itself and, in many ways, confirms the belief of my architecture.[34]

Diary as Archive: *Biome Diaries: Now; Then; Emergence*

Somaya and Kalappa's commitments to research, discourse, exhibition, and community work are, as Parikh notes, more characteristic of an alternative rather than a mainstream practice. Chitra Vishwanath is one of the founders of Biome Environmental Solutions based in Bangalore. It designs sustainable architecture and water and waste management systems there and across India. Because she first built with earth (using rammed construction and compression stabilized blocks), her practice is still often described as alternative despite its having built more than 700 affordable homes for middle-class clients since 1990.[35]

While De Silva was raised during the tumultuous decades of the independence struggle, Somaya grew up amidst the idealism and optimism of post-independence. Vishwanath came of age after the Emergency Period when Prime Minister Indira Gandhi suspended civil liberties and imprisoned opponents between 1975 and 1977; the Emergency also underscored the failures of centralized planning and modern architecture to overcome poverty, corruption, and sectarianism in India. According to architect Rahul Mehrotra, alternative practices based on traditional materials and methods arose in its wake just as Vishwanath began her design studies.[36]

In the early 1990s Vishwanath first experimented with earth, "quarrying" it from her building sites to build basements. Excavation created not only the building material but also more livable spaces in her early small houses. Earth was an ideal building material; it was readily available, easily worked, and labor intensive. By harvesting rainwater and recycling waste for roof gardens and agriculture, these buildings nurtured biodiverse habitats and seeded surrounding ecosystems too.[37]

Founded in 2008, Biome emerged from Vishwanath's architecture and the water and waste management expertise of planner Vishwanath S., her partner and husband. Just as the term biome refers to a rich ecosystem of plants and animals responsive to their environment, Biome arises from a diverse team of designers, engineers, and builders responding to the site and context. Regardless of whether the project is a home, office, resort, or school, it is also a self-sustaining ecosystem. The Covid pandemic and rapid pace of climate change convinced Vishwanath and her colleagues to "mainstream [Biome's] ecological sensitivity and alternative ways of architecting" through a publication. In turn the publication itself became an alternative to the usual monograph.[38]

When construction ceased with the Covid lock-down in 2020, Biome now had the time and space to reflect critically on its work and proposed publication. Moreover, the office team could now devote itself to designing and producing the publication in-house.[39] Instead of the large and heavy tomes typical of architectural monographs Vishwanath envisioned a small footprint for the Biome publication just like its many houses. Intended to be personal and open-ended it became a series of diaries small enough to "be carried in a handbag and read anywhere."[40]

Subtitled *Now, Then*, and *Emergence*, the diaries begin in the present, look back to the past, and then speculate on the future (Figure 5.6). While Biome partners and staff (past and present) created work for the diaries, a lawyer, client, engineer, contractor, psychiatrist, photographer, social entrepreneur, and historian (myself) contributed too. The entries and captions are in English but also Kannada, Hindi, and Tamil. Each diary concludes with an appendix of architectural drawings of selected works. While the diaries have essays, they are also rich in comics, artwork, poetry, interviews, and photoessays. Inspired by his love of comics and poetry, senior architect Siddharth Achaya guides us through Sans Souci (the house and architectural laboratory Vishwanath and Vishwanath S. built for themselves). His poem of alternating rhymes and playful drawings (showing the Biome founders at play, rest, and work) makes clear the design

FIGURE 5.6 *Biome Diary 01 NOW*, *Biome Diary 02 THEN*, and *Biome Diary 03 EMERGENCE*, editorial team: Chitra Vishwanath, Sharath Nayak, Anurag Tamhankar, and Ishita Shah, Bangalore: Grafiprint Pvt. Ltd, 2021 (© Biome Environmental Solutions Pvt. Ltd.)

thinking behind the house from basement to roof terrace. Vivek Muthuramalingam, a visual story teller and architectural photographer, created salt prints of Biome interiors filled with a haunting chiaroscuro. He chose this nineteenth-century process for its sepia tones and intensive craft to echo Biome's earthen palette and emphasis on handiwork.[41] There are also pages in the diaries left intentionally blank for readers to fill as they choose.

The diary editors note that rammed earth, earthen blocks, and water and waste management systems were not considered architectural when Vishwanath began her practice. Thus architects, contractors, and workers learned together and collaborated on site. Even estimating costs for alternative methods and materials, architect Sharath Nayak wrote, takes on a different meaning when understood in the context of such collaborations. "No longer could the architect just draw," he and the other editors emphasized, "and expect it to be made" [42] In the diary entry "The Ones Who Build" Vidushi Gupta and Visalakshi Ramanathan foreground the usually untold stories of Biome's workers, masons, and contractors. Gupta narrates the lives and work of Ravi Maistry, a helper who rose to become a mason and then contractor, and contractor Muralidhar who now corrects the junior architects' drawings after more than thirty years of working with Vishwanath. Unfolding like a scroll painting Ramanathan's elegant line drawings depict them and other builders working out ideas and designs on site, living in temporary dwellings they and their families build there, and adding extensions to their homes in the villages. Captions in English, Kannada, Hindi and Tamil reflect the multiple languages spoken by these migrant workers from across India. Here the agency and identities of the masons and contractors are highlighted instead of the architects (Figure 5.7).

The Ones Who Build

Vidushi Gupta

There is a long arduous journey from a few thoughts on paper to realization in a built form. Good design has the responsibility to translate into a great building. And for a practice like Biome, construction is not just the conclusion, but also a strong informant of design. Local techniques of building are in fact the primary drivers for an ongoing project in remote villages of Madhya Pradesh.

In one of the villages, a little extension is to be built for Rakeshji's house. He, himself, is the mason. He has built the walls, slamming each blob of cob, over weeks altogether. His cousin makes country roof tiles and has even arranged for timber for this project. Together, they have put up the roof in a matter of days.The women of the house have plastered each wall, achieving a finish unparalleled by some of the best machines. They have made a variety of murals, solely from their imaginations, without the need for any drawings.

The architects have shared a basic plan drawing. Rakeshji has seen it and made minor improvisations. By flipping the very orientation of the little building. So now one gets a fleeting glimpse of the lush green fields from the toilet. While the room has an uninterrupted view (and smell) of a dysfunctional to let and fully functional cowshed.

There is another electrical drawing. The neighbour's nephew, an electrician, can read it. He even lists out the items needed to be procured. But it's too late now. The walls are already plastered. So it's either the banal switch board, or the stunning mural. The plumber says he doesn't even need a drawing to do the work. Except the sloping roof is done and dusted. There is no place to put the water tank.

When you see a team working diligently, regardless of the project's scale, the shortcomings become all the more prominent. The smooth functioning of basic site work like timely procurement of materials, proper sequencing of works, ability to read and execute drawings, is often taken for granted. Perhaps the work is not as simple as it looks. This underlines the need for contractors.

Meanwhile in the capital city, Bhopal, a batch of 8000 custom made bricks has been rejected, despite a contractor's involvement. Maybe mere presence is not enough. The contractor here, Soniji, thinks quickly on his feet. A person is deployed to ensure quality and correct proportions of materials being used for making the bricks. Subsequent orders are smaller batches that are rigorously tested and the site work continues without a hitch.

20

FIGURE 5.7 Vidushi Gupta, concept and idea, and Visalakshi Ramanathan, illustrator, "The Ones Who Build", *Biome Diary 03 EMERGENCE*, editorial team: Chitra Vishwanath, Sharath Nayak, Anurag Tamhankar, and Ishita Shah, Bangalore: Biome Environmental Solutions Pvt. Ltd, 2021), pp. 26–27 (© Biome Environmental Solutions Pvt. Ltd.)

Similarly, Vishwanath braids together other untold stories in a personal diary entry "My Life and Others," Here she pays tribute to her father, a sculptor and arts educator, who guided her into architecture because of his love for design. Pursuing architectural studies at the Centre for Environmental Planning and Technology (CEPT), she met fellow student Vishwanath S., her aforementioned husband and partner, who encouraged her to explore the work of alternative designers like Laurie Baker.[43] But her last words are for her mother and mother-in-law whose work "looks normal and expected [and] therefore remains unacknowledged." However, "mothers pass on invaluable life lessons," she continues, "without these lessons balancing professional and home life would have been close to impossible for me . . . . Their role has been priceless"[44]

Almost fifty years ago Ellen Perry Berkeley opined the "real problem for a thoughtful woman [architect] *is* not whether she is accepted into the profession, but whether she *wants* to be accepted into the profession as it is now." [emphasis in the original]. And that is still the problem today. Paraphrasing Berkeley , my question is whether a thoughtful woman architect wants to appear in the archive and monograph as they are now. More recently Nora Wendl asks, "what other modes of writing can better speak to a woman's whole human life as an architect" rather than biographies of exceptional women designers?[45] The publications of De Silva, Somaya, and Vishwanath all respond to these two queries. Each woman interweaves the personal with the professional while opening up spaces for different narratives written and illustrated in often unconventional ways. Equally important is that these publications speak to more inclusive ways of understanding architecture and other modalities of practice.

Other Archives

Geraldine Forbes, a pioneering historian of Indian women in the colonial and modern eras, began searching for archival materials for these women in the late 1960s. And she was still writing about the need to locate and preserve such documents in 2003.[46] That was the year I began researching women architects in Mumbai and Delhi. Then the Council of Architecture, India's regulatory body for professional education and practice, did not even collect statistics on architectural students and professionals according to gender. Several of the first women architects in India were deceased when I started my project. When their offices closed, papers, drawings, and models documenting their practices were discarded. State, educational, and organizational archives either held no trace of these women architects or were inaccessible to me.

Oral history, a method totally unfamiliar to me, now became my primary research tool. I pursued the friends, families, colleagues, and former students and assistants of these pioneering architects. They were all incredibly generous with their time and memories. I had a Burton "dwelling-in-the-archive" moment with Dr. Malvika Chari, the sister of architect Pravina Mehta. Dr. Chari warned she had no materials relating to her deceased sister's practice. After a few interviews she brought out a box of family photographs. Inside were not only pictures of a young Mehta but also photographs of some of her buildings, drawings, and models. A chance remark to Nazir Hoosein, owner of the Liberty picture palace, led me to more material about Mehta. His friend Uma Patel, a single woman who bred poultry, shared her memories, photographs, and publications about the residence she commissioned from Mehta in the early 1960s.

Interviewing these two women and examining their personal collections with them was a very different experience from my solitary explorations in institutional archives. Forbes explained how different this kind of research can be:

> When I work with an individual who is showing me her family collection, it becomes a joint project. When examining photographs, I am not the one in control—it is the keeper of the collection who sets the time, place, and pace; determines which photographs I will see; selects the questions she likes and answers them; and decides how the images will be framed. My questions guide and probe but they never dominate—the interviewee is in charge.
>
> In the course of these interviews, I have had to change my questions and invent new ones to keep pace with my subjects. And the exchange does not end with the interview. Many of these women I have met continued to revise their versions of their lives, search for new evidence and information, and add to my collection of data on their lives through letters and conversation. In other words, my project is no longer mine—the subjects have become participants and collaborators. When this collaboration occurs, I feel that I am the closest I will ever be to doing feminist women's history.[47]

Milka Bliznakov (1927–2010), architecture professor at Virginia Tech University, began locating and preserving women's documents too when she opened the International Archive of Women in Architecture (IAWA) there in 1985. Bliznakov sought to build more than an archive of women who excelled in architectural design. She emphasized collecting materials of women from around the world who were also innovators in: materials; technology; management; planning; landscape; history; and criticism. Professor Donna Dunay, the current IAWA director, expanded the archive's reach further with the "Seminal Piece Project" she launched in 2018.[48] Any woman anywhere in the world can donate what she considers a seminal drawing or design to IAWA. Women who are typical, not just exceptional, can contribute to what then is really an open archive. Studied collectively such materials can reveal norms and differences of architectural practice in disparate places and times.

Other leading architectural archives in the West also have diverse women represented in their collections. The Royal Institute of British Architects (RIBA) has maintained archives since its foundation in 1834 (at first primarily membership applications). Melanie Bailey-Melouney, its archivist, counted thirty-eight women (including two from the 1500s and 1600s) in its 880 individual collections. There are materials of women patrons, designers, planners, partners (including a sister partnership), single practitioners and a feminist collective. The Avery Drawings and Archives at Columbia University were founded in 1890. However, curator Janet S. Parks acquired ninety-five percent of its collections in her thirty-six years there that ended in 2017. There are thirty-six women listed as primary creators in Avery's approximately 539 unique collections. In addition to architects there are also: students; artists; planners; interior and landscape designers; community activists; and researchers/historians. The collection is especially rich in the latter's papers, underscoring the importance Parks placed on women's contributions to scholarship.[49]

Phyllis Lambert is an architect, curator, scholar, collector, and preservationist who has profoundly shaped architectural design, culture, and knowledge. She is also the first woman to create an architectural museum and research institute, the Canadian Centre for Architecture (CCA), in 1979. Its online guide lists papers for some of modern and contemporary architecture's most important women like Jane Drew. However, as Anna Hayward, CCA archivist, notes, its first accessions were catalogued only under the names of those who compiled them (typically white male architects). Erased or obscured are the contributions of women and others who were partners, colleagues, students, and spouses. Consequently, she believes there are more than the nineteen collections related to women I counted on the CCA archives website. Although all these archives have accessioned more women's papers in the last few decades, they still account for only a very small percentage of the overall collections.[50]

Going forward, as Maristella Casciato (senior curator and head of architectural collections at the Getty Research Institute) stressed, archives must proactively seek out women's papers. Moreover, they need to create finely grained metadata and finding aids so women do not disappear into larger collections. In this regard RIBA's research website is a valuable model. It highlights women already in its collections, acknowledges their still limited numbers, and discusses how to address the problem of women forgotten by the archives.[51]

Writer and scholar C. S. Lakshmi was instrumental in creating another kind of archive for women. SPARROW (Sound and Picture Archives for Research on Women) is a community archive she helped to found in 1988. Lakshmi has resisted affiliation with any academic institution to preserve SPARROW's freedom to collect any materials. "Every woman has achieved something through acts of assertion," she said, "I don't think there is any history that is not worth being seen and retrieved."[52] As one of the first collections in India focusing on women, SPARROW interviews and films women who make history but are rarely the subjects of history.

Lakshmi is another woman who has literally dwelt in the archive; SPARROW was originally housed in her Mumbai apartment. Its collections document the lives and work of the following: poets; writers; artists; actors; dancers; educators; scientists; traditional healers; freedom fighters; policy makers; and community activists. There are, however, no videos or oral histories of women architects or builders. Because SPARROW empowers women of all castes, classes, and communities to tell stories in their own languages,[53] women artisans and headloaders as well as architects could find a place there too. When even national archives around the world now struggle to finance more diverse and inclusive collections, community archives like SPARROW with their limited staffs and uncertain finances have long lived with precarity. In 2019, the Mellon Foundation took notice, sponsoring a conference to explore funding models for community archives. As Lakshmi knows all too well, how to preserve community archives' autonomy and control of their collections is crucial when powerful institutions become involved.[54]

The first archive for modern architecture, planning, and design in India was established at CEPT in 2015. And Hema Sankalia (1934–2015) was the first woman architect whose papers it acquired.[55] She had extensive experience designing institutions and government buildings in the state of Madhya Pradesh. Architect Charles Correa wisely chose her as his associate architect for the legislative assembly he was designing in Bhopal, the state capital. Because CEPT subscribed to Correa's digitized archive with its 15,000 writings, drawings, and photographs, it is now possible to consult Sankalia's analog and Correa's digitized materials in one place. As historian Gwendolyn Wright discerned, only with such intersectional research can we begin to understand architects not as isolated stars but as parts of constellations illuminating larger patterns of meaning.[56]

Ishita Shah (historian, designer, and former CEPT archivist) coordinated the accession of the Sankalia papers. Since then, she has curated Biome's professional archive and edited and contributed to its diaries. Shah is also a founder of Curating for Culture, a collective dedicated to community activism and cultural and historical preservation. Making online archives and digital humanities more visual, engaging, and interactive is one of its goals. In 2020, the Graham

Foundation supported Shah's project to record oral histories with Indian women architects from the twentieth century for an open-access online archive. Three years later she and Curating for Culture launched the website "Women of Vaastukala/Women of Indian Architecture" with the first tranche of twenty-one interviews.[57] Given Curating for Culture's and SPARROW's commitment to audio and visual archiving, a partnership or collaboration might enrich and enhance each collection. Moreover, SPARROW is a model for Vaastukala to curate a more inclusive archive of women from different castes, classes, and communities. Finding the funds to sustain itself for thirty-five years, SPARROW can teach Curating Culture how to defy the odds against community archives.

The Archive and Me

In a 2019 interview, Dunay told me the IAWA's greatest challenge is women's reluctance to donate their papers. Some are disinclined because they are still actively working. Others believe their materials have little historical value. Since I was retiring soon, Dunay asked me what I planned to do with my papers. I suddenly understood the reluctance she had just described. After researching and writing this chapter, I am now planning for the disposition of my own papers. I am a footnote in the history of architectural education as the first woman tenured in Cornell's architecture program, only 120 years after it was established. My course materials may be of interest because they include the first classes on race and gender in architecture and on film, the city, and architecture taught at Cornell. I also have documents for the first women's organization in my college. Here my colleagues and I brought together female faculty and students from Cornell's still too siloed departments of architecture, art, and planning. There are also research notes, drafts, photographs, and slides for my dissertation, books, and articles.

Apart from my own papers, I have an obligation to care for other women's histories. I deeply regret never discussing with Dr. Malvika Chari what she might do with the photographs and publications related to her sister Pravina Mehta's career. Dr. Chari died in 2019, and I have no idea what happened to the materials she so generously shared with me. The photographs I made of them may be the only traces left.[58] Architects, curators, and scholars like myself who have made creative or intellectual capital from pioneers like Minnette De Silva and Pravina Mehta must support their families and colleagues to find and preserve these women's legacies. Helga De Silva Blow Perera, the architect's niece, is working to do just that at the immersive artwork she has created and curated at her Helga's Folly Art Museum Heritage Anti-Hotel Kandy. Here she plans to establish research fellowships and educational programs. And we should also help community archives like SPARROW and Women of Vaastukala to thrive and institutional collections to become more diverse and inclusive.

Archives are about ways of knowing and ways of forgetting. They have the power to project stories from the past into the future. And they can erase stories. Women have long been absent or elusive figures in state and institutional archives. Undeterred, the women architects discussed here reread and reimagined archives and monographs to tell more diverse and inclusive stories about architecture. All this matters as Donna Haraway reminded us in her tongue-twisting yet rhythmical prose:

> It matters what matters we use to think other matters with; it matters what stories we tell to tell other stories with; it matters what knots knot knots, what thoughts think thoughts, what descriptions describe descriptions, what ties tie ties. It matters what stories make worlds, what worlds make stories.[59]

Acknowledgments

Many thanks to Brinda Somaya, Nandini Somaya Sampat, and Ruturaj Parikh for their invitation to present a paper on women in the archives for the Women in Design 2020 + conference held in Mumbai, January 8, 9, and 10, 2020. I am very grateful to Somaya, Sampat, Chitra Vishwanath and her Biome colleagues, Helga De Silva Blow Perera, Ashley De Vos, Anooradha Iyer Siddiqi, Janet S. Parks, Jeff Cody, Carla Bahn, Dana Arnold, and Clare Barry for their help with this chapter. Michael (Mike) Radow, my late partner, made this project and all my work possible with his unwavering support, research skills, and knowledge of all things.

Notes

1 Jacques Derrida "Archive Fever: A Freudian Impression," *Diacritics*, 25, no. 2 (Summer 1995): 9.
2 Today many librarians advise against handling rare books with white gloves because they can cause more damage than bare hands. See Jennifer Schuessler "For Rare Book Librarians, It's Gloves Off. Seriously," *New York Times*, March 11, 2023, C1 and C4.
3 Mary N. Woods, *From Craft to Profession: The Practice of Architecture in Nineteenth-Century America* (Berkeley, Los Angeles, and London: University of California Press, 1999); Woods, *Beyond the Architect's Eye: Photographs of the American Built Environment* (Philadelphia: Penn Press, 2009); Woods, *Women Architects in Mumbai and Delhi: Histories of Education and Practice* (Abingdon, Oxon and New York: Routledge, 2017); and *Cinema Pe Cinema: The Theatres. The Movies, And Us*, directed by Vani Subramanian and produced by Mary N. Woods (New Delhi, 2024). This documentary film about India's single-screen theatres features women and gender issues on, behind, and in front of the screen. See https://www.vanishes.in/cinemapecinema. I am now working with Nipun Prabhakar and Annie Schentag on a book about postindustrial landscapes in the United States and India. Among the women we plan to discuss are the Begums of Bhopal, female rulers who were patrons of the arts, industry, photography, and architecture there from 1819 until 1926.
4 Quoted in Mary N. Woods, *Women Architects in India: Histories of Practice in Mumbai and Delhi* (Abingdon, Oxon and New York: Routledge, 2017), 207.
5 Alice Gregory, "Body of Work," *The New Yorker*, August 1, 2016, 30. See also Anon., Luis Barragán Foundation website, n.d., accessed August 18, 2022, https://www.barragán-foundation.org/foundation; and Anon., "The Foundation Is Transferred to the Vitra Design Museum," *NDION*, May 11, 2022, accessed August 18, 2022, https://ndion.de/en/barragán-archive-is-transferred-to-the-vitra-design-museum/
6 Ibid., 27, 30, and 31; Jill Magid, "Jill Magid Biography," n.d., accessed August 19, 2022, http://www.jillmagid.com/info; and Anon., "Foundation Barragán"; *NDION*; and Jacques Derrida, "Archive Fever," A Freudian Impression," *Diacritics*, 25, no. 2 (Summer 1995): 14–15.
7 Although archivists were originally male historians, professionally trained women came to dominate the field by the 1990s. Women were 69% of American archivists by 1996 and 82.1% in 2017. Alexandra A. A. Orchard et al. "The Archival Mystique: Women Archivists Are Professional Archivists," *The American Archivist*, 82, no. 1 (Spring/Summer 2019): 56, 62, and 63.
8 Griselda Pollock, 'Modernity and the Spaces of Femininity,' in *Vision and Difference: Femininity, Feminism, and the Histories of Art* (London and New York: Routledge, 1988), 125–26.
9 Antoinette Burton, *Dwelling in the Archive: Women Writing House, Home, and History in Late Colonial India* (Oxford and New York: Oxford University Press, 2003), 4, 6, and 18–21.
10 Linda Colley, *The Ordeal of Elizabeth March: A Woman in World History* (New York: Anchor Books, 2007), 262.
11 Joumana Khatib, "Still Staying the Course: How Covid Caused the Author Gish Jen to Reflect on China," *New York Times*, January 31, 2022: C1 and C7.
12 Debra Kamin, "They Wanted Good Light and a Dog Park. But the Front Door Could Not Face South," *New York Times*, September 22, 2022, accessed September 30, 2022, https://www.nytimes.com/interactive/2022/09/22/realestate/three-bedroom-brooklyn-williamsburg-dumbo.html.
13 William MacDonald, "Roman Architects," and Catherine Wilkinson, "The New Professionalism of the Renaissance," in *The Architect: Chapters in the History of the Profession*, ed. Spiro Kostof (New York: Oxford University Press, 1977), 33, and 36–38 and 153–56.

14 Mrinal Rammohan, "The Architectural Monograph Is Here to Stay," *ArchDaily*, June 16, 2015, accessed September 19, 2022, https://www.archdaily.com/640615/the-monograph-is-here-to-stay.
15 Woods, *Women Architects in India*, 23-24. MARS (Modern Architectural Research Group), created by British architectural modernists in 1933, inspired De Silva and the other MARG founders.
16 Woods, *Women Architects in India*, 9, 12, 21, and 23–24; Anooradha Iyer Siddiqi, "Crafting the Archive: Minnette De Silva, Architecture, and History," *The Journal of Architecture*, 22, no. 8 (2017): 1310–11 and 1320–22. See also, Mary N. Woods and Namita Dharia, "Women Architects in India: Dreaming through Design," *MARG*, 72, no. 1 (September 2020): 76–77.
17 Minnette De Silva, Ashley De Vos, and Susil Sirivardana, eds, *Minnette De Silva: The Life and Work of an Asian Woman Architect* (Colombo: Smart Media Publications, 1998), 32–33, 61, and 70, and 78–79.
18 Burton, *Dwelling in the Archive*, 4.
19 Woods, *Women Architects*, 6. Interviewing women architects in India, I learned several objected to being identified by gender. They preferred to be known as Indian architects.
20 Ibid., vi.
21 Ibid.
22 "The History of Scrapbooks," Special Collections and Archives, California State University Northridge, October 22, 2019, accessed September 24, 2022, https://library.csun.edu/SCA/Peek-in-the-Stacks/scrapbooking.
23 Quoted in Iyer Siddiqi, "Crafting the Archive," 1313.
24 Ibid., 1301 and De Silva et al., *Minnette De Silva: The Life and Work*, vii. After she conducted many oral histories with De Silva's family, friends, and colleagues, Iyer Siddiqi concluded: "Artifacts and works that appear in photographs or were seen by the Author in person are not located in any public archive, neither are their rumoured whereabouts in private collections conclusive," 1327 n8.
25 Brinda Somaya and Nandini Somaya Sampat, zoom call with author, August 23, 2022.
26 Quoted in Woods, *Women Architects*, 68.
27 Peggy Deamer, Introduction, in *Architecture and Labor*, ed. Peggy Deamer (New York: Routledge, 2020), 2; Noam Scheiber, "Architects Are the Latest White-Collar Workers to Confront Bosses," and Noam Scheiber, "Architects at Prominent New York Firm Drop Their Unionization Drive," *New York Times*, December 21, 2021 and February 4, 2022, accessed September 28, 2022, https://www.nytimes.com/2021/12/21/business/architects-white-collar-union.html and https://www.nytimes.com/2022/02/04/business/economy/shop-architects-union.html.
28 Nandini Somaya Sampat, Introduction, *Brinda Somaya: Works and Continuities. An Architectural Monograph*, curator, Ruturaj Parikh and editor, Nandini Somaya Sampat (Ahmedabad and Mumbai: Mapin Publishing in association with The Hecar Foundation, 2018), 23.
29 Mary N. Woods, "Working from Mumbai—Mary Norman Woods, Kamu Iyer, and Brinda Somaya," and Mary N. Woods, "An Empathetic Architect," in *Brinda Somaya: Works and Continuities. An Architectural Monograph* (Ahmedabad and Mumbai: Mapin Publishing in association with The Hecar Foundation, 2018), 153–61 and 441–44.
30 Ibid., 454–77 and 480–88.
31 "Campus for Goa Institute of Management" and Woods, "Working from Mumbai," in *Brinda Somaya: Works and Continuities. An Architectural Monograph*, 415 and 156; and Shilpa Phadke, Sameera Khan, and Shilpa Ranade, *Why Loiter? Women and Risk on Mumbai Streets* (New Delhi: Penguin, 2011).
32 Ruturaj Parikh, Preface, *Brinda Somaya: Works and Continuities: An Architectural Monograph*, 12.
33 Ibid., 156, 415, 454, and 477.
34 Ibid., 230–31.
35 G. Manish, "Building Small: Conversations with Chitra Vishwanath", n.d. (2017? or 2019?), accessed August 1, 2023, https://www.e-coexist.com/mailchimp/building-small-chitra-vishwanath.html. Sharath Nayak notes Biome uses earth for "its versatility and appropriateness in most contexts but we are material agnostic." See his "Mainstreaming Ecological Architecture," *Biome Diary 01: Now* (Bangalore: Biome Environmental Solutions, 2021), 25.
36 Rahul Mehrotra, Foreword, *Biome Diary 01: Now*, 7.
37 "Chitra Vishwanath," *Women in Design 2020+ Proceedings* (Mumbai: Hecar Foundation, 2020), 90; and Mary N. Woods, Afterword, *Biome Diary 03: Emergence*, 77.
38 Woods and Dharia, "Women Architects in India," 76, 79, and 82; and Sharath Nayak, "Mainstreaming Ecological Architecture," ," *Biome Diary 01: Now* 23.

39 De Silva's and Somaya's monographs were also in-house productions. The foundation created by De Silva's parents funded her publication. The Hecar Foundation, which Somaya helped to found, and Mapin, an Ahmedabad imprint, published and distributed her monograph

40 Chitra Vishwanath, Ishita Shah, Sharath Nayak, Anurag Tamhankar, Siddharth Achaya, Abhinav Agarwal, and Ravi Umraniya, zoom call with author, June 18, 2020.

41 Siddharth Achaya, "Design Thinking II,", *Biome Diary 02: Then*, 26–31; and Vivek Muthuramalingam, "Biome's Architecture, with a Pinch of Salt," *Biome Diary 03: Emergence*, 32–41.

42 Chitra Vishwanath, Sharath Nayak, Anurag Tamhankar, and Ishita Shah, eds., endpaper text and Nayak, "Mainstreaming Ecological Architecture," n.p., and 32.

43 Vishwanath, "My Life and Others," *Biome Diary 02: Then*, 5 and 7.

44 Ibid., 8.

45 Ellen Perry Berkeley "Architecture: Toward a Feminist Critique," in *Feminist Collage: Educating Women in the Visual Arts*, ed. Judy Loeb (New York: Teachers College Press, 1979), 270; and Nora Wendl, review of *The Women Who Changed Architecture*, ed. Jan Cigliano Hartman, *Journal of the Society of Architectural Historians*, 82, no. 2 (June 2023): 222–23. The criteria for inclusion in the book Wendl reviewed were "design excellence and distinction, cultural and social progressiveness, and leadership in architectural practice." Therefore, Wendl notes, women educators, historians, and activists like those in the #MeToo movement were not even considered.

46 Geraldine Forbes, "Locating and Preserving Documents: The First Step in Writing Women's History," *Journal of Women's History* 14, no. 4 (Winter 2003): 169–78.

47 Ibid., 176.

48 Anon. "International Archive of Women in Architecture (IAWA)," n.d., accessed October 12, 2022, https://spec.lib.vt.edu/iawa/; and Anon. "Racing to Save—and Celebrate—the Work of Women Architects," *Virginia Tech News*, November 2, 2018, accessed October 12, 2022, https://vtnews.vt.edu/articles/2018/10/unirel_iawa.html.

49 I am very grateful to the following archivists who responded with such candor, detail, and thoughtfulness to my queries about women in their collections: Melanie Bailey-Melouney; Cynthia Wilson; and Rachel Costello at RIBA; Janet S. Parks and Shelley Hayreh, Avery Drawings and Archives, Columbia University; and Anna Haywood, Canadian Centre for Architecture. Parks, email messages to author, June 13 and 14, 2023; Bailey-Melouney, email message to author, July 31, 2023; and Hayreh, email message to author, August 2, 2023. See also Janet Parks and Mariana Mogilevich, "Architecture in the Basement," *Urban Omnibus*, April 26, 2017, accessed August 12, 2023, https://urbanomnibus.net/2017/04/architecture-in-the-basement/.

50 Haywood, email messages to author, August 2 and 9, 2023.

51 Maristella Casciato, "Collective Memory of Diverse Women Architects," Women Who Design, panel organized by Meral Ekincioglu, May 7, 2021, accessed August 12, 2023, https://www.youtube.com/watch?v=QKI8TX3GI3c; "RIBA Collections Research Guide: Women in Architecture," and Sarah Ackland, "Revisiting the Collections: The Forgotten Woman," n.d., accessed August 12, 2023, https://www.architecture.com/explore-architecture/inside-the-riba-collections/research-guide-women-in-architecture and https://www.architecture.com/explore-architecture/inside-the-riba-collections/revisiting-the-collections-the-forgotten-women.

52 "Profile—SPARROW," n.d., accessed October 12, 2022, https://www.sparrowonline.org/profile/; and Dhamini Ratnam, 'C. S. Lakshmi: The Her Story', *Livemint*, August 9, 2014, accessed October 12, 2022, https://www.livemint.com/Leisure/jsUXD0QSY9iDYKXPXoh7ZP/CS-Lakshmi--The-her-story.html.

53 There are some newspaper articles about women architects at SPARROW. I am grateful for the help of Sharmila Sontakke, Senior Librarian, SPARROW. Sontakke email message to author, August 14, 2023; and Forbes, "Locating and Preserving Documents," 173.

54 Dr. Oya Rieger conversation with author, June 24, 2023; Rieger was involved with the survey of national institutions for Ithaka, a non-profit research group making knowledge more accessible to students and researchers. Jules Bergis, *Architecting Sustainable Futures: Exploring Funding Models in Community-Based Archives* (n.p.: Shift Design with support of Andrew W. Mellon Foundation, 2019).

55 Anon., "Hema Sankalia," CEPT Archives, June 23, 2015, accessed October 10, 2022, https://cept.ac.in/news/hema-sankalia-the-first-woman-architect-s-work-at-cept-archives. CEPT has added only a few women to its archives since Sankalia's papers were accessioned in 2015.

56 Gwendolyn Wright, "A Partnership: Catherine Bauer and William Wurster," in *An Everyday Modernism: The Houses of William Wurster*, ed. Marc Treib (Berkeley: University of California Press, 1996), 199.

57 Anon., “Vandalizing the Indian Atelier: A Search for Stories of Women Practitioners,” in Curating for Culture and Fiona Evangeline, Pornima Francis, and Ishita Shah, “Visualization of Oral Histories: Tracing Journeys of Women Practitioners in India,” n.d. (2022?), accessed August 12, 2023, https://sites.google.com/curatingforculture.com/curatingforculture and Anon., “Women of Vaastukala,” n.d., accessed August 12, 2023, https://womenofvaastukala.com/. Vaastukala translates as architecture, the art of designing and constructing buildings. I contributed closing remarks for a July 16, 2023 workshop for the Vaastukala website. Young scholars like Theertha Gangadharan and Anuradha Kumar are also publishing illuminating articles about pioneering women architects like the aforementioned Perin Mistri and Urmila Eulie Chowdhury. The latter worked with Le Corbusier and Pierre Jeanneret at Chandigarh and became chief architect of Haryana, Chandigarh, and Punjab. See Theertha Gangadharan, “India’s First Woman Architect – a Tribute to Perin J. Mistri,” Art Deco Mumbai Trust, May 24, 2021, accessed August 25, 2023, https://www.artdecomumbai.com/research/perin-j-mistri/; and Anuradha Kumar, “Eulie,” *FiftyTwo*, July 2, 2022, accessed August 25, 2023, https://fiftytwo.in/story/eulie/. Vikramaditya Prakash, architecture professor at University of Washington, is writing a biography of Urmila Eulie Chowdhury.

58 I plan to offer my digitized photographs of the Pravina Mehta materials to architectural archives like CEPT, SPARROW, and Women of Vaastukala. They would also be in collections I donate my papers too. However, there may be problems with publishing them until issues of copyright are resolved.

59 Donna Haraway, *Staying with the Trouble: Making Kin in the Chthulucene* (Durham and London: Duke University Press, 2016), 12.

6

IN PLAIN SIGHT

Women In and Around the Archive

Elizabeth Darling

To write about art or architecture in terms of an individual life is a technique as old as the discipline of art history. Pragmatically, it is as good a device as any around which to organise and construct a piece of writing. More problematically, such an approach can unduly simplify how a painting or building comes into being and, as Michael Freeden has observed, perpetuate what he calls 'the individualistic fallacy', which 'overstresses the function of a particular individual as the creator of a system...'.[1]

In this chapter, my aim is to reflect on how my personal experience of embarking on research in architectural history through the lens of one individual led to the subversion of that monographical approach. It turned out that the nature of my subject revealed the set of suppositions on which the architectural history in which I had been trained was based, about what constitutes architecture, and about who is worth seeing in its past, and who is not. The consequence for me was a concern to re-frame the discipline, which aimed, and still aims, to better represent and understand the processes and media through which architecture is made, and re-made.

Catalyst

The starting point for this re-framing was my doctoral research on the housing consultant Elizabeth Denby (1894–1965). I had first become aware of her as a Master's student. One of the modules I took was on Social Housing and among the case studies was Kensal House, west London (1937). In reading around this topic I came across an article which featured a perspective of the scheme and an unusually long credit line (Figure 6.1).[2] At the time (1990), I was most interested in the fact that it was an example of British modernism from before the Second World War (which I was then led to understand was unusual) and of social housing; as someone who had an undergraduate degree in Art History in a programme dedicated to the social history of art (to such an extent we rarely talked about style) and who had specialised in the modern period, Kensal House therefore ticked several boxes. I had also come out of that degree with a strong interest in feminist approaches to my subject but, as yet, the final name in that list, and its qualifier, were something I noted (I remember writing her name down in my notebook) but did not actively pursue.

DOI: 10.4324/9781003224662-9

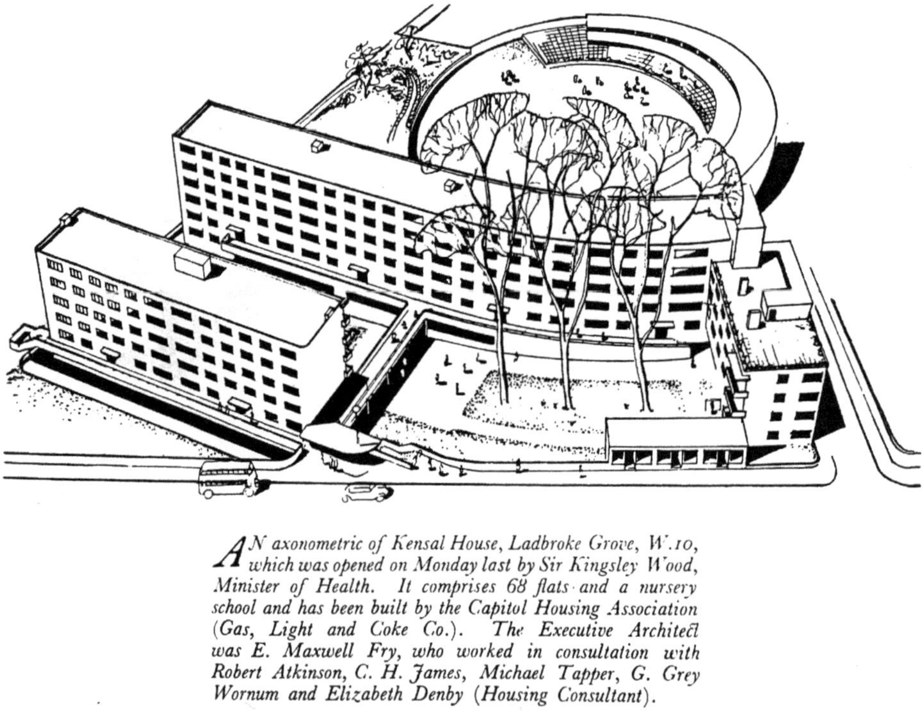

FIGURE 6.1 The Kensal House Credit Line from the *Architects' Journal* of 18th March, 1938.

It was another five years before I was in a position to embark on a PhD. By that point I was much more interested in exploring women in/and architecture. Initially, and as I shall go on to explore, I made the typical move of thinking of this in terms of looking at women architects generally or, perhaps, one in particular. I recall struggling to find one on whom I could productively focus (there seemed to be no woman practitioner with an archive of the extent and scope of say Ernö Goldfinger's) while looking at several seemed too generalist an approach, and one which would not be conducive to the fine historical work I wanted to do. It was at that point that I recalled that name I had jotted down. Here, potentially, was a topic which would allow me to explore modernism, social architecture and someone female involved (somehow) in its making. I therefore set about doing an initial trawl for information about Denby, her work and her life.

Quite quickly it became apparent that, for a woman in architecture, she was not unknown (in fact more so than many of the women architects who were her contemporaries). In the early 1990s, her name invariably led to a nod of recognition and perhaps a reference to her book *Europe Rehoused* (which was published in 1938, and on my Social Housing module's reading list) or the other work which she is most associated, the aforementioned Kensal House, the block of model flats at Ladbroke Grove, west London of 1937. Mention of her, although not much more than that, could also be found in the architectural historical literature. Lionel Esher wrote of her as '...the most level headed of the housing experts of the thirties...';[3] Judith Attfield described her as 'an influential adviser on working class housing',[4] others called her a 'journalist',[5] or 'housing reformer'.[6] Such analysis as there was tended to place her in the category of middle-class do-gooders. Jules Lubbock cast her among those who sought to tyrannise the working classes in the 1930s with the imposition of good design in their homes,[7] an interpretation shared by Jonathan Woodham.[8] At the same time, what also became clear was how her name (and the others on the credit line) was gradually removed from the attribution of Kensal House, with Max Fry being awarded sole authorships of the scheme.

From that initial survey, I drew three conclusions. First that she was worthy of further study. Second, that her (relative) predominance in architecture and design histories was because of her role in Kensal House, which, alongside a handful of other projects built in the 1930s, formed a small canon of British modernist buildings (I will return to the theme of the canon later in this chapter). And finally and rather curiously, despite that familiarity and frequency of presence in the literature, there was no attempt to look at her work in detail, nor, and in particular, to consider why a woman might have called herself a housing consultant in Britain at that date.

Further preliminary research, this time into more contemporary sources, showed me that her career encompassed much more than the writing of a book and collaboration on one block of social housing. In fact (and to name but a few of her achievements), she was responsible for a second block of flats (R.E. Sassoon House, south London, 1934) and involved in projects such as the Pioneer Health Centre. She was a leading figure in the voluntary housing movement, and one of the founders of the Housing Centre in 1934. She served on the Utility Furniture Advisory Committee in wartime, gave evidence to wartime reconstruction investigations, and wrote extensively for both the architectural and lay press. In her own day, she was held in much esteem. In 1936, for example, the *Architect's Journal* columnist, Astragal, wrote 'in our little world Miss Denby...wields more influence – and gets more done – than any six pompous or prating males.'[9] Six years later, reporting the award of an Honorary Associateship of the RIBA (another sign of her contemporary standing) the same journal noted:

> ... the RIBA has conferred well-deserved recognition on one who occupies a unique position in the architecture world. Her experience in flat management and her researches abroad, which were embodied in her remarkable book *Europe Rehoused*, have enabled her to make important contributions to a number of housing schemes. Elizabeth Denby is the star in the profession she invented for herself, "Consultant in Low-Rental Housing.[10]

Denby's status in her lifetime, and the range of projects with which she was associated, and for which archival material survived, made it clear that she was a subject ripe for doctoral study. And so I began. At that point, my focus was on the primary research that was core to my approach, and I experienced that peculiar pleasure of being the first person to open a minute book, or file, since it was signed off sixty or seventy years previously. At a more conceptual level, I thought of this as a feminist project in some sense, if only because I had very determinedly chosen to focus on a woman's agency in architectural culture (although I do not think I would have expressed it thus at the time). It would be some time, however, before I fully grasped the implications that focus would have when it came to framing and writing historically about Denby.

Going into the thesis my main methodological influences came from feminist art history, specifically the writings of Griselda Pollock and Rozsika Parker. Their *Old Mistresses. Women, Art and Ideology* (1981) and Pollock's *Vision and Difference* (1988) were particularly important because their emphasis was historiographical and concerned to demonstrate and challenge the precepts on which the discipline was based. They wrote:

> We have been caught too often in reacting against the dominant notions about women's art and have tended only to exchange one set of stereotypes for another...We have submerged them [women artists] once again in a slightly reformed but still traditional notion of history.[11]

Pollock reiterated the point in 1988, asking, 'Is adding women to art history the same as producing feminist art history?'[12] This eschewal of the reclamation mode of feminist art history, already articulated in Linda Nochlin's germinal essay of 1971 'Why have there been no great women artists', encouraged me to resist the temptation to cast Denby as a lost heroine.[13] In addition, Nochlin's advocacy of an empirically-based art history that explored the conditions in which women who were artists produced their work, informed my reliance on using the archive, and contemporary sources, to challenge the masculine-centred narratives which dominated art history as written.

These were significant influences not least – and it may seem obvious to say this – because they demonstrated the constructed-ness of history. And hence the realisation that if histories could be written to privilege and value certain people and things, then they could also be written to privilege and value other people and other things. What I also came to realise was that at the same time as they pointed to a different way of doing history, these women's critiques were grounded within the concerns of art history. They applied their re-thinking, for the most part, to painters and painting, but I was writing about a woman in architecture, did the same (re-written) rules apply?

Architectural history is a curious discipline. Nomadic, in the UK it is found in architecture schools, university art history departments, the heritage sector. This has important legacies for how it is practised and researched. The connection to practice often leads to an approach framed by the concerns of the profession, to support a specific architectural praxis, and, very often, also a focus on the primary figure of the architect. The heritage and conservation sector tend to an emphasis on style history and a concern for status tied to an individual practitioner or the building as some sort of 'first.' In an academic context, the discipline has often been framed by the preoccupations of art history. As an undergraduate, I was encouraged to look at buildings as visual rather than spatial, in terms of stylistic progression, and as the product of one creative force who had some form of professional (or proto-professional) training. Postgraduate teaching was more sophisticated, insofar as it took a social-historical approach to architecture, but it retained a focus on buildings and on architects as their makers. My subject, however, seemed to contravene at least some of these parameters and, as time went on, suggested there were other values which might lead to a more interesting history than one preoccupied with style and pioneers.

In 1995, there seemed not to be many models at hand that dealt both specifically with the British context and which might help me with my awkward subject. There was Lynne Walker's essay on 'Women Architects' in Attfield and Kirkham's *A View from the Interior* (1989), in which she placed women within the amateur tradition of the sixteenth to nineteenth century and then, following professionalisation, as what she called 'conventional professional architects.'[14] Walker's periodisation remains valid, although it is notable how many of the practitioners she mentioned over forty years ago (and has explored since in other publications) still pop up as new 'discoveries' today. Her 1989 essay also made reference to a then contemporary practice, Matrix. This feminist architectural cooperative construed its work broadly and, alongside design, had also produced a book, *Making Space, Women and the Manmade Environment*, published in 1984. This had been on my Social Housing module reading list for the essay by Barbara McFarlane, which explored the role of the Women's Housing Sub-Committee in shaping the design of council housing after the First World War.[15] Here was an inkling of a proposition that I would later develop more thoroughly, that women could make space without being professionally trained, but at that date such studies were (and for a long time, at least in the British context) outnumbered by the reclamation model.

Initially, therefore, it was Denby herself who was the key to how I framed my analysis. Although she had left traces that gave a sense of how she wished to be seen, such as her entry in *Who's Who*, she had also left no personal papers (they were burnt on her instruction after her death) and the business papers she did leave (then housed in the library of the Building Research Establishment) amounted to very little of value, comprising mostly of newspaper cuttings and a few typescripts of her writing. This meant that her historian was left to write, as Beatriz Colomina put it '... in, on or around the gaps'.[16] Thus, I looked for her in the archives of the spaces she occupied, the people and organisations she worked with, on the pages of the architectural and other press where projects with which she was involved were mentioned or where I might come across something she herself might have written. This was a relevatory process because it so very clearly, and empirically, belied the individualist model in which I had been schooled. It placed Denby firmly within the contexts in which she studied, trained, and worked, and showed how her practice as what she came to call a housing consultant emerged from these contexts. Moreover, by tracing her work, for example, in the voluntary housing world of the 1920s (which was where she learnt her trade), it became clear that far from being remarkable, which was the implication of the way she then featured in the historical literature, she was, in fact, one of the many women who (as my thesis went on to argue) were integral to the framing of debates about the modernisation of housing (and, indeed, about shaping a modern nation more generally) in the twentieth century.

It was about halfway through my research, and as my thinking about an expanded notion of architecture and its making began to cohere, that Alice Friedman's book, *Women and the Making of the Modern House* was published (1998).[17] Here was a counter history of modernism, which argued that it was the modern, progressive subjectivity of women clients such as Truus Schroder-Schrader and Edith Farnsworth which was central to the creation of a new twentieth-century architectural language. It was also at this point that I revisited Dolores Hayden's work on material feminism, and, in particular, Gwendolyn Wright and Susanne Stephen's propositions.[18] Wright argued that women's engagement with architecture entailed a 'quandary of roles': the exceptional woman; the anonymous designer; the adjunct (planner, critic, journalist); reformer.'[19] Stephens developed the idea further in her discussion of some of the 'adjuncts'. She wrote:

> 'although none of these women was trained as an architect, each was able to postulate and communicate trenchant and prophetic issues both to the profession and to the general public. Their discourse was to influence the decisions that gave shape to evolving landscapes.[20]

Taken together with what my empirical research was telling me about Denby, this led me to an understanding of architecture as process rather than 'actual monument' and from that a mode of architectural historical writing that sought to simulate that process. This was exemplified in Denby's polymathy which showed how many were the practices which could result in a building or which, purely as discourse, could also be understood as architecture. A consequence of this was what I later characterised as 'decentring' the architect as I moved them from the apex of any discussion to a place on a continuum. That might span a committee meeting to discuss the need for a building, the networks that brought together architect and client, those whose ideas influenced the conceptualisation of a building, drawings, the building itself, those who inhabited it, the reception and mediation of that building in the architectural and other press and later in architectural histories. All these constituted architecture. Such a standpoint also moved away from architectural history as style history, which, in the modernist case, tended to devolve into arguments about how modernist or otherwise a building really was.

To conceptualise architecture thus was not only, in my view, a more accurate representation of how buildings come about but, perhaps more importantly, a vital technique to move beyond a reclamation model which focused on 'finding' women architects, which, as Pollock noted in 1988, would not have changed fundamentally the epistemology. Opening up definitions of design on the lines of Denby's polymathy, introduced a raft of new actors into the researcher's purview, and normalised the presence of women in architectural history. Indeed, and this is where I moved beyond Wright and Friedman, if only to be provocative and to confront deeply-held assumptions, my concern was to posit such women as designers too.[21]

The challenge in writing the thesis became how to marry this episteme alongside a study that was ostensibly focused on an individual. This became a first attempt to do this, and as I wrote at the time, the text comprised a biographical element to the extent that it gave dates of Denby's birth and death and charted her main activities, but it did not, as many biographies do, stop there. Rather these details were a means to an end, and my focus was equally on the spaces which she occupied and the people and discourses with whom she interacted as an individual. I did not want to privilege her, rather, as Freeden put it, to note how '...constant interaction among individuals may point to the existence of regularities of thinking reinforced by that very interaction.'[22] It was the regularities of thinking as much as Denby herself which were the subject of the thesis.

As noted above, this approach meant that my study of Denby allowed me to say much about her activities but, perhaps more importantly, it achieved two further things. First, by situating her historically, it showed the ways in which women participated in and contributed to the creation of the built environment in Britain for much of the twentieth century (and indeed beyond it). Second, it started a process of revisionism of histories about the nature and evolution of modernism in Britain.

Decentring

I have emphasised the fact that mine was a historical study of Denby. This might seem a strange thing for an architectural historian to state, and it is, perhaps, a peculiarity unique to a historian whose work focuses on modernism. Nevertheless, as I have explored elsewhere, when I embarked on my research the existing historiography was dominated by accounts that were concerned to advocate for modernism as the defining style of the age rather than to understand it as a specific and transnational response to the condition of modernity in the twentieth century as later historians (including myself) have done.[23] Standard accounts were of an 'ur' modernism generated in continental Europe, which was then exported to countries which had not been sufficiently modern to generate it themselves. This importation narrative was particularly strong in the British context. A remarkably tenacious chronology was established as early as the 1930s which saw modernism 'start' here with the arrival of architects from overseas (both economic migrants and bona fide émigrés) and which was bookended with Amyas Connell's house for Bernard Ashmole, 'High and Over' (1929–30) and the Finsbury Health Centre (Tecton for Finsbury Borough Council, 1939). These 'pioneering' first steps, often criticised for their derivative styling, then gave way, after the end of war in 1945, to a full-blown modernism, which prevailed until the late 1970s. No one gave consideration, for example, to why there should be a demand for such buildings, nor had anyone quite accounted for how pre-war pioneering gave way to post-war hegemony.

Emerging from the completion of my thesis, and shaped by the methodology it had honed, it was that task I set myself. To paraphrase Lisa Tickner, I sought to write 'a non-modernist history of [architectural] modernism.'[24] I wanted to develop further what my work on Denby had shown: that the conditions in which a demand for new forms of architecture emerged were well-established in Britain before the 1930s, and that women were vital actors in these contexts. Moreover, the decentring of the architect and the understanding of architecture as a multitude of practices and processes, pointed to modernism's existence as a set of discourses, debates, interior spaces (to name but a few) throughout the inter-war decades. There may not have been a substantial number of actual modernist buildings but modernism there was, and it was generated within an ongoing set of conversations and arena as progressives sought to re-shape Britain in an emerging post-imperial modernity. Certainly, it was by no means hegemonic before 1939 but, and this conclusion came from that broad construing of architecture, it became hegemonic by virtue of its command of discourse, in which the exploitation of the building's image was central. This is a point that takes me back to the representation of Kensal House referred to at the start of this paper. This block of flats, which sits at the top of Ladbroke Grove in west London, and was completed in late 1936, was, even before the tenants moved in, a building which existed as re-produced image as much (if not more so) as a three-dimensional material thing. It featured in documentary films, in advertising, in the architectural and lay press and on wartime posters and, as a deliberate gesture towards this constant process of mediation, it was also put on the cover of the book that became my non-modernist history of British modernism. *Re-forming Britain, Narratives of Modernity before Reconstruction.*[25]

Re-forming Britain began by exploring, in a phrase borrowed from the architect Wells Coates, 'the conditions for an architecture for to-day', which explored 'sites of campaign' and 'sites of encounter'. The former were locations such as the voluntary housing sector and the architectural media, which advocated for a re-formed architecture more in keeping with a Britain experiencing a new wave of modernisation; the latter, the spaces in which the progressively inclined began to meet and gather critical mass in the 1920s, such as the bedsits and clubs of Bohemian Fitzrovia (the 'anti-Bloomsbury' as I like to think of it, and far more influential on built form). The main part of the book explored the concept of Rhetorical Modernism, a term that did not take off in the way I should have liked, but which referred to that idea of modernism as existing at multiple levels. Themed around health and housing this explored projects including the Finsbury and Pioneer Health Centres, the Lawn Road Flats, and social housing schemes including Kensal House and Sassoon House, as well as Kent House, designed for the Northern branch of the Saint Pancras House Improvement Society, chaired by Lady Marjorie Pentland, by Connell, Ward, and Lucas. The final part of the book 'Towards a New Britain', explored how modernism began to be absorbed into academic architectural training, and also followed pre-war protagonists and 'sites' into wartime and their advocacy for it as integral to the nation's reconstruction after the end of hostilities.

I understood *Re-forming* as a piece of feminist architectural history. In its redefinition of architecture, women became imbricated into an account of modernism's emergence and form in Britain; ordinary rather than extraordinary. From clients (and in my view co-designers) such as Molly Pritchard for the Lawn Road Flats, theorists such as Denby, campaigners such as Pentland, writers on domesticity such as Mrs C.S. Peel, and residents, such as Elsie Winborn of Kensal House, this was a history which evidenced, through painstaking archival work, the diversity of women's presence in architecture. That was, undoubtedly, my primary concern at the time, but it is worth remarking that in decentring the figure of the architect (invariably white, male and middle or upper class) my purview also extended to male 'makers' who did not fit such categories, such as Mansfield Forbes, a gay Cambridge don, whose home, Finella (co-designed with Raymond McGrath) was a significant site of encounter for all those engaged with the modern in the late 1920s.

In the same year that *Re-forming Britain* was published, a more obviously feminist book that I co-edited with Lesley Whitworth, also came out. In *Women and the Making of Built Space in England, 1870–1950,* we used the term 'built space' as a way to further emphasise that the formation of built environments has always been a female affair and that a focus on professionally-trained designers is a reductive rather than productive approach.[26] Our contributors explored women as housing managers and rent collectors, as rent strikers, members of the Women's Cooperative Guild and the Housewives' Committee of the post-war Council of Industrial Design. This Pandora's box, we hoped, would further set the cat among the historiographical pigeons.

Seeing/Not Seeing

Methodologically, my work continues to take this approach. A 2012 study of Wells Coates, for example, despite being focused on a male architect, was careful not to paint him as a pioneer outsider.[27] Instead, attentive reading of sources, archival and otherwise, placed him within a broader progressive scene (Freeden's 'regularities of thinking') as early as 1922 (when he settled in England), which was already 'making it new' and which shaped his approach to architecture and, in due course, brought him his first commissions. More recent work has taken my interest in women as spatial reformers and the significance of the voluntary sector as a site where new spatial ideas were developed, back to Edwardian Edinburgh. There I have traced the networks of women of all classes who worked together to transform the urban environment especially in the city's Old Town.[28]

In pursuing that work, I found myself in a familiar position. Just as Max Fry's name had come to supplant all others on the Kensal House credit line, the name of Patrick Geddes dominates accounts of urban reform in late-nineteenth and twentieth-century Scotland. There was some work on another (male) figure – H.D. Littlejohn, Edinburgh's Medical Officer of Health – but Geddes was the pure embodiment of the individualist fallacy.[29] Even a cursory glance at minute books or reports of organisations with which he was involved, however, revealed scores of other names, often predominantly female, who seemed to be doing quite significant work. More detailed research confirmed the existing reform work, much by women, onto which Geddes grafted himself and on which he drew for ideas, as well as the day-to-day administration and research, again by women, that powered the Outlook Tower which was his Edinburgh power base.

Both the post-history of the credit line, and the veneration of Patrick Geddes, point to a fascinating phenomenon in which things that are there are not seen. It is the historiographical equivalent of the way in which women are overlooked in social situations when a man comes into view, or when an idea that they have mooted in a meeting is ignored until stolen and repeated by a male colleague at which point everyone agrees that it is a brilliant proposition. My decision to see Denby's name led, as I have outlined, to a revisionist methodology which has allowed a more diverse and representative historical account of twentieth-century architecture and urbanism. It is an approach which has had some influence and there is now a definite impulse in academic histories of twentieth-century British architecture to think more expansively and write from the archive, rather than to the demands of a profession.[30] Importantly, these studies see things that I did not. Most obviously, reflecting a shift as significant as that instigated by feminist historiography, this is the premise that coloniality sits firmly within modernity and its cultural formulations. More simply there is a desire to move, at least for inter-war architecture, beyond the canonical examples and to postulate a number of modern architectures in this period.[31]

Nevertheless, the pull to link history to a specific 'name' is incredibly tenacious. It is, perhaps because of the sites in which architectural history is practised, that this should be so. In the case of Geddes, an entire heritage industry has been built up around him in Edinburgh (not dissimilar from the way that a 'rediscovered' Charles Rennie Mackintosh became a cipher for Glasgow's post-industrial reinvention in the mid-1980s) and a mode of history which is pluralist and decentred does not support such branding. Similarly, architectural history's links to professional practice again means that a methodology that seeks not to prioritise the individual – and, indeed, shows how the architect (male or female) is produced structurally as white and male – is deemed problematic and as raising some awkward truths. It is in tension with a desire, especially from women professional architects, for role models and a genealogy.

A sense of this tension became apparent during the project to commemorate the centenary of women's admission to professional training at London's Architectural Association School of Architecture (AA) in 1917. This was a significant moment in the history of the profession generally, and for women especially, not least because the AA trained a good majority of the first generation to practise professionally en masse. Of the wider team, Lynne Walker and I had specific responsibility for what became the project's centenary year outputs: an international conference, a book and an exhibition.[32] For the latter, and indeed the book, it became clear that there was a strong, if never fully expressed, desire that we focus on specific women (a gallery of starchitects). We resisted this and instead organised both thematically, so that women's presence in the AA was understood within broader currents in twentieth-century architecture. Individual women were mentioned but none given special treatment, except for Zaha Hadid, whose early death coincided with the exhibition, and which we felt we must acknowledge in some way.

Many of those featured in the exhibition were women whose work Lynne Walker had first mentioned in her writings from the 1980s onwards, and I and other scholars had published about since the late 1990s. Decades of feminist scholarship went into the exhibition and book. It was a shock, therefore, to hear visitors saying: 'how did I not know about this history?' Three years on we heard a similar refrain when Walker and I spoke at an event, organised by the Part W campaign group, about architectural women including Mary Medd, Justin Blanco White, Sadie Speight and Elizabeth Denby.[33] This was held at the RIBA's headquarters in a Florence Hall full of women, yet, when asked, the majority of them declared they have never heard of any of the designers under discussion.

It seems that a sort of double-not-seeing is at play here. Women historians' work is not seen while the epistemological shifts I have outlined here are not seen either. Thus, women's presence in architecture and its histories in turn remain something to be 'discovered' and interpreted as surprising and extraordinary; women remain as 'guests' in architectural history (a role currently played by Eileen Gray, Jane Drew, Minnette de Silva, Lina Bo Bardi among others) because as professionals, they are relatively few. The same tendency tends to play out as other identities seek a genealogy, whether that be architects of colour or LGBTQIA+ practitioners.

Again, such questions point to architectural history's interweaving with the concerns of practice, and the domination, at least in more popular contexts, of the reclamation approach. It may be that the sheer critical mass of interest in non-male architects means a grassroots and structural shift in conceptions of architecture will ensue. In the meantime, it is interesting to consider what can be learnt from those whom the reclamation model tends to favour and to offer some final reflections on how this affects the architectural archive.

Returning for a last time to the Kensal House credit line, it was not simply Denby who was edited from the list, but the other male architects too. Unlike Denby they have never made it back (partly because my research showed that they had little if anything to do with the project; the credit line was there to show the client's modernity in having a team of experts to advise it on its buildings). Nevertheless, their continued disregard is a reminder of what were engrained (I hope now gone) biases in twentieth-century architectural history which established a canon of buildings and architects, largely benchmarked against the 'ur' European standard as re-formulated by Henry Russell Hitchcock as the International Style. C. H. James, Michael Tapper et al did not design buildings that had flat roofs, large windows and so on, therefore they were not worthy of attention. Denby was because she had a clearer association with modernism more generally. My interest in writing a history which included canonical buildings was to demonstrate the partiality of existing accounts and, by re-framing debates around demand and circumstance, move beyond the stultifying strictures of stylistic debate.

I was reminded of this game of acceptability/unacceptability when writing the *Oxford Dictionary of National Biography* (ODNB) entry for the architect Jane Durham who died in 2019. Since 2012, I have written a number of entries on women architects for the ODNB as it seeks to diversify its content. Until Durham, nearly all of these had been women added retrospectively. This time, I was writing the entry in the normal fashion: 2019 deaths were being commissioned, and she died that year. From my research, Durham emerged as an exceptionally interesting person: co-founder of Chapman Taylor Partners in 1959, and through her skills both as a designer and as manager and finance director, core to its success as what is now a global practice. Yet, in the short amount of time I had to work on her, it was clear that Durham and her practice had not troubled the architectural histories nor the archives, and that this was because she and they did not fit the standard account of twentieth-century British architectural history. This focused (to put it simply) on a progression to various forms of modernism practised in the public sector. Chapman Taylor worked for commercial clients, was stylistically diverse in its output, and therefore disrupted this narrative and so were ignored. Durham's gender – unlike Denby's – could not outweigh her non-canonical connections.

Durham's problematic status contrasted with the entry which I had completed just before hers, which was on Rosemary Stjernstedt. This was an addition to the *Dictionary* and reflected the fact that she has become better known in recent years. Like Denby, she was a woman *and* a modernist. She was the first woman group leader in the post-war London County Council Architect's Department, where she worked on the development of the point block and led the team that designed the Alton East estate, west London. Later projects included the Central Hill Estate for Lambeth Council, which is currently under threat of demolition.

It was easier to research Stjernstedt than Durham, but both revealed the way the archive has historically been gendered and the tactics that are needed to see what the material can tell us about our subject. Although Stjernstedt was a 'name' in her day, like Denby, that name tended to get effaced as time went on with her male colleagues being accorded more attention by historians. This means she was not included in the Architects' Lives series of recordings produced by the British Library and it was only in 1984, alongside Lynne Walker's first exhibition on women architects at the RIBA, that she began to be 'discovered'. Even then, she did not consider her legacy sufficient to leave her papers to an archive and they remain in private hands. Nevertheless, as a woman in public practice, it was possible to trace her projects through papers in the London Metropolitan Archives which holds the LCC's records (these, incidentally, document a whole host of names of architects, men and women, who also worked on landmark schemes, but, because of that desire to individualise, do not get a mention in current histories). For Durham, no personal papers survive, nor does the practice have a formal archive. There were some interviews with her and her partners and a practice monograph, but very little else. Although she will have her individual entry, and it feels important that she will be in the national dictionary of record, what struck me as I sent my manuscript off was that a more representative entry would have been a collective one on the three founding partners.

Conclusion: In and Around the Archive

Throughout this chapter, I have discussed a tension between individual and collective histories and between reclamation and revision. I have also noted a frustration that these tensions still prevail decades after Nochlin, Pollock and Parker first articulated them. Moving forward, an historical architectural history which construes design expansively remains the most productive, and transformative, path. It is one which normalises and makes women's (and other under-represented groups') presence visible. This does not make for an ease of writing or researching, but it does make good history as the historian has to move beyond an individual's papers (if they exist) and explore more and diverse archives and focus on contemporary sources.

A corollary of this, and another theme of this chapter, has been an insistence on the researcher being willing to see what is in plain sight. It is not that women are not in the historical record at all, but that a certain adjustment of vision is required, in order that they are seen. This might be reading a document 'against the grain', focusing on what is not said as much as what is, or, as noted, looking beyond architectural archives and sources (here, again, that expanded view of architecture is a powerful revisionist tool). Within the architectural archive we can remember that women's presence might take many forms: a practitioner certainly, but also a client, the office secretary who holds things together and so on. We can find women everywhere if we are willing to see. At the same time, however, the nature of this seeing draws attention to the biases of the archival process.

And what of the architectural archive? As currently constituted most focus – almost invariably – on the architect as individual. Is it enough to ensure that more women and women-led practices leave their papers, something for which projects such as Voices of Experience and Women and the Welfare Landscape have, among other concerns, been advocating (though what of the lost papers of the many women who did not consider their legacy worth preserving)?[34] On the other hand, as Marika Cifor and Stacey Wood have noted, the invariable linking of the archive both in origin, and in attempts to reform it, as embedded in representational politics might not get us far. If the goal of a critical feminist position is, in their words, 'the dismantling of heteronormative, capitalist, racist patriarchy' then in the archive as in the practice of history, we need a praxis that is 'aimed at more than better representation of women in archives.'[35]

Is there a way to work towards an architectural archive without the architect at its centre? This might entail a re-thinking of who the archive is for. Is it a memorial to a profession, its self-image and self-perpetuation; how many architectural archives from part of professional bodies? Can we diversify how the archive is catalogued so that it better signals the collaborative nature of architecture and brings all of its protagonists into the light. An expanded archive and an expanded history could prove a powerful transformative force for an inclusive intersectional understanding of our pasts. Moreover, it might also and not before time, similarly transform the colonial metaphors that emerge from the reclamation model – 'pioneers' are sought, 'discoveries' are made, and existing traces not seen.

Notes

1 Michael Freeden, 'The Stranger at the Feast: Ideology and Public Policy in 20th Century Britain,' *Twentieth Century British History* 1:1 (1990), 19.
2 See 'Opened Last Monday', *Architects' Journal* (18 March 1937), 453 (and also the *Architect and Building News* 149 (1937), 381, *Architectural Review* (March 1937), 207).
3 Lionel Esher, *A Broken Wave. The Rebuilding of England, 1940–1980* (London: Allen Lane, 1981), 28.
4 Judith Attfield, 'Inside Pram Town', in Judith Attfield and Pat Kirkham (eds.), *A View from the Interior, Feminism, Women and Design* (London: Women's Press, 1989), 217.
5 Christine Boydell, 'Women Textile Designers in the 1920s and 1930s', in Attfield and Kirkham, *A View from the Interior*, 63.
6 Miles Glendinning and Stefan Muthesius, *Tower Block, Modern Public Housing in England, Scotland, Wales and Northern Ireland* (New Haven & London: Yale University Press, 1994), 2.
7 Jules Lubbock, *The Tyranny of Taste* (New Haven & London: Yale University Press, 1995), 299.
8 Jonathan Woodham, 'Women, Design and the State in the Interwar Period', in Jill Seddon and Suzette Worden (eds.), *Women Designing, Redefining Design in Britain between the Wars* (Brighton: University of Brighton Press, 1994), *passim*.
9 Astragal, 'New Homes for Old,' *Architects' Journal* 75 (1936), 726.
10 Anon, 'Miss Elizabeth Denby,' *Architects' Journal* 95 (1942), 400.
11 Rozsika Parker and Griselda Pollock, *Old Mistresses. Women, Art and Ideology* (London: Pandora, 1981), 45.
12 Griselda Pollock, *Vision and Difference, Femininity, Feminism and the Histories of Art* (London: Routledge, 1988), 1.
13 Nochlin's article was originally published in *ARTnews* (January 1971): 22–39, 69–71.
14 Lynne Walker, 'Women Architects', in Attfield and Kirkham, *A View from the Interior*, 90–105, quotation on 104.
15 Barbara McFarlane, 'Homes Fit for Heroines', in Matrix, *Making Space, Women and the Manmade Environment* (London: Pluto Press, 1984), 26–36. It is notable that this book, *Old Mistresses* and *A View from the Interior* were not published by presses who specialised in art/architectural history.
16 See Beatriz Colomina, *Privacy and Publicity, Modern Architecture as Mass Media* (Cambridge, MA: MIT Press, 1996), 1 and her description of the position she was forced to adopt in her study of Adolf Loos who, like Denby, destroyed all traces of his personal life.
17 Alice T. Friedman, *Women and Making of the Modern Home, A Social and Architectural History* (New York: Harry N. Abrams, 1998).
18 Dolores Hayden, *The Grand Domestic Revolution, A History of Feminist Designs for American Homes, Neighbourhoods and Cities* (Cambridge, MA: MIT Press, 1981); Gwendolyn Wright, 'On the Fringe of the Profession: Women in American Architecture', in Spiro Kostoff (ed.), *The Architect, Chapters in the History of a Profession* (Oxford: Oxford University Press, 1977), 280–307.
19 Wright, 'On the Fringe of the Profession: Women in American Architecture', 283–84.
20 Susanne Stephens, 'Voices of Consequence: Four Architectural Critics', in Suzanne Torre (ed.), *Women in American Architecture: A History and Contemporary Perspective* (New York: Whitney Library of Design, 1977), 136.
21 I developed this idea in the chapter 'Elizabeth Denby or Maxwell Fry? A Matter of Attribution', in Brenda Martin and Penny Sparke (eds.), *Women's Places: Architecture and Design 1860–1900* (London: Routledge, 2003), 149–70. The thesis was 'Elizabeth Denby, Housing Consultant: Housing Reform and Cultural Politics in the inter-war Period, University College London, 2000.
22 Freeden, 'The Stranger at the Feast', 22.
23 See the introduction of my 2007 book, *Re-forming Britain, Narratives of Modernity before Reconstruction* (London: Routledge) and for a further reflection my 'Foreword: Narratives of Modernity After Reconstruction', in Neal Shasore and Jessica Kelly (eds.), *Reconstruction: Architecture, Society and the Aftermath of the First World War* (London: Bloomsbury Academic, 2023).

24 Lisa Tickner, *Modern Life and Modern Subjects. British Art in the Early Twentieth Century* (New Haven & London: Yale University Press, 2000), 189.

25 Published by Routledge in 2007.

26 Published by Ashgate in 2007.

27 Elizabeth Darling, *Wells Coates, Architect Engineer* (London: RIBA Publishing, 2012).

28 See Elizabeth Darling, 'Womanliness in the Slums: A Free Kindergarten in Early Twentieth-Century Edinburgh,' *Gender & History* 29:2 (2017), 1–28 and idem, 'An Urban Experiment in Spiritual Motherhood: Gender, Class and Reform in Edwardian Edinburgh,' in *Suffragette City, Women, Politics, and the Built Environment* (Routledge, 2020) co-edited with Nathaniel Robert Walker, 9–32.

29 See Paul Laxton and Richard Rodger, *Insanitary City. Henry Littlejohn and the Condition of Edinburgh* (Lancaster: Carnegie Publishing, 2013).

30 See for example, the range of essays in Shasore and Jessica Kelly, *Reconstruction.*

31 See Neal Shasore, *Designs on Democracy, Architecture and the Public in Interwar London* (Oxford: Oxford University Press, 2023).

32 See Elizabeth Darling and Lynne Walker, *AA Women in Architecture 1917–2017* (London: AA Publications, 2012); the exhibition *AA XX 100 AA Women in Architecture 1917–2017* was held at the AA from October–December 2017 with the international conference held in the November.

33 'Pioneering Modernist Women' held at the RIBA, 21 January 2020, RIBA, and organised by Part W (https://www.part-w.com) with the RIBA.

34 See https://voices-architecture.com and https://www.liverpool.ac.uk/architecture/research/women-welfare-landscape/.

35 Marika Cifor and Stacey Wood, 'Critical Feminism in the Archive,' *Journal of Critical Library and Information Studies* (March 2017), 2.

7

MAKING THE ZAHA HADID FOUNDATION

Jane Pavitt

Introduction

This essay explores the opportunities and challenges involved in establishing a Foundation devoted to a female architect – Dame Zaha Hadid (1950–2016) who described herself (Figure 7.1):

> I'm a woman. I'm an Arab. I'm an architect. Biology and geography define the first two; the third has taken forty years of hard work. But hard work is not always enough. For a large part of those forty years, some of the biggest difficulties that I faced were brought about not by my work, but by my existence as a woman, or as an Arab, or indeed, as an 'Arab Woman'. Ignorance and injustices, large or small, blatant or subtle, deliberate or – and perhaps worse – casual, not even recognised by their perpetrators.[1]

Zaha Hadid trained at the Architectural Association (AA) in London, and she established her eponymous practice in 1979 (known first as the Office of Zaha Hadid). At the point of her untimely death in 2016, Hadid was the world's most prominent female architect. She was the first woman to be awarded the Pritzker Prize (2004) and the Royal Gold Medal (2015) and was twice-winner of the Stirling Prize for architecture (the MAXXI National Museum of 21st Century Art, Rome 2010 and Evelyn Grace Academy School in Brixton, London 2011). She registered a Foundation in her name in 2013. Its mission is to preserve her legacy, archives and collections and to pursue research, educational and curatorial activities in support of this, and in the area of modern architecture and its related disciplines more broadly. Following the settlement of Hadid's estate and the appointment of its inaugural director (Professor Paul Greenhalgh) in late 2021, the Foundation became operational at the start of 2022 with the appointment of a senior team. The first stage of our work is to undertake a comprehensive cataloguing of the collection of Hadid and the works of her office, Zaha Hadid Architects (ZHA) during her lifetime. Our holdings comprise around 15,000 works, including architectural models, drawings, paintings as well as product and digital design, her personal archive and her substantial fashion collection.

DOI: 10.4324/9781003224662-10

FIGURE 7.1 Zaha Hadid in her London office, 1985 (© Christopher Pillitz, courtesy of Getty Images).

Hadid achieved considerable recognition in avant-garde architectural circles early on, and her work was exhibited widely, including at the AA, where she taught and from where some of her students were chosen to work on competition projects. She established herself as a creative and social presence within the international architectural scene in the 1980s, known for her distinctive painting and drawing method inspired by Russian Suprematism which led to her to be aligned with the so-called 'Deconstructivist' tendency of the 1980s.[2] Her first completed building was the Vitra Fire Station in Weil-am-Rhein, Germany (1990–94). Over the course of her career, her repertoire included buildings for science and technology (Phaeno Science Center, Wolfsburg, 2000–05) and arts and culture (Dongdaemun Design Plaza, Seoul, 2007–14; Heydar Aliyev Centre, Baku, 2007–12), major works of infrastructure (Napoli-Afragola High Speed Train Station, 2003–17; Salerno Maritime Terminal, 2000–16) and commerce (Galaxy Soho, Beijing, 2009–12). The work of her practice was lauded for its engineering and technological innovation, and for being at the forefront of computational modelling. She also succeeded in parts of the world where women traditionally experience severe restrictions in professional and public life, namely the Middle East, including Qatar and Saudi Arabia. Her 'exception' status as an Arab woman architect was a factor here (and even a benefit later on as it helped her to secure patronage); she was astute in the ways in which the office did business, building and maintaining strong client relationships with herself and her team despite several high-profile setbacks.

The Zaha Hadid Foundation is based at two sites in London: the first, Hadid's former office (originally a Victorian school) is at Bowling Green Lane in Clerkenwell, which now houses the Foundation's office, research and learning facilities and a gallery for temporary exhibitions.

The local area is also home to Zaha Hadid Architects, which has continued since her death under the direction of Patrik Schumacher.[3] Bowling Green Lane was the main site of Hadid's practice from her early career until her death. During the 1980s, the former school was in use as small business rental units (many occupants were design companies), when Hadid rented a single studio ('Studio 9') for her fledgling practice in 1985, gradually taking over more studio space until she was the sole occupant. She bought the building in the early 2000s. During this period Zaha Hadid Architects grew from around 10 to 400 employees worldwide. One major aspect of the Foundation's research is to understand the collections as evidence of team-work, identifying how the practice operated and identifying the contribution of other architects in her office, as well as painters, model-makers, engineers and other specialists and external collaborators.

Our second site, a converted warehouse in Shad Thames, is the former London Design Museum, which Hadid acquired in 2013 (the same year she registered the Foundation) and prior to the Museum moving to a new site in Kensington in 2016.[4] Currently, the Shad Thames building operates as our archive and collections store. Hadid's purchase of the former museum gives us some indication of her intentions regards her planned Foundation and its intention to serve as a museum or gallery. Since early on, her office had a practice of making and touring exhibitions and the active use of its historical and contemporary collections. In an interview with the *Architect's Journal* at the time, Hadid stated that the acquisition of the former museum would "give an opportunity to consolidate our archive in a single location and also engage in a collective dialogue by exhibiting the research and innovation of global collaborations in art, architecture and design."[5]

Over the course of the next few years, our premises will be enhanced to provide accessible museum-grade collections and archive storage, a larger exhibition gallery and research institute. In the process, we are also planning a major retrospective exhibition. These activities afford us the opportunity to explore what it means to create a Foundation 'from the ground up' and especially in keeping with the unique status and career trajectory of a singular figure like Zaha Hadid.

Writing this essay at such an early stage in the Foundation's development (in its first year) has been an unusual and interesting challenge – it is not the honed reflection of a historian (or archivist) who has spent many years with her subject. In part, a practical account of the early set-up of an organisation devoted to a female subject, the essay also provoked a negotiation with the layers of legacy and interpretation which have accrued around Hadid over forty years. The first read-through of (uncatalogued) archive boxes, comprised not only of drawings but also (for instance) post-it notes, faxed correspondence, itineraries, notebooks and shopping lists, shows a busy office with a charismatic woman at the helm, whose professional and social life are blended, and for whom work involves long hours and numerous airmiles. The archive holds all the traces of its 'authentic' subject (Hadid) as well as those of dozens, if not hundreds, of collaborators and employees over time. So it also begs questions such as: Whose hand is this? Whose scribble or sketch? Whose comment or amendment? It may take years of archival study, coupled with detailed oral histories, to resolve authorship in such detail. The other aspect of archival research is the volume of published and broadcast material related to Hadid as a person – not only in the specialist architectural press, but also the mainstream and lifestyle press and numerous filmed appearances. There are relatively few scholarly studies of Hadid and her work, and only a limited amount of published words written by Hadid herself. She preferred to talk – in interviews, lectures and other public appearances. Her tone is informal – warm, funny, imperious at times. It was part of her brand image and often differentiated her from her male counterparts in architecture. This, then, is evidence of 'the empowerment of otherness' which Hadid so uniquely demonstrated. On the other hand, the persistent and at times aggressive interest in her person (not only in the work of the office) was a constant battleground for her. For a foundation devoted to her legacy, this is interesting territory to negotiate –and begs the question, to what extent is our mission to explore the life's work, or the life and work, of its female subject?

Planning a Legacy

> I leave everything I possess to an administrative entity, "the Fondation Le Corbusier", or any other meaningful form which shall become a spiritual entity, that is, a continuation of the endeavour pursued throughout a lifetime.[6]

So what makes an architectural foundation? Planned legacy projects may be the designed intention of architects' themselves, or of their families or executors. They often go beyond arrangements for the safeguarding of an archive, to add educational, philanthropic and research ambitions. Take the example of Le Corbusier, quoted above, whose plan for his 'spiritual entity' was devised over the course of fifteen years, with the architect setting out in considerable detail the philosophical as well as the operational logic behind his legacy organisation.

As Albena Yaneva has shown, the transition of an architectural archive from an office to a museum is a complex process involving many actors and also the recoding of works as they move from one designation to another.[7] Generally though, an archive passing into museum 'hands' will become subject to the wider requirements and processes of a public collection. A foundation does this too according to its non-profit and cultural status as a museum, and this is often also within the wider intention of preserving and enacting the architect's vision and philosophy. An architect, practice or estate may choose to gift or sell their archive to a museum, library or a similar professional or academic organisation. Archives may be handed on with the stated intention of keeping the body material together as one, in other instances they may be 'cherry-picked', broken or parcelled up for distributed sale or bequest.

A foundation created to manage and promote the legacy of an architect according to their wishes and in perpetuity is a rare venture. Like artists' foundations and estates, whilst their purpose may be varied, most or all would consider their core business to be collections and research, granting access for researchers and managing loans, copyright and licensing, for instance. Additional social, educational, philanthropic and research activities may include working with schools and universities, funding and promoting critical agendas which align with their subject (for instance, environmental or social concerns). They may award grants, bursaries, scholarships or prizes in support of their stated mission. Like museums, their collections may be open or closed, usually with future acquisition confined to works by their subject or their subjects' contemporaries or associates, according to the original statute of the organisation. Frequently, they will interact with other museums, dealers or collectors in areas such as authentication, provenance, loans and touring exhibitions. Over time, the mission of a foundation may change or expand – perhaps through the broadening of its collecting remit or by addressing contemporary concerns that pertain to the original mission. Like the cultural sector as a whole, many charitable foundations have begun addressing questions of diversity and visibility in terms of race, gender, etc., through their programmes, statutes and funding.

Legacy projects may also differ in the degree to which they promote an 'authorised' version of a subject's life and work. Although legacy-management and authorisation are often taken to mean the protection of reputation and the authentication of works for instance, the archival holdings of a singular estate can create multiple opportunities for revision and reassessment.

In the case of women architect/designers such as Eileen Gray or Ray Eames, archival evidence has repositioned them as equal partners with their male collaborators. In Hadid's case, material related to her life and work may challenge numerous assumptions about her, her creative methods, her collaborations and her client-relationships, for instance. But this is still work for the future.

The mission of Hadid's Foundation is described in its 2015 Charities Commission registration statement as follows:

1 The advancement of education and the promotion of useful knowledge related to architecture especially modern architecture, design and related disciplines by such charitable means as the Trustees shall think fit including without prejudice to the generality of the foregoing:

 1.1 Advancing the education of students and young persons in the fields of architecture, design and related disciplines;
 1.2 For the public benefit, establishing, providing and/or maintaining archives and permanent or temporary exhibitions of the works of Zaha Hadid (whether comprising models, furniture, jewellery, fashion, drawings, paintings or other related works) and such other architects or practitioners in related disciplines as the trustees may determine;
 1.3 For the public benefit, the establishment and maintenance and/or support of a museum and/or art gallery; and

2 The advancement of such other charitable objects as the Trustees may determine.[8]

Clearly, her intention for the Foundation was to extend beyond management of her collections into areas of wider education and research, and also to situate her work within a broader interdisciplinary field and in relation to the works of other practitioners. Publics – whether students or wider audiences for architecture and design – were central to her intention. The plan was in keeping with an architect who was also a prominent teacher in architectural schools around the world throughout her career, and for whom exhibition-making had been core to her practice from her very early days. Hadid's Foundation was not intended to be only posthumous. Like many architects engaged in legacy planning, this was begun when her career was at a peak and with no intention that it signalled retirement from commercial practice. Her untimely death at age sixty-five was followed by a legal case to settle her estate, after which her trustees could begin the process of enacting the Foundation's intended purpose.

It is useful to compare this to other legacy projects in architecture, and to differentiate from archives held by large-scale specialist organisations, such as RIBA, the Getty Institute, the Canadian Centre for Architecture (CCA), the FRAC (Fonds Régional d'Art Contemporain) in France; and Het Nieuwe Institut, Rotterdam. These organisations lead the field in thinking about architectural archiving and curatorship; including major research initiatives in conservation, documentation and the digital. They are also addressing questions of female representation and decolonisation (amongst others) through reassessment of their collecting and curatorial practices. The singular Foundation devoted to a named individual (or practice) is a rarer occurrence. A few have the benefit of a studio or house museum as their base, like the Sir John Soane Museum (the first architect to create such a unique legacy) or its modern parallel, the Cosmic House in Ladbroke Grove, London – home to the Charles Jencks Foundation. In the case of the Zaha Hadid Foundation, we are based in her original office which bears still traces of her practice's occupancy, although it is not a building designed by her.

The expansion of architectural practice in the late twentieth century saw the growth of 'mega practices' whose global scale and influence have supported independent legacy organisations. Possibly the most influential architectural foundation established by a living architect in recent years is the Norman Foster Foundation (NFF), based in Madrid and London, and chaired by Foster himself.[9] The NFF was formed in 1999 (after Foster won the Pritzker Prize) with the initial intention to fund travel and study opportunities for architectural students. Foster has acknowledged the enormous influence of a travel scholarship (the Henry Fellowship) which allowed him to travel to the US in the early 1960s where he studied at Yale and met fellow student Richard Rogers (himself the beneficiary of a Fulbright Scholarship). Since then, the Foundation has become the repository for archives and collections related to Foster himself and his various practices and is based in a restored Beaux Arts palace of 1914 in Madrid. As well as collections, it houses library, education and research spaces, and has a Foster-designed glass annexe which functions as an exhibition space.[10] Its collections include works by other architects and engineers admired by Foster (including Le Corbusier and Buckminster Fuller). The NFF combines its role preserving collections and interpreting Foster's work historically with a future-facing research agenda in areas of architecture, design, technology and the arts. Given Foster and Hadid were friends, the model of his foundation is likely to have informed her thinking, too.

Despite the exemplars mentioned here, there is still no particular road-map for the establishment of an architectural foundation devoted to a singular legacy. One thing is clear, however – the monographic architectural foundation is usually male, white and so forth. There are few, if any, in the name of a solo woman practitioner.[11] How should this matter? What framing does it create for the Foundation's mission and activities? To what extent will it shape its operations? Hadid's legacy, like her career, is an exceptional undertaking, not least in the ways in which it might address a life and a practice by thinking through questions of biography, agency and authorship. A female architect of Hadid's renown was expected to be both exceptional and typical – achieving heights no other woman has achieved in her profession, whilst asked to speak, though her own experience, for that of all women in her field. In the wider context of architectural history (and as her career becomes a historical subject rather than a contemporary concern), her use as bellwether, harbinger or exemplar of women's practice in architecture is likely to change, according to historical specificity and in light of thinking about intersectionality, for instance. Kathleen James-Chakraborty's recent essay comparing the careers of Hadid and Denise Scott-Brown, to take one example, explores the migratory experiences of both architects – Scott-Brown as a South African, Hadid as an Iraqi – and how this affected their own positionality in relation to mainstream practice.[12]

Gender in the Context of Legacy Planning

"I don't go around thinking of myself as a woman on a daily basis."[13]

An Iraqi woman who came to the UK in the 1970s and who established a practice in her sole name whilst still in her 20s, Hadid's rise to international prominence was not easy. She frequently encountered racism and sexism, especially during the early stages of her career. During her life, and increasingly since she passed away, Hadid has become a symbol of female achievement and inspiration. This has led to an unprecedented number of popular and professional accolades, from children's books and films made about her to awards in her name[14]. Since at least the early 2000s, it is extremely unlikely that any publication dealing with women in architecture would fail to mention her. In debates that highlight the lack of diversity within the architectural profession, she is regularly cited as the exception that proves the rule. Rather, qualifiers like '*even* Zaha Hadid' and '*despite* Zaha Hadid' are employed as means to describe women's continuing experience of inequality within architecture. Nevertheless, and rather obviously, this is not to say that her exceptional status put her beyond gendered categorisation. Burns and Brown, writing in 2020, observed that 'even when women's buildings meet the norms of 'exceptional building' status, the commentaries and histories on their lives and the explanations of their career paths do not conform to the exceptional architect narrative because the discourse of their achievements is frequently gendered. Pace Zaha Hadid'.[15]

When exceptionality was conferred upon Hadid through numerous prizes and awards, gender was inevitably the primary lens through which her success was evaluated in the press. As the first female recipient of the profession's top prizes; her ubiquity also highlighted the lack of general visibility for women in architecture generally. In 2016, Joe Kerr commented that whilst

> it is an inarguably good thing that a number of the great national and international prizes have in recent years finally been awarded outright to a woman for the first time, including the Pritzker Prize (2004), the RIBA Stirling Prize (2010, 2011), and the RIBA Gold Medal just this year … it is equally unfortunate that all three have gone first to the late Zaha Hadid, suggesting that architecture has indeed become more inclusive, but only to the sum total of one individual.[16]

The insistent gendering of her career success and her architectural practice was a regular source of frustration for Hadid, as will be explored later in this essay. Whilst honoured to accept awards for female achievement and who would speak on inequality in the profession when asked, she did not elect herself a spokesperson for the subject. In her study of gendered identities articulated by architects in interviews, Karen Burns identifies the 'tendency of female practitioners to self-identify as architects rather than women architects'.[17] This was absolutely the case for Hadid. Burns was referring to sociological studies since 2000, including Fowler and Wilson's 2004 study 'Women Architects and their Discontents'[18] where a feminist approach to describing the lived experience of women in the profession came up against an apparent reluctance on the part of interviewees to discuss gender as the sole or even primary reason for disadvantage. Instead, interviewees describing their experiences would focus on the constraints or complexities within the profession which led them to make certain choices to work full-time or part-time, to be self-employed or in work in education, for example. As Burns notes, ideas of individuality, agency and meritocracy are 'hard-wired' into the discipline and profession of architecture through education. Hadid, too, emphasised hard work and hard choices made throughout her career in order to succeed, whilst speaking out against the lack of opportunity for women to lead large-scale projects or be recognised by their profession, even though she managed both.

When equality gaps have been exposed, through studies which lay bare the bias and economic disparity experienced by women in architecture[19], one tendency is to focus on the lack of representation of women in architecture's prizes and awards. Despina Stratigakos discusses this in her essay 'Architecture Prizes and the Boys Club', recounting both Hadid's glass-ceiling shattering Pritzker win of 2004, and the sorry story of Denise Scott Brown's exclusion from her own Pritzker in 1991 when the Prize was solely awarded to her partner-in-business and husband Robert Venturi, and which, in 2013, prompted a major campaign to acknowledge her joint right to the prize.[20] Stratigakos notes the negative press and personal comments directed at both female architects for winning as well as not winning awards. She describes how recent criticism of the Awards 'Boys Club' has opened the door not only to wider debate about discrimination in the profession and has also led to the establishment of women-only prizes. It has also generated calls to recognise the collaborative nature of architectural practice, rather than the 'outmoded focus on a single star player'.[21]

Hadid, of course, was a regular recipient of both gender-neutral (sic) and women-only awards. And when she won, the criticism was often, as Kerr indicated, that she was too 'easy' a choice or, as others grumbled, that she was not the 'right' kind of woman architect. Take Vanessa Quirke, for example, writing in ArchDaily on the occasion of Hadid being awarded the 2012 Jane Drew Prize for 'outstanding contribution to the status of women in architecture'. Quinn's suggestion (in answer to her own question 'Is Zaha's latest prize really an advancement for women?') was that Hadid was not an architect 'revolutionising the profession for women' unlike Drew, the prize's namesake: 'because Drew represents an architect who sees architecture as an instrument of good; Hadid represents the epitome of an architect who practices architecture as High Art'.[22]

This all seems to be a case of 'damned if you do, damned if you don't'. Hadid won too many prizes, in a profession which didn't award enough to women. Her success as a role model did not prevent frequent assertions that her experience was too far removed from that of most women in architecture. She 'played the profession on its own terms and won' (in Quinn's words) whilst experiencing extreme bias based on her gender and ethnicity throughout her career. Little wonder that she was sometimes reluctant to speak on the matter of her gender as it was raised so frequently, and insidiously, in interviews with journalists.

In fact, Hadid was quite clear on the challenges faced by women in the workplace and in the profession, from the perspective of an employer as well as an architect. In 2012, the *Architects Journal* (AJ) published a damning report into sexism within the profession which highlighted (amongst other things), extreme disparity in professional advancement, higher drop-out rates and lower pay for women with children, male bullying in the workplace, and a lack of recognition for women's authority within the building industry.[23] Asked to comment, Hadid acknowledged the 'tough, male-dominated' environment and the systemic nature of architecture's inequalities:

> Society has not been set up in a way that allows women to go back to work after taking time off. Many women now have to work as well as do everything at home and no one can do everything. Society needs to find a way of relieving women. It may be a little easier now, with new technology, for a woman to take off six months or a year and then come back .... Like men, women have to be diligent and work hard. I have quite a few senior architects in the office and they are extremely reliable and very talented, but, when I taught, all my best students were women. Then they drift off.[24]

Hadid's office (like many other prominent architectural practices of this generation) was known for its long hours and late-night working culture. It grew rapidly, from a handful of close colleagues and former students working first at Hadid's kitchen table and then in a one-room studio, to a practice employing hundreds. The early years were precarious, in the sense that income was sporadic, competitions would involve working to the wire to complete entries, and there were regular setbacks when projects were lost or foundered due to funding. Strong personalities, not least that of Hadid herself, made for a heated environment at times. For many years, the office was sustained by Hadid's teaching and by exhibitions – both of which fuelled her growing recognition long before there was a significant body of built work. In later years, the extraordinary success and global workload of the practice created an intense demand for its figurehead to be 'seen' and whose public profile also sustained and attracted business.

Reading the Buildings: Berlin and Cardiff as Examples

What approach to the archive might we take when considering the intersection of gender with the process of making buildings? How did Hadid operate – in business as well as creatively – to see projects through? Through brief example of two early projects, I want to consider the various conditions under which gender became a factor, and how Hadid responded. The first is a lesser-known project in Berlin – a housing block designed as part of the 1987 International Building Exhibition (*Internationale Bauausstellung Berlin* or IBA) and completed in 1993. (Figures 7.2 and 7.3).The second is the competition project to build the Cardiff Bay Opera House between 1992 and 1997, a high-profile project where she experienced profound discrimination which contributed to the project's ultimate failure (Figure 7.4).

The International Building Exhibition in Berlin was initiated in 1979 to mark the city's 750th anniversary in 1987. Josef Paul Kleihues was chosen as its director. International participants included Peter Eisenmann, Rem Koolhaas, Alvaro Siza, Aldo Rossi, James Stirling and John Hejduk. IBA 1987 was a significant moment in Berlin's architectural history for a variety of reasons, too complex to explore fully here.[25] For a start, it instigated discussion of how to deal with the historical fabric of the city through 'infill and repair' and 'critical reconstruction' as a means of dealing with its interrupted political history which had left absences, scars and abrasions. Many participants were critical of Kleihues's approach, and also of the complexity of Berlin's building regulations, and it was hotly debated over the years of its development – the construction of IBA works ran into the 1990s and after German reunification.

Although its international range of architects was impressively broad, there was one startling fact- the lack of women. Criticism of this was led by the group FOPA (Feministische Organisation von Planerinnen und Architektinnen), who had formed to protest IBA. Under pressure from FOPA and also the International Union of Women Architects (L'Union Internationale des Femmes Architectes or UIFA, formed Paris 1963), IBA ran a series of design seminars in 1986 with the twin objectives of tackling the lack of female representation in practice as well as the lack of women-specific objectives in the planning process. A token solution was found – a site was identified on the corner of Stresemannstrasse and Dessauer Strasse (Block 2 or the 'women's block' as it was referred to), which became the focus of workshops on the topics. Three housing projects, arranged around three inner courtyards, were eventually commissioned, on the theme of 'emancipatory living'. The architects proposed by FOPA were Myra Warhaftig, Christine Jachmann and Zaha Hadid. Requirements included provision for disabled occupants and single women with children, including wheelchair accessibility and access for prams. Progress was inevitably slow given political events and the initiation of reunification. Post-IBA, management of the Block 2 housing projects passed into the hands of DeGeWo, the state-owned Berlin housing company.

Of the three female architects, Myra Warhaftig was an obvious choice– a German-Israeli architect who worked for Hans Scharoun in Berlin in the 1950s and 1960s, and who had completed a research project on housing and the emancipation of women in 1978. A single mother, she moved into the IBA block she had designed on completion and remained there for the rest of her life. Christine Jachmann had established her practice in Berlin in 1972 and specialised in housing. Hadid was an unusual choice, however. Despite coming to attention for her winning

FIGURE 7.2 IBA Housing, Berlin, completed 1993. Zaha Hadid Architects (Zaha Hadid with Michael Wolfson, Piers Smerin, David Gomersall, David Winslow, Paivi Jaaskelainen) Co-architect: Stefan Schroth. Client: Dewego AG. Photograph by Christian Richters. Courtesy of Zaha Hadid Foundation.

project for the Hong Kong Peak Project (1982–83), which was widely published, she hadn't built anything. She wasn't known for housing projects either. But she was beginning to be a prominent name, and in 1986, the year of the IBA commission, she had completed a proposal for an office building on Kurfurstendamm, Berlin. Still, she was apparently considered a risk by Kleihues[26] and was paired with a Berlin-based co-architect, Stefan Schroth.[27]

The project was a long-drawn out affair (with periods of inactivity), which put pressure on Hadid's small office. According to Hadid, her designs were being interpreted in Berlin in ways she could not control. Secondly, the building regulations limited the scope for experimentation. The regulations stated a required average height of five storeys in line with Kleihues' 'small-scale' vision. Hadid responded with a block in two halves, one tall and one much smaller,

FIGURE 7.3 Drawing (Perspective View), IBA Housing, Berlin, 1986–93. Collection of the Zaha Hadid Foundation. (©Zaha Hadid Foundation).

FIGURE 7.4 Cardiff Bay Opera House, Painting (acrylic on cartridge paper), 1994–96. Zaha Hadid Architects (Design: Zaha Hadid, Project Architect: Brian Ma Siy). Client: Cardiff Bay Opera House Trust. Collection of the Zaha Hadid Foundation. (©Zaha Hadid Foundation).

where the average would be five. This was accepted, but other regulations about apartment layout were also restricting. Furthermore, as reunification occurred (and the borders between East and West were removed), the site 'changed' from being a marginal one to a central site, but the brief didn't follow suit. Finally, the choice of materials was severely limited by cost and the colour scheme for the building was difficult to oversee from the London office.[28] Hadid's frustrations were, as she later stated, a 'struggle on two fronts, first against the IBA strategy of infill and repair, secondly against the tight building regulations of social housing'[29] She later alluded to a third, and that was her relegation to a 'women-architect only' project which she was reported as saying was 'like being told you had leprosy'.[30] Her principle objection appeared to have more to do with the IBA commissioning process for (women) architects, rather than the nature of the brief to design social housing for women (her project made sensitive provision for its inhabitants and, as Esra Akcan has recounted through interviews, is considered successful by long-term residents).[31] It has also weathered well and stands as a good example of her early work. However, the IBA project has never featured strongly in the Office's own history of its rise to prominence. It was eventually completed at roughly the same time as the Vitra Fire Station – the latter has always been claimed as her 'first' built work.[32] What this points to, on Hadid's part, is a strong desire to control the narrative of her career rise and to ensure that 'hero' projects like Vitra were centre stage.

The project to design a new centre for the performing arts in Cardiff was one of the architectural *causes célèbres* of the 1990s. Whilst the circumstances of this project have been described in detail elsewhere, they deserve a little recounting here.[33] The 1994 scheme to design a new home for the Welsh National Opera, as part of the Cardiff Bay Development scheme, a regeneration project for a large swathe of the Welsh capital city's docklands area, was planned to attract funding from the newly established Millennium Commission of the National Lottery Fund. Hadid was the outright winner of the international competition, organised by the Cardiff Opera House Trust (chaired by Nicholas Crickhowell), which attracted 268 entries. Hadid's design was for a glass-fronted complex 'like jewels in a necklace' arranged around a piazza. Despite her competition success, from the outset there was some open hostility to her and her project from local business and political interest, amid the complex of organisations with interest in the city's regeneration. A misconceived public consultation attracted a mixed reaction to Hadid's winning design. The organisers arranged a second competition round of eight resubmissions, which she won again (and then a third time, after another submission was arranged). The campaign against her intensified. Objections included her perceived lack of status in comparison to such names as Norman Foster and also the cost of the project, which was strongly defended. Critics described her project as 'an absurd architectural arrogance' and 'a monumental folly at taxpayers expense'.[34] Even more insidious, however, were the attempts to undermine the project on the basis of her being a foreigner and a woman, and the intense and personal behind-the-scenes briefing against her. The Welsh media stoked the debate by pitting the Opera House project against another bid to build a new national rugby stadium. The Opera House which, despite its name, was intended as a venue for a wide range of cultural activity, was branded 'elitist' in the press, in comparison to the national sport. Eventually the promise of funding by the Millennium Commission was withdrawn and the project was cancelled in late 1995. The cancellation, and the widely publicised treatment of Hadid sent shockwaves through the architectural profession, who saw the shambolic process as a threat to the integrity of architectural competitions and a 'dirty' campaign against a worthy winner. A number of prominent architects, including Richard Rogers, came to Hadid's defence, but overall, the episode reflected poorly on architecture's process of competitive 'trophy' building, and on this national project in particular.

The cancellation of the Cardiff Bay Opera House was undoubtedly the most difficult episode in Hadid's career, and one that apparently giving up architecture all together. She would refer to its negative effects in interview throughout the rest of her life. Fifteen years later, in 2010, Hadid's widely admired Guangzhou Opera House opened in China, with a clear debt to its Welsh forerunner. Hadid's career recovered, and she later would speak candidly about her experience, and the discriminatory treatment she felt she received.

What these two projects tell us about the gendered experience of working in architecture? First, that the process of commissioning, competing for and delivering architectural projects over many years is so complex that discrimination is just as likely to be buried in the bureaucratic detail of a project as it is performed in public. Secondly, that the necessary control of image and reputation by any 'brand' – in this case, an architect – is made ever more difficult when each wave of failure and success is accompanied by a kind of misogyny. Hadid's rough treatment at the hands of the media came during prize-winning success, just as it did during periods of struggle or failure. That she came through this and arguably used it to strengthen her career is an important feature of her legacy.

Conclusion

As Karen Burns has said:

> an almost unbearable contradiction exists in the public lives of women who cannot entirely control their public image but operate amidst a culture of fetishisation of the individual's capacity to shape her actions, mould her identity and receive merit-based assessment.[35]

This seems particularly applicable to Hadid, whose success (and charisma) afforded her a celebrity status and public profile unlike no other female architect in history – or almost any male architect, for that matter. From the early 2000s she featured frequently in media 'Power' lists of influential people, including BBC Women's Hour Power 100 (2013), Glamour Magazine 'Woman of the Year' (2012), Time Magazine '100 Most Influential People in the World' (2010) and Forbes '100 Most Powerful Women' (2007, 2008). However, these years also saw an increasing number of media profiles and interviews with her where the treatment she received was deeply intrusive.

It is hard to find an instance of Hadid's portrayal in the media where her appearance and personality were not scrutinised, or where she was not intimately questioned about her work/life balance and at what cost her exceptional career success had been achieved. For example, Marcus Fairs' *Icon* profile of her in 2003 made sure to mention: 'She does not have a boyfriend ("Where is the time for me to have a boyfriend?") and she has stopped going to the ballet – a passion of hers – for the same reason'. Fairs seemed particularly keen to emphasise what her saw as her 'extremes' of character: 'she's a temperamental figure with a reputation for tantrums and sulks. Yet she's simultaneously a woman of magnetic charisma who sucks flirtatiously on her Starbucks Frappuccino while *icon*'s photographer changes film'. Quite difficult to imagine interviews where it is suggested that Norman Foster or Daniel Libeskind managed some light flirtation through the medium of iced coffee.

Simon Hattenstone's 2010 interview in *The Guardian* is typical of the relentless questioning that she received about personal matters, Hattenstone's quick fire questions include 'Is there a man in her life?', 'When was the last time she had a boyfriend?' and 'Does she think men are scared of her?' Despite professing admiration for her, the interview is loaded with cliches – she is a 'mouthy diva', the 'Wife of Bath', and a 'fantastic monster'. It is also cruel: 'I could see her as an earth mother, but she has no children and lives alone in (her) flat'.[36]

Her apartment in Clerkenwell – a gallery-like white space filled with her own paintings and designs, regularly featured in magazines as a means of promoting her business – and was often the focus of gender analysis, in terms of its décor and assumed single occupancy.[37] 'Living alone' held a particular fascination for journalists. Xan Brooks, also writing in *The Guardian*, wrote in 2013: 'Hadid isn't married and doesn't have children. She lives alone in what visitors have described as a stark and impersonal flat down the road from her office. No doubt it works for her, though it sounds a little bleak'.[38] It was sometimes mentioned that her home did not have a kitchen as she usually ate out or was travelling (this is not entirely true) and this perceived lack of a domestic life seems to antagonise journalists keen for a story. It is also at odds, by the way, with the many personal recollections about her cooking and entertaining friends and colleagues.[39] Lynn Barber's 2008 interview for *The Observer* is a mean-spirited deployment of the usual tropes: a flat with 'the intimacy of a car showroom', a 'difficult woman' with an 'almost incomprehensible accent', who has 'sacrificed her private life' to 'rise to the top of her profession'. Barber's article ends harshly by saying: 'I came away feeling obscurely sorry for her and thinking how sad for her to have to go home alone to that awful bare comfortless flat'.

Whilst the Zaha Hadid Foundation's role is, first and foremost, to present the legacy of Hadid the architect, the nature of her celebrity affords us further opportunities for analysis and reassessment. First, by considering the ways in which design *in all its aspects* was part of her persona – not only her buildings and products, but also through consideration of her personal use of style and fashion and the environments in which she lived and worked. Like her much-photographed apartment, her signature 'look' – wearing labels like Issey Miyake and Prada, with dramatic jewellery and elegantly coiffed hair – was an important business tool as well as an extension of her lifelong interest in fashion. Her archives and sketchbooks contain numerous designs for outfits from an early age. She frequently collaborated with fashion designers and saw the design of accessories as an extension of her architectural practice. Certainly, she was not the first architect to show such interest, or the first to curate her image so carefully. Analysing her uses of style in this way might lead us to consider how other architects (male and female) orchestrate their own images. Her public persona – fearsome, dramatic and humorous – can be read as part of her brand image too, and an important tool in her client-relationships.

Curating a life's work inevitably leads to reflection on the entanglements of the personal with the professional, especially when, in the case of Hadid, they were so deeply intertwined. One task for the Foundation is perhaps to resist the drive to render her life in aspic through only one 'official' biography, but rather to afford researchers the opportunity to evolve multiple narratives. The day-to-day life of the office is revealed through the archive – not only in the sheaves of drawings which bear the marks of many different hands, on projects that would eventually be assigned, in public minds and in print at least, to only one name (Hadid). It's also there in the notebooks, itineraries and copies of faxes which detail business transactions and meetings with clients and as well as bearing scribbled notes about hair appointments and dinner dates. There is certainly a higher degree of fascination in the personal when the subject is a woman like Hadid. A task for the Foundation is to make the archive not only accessible, but also to do justice to its complex cultural relevance as well as its material actuality.

Notes

1 Interview with Zaha Hadid by Sophie Lovell, Uncube Magazine, https://www.uncubemagazine.com/sixcms/detail.php?id=15927105&articleid=art-1441185293554-a9de40e6-7535-46c2-91f2-0a07eb065c4f#!/page7.
2 The label 'deconstructivism' in architecture was promoted by Mark Wigley and Philip Johnson in their 1988 MOMA exhibition 'Deconstructivist Architecture' which included Hadid, Frank Gehry, Rem Koolhaas, Daniel Libeskind, Peter Eisenman, Bernard Tschumi and Coop Himmelb(l)au with works by the early Russian avantgarde.
3 Zaha Hadid Architects (ZHA) is a global architectural practice, headquartered in London and owned by an Employee Benefit Trust. Patrik Schumacher worked with Hadid from the late 1980s and assumed the role of ZHA principal director after her death. He is Chairman for life of the Trust. ZHA is a separate entity from Zaha Hadid Foundation.
4 https://www.dezeen.com/2013/07/09/zaha-hadid-buys-londons-design-museum/.
5 Zaha Hadid, quoted in Architects Journal, 9 July 2013 https://www.architectsjournal.co.uk/archive/zaha-buys-design-museum-to-house-her-archive
6 Le Corbusier, note dated 13 January 1960, http://www.fondationlecorbusier.fr/corbuweb/morpheus.aspx?sysId=19&IrisObjectId=7778&sysLanguage=en-en&itemPos=1&sysParentId=19&clearQuery=1
7 Albena Yaneva, *Crafting History: Archiving and the Quest for Architectural Legacy*, Cornell University, New York, 2016.
8 Zaha Hadid Foundation Mission Statement, 2013.
9 https://normanfosterfoundation.org/about/mission/
10 Paul Goldberger, 'The Norman Foster Foundation opens in Madrid – A legacy of the future', *Arquitectaviva*, 30.09.2017, https://arquitecturaviva.com/articles/a-legacy-of-the-future
11 Examples of design and architecture foundations in the name of women include several devoted to married partnerships, such as the Instituto Bardi, set up in 1990 by Lina Bo Bardi and her husband Pietro Maria Bardi and the Eames Foundation, devoted to the legacy of Charles and Ray Eames. Both also manage the historic houses designed by their protagonists.
12 https://www.transcript-verlag.de/978-3-8376-5630-5/women-architects-and-politics/
13 Zaha Hadid, quoted in the New Yorker, Dec 13, 2009. https://www.newyorker.com/magazine/2009/12/21/the-abstractionist.
14 In 2022, we recorded seven children's books devoted to Hadid (authorised and unauthorised) published in Europe and North America. To give comparison, the Frank Lloyd Wright Foundation lists eleven books devoted to its subject. https://shop.franklloydwright.org/collections/kids-books. Accessed 07/11/2022 15:07.
15 Karen Burns and Lori Brown, 'Telling Transnational Histories of Women in Architecture, 1960–2015'. *Architectural Histories*, 8, no. 1 (2020), 15, pp. 1–11. DOI: https://doi.org/10.5334/ah.403.
16 Joe Kerr, 'Designers of the World Unite: Why Trade Union Organisation Is Essential in the Fightback against Inequality and Discrimination within Architectural Practice', in Brown, Harriss, Morrow & Soane (eds.), *A Gendered Profession: The Question of Representation in Space Making*, RIBA Publishing, London, 2016, pp. 139–40.
17 Karen Burns, 'The Woman/Architect Distinction'. *Architectural Theory Review*, 17, nos. 2–3 (2012), 234–44, DOI: 10.1080/13264826.2012.730537, https://doi.org/10.1080/13264826.2012.730537.
18 Bridget Fowler and Fiona M. Wilson, 'Women Architects and Their Discontents'. *Sociology*, 38, no. 1 (2004), 114.
19 An important study in the UK was the 2012 AJ survey of women working in architecture and construction, which led to the establishment of the AJ awards for women.
20 Despina Stratigakos, 'Architecture Prizes and the Boys Club', Chapter 4 in *Where Are the Women Architects'*, Places Books/ Princeton University Press, Princeton and Oxford, 2016, pp. 50–64.
21 Stratigakos, p. 60.
22 Vanessa Quinn, 'Is Zaha's latest prize really an advancement for women?". *ArchDaily*, 12 April 2012, https://www.archdaily.com/225789/is-zahas-latest-prize-really-an-advancement-for-women?trashed=1&ids=2106029.
23 The AJ's first women in architecture survey, 2012. https://www.architectsjournal.co.uk/archive/shock-survey-results-as-the-aj-launches-campaign-to-raise-women-architects-status.
24 https://www.theguardian.com/artanddesign/2013/feb/17/architecture-misogyny-zaha-hadid.

25 For a forensic examination of IBA in the context of its user-communities as well as its architectural legacy, see Esra Akcan, *Open Architecture: Migration, Citizenship and the Urban Renewal of Berlin-Kreuzberg by IBA 1984/87*, Birkhäuser, Basel, 2018.

26 This is recounted by Esra Akcan (2018) through an interview with IBA architect Hildebrand Machleidt, who was involved in discussions with both Hadid and Kleihues (pp. 153–54).

27 Schroth also worked with Oswald Mathias Ungers on the 1987 Tiergarten Pumping Station in Berlin, also for IBA.

28 Hadid's account of the building process can be found in Yukio Futagawa, *Zaha M. Hadid*, GA Document Extra 03, Tokyo, 1995, pp. 24–30.

29 Zaha Hadid, *IBA Housing*, A+U 299, no. 8 (1995), 38, quoted in Akcan, p. 153.

30 Quoted in Deborah Dietsch, 'Beyond the Peak: Three Projects by Zaha Hadid'. *Architectural Record*, 175, no. 7 (1987), 118–29, p. 118.

31 Akcan, p. 156.

32 For example, see project information in *The Complete Zaha Hadid* (Expanded and Updated), Thames and Hudson, London, 1998, pp. 304–5. Dates for IBA Block 2 are listed as 1986–993, and for Vitra are listed as 1990–94. Verification of exact completion dates in archive papers has not been possible to date.

33 Nicolas Crickhowell, *Opera House Lottery: Zaha Hadid and the Cardiff Bay Opera House*, University of Wales Press, Cardiff, 1997.

34 Joseph Giovannini, 'Architecture's New Diva Makes an International Scene'. *Architectural Digest*, 53, no. 1 (Jan. 1996), 00038520.

35 Burns, p. 242.

36 Simon Hattenstone, 'Saturday interview: Zaha Hadid: I'm happy to be on the outside", *The Guardian*, Sat. 9 Oct. 2010, https://www.theguardian.com/artanddesign/2010/oct/09/zaha-hadid.

37 For an analysis of the apartment's design and its appearance in media, see Igea Santina Troiani, Zaha Hadid's Penthouse: Gender, creativity and 'biopolitics' in the neoliberal workplace in *The Routledge Companion to Modernity, Space and Gender*, Routledge, 2018.

38 Zan Brooks, 'The G2 interview: Zaha Hadid: I don't make nice little buildings', *The Guardian Sun*, '22 Sept. 2013, https://www.theguardian.com/artanddesign/2013/sep/22/zaha-hadid-dont-make-nice-little-buildings.

39 Many recollections of Hadid note her love of entertaining, of food and, especially in the early years, cooking for friends.

PART III

Social and Cultural Flows

8

FEMINIST ARCHITECTURAL HISTORY 2.0

Alice T. Friedman and Nora Wendl

This collaborative essay is the result of an extended conversation that began in March 2020. For some time, Nora Wendl had been working with Scott Mehaffey, the Director of the Farnsworth House in Plano, Illinois to re-focus the narrative about that extraordinary house and its history, paying closer attention to the role of Dr. Edith Farnsworth—a gifted nephrologist, medical researcher, musician, and poet—who was the client, and giving less time to the well-known, hero-worshipping stories about the architect, Mies van der Rohe. The resulting onsite exhibition, "Edith Farnsworth, Reconsidered," which briefly returned its first occupant to her weekend home through furnishings, books, and other personal details, was intended to open in March 2020, but was delayed by the pandemic; thus we decided to record a short, online dialogue, focusing on our research and our efforts as scholars to "shift the paradigm" toward a view that allowed for collaboration, creativity, and stories told by multiple voices—teaching by example, perhaps. Moreover, for both of us, the evolution of feminist architectural history over the course of the last half century, so clearly visible in our differing voices and approaches, and the emergence of new ways of seeing and speaking about buildings are key elements in the story, not just of our own work about the Farnsworth House, but for our research methodologies and treatment of evidence. We wanted to highlight these by foregrounding our individual voices and concerns, even as we point to the many areas of congruence in our work.

Part I: Friedman: Discovering the Farnsworth House: New Voices, New Audiences

In 1994, I published a short essay called "In this cold barn we dream," in the *Art Bulletin*'s compilation of critical perspectives on "The Subject of/in Art History," borrowing a line from the lesbian feminist poet and theorist Adrienne Rich for my title.[1] Grouped with contributions from cutting-edge thinkers in the field of art history such as Whitney Davis, Rosalind Krauss, and Lowery Stokes Sims, my article tried to make the case for a feminist, interdisciplinary, poetics of architectural history, focused not only on monuments or "canonical images" (such as the photo of Mies van der Rohe's Farnsworth House included in the still-in-use study set of University Prints) (Figure 8.1), but instead on houses, domestic spaces and ordinary places, drawing

DOI: 10.4324/9781003224662-12

FIGURE 8.1 Mies van der Rohe, Farnsworth House, December 1951, photograph: Hedrich-Blessing, Chicago History Museum.

on new sources of evidence, the small things and "fragments, pentimenti, bricked-up doors, erasures on drawings, snap-shots of rooms, household inventories, [and] private letters"—the "things by women saved" as Rich put it in her poem—that connect us to the everyday experiences and memories of the people, especially women, who lived in these buildings before our time.[2] In this way, our histories of the built environment might begin to create new narratives, attending to those whose voices had rarely been heard by historians (Figure 8.2).

Foregrounding issues of gender and power, the changes that I and other feminists sought for our discipline were ambitious, and I tried to make the case in my essay:

> Just as the art of architecture cannot be an end in itself, but is rather a starting point in the unfolding experience of body and memory, so buildings are the subject of architectural history only in the narrowest and most preliminary sense. This does not deny the poetry of built form but shifts attention from cause to effect, acknowledging the varieties of experience and the central role of the spectator, the "inhabitant" (for lack of a better term) or the historian in the process through which meaning is construed and value assigned. What we have learned from twenty years of feminist theory – from writers such as Laura Mulvey, Teresa de Lauretis, and bell hooks – is that the eye is connected not only to the mind but also to the heart, to an identity constructed across time and space, which shapes, deletes, foregrounds, represses, and selects what we see.[3]

Inspired by the political language and activism of the feminist movement around us, we turned away from architectural histories that focused exclusively on male architects and the well-worn

FIGURE 8.2 Farnsworth House, undated, back of photograph stamped "Gorman Child Photography," Farnsworth Collection, Newberry Library, Chicago.

narratives of their heroic efforts to replace old forms with new ones of their own design, histories that we had all learned when we studied avant-garde Modernism. We wanted to ask new questions, not by jettisoning the study of building design per se—as we were sometimes accused of doing—but instead by focusing on buildings as manifestations of structures of power, cultural values, and access to spatial environments that separated people by gender, race, and sexuality, as well as social and economic status.

As feminists, we also wanted to create new methodologies that would help us analyze the values and functions—literal and symbolic—that shaped the built environment, and develop new research initiatives that would enable us to reconstruct the ways in which architects, builders, clients, and patrons worked together in "constellations" of actors who created new buildings and spaces. In short, we wanted to shift our focus from the static forms of buildings per se to the dynamic relationships encoded in building programs—the real or imagined lists of a building's functions, and the maps of relational, lived experiences—with gender and power highlighted, hoping to better understand both the creative design process and the work of shaping and sorting that buildings do.

A number of pioneering feminist historians led the way. Each of these women made a distinctive contribution by asking new questions and finding new evidence on which to base their answers. For Iris Origo, whose beautiful 1959 book, *The Merchant of Prato*, became a staple of interdisciplinary teaching in the 1960s and 1970s, the catalyst was her discovery of a large archive of personal letters, account books, inventories, and business instructions; her goal, she said, was to discover what it "felt like" to be the merchant Francesco Datini or, notably, his wife and de facto business partner Margherita, who was the frequent recipient of his letters.[4]

Origo had come upon the archive in connection with her research on slavery in Renaissance Tuscany, leading not only to a 1955 article in *Speculum*, but also to a lifelong fascination with the Datinis and their relationship: "What emerges from these unliterary, unpolished, unromantic, self-repetitive letters," Origo wrote, "is the portrait of a man and a woman, so clearly outlined that we could hardly fail to recognize them if we met them in the streets of Prato today."[5] Her gripping story, with its focus on the details of food stuffs, fabrics, and household goods, inspired many readers to want to look further; the clues she offered about where events took place, together with hints about the character of the spaces, objects, and sense perceptions opened up a whole new world for historians of architecture.

In the 1970s and 1980s, new work on historical and institutional mechanisms of gender and power pushed the conversation forward. When Joan Kelly-Gadol's "Did Women Have a Renaissance?" first appeared in 1977, it asked a question that seemed obvious but had never been asked before.[6] That her answer, which emerged from her analysis of the lives of upper-class women within the context of writings by Renaissance Humanists like Leon Battista Alberti (on whose writings she had based her PhD thesis), was a resounding "no" was not surprising, but what was shocking was how little historians knew about women's lives in that period or in any other. Here again, new work followed in the wake of these discoveries.

Books and articles published in the early 1980s—like Dolores Hayden's *The Grand Domestic Revolution: A History of Feminist Designs for American Homes, Neighborhoods and Cities* (MIT Press, 1981) and Lizabeth Cohen's "Embellishing a Life of Labor: An Interpretation of the Material Culture of American Working Class Homes" (1980)—grew out of these initiatives: these scholarly studies foregrounded the significance of gender in shaping both program and built form while foregrounding the significant roles played by women (as documented in letters, photographs, and political writings) who responded to institutional and social constraints with creative agency.[7] Hayden and Cohen both focused on the domestic realm, a neglected area of study obviously closely tied to women's experiences, and investigated new forms of evidence, from period photographs to feminist tracts. Thus, through research into women's interventions at both the large scale of innovative planning and the small scale of "embellishing" individual tenement interiors, these historians clearly demonstrated the significance of feminist studies for architecture and the built environment. Like Kelly-Gadol, these historians also pointed to the longstanding gender and racial hierarchies that had created huge gaps within the discipline of history itself.

My own experiments with writing in this new way began to appear in the early 1990s. The first was grounded in a "test case" that focused on two Elizabethan country houses, Wollaton Hall (1580–88) and Hardwick Hall (1590–97), built by the same architect, Robert Smythson, for prominent members of the gentry with significant connections to the court of Elizabeth I, and located about forty miles apart in the English Midlands.[8] The former was commissioned by a man named Sir Francis Willoughby about whom I'd written in my Ph.D. dissertation, and the latter by a woman named "Bess of Hardwick," the Countess of Shrewsbury. What distinguished these two examples were the profound differences in their planning and execution. Wollaton had all of the signifiers of a fortified manor house or castle: a gatehouse, porters lodge, Screens Passage, Great Hall, and the circuitous access sequence—marked by frequent ninety degree turns and screened or blocked visual access—that were characteristic of traditional planning. Hardwick, on the other hand, was clearly influenced by Andrea Palladio's *Four Books on Architecture* (1570): it had a centralized plan, an open approach through a garden, a permeable hall screen and large, rectangular windows, and an elaborately staged sequence of processional routes and monumental spaces on upper floors that drew the focus of the household away from the real and symbolic uses of the Great Hall. Wollaton is traditional, Hardwick is innovative and forward-looking, reflecting classical principles of design that were frequently adopted in the seventeenth and eighteenth centuries.

The question I wanted to answer was whether these differences in any way reflected the gender of the two clients, yet what I found was not at all what I expected: gender did indeed play a role in the new strategies for design and everyday life that characterized Hardwick, not because Bess was a woman per se, but because designing for a woman client was such an anomaly in the experience of all concerned. Put simply, at Hardwick the client lived very differently by virtue of her gender, and her program—what she wanted to do in her house—could not be accommodated by conventional planning. Hence the new approach and the borrowing from printed and other professional sources which would have been of interest to the architect and to followers of new trends in design.

Perhaps unsurprisingly, none of the scholarly journals focusing on History, Elizabethan Studies, or Architectural History in the U.S. or the UK had any interest in a "radical," interdisciplinary, feminist study that focused on such little-known, non-canonical, and stylistically unusual buildings. The article was instead published in *Assemblage*, an experimental journal focusing on modern and contemporary architecture and theory. With few ties to the academic establishment or its rigid categories of periodization, the editorial board (and its much-admired editor K. Michael Hays, an architect and critic at Harvard) could afford to break with tradition and take on quirky, controversial questions. That bold move opened the way for more extended discussion of these issues.

Indeed, it was that interest that motivated me to turn to twentieth-century houses in search of test cases with which to explore the "Hardwick hypothesis." The result was the publication of *Women and the Making of the Modern House: A Social and Architectural History* (Abrams) in 1998. The book began by asking a simple question: why had the most significant modern houses been built for women clients? Through a series of case studies that focused on many of the most noteworthy modern houses of the twentieth century—Mies van der Rohe's Farnsworth House in Plano, Illinois, Gerrit Rietveld's Schroeder House (1923), Le Corbusier's Villa Stein-de Monzie (1926), and Richard Neutra's Perkins House in Pasadena, CA (1955), among others—I examined the ambitions and goals of the major players in the making of each building, bringing women clients and their concerns back into the story. Using letters and diaries, memoirs and recorded interviews as well as plans, photographs, and models—and of course drawing on the research and analysis of others—I tried to create new narratives that balanced the objectives of each of the major figures, focusing on program, etiquette, economics, and individual aspirations as well on the histories of architectural design, building construction techniques and style.

What my studies revealed was surprising to me and to those critics who had imagined that my project was simply intended to construct an essentialist argument about the superiority of women: as with Hardwick, the originality of these projects had far less to do with the fact that they were all built for women clients than it did with the social and architectural reality that women clients, and especially women heads of households, were, and still are, highly anomalous in the U.S. and Europe. When dealing with the spatial or functional requirements of these clients, none of the architects I studied could just turn to conventional paradigms or familiar planning strategies. Indeed, the new domesticities that these women clients were proposing—and willing to pay for—often involved hybrid programs and planning that combined living with work, or political activism, or artistic production and theatrical performance. These factors were the catalysts for change and creativity that produced the extraordinary modern houses included in *Women and the Making of the Modern House.*

In the case of Mies van der Rohe's Farnsworth House in Plano, Illinois of 1945–51, built for a Chicago nephrologist and recently renamed the "Edith Farnsworth House" by the National Trust in 2021, the client clearly wanted to boost her cultural cachet by hiring Mies to design her weekend house. We know from her memoirs in the Newberry Library that what she asked Mies for was a house in the country where she could live alone and spend her time doing ordinary leisure activities in a space beyond social surveillance and judgment, including gardening with her dog, listening to music, reading and translating Italian poetry, or entertaining friends. In the eyes of most American members of white, middle-class, postwar society, Farnsworth was clearly an outsider, someone whose single status and professional ambitions were decidedly "queer" in the language of the time—too tall, too artsy, too outspoken. Mies recognized this, and he used it to his advantage: after all, he had aspirations of his own, among them a desire to build an ideal modern dwelling that could exist as a diagram of domesticity, floating in universal space outside of time and place. Farnsworth hated the high cost, which ballooned to nearly double the estimate, and she was ridiculed by some of her family and neighbors, but it she appreciated her status as patron of modern architecture and the cultural platform this afforded her. The well-known court case in which Farnworth expressed her frustration and anxiety with Mies's office doesn't erase the fact that Farnsworth lived there for twenty mostly happy years before selling the property to the collector Peter Palumbo and moving to Italy.

My research on the Edith Farnsworth House essentially stopped there, leaving a handful of questions unanswered. That was the point at which Nora Wendl's work began: she tells her own story in Part II of this essay, outlining not only new ways of looking, but also new evidence and new audiences.[9] We know so much more now than we did twenty-five years ago, especially about gender and sexuality, conformity and indeterminacy, fluidity and trans identities. We also know more about the ways in which the persistence of homophobia limits and excludes queer—used here in our contemporary sense—clients and designers, and we are far more aware of the ways in which "whiteness" is invisible and needs to be called out. Viewed across the distance of nearly two decades, it seems obvious that by limiting my analysis to the most "outstanding" or "significant" modern houses—sticking to the Modernist canon of "quality" as the focus of my formal analysis—I had marginalized or ignored both a large group of unconventional women and queer clients as well as the work of architects whose projects remained screened, hidden, or interiorized.

Looking back, I have to admit that although I was able to expand both the formal and programmatic analysis of Edith Farnsworth's project through a comparison with Philip Johnson's Glass House/Guest House complex in New Canaan, CT, my treatment of Johnson's project was too cautious about his status as a queer architect, though clearly not in comparison with the dominant voices in architectural history which refused to make Johnson's sexuality a point of discussion despite his own late-in-life desire to "come out." What I was able to do with the Farnsworth/Johnson comparison was to highlight issues of privacy and the body, not only by looking at Farnsworth's comments in her interview with *House Beautiful* editor Elizabeth Gordon—she claimed that the house felt like an x-ray, a cage, or a sort of fun house in which she appeared behind awkwardly scaled partitions as a headless body—but also by comparing her experience, and Mies's strategies, with the role and status of middle- and upper-class white women in the U.S. in the late 1940s and 1950s.[10]

Indeed, the Farnsworth/Johnson comparison and the structural homophobia that shaped both the Farnsworth and Glass House/Guest House projects have led me to think more carefully about interior spaces in the history of queer architecture. Thanks to books like John Potvin's *Bachelors of a Different Sort: Queer Aesthetics, Material Culture and the Modern Interior in Britain* (Manchester University Press, 2014), which highlights the significance of interiors in the spatial landscapes and imaginaries of queer clients, it is possible to frame a new set of questions about the dynamic relationships between non-conforming clients and Modernist design. Equally important in this evolution of feminist architectural history is the work of my colleagues at the Modern Interiors Research Center at Kingston University, where historians like Professor Penny Sparke and Professor Pat Kirkham (formerly of the Bard Graduate Center) and their colleagues have for over twenty years foregrounded the imbrication of interior design with the study of gender and sexuality.

> Now I have begun to ask new questions: what kinds of modern houses did queer people build, and what kinds of spaces did queer people occupy in the 20th-century? What might these tell us about how we might design new spaces for queer households and individuals in U.S., European, or other contemporary contexts? Many people tell me now that they assumed that all of the women in *Women and the Making of the Modern House* were gay or bi-sexual – why else would they live independently of men? – although it is very clear that most "performed" flagrantly heterosexual and male-centered social narratives, having children with male husbands and partners and identifying themselves with male mentors and sponsors. While all of these women were clearly social non-conformists and outsiders in one way or another, and all of them were white and privileged, and all used their patronage of Modern art and architecture to distinguish themselves from the people around them. Were they also protected from further exclusion by their apparently "normal" gender identity and sexuality? I never really stopped to ask.

To answer those questions, I began by looking again at the "outtakes" for *Women and the Making of the Modern House*, case studies of houses built for women clients that I'd discarded over the course of my research and writing, with the idea of developing a new typological category called "Poker Faces," which would group together houses (or buildings more generally, like the church of "Our Lord in the Attic" in Amsterdam that, from the street, appears to be a typical canal house) that present a blank or misleading face to public view while concealing their interior spaces and functions. As a group, Poker Faces highlight the contradictions between how buildings look from the outside—or how they are "read" and interpreted by observers—and how they function as interior spaces. In a short 2014 essay titled "Poker Faces: Seeing Behind the Mask of Convention" (*Docomomo* 51) I began to explore this idea and tried to tell a new story about twentieth-century houses as an alternative to the celebratory and heroic narrative of my earlier work.[11] Many examples among the outtakes were houses designed in traditional and vernacular styles, and many had initially struck me as ordinary and in some cases quite ugly. However, when I looked again through the lens of queer studies, I saw something else: I recognized that most of these houses were designed for closeted, secretive, or queer women, or for "single" people who didn't want to have to answer questions about themselves or their sexuality. Obviously, these were people with very different motives from Farnsworth, or Schroeder, Barnsdall or the Steins. The ordinary, camouflaged, or non-descript examples I pulled together began to suggest new paradigms for the study of domestic architecture, and a new domestic typology that emerged in opposition to conventional Modernism, with its suburban or rural settings, its stand-alone monumentality, its glass walls and open-planned interiors.

Given the social conservatism and heteronormative values of many members of the avant-garde—which, as a number of commentators have shown, opened the way for an unquestioning, utopian acceptance of surveillance and conformity, despite the rise of Nazism, anti-Semitism, and homophobia—these "poker faces" suggested an alternative, protective modernism and interiority more prevalent, and more creatively innovative, than previously recognized.[12] As John Potvin discussed in his recent book, *Deco Dandy*, for both Adolf Loos and Le Corbusier, Modern architecture's clarion calls for change were fundamentally grounded in hierarchies of sexuality and race, hierarchies which placed interiors, decor, decoration, and ornament into debased categories that encompassed all that was "savage," feminine, and queer: "the time has passed," as Le Corbusier wrote,

> when we – men of vigor in a heroic age awakening from the powers of the spirit – can lounge on ottomans and divans among orchids in the scented atmosphere of the harem and behave like so many ornamental animals or hummingbirds in impeccable evening dress.[13]

No small wonder that "poker-faced" houses, like the churches of non-conforming believers in Protestant Holland, used architecture to conceal and mislead their oppressors.

The new category ultimately came to include examples in two different modes. On one side are vernacular or stylistically camouflaged examples like William Brainerd's Colonial Revival "Scarab" in Wellesley, MA (1907), built as a home for Wellesley Professor Katharine Lee Bates and her life partner, Professor Katharine Coman or Eleanor Raymond's Natalie Hammond Compound (1942), a cluster of four New England-style wood-frame houses built as living and work space for a group of queer women on the coast in Gloucester, MA.[14] In this category we can also place urban apartments and secluded compounds like those inhabited by such well-known queer clients as Gertrude Stein and Alice B. Toklas, Natalie Barney, and the hotel-dwelling Janet Flanner in Paris; in New York she shared an upper-east side apartment with her lover Natalia Murray, while in France she divided her time between her hotel and the sprawling manor house in the village of Orgeval owned and maintained by another woman (also her long-term lover) Noel Murphy.[15] On the other side is a different type of "poker-faced" house entirely: modern-looking yet closed off and blank-walled, revealing little or nothing. Examples like Frank Lloyd Wright's Goetsch-Winkler House in Okemos, Michigan (1940), Richard Neutra's Constance Perkins House, in Pasadena, CA (1955), Paul Rudolph's Hirsch-Turner House (better known as the "Halston House") on E. 63rd Street in Manhattan (1963), or Michael Maltzan's 2010 Pittman-Dowell House in La Crescenta, CA, north of Los Angeles are all examples of this type.[16]

A brief look at the Pittman-Dowell House makes clear why this sort of "modern/not Modern" example and the questions it raises offer such an exciting next phase for my work. In 1997, Lari Pittman and Roy Dowell, both successful artists and educators, purchased the 1952 Dorothy Serulnic House, a mid-century, suburban-style glass house with an open plan designed by Richard Neutra for his secretary and her husband. The Serulnic house occupies one of three plots in a six-acre compound thirteen miles north of Los Angeles, land intended by Neutra and his clients to accommodate future growth and investment by the original client. As it happened, the site remained undeveloped until one of the adjacent parcels was transformed by Pittman and Dowell into an extensive garden and outdoor pavilion.

The last parcel was given over to their new 2500 sq. foot house, which responds to both the increased density of the suburban California site and to the steep hillside with thick diagonal walls, layered openings, and a substantial interior courtyard that turns the logic of Neutra's translucent and permeable design on its head. Here the focus is again on boundary and enclosure, and while there are dramatic views to the valley and surrounding landscape via carefully choreographed exterior platforms and window openings, there are few opportunities for visual or physical access to the private space of the home. High, clerestory windows and small, randomly-placed circular openings offer little relief from the mute, futuristic form of the plain, white exterior. On the interior, however, the house opens up in a series of animated, light-filled vistas that crisscross along oblique lines passing through the glass walls of the court. Only one room, the guest bathroom, has a door that closes, while a luxurious, tiled bathroom/spa—nicknamed "the car wash"—with a generously scaled shower, bidet, and deep soaking tub, not only occupy a third of the interior, but are clearly visible from the interior threshold of the front door. Here domesticity is reinvented through the elimination of thresholds and boundaries: clearly no children or servants intrude into the cool order of the elegant living room, study, and master bedroom, and the notion of privacy gives way to a celebration of the male body that is choreographed, foregrounded, and staged by Maltzan's architecture.

In a number of interviews, the couple talked about their desire to "reorder the hierarchies" of traditional American houses, increasing visual access and reducing the kitchen to a secondary, functional space. As Pittman noted in *Architectural Record*: "As a same-sex couple, we felt that the old nomenclature of residential space didn't apply to us." Instead, they eliminated interior walls and partitions, and asked Maltzan to "disrupt and dismantle the hierarchy of spaces." According to Roy Dowell, they wanted to do away with both Neutra's tiny, "punishing" bathrooms, which responded to outdated ideas of family and privacy, and the space-hogging bourgeois kitchen in favor or a functional workspace for cooking.[17] This opened the way for the production of a new type of house: an enclosed cluster of spaces forming an interior that not only responded to, but also staged, queer domesticity. That this came about through a collaboration between architect and clients—noting here that Maltzan's focus on designing alternative domesticities has also yielded significant results in congregate housing for Los Angeles's Skid Row Housing Trust and new student housing at MIT—is particularly noteworthy.

The house built for Lari Pittman and Roy Dowell thus suggests a stark contrast to most twentieth and twenty-first-century American examples, offering instead a private, "poker-faced" domesticity. It is also a vibrant example of a new kind of modernism, one less indebted to the old heteronormative hierarchies and more open to experimentation and difference. Here again the image of Johnson's Guest House and its camp interior comes to mind and takes us back to the comparison with Mies's Dr. Edith Farnsworth house. Viewed through the lens of feminist architectural history, these important buildings acquire new meanings, becoming more compelling, more inclusive, and less constrained by convention than ever before. We have much to look forward to as a new generation finds their own voices and shapes their own methodologies, producing creative new ways to explore and interpret these houses and their evolving stories for new audiences.

Part II Wendl: Leaving the Farnsworth House

The last time I saw the on-site exhibition "Edith Farnsworth, Reconsidered," I was leaving the Farnsworth House. It was a late afternoon in November and the sun was setting. I'd spent the last two days at the house shooting a film that I hoped would translate what it might have been like to inhabit this house as Dr. Farnsworth did—the possibility of experiencing this house as a place, not as a heroic architectural form. For hours, I had documented what might seem like

FIGURE 8.3 *The wind has left you a clear echo* (2022), Nora Wendl, Video still courtesy of the author.

peripheral information: the slight movement of interior curtains, the way the waning sunlight ignited the edge of a pile of autumn leaves as a gust of wind swept them into the space under the house. The stark contrast of these decaying leaves against the white travertine marble was something I wanted to record alongside what occupied the interior of the house—recreations and approximations of the furniture that Dr. Farnsworth selected for this house, all put into place just as the COVID-19 pandemic was declared a U.S. national emergency in March 2020 and this installation was shut away in the house for months (Figure 8.3).

From March until June 2020, the house waited, suspended in time, full of those reproductions, but not yet open to the public. It flooded, briefly, in June. As friends and colleagues emailed me images of the river swirling around the house, I believed that everything we'd been planning for would be lost. The flood water eventually receded, and the house opened for visitors in July. I drove from New Mexico to see the installation in rural Illinois in those pre-vaccination days of the pandemic, and again a year later, in November 2021, when the pandemic was familiar and unceasing, and the installation was about to close for good.

The project of documenting this installation in film felt absolutely critical. Visual documentation of how Farnsworth occupied her house during her tenure there from 1951 to approximately 1968 is scarce: there is the series of photographs that were first taken by photographer William Hedrich without Farnsworth's permission—an event organized by *Architectural Forum* editor Douglas Haskell in late August 1951, just before he published the first review of the Farnsworth House, and just before Farnsworth received notice of the lawsuit *van der Rohe vs. Farnsworth.* These photographs were the first published images of the house—an agonizing series in which her mattress is on the floor and just a few simple chairs and one Florence Knoll table cluster in the living room. In a separate and undated series of photographs in her Newberry archive, Farnsworth reproduced these same exact photographs herself years later, with more furniture—much of which she purchased at the Chicago women-owned furniture store, Baldwin-Kingrey:

FIGURE 8.4 Top: Farnsworth House, 1951. Photograph by Bill Hedrich. Courtesy of the Newberry Library. Bottom: Farnsworth House, undated, back of photograph stamped "Gorman Child Photography," Farnsworth Collection, Newberry Library, Chicago.

Bruno Mathsson lounge chairs, Angelo Lelli lamp, low slipper chairs, and a Franco Albini table which shows up in one particularly memorable photograph: a neighbor's young daughter eats a sandwich there. From these photographs and from photographs that were shared with us by the families of her former neighbors and friends and the families of Mies's employees, we were able to piece together a visual history of how Farnsworth really lived here in and around the year 1955—and a completely different image of Farnsworth emerged, a woman who enjoyed coffee in the morning on the front steps of the house with a friend, Beth Dunlap (wife of William Dunlap, who worked in the Office of Mies van der Rohe), her poodles lounging beside her (Figures 8.4 and 8.5).[18]

FIGURE 8.5 Edith Farnsworth and Beth Dunlap. Photograph by William Dunlap, c.1951. Courtesy of David W. Dunlap.

As I entered this installation for the last time, I thought about the radical act of documenting so many details that are not explicitly the subject of architectural history. At the outset of the project, I'd been advised by a colleague that "the only thing we have to learn from is the building itself," that to re-furnish it was somehow superfluous or beside the point. Though dismissed as non-architectural, the shift in furnishing is a contentious act because it interrupts the assumption that the house is a complete, "Miesian" experience. Visitors are by now used to seeing the house full of furniture that the architect designed for pavilions and houses in Europe in the 1920s and 1930s: Barcelona chairs, Barcelona tables, MR chaise lounges, leather-corseted side-chairs, and two notable and patrilineal exceptions—a bed and a desk designed by his grandson, architect Dirk Lohan. But this notion of authorial continuity is at best fantasy: even the interpretation of this assemblage of pieces as "Miesian" is an error, and erases the unmistakable fact of the influence of designer Lilly Reich upon them.

For the last time, I walked through the south-facing sitting room in its configuration as Farnsworth occupied it in 1954. In place of the Barcelona chairs were slipper chairs that sidled up to the fireplace, a Florence Knoll table under a wild assortment of local flowers, and a recreation of that infamous daybed on which a woman—often mistakenly identified as Dr. Farnsworth—languished while a photographer snapped an image: the photograph that historians have often used to tell the story that she was miserable, defeated in her own house. The photograph that is not of her, but another woman, and yet stands in for her in that version of history in which women are indistinguishable from one another (Figure 8.6).

"Edith Farnsworth, Reconsidered," sought to unseat that type of history, and yet its genre—the house re-constructed for a tour—could not, even with a new tour script, truly subvert the history of the Farnsworth House. I had joined a tour out of curiosity during what Mehaffey and

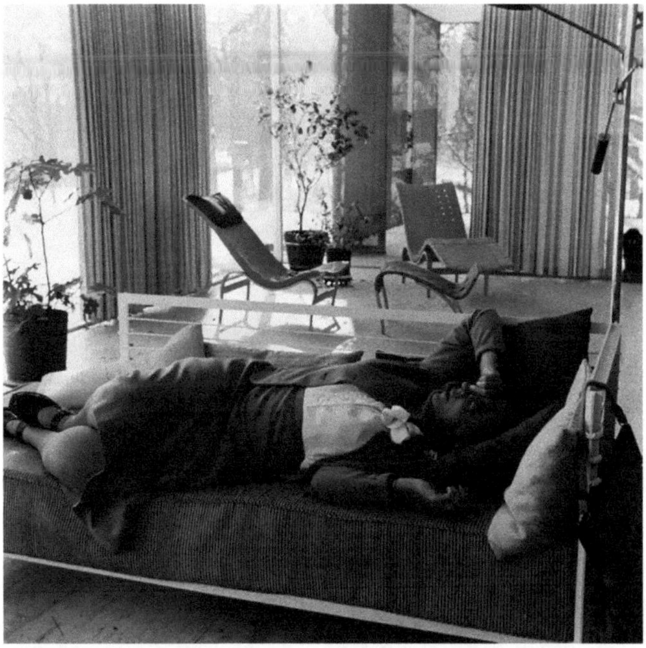

FIGURE 8.6 Photograph of unknown woman in the Farnsworth House, undated, back of photograph stamped "Gorman Child Photography," Farnsworth Collection, Newberry Library, Chicago.

I began to call the "Year of Edith," and though the docent expertly presented a totally new narrative, the same, familiar questions came up—*was she in love with Mies, were they lovers, she was a tough lady, wasn't she, haha?* History is never just history, but a power dynamic—and even the re-telling of events and the introduction of objects connected to the actual, lived history of the house (rather than the fantasized version) cannot override how that history is interpreted if the power dynamic itself is not challenged. The staging of the house with Farnsworth's furniture lasted only as long as the National Trust for Historic Preservation's "Where Women Made History" campaign, launched in 2020.[19] By 2022, that initiative ended and, with it, this installation at the Farnsworth House. I sat on the opposite bank of the Fox River the morning that the installation began to be altered and watched as a Christmas tree and other holiday decorations were placed inside. For the NTHP, the institution that owns the structure, the year of women—unfortunately coinciding with the COVID pandemic and therefore extended to two years—was over. The NTHP officially changed the name of the house from the Farnsworth House to the Edith B. Farnsworth House in November 2021 to celebrate her 118th birthday. However, by January 2022, the house was staged once again with Barcelona chairs and other objects attributed to the architect's legacy, this time presented as Lord Peter Palumbo had infrequently inhabited it after he purchased it from Dr. Farnsworth in the 1970s (Figure 8.7).

The power dynamic of the history of the Farnsworth House—one that has repeatedly dismissed and erased Dr. Farnsworth—would not exist had the house not been Mies van der Rohe's first fully-realized private commission in the United States. Had he not been so desperate for it to secure his career in the U.S., would he have brought up with her his architect's fee ahead of time? Would he have added to the lawsuit—in addition to the two fees they'd never discussed, his architect's fee and his contractor's fee—the lien that would allow him to seize the house if

FIGURE 8.7 Edith Farnsworth, Reconsidered, On View at Farnsworth House, 2020–22, Photography by author.

he won the case? In fact, from the first time this house was reviewed in the press, Dr. Farnsworth was imagined as gone—viewed not as a client or patron, but an unfortunate nuisance (who had paid over $70,000 to realize the structure). In the October 1951 issue of *Architectural Forum*, she is described as a temporary tenant whose eventual disappearance is in fact necessary for the house to be truly culturally valued:

> Mies is convinced that architecture should be no more than the shell within which each occupant produces his or her own dwelling. To put it another way: no romantic self-portraits of the architect, **no inflexible portrayals of clients (who, in the long view, may turn out to have been only temporary tenants)**. Mies believes that his architecture must be objective, impersonal, a quiet and simple space, a backdrop against which each individual and all human life in its great complexities can develop freely—and develop in changing ways, from generation to generation, **long after such striking clients as Dr. Edith Farnsworth are gone.**[20]

In my 2015 essay, "A Story of Sex and Real Estate, Reconsidered: Uncompromising Reasons for Going West," (2015), I'd carefully traced how the desire to erase Farnsworth in this way took the form of several rumors about her over the decades—the most-cited one being the accusation of her unhinged lust for the architect, which can be traced to an early quip by an editor at *Newsweek* in September 1969, just weeks after Mies died, claiming that Mies had said, "the client expected the architect to go along with the house" (implying that this was at the center of their disagreement, not money).[21] This quip mutated into a historical fact when Franz Schulze chose it for his *Mies van der Rohe: A Critical Biography* (1985), and interviewed her sister, Marion Carpenter, who claimed the now-deceased Farnsworth had been "obsessed" with the architect.[22] After Schulze, several historians including Maritz Vandenberg, Edward Windhorst, and writer Alex Beam adapted this pseudo-historical rumor to their own narratives, and the stories about Farnsworth multiplied, from her (unreturned) romantic interest in the architect to her deranged housekeeping—piles of filthy dishes in the sink, a rifle to chase off visitors, and her desire to destroy the very house in which she lived. And, in fact, much of Farnsworth's history does seem to center on her conflicts with men and institutions—perhaps, largely, because these are so well-documented. From *van der Rohe vs. Farnsworth,* which lasted from 1951 to 1954, *Kendall County vs. Mae C. Feeney, Edith B. Farnsworth,* in 1967 in which the county condemned three acres of her land to widen a road, to an accusation in 1966 by a colleague at Northwestern University Medical School of improper treatment of a patient (though the patient never complained), after which she simply resigned from her medical practice and teaching. And yet, beyond this conflict, Farnsworth lived an entire life. How does one register *that* as history? Where is *that* documented? What *counts* as a form of documentation? And *in what form* could we tell that history? Could we tell it without a plot, without a protagonist or an antagonist?

In her 1994 essay, "In this cold barn we dream"—referenced in Part I of this chapter—Alice T. Friedman makes the case for what she aptly describes earlier in this paired essay as a "feminist, interdisciplinary, poetics of architectural history." In this essay, she acknowledges the amount of interpretation that constructing history typically involves:

> Fantasy is as much a part of the process of reconstruction and interpretation as memory. Projecting ourselves into places we cannot go, we move through them in plan, on maps, in films and photographs, imagining their spatial qualities and the sensations they inspire. Desire motivates the searcher.[23]

Though I did not know it until our conversations in 2020 and 2021, Friedman had encouraged Farnsworth's nephew to give her papers to the Newberry Library to create the archive. And Farnsworth's archive is largely organized around her desire, rather than her conflicts. In the many hours that I spent sifting through the correspondence, photographs, memoirs, and poetry translations in her collected papers, I continued to gravitate toward Farnsworth's memoirs, in particular. Here, I could read how she saw herself in the world, how she imagined herself—a desire for a certain kind of life, her formative friendships with queer women, and her desire to build a house. In traveling alone for the first time as a young woman, she recorded how she felt:

> released
> from dimensions that I was used to thinking of as mine.
> So wide, so long, so thick and with certain traits thrown in,
> always through the refractions of other people's eyes.

But now
there was nothing to limit one's transcending.[24]

I found in these words an acknowledgment that I'd been seeking. Most historians—and in the case of Farnsworth's historians, primarily white men before Alice T. Friedman stepped in to contribute her scholarship—had the power to simply wield their voice and interpretation of her life and to be believed. Voice after voice, text after text, unquestioned authority. But one is only readily believed when they are *already* in a position of power. For the rest of us, those whose bodies are the thing that precedes us—the vehicle through which we are marked as other, different, those who are not trusted to be adequate witnesses of our own lives, let alone trusted to be witnesses or creators of history—the work that we do must be made physical, undeniable. For myself, and for many emerging contemporary practitioners engaging in writing and creating architectural history, the body joins the voice in the construction of architectural history.

There are rules about the physical engagement with canonical architecture that organize its separation from the body: the mandatory medical booties worn by visitors, the long list of things that cannot be touched. I encountered such a list on my first visit to the Farnsworth House in 2005, just two years after it had been purchased by the Landmarks Preservation Council of Illinois and the National Trust for Historic Preservation in a joint venture to purchase the house at that infamous Sotheby's auction. There were rules against touching the curtains or opening cabinets, but no rules against lying down on the travertine floor, feeling the radiant heat through my own body. There were no rules against lying in the grass under the house, either, or photographing the bubbling paint or the twigs littered across the surface of the travertine floor outside. There were no rules against anything that could not be imagined—and so, I think, that's where my practice emerged, in that space where, because it's slightly unimaginable, no rule has yet been constructed for "proper" engagement. In the space where the body touches architecture, anything is possible—and from this space, the whole history of architecture emerges.

Brennan Gerard and Ryan Kelly argue that institutions cannot transmit history, that only humans can do this. In their performance project, "Modern Living" (2016–present), they tell the histories of modern houses whose architects or patrons were queer: the Glass House (New Canaan, Connecticut, U.S., 1949) which was (sometimes) home to a homosexual couple, architect Philip Johnson and his partner David Whitney; Eileen Gray's E-1027 (Roquebrune-Cap-Martin, France, 1929), which was home to bisexual Gray and her lover at the time, Jean Badovici; the R.M. Schindler House (West Hollywood, California, U.S., 1922) which was home to Rudolph and Pauline Schindler as well as Clyde and Marian Chace—a co-living arrangement that emphasized private studios within the house and more public "sleeping baskets" on the roof of the structure rather than typical bedrooms. Their approach is to center the autobiographies of their performers alongside autobiographical elements drawn from the archives and histories of the clients and architects. They bring performers to the site of their performance well in advance—having them reflect on and write the personal memories that the architecture and its setting brings up. These are joined together in a script that moves from a historical lens to one in the present tense, often focusing on an interior, emotional landscape of memories of loved ones, past lovers, and self. By using what they call a "clock"—which orients each performers' spoken memories to a particular moment and specific directional focus—they translate these memories into autobiography. Gerard and Kelly research the lives that unfolded in these spaces,

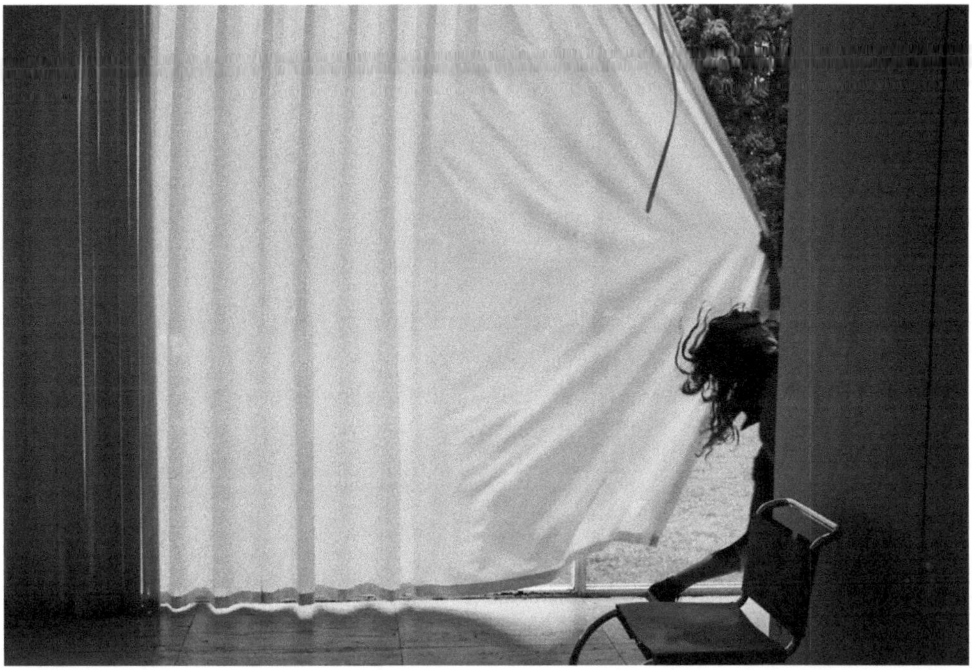

FIGURE 8.8 Gerard & Kelly, Modern Living, 2017. Performance view: Farnsworth House, Plano, Illinois, presented by the 2017 Chicago Architectural Biennial. Pictured: Julia Eichten. Photo: Robert Hickerson. Courtesy of the artists.

drawing from historic letters, photographs, essays, and other archival materials of the patrons of the structures and perform episodic choreographies—both movement and spoken word—that reveal the relationship dynamics that were once at play in them. Drawing from historic letters, photographs, essays, and other archival materials of the former occupants of each house, they speak (sometimes repetitively) words and phrases that encapsulate the relationships sponsored by the structure.[25] The result is an architectural history that is at once institutional and personal, historic and contemporary, openly queer and also ambiguous as the gender and orientation of the author—if speaking the historical words of a client or architect—dissolves in the present-day body and voice of the performer (Figure 8.8).

The idea of being firmly embedded, as an author, in one's theorizing and historicizing is not new. Stacey Young is the first to describe this as "autotheory."[26] She defines autotheory as a "genre of writing that emerges from the women's liberation and civil rights movement…" that "combine[s] autobiography with theoretical reflection and the author's insistence on situating themselves within histories of oppression and resistance."[27] For the purposes of this essay and my view of those engaging telling architectural history in an embodied way, this means creating history out of and through the medium of resistance, making that opposition to a counter-discourse not just intellectually understood, but *felt* by an audience.

I performed this in one of my own non-institutional engagements with constructing a history of/related to the Farnsworth House when I redacted every line in the trial transcript *van der Rohe vs. Farnsworth* during an artist residency at the Santa Fe Art Institute. In this act, I acknowledged the bodily pain of obliterating a document that Mies's estate allowed me to access as long

FIGURE 8.9 *Guard Everything Appropriately and All Will be Well* (2018) Nora Wendl and Melinda Frame. Video still courtesy of the author.

as I promised to "guard everything appropriately," to ensure that "all will be well."[28] Under these vague instructions and the even vaguer threat of what would happen should I disseminate this transcript, I performed what that silencing meant, the rote and banal violence of archival and institutional power that allows a woman researcher access a document, but denies her the pleasure of sharing that access with others. *Guard Everything Appropriately and All Will be Well* is a twelve-minute film shot and edited by New Mexico filmmaker Melinda Frame, the soundtrack of which is the squeaking rasp of redaction pens against paper. By enacting this by hand, I perform the physical burden of what was meant to be silent, and I resist internalizing the threat (Figure 8.9).

At the center of this work is a distinction that American historian Hayden White has made between "the practical past"—one's own life experiences, or "the situational account related to our everyday lives"—and the larger rubric of history that White calls "the historical past," the official account of an event based upon witness statements and other facts.[29] In autotheoretical projects, the two merge—author and subject become one, with even the singular, first-person pronoun, *I*, being used interchangeably. The embeddedness of the author in the theory that she writes is palpable in the words of bell hooks, who writes that theory was, for her, a form of liberation: "I found a sanctuary in 'theorizing,' in making sense out of what was happening. I found a place where I could imagine possible futures, a place where life could be lived differently."[30] And, Lauren Fournier argues, citing Stacey Young, that it is in fact the legacy of women of color and lesbian women who wrote theory from their own perspectives that began to address intersectionality as a feminist imperative.[31] This is present in the work of Saidiya Hartman, whose essay "Venus in Two Acts" focuses on the girls and women whose lives, records, and names were lost in the evil brutality of the transatlantic slave trade; Hartman writes that the work of recovering them is personal to her because "this history has engendered me, because 'the knowledge of the other marks me.'"[32]

A feminist, interdisciplinary poetics of architectural history can and should belie institutions; can and should transform how those very institutions operate from the inside, if only temporarily. This is perhaps the only future for architectural history. Sherry Ortner writes that

> [a]lthough patriarchy is a system of social power, it is also a system of cultural categories and personal identities. As a system of cultural categories, it is grounded in a conceptual division of the world into two (and only two) kinds of gendered persons, "women" and "men," defined as both different and unequal.[33]

To describe the installation "Edith Farnsworth, Reconsidered" as "her story"—in the words of the National Trust—in relation to Mies's "history" rehearses the very structures handed to us by patriarchy. And to remove the installation reinforces, once again, the power imbalance. Institutions cannot enact social change—institutions are organizations of power. Particularly, in the US, in which patriarchy walks hand-in-hand with white supremacy, in which the bodily autonomy and civil and human rights of girls, women, the LGBTQ+ community, trans-people, and people of color is a continuous question of partisan "politics"—in a country like this, organizations cannot be expected to overturn the very power that created them, within which they operate. The capital upon which these institutions depend—whether government grants or private donations—flows along these very lines of power.

Which returns us again to the Farnsworth House: visiting the Farnsworth House for the last time, I believed I was there to simply document the installation "Edith Farnsworth, Reconsidered"; perhaps I was also there to reconcile myself to the fact that this simple, temporary installation would be gone soon. Perhaps it was also a sort of grieving. I went alone, and while the sky darkened, I moved to the interior of the house. The tour guides and Director had kindly provided me with the keys. I turned them over in my hand, playing with the idea of staying the night here, of recreating what Farnsworth described as an uncanny and uncomfortable experience. I turned on the lights, thinking this would allow me a chance to document the interior as it might have appeared during Farnsworth's time. But instead, the light within the house turned the glass walls into a mirror-like surface, made me hyper-visible. I saw my own ghostly outlines in the surface of the glass wherever I turned. I also heard the hum of motors, saw the flash of headlights, and watched as two all-terrain vehicles made their way up the river bank, toward the house. Instinctively, I turned off the lights so that, in the dark, I could not be seen. From the house, five feet above the meadow floor, I watched as the ATVs made their way onto the National Trust's property. Later, talking with Mehaffey about it over dinner, he explained that the grounds had been used by illegal night hunters, and that it was deer season. The deer, over time, had learned that the NTHP land was safe for them: and by now, hunters simply stalked them onto the property at night.

I will never be able to disentangle my last experience of the house with this awareness—that, had I moved wrong, I could have been mistaken as prey myself. That, despite the expertise, knowledge, and hard work required to stage even a temporary exhibition at the Farnsworth House, to the surrounding community, this landscape was a place to illegally hunt. And that perhaps, as a local community, they had a right to that. That I could not dwell in the house for a final moment without being aware of the power of violence all around me. That the house does not live in an empty world, devoid of these things, but squarely within it—a flooding river, wrought by over-development and climate change, bullets whizzing by in pursuit of deer who've migrated to the area as their ecosystems have been displaced. We're part of this world, and our histories ought to be as well.

Notes

1 *The Art Bulletin*, 76, no. 4 (Dec., 1994), 570–95. Rich's poem is called "Natural Resources."
2 Ibid., 577.
3 Ibid., 575.
4 Iris Origo, *The Merchant of Prato* (London: Cape, 1957 and New York: Knopf, 1957); reprint of 1957 edition, New York Review, 2020, forward by Charles Nicholl, xviii.
5 Origo, *Merchant*, 11. Iris Origo, "The Domestic Enemy: Eastern Slaves in Tuscany in the Fourteenth and Fifteenth Centuries," *Speculum* XXXIX (July 1955), 321–66.
6 Joan Kelly-Gadol, "Did Women Have a Renaissance," in *Becoming Visible: Women and European History* (Boston: Houghton €Mifflin, 1977), 137–64.
7 Lizabeth Cohen, "Embellishing a Life of Labor: An Interpretation of the Material Culture of American Working-Class Homes, 1885–1915," *Journal of American Culture* (Winter 1980), 752–75.
8 The piece was published as Alice T. Friedman, "Architecture, Authority and the Female Gaze: Planning and Representation in the Early Modern Country House," *Assemblage* 18 (1992), 40–61.
9 This work resulted in a book manuscript, numerous new discoveries, and public exhibition held in the house from July 2020 to December 2021. These are described in an online talk, "Edith Farnsworth Reconsidered" recorded by Nora Wendl for The Glass House online site, https://theglasshouse.org/media/edith-farnsworth-reconsidered/ and in the second part of this article.
10 Alice T. Friedman, *Women and the Making of the Modern House: A Social and Architectural History* (New York: Harry N. Abrams, 1998), Chapter 4.
11 Alice T. Friedman, "Poker Faces: Seeing Behind the Mask of Convention," *Docomomo Journal* 51, no. 2 (2014), 22–27.
12 See Joan Ockman, "A Crystal World: Between Reason and Spectacle," in *Engineered Transparency: The Technical, Visual and Spatial Effects of Glass*, eds. Michael Bell and Jeannie Kim (New York: Princeton Architectural Press, 2009), 45–54.
13 John Potvin, *Deco Dandy: Designing Masculinity in 1920s Paris* (Manchester: MUP, 2020), 182, quoting Le Corbusier, *The Decorative Art of Today* (Cambridge, MA: MIT Press, 1987), 192.
14 Alice T. Friedman, "Hiding in Plain Sight: Life, Love and the Queering of Domesticity," *Home Cultures*, special issue on *Gay Domesticity*, ed. Brent Pilkey, 12, no. 2 (2015), 1–22.
15 Alice T. Friedman, "Queer Old Things: Glamour, Memory, and Spatial Imagination," *Places Journal* (Feb., 2015); see also "F the U-Haul: Janet Flanner's Paris and the Varieties of Lesbian Domesticity," in *Sexuality and Gender at Home: Experience, Politics, Transgression*, ed. B. Carnell (2017), 88–105.
16 Alice T. Friedman, "Public Face and Private Space in the Design of Contemporary Houses," in *The Routledge Companion to Critical Approaches to Contemporary Architecture*, eds. S. Chattopadhyay and J. White (New York and London: Routledge, 2019), 11–24.
17 Roy Dowell, Interview with Alice T. Friedman, March 23, 2020.
18 Scott Mehaffey, Director of the Farnsworth House, and architect Rob Kleinschmidt were collaborators in this project and bravely installed it in the Farnsworth House during a very uncertain time. They were also co-authors on the 2019–21 Graham Foundation Grant that made this very exhibition possible.
19 Anon., "Her Turn: A Campaign for Where Women Made History," *National Trust for Historic Preservation Pamphlet* (2020), 3.
20 Anon., "Houses: Architect & Client," *Architectural Forum: The Magazine of Building* (October 1951), 160. Emphasis is my own.
21 Nora Wendl, "Uncompromising Reasons for Going West: A Story of Sex and Real Estate, Reconsidered," in *Thresholds Vol. 43, Issue: Scandalous* (Cambridge, MA: The MIT Press, 2014). For quip, see *Newsweek*, September 29, 1969, under the headline "House Yes, Architect No." The editor's reply states: "Mies and Dr. Farnsworth were good friends and Mies once cracked that Dr. Farnsworth's discontent occurred because 'the lady expected the architect to go along with the house.'"
22 Franz Schulze, *Mies van der Rohe: A Critical Biography* (Chicago: University of Chicago Press, 1985), 253.
23 Alice T. Friedman, "In This Cold Barn We Dream," in *The Art Bulletin* 76, no. 4 (Dec., 1994), 577.
24 Edith Farnsworth, "Memoir," unpublished ms in three notebooks, Farnsworth Collection, Newberry Library, Chicago, unpag.
25 For more on this performance project, see Nora Wendl, "I remember: On *Modern Living*," in *Ventriloquism, Performance, and Contemporary Art*, eds. Jennie Hirsch and Isabelle Loring Wallace (New York and London: Routledge, 2022).

26 Stacey Young, *Changing the Wor(l)d: Discourse, Politics, and the Feminist Movement* (1997). Cited by Lauren Fornier, *Autotheory as Feminist Practice in Art, Writing, and Criticism* (Cambridge, MA: The MIT Press, 2021), 24.
27 Ibid.
28 Email exchange between the author and Architect X, October to December 2014.
29 Juli Carson, "Aesthetics of an Untethered Past," in *Mary Kelly: The Voice Remains (Works in Compressed Lint 1999–2017)* (New York: Mitchell-Innes & Nash, 2017), 164.
30 bell hooks, *Teaching to Transgress: Education as the Practice of Freedom* (New York and London: Routledge, 1994), 61.
31 Lauren Fornier, *Autotheory as Feminist Practice in Art, Writing, and Criticism* (Cambridge, MA: The MIT Press), 24. Fournier identifies that Young cites Minnie Bruce Pratt's *Rebellion: Essays 1980–1991,* Rosario Morales and Aurora Morales's *Getting Home Alive* (1986), and the 1981 anthology *This Bridge Called My Back: Writings by Radical Women of Color*, edited by Gloria Anzaldua and Cherri Moraga, as original examples of autotheoretical texts.
32 Saidiya Hartman, "Venus in Two Acts," in *Small Axe*, Vol. 26 (June 2008), 4. Hartman quotes Veena Das, *Life and Words: Violence and the Descent into the Ordinary* (Berkeley, CA: University of California Press, 2007).
33 Sherry B. Ortner, "Too Soon for Post-Feminism: The Ongoing Life of Patriarchy in Neoliberal America," in *History and Anthropology* (New York and London: Routledge, 2014), 5.

9

EXPANDING AGENCY

Ethel Power, *House Beautiful*, and the Writing of the History of American Architecture

Kathleen James-Chakraborty

When I was a college senior, my thesis advisor required me to skim two decades of *Harper's Magazine*, which he upheld as a key source for understanding the upper middle class American culture in which the building I was studying was embedded. It took me forty years, however, to move beyond using newspapers to supplement the stories I and my colleagues easily found in professional architectural journals and turn my attention to the shelter press, that is to journals that target consumers of architecture and design, most of whom its editors presume to be female. Why so long? Did I presume that middle-class women were not as worthy subjects as the male makers upon whom I focused for much of my career as an architectural historian? Certainly, I was less interested in studying the taste of my grandmothers, their sisters, and their sisters-in-law than in modernist alternatives to their familiar approaches to the decoration of their homes. Yet once I scanned the pages of *House Beautiful* in the years it was edited by Ethel Power, and the contributions she made to its pages immediately afterwards, it became clear that I had greatly underestimated the impact women had in shaping taste in the United States in the 1920s and early 1930s. This included – but was by no means limited to – their reception of modern European architecture and their creation of networks, often fostered by same-sex relationships, that supported women's professional careers as architects, interior decorators, and landscape architects. Furthermore, Power sought to educate women to be able to commission, renovate, and decorate houses as well as maintain their gardens. She also presumed that women would be interested in gentrifying neighborhoods, preserving historic architecture, and staying abreast of new approaches to housing. The purpose of these activities, at least as defined by the editorial content rather than ads, was not an extension of caring for husbands or children. Readers were to find intellectual fulfillment through creating and inhabiting well-designed alternatives to what were understood to be outmoded late Victorian paradigms. While the assistance of professional architects, landscape architects, and decorators was presumed to be key, *House Beautiful's* female readers were expected to want to be able to read plans, to learn to understand modern appliances and mechanical systems, and to be familiar with the history of architecture and decorative arts in Europe, the United States, and beyond.

Ethel Power was one of the first students to enroll at the Cambridge School of Architecture and Landscape Architecture, the only all-female degree program in architecture ever offered

DOI: 10.4324/9781003224662-13

FIGURE 9.1 *House Beautiful* illustration by E.J. Munro, July 1925, 12.5 × 9.75″. Vintage Magazine Covers collection, Rhode Island School of Design, Fleet Library, Picture Collection.

in the United States; she would later serve on its Board of Trustees.[1] In 1922, she became the editor of *House Beautiful*, a position she resigned at the end of 1933, although she continued to contribute articles in 1934 and 1935 (Figure 9.1). Established in Chicago in 1896, *House Beautiful* was the earliest consumer-oriented publication in the United States to focus exclusively on architecture, interior decoration, and design. It also covered gardening. Left out, however, were fashion, fiction, and the housekeeping advice included in the magazines targeted at women, such as *Ladies Home Journal* and *Good Housekeeping*, that were already well established by this point and, with circulations that could surpass one million, ten times what *House Beautiful* achieved under Power's stewardship, were the country's most widely read periodicals.

Journalism, far more than architecture, had for nearly a century at the time of Power's appointment been a well-worn path for well-educated unmarried or widowed New England women to achieve economic independence. Female readership supported women writers. Sarah Hale, the editor of *Godey's Lady's Book* from 1837 to 1877, was the first of a series of influential female editors. By the 1920s, a quarter of the country's journalists were women.[2] Women were presumed to be especially suited to judging buildings, and not just houses. Women writing about architecture and interior design in the nineteenth century in the United States included Louise Tuthill, the author of the first survey of architectural history published in the country; Mariana Griswold van Rensselaer, the country's first architecture critic, and the novelists Harriet Beecher Stowe and Edith Wharton.[3]

House Beautiful already had a remarkable history before Power took the helm. In 1897, a year after it was founded, it became the first journal of any kind to publish the work of Frank Lloyd Wright; it continued to offer key support to the Prairie Style until moving east to Boston in 1910.[4] Power was well positioned to reconfigure the magazine's progressive outlook in relation to New England's architectural heritage. Although not a native of Boston, she came from a family that had roots in nearby Salem and Marblehead. Her father died when she was still in her early teens; her mother followed just over a decade later.[5] The family was well-established in the region but probably not wealthy enough so that Power did not need to have to support herself. Through the Cambridge School, Power belonged to a network of women who had similar backgrounds and were also engaged in building careers as architects, landscape architects, and journalists. These included the architects Lois Howe and Eleanor Raymond. Howe, one of the first women to receive a degree in architecture from the Massachusetts Institute of Technology, injected her comprehensive knowledge of the region's seventeenth- and eighteenth-century architecture into her designs for houses.[6] Power met Raymond, her life partner and a fellow graduate of the Cambridge School, through their shared commitment to women's suffrage. Relationships like theirs were not unusual in these circles, or among educated Bostonian women more generally, and were accepted as long as they did not openly flout convention.[7] Instead, these women shaped it, above all by redefining the Colonial Revival in terms of modern comfort and simplicity in a way that eventually morphed into an early acceptance of new architectural styles from Europe.

I began to scroll through digitized issues of *House Beautiful* from the 1920s while sitting in the living room of my mother's house in New Hampshire's White Mountains. A modest farmhouse erected just before the start of the Civil War; it was later extended to serve as a summer house. The furnishings that surrounded me, most of which dated to the second quarter of the nineteenth century, were amassed by my stepfather's grandmother, who was Power's exact contemporary; both were born in 1881. Although I first visited the house only in 2015, it felt uncannily familiar, as the style of decoration was that of my mother's and grandmother's generations of my own family. While my mother assured me that her mother's apparently innate good taste had not been dependent on perusing a home decorating magazine, it is inconceivable to me that these women had been unaware of the issues Power edited in the 1920s.

My grandmothers and great aunts who could have read these issues had much in common with Power and the decorating strategies she favored. Younger than Power, they were born between 1892 and 1916. Although several spent their adult lives in New England, most grew up in Baltimore, where many were educated at the Bryn Mawr School; only one, a great-aunt by marriage, graduated from college.[8] Book-lined walls were not surprisingly a favorite decorating motif, and few of the classic and contemporary novels, volumes of poetry, museum exhibition catalogues, and popular works of history on their shelves were there simply for show.

Books aside, the decorating choices these women made were indisputably statements of whiteness, but also of very particular class and ethnic identities. Like Power, these women, except for one émigré from Germany, could trace their family's presence on the Eastern Seaboard to the eighteenth century. Well enough off to express themselves through the objects with which they surrounded themselves, they shared Power's use of interior decoration to establish visual continuity between the present and the history of that part of the world from the middle of the eighteenth to the middle of the nineteenth centuries. This distinguished them not only from the Catholic and Jewish immigrants who poured into the United States after the Civil War, but also from what they saw as the old-fashioned, stilted formality of their parents, as well as the ostentation of those whose greater wealth most could not afford to match.

Already in 1922, Rose Greely, a fellow graduate of the Cambridge School who would be one of Power's most regular contributors, defended a colonial revival house in *House Beautiful's* pages by noting, "In the Victorian age, convenience would have been considered an enemy of beauty. But now, fortunately, we see beauty in simplicity, rather than elaboration" (Figure 9.2).[9] Ideally, the understated American-made furniture these women displayed in their living and dining rooms, along with the porcelain, prints, and silver, were family heirlooms whose manufacture showed few traces of industrial production or of the rich ornament it made more easily possible; just as often they were chosen to imply that this was the case. Persian rugs and chintz curtains were of more recent manufacture, but their Asian patterns were presumed to be timeless. The comfortable seating that supplemented these references to the past and other cultures had little discernable style. The intention was that these rooms look as if they had always been there. And indeed, by the time I first visited them in the 1960s, many had probably changed little for several decades; one remained reassuringly familiar into the twenty-first century.

As a historian of architecture, however, I am well aware that this intended sense of permanence was very much products of a particular time and class. Growing up in the early years of the twentieth century, these women were surrounded by what they regarded as stodgier furniture from the second half of the nineteenth century, much of which survived in less privileged positions in the dwellings they inhabited as adults. Power did not define the aesthetic that pushed these pieces out of public view on her own, but it did emerge in the first three – and especially the third – decades of the twentieth century out of the milieu of which she became a prominent representative and for which she served as an influential tastemaker. What impressed me reading these volumes of *House Beautiful* was the degree to which, building on nearly a century of advice literature published in the United States and targeted at precisely such readers as my grandmothers and great aunts, Power focused on education and empowerment. Betty Friedan would later chastise postwar women's magazines as a source for what she termed the "feminine mystique," but domesticity was not presented in *House Beautiful* as necessarily paired with caring for a husband and children, but instead as a possible means of self-expression, including on the part of career women (Figure 9.3).[10] And although Richard Ohmann has described how the emergence of mass-marketed periodicals in the country at the end of the nineteenth century occurred as editors sold their reader's attention to advertisers, the many pages of full-page ads for building materials, bathroom fixtures, and heating systems appeared only loosely tied to the articles.[11] Overt product placement simply did not happen.

Instead, Power's purpose was to train her presumably female readers to become informed consumers. A regular reader of *House Beautiful* was presented with the plans as well as the information about the latest building materials and mechanical systems, plus styles and their sources, available to her to build and furnish new houses, update Victorian ones, or renovate historic ones. Thus empowered, she could make decisions governed by a commitment to simplicity and relative informality understood to be appropriate to the descendants of early white settlers of New England and California while also taking advantage of the technology that increasingly

422 *THE HOUSE BEAUTIFUL*

THE BREAKFAST-ROOM SHOWING THE WIDE DUTCH DOOR OPENING ON THE TERRACE, AND THE CHINA CABINET AND SLIDING DOORS BENEATH OPENING BOTH INTO THIS ROOM AND THE KITCHEN

THE KITCHEN IS BY NO MEANS THE LEAST ATTRACTIVE ROOM, WITH ITS DOVE-GRAY WOODWORK, BLACK AND WHITE LINOLEUM AND UN-BLEACHED COTTON CURTAINS EDGED WITH BLUE AND WHITE CHINTZ

THE FIREPLACE, WITH ITS SIMPLE MOULDING AND PANELING AND BLACK CEMENT FACING, SHOWS THE CAREFUL ATTENTION WHICH HAS BEEN PAID TO EVERY DETAIL. THE LIGHTING FIXTURES ARE BLACK AND GILT

FIGURE 9.2 Excerpt from an article "A Small House of Distinction" by Rose Greely exemplify an interior design of an American home, *House Beautiful* 52 (1922): 422. Public domain, courtesy of HathiTrust.

THE HOUSE BEAUTIFUL

A House Designed *for the* Business Woman

This house, *designed by the* house beautiful home builders' service bureau, *is planned for either the small family of two or three or for one or two business women who prefer a single house to an apartment, but who want the same convenience that an apartment affords. A separate hallway which, although very small, contains a coat closet, a breakfast-room large enough for dining on ordinary occasions, an ample living-room and a well-arranged kitchen, on the first floor, with two bedrooms and a bath upstairs, constitute a well-organized plan which has also such convenient features as a separate telephone closet, a closet near the porch which can be used for garden tools if desired, and the now essential attached garage. The house has shingles on three sides and matched boarding on the front*

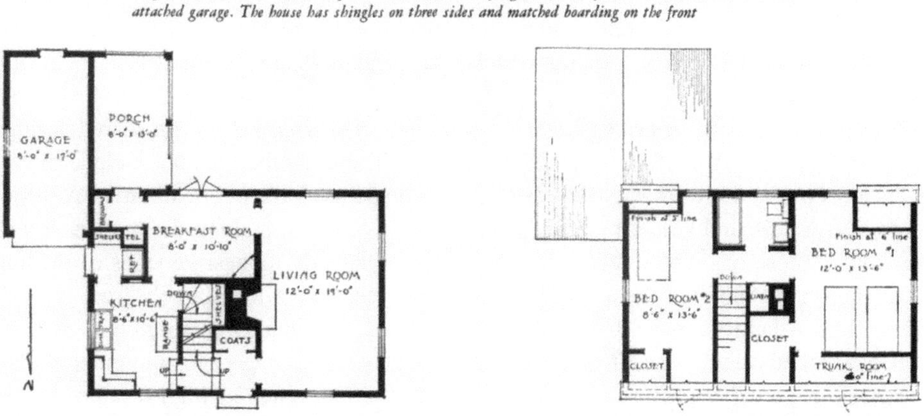

[160]

FIGURE 9.3 "A House Designed for the Business Woman" excerpt from *House Beautiful* 69 (1931): 160. Public domain, Internet Archive.

replaced domestic servants. Power also enabled her to participate as a well-informed citizen in discussions about community planning with the same critical skills readers gained in recognizing the motifs in an antique palampore from India or a carpet from Iran.[12] Simply being fashionable ("Good taste is quite another thing from fashion," an unidentified author, who may have been Power herself, quipped in 1923) was actively discouraged as was, excepting in the many advertisements for silver cutlery and for automobiles, overt luxury.[13] Although the magazine regularly featured mansions alongside ample urban apartments, Power was committed to publishing relatively economical houses of two to four bedrooms. For many years the magazine ran an annual Small House Competition, won in 1931 by William Wurster's self-consciously unshowy house for Sadie Gregory.[14] Power's book *The Smaller American Home*, of 1927, further buttressed her reputation as an expert in this area.[15]

Crucially, *House Beautiful* also showed women how they could support themselves through such efforts. The work of architects Howe, Raymond, and Verna Cook Salomonsky featured regularly in its pages.[16] So did that of Ellen Shipman and other female landscape architects, not to mention women who supported themselves as decorators, such as Raymond's sister Rachel, or who designed textiles and furnishings, including the Hungarian-born sisters Ilonka and Marisha Karasz.[17] The majority of the magazine's writers were female; some such as Sophie Kerr and Catherine Drinker Bowen were or became well-known writers; others, including Greely, the first female architect licensed to practice in Washington, or Isabel Goodwin, who contributed a series on gardens in the city's gentrifying Georgetown neighborhood, undoubtedly welcomed the income and publicity such contributions generated.[18] Probably the majority of the books reviewed in the magazine were by women authors, some of them familiar to readers as regular contributors.[19] Many of those who wrote or whose work was illustrated in the magazine's pages had studied at the Cambridge School, but Power was also alert to new talent, and especially on the lookout for women who could address their readers in the slightly chatty style she clearly favored. She herself wrote of one contributor,

> Mrs. Elizabeth Macdonald has a husband and three children. She also has a ten-room house and a garden in which she raised twenty-seven pumpkins. Moreover, she not only runs her home according to the very excellent advice that she gives, but in addition she is professor of Economics at Boston University, and a writer (her book *Home-Making, A Profession for Men and Women*, written in collaboration with her husband, will soon be published).[20]

Power herself was an astute professional. The circulation of *House Beautiful* soared during her editorship from 63,662 in 1924 to 105,972 in 1933.[21] These numbers do not include the many readers to whom copies were passed by friends, or who perused it in public libraries. A subscription cost $3 a year; individual monthly issues thirty-five cents, making the magazine widely affordable to those who could afford to inhabit even relatively modest versions of the homes Power published. Although the examples Power focused were drawn largely from New England, the Mid-Atlantic, and California, the magazine had a national circulation. Except in 1932, numbers climbed steadily despite the Depression when advertising pages plummeted; during these years, it probably provided an aspirational distraction, much as high fashion monthlies do for those who will never buy a couture dress but might easily splurge on a designer lipstick. This fall in revenue sparked the sale of what had been an independent business to Hearst; Power resigned rather than move to New York. She continued to be a contributor but was unwilling to leave Raymond and the apartment they shared on Boston's Beacon Hill or their summer house in Gloucester behind. The journal's circulation numbers immediately slipped, but not by much. It remains a Hearst publication to this day.

One of the inherent tensions during Power's years at the helm was between her belief, shared by many of those who wrote for her and many whose designs for houses, gardens, interiors, and objects she published, in transcending fashion, and the fact that such publications earn their keep by marketing the new. Today we recognize that the version of the colonial revival presented in her pages was, like that presented in museum period rooms of the day, far from historically accurate.[22] Its appeal at the time, like that of the Native American (declared in 1932 to be "modernists in the true sense") and Mexican designs Power also included, was undoubtedly tied to the way in which such articles combined a respect for a past that implied stability at a time when most of the new houses illustrated in the magazine were actually located either in new high-rise apartment towers or, more commonly, in rapidly growing suburbs.[23] The magazine's focus also encompassed the gentrification of older urban neighborhoods as well as the renovation of historic homes in rural and small town New England, including their transformation into vacation homes.[24] These, including the one in which my mother now lives, provided appropriately modest alternatives to the typically much larger "cottages" erected across the region during the last two decades of the previous century. There was, however, little nostalgia in *House Beautiful* for plantation slavery.[25] Instead, the editorial tone established that, unlike the mid and late Victorian designs that they superseded, New England houses built before the Industrial Revolution in particular offered a uniquely American – if well informed regarding European, especially English precedents – and thus practical way of life, one moreover that usually had clearly identifiable roots in the farmstead, even if it was now being transplanted to the suburb.

This emphasis on informality and pragmatism encompassed, of course, the innovations that made the houses published in *House Beautiful* in these years up to date. These included improvements in heating and cooking provided by the switch away from coal and gas, presented as dirty and outmoded, as well as the provision of hot running water and electricity that transformed the cleaning of clothes, dishes, and houses, not to mention food storage and preparation. Contributors and advertisers alike presumed that knowledge of these was the responsibility of the woman of the household as much or more so than of her husband. Although probably only a minority of the magazine's readers relied on servants, these forms of modernity were presented as providing efficient alternatives to the country's declining supply of women willing to work as maids and cooks as well as of households, even in the booming economy of the 1920s, that could afford to pay them.[26] The so-called "servant problem" was also identified as the excuse for dwellings that do not necessarily appear modest today, especially in comparison to those erected in the 1930s through the 1950s, but which were often smaller than the ones in which their more prosperous inhabitants had been raised. The new homes could be apartments as well as houses. Edward Stratton Holloway argued for the latter, writing that "the cares of even the small house involve a slavery to which many refined and intelligent women are now forced to devote their lives to the exclusion of intellectual interests and needful recreation of body, mind, and spirit."[27]

In the 1930s, two of my great-aunts would, with their husbands, commission International Style homes, although by the time I knew them, both households had retreated to more conventional quarters (one of the pair was even published in *House Beautiful*).[28] This left me free in the 1970s and 1980s to discover modern architecture as a liberating alternative to the environments in which I grew up, furnished in a style of which Power would have approved. The longevity of her version of the colonial revival belies the role she and they played in pioneering alternatives to it. Masculinist histories of modern architecture tell us that in 1932 the International Style architecture. The plan is thought out to suit the person who will live in the house rather than to meet a preconceived idea of what the outside should look like. With the plan settled upon first, the architect then builds around it a simple and graceful exterior. Hence the practical advantages are many.

In the Lindbergh house, for example, the orientation is a prime consideration. The house is very long, nearly two hundred feet. All the rooms are on the south side. Corridors, servants' quarters, service entrance, and garage face the north. The house is generous in window area, making dark winter days brighter. In summer the house is cool and delightfully open, especially in the late afternoon and evening. To regulate the light, or for privacy, curtains covering the whole window surface can be drawn. Awnings keep the glare of sunlight off the glass. The windows on the ground floor are really glass doors, which, when thrown open, make the living-room a veritable porch.

So great an expanse of windows was not possible in the last century. Modern steel or reënforced concrete construction makes potentially possible a house without any solid walls, one which can therefore be as free and open as modern life requires. One concomitant of this type of construction is the flat roof. It can be better built and better insulated against sun, snow, or rain, with the same expenditure of money and effort, than any other type of roof. In addition, the roof of the lower story can be used as a terrace. The Lindbergh house has both an open and a covered terrace on each floor. The (*Continued on page* 356)

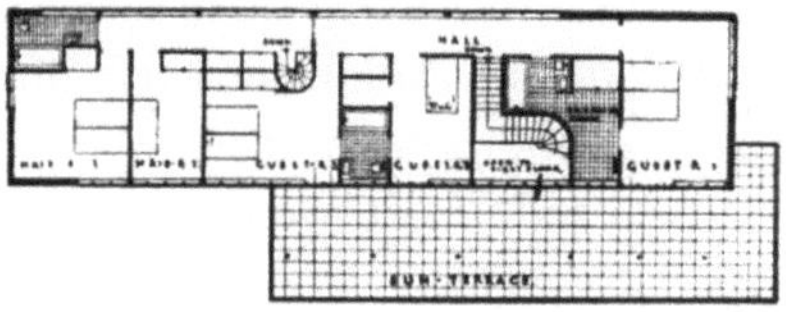

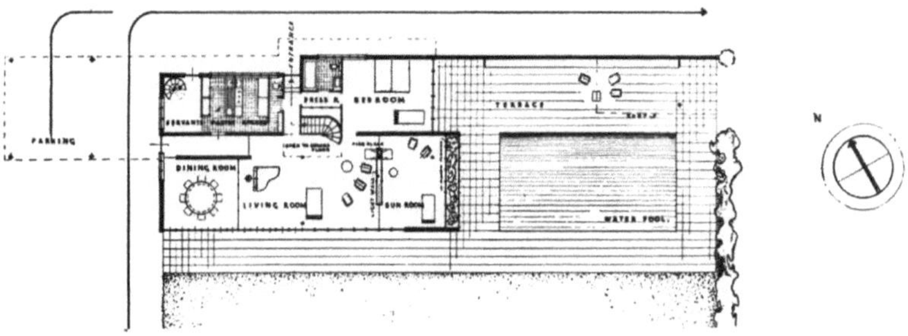

This house, designed for Mrs. Homer H. Johnson by the same architects, is being built in Pinehurst, North Carolina. It is planned to be placed on the extreme northeast corner of the lot close to the house behind, from which it is screened by a wall, which also serves as a windbreak. The plentiful use of glass is desirable for the Southern climate

FIGURE 9.4 Philip Johnson, "Two Houses in the International Style" excerpt from *House Beautiful* 70 (1931): 309. Public domain, Internet Archive.

was introduced to audiences in the United States through a traveling exhibition organized by the Museum of Modern Art in New York and curated by Henry Russell Hitchcock and Philip Johnson.[29] Putting aside the involvement of Catherine Bauer and Lewis Mumford in organizing "Modern Architecture: International Exhibition," a display that featured a great deal of new European housing not included in Hitchcock and Johnson's book *The International Style*, this story is demonstrably false.[30] No one knew better than Hitchcock and Johnson themselves that much of the credit they took was unwarranted, and that one of the people with whom it should have been shared was Power. She had, after all, allowed the two then entirely unknown young gay men, neither of whom had yet turned thirty, to trial their arguments in the pages of *House Beautiful*, whose readership far exceeded the number who saw the show in New York or indeed, the size of the architectural profession in the United States at the time (Figure 9.4). That their exhibition, which almost certainly had almost no impact on the way in which architecture was practiced in the United States across the next decade and a half, continues to be credited with introducing into the country architecture that was already well known there is a testament to the willingness of generations of architectural historians to take male hubris at face value as well as to the power both men held over the discipline in the second half of the twentieth century.[31]

Hitchcock published the work of Le Corbusier and other modernists in *House Beautiful* in 1928, the year before his book *Modern Architecture: Romanticism and Reintegration* appeared. He was careful to ally the European work he showed with the ethos of the magazine and the tastes of its readers:

> The . . . houses here illustrated have indeed in their general lines much in common with the simplest of our own. They depend for their effect on the excellence of their brickwork and the skilled arrangement of their essential parts. If they differ from American work it is in the very pointed avoidance of all inherited ornament and in a certain rather successful attempt to make the essential parts form a scheme of design which is new and perhaps even a little unnecessarily novel. In other words, where our simplicity is largely negative theirs is for good or ill distinctly positive.[32]

Johnson introduced the term International Style, which he borrowed without attribution from Frederick Kiesler, to the magazine's readers in 1931.[33] As exemplars he illustrated two projects by now largely forgotten firm of Clauss and Daub, one a design that pioneering aviator Charles Lindbergh had already rejected, and another that Johnson's mother failed to build. Both had been featured in a recent exhibition in New York of work that the Architectural League had refused to show. This was one of the many exhibitions to which Power, who would completely ignore the 1932 MoMA display, alerted her readers. But the work of women writers and women architects played a more substantial role in Power's efforts to publicize developments of which she believed her readers should be aware, even if she never focused exclusively upon them. Dorothy Todd, the former editor of the British edition of *Vogue*, tutored readers on the difference between the International Style and Art Deco, advocating the work of Le Corbusier, Marcel Breuer, and Walter Gropius over that of figures like Jean Frank.[34] Ise Gropius, whom Power met in Berlin when she traveled there with Raymond in 1930, defended standardization.[35] Katherine Morrison, who mostly authored articles on medieval or revivalist British houses, introduced readers to the London apartment of Serge Chermayeff.[36] Later in 1932, Power published the Raymond House which her partner Eleanor had built in Belmont, Massachusetts, for Eleanor's sister Rachel, almost certainly the first International Style house erected on the East Coast of the United States.[37]

What did modernism offer Power, her readers, and my foremothers? First and foremost, modern technology was convenient. Heating systems, kitchens, and bathrooms are not the modernism on which the Museum of Modern Art focused, but they transformed the daily lives of those who could afford them.[38] Fashion also mattered more than these women cared to admit. Male and female *House Beautiful* authors who advocated the International Style frequently equated it with the change in women's dress that occurred in the 1920s.[39] The introduction of bobbed hair, uncorseted waists, and knee-length skirts was one of the most abrupt and transformational revolutions in the entire history of women's dress. Women who had been physically emancipated in this way were more likely to appreciate other dramatic changes, even if they were also being constantly encouraged to dismiss mere fads. And for Power, modernism increasingly fulfilled a desire for comfort that previous styles were less able to fulfill. In an article published in June 1934, after she had resigned as editor but at a time when continued to contribute two articles on average to each issue, she summarized her position:

> Our way of living has radically changed. Today the automobile, the several bathrooms, the telephone, the electric refrigerator, the oil heater, the gas-fired incinerator, the radio and other mechanical equipment all have to be taken care of. Our early houses – the houses we are still copying – had little to do but provide shelter, and if we would build as sincerely as our forefathers, we will face facts as squarely as they did . . . The modern house is an effort to meet modern requirements with a sincerity equal to theirs. Indeed, the very essence of the modern house is its straightforwardness in meeting our complicated modern problems . . . The modern house is, therefore . . . restful, for it promotes the comfort that comes from ease of operating and lack of fussy, meaningless detail . . . This characteristic appearance of the modern house, which is so largely influenced by the plan, is also due to some extent to the increased use of new materials or to a new use of old ones.[40]

My two great aunts who traveled to Los Angeles in the early 1930s in search of an alternative to the taste of the formidable mother-in-law of the elder of the pair undoubtedly agreed. So did the one who a decade later supervised the encasing of a Queen Anne staircase in a sleeker, streamlined version. Like Ise Gropius, who was nine years her senior and grew up less than forty miles away from her, she believed in standardization. By the time I knew her, her wardrobe consisted almost exclusively of the same dress design. She wore new ones on special occasions, such as when she was honored for her pioneering epilepsy research; less new ones when busy at work; and old ones for tending her garden. But, like Power, these women agreed that the International Style was just one of a number of legitimate choices and that the new could often be convincingly combined with whatever one already had to hand. To deftly transfer an omelet from a Teflon frying pan onto an earthenware plate decorated with jaunty flowers, a memento of a trip to Italy, represented the perfect pairing of progress and prettiness.

Although Power, who died in 1969, gradually faded out of view after working in the 1930s as a kitchen consultant, *House Beautiful* continued to flourish.[41] So did the importance of female editors, designers, and consumers in defining the material culture of domesticity in the United States. Historians of architecture have been most willing to acknowledge female agency when it allows them to blame women for the rejection of self-proclaimed male genius. For instance, H. Alan Brooks denounced the readers of *House Beautiful* for the shift in taste in the early 1910s away from the Prairie Style.[42] Elizabeth Gordon, editor of *House Beautiful* from 1941 to 1964, hardly endeared herself to the upper echelons of the architectural establishment when she notoriously labeled the International Style "The Threat to the Next America." At stake was not just Cold War politics, but whether a male architect, Ludwig Mies van der Rohe, or his female client, Edith Farnsworth, would call the shots. Selling advertising for more affordable middle brow furnishings may have also played a role, but it could hardly have been the determining factor.[43] Meanwhile, Power's partner Raymond was a pioneer designer of solar houses.[44]

My grandmothers and my great-aunts probably ignored the debate over "The Threat to the Next America." By that time, they had made most of their home decorating decisions, although in the 1960s one would with her husband erect an informal hillside retreat in which floor to ceiling glazing was placed perpendicular to the usual wall of books, while electric blankets added a space age note. Many of their daughters moved into conventional suburban ranch and split-level houses, but the chintz curtains, Chinese export porcelain, and antique or reproduction furnishings remained a constant. I grew up amidst the slightly shabby disarray of an actual eighteenth-century house. My mother, the "handy man" in the family, oversaw its ongoing repair, about which she spoke in much the same tone of humor mixed with exasperation adopted by the authors of the *House Beautiful* articles her own mother apparently never read. The major concession to the twentieth century, besides the not always robust heating and hot water systems, was a mid-century modern Danish chair, a wedding present from an eccentric great-uncle who had settled south of San Francisco.

Neither the International Style nor avant-garde alternatives to it ever captured the hearts of most American consumers. The architects whom Hitchcock and Johnson lauded defended their designs as capturing the spirit of a time defined by airplanes and automobiles, but Power was in many ways more astute in judging that mass production coupled to an increasingly equitable distribution of wealth could generate greater simplicity in ways that leapfrogged over the Victorians to respect a more distant past. She also understood the appeal of emotional as well as physical comfort. The niches among which modern architecture and home décor had the largest degree of acceptance in the United States included Jewish professionals and migrants to the sun belt, but even among these groups, enthusiasm for it was far from universal.[45] The degree to which historians of architecture have focused on architects such as Le Corbusier and Mies van der Rohe, and on the writings of the men such as Hitchcock and Johnson who championed them, ignores the degree to which mainstream taste was largely shaped outside circles controlled by professional architects and yet was very much the product of its times. While there has been much scholarship on the postwar American suburb, less attention has been paid to the popularity of Ethan Allen-style reproductions sold through Sears Roebuck catalogues that filled the living and dining rooms of many of the kids, Black as well as white, with whom I went to school.[46] More needs to be done not just to identify the overlooked role women played in championing the International Style, but to understand why alternatives to it remained so popular across the twentieth century among so many different social groups, including those with the knowledge and economic means to know about and be able to afford the alternatives. Nor can it be an accident that Jane Jacobs and Denise Scott Brown, two champions in their different ways of the everyday, numbered among the most astute and influential critics of International Style architecture and urbanism, despite in Scott Brown's case having grown up in a modernist showpiece.[47]

The women who resisted the International Style were not necessarily beholden to nostalgia for a vanished past. In the 1920s, Power, my grandmothers, and my great-aunts appreciated the association of the colonial revival with what they viewed as enduring democratic values, very much including their own recently won right to vote.[48] While not all of these women were politically progressive, many shared a real commitment to social change. My step-great grandmother regularly rented her New Hampshire cottage to her good friend, Frances Perkins, the first woman to serve as a member of the cabinet and a key figure in the implementation of the New Deal. Even women who did not have their (or my) degree of privilege, however, often preferred alternatives, as my research into the career of Edith Bailey Madison Furman demonstrates.[49] Furman, whose lifespan overlapped almost exactly with that of my eldest great aunt, spent her career designing houses and churches for fellow African Americans in and around Richmond. In the postwar years these houses typically conveyed their owner's aspirations for the same sort of dwellings that were so much more easily attainable by white contemporaries moving to postwar suburbs from urban working-class neighborhoods. Nor, as numerous exposes of conditions in architecture schools and practices across the United States and Europe have demonstrated, does ownership of Wassily or Barcelona chairs equate with a sense of responsibility for mitigating inequalities rooted in class, gender, or race.

Reading *House Beautiful* explained to me a great deal about myself. I began this research in my mother's living room, but I am writing this article in my own flat in Dublin, where I am surrounded not by the aesthetic that I study, but by furniture I inherited. My step-grandmother proudly purchased most of my best antiques in the 1940s with her earnings as a nurse; much of the rest belonged to my great-grandparents. As a historian of modernism, why did I not exchange any of it, especially before its value plummeted as the taste for brown furniture finally declined, for the objects I teach? In questioning myself about this, I thought long and hard about what these objects embodied to me as well as the importance to me of the women in my family who had cherished them. They had little if any time for the feminine mystique. Particularly proud of me when I took advantage of opportunities that had not been available to them, they passed on as well the pleasure they derived from their skill in visual discernment. All could see distinctions not everyone else noticed and in ways that stretched far beyond the expression of their social status. In addition to the epilepsy expert, one birthed calves and churned butter, another was a military historian, a third was instrumental in raising the salaries of American orchestra musicians, while a fourth was a spy. Yet their taste for the new, when it existed at all, was tempered to no small degree by an appreciation for precisely the past that Power had often championed, and which, like her, my grandmother and great-aunts were often adept at folding into a forward-looking present. It is impossible to relinquish the privilege they bestowed upon me. If I also renounced the objects that had meant so much to them, I would also be sacrificing the material evidence of the sustenance their example had provided across the course of the career they had so strongly encouraged me to undertake. Furthermore, it was precisely this support that enabled me to mentor others, few of whom had such imposing precedents to draw upon. Even, however, when I leave their taste behind, Power was there first. My most treasured example of twentieth-century design, a set of half a dozen Georg Jensen silver demitasse spoons presented to my mother by a Jewish friend of the family upon the occasion of her christening, was advertised in *House Beautiful* in 1928 for $13.50.[50]

In the context of the Cold War, Hitchcock and Johnson's formalist interpretation of modern architecture did eventually triumph, along with the myth that they had been responsible for introducing the architecture that embodied it to American shores.[51] Since the 1990s, I have belonged to the generation of scholars who have challenged the primacy of their perspective. Formalism could account up to a point for the best of the buildings in which I was educated once I left home but not for the environments in which I grew up. Although I have only come recently to wrestle with the discrepancy between the two, I have always explored architecture as the intersection of form and identity and been interested in spaces crafted to shape experiences in ways that can be profoundly political and also spiritual.[52] Unlike Hitchcock and Johnson, I have never been afraid to admit that consumer choice, including that of the clients for the buildings I study and also for the audiences they intended to reach, matters enormously. This is something of which both Power and Erich Mendelsohn, the German Jewish architect who was the subject of much of my early scholarship, were acutely aware.[53] Moreover, whereas Philip Johnson attempted to start a fascist movement in the United States and Hitchcock was a Cold War warrior, the same women in my family who decorated in a style of which Power would have approved also encouraged me to understand that ours was not the only heritage that mattered.[54] Many supported the integration that ensured that I had African-American classmates and, in school teachers and principals, real figures of authority. This and their openness to other religions and cultures paved the way for my engagement with India and my commitment to global histories of architecture that countered the emphasis on the movement of ideas from what Hitchcock and Johnson believed to be the center to the periphery and that address issues like slavery and colonialism, whose impact they studiously ignored.[55] Finally, without the example of my female relatives, I would not have been fortunate enough to grow up knowing that women had long made a difference, the idea at the core of my current project exploring the role of female and non-white taste in the global dissemination of modern architecture and design between 1920 and 1970.[56] They primed me to be able to take Power seriously, and thus to be able to contribute to the liberation of the International Style, if not its most self-serving defenders, from being understood as inherently masculinist.[57]

Acknowledgements

This research was undertaken while I was an Ailsa Mellon Bruce Senior Fellow at the Center for Advanced Study in the Visual Arts at the National Gallery of Art. This project has received funding from the European Research Council (ERC) under the European Union's Horizon 2020 research and innovation program (grant agreement No. 1010119419). I would also like to thank Weronika Kocurkiewicz for sourcing the illustrations.

Notes

1 Dorothy May Anderson, *Women, Design, and the Cambridge School* (West Lafayette: PDA Publishers, 1980).
2 Mary Ellen Zuckerman, *A History of Popular Women's Magazines in the United States, 1792–1995* (Westport: Greenwood Press, 1998).
3 Louisa Tuthill, *History of Architecture, from the Earliest Times; Its Present Condition in Europe and the United States; With a Biography of Eminent Architects, and a Glossary of Architectural Terms* (Philadelphia: Lindsay and Blakiston, 1848); Judith Major, *Mariana Griswold Van Rensselaer: A Landscape Critic in the Gilded Age* (Charlottesville: University of Virginia Press, 2013); Catherine Beecher and Harriet Beecher Stowe, *The American Woman's Home* (New York: J. B. Ford, 1869); Edith Wharton and Ogden Codman, *The Decoration of Houses* (New York: Charles Scribner's Sons, 1897).
4 H. Alan Brooks, *The Prairie School: Frank Lloyd Wright and His Midwest Contemporaries* (New York: W. W. Norton, 1972), 23–24, 294.
5 https://www.findagrave.com/memorial/117941223/ethel-b-power, accessed 15 August 2022, for the family monument in Waterside Cemetery, Marblehead, Massachusetts that lists Power, her parents, and five of her siblings.
6 Maureen Meister, *Arts and Crafts Architecture: History and Heritage in New England* (Hanover: University Press of New England, 2014), 20–22; 159–60; 172–202.
7 Sarah Deutsch, *Women and the City: Gender, Space, and Power in Boston, 1870–1940* (Oxford: Oxford University Press, 2000) for the milieu in which Power lived and worked.

8 Kathleen Waters Sander, *Mary Elizabeth Garrett: Society and Philanthropy in the Gilded Age* (Baltimore: Johns Hopkins University Press, 2008).
9 Rose Greely, "A Small House of Distinction," *House Beautiful* 52 (1922): 420. This is an up-market version of the advice that was being dispensed to school girls at the time through home economics. See Carma Gorman, "Educating the Eye: Body Mechanics and Streamlining in the U.S., 1925–1950," *American Quarterly* 58 (2006): 839–68.
10 Betty Friedan, *The Feminine Mystique* (New York: W. W. Norton, 1963). See also Joanne Meyerowitz, *Not Just June Cleaver: Women and Gender in Postwar America, 1945–1960* (Philadelphia: Temple University Press, 1994); and "A House Designed for a Business Woman," *House Beautiful* 69 (1931): 160.
11 Richard Ohmann, *Selling Culture: Magazines, Markets, and Class at the Turn of the Century* (London: Verso, 1996).
12 Agnes Warbase, "Real Coöperative Housing," *House Beautiful* 59 (1926): 29, 78; Lucy D. Taylor, "Oriental Rugs," *House Beautiful* 59 (1926): 142–43, 197; Nancy Cooper, "Indian Palampores," *House Beautiful* 62 (1927): 650–51; 693–96.
13 "Our Fifth Avenue Looking Glass," *House Beautiful* 53 (1923): 338.
14 "Our First Prize House," *House Beautiful* 69 (1931): 238–40.
15 Ethel B. Power, *The Smaller American Home* (1927, Altigen: Shiffer, 2007).
16 For instance, Mary Kellogg, "Expanding a Cape Cod Cottage," *House Beautiful* 53 (1923): 624–25, 660–62, emphasizes that the architects, Howe & Manning, were both women. See Catherine R. Ettinger, "Designing Houses Is Like Having Babies: Verna Cook and the Practice of Architecture in the 1920s and 1930s," in Anna Sokolina, ed., *Routledge Guide to Women in Architecture* (London: Routledge, 2021), 57–69, for an analysis of *House Beautiful's* coverage of Cook Salomonsky.
17 For example, "Sunshine and Shadow," *House Beautiful* 57 (1925): 543; showcased a garden designed by Marian Coffin, while "The Garden of Mrs. Robert A. Franks," *House Beautiful* 60 (1926): 166–67 focused on a design by Shipman. See also Thaïsa Way, *Unbounded Practice: Women and Landscape Architecture in the Early Twentieth Century* (Charlottesville: University of Virginia Press, 2013); "The House in Good Taste," *House Beautiful* 64 (1928): 149–52, for the work of the Karasz sisters.
18 Mrs. Ezra Bowen, "The Amenities of Home Building," *House Beautiful* 53 (1923): 497, 534, for the first in a series by the author; Sophie Kerr, "Other People's Houses," *House Beautiful* 54 (1923): 472, 516; Rose Greely, "Tudor Place," *House Beautiful* 57 (1925): 141; and Isabel M. G. Goodwin, "Gardens of Old Georgetown," *House Beautiful* 62 (1927): 368–71.
19 For instance, Rose Standish Nichols's *Italian Pleasure Gardens*, was reviewed in "Book & Lamp," *House Beautiful* 65 (1929): 774.
20 [Ethel B. Power], "Overheard in the Editor's Office," *House Beautiful* 61 (1927): 20.
21 The figures are from the Audit Bureau of Circulation and were supplied to me by Kathy Woodrell of the Researcher and Reference Services Division of the Library of Congress.
22 Kathleen Curran, *The Invention of the American Art Museum: From Craft to Kulturgeschichte, 1870–1930* (Santa Monica: Getty Research Institute, 2016).
23 "Table of Contents," *House Beautiful* 71 (1932) 251; See "Style Notes," *House Beautiful* 71 (1932): 14, however, for the racist tone that could mar such appreciations. The unidentified author, perhaps Power herself, notes

> This is not to assume that primitive objects and motives [from Mexico and Central America] are being copied outright. Being sophisticated people living in a sophisticated age, we adapt and modify what we take from other sources to suit our own needs and tastes, but the clear, intense hues associated with tropical suns, and the naïve designs of childlike people, can be found in increasing numbers in our textiles and other furnishings.

24 For example, Elizabeth Bootes Clar, "What Philadelphia Is Doing with Her Alleys," *House Beautiful* 56 (1924): 478–79, 528; and Dale Warren, "The Minettas," *House Beautiful* 60 (1926): 568–69, 626–30.
25 Delos H. Schmit, "And Other," *House Beautiful* 64 (1928): 558 noted in an account of early colonial architecture in Maryland that "The negro slave was introduced at an early period, and we may not omit our word of admiration for his part in the erection of the early Tidewater house."
26 For example Elva D. Hoover, "Do You Hate Dishwashing?," *House Beautiful* 56 (1924): 59, 87; Gladys Beckett Jones and Jenoise Brown Short, "New Electrical Appliances," *House Beautiful* 56 (1924):

248, 284–86; and F. J. St. John, "Artificial Refrigeration," *House Beautiful* 57 (1925), 404, 435. See also Deutsch, *Women and the City*.

27 Edward Stratton Holloway, "Apartments and How to Furnish Them," *House Beautiful* 56 (1924): 130.

28 Dietrich Neumann, ed., *Richard Neutra's Windshield House* (New Haven: Yale University Press, 2002) for both Windshield and the Gibbs House in Brookline, Massachusetts. See also "New Angles on the Boston Scene," *House Beautiful* (April 1939): 60–61.

29 For instance, Alan Colquhoun, *Modern Architecture* (Oxford: Oxford University Press, 2002), 231, writes "The defining moment for the introduction of the Modern Movement into America is usually seen to have been the exhibition . . ."

30 Greg Castillo, "German Lessons," *Places Journal*, August 2022. Accessed 26 Aug. 2022. https://placesjournal.org/article/philip-johnson-catherine-bauer-and-modernism-at-moma/ on Bauer's role.

31 For my earlier critique of this narrative see Kathleen James-Chakraborty, "From Isolationism to Internationalism: American Acceptance of the Bauhaus," in Kathleen James-Chakraborty, ed., *Bauhaus Culture from Weimar to the Cold War* (Minneapolis: University of Minnesota Press, 2006), 153–70; for recent insistence, as usual without supporting documentation, on the importance of the exhibition, Patricio del Real, *Constructing Latin America: Architecture, Politics, and Race at the Museum of Modern Art* (New Haven: Yale University Press, 2022), 1.

32 Henry-Russell Hitchcock, "Six Modern European Houses," *House Beautiful* 64 (1928): 253. A house by Le Corbusier had already appeared in Simon de Vaulchier, "The Style Moderne in France," *House Beautiful* 63 (1928): 606–07, 670–72.

33 Philip Johnson, "Two Houses in the International Style," *House Beautiful* 70 (1931): 307–09, 356; and Frederick J. Kiesler, *Contemporary Art Applied to the Store and Its Display* (New York: Brentano's, 1930).

34 Dorothy Todd, "Some Reflections on Modernism," *House Beautiful* 66 (1929): 416–17, 470–76.

35 Ise Gropius, "Modern Dwellings for Modern People," *House Beautiful* 69 (1941): 506, 532–34.

36 Katherine Morrison, "Where Furniture Is Based on Function," *House Beautiful* 69 (1931): 56–60, 83.

37 It graced the cover of the September issue and was the subject of the lead article the following month, Edith Kingsbury, "Spring Pasture – Our Experiment in the Country," *House Beautiful* 72 (1932): 200–07, 263. For more on the house see Kevin D. Murphy, "The Vernacular Moment: Eleanor Raymond, Walter Gropius, and New England Modernism Between the Wars," *Journal of the Society of Architectural Historians* 70 (2011): 308–29.

38 Judy Giles, *The Parlor and the Suburb: Domestic Identities, Class, Femininity and Modernity* (Oxford: Berg, 2004).

39 Charles R. Richards, "Is There a Modern Style in Decorative Art?," *House Beautiful* 62 (1927): 374–76, 429–30; and Todd, "Some Reflections on Modernism," 416. Interestingly, before Power became editor, Chester H. Walcott, "Domestic Architecture in the Middle West," *House Beautiful* 22 (1922), 13, defended historicism as opposed to the prairie style which he described as "passing into limbo, with last season's style of clothes."

40 Ethel Power, "Talking Points on Modernism," *House Beautiful* 75 (1934), 61.

41 Dorothy G. Wayman, "Women Who Made Jobs for Themselves," *Boston Globe*, 16 May 1938, 1, 7.

42 Brooks, *The Prairie School*.

43 Alice T. Friedman, *Women and the Making of the Modern House: A Social and Architectural History* (New York: Harry N. Abrams, 1998) and Monica Pennick, *Tastemaker: Elizabeth Gordon, House Beautiful, and the Postwar American Home* (New Haven: Yale University Press, 2017).

44 Daniel A. Barber, *A House in the Sun: Modern Architecture and Solar Energy in the Cold War* (Oxford: Oxford University Press, 2016).

45 Donald Albrecht, ed., *Designing Home: Jews and Mid-Century Modernism* (San Francisco: The Contemporary Jewish Museum, 2014).

46 Kristina Wilson, *Mid-Century Modernism and the American Body: Race, Gender, and the Politics of Power in Design* (Princeton: Princeton University Press, 2021) is very astute regarding African American resistance to mid-century modernism, but almost certainly exaggerates the hold that firms like Herman Miller had on white upper middle-class families.

47 Jane Jacobs, *The Death and Life of Great American Cities* (New York: Random House, 1961), and Robert Venturi, Denise Scott Brown, and Steven Izenour, *Learning from Las Vegas* (Cambridge: MIT Press, 1972).

48 Highlighted in a General Electric advertisement, *House Beautiful* 54 (1923): 644.

49 Kathleen James-Chakraborty, "Ethel Madison Bailey Furman: Building Community in Richmond, Virginia," forthcoming in Felipe Hernández and Itohan Osayimwese, *Routledge Companion to Race and Architecture* (London: Routledge, 2024).
50 Mary Jackson Lee, "Window Shopping," *House Beautiful* 64 (1928): 494.
51 Del Real, *Constructing Latin America*, does an excellent job of tracing the emergence of this formalist position in relation to race.
52 Kathleen James-Chakraborty, *German Architecture for a Mass Audience* (London: Routledge, 2000).
53 Kathleen James, *Erich Mendelsohn and the Architecture of German Modernism* (Cambridge: Cambridge University Press, 1997).
54 Franz Schultze, *Philip Johnson: Life and Work* (Chicago: University of Chicago Press, 1994); Walter Nichols as quoted in Henry-Russell Hitchcock, letter to Louis I. Kahn, March 13, 1960, in "Voice of America -- Louis I. Kahn, Recorded November 16, 1960," Box LIK 55, Louis I. Kahn Collection, University of Pennsylvania and Pennsylvania Historical and Museum Commission, Philadelphia, for the purpose of a series of Voice of America talks on architecture that Hitchcock organized.
55 Kathleen James-Chakraborty, *Architecture since 1400* (Minneapolis: University of Minnesota Press, 2014).
56 Kathleen James-Chakraborty, "Agenda expandida: Mujeres, raza y la diffusion de la Arquitectura moderna," *ZARCH: Journal of Interdisciplinary Studies in Architecture and Urbanism* 18 (2022): 16–29. https://doi.org/10.26754/ojs_zarch/zarch.2022186967
57 Power's example, and that of many of her writers, counters the argument for the modern architecture and design as masculinist made by Penny Sparke, *As Long as its Pink: The Sexual Politics of Taste* (London: Pandora, 1995).

PART IV

Spatial Experience

10

BEYOND THE WALLS

Traversing the Boundaries of Architectural History

Elizabeth McKellar

> *Before I built a wall I'd ask to know*
> *What I was walling in or walling out,*
> *And to whom I was like to give offense.*
>
> (Robert Frost, Mending Walls, 1914)

Communing with Walls

I am sitting looking out from my study on the type of suburban scene which has been my subject matter for much of the past thirty-five years. I wrote about this study and the rest of my house in an article which is the nearest I have ever come before to mixing the personal and the academic.[1] This essay will continue that process as I reflect back on my career in architectural history focussing on my two major monographs and my current biographical project, as well as the settings and experiences that have shaped my professional life.

I decided that I wanted to be an architectural historian from my very early encounters with the subject. But until relatively recently I have always felt on the margins of the discipline. This was largely due to the interdisciplinary nature of my work concerned with everyday architecture, housing and urbanism but also due to a temperamental and intellectual contrariness. I've never wanted to be part of a pack, have an instinctive distrust of the latest academic fashions and have always felt myself to be an outsider to the mainstream. This is reflected in my attitude to feminism, whose principles have informed my life and work although I have not specialised in gender-related topics in architectural history.

My historical and architectural education began while a student reading History at Oxford. Although I went there in the early 1980s, the university was still untouched by post-modernism. History was dominated by 'big history'. E. H. Carr's history as the movement of large social forces and the statistical revolution of the 1970s brought in from Social Sciences held sway.[2] Although social history was becoming more prominent, it was still primarily through the prisms of political, intellectual and economic history that the past was viewed. I did encounter a tiny amount of what was then called 'women's history' as an undergraduate and I was certainly exposed to a more radical political agenda and socially-informed understanding of architecture

DOI: 10.4324/9781003224662-15

at the Bartlett, where I did my Masters. But history was still essentially an interplay of the socio-economic and the political in which the current issues of identity played little part.

I had grown up in Metroland, the outer London suburbs and home counties green belt. I discounted its rows of identical semi-detached houses or even the more distinctive 1920s detached models as being of any great interest – ironically in the light of my later fascination with the quotidian – preferring to explore the surrounding countryside instead. Once in Oxford, like thousands before me, I fell in love with the city and its architecture. With the play of sun and shade as it encountered stone and moss. With the effect of soft lights shining out on paved quads in the dark evenings and of the glow of lamplight in the streets and back lanes of the city. I would take different routes on my bike to explore all its hidden corners and treasures and so when an opportunity arose to study architectural history in my final year, the city itself had already prompted my enthusiasm for the subject. A few years ago on the radio I heard the new reforming Master of Jesus College, Cambridge, as part of her laudable attempts to widen access, seeking to downplay the historic environment. Her remarks were words to the effect that 'no one ever learnt anything from an old wall'. How wrong she was. When I think of Oxford for all its wonderful individual buildings, it is essentially the walls and the relationships that they create, the buildings and green spaces that they define, and the pathways through the city that they carve out which have remained my passion ever since.

When I moved to London to continue my studies, my trusty bicycle continued to play a key part in my architectural education. My first job after the Bartlett was as a researcher for the Hackney Society. In some ways it was the best job I ever had – albeit the worst paid and the least prestigious – but it was the right job at the right time. I spent my days cycling around Hackney and learning about a very different urban environment but still reading it with the same attention to materials, typology and spatiality as the honeyed stones of my *alma mater*. I was still learning from walls but now they were of London stock, terracotta, steel and concrete. Hackney in the 1980s was a by-word for poverty, crime and deprivation epitomised in a notorious book of the time *Inside the Inner City.*[3] However, as befitting its much longer history as one of the most desirable outer London suburbs (which I was later to explore in *Landscapes of London*), it was stuffed with historic buildings mainly in various states of decay and had at that time the highest number of listed buildings outside of Westminster. The Hackney Society, led by the energetic Pat Hammill and able to employ staff through money from the Urban Renewal Fund, was ahead of its time in seeing beyond the dilapidation and attempting to catalogue and publicise the large number of significant buildings on its patch. It was the first to realise the potential for renovating the empty furniture warehouses in Shoreditch and was instrumental in campaigning for the renovation and reuse of many important sites including the National Trust's Sutton House and the Round Chapel, Clapton.[4] Even the Hackney Society's most zealous advocates for urban renewal would probably not have foreseen the transformation that has subsequently taken place of other unpromising destinations such as Hackney Wick whose sludge-coloured landscape of scrap merchants and industrial waste processes were re-shaped by the 2010 Olympics, for better or worse. These landscapes of desolation and detritus, that have been so well-documented by artists such as Jock MacFayden and writers like Iain Sinclair, became my everyday working beat.[5]

Meanwhile at the southern end of the borough the effects of Thatcher's Big Bang of 1986 were being felt. Here adjacent to the City large commercial developments such as Stuart Lipton's Broadgate were going up, while beyond the regenerated Docklands and the towers of Canary Wharf began to emerge. Hackney had it all from abandoned Tudor mansions to Georgian terraces, from Victorian villas and mission churches to twentieth-century tower blocks. These behemoths were scattered across the borough in clumps forming mini-citadels in their own right, around which I carefully skirted on my bike. Working in Hackney taught me to see both the surface evidence of architecture in all its glorious variety as well as to trace the social and economic forces that left their own marks on the environment whether the empty lot, the arterial road or the shiny new development. I once spent a day going round the then largely empty government-designated Docklands Development Area with an estate agent pointing out the different sites and their relative potential and merits which gave me an insight into the property developer's way of evaluating the urban landscape as one of profit and loss, of margins and calculations.

At the same time, I was learning a huge amount from teaching in architecture schools mainly at Kingston and then North London universities (now London Metropolitan). North London was the home of the Women's Access Course, the first such programme in the country aimed at increasing the number of women on architecture degrees. Here I met and worked with some of the pioneers of feminist architectural practice such as Jos Boys (of the feminist collective Matrix) and Yvonne Dean who helped to open my eyes to the then very new explorations of feminist practice. There were very few available texts at that time, the 1986 Matrix book *Making Space: Women and the Man-Made Environment* being an honourable exception, but I introduced what came to be known as gender studies in my teaching wherever possible.[6] We would purloin feminist texts from Art or Design History where the historiography was more advanced; favourites included the edited collection *A View from the Interior* and Anthea Callen's *Angel in the Studio*.[7] Many of my women architecture students seized on these avidly in an environment over which the hand of architectural masculinity still hung heavily. Another important influence in North London was Elizabeth Wilson then at the height of her powers producing the revelatory *Sphinx in the City* (1992). Elizabeth's work was really my first encounter with feminist writing which went beyond documenting absences or providing insertions into existing narratives but rather provided a radical account of women's experiences and understandings of the city. She was based in Social Studies with whom the Architecture Department was merged at some point and she proved an important role model, not just intellectually, but in terms of her professional status and *modus operandi*. Here she was a leader in her field with a formidable presence – enhanced by her remarkable physical resemblance to her namesake Elizabeth I – but one who was operating outside the mainstream from a non-elite institution. The American feminist Camille Paglia, also a social scientist, made similar remarks about her own career trajectory and from them I learned that it was possible with a strong enough sense of academic direction and purpose to plough your own furrow even in unpromising institutional terrain.

My eight years or so in architecture schools were great fun and hugely instructive in learning about how designers think and see the world. So while I was ostensibly teaching architecture students about history I was at the same time learning a huge amount from them and from my colleagues. But I never became assimilated into the prevailing studio culture and indeed was somewhat critical of it as can be seen in an article I wrote at the time stating: 'architecture schools still create part of their identity from a notion of the avant-garde in a way which I find both inspiring and exasperating .... Exasperating in its perpetuation of the idea of architect as hero'. I might have added and a male hero at that.[8] The article was called 'Architectural History: the Invisible subject' and traced the marginal position of the discipline within architecture, historical studies and the humanities more widely. It addressed the theme of the failure of architectural history

> to establish itself as a significant subject within the academic sphere ... the failure to create a credible and distinctive area of academic enquiry, which can attract new students and

> research grants, sustain significant research projects, and provide the weight within institutions to develop centres of excellence.[9]

I discussed the contingent nature of architectural history within architecture schools, art history and in the then burgeoning design history, as well as in relation to conservation studies.

Much of what I wrote nearly thirty years ago, at least the central premise, is still sadly all too true today. But how far was my sense of marginality informed by being a woman? Certainly, British eighteenth-century architectural history was very male dominated when I started out in the 1980s. Doing a PhD attached to the fledgling V&A/RCA History of Design course placed me further outside the canonical fold. A North American colleague once asked me how I could stand what she saw as a 'Georgian boys club' and the answer was that I didn't really engage with them. I attended conferences, I made allies where I could but for the most part I followed Elizabeth Wilson's lead and pursued my own agenda and research interests. In so far as I was making a feminist stand, it was by trying to be a competent, professional woman in a male-dominated world. Once I moved out of architecture schools and under the umbrella of Art History from the mid-1990s at Birkbeck College, University of London and then the Open University the departmental culture shifted – if not the wider university one – and the majority of my colleagues were female. As an architectural historian, I was still in a minority and had to fight my corner but as a woman I was no longer such a rarity.

Modern Londons – Old and New

When I started my PhD in 1987, which I wrote part-time while teaching at North London, I returned to my Oxford roots in terms of period, if little else. As I wrote of Oxford in the subsequent book of the thesis

> my investigations into the topic of urban housing are attributable to a stubborn intellectual perversity ... when I was informed ... that architectural history was only concerned with the great buildings of the past, I immediately began to explore their opposite.[10]

My theme was speculative building in London in the period 1660–1720; a topic that had intrigued me since my undergraduate days when I wondered to what extent Summerson's account of its operations in *Georgian London,* as primarily initiated by aristocratic landowners, was correct. Although I was unaware of it at the time, the subject encompassed all the issues which were to dominate my research over the following thirty years: London's development, suburban housing and the processes which shape and form the built environment. At the time I phrased it in more overtly ideological terms, the legacy of my time at the Bartlett, as investigating the impact of capitalism on the building process. This was a subject which was explicitly explored by Linda Clarke in *Building Capitalism: Historical Change and the Labour Process in the Production of the Built Environment* which came out in 1992, the same year that I finished my doctorate. One reviewer called my book Marxist, which surprised me, but really revealed how far accepted tenets of causality in mainstream history and ideas about the social production of culture had still to penetrate architectural history at that time.[11]

My research was based on traditional primary sources, mainly manuscripts plus some maps and drawings, supplemented by field work into surviving examples. In terms of the use of evidence it was textbook Colvinism, that is documentary-based architectural history. But in terms of approach, it was the polar opposite. Inspired by my MA studies under Mark Swenarton and

Adrian Forty, particularly a revelatory course on 'Architectural and Building Practice' spanning from the classical period to the modern, I launched a full-on revisionist critique of Summerson. I was particularly concerned to challenge his rather fuzzy notion of how builders operated in a construction industry turbo-charged by the recent widespread availability of credit in the form of mortgages. Summerson was clearly attuned to the new capitalistic framework in which tradesmen were operating, as he demonstrated most memorably in his unforgettable portrait of Nicholas Barbon the foremost developer of his day, as well as in his famous dissection of the building lease system with its separation of land and financing. Nevertheless, acute as his analysis was, he was unable to take the next step in explaining how the building system worked at the lower levels falling back on craft-derived assumptions of 'barter' as a form of sub-contracting, reducing such workers as I wrote to the level of 'economic virgins'. Through a study of a selection of cases from the Court of Chancery, I was able to show that the competitive capitalism evident for the large-scale operations did in fact permeate right through the system; facilitated by new forms of contracting combined with the widespread use of mortgages as a means of finance. Bolstered by my experience of seeing the fringes of the City of London and Docklands being transformed before my eyes, as the Thatcherite Big Bang revolutionised the City's financial practices and environment, the issue of property development was very much a hot topic. It also offered a corrective to the over-sentimentalisation of Georgian architecture, under the impact of the New Classicism movement, a mythology which I was eager to dispel.

And where were women in this relentless slaying of holy cows? I'm afraid to say that they were largely absent and have remained so in accounts of building practice in the long eighteenth century until very recently. Wherever I came across activities by women, I was keen to include them, so that the new information on women as investors and property managers was highlighted. I found no evidence of women acting as builders or designers directly although soon after two important articles appeared in the *Georgian Group Journal* by Richard Hewlings and Peter Guillery. This work has subsequently been expanded by Chris Wall and Linda Clarke and has been added to added to further in an important article by Conor Lucey.[12]

My thesis and the book that followed, *The Birth of Modern London: the development and design of the city, 1660–1720* was also shaped by the astonishing renaissance of eighteenth-century studies in the 1980s and 1990s which transformed understandings of Britain in the period from being seen as a byword for stasis into the birthplace of the consumer society and the beginnings of the modern world commercially, socially and culturally.[13] I imbibed this new approach during the five years studying for my PhD attached to the V&A/RCA Course which under Charles Saumarez Smith and John Styles proselytised for a radical reformulation of design and culture in the period. I was spurred on by existing accounts, such as that of Frank Kelsall, of the idiosyncrasies in typology of London housing stock before its increasing codification under Palladianism.[14] My experiences in Hackney also stood me in good stead for my field work, which increasingly found me in the outskirts of the city core where surviving examples of late seventeenth and early eighteenth-century housing of the middling sort were more likely to be found, such as in Hoxton just north of Shoreditch which became one of my case-studies. Where houses did survive in inner-city locations, which for one reason or another had not been re-modelled or 'improved' to use a good eighteenth-century term, they were often to be found in louche locations such as 'Tin Pan Alley' aka Great Denmark Street, St Giles or odd houses in Soho, still in its old seedy days (Figure 10.1).

In these insalubrious surroundings, I began to uncover the surprisingly wide range of approaches to the basic model of the brick box. This led me in turn to seek further enlightenment

FIGURE 10.1 32 Hoxton Square, London, N1, 1680s/90s: photo Author. A rare survival from the original development of the square from 1683 onwards.

through the medium of print, particularly contemporary books aimed at builders and craftsmen, rather than the architectural treatises which predominated in architectural history at the time. These books, mostly written as trade manuals, opened the door to a new world showing how everyday architectural practice could exist in a parallel world of text through which both object and word were mutually reinforcing of contemporary cultural understandings and norms. There is only one chapter on books as a means of architectural discourse specifically in *The Birth of Modern London* but my new appreciation of the importance of printed materials as another form of primary source alongside manuscripts was to be of huge importance in my next major work on London. My understanding of print culture was later boosted by teaching alongside Michael Harris at Birkbeck, one of the pioneers of the subject, on the late lamented MA in London History.

The idea for my subsequent book was partly the result of reviews of *The Birth of Modern London*. At my publisher's insistence I had reluctantly added a final chapter on 'Open Spaces

In London', a topic which did not feature in my doctoral thesis. This covered aspects such as squares and gardens as well as what I described as an intermediate zone around the centre which was neither city nor country. Many reviewers praised the originality of this last chapter and so the theme of *Landscapes of London: The City, The Country and the Suburbs 1660–1840* was born in which I expanded the focus both temporally and spatially. I then spent the next fifteen years researching and writing the book with some major interruptions due to work and life events along the way.

Expanding Horizons: The Extra-Mural City

By the time of *Landscapes of London* (2013) it was no longer inner-city regeneration that was current but rather attention had shifted to the post-modern global megacity and the post-suburban sprawling conurbations of the late twentieth century and early twenty-first centuries.[15] It became increasingly apparent to me that London in the long eighteenth century had its edge city or exopolis also. These ideas of new types of urban landscapes overturned the normal centre-periphery paradigm in which the relationship between towns and the surrounding countryside or suburbs is taken as axiomatic, with the latter dependent on the former for goods, services and, most importantly for my purposes, culture. Using a wide range of sources both textual – urban literature and guidebooks, poems, songs and plays – and visual and material – maps, prints, paintings, buildings and ephemera – I discovered powerful and compelling evidence that outer London's growth in the eighteenth century was far more vigorous and complex than the normal catch-all term 'satellite development' conveys (Figure 10.2).

In approaching the topic, I was influenced by theorists such as de Certeau and Soja in exploring the connections between the landscape and the lives lived within it.[16] It was in tracing the connections between 'spaces' whether metaphorical or physical and 'existences' that was at the heart of my work. I also reconsidered Raymond Williams's classic work *The Country and the City* (1973). His central theme of the distinction between the pastoral ideal versus a corrupting urban environment has been enthusiastically embraced by subsequent generations of scholars leading to a bifurcation in cultural studies between urban and rural scholarship. More recently there have been a number of works which have begun to unpick these two binaries and explore the connections and interstices between city and country. In relation to early nineteenth-century London, Dana Arnold offered an important re-conceptualisation of urban and rural as having a commonality of values rooted in land and its associated values, arising from the practices of land ownership and development by the great estates.[17] My book by contrast suggested that middle-class practices and culture were central to the creation of a new urban-rural configuration in the environs; a zone with a far more fragmented pattern of land ownership and no history of large-scale estate development until the second quarter of the nineteenth century. This was a novel landscape arising not out of aristocratic ownership but out of the commercial society of the metropolitan middle classes in the long eighteenth century which created something neither city nor country, but rather something in-between, a new suburban culture in which dwelling, leisure and commerce were all inter-twined.

I was particularly concerned to explore the transformation of the suburbs in the eighteenth century from the despised extra-mural overspill of the poor of earlier centuries to their modern status as a distinct zone of settlement contiguous to but different from the urban core. It was in eighteenth-century London, as had been argued by two Americans Fishman and Archer, that this first occurred. They saw the wealthy settlements of south and south-west London as the

FIGURE 10.2 Lauderdale House, Highgate, London, N6, 1582–1760: photo Author. An outer London mansion whose continuous updating is shown in the original timber-framed structure given a Georgian make-over in 1760.

beginning of the modern suburb.[18] I was keen to show that this development also happened in the middle-class northern and eastern suburbs and was not just an elite phenomenon. These early suburbs were not simply dormitories, as with their later nineteenth and twentieth-century counterparts. They were also important commercial, agricultural and industrial centres. This mixture of spaces led to the creation of a new type of environment distinct from that of city centre in its greater architectural variety, spaciousness and greenery but at the same time inextricably bound to it culturally, socially and economically.

In exploring the middle-class culture of these outer areas, I was continuing my examination of the demotic – whether structures, places or people – in an attempt to expand the traditional narratives of architectural and landscape history. Even when I dealt with the canonical in Regent's Park I did so against the grain using the figure of John White, the Duke of Portland's surveyor, to consider an alternative version of the scheme's genesis and to explore issues of architectural practice through his position as a designer, developer and timber entrepreneur in the greater London area. I was keen to overturn a series of oppositions, not just city and country, but also polite and vernacular or builders and architects which were both inaccurate and unhelpful as a means of taxonomy in this inherently hybrid landscape.

If women were just present in *The Birth of Modern London*, they played a larger part in *Landscapes of London* as I wove together a topographical approach in which spatiality, gender and class all came together to provide a new reading of the middle-class landscape. It was an environment in which one can see some of the new social freedoms that women enjoyed in the period but also the brutal realities of the sexual and reproductive politics which simultaneously severely constrained their lives. The London countryside was a playground and residential retreat, but also a zone of marginality and displacement. Marginality was not confined to the destitute or the dying, it also embraced other groups, less immediately threatening but nonetheless still tangential to normal society, notably children and fallen women. The conjunction of these latter two was exemplified by the Foundling Hospital (1741) for abandoned infants, situated just beyond the northern edge of the city in the fields of Bloomsbury. The environs, as they were known, also functioned as a zone of liminality for women in the many pleasure gardens and spas that surrounded the capital. These have long been hailed in the secondary literature as sites of the new Habermasian sociability in which people from all classes mixed together. But unlike the coffeehouses and clubs of the city centre they were establishments which both sexes attended and as the textual and visual sources revealed, this created a new spatiality in which women as well as men might experiment with different personas. A space neither town nor country, neither wholly occupied by the polite nor the impolite, an ambiguous arena in which it is suggested the normal moral and social codes of conduct might be suspended.

Such a characterisation of the metropolis as a multivalent, de-centred conurbation has been a theme which has developed across disciplines. I benefitted hugely from the burgeoning studies on London from the 1990s onwards, including a very valuable stint on the multi-disciplinary Editorial Committee of *The London Journal* alongside leading eighteenth-century scholars such as the social historian Tim Hitchcock and the cultural geographer Miles Ogborn. However, much as my work has been informed by this scholarship *Landscapes of London* was also borne out of a frustration at the somewhat nebulous way in which the 'suburbs' were often portrayed. I wanted to inject some architectural and topographical specificity while at the same time showing social and cultural historians how the material evidence of buildings and landscapes can contribute distinctive insights into discussions of life and culture. I was staking out a challenge to consider a conception of the landscape as both metaphor and product of material culture relevant to a specific time and place.

My work on *Landscapes of London* tracked my own journey across the capital moving ever further out from the centre in search of more greenery and space. Luckily this coincided with the development of the first online sources and digitised collections such as EEBO and ECCO,[19] which opened up a whole new world of non-elite printed sources which contributed enormously to the richness and diversity of the project and allowed me to work anywhere.[20] By the time I finished the book, I was no longer living in London and I would write about it no more.

Biographical Studies: A Shift to the Centre?

The use of individual stories in *Landscapes of London* as a means of evidencing middle-class culture made me increasing sympathetic to the use of micro-histories and biography as a means of historical explication.[21] If you had told me as a student that I would one day write a biography I would have been incredulous. I was part of the generation who believed firmly that architectural history had to rid itself of its obsession with individuals whether practitioners or patrons, and looked down with disdain on biographical treatments of the subject, whether in Colvin's great dictionary or individual monographs; as Dana Arnold wrote 'in recent times ... the wish to imbue historical narrative with the notion of causation gives the actions of individuals a fairly low priority'.[22] Given this methodological legacy and my interest in broad social and cultural patterns how did I end up not only researching a biography but also branching out into late nineteenth and twentieth-century studies, largely through examining a series of individuals? And one might add shaping this chapter through a largely autobiographical lens?

By the later twentieth century biography had gone through a renaissance – in no small part due to the feminist assertion of the power of the personal – and became a respectable intellectual approach as well as the dominant form of popular history. Spearheaded in Britain by figures such as Michael Holroyd it threw off its fusty image and became a means of offering social and cultural history through the prism of an individual life. As time went on experimentation burgeoned so that in the hands of scholars like Hermione Lee the biography no longer had to be chronological or even attempt to be comprehensive in its coverage. Group biographies, family biographies and eventually life writing, the exploration of the world through one's own personal narratives, have come to prevail as one of the dominant genres in contemporary writing practice.[23] Architectural historians too began breathing new life into the genre, outstanding British examples being Rosemary Hill's *Pugin* (2007) and Fiona MacCarthy's *Morris* (2010). This trend was further galvanised by what we might call 'the historiographical turn' in the twenty-first century whereby all academic disciplines began to explore their own recent history.[24] My forthcoming book on John Summerson (1904–92) follows on from biographies of two of the other leading stars in the Anglo-American firmament, Nikolaus Pevsner and Reyner Banham.[25] It has as a central concern the role of architecture and architectural history in shaping national identity in the inter-War and post-World War Two eras. The publication of the two Pevsner biographies brought these themes to wide public and scholarly attention, as *The Guardian* reviewer commented: 'the very fact that an architectural historian … has inspired two such thorough-going biographies is an indication of just how central Pevsner was to postwar British cultural life' (2011).[26] My book will show how Summerson played an equally vital part and one of greater longevity in the cultural landscape of that era (Pevsner died in 1974).

I first returned to Summerson as a subject after *The Birth of Modern London* in a book I co-edited with Barbara Arciszewska, *Articulating British Classicism,* which explored new approaches to eighteenth-century architecture. In my contribution I investigated perceptions of the Georgian in British twentieth-century culture.[27] I started with the theme of Palladianism but I quickly discovered that it played only a minor part in the wider rehabilitation of classicism in the early twentieth century. It was not until the 1930s that Palladian or 'Georgian' architecture, as it was by then known, became fashionable in architectural circles and furthermore allied to modernism by its proponents. I amassed vast amounts of information but when the time came to write the article the best means of focussing the topic seemed to be through a return to Summerson; who exemplified the dual Georgian-Modernist theme through his founding membership of both the MARS Group (1933) and the Georgian Group (1937). The ensuing chapter showed the shifts in his thinking about classicism up until the 1970s in works such as *Georgian London* (1945) and the various editions of *Architecture in Britain 1530–1830* (1953) as well as his attitudes to the burgeoning conservation movement of the late 1960s and 1970s.

Out of the same great pile of material, including extensive trawls through the *Architectural Review*, two further articles arose. One was on C. H. B. Quennell who I first encountered writing about the importance of Georgian architecture as a precedent for the modern world just after the First World War. Another was on Annabel Dott who I came across in an article on 'The Woman Architect' in the *Architectural Review* sitting on the upper floor of the RIBA Library in the late 1990s. My interest was piqued not only by the reference to an unknown woman designer but also by the fact that she was describing housing for disabled veterans from the First World War,

FIGURE 10.3 The Orchards, Goathland, North Yorkshire, Annabel Dott, c.1912: photo Author. The cottages by Dott donated by her for use by disabled officers after the War.

another topic which I had never seen discussed but which attracted me as my own grandfather had lost a leg at Gallipoli. I returned to Quennell not long after and found him to be an intriguing figure, well-known as the co-author with his wife Marjorie of the *Everyday Things* books, but also a wonderfully diverse architect and proponent of standardisation pre-1918.[28]

It took me another twenty years to get back to Dott following an invitation to contribute to a conference on 'Architecture and the Aftermath of the First World War' at the Institute of Historical Research, London in 2018 (Figures 10.3 and 10.4). My first task was to try to find the cottages for the disabled that Dott had described in her article at Goathland, North Yorkshire. Maps and all the usual topographical aides proved no use but the indefatigable Jane Grenville, who was researching the revised Pevsner volume for the area, tracked the row down for me and aided by her introduction to a splendid group of local historians who were working on Dott, I was off and running. Dott turned out to be the most remarkable figure, more of a builder than an architect, but one who financed and built several major projects including an ideal community at East Hoathly Sussex as well as several church projects and houses in South Africa, London and Wiltshire. She was a leader in providing housing for working women in the inter-war period as part of the Women's Pioneer Housing Association and in her own ventures.[29] Discussions of such women benefactors I discovered are in danger of becoming caught between, on the one hand an architectural historiography which celebrates their achievements with Pevsnerian pioneering rhetoric; something which is understandable in a discipline in which new women contributors – whether as designers, patrons or other agents – are still being disinterred from the historical record.[30] On the other hand, there has been a strongly entrenched strand in twentieth-century social history which tends to dismiss the efforts of middle or upper-class women as

FIGURE 10.4 The Stone House, Goathland, North Yorkshire, Annabel Dott, c.1912–15: photo Author. The house Dott designed for herself and where she lived until 1919.

paternalistic, classist and localised.[31] This gender discrimination further reinforces a prejudice against small-scale, local initiatives in twentieth-century historiography, in favour of national state intervention, which is only now being challenged in recent scholarship. Eve Colpus has powerfully demonstrated how such female philanthropy might be reconceived as 'part of the reflex and communicative practices individuals used in the inter-war years to make sense of the social, political and cultural changes in the world around them'.[32]

In both these articles on individuals, I came to see the value in biographical studies which uncover overlooked figures from the past and help to challenge and broaden accepted historical narratives. There was no deposited archive for either Quennell or Dott but luckily both of them were prolific journalists and propogandists in print which provided alternative sources, alongside their built works, for exploring their ideas and achievements. As I have already discussed the broadening of the evidential base beyond the traditional archive is essential in the creation of an expanded field of architectural history and particularly so for exploring women's narratives. In Dott's case she asserted herself in the public sphere with a string of articles and interviews in the architectural, national and international press promoting social reform in relation to a number of contemporary debates regarding gender, domestic space, housing and rural society. Quennell was a key figure in the pre-1918 architectural landscape but his career never fully recovered after the War and so he turned to writing the hugely successful *Everyday Things* series. The stories of those who failed to capture the heights of the architectural profession can be as illuminating of the culture of the time as the minority who did.[33] In a similar way a later article I wrote on the architect Peter Boston, who was active from the 1950s onwards, sought to examine an overlooked architect and explore the workings of the small-scale practitioner in the mid- to late twentieth century at a time when architectural practice shifted from an individualistic to an increasingly corporate model.[34]

This bring me on to my current writing about Sir John Summerson, someone who is extremely well known, which brings with it different challenges and issues. *Georgian London* had been the impetus for my doctorate but my relationship with the text evolved as the project progressed and, as I wrote, 'as time went on I found my work taking on the form of a sustained dialogue with him. Sometimes he provided the source of inspiration, at others he became the point of opposition'.[35] I know I was not alone among British specialists in feeling this way, although to my surprise nobody else seemed to be following this continuing debate with Summerson through to its logical conclusion in the form of a biography.

Most studies to date have focussed on Summerson's intellectual formation, his attitudes to modernism, conservation and urban history and his role in creating period and geographical canons.[36] His career as an architectural critic, journalist and historian has been discussed from various angles and for different periods but there has not been a biography which seeks to draw the strands of his life together to date and which utilises all the primary sources.[37] Summerson's working life from the 1920s to the 1980s traces the arc of the rise and fall of modernism in Britain while his complicated relationship with the conservation movement and postmodernism in the 1970s and 1980s foreshadowed many of the heritage debates of the late twentieth and early twenty-first century. In between he wrote numerous articles, essays and books including some of the foundational texts of modern British architectural history such as: *Georgian London* (1945), *Architecture in Britain 1530–1830* (1953) in the Pelican *History of Art* series, and the volumes covering the period 1558–1660 in the *History of the King's Works* (1975, 1982). As well as being a leading scholar Summerson played a major role in public life sitting on numerous public bodies and committees, including the Royal Fine Arts Commission (1947–54), the Royal Commission on Historical Monuments (1953–74), and the Historic Buildings Council (1953–78).

I am attempting to write a cultural biography tracing Summerson's important position at the centre of British artistic life over six decades following Roger Chartier's proposition that 'we move from intellectual history to a cultural history of intellectuals'.[38] It will be based on extensive research in all relevant archives, including the voluminous one he left to the RIBA, and will have as a central concern the role of architecture and architectural history in shaping national identity. I explore architectural history's important position in relation to the post-1945 rebuilding project in its broadest sense – physical, spiritual and intellectual – in creating, what David Matless has called, 'landscapes of Reconstruction'.[39] I then extend the discussion into the critical decades of the 1970s and 1980s when much of the post-war consensus was dramatically overturned. Using the interdisciplinary approach, which has characterised nearly all of my work, I aim to bring together the areas of architectural history with social and cultural history and its sub-genres of public history and heritage studies. The topic demands a wide knowledge of British architecture and culture from the early modern period to the late twentieth century and feels like a summation, and at times a test, of my reading over many years. I could not have done justice to the subject even ten years ago and as with the Hackney Society post this is the right project at the right time.

Although biography is not a young person's game, I am sufficiently youthful not to have known or worked with Summerson, although I know plenty of people who did so. I am thus of a generation near enough to engage with and be inspired by the man but sufficiently distant to be able to assess his methods and assumptions. I would not claim that mine will be a feminist biography of Summerson but it will be one in which the gender politics of his domestic and professional arrangements will feature, as well as an awareness of the male-dominated spaces that he inhabited in academia, public life, journalism and publishing. The BBC surprisingly was something of an exception having large numbers of female senior producers, the people with whom Summerson principally engaged. I hope to contribute to the use of biography as a means of academic writing by creating a dynamic interplay between the biographical subject and the wider historical and cultural context; an issue with which Summerson himself was much concerned. Through it I aim to show how architectural studies can contribute to debates about national culture and public memory. The biography will therefore sit alongside not just studies of other historiographical works but also recent reassessments of British artistic culture in the twentieth century.[40]

Within the Walls?

I was elected as the first woman President of the Society of Architectural Historians of Great Britain in 2021 and so can no longer claim to be an outsider. I am now part of the institutional scaffolding of the subject and furthermore researching the ultimate establishment figure. Nevertheless, I feel that the discipline is perhaps more de-centred than ever. In some ways this is borne out of positive developments even though there is a continuing lack of opportunities and funding. Architectural history in the United Kingdom has very belatedly become broader and more diverse in recent years and this inevitably leads to a greater plurality of ways and places, including crucially electronically, where architectural history is propagated.[41] At the same time, the Heritage sector has increased its scope and range enormously since I wrote my article in 1996 forming an important locus for the investigation and explication of historic buildings in both the public and private sectors. However, what I have come to realise over time is that the sense of being a beleaguered outsider whether in Art History or Architecture departments is something that is widely shared by other architectural historians even among the most senior ranks. While we will continue to lobby for our right to a share of the available resources at the same time, for my own part at least, I have to admit that the malleability and marginality of the subject has suited me both intellectually and temperamentally. Is this to do with my being a woman? I'm not sure although I have been largely content for the template of my career to run outside the traditional channels. So while my attraction to the peripheries of the discipline and to subjects that sit astride the polite/vernacular divide might be attributed to a feminist aversion to the male mainstream of architectural history it also comes out of a wish to explore the connections between the social and the cultural influenced by long-standing approaches in urban, design and housing histories. I have tried to use my peripheral position as a strength drawing on a wide range of subject areas and sources to take architectural history beyond its usual methodological bases and preoccupations, particularly in creating a landscape approach to urban history. For me paradoxically in an object-led subject it is the de-centred nature of architectural history which provides its fascination and its strength. I hope I have shown how the intersectionality and inherently interdisciplinary nature of architectural history can be used creatively to form new narratives and areas of investigation. It is the urge to take Frost's 'less travelled path', to go outside the known walls and trample down boundaries, which sparks curiosity and propels one forward to expand the subject and traverse its limits.[42]

Notes

1 Elizabeth McKellar, 'All Roof, No Walls: Peter Boston, A-Frames and the Primitive Hut in Twentieth-century British Architecture c. 1890–1970.' *Architectural History* 62 (2019): 237–69.
2 Edward Hallett Carr, *What Is History* (Harmondsworth: Penguin, 1964).
3 Paul Harrison, *Inside the Inner City: Life Under the Cutting Edge* (Harmondsworth: Penguin, 1983).
4 Elizabeth McKellar, *Buildings at Risk in Hackney* (London: Hackney Society, 1987); Hackney Society, *South Shoreditch: Historic and Industrial Buildings* (London: Hackney Society, 1986).
5 Iain Sinclair, *Hackney, That Rose-Red Empire: A Confidential Report* (London: Penguin, 2009); Iain Sinclair, *Ghost Milk: Recent Adventures among the Future Ruins of London on the Eve of the Olympics* (London: Penguin, 2012).
6 Matrix eds., *Making Space: Women and the Man-Made Environment* (London: Pluto Press, 1986).
7 Judy Attfield and Pat Kirkham eds., *A View from the Interior: Feminism, Women and Design* (London: The Women's Press, 1989); Anthea Callen, *Angel in the Studio. Women in the Arts and Crafts Movement, 1870–1914* (London: Astragal Books, 1979).
8 This critique has been publicly aired recently following a scandal over a toxic culture at the Bartlett in 2022, see Ben Flatman, 'Bartlett Report Sheds Much Needed Light on Our Profession's Wider Failings.' *Building Design* (15 June 2022).
9 Elizabeth McKellar, 'Architectural History: The Invisible Subject.' *The Journal of Architecture* 1 (1996): 159–64 (159).
10 Elizabeth McKellar, *The Birth of Modern London: The Development and Design of the City 1660–1720* (Manchester, Manchester University Press), xi.
11 Chris Miele, Review 'The Birth of Modern London: The Development and Design of the City 1660–1720.' *London Journal* 24 no. 2 (1999): 82–83.
12 Richard Hewlings, 'Women in the Building Trades, 1600–1850.' *Georgian Group Journal* 10 (2000): 70–83; Peter Guillery, 'The Further Adventures of Mary Lacy.' *Georgian Group Journal* 10 (2000); Linda Clarke and Chris Wall, 'Omitted from History: Women in the Building Trades', in ed. M. Dunkeld et al. *Proceedings of the Second International Congress on Construction History* (Cambridge: Cambridge University Press, 2006); Conor Lucey, 'Women and the Construction Industry in Georgian Britain and Ireland.' *Architectural History* 66 (2023): 127–154.
13 Neil McKendrick and John Harold Plumb, *The Birth of a Consumer Society: The Commercialization of Eighteenth-Century England* (London: Europa, 1992).
14 Frank Kelsall, 'The London House Plan in the Later 17th Century.' *Post-Medieval Archaeology* 8 (1974): 80–91.
15 Joel Garreau, *Edge City: Life on the New Frontier* (New York: Anchor Books, 1992).
16 Edward W. Soja, *Postmetropolis: Critical Studies of Cities and Regions* (Malden, MA & Oxford: Blackwell, 2000); Michel de Certeau, *The Practice of Everyday Life*, trans. Steven Rendall (Berkeley, Los Angeles & London: University of California Press, 1984).
17 Dana Arnold, *Rural Urbanism: London Landscapes in the Early Nineteenth Century* (Manchester: Manchester University Press, 2005).
18 Robert Fishman, *Bourgeois Utopias: The Rise and Fall of Suburbia* (New York: Basic Books Inc., 1987); John Archer, *Architecture and Suburbia: From English Villa to American Dream House, 1690–2000* (Minneapolis & London: University of Minnesota Press, 2005).
19 Early English Books Online and Eighteenth-Century Books Online.
20 Tim Hitchcock and Robert Shoemaker, 'Editors' Introduction.' *London Journal* 30, no. 11 (2005): 2–4.
21 Jill Lepore, 'Historians Who Love Too Much: Reflections on Microhistory and Biography.' *The Journal of American History* 88, no. 1 (June 2001): 129–44.
22 Dana Arnold, *Reading Architectural History* (London & New York: Routledge, 2002): 35.
23 Hermione Lee, *Body Parts: Essays on Life Writing* (London: Pimlico, 2005).
24 David Watkin, *The Rise of Architectural History* (London: Architectural Press, 1980).
25 Stephen Games, *Pevsner - The Early Life; Germany and Art* (London & New York: Continuum, 2010); Susie Harries, *Nikolaus Pevsner: The Life* (London: Chatto & Windus, 2011); Nigel Whitely, *Reyner Banham: Historian of the Immediate Future* (Cambridge, MA: MIT Press, 2002).
26 Michael Prodger, *The Guardian,* 9.9.2011. https://www.theguardian.com/books/2011/sep/09/nikolaus-pevsner-life-harries-review (accessed 09/01/2023).
27 Elizabeth McKellar, 'Populism versus Professionalism: John Summerson and the Creation of "The Georgian"', in *Articulating British Classicism: New Approaches in Eighteenth-Century Architecture*, eds. Elizabeth McKellar and Barbara Arciszewska (Aldershot: Ashgate, 2004): 35–56.

28 Elizabeth McKellar, 'C. H. B. Quennell (1872–1935): Architecture, History and the Quest for the Modern.' *Architectural History*, 50 (2007): 211–46.
29 Elizabeth McKellar, 'Annabel Dott and Colonial, Metropolitan and Rural Communities', in *Reconstruction: Architecture, Society and the Aftermath of the First World War*, eds. Neal Shasore and Jessica Kelly (London: Bloomsbury, 2023), 219–240.
30 For a more nuanced discussion of women's agency in building in this period see: Elizabeth Darling and Lesley Whitworth, eds. 'Introduction', in *Women and the Making of Built Space in England, 1870–1950* (Ashgate: Aldershot, 2007).
31 See Alison Creedon, 'A Benevolent Tyrant? The Principles and Practices of Henrietta Barnett (1851–936), Social Reformer and Founder of Hampstead Garden Suburb.' *Women's History Review* 11, no. 2 (2002): 231–52; Eileen Janes Yeo, ed. *Radical Femininity: Women's Self-Presentation in the Public Sphere* (Manchester: Manchester University Press, 1998).
32 Eve Colpus, *Female Philanthropy in the Interwar World: Between Self and Other* (London: Bloomsbury, 2018), 2.
33 Timothy J. Brittain-Catlin, *Bleak Houses: Disappointment and Failure in Architecture* (Cambridge, MA & London: MIT Press, 2014).
34 McKellar, 'All Roof, No Walls', 237–69.
35 McKellar, *The Birth of Modern London*, xii.
36 Jane Pavitt, 'The Georgians and the Moderns: Preservation and Modernism in Britain in the 1930s.' London: MA Thesis, Royal College of Art (1991); Peter Mandler, 'John Summerson (1904–92): The Architectural Critic and the Quest for the Modern', in *After the Victorians: Private Conscience and Public Duty in Modern Britain*, eds. Susan Pedersen and Peter Mandler (London & New York: Routledge, 1994): 229–46; Alan Powers, 'John Summerson and Modernism.' *Twentieth-Century Architecture and Its Histories* (Society of Architectural Historians of Great Britain Millennial Volume, 2000), 153–76; Michela Rosso, *La Storia utile; Patrimonio e modernita nel lavoro di John Summerson e Nikolaus Pevsner: Londra 1928–55* (Torina: Edizioni di Comunita, 2001).
37 Frank Salmon, ed. *Summerson and Hitchcock: Centenary Essays on Architectural Historiography* (London & New Haven: Yale University Press, 2006), 'Introduction', xxv.
38 See Hèlène Lipstadt, 'Celebrating the Centenaries of Summerson and Hitchcock: Finding a Historiography for the Architect-Historian', in *Summerson and Hitchcock*, ed. Salmon, 345.
39 David Matless, *Landscape and Englishness* (London: Reaktion, 1998, 2016).
40 Elizabeth Darling, *Re-forming Britain: Narratives of Modernity Before Reconstruction* (London: Routledge, 2006); Alexandra Harris, *Romantic Moderns: English Writers, Artists and the Imagination from Virginia Woolf to John Piper* (London: Thames & Hudson, 2010); Kitty Hauser, *Shadow Sites: Photography, Archaeology & the British Landscape 1927–1955* (Oxford: Oxford University Press, 2007).
41 Nancy Stieber, 'Architecture between Disciplines.' *Journal of the Society of Architectural Historians* 62, no. 2 (2003): 176–77.
42 Robert Frost, *The Road Not Taken*, 1915. https://www.poetryfoundation.org/poems/44272/the-road-not-taken

11

LOOKING SOFTLY AT ARCHITECTURAL HISTORY

Eroding the Hegemony of Formalism

Joan Coutu

Identity, home, domesticity, nostalgia, nuance, tradition. Such 'soft' concepts are central to people's lives and condition the spaces we build and how we interact with them. They are also familiar tropes now regularly used in Western universities to study the history of architecture and built environments more generally.[1] They have displaced formalism – the aesthetics of form and style without consideration of the use or social implications of architecture – as the primary, and what was often the only, mode of analysis. In contrast to most other humanities-oriented disciplines which were grounded in comparable formalist methodologies in the mid-twentieth century, the shift away from formalism in architectural history came late, and, when it did come, it happened quickly. One reason might be that the tangibility and presence of a building promotes close scrutiny of its form to the exclusion of anything else, making it harder to 'read' the building any other way. It also, of course, depends on who is doing the reading.[2]

The slow-to-change evolution of architectural history has been acknowledged by many scholars, including many female architectural historians, who were keenly aware of the strictures of the traditional architectural history canon, which is the similarly intractable soulmate of formalism.[3] Postcolonial scholars also joined the conversation, but, likewise, later than in other disciplines.[4] Like formalism and the canon, imperialism and imperial studies exuded an intransigent hegemony that was, and continues to be, a monolith to overcome.

As a woman who has worked on aspects of the British imperial enterprise for over three decades, I have long been interested in the synergies between these non-formalist perspectives. As such, I have used the opportunity to contribute to this volume to highlight the work of female scholars – whether distinctly feminist or less paradigmatic in approach – with other modes of scholarship that have collectively recalibrated how we consider the architectural history of the British Empire. Rather than taking on the scholarship of the whole of the British Empire, a task that is both unwieldy and runs counter to postcolonial and decolonial thought of accentuating the individual circumstances of each facet of the empire, I have chosen to concentrate on two genres, eighteenth-century British country houses and settler-built environments in Canada. The essay ends with a brief discussion of attempts to actively decolonise the study of architecture, also with a particular focus on Canada. In terms of my goal, the aim is to articulate the moments when the work, and indeed the presence, of women fundamentally disrupted, dislodged, and eroded the

DOI: 10.4324/9781003224662-16

hegemony of formalism in imperial contexts. I also wish to leave the reader to reflect upon the often quiet but incremental work of women – essentially a slow fuse effect – that was a sort of harbinger of what would become an unprecedented drive for institutional and systemic change.

Two of the more profound lessons we have learned from decolonisation are the value and significance of lived experience and the recognition of relationships and the relational. Both guide this project. British country houses and settler-built environments in Canada are the ongoing foci of my research career and, as such, they are part of my lived experience. In terms of the relational, when we consider how these buildings and spaces were used, by whom, and why, they and their legacies become more vital, in good ways and bad. This is especially true of the settler spaces. They exist in an in-between. This is not the in-between of Homi K. Bhabha's third space of imperial-colonial subaltern antagonism. Rather, these are actual spaces in the 'new world' first claimed by imperial-colonists beginning in the seventeenth century that, with the move toward self-governance in the late nineteenth and early twentieth centuries (Canada in 1867, Australia in 1901, New Zealand in 1907, and South Africa in 1910) underpinned by the capitalist fervour of this era of New Imperialism, came to carry metonymic or explicit nation-building identity as the former colonists sought to define themselves culturally against, but entangled with, Britain, Europe more generally, and the United States. Such spaces speak of imbrication and are untidy, blurry, and evanescent, full of undercurrents, nuance, and edges. By contrast, defining themselves against the Indigenous 'Other' was straightforward, although perverse: while the colonial elite brutally effaced Indigenous peoples through displacement, assimilation, and death, they simultaneously wrote Indigenous peoples into the 'official' teleological settler history through prose, poetry, lyrics, paintings, posters, murals, schoolbook illustrations, and more.[5]

Within a personal context, the historical settler edge and the settler in-between I describe above are the spaces of my identity, my work, and where I live. I am of French-Scottish-Irish-Canadian heritage, which means I am not French, Scottish, or Irish, nor am I Indigenous. I grew up in Toronto, a city that is largely a product of the turn of the twentieth-century emergent Canadian nation-state and was vociferously WASP until the 1980s.[6] Now, I live and work about 100 kilometres west of Toronto, in Waterloo Region – the name speaks volumes – on land that is the traditional territory of the Neutral, Anishinaabeg, and Haudenosaunee peoples. Claimed by the British, the land was then presumptuously granted back under the title of the Haldimand Tract to the Six Nations of the Iroquois Confederacy in 1784.[7] Within the context of my work on Britain and the British Empire, my hereditary identity and where I live place me on the edge, but because I did my postgraduate studies in England, I am somewhere in-between. In terms of architectural history, my research also lies on the edge since much of it is about sculpture – monuments, statues, and busts – that I consider within the built environments in which they exist. Within the context of this volume, although I am attuned to women living in the spaces which I explore and I employ aspects of feminist theory, my research neither concentrates on women nor is feminist *per se*.

The edge and the in-between are interesting spaces. They at once provide distance but are not truly distant and like synergies and imbrication they are blurry and untidy and are spaces where categories breakdown: here nor there, belonging to but not. Because of this, they have long been ignored or neglected. Remarkably, like women and sculpture, one of the quips about Canada and Canadians is that they often go unnoticed. However, the edge and the in-between can also be privileged spaces. Inclusion-exclusion allows for observation, and it is from the edge, as we know from feminist and postcolonial studies, that imperial hegemonies often began to be picked at, disrupted, and ultimately destabilised.

The narrative arc of the study of architectural history over the last fifty years is a familiar one, from the absolute dominance of formalism in the mid-to-late twentieth century to the proliferation of contextual 'isms' and relational explorations. The shift away from formalism, like imperial centrism, was fraught with resistance. Architectural history was further beset, like art history, by the tyranny of the aesthetic object, with the magnitude and phenomenological presence of grand buildings making it especially difficult to overcome their enthralling allure. For much of the twentieth century, Western university architectural history programmes, and scholarship, were about the study of mostly European big buildings and assessing them in terms of the purity of their form: measuring distances between columns; scrutinising the correct use of the classical orders; analysing the evolution of Gothic vaulting; and so on. When smaller or somehow less portentous buildings were included, these were hived off, usually relegated to a single class at the end of the course and discussed in terms of their less auspicious vernacular status. Whilst useful for understanding style, this hagiographic aesthetic approach offered little, if any, social context. Furthermore, it was underpinned by the inherent pre-supposition of European superiority and civilisation.

Yet, there were rumblings of other ways to think about architecture. Some of these came from outside the discipline. A well-known example is the French social and economic historian Georges Duby and his transformative study, *The Age of Cathedrals* (1976), which placed French Gothic cathedrals in the context of people and at the heart of communities.[8] In British country house studies, the shift was less seismic, but nonetheless began around the same time, and was associated with the wholesale destruction of country houses. This was sparked by the highly visible exhibition, *The Destruction of the Country House,* at the Victoria and Albert Museum in 1974, curated by John Harris, Sir Roy Strong, and Marcus Binney, and the primary strategy was to emphasise aesthetic formalist significance infused with a nationalistic resolve to protect the country's physical heritage. This was followed by Mark Girouard's 1978 book, *Life in the English Country House: A Social and Architectural History.*[9] The sub-title is telling as it stresses a union of what were otherwise considered two different modes of history that had grown apart under the aegis of formalism. Girouard took this further in his short essay on the country house as power house in the catalogue associated with the enormous exhibition at the National Gallery in Washington, D.C. in 1985–1986, *The Treasure Houses of Britain,* curated by Gervase Jackson-Stops.[10] A product of mutual British-American appreciation politics, the exhibition was an extraordinary celebration of precious books and aesthetic objects from the houses and of the houses themselves, an affirmation of Britain's cultural – if no longer political or economic – superiority.[11] Specifically, Girouard's essay focused on the owners of the houses and their role, as well as that of the house in the economic and social infrastructure of bygone eras. This was accompanied by a wave of well-researched but ultimately adulatory landscape garden biographies.

The coupling of hagiographic formalism and anxiety about disappearing physical patrimony proved difficult to overcome and alternative ways of exploring the country house were slow to materialise. Two of the first to do so are edited volumes by Dana Arnold, *The Georgian Villa,* published in 1996, followed by *The Georgian Country House: Architecture, Landscape, and Society* in 1998.[12] The latter especially embraces a range of critical themes that include dissemination of the house to various publics and via the press, a critical analysis of the idea of grandeur, a study of the relationship between surrounding landscape and the house, and, most relevant to this volume, a discussion – by Arnold – of the role of women in the country house. As Arnold points out, such a study came years after comparable interventions in the history of art by Linda Nochlin, Deborah Cherry, Rozsika Parker, and Griselda Pollock.[13] A third volume edited by Arnold, *Reading Architectural History,* published in 2002, in which country house studies also figure prominently, critically examines the historiography of British architectural history, articulating and contextualising the predominance of the intertwined formalist, aesthetic, 'great architect/Roarkist' canon whilst championing the validity of relevant theoretical discourses, including narrative, authorship, class, social, and gender. Collectively, these volumes, while initially outliers, were central to fundamentally shifting the scholarly discourse.[14]

Consideration of the country house by scholars from other disciplines and fields would also broaden, and deepen, the discourse. Some of this groundbreaking work was, and is being, done by women. The social historian Amanda Vickery published *The Gentleman's Daughter; Women's Lives in Georgian England* in 1998, which became a benchmark analysis of women and material culture largely within the country house setting.[15] This was followed a decade later by *Behind Closed Doors: At Home in Georgian England* (2009).[16] Both books won multiple prizes and the latter formed the basis of a three-part BBC television series in 2010, *At Home with the Georgians*. Together, these became foundational studies for the analysis of gender, social, and material culture in the country house.[17] Coming from art history, Kate Retford has likewise firmly placed people, especially women, within the country house, in her discussions of family portraits (2006) and the conversation piece (2017).[18] Notably, both Vickery and Retford draw upon a range of historical and conceptual themes, including gender, domesticity, status, material culture, and consumption, all of which lie outside the traditional formalist canon of architectural history. These, in turn, have spurred new and revisionist studies of female patrons in country house studies, of which Sarah, Duchess of Marlborough takes centre stage.[19]

By the middle of the 2010s, the country house had finally been broken into with multiple diverse and imbricated lines of inquiry. The result was much more critical discussion of the meaning and phenomenology of the country house. My own work on monuments and empire (2006) and sculpture collections and politics (2015) falls within this sphere, but the impact was glancing, partly because monuments, copies, and casts have less cachet in art history studies.[20] The house was more emphatically centred in the context of the British Empire with ground-breaking texts by Stephanie Barczewski, *Country Houses and the British Empire, 1700–1930* (2014), and Margot Finn and Kate Smith's edited volume, *The East India Company at Home, 1757–1857* (2018).[21] Notably, none of Barczewski, Finn, and Smith are architectural historians and only one contributor to Finn and Smith's book identifies as an architectural historian. Then came the National Trust's *Interim Report on the Connections between Colonialism and Properties now in the care of the National Trust, including links with Historic Slavery*, published in September 2020. Whilst Barczewski's book and Finn and Smith's volume were generally enthusiastically received within the narrow scholarly world in which they live, the National Trust's much more public report was alternately praised and vehemently criticised. The latter came mostly from people who keenly believed that the nation's heritage was being besmirched and who already felt threatened by what they saw as attacks on monuments during the Black Lives Matter protests in the summer of 2020, including the toppling of the Edward Colston statue in Bristol and the spray-painting of 'was a racist' on the base of the Winston Churchill statue outside the Houses of Parliament.[22] Collectively, these were large sparks in Britain's culture wars. Moving forward, responsible country house scholarship will need to acknowledge this transformative moment. One example is a volume of essays about politics and the country house, edited by me, Jon Stobart, and Peter Lindfield, published in early 2023. The essays, all of which were written during 2020, explore the relationship between country houses and ownership and the mutable nature of politics and imperialism in the eighteenth century.[23]

Looking at the broader field of architectural history, the trajectory was similar. Consistent with second-wave feminism, attempts were made to write women architects into the canonical histories of architecture.[24] As in country house studies, these came later than comparable interventions in art history and other humanities disciplines. However, as hindsight has shown, such an approach, whilst highlighting the work of 'forgotten' women, perversely diminishes their contribution because they were defined by the terms of the canon. Nevertheless, these studies succeeded in exposing the infrastructure of the Western profession of architecture – training, professional designations, industry resources – as well as the strictures of its canonical historical study that stymied women both in the practice of architecture and in the history of it. One of the more often cited texts in this regard is *Designing Women: Gender and the Architectural Profession* by Annmarie Adams and Peta Tancred, published in 2000. The book rumbles the exclusionary presumptions of the canon and questions the conventional idea of the profession.[25] Notably, this challenge came from within and without, as Adams is both an architect and an architectural historian and Tancred was a sociologist (both based at McGill University in Montréal).[26]

Meanwhile, the surge of postcolonial studies in the 1980s and 1990s also made an impact, although the Eurocentric canon retained its dominance particularly in conjunction with the spread of modernism. As Kathleen James-Chakraborty has observed, the focus was initially on the imposition of style as sites of oppression with the devaluation of local expertise – essentially a variant on formalism – but this was soon replaced by a more critical analysis of the impact of the use of local building materials and, more significantly, the flow of information, material culture, and people.[27] As James-Chakraborty also notes, postcolonial approaches were entangled and subsumed in the more generic phrase 'global approaches' that was widely adopted in Western institutions' curricula in the early 2000s.[28] In concert with history programmes throughout Western universities, the requisite Africanist, Latin Americanist, and Asianist were hired, which, like feminist scholars, was a form of being outside whilst being within. Nevertheless, these scholars brought with them critical consideration of abstract and soft concepts of place, tradition, identity, and intersectionality, now widely used in analysis and inquiry. Furthermore, the phrase 'built environment' came into common scholarly usage and suggests something far more malleable and inclusive than the intangible bricks and mortar of 'architecture'. Although big buildings still drive much of the architectural history curriculum, the space around and inside them, as well as housing, town planning, landscapes, parks, and even monuments now figure in the discussion. Jürgen Habermas's consideration of space, Michel Foucault's power relations, Henri Lefebvre's social space, Nicolas Bourriaud's relational aesthetics, and Pierre Bourdieu's habitus have become regular intellectual touchstones. Although all these men are European and their writing is Eurocentric in focus, the concepts they explore are malleable and adaptive. Likewise, underpinned by postcolonial scholarship, Édouard Glissant's *Poetics of Relation* offers a template for the analysis of the built environment in many of the former European imperial colonies.[29] And finally, as many Western institutions seek, or at least aim, to decolonise, the door has begun to creak open for Indigenous ways of knowing, particularly of time, land, tradition, spirit, and place.

The foregoing survey of the parallel yet often imbricated threads in recent country house scholarship, and architectural history more broadly, lays the groundwork for my second point of focus, that of architectural history in the context of the settler society of Canada. Using a case study approach to consider the various societies and cultures created or otherwise impacted by imperialism articulates characteristics that might be shared by each entity but are also, equally important, unique to each, both during the empire and in its afterlife. Furthermore, concentrating on the idiosyncrasy of each situation demonstrates a complexity that destabilises monolithic imperial histories. Some key delineators include the economic viability of colonised lands, their size, proximity to Britain and to other societies and cultures, patterns of settlement, ethnic origins of settlers, reasons for immigration, interactions between settlers and Indigenous peoples and with other Europeans, and the very strong cultural ties that bound colony and then independent nation to 'mother' country. These, in turn, shaped, and continue to shape settler and often Indigenous building practices and built environments and have also determined both how and how much those built environments have been studied.

In contrast to European countries and the United States where the built heritage is a highly valued and celebrated subject, the level of study directed at built environments within settler societies has typically been erratic, especially within the university environment. This too is a condition of the settler society. In Canada, throughout much of the twentieth century, settler architecture was either ignored or celebrated, and Indigenous spaces were, for the most part, deemed to be outside the purview of architectural history. The reasons for this bifurcation and erasure are multifold. They have much to do with when and who established the academic programmes and courses, as well as the precarity of being on the edge, at once the 'less-civilised inferior' edge to Britain and to the United States yet also the dominant superior edge to the subaltern Indigenous other. In that sense, the settler society is an unstable and insecure in-between, a place where architecture and the built environment can, consequently, play a powerful metaphorical role. This 'on the edge-ness' seems also to have perpetuated the persistence of formalism as a dominant methodology, well past when it had been eroded in Europe and the United States. To explore the reasons for this tenacity, I have foregrounded the teaching of Canadian architectural history in Canadian universities, since the teaching – and the pedagogy more broadly – speak to the instructors and students involved over several generations. The academic scholarship has, in turn, tended to mirror the topics and methodologies in the classroom.

Historically, as with other Western countries, there have been two primary streams of architectural history study in Canadian universities. One is in the schools of architecture, of which there were eleven distributed across the country in the twentieth century.[30] Here, architectural history served as context for the practice of architecture. For the most part, these courses were European and American in content, indicative of the desire by the schools to participate on the world stage. Because they were the only required history courses in the professional programmes, they also had a broad remit. Meanwhile, architectural history lived in some of the art history departments spread across the country. Here, its position was somewhat precarious, made more so by the introduction of new methodologies in art history – including feminist approaches – in the latter part of the century. Nevertheless, some significant nodes of architectural history held their own. In these, the content was also almost exclusively European and American architecture.

In 2003 Annmarie Adams and Martin Bressani, both faculty members in the school of architecture at McGill University, published "Canada: The Edge Condition". This was a status survey of architectural history in Canada situated within the then current centre-periphery trope of postcolonial studies.[31] As they indicate, such emphasis on European and American architecture had much to do with demographics since the professors were either European or American or, if they were Canadian, they had done their postgraduate studies in another country.[32] This had consequences on the way Canadian architecture was studied, if it was at all, and by whom. This concept of 'abroad-ness' is a critical factor in settler societies, especially those that have smaller populations. In Canada, initially this was a circumstance driven by the lack of postgraduate programmes.[33] In this sense, it attests to the time required for academic programmes to grow and the corresponding reliance on faculty members who come from abroad. But it also contributes to generating inherent biases that can perpetuate down through generations in departments, in terms of subject matter taught, methodological approaches, and an ongoing predisposition to hire scholars who have trained outside the country. The last point continues to be a factor in some Canadian universities today, especially those that emphasise their 'world-class' status and global nature of their postgraduate programmes.

Not surprisingly, the faculty members of the earliest schools of architecture in Canada – founded around the turn of the twentieth century – were initially caught up in the choice of styles. This was consistent with the contemporaneous reigning influence of the French and American variants of the Beaux Arts aesthetic and principles, combined with the British Arts and Crafts tradition. British imperial zeal was also a strong defining current. By way of example is Ramsay Traquair, a Scottish architect originally based in Edinburgh who emigrated to Canada in 1913 to become the third director of McGill's school of architecture, which at the time consisted of one full-time instructor and two students.[34] Traquair developed a fascination for the style of vernacular Québecois architecture which he rigorously documented through careful measured drawings made by himself and his students, consistent with the practical curriculum of a school of architecture. Such deep observation of form is, of course, also the guiding principle of formalism. Traquair remained at the helm of the school until 1939 by which time his focus on tradition, history, and style had evolved into implacable anti-modernism. This he promulgated with the same ferocity with which he voiced his anti-woman stance and anti-Black racism.[35] Although such repellent prejudice was typically more mutedly expressed after Traquair's time, as we know it was systemically entrenched in Western universities generally. Likewise, although not an exclusive relationship nor one necessarily being the condition of the other, resistance towards women and visible minorities was often imbricated with anti-modernist sentiment, and this predilection would perpetuate in architecture and the arts generally in Canada for decades, as much of the nation would continue to revel in an antediluvian relational identity with Britain.[36]

However, by the 1960s the modernist ethos had begun to seep in. In terms of architectural history, the pioneer was Eric Arthur, a New Zealander who was a generation younger than Traquair but who studied essentially in the same genre – in his case with Sir Edwin Lutyens in England. Arthur emigrated to Toronto in 1923 to take up a post at the school of architecture at the University of Toronto. He too turned his eye to Canada's architectural history but unlike Traquair and other anti-modernist zealots, he stridently embraced modernism whilst ironically also celebrating the architecture of the past. This culminated in his influential book *Toronto: No Mean City*, first published in 1964, which, in turn, would help to spark the preservation movement in many Canadian cities against the mid-twentieth century wrecking ball of progress. As with the drive to save British country houses and similar campaigns throughout the Western world, preservation activists included both men and women, although the rationales for preservation often fell along gender lines. In Canada, in terms of the university architectural history professoriate – which was almost exclusively male in the 1970s – some young professors joined the cause. Many were Americans or Canadians who had studied in American Ivy League schools where formalism held sway.[37] Their core tactic was aesthetic formalism wrapped up with cultural loss. In other words, they knew the Euro-American canon, and, for them, the threatened Canadian buildings 'measured up'. Because these professors were the *de facto* experts – further legitimised by their coming from abroad – the idea that these buildings were worth saving gained greater traction within the broader public. By contrast, several women led the preservationist charge by focusing on the social dimension of neighbourhoods and communities.

Toronto provides an especially sharply defined example of this bifurcated approach. Whilst Douglas Richardson, a Canadian-born Princeton-trained architectural history professor based at the University of Toronto, was instrumental in saving the city's monolithic Beaux Arts Union Station (1914, Ross and Macdonald with John M. Lyle), community activists Bobbi Speck and Lorraine Van Riet with Jane Jacobs – who had moved to Toronto in 1971 – successfully led the campaign to stop the construction of the Spadina Expressway which would have torn apart several neighbourhoods. As we know of Jacobs, she was beyond the edge; she was profoundly from the outside.[38] Meanwhile, the division between style/'big' architecture versus social community was less pronounced in Montréal. There, two of the core defenders were two female architects – Phyllis Lambert and Blanche Lemco van Ginkel – who were both committed modernists but who also understood the social relevance of aesthetics and community. Lambert, daughter of Samuel and Saidye Bronfman and owner of a controlling stake in the family's Seagram distillery empire, had begun her architectural career by – as the now famous story goes – convincing her father to hire Ludwig Mies van der Rohe to design the Seagram Building in New York. In the 1970s, she turned her attention to some of the threatened older 'villages' and buildings of Montréal and founded Heritage Montréal to facilitate fundraising for grassroots conservation groups. Lemco van Ginkel, meanwhile, was one of the first women admitted to McGill's school of architecture, in 1940 just a year after the end of Traquair's reign. After graduation she worked with Le Corbusier and designed aspects of the rooftop terrace of Unité d'Habitation in Marseille and then co-founded (with Robert Geddes) a branch of the Congrès Internationaux d'architecture Moderne (CIAM) in Philadelphia in the 1950s before returning to Canada in the early 1960s. With her husband, Sandy van Ginkel, she concentrated on urban planning and modernist subdivisions which aligned with their emphasis on societal values whilst offering a path forward for Blanche in a male-dominated profession and the masculine milieu of modernism. In Montréal, the van Ginkels developed the initial plans for the hyper-modern Expo'67 before also leading the campaign to save the district of Old Montréal that was threatened by an overground expressway.[39] Lemco van Ginkel also had an immense impact pedagogically as she offered the first courses in urban design in Montréal in the 1960s and 1970s, first at the Université de Montréal and then at McGill, before joining the faculty of the school of architecture at the University of Toronto in 1977 where she was soon appointed dean.[40]

This brings our discussion back to the study of architectural history in Canada. The convoluted tensions infused with aesthetic formalism which made up the Canadian architectural identity in the mid-twentieth century played out in university architectural history curricula for decades, with their continued emphasis on the Euro-American canon. This was especially true in the architectural history courses in art history departments (as opposed to schools of architecture). One reason was the resilience of the canon but this was further accentuated by the intense focus on media-specificity in art history, where painting, sculpture, and architecture were rigorously defined and separated. This would perpetuate in departments that tended, over generations, to hire faculty who had trained in mostly American Ivy League schools where stylistic formalism remained engrained. By contrast, in the schools of architecture, after the turn away from historicising design, formalism more quickly lost its unconditional hegemony, becoming first a subject of intellectual inquiry within the purview of modernism, evidenced by Peter Collins's intensive scrutiny of formalism as he advanced his own system for seeing (which he called 'parallax') in the 1960s and 1970s at McGill, and then contextualised within Lemco van Ginkel's social consideration of modernism. Both approaches would persist, especially as new faculty were hired who had trained outside of the Ivy League schools.[41] Of these is Annmarie Adams who studied at the more socially-oriented University of California, Berkeley in the 1980s and who joined McGill in 1993, where she remained the only female faculty member for fifteen years. Another is Anne Bordeleau whose research focuses on the temporal and mnemonic aspects of architecture. She was hired at the University of Waterloo soon after receiving her PhD from the Bartlett School at University College, London in 2007. Both Adams and Bordeleau would go on to serve as director of their respective schools. This brings us to a remarkable statistic: within the last fifteen years most of the twelve schools of architecture in Canada have had a female director or currently have one now.[42] Whilst harkening back to Lemco van Ginkel's tenure as dean at the University of Toronto and a testament to each woman's extraordinary professional achievements and administrative prowess, such a statistic is noteworthy in the context of a profession that continues to be dominated by men, in that it rings of an exemplary demonstration of equity that is nevertheless tinged with a form of gendered labour by which women are deemed 'natural' administrators. This is particularly amplified in academe where administrative ineptitude is easily feigned.[43]

Turning our attention to the architectural history courses offered in art history departments in the second half of the twentieth century: if we look to the United States, courses about the history of American architecture are numerous and central to the curriculum. The same is true in France with courses about French architecture, in Britain with courses on British architecture, in Italy with courses on Italian architecture, and so on. Not so in Canada. If there were courses on Canadian architecture, they usually hovered on the edge of the Euro-American canon and were rarely required for completion of the degree. (The same was also often true of courses on Canadian art.) This is consistent with the diminution of the value of things Canadian and is a condition of a settler society that relies on outside expertise. Within the courses that did exist, two threads were evident. One, taught by Alan Gowans at the University of Victoria in British Columbia, was characterised by an emphasis on cultural and social vernacularism. Gowans had studied at Princeton with Donald Drew Egbert, whose medievalist training and fascination for socialism and radicalism ensured he was on the edge of mainstream formalist architectural history. Gowans took a similar approach, minus the political ideology; as he said in the byline and preface to his 1958 publication *Looking at Architecture in Canada* – one of the first on the subject – 'you will not find in Canada much of what is commonly considered Great or Original architecture'.[44] The book, and presumably his course, is set up primarily according to styles, but integrates modest homes and large structures, considering them according to culture and ethnicity – what we now call diaspora – and the physical and social conditions of the Canadian environment. He would go on to found a uniquely international history of art department, calling it the 'History in Art' department, a moniker it still retains.

However, Gowans, like Egbert, were relegated to the margins of acceptable academic study, sidelined by the teleological march of aesthetic formalism and accompanying articulation of a canon that ultimately culminated in modernist and post-modernist examples of 'big' architecture. This did not mean that the vernacular disappeared from other Canadian courses. Instead, these courses were something of a hybrid, positioning historical Canadian architecture as derivative yet also infusing it with a sense of what had been achieved against seemingly insurmountable odds in a 'new' world. This dualism is a consistent feature of the settler society narrative. The narrative arc was heady, first about the taming of the land and building a new world and then from the 1950s onward about moving on from colonial roots and taking a place on the world stage.[45] As such, the content typically unfolded along the lines of European settlement and Anglo dominance: Jesuit missions; forts of the fur trade; pioneer log cabins and sod houses; Québecois *habitant* homesteads and churches; and then the 'here-to-stay' classical and gothic revival superlative houses and big buildings. A certain utopian inevitability reached a zenith around 1867 when Canada became a dominion of the British Crown that still proudly (in contrast to the United States) retained its strong cultural, social, and economic ties with the 'mother country'. From the 1880s until after the Second World War, the theme was about progress and civilisation, and the focus was more emphatically on the big buildings: the instantly famous Canadian Pacific Railway château hotels; the federal capital buildings in Ottawa; the enormous provincial legislatures in the mostly unpopulated-by-settlers yet expansive new Prairie cities; and the early commercial skyscrapers and banks. Occasionally, a glimpse of the non-Anglo and non-French European diaspora was included, usually summarily with early twentieth-century Ukrainian Orthodox churches on the Prairies. Finally came the turn toward modernism when modernist and then post-modernist examples were measured against the icons of the International Style and American Post-Modernism, respectively. Some examples, such as Toronto's New City Hall (Viljo Revell, completed 1965) and the Mississauga Civic Centre (Jones and Kirkland, opened 1987) still retain such a 'world-class' aura. Told through this uncritical lens, the tale was in lockstep with the exhilarating nationalism that infused the country around its centennial in 1967, so evocatively expressed in the modernist extravaganza of Expo'67 in Montréal.

Consistent with the buildings and settlements themselves, such a teleological juggernaut of a course typically pushed aside Indigenous peoples and their environments. If any Indigenous content was included, it was exoticised with observations on Indigenous ingenuity in the design of portable teepees or in the construction of long houses with 'unsophisticated' tools. But, for the most part, a thorough study of Indigenous structures was considered the domain of archaeology and anthropology where, with the rest of Indigenous culture, they were usually rendered dead. And where were the women in this narrative? Indigenous women might pop up assembling the teepees in the Prairies – another mark of exoticisation – or, in the settler context, they were heartily heaving sod along with their similarly hearty husbands, or clearing land and 'roughing it in the bush' like the displaced gentlewoman Susannah Moodie.[46] As such, they either did not fit the Eurocentric canon or they teetered on the edge.

Approaching the end of the twentieth century, architectural history retained its status in schools of architecture and even expanded to include vigorous postgraduate programmes. However, architectural history fared less well in art history departments. As art history evolved more quickly than architectural history and embraced multiple methodologies and global perspectives, architectural history – whether Canadian or not – became evanescent, with its continued existence increasingly precariously tied to individual ageing (male) faculty members' areas of research and their propensity toward style. For example, the ongoing intense enthusiasm for gothic revival architecture in Canada coincides with a few scholars' expertise in European medieval architecture. Likewise, modernist architecture also retains its status, driven by the legacy of the narrative outlined above as well as individual faculty members' interests.[47]

Within the schools of architecture, students taking architectural history courses were mostly male, in line with the gender imbalance within the profession. By contrast, far more women populated architectural history courses within art history departments, and several went on to pursue postgraduate studies either in Canada or abroad. Yet despite the turn toward equity in hiring, this rarely translated to more female architectural historians finding secure employment in universities. This was largely because of the turn away from architectural history as a distinct sub-discipline as described above but also compounded by the fantastically few positions in art history generally that were available in Canada during the 1990s. By way of example, when I was on the job market from 1993 to 1996, there were only three, possibly four, positions in any area of art history in all of English-speaking Canada.[48] For women who had chosen to do their postgraduate work in Canada and/or focus on a Canadian topic, the hurdles were higher as disparagement of the Canadian built environment (and Canadian art) continued to linger in some departments across academic generations. To misuse Gowans's phrase, within university circles 'Canadian' continued to be neither 'Great [n]or Original'.

This begs the question of where did these women go? Whilst the overarching narrative is the familiar one of eking out a living as a contract instructor and/or leaving the field altogether, two areas of the country stand out both for their vigorous study of Canadian architectural history and prominence of women working in the field. One is Québec where, in addition to the schools of architecture (at McGill and the Université de Montréal in Montréal and the Université de Laval in Québec City), the study of the architectural history of Québec is a core focus in art history departments as well as urban studies and tourism programmes. Some of the work includes Lucie Morisset's projects on resource extraction company towns and Christina Contandriopoulos's study of the relationships between cartography, utopia, and settlement in eighteenth- and nineteenth-century Québec. Morisset and Contandriopoulos, in turn, are members of larger thematic networks that transcend institutional and disciplinary boundaries in Québec, something that is relatively unique within the Canadian university context; Morisset is part of DePOT (Deindustrialization and the Politics of our Time) whilst Contandriopoulos is connected with the Laboratoire d'histoire et de patrimoine de Montréal.[49] Meanwhile, the art history department at Concordia University in Montréal has strong ties with The Gail and Stephen A. Jarislowsky Institute for Studies in Canadian Art and the Centre for Oral History and Digital Storytelling and several art historians have architectural research projects associated with both. For example, Cynthia Hammond has ongoing projects about industrial landscapes and garden design in Montréal whilst Johanne Sloan – a scholar of modernist painting by training – has focused on comparative perceptions of Montréal and Toronto and co-edited an in-depth study of Expo'67.[50] All of these scholars have brought spatial theory, oral history, and memory and identity studies to the study and teaching of the built environment and the Canadian condition.[51] Many reasons contribute to this robust inquiry in Québec. One goes back to Traquair's era, of acknowledging the distinctiveness of Québécois architecture. Another is the relative prominence of *patrimoine* in Québec, which is a vigorous cultural heritage infused with a heightened sense of identity that has been exacerbated by the French-Canadian/Québécois condition within Canadian society, both past and present. Other factors include the legacy of the campaigns to save Old Montréal, the pedagogical legacy of first Lemco van Ginkel and now the presence of Adams, the existence of the three schools of architecture, and, last but not least, the vibrant presence of the Canadian Centre for Architecture (CCA). Established by Phyllis Lambert in 1979 and opened to the public in 1989, the CCA is an extraordinary independent institution with a vast library and archive. With its commitment to critical scholarship and exhibition, it sits at the intersection of academe and public engagement. Although its outlook is international and, until recently, has focused largely on high-style architecture with a biographical approach to architects and architecture, the CCA has always embraced Canadian architectural histories as part of its purview, especially that of Montréal. A glance at the CCA's exhibition timeline, which begins in 1982, offers a fascinating overview of the evolution of the idea of architecture and emergence of approaches.[52]

The other area is Ottawa, the nation's capital. Carleton University has long had a robust Canadian Studies programme that aligns with various national institutions in the city, such as the National Gallery of Canada and Library and Archives Canada. Its art and architecture history department is also distinctive for retaining 'architectural' in its name and was the first English-language university in Canada to hire a female architectural historian (in the 1990s) who had both trained at a Canadian university and focused on a Canadian topic.[53] Of even more significance is Parks Canada, the federal government department responsible for national heritage. Since the 1960s, Parks Canada has been the single largest employer of Canadian architectural historians, with a particular focus on women. Barbara Humphreys was the first and the lynchpin for subsequent hires. She was another of Canada's earliest female architects, having graduated from the school of architecture at the University of Manitoba in 1941. In the 1960s, after working for various government agencies and in her own practice, she joined Parks Canada where she co-ordinated a sites registry project that was the pilot for the Canadian Inventory of Historic Buildings programme (CIHB), which she also co-founded. The CIHB was the world's first computer database of historic sites and would grow to list over 169,000 buildings and go on to be the model for other heritage organisations elsewhere in the world, including UNESCO.[54] In turn, one of Humphreys's early hires, Christina Cameron, would go on to become the Director General of National Historic Sites in Canada and the Head of Canada's Delegation to UNESCO's World Heritage Commission for nearly twenty years (1990–2008).[55] In addition to such thorough registries – the CIHB and its more fulsomely detailed companion, the Historic Sites and Monuments Board of Canada – Parks Canada published a series of style-oriented guides to architecture in Canada in the 1980s, all of which were written by women.[56] These were aimed at a non-scholarly general audience and were instantly successful, selling out immediately. Thus, it was a group of women who had been largely ostracised from the architecture profession and the university sector who were responsible for comprehensively documenting Canada's architectural history and bringing it to the attention of Canadians and the world. Initially, the emphasis was on style, consistent with academic study, but in the 1990s, Parks Canada's approach began to shift more emphatically to societies and cultures, in line with the nationalist verve that had been carefully honed by successive federal governments since the 1970s of Canada as a multicultural, tolerant, and peace-loving nation. This led to less discrimination in terms of building types, ethnic diversity, and Indigenous structures and spaces whilst also mitigating stereotypes and outright racism embedded in some historic sites and living history sites created in the mid-twentieth century.[57] Such a shift recalled Gowans's cultural value of the vernacular whilst aligning with the simultaneous turn towards social and feminist approaches within history and art history.[58]

Going back to the 1970s, the generally demographically disparate and precarious state of architectural history in Canada also prompted the creation of the Society for the Study of Architecture in Canada | Société de l'étude d'architecture au Canada (SSAC) in 1974. In contrast to the broad remits of the Society of Architectural Historians or the Society of Architectural Historians of Great Britain, the SSAC's sole focus is on Canadian built environments, and its membership cuts across academic disciplines, heritage and professional organisations, as well as interested members of the public. Nearly fifty years on, the SSAC is still a small but feisty association that has maintained its independence and expansive purview of Canadian architecture, and its journal also remains the single most valuable resource for the study of architecture in Canada. Perhaps not surprisingly, Humphreys was one of the founders of the SSAC, and today, half of the board of directors are women.[59]

In many ways, the loosening of the grip of formalism in universities and heritage organisations across Canada, in which women played key roles as chronicled above, has been instrumental in easing the path to more profound change that has come in the wake of the Truth and Reconciliation Commission (TRC). Established in 2008, the TRC's mandate is to gather stories and experiences of Indigenous peoples who were forcibly assimilated via government-funded and church-administrated residential schools between 1894 and 1997. In response to the TRC's Calls to Action, published in 2015, and at the behest of provincial and federal governments, Canadian universities (which are almost all publicly-funded institutions) have begun the process of decolonising their infrastructure and curricula. With the simultaneous decolonisation of elementary and secondary school curricula, students – Indigenous and not – are entering universities more culturally aware and attuned to multiple ways of knowing. The #MeTooMovement, Black Lives Matter, and the National Inquiry into Missing and Murdered Indigenous Women and Girls have also spurred seemingly inert institutions to change.

Although full systemic transformation is still a long way off, and is dependent upon continuing momentum, at the very least the concept of cultural erasure has come to the fore. In terms of the relatively narrow parameters of architectural history, after tentative efforts coinciding with the start of the TRC's investigations to insert Indigenous built environments into the conversation using such vital Indigenous ontologies as memory, orality, tradition, identity, and place, the space is now much more open.[60] Likewise, imperial-settler structures built to contain and/or forcibly assimilate Indigenous populations have also come under similar scrutiny.[61] The most evocative and traumatic are the residential school buildings themselves, whose monolithic structure and design fundamentally implicate them in effecting such assimilation and horrific abuse. Previously not a topic in Canadian architectural history courses nor of research, they are now the subject of much attention and the modes by which they are considered include collective memory and grief, as well as hubris, dominance, disruption, and control. These concepts and approaches stand well outside the formalist playbook and, as such, offer ways to grasp the unconscionable impact of these intransigent structures and spaces. Of these, Geoffrey Carr's 2011 PhD dissertation on the schools in British Columbia was ground-breaking and Magdalena Miłosz, who is completing her PhD under the direction of Adams at McGill, is looking at the schools in conjunction with other colonial structures and environments imposed on Indigenous peoples in Canada. The titles of the two authors' respective articles in the SSAC journal speak to the 'tools' used to analyse these spaces: "Educating Memory: Regarding the remnant of the Indian Residential School" (Carr, 2009) and "Instruments as Evidence: An archive of the Architecture of Assimilation" (Miłosz, 2016).[62] In the context of this essay, it is worth noting that Miłosz – who is also a trained architect – has recently joined Parks Canada, following a path blazed by several other remarkable women. She also has an active exhibition record, including at the Canadian Centre for Architecture. Miłosz's work, along with several other projects coming out of the university sector, demonstrate the increasing synergy across universities, the heritage sector, and Indigenous and other communities. These projects also signify the significant erosion of the longstanding prejudice against things Canadian within university art departments, although traces do linger.

Although not specifically about women, these incipient acts of decolonisation also demonstrate that universities as institutions – rather than just individual faculty members – are now shouldering some of the shared responsibility of redressing social injustice and are working toward reconciliation. In terms of the pedagogy and study of the built environment, the change began with a slow fuse, its delay and then halting progress exacerbated by distinctive idiosyncrasies of the Canadian settler condition, further hampered by the phenomenological authority of the buildings themselves. As with the study of British country houses that lie at the centre of the empire, the impetus to change has often come from outside the traditional formal discipline of architectural history. In line with the focus of this volume, the work of many women who offered alternative ways of seeing, reading, and experiencing has been central to disrupting the hegemony of formalism and the canon. Most of these women were sidelined, either within the profession or the university, yet they found their way forward and ironically have left lasting impacts. A few were paradigmatically louder but most quietly contributed to effecting the sea change. A plurality of approaches is now the starting point for the perception and study of built environments. Like Eurocentrism more broadly, aesthetic formalism has lost its monopoly; it now sits in the toolbox alongside other approaches where it might or might not be picked up to query the function and role of buildings and spaces within our societies.

Notes

1 I use the term 'Western' as short-hand for European, Eurocentric, and the European imperial diaspora.

2 I am grateful to Annmarie Adams and Jessica Mace for their comments on an early draft of this paper, also for Adams's numerous publications that have provided a firm foundation for this paper, and Mace for her confirmation of some of the key players involved in the practice of architectural history in Canada.

3 This includes several contributors to this volume. See also Sarah Bassnett, "Measuring Milestones: Feminist Histories of Architecture in Canada and the United States (Discussion Papers/Documents De Travail)," *Resources for Feminist Research* (Toronto: Ontario Institute for Studies in Education) 29, no. 3/4 (Fall 2002): 233–43.

4 See Kathleen James-Chakraborty, "Postcolonial Thought and the Emergence of Global Architectural Histories," *Oxford Research Encyclopedias* (29 September 2021): 4. https://doi.org/10.1093/acrefore/9780190201098.013.1282, last accessed 20 October 2022.

5 The New Zealand-born cultural historian J.G.A. Pocock coined the term 'Neo-Britain' to define such emergent national identity in former settler colonies. See J.G.A. Pocock, "The Neo-Britains and the Three Empires," in J.G.A. Pocock, ed., *The Discovery of Islands: Essays in British History*, 181–98 (Cambridge: Cambridge University Press, 2005). See also Cecelia Morgan, *Building Better Britains? Settler Societies within the British Empire, 1793–1920* (Toronto: University of Toronto Press, 2017). Bhabha defined his third space in his *The Location of Culture* in 1994 (London: Routledge). The phrase has since broadened to embrace a much wider range and spaces of cultural hybridity. Memory studies are also central to these and imperial, postcolonial, and decolonial theory generally and, as such, also figure in my work.

6 By way of example, every mayor of Toronto was a member of the Orange Order until Nathan Phillips, who was Jewish, was elected in 1955. The WASP stranglehold on Toronto began to erode more fundamentally in the 1980s in line with significant waves of immigrants from around the world, although powerful residue of that WASP heritage continue to resonate, especially at the provincial government level.

7 The following is the University of Waterloo's formal territorial acknowledgement:

> The University of Waterloo acknowledges that much of our work takes place on the traditional territory of the Neutral, Anishinaabeg and Haudenosaunee peoples. Our main campus is situated on the Haldimand Tract, the land granted to the Six Nations that includes six miles on each side of the Grand River. Our active work toward reconciliation takes place across our campuses through research, learning, teaching, and community building, and is co-ordinated within the Office of Indigenous Relations.
>
> See https://uwaterloo.ca/indigenous/knowledge-building/territorial-acknowledgement.

8 Georges Duby, *The Age of Cathedrals: Art and Society, 980–1420*, translated by E. Levieux and B. Thompson (Chicago: University of Chicago Press, 1976 & 1981).

9 Mark Girouard, *Life in the English Country House: A Social and Architectural History* (New Haven: Yale University Press, 1978).

10 Mark Girouard, "The Power House," in *The Treasure Houses of Britain: Five Hundred Years of Private Patronage and Collecting*, edited by G. Jackson-Stops, 22–27 (Washington, DC, New Haven, and London: National Gallery of Art, Washington, and Yale University Press, 1985).
11 The exhibition attracted nearly one million visitors and Prince Charles and Princess Diana were the patrons. A three-part television series was also produced in conjunction with the exhibition. See Peter Newington, *Treasure Houses of Britain* (Saffron Waldon, Essex: Michael Gill, producer, 1985).
12 Dana Arnold, ed., *The Georgian Villa* (first published by Alan Sutton (Stroud, UK) in 1996; re-issued by the History Press (Cheltenham, Glouc.) in 2011); Dana Arnold, ed., *The Georgian Country House: Architecture, Landscape and Society* (first published by Alan Sutton (Stroud, U.K.) in 1998; re-issued by the History Press (Cheltenham, Glouc.) in 2003).
13 Arnold, *Georgian Country House*, 79–99 & 196n1.
14 Dana Arnold, ed., *Reading Architectural History* (London: Routledge, 2002). The term 'Roarkist' derives from Howard Roark, the genius-architect protagonist of Ayn Rand's *The Fountainhead*, published in 1943 at the height of the celebration of the swaggering male modernist hero. In an early draft of this essay, I had inaccurately downplayed the impact of Arnold's volumes which, in itself, is interesting in the context of the persistence of formalism in architectural history studies in Canada, something that I address later in this essay. As a scholar working in Canada, my perception of the impact of Arnold's volumes was informed by my memory of the lack of attention given to them by architectural historians based in Canada at the time.
15 Amanda Vickery, *The Gentleman's Daughter: Women's Lives in Georgian England* (New Haven: Yale University Press, 1998).
16 Amanda Vickery, *Behind Closed Doors: At Home in Georgian England* (New Haven: Yale University Press, 2009).
17 Amanda Vickery, *At Home with the Georgians,* three-episode video documentary series (London: BBC 2, 2010). See for, example, Jon Stobart and Mark Rothery, *Consumption and the Country House* (Oxford: Oxford University Press, 2016); Henry French and Mark Rothery, *Man's Estate: Landed Gentry Masculinities, 1660–1900* (Oxford: Oxford University Press, 2012).
18 Kate Retford, *The Art of Domestic Life: Family Portraiture in Eighteenth-century England* (New Haven and London: Yale University Press, 2006); Kate Retford, *The Conversation Piece: Making Modern Art in Eighteenth-century Britain* (New Haven and London: Yale University Press, 2017). Both Vickery and Retford also bring the Georgian townhouse into the conversation. See also Susan Avery-Quash and Kate Retford, eds., *The Georgian London Town House: Building, Collecting and Display* (London and New York: Bloomsbury, 2019); Elizabeth McKellar, *Landscapes of London: The City, the Country and the Suburbs, 1660–1840* (New Haven and London: Yale University Press, 2013).
19 See, for example, Juliet Learmouth, "Holding Court at Marlborough House: The London Residence of Sarah, Duchess of Marlborough," in *Politics and the English Country House*, edited by Joan Coutu, Jon Stobart, and Peter Lindfield, 47–69 (Montréal and Kingston: McGill-Queen's University Press, 2023). These also build on several biographies of female aristocrats that were published in the 1990s, of which Frances Harris, *A Passion for Government: The Life of Sarah, Duchess of Marlborough* (Oxford: Clarendon Press, 1991) looks at the patronage of Marlborough. See also Terence Dooley, Maeve O'Riordan, and Christopher Ridgeway, *Women and the Country House in Ireland and Britain* (Dublin: Four Courts Press, 2018); Judith S. Lewis, "When a House Is Not a Home: Elite English Women and the Eighteenth-Century Country House," *Journal of British Studies* 48, no. 2 (2009): 336–63; Briony McDonagh, *Elite Women and the Agricultural Landscape, 1700–1830* (London: Routledge, 2019).
20 Joan Coutu, *Persuasion and Propaganda: Monuments and the Eighteenth-century British Empire* (Montréal and Kingston: McGill-Queen's University Press, 2006); Joan Coutu, *Then and Now: Classicism and Collecting in Eighteenth-century England* (Montréal and Kingston: McGill-Queen's University Press, 2015).
21 Stephanie Barczewski, *Country Houses and the British Empire, 1700–1930* (Manchester: Manchester University Press, 2014); Margot Finn and Kate Smith, eds., *The East India Company at Home, 1757–1857* (London: UCL Press, 2018).
22 See Sally-Anne Huxtable, Corinne Fowler, Christo Kefalas, and Emma Slocombe, eds., *Interim Report on the Connections between Colonialism and Properties Now in the Care of the National Trust, Including Links with Historic Slavery* (Swindon: National Trust, 2020). https://nt.global.ssl.fastly.net/documents/colonialism-and-historic-slavery-report.pdf, last accessed 26 July 2022. For reactions from newspapers of various political persuasion, see Peter Mitchell, "The National Trust Is under Attack

Because It Cares about History, Not Fantasy," *The Guardian* (12 November 2020): https://www.theguardian.com/commentisfree/2020/nov/12/national-trust-history-slavery, last accessed 26 July 2022; Christopher Hope, "National Trust Could Face Inquiry into Its "Purpose",' *The Telegraph* (23 October 2020): https://www.telegraph.co.uk/politics/2020/10/23/national-trust-could-face-inquiry-purpose/, last accessed 26 July 2022; Vanessa Allen, "National Trust Includes Former Homes of Winston Churchill and Rudyard Kipling on 'List of Shame' of a Hundred Properties It Believes Have 'Links to Slavery and Colonialism'," *The Daily Mail* (21 September 2020): https://www.dailymail.co.uk/news/article-8757745/National-Trust-lists-properties-believes-links-slavery-colonialism.html, last accessed 26 July 2022. For a broader discussion of the state of country house research now, see Jon Stobart's contribution to the 'Introduction' in Coutu, Stobart, and Lindfield, *Politics,* 5–12.

23 Coutu, Stobart, and Lindfield, *Politics.*

24 See Elizabeth Darling's essay in this volume, "In plain sight: women in and around the archive". Bassnett's "Measuring Milestones" also provides a helpful overview up until its publication in 2002.

25 Annmarie Adams and Peta Tancred, *Designing Women: Gender and the Architecture Profession* (Toronto: University of Toronto Press, 2000).

26 For Adams's profile see https://www.mcgill.ca/architecture/annmarie-adams; for Tancred, see, Annmarie Adams, "Peta Tancred's Important Contribution to Feminist Scholarship," *McGill Reporter* (28 September 2017): https://reporter.mcgill.ca/peta-tancreds-important-contribution-to-feminist-scholarship/, last accessed 26 July 2022. Adams's ongoing work on women, and gender more broadly, which she has dovetailed with the study of the architecture of health, has profoundly reshaped the consideration of the built environment of healthcare, both historically and into the future. Central to her study are soft concepts such as social identities of doctors and nurses, home, domesticity, and wellbeing.

27 James-Chakraborty, "Postcolonial," 3–5.

28 James-Chakraborty, "Postcolonial," 4

29 Édouard Glissant, *Poetics of Relation*, translated by B. Wing (Ann Arbor: University of Michigan Press, 1997).

30 See the Canadian Architectural Certification Board website: https://cacb.ca/accredited-programs/. The programme at Laurentian University in Ontario was established in 2013.

31 Annmarie Adams and Martin Bressani, "Canada: The Edge Condition," *Journal of the Society of Architectural Historians* 62, no. 1 (2003): 75–83. In 2001, Adams also published an essay about the state of literature on Canadian architecture, which also informs my discussion here. Annmarie Adams, "The Monumental and the Mundane: Architectural History in Canada," *Acadiensis* 30, no. 2 (Spring 2001): 149–59.

32 Adams and Bressani, "Canada."

33 Note: rather confusingly, the word 'graduate' in the context of 'graduate programmes' and 'graduate degrees' in North America corresponds to 'postgraduate' in the United Kingdom. In terms of art history, the first MA began in the late 1950s and the first PhD programme, at the University of Toronto, was established in 1968.

34 Annmarie Adams, "Picturing *The Old Architecture of Quebec*: Ramsay Traquair and Cultural Conservatism, 1913–39," in *Photogenic Montreal: Activisms and Archives in a Post-industrial City*, edited by Martha Langford and Johanne Sloan, 164–86 (Montréal and Kingston: McGill-Queen's University Press, 2021), 152.

35 Traquair used the words 'contamination' and 'contaminate' to describe the effect of women in architecture and of Black people on white people. He was also anti-American. See Adams, "Picturing *The Old Architecture of Quebec*," 153, 166; Isabelle Gournay, "The First Leaders of McGill's School of Architecture: Stewart Henbest Capper, Percy Erskine Nobbs, and Ramsay Traquair," *Bulletin – Society for the Study of Architecture in Canada* 21, no. 3 (1996): 63–64. For a detailed discussion of Traquair's anti-modernist stance, see Nicola Spasoff, "Building on Social Power: Percy Erskine Nobbs, Ramsay Traquair, and the project of constructing a Canadian national culture in the early decades of the twentieth century," PhD dissertation, Queen's University, Canada, 2002.

36 For historical settler identity up to 1920, see Morgan, *Building Better*, 133–69. See also Pocock, "Neo-Britains."

37 Adams and Bressani, "Canada," 78–79.

38 On Richardson and Union Station see his contribution, "'A Blessed Sense of Civic Excess': The Architecture of Union Station," in *The Open Gate: Toronto's Union Station*, edited by Richard Bébout (Toronto: P. Martin Associates, 1972), 67–96. On the Spadina Expressway, see Danielle Robinson, "Modernism at a Crossroad: The Spadina Expressway Controversy," *The Canadian Historical Review* 92/2 (June 2011): 295–322.

39 The expressway was ultimately built below ground. See Annmarie Adams and Tanya Southcott, "Blanche Lemco van Ginkel," *Pioneering Woman of American Architecture* (Beverley Willis Foundation): https://pioneeringwomen.bwaf.org/blanche-lemco-van-ginkel/, last accessed 3 May 2023. An adaptation of this article was used for Lemco van Ginkel's obituary in *The Canadian Architect*: "In Memoriam: Blanche Lemco van Ginkel, 1923–2022," *The Canadian Architect* (21 October 2022): https://www.canadianarchitect.com/in-memoriam-blanche-lemco-van-ginkel-1923-2022/, last accessed 3 May 2023.

40 A good overview resources for the careers of Lambert and Lemco van Ginkel is the 2018 film *City Dreamers* directed by Joseph Hillel (Montréal: Ziad Touma, Couzin Films). For Lemco van Ginkel, see also Adams and Southcott, "Blanche Lemco van Ginkel" and the 2020 symposium, "For Her Record: Notes on the Work of Blanche Lemco van Ginkel," co-hosted by the Daniels School of Architecture, University of Toronto and the Peter Guo-hua Fu School of Architecture, McGill University, Montréal, https://www.youtube.com/watch?v=uNIiIX4swio&t=16s, last accessed 3 May 2023.

41 For Collins, see Peter Collins, *Changing Ideals in Modern Architecture, 1750–1950* (Montréal and Kingston: McGill-Queen's University Press, 1965); Annmarie Adams, "Peter Collins: A Study in Parallax," *Journal of Architectural Education* 59, no. 2 (2005): 22–31.

42 Bordeleau moved from Waterloo in 2022 to be director of the school of architecture at Carleton University in Ottawa.

43 This is a variant of Arlie Russell Hochschild's emotional labour and Silvia Federici's social reproduction labour theories in a capitalist world. Statistics from 2017 indicate that in Ontario, for example, whilst over 50% of graduates from schools of architecture are female, only about 30% stay in the profession. See Rhys Phillips, "Because It's 2017: Gender Diversity in Canada's Architecture Profession," *Canadian Architect* (January 2017): https://www.canadianarchitect.com/gender-diversity-in-canadas-architecture-profession/, last accessed 24 March 2023. The gap is closing but almost imperceptibly. See also BEA (Building Equity in Architecture) with chapters across the country, e.g. BEAT in Toronto: http://www.beatoronto.com/, last accessed 24 March 2023.

44 Alan Gowans, *Looking at Architecture in Canada* (Toronto: University of Oxford Press, 1958), 15. See also Harold Kalman, "Alan Gowans [1923–2001]: A Tribute," *Journal for the Society of the Study of Architecture in Canada* 42, no. 1 (2017): 3–5. Gowans's book was revised and re-issued in 1964 with the title *Building Canada: An Architectural History of Canadian Life* (Toronto: University of Toronto Press).

45 Many of the older buildings, such as the railway château hotels and the Parliament Buildings in Ottawa, were also routinely compared to the grandeur of the surrounding landscapes, which corresponds to another Eurocentric trope, that of the picturesque and the sublime.

46 Moodie's account of her settler life in Canada, *Roughing it in the Bush: or, Forest Life in Canada*, was published in London in 1852 and received much acclaim in Britain and the United States.

47 Here I am thinking about Malcolm Thurlby at York University in Toronto and Rhodri Windsor Liscombe at the University of British Columbia in Vancouver. The "Reading List" on the Society for the Study of Architecture in Canada website (https://canada-architecture.org/reading-list/) provides an excellent snapshot of the areas of concentration, although the list has not been updated since 2015. See also Adams, "The Monumental." Some of the gap was filled by scholars in historical geography and town planning – another instance of originating outside the discipline – who concentrated on Canada's architectural history, but this too was often linked to individual professors' areas of research. Some examples include James T. Lemon at the University of Toronto who was also a key player in the campaign against the Spadina Expressway, and the more comprehensive work of Brian Osborne in the Department of Geography and Planning at Queen's University in Kingston. David L. Gordon has taken up that mantle since Osborne's retirement.

48 In my case, I was not hired either in a school of architecture or an art history department. Instead, after a few terms of single-course contracts, I was hired in 1996 to be the only art historian in a studio-based department at the University of Waterloo. My purview was (and is) to teach art history to studio students, students from other disciplines, and oversee a small art history programme. For the hiring committee, my area of research was less of a concern, with the key question being "What areas of [Western] art history are you not comfortable teaching?"

49 See the official websites for Lucie Morisset (https://patrimoine.uqam.ca/membre/morisset-lucie/); Christina Contandriopoulos (https://lhpm.uqam.ca/christina-contandriopoulos/); The Départmente d'études urbaines et touristiques at the Université de Québec à Montréal (Department of Urban Studies

and Tourism, https://deut.esg.uqam.ca/); and the Laboratoire d'histoire et de patrimoine de Montréal at the Université de Québec à Montréal (https://lhpm.uqam.ca/).

50 For Cynthia Hammond, see https://www.concordia.ca/faculty/cynthia-hammond.html; for Johanne Sloan, see https://www.concordia.ca/faculty/johanne-sloan.html.

51 A new initiative, called "Canada Constructed," has been launched by Christy Anderson with Joseph L. Clarke and Jessica Mace in the Department of Art History at the University of Toronto: https://canadaconstructed.ca/. It remains to be seen if it will become firmly tethered, particularly within a department that has had a long ambivalent relationship with Canadian studies.

52 See "Overview" and "Exhibitions" at the Canadian Centre for Architecture: https://www.cca.qc.ca/en/.

53 This is Angela Carr, who completed her PhD at the University of Toronto in 1990. The next to be hired at an English-speaking university was Marie-Josée Therrien at the Ontario College of Art and Design University in Toronto in the mid-2000s.

54 See "Pioneers in Architectural History at Parks Canada!" *Canada's Historic Places* [2011]: https://www.historicplaces.ca/en/pages/23_histoire_architecturale_history.aspx, last accessed 5 May 2023; Andrew Waldron, "Remembering Barbara Humphreys (1919–2017): A Pillar of Heritage Conservation in Ottawa," *Heritage Ottawa | Patrimoine Ottawa* (28 February 2017): https://heritageottawa.org/news/remembering-barbara-humphreys-heritage-conservation-canada, last accessed 5 May 2023.

55 Cameron had just completed a Masters in Art History from Brown University when she was hired by Humphreys in 1970. She had done undergraduate studies at the University of Toronto. Cameron would go on to do a PhD in art history at the Université de Laval, focusing on the historic architecture of Québec. In 2005, nearing the end of her career, she took up a Canada Research Chair in *Gestion, conservation et mise en valeur du patrimoine bâti* (Built Heritage) at the Université de Montréal. The federal government's Canadian Research Chairs programme is meant to attract and retain intensive researchers and foster research at the postgraduate level. Unfortunately, since CRCs teach few undergraduate students, the pedagogical impact of their expertise is somewhat muted. Notably, a short biography of Cameron published online by an academic history education network THEN | HiER described heritage studies as an 'emerging field' as late as 2011; see "Heritage Studies: An Emerging Field (Christina Cameron)," *THEN | HiER* (2011): http://thenhier.ca/en/content/heritage-studies-emerging-field-christina-cameron.html, last accessed 5 May 2023.

56 The style guides include, Nathalie Clerk, *Palladian Style in Canada* (Ottawa: Parks Canada, 1984); Janet Wright, *Architecture of the Picturesque in Canada* (Ottawa: Parks Canada, 1984); Leslie Maitland, *Queen Anne Revival in Canada* (Ottawa: National Historic Parks and Sites, Parks Service, Environment Canada, 1990).

57 For living history sites in Canada, see Alan Gordon, *Time Travel: Tourism and the Rise of the Living History Museum in Mid-twentieth-century Canada* (Vancouver: UBC Press, 2016).

58 A tiny number of architectural historians also found employment in the very few architecture firms that specialise in historic preservation in Canada.

59 See the Society for the Study of Architecture in Canada, https://canada-architecture.org/.

60 One such early foray is included in a survey of Canadian architecture published in 2011. It comes at the end, after eighteen other essays that explore imperial-settler spaces and themes. See Daniel Millette, "Memory, the Architecture of First Nations, and the Problem with History," in *Architecture and the Canadian Fabric*, edited by R. Windsor Liscombe, 467–79 (Vancouver: University of British Columbia Press, 2011). For more of this work, see "Indigenous Architecture" in the SSAC's "Reading List" and for an early discussion of the problems of the Eurocentric canon and Eurocentric history, see Daniel Millette and Amy Oliver, "The First Nation Architectural Landscape: Considering a Neglected Architectural History," *Journal of the Society for the Study of Architecture in Canada* 37, no. 1 (2012): 57–66.

61 See for example, Stephanie Weber, "'A City of the Future': Thomas Mawson's Preliminary Scheme for Calgary as Imperial Map" and Samuel Dubois, "Classicism and Indigeneity: Looking into Montreal's Kondiaronk Lookout," both in *Utopia and Hubris: Classicism and Canadian Architecture, c. 1900–1939*, edited by Joan Coutu and David Galbraith (currently under review).

62 Geoffrey Carr, "Educating Memory: Regarding the remnant of the Indian Residential School," *Journal for the Society of the Study of Architecture in Canada* 34, no. 2 (2009): 87–99; Magdalena Miłosz, "Instruments as Evidence: An archive of the Architecture of Assimilation," *Journal for the Society of the Study of Architecture in Canada* 41, no. 2 (2016): 3–10. Miłosz's essay also won the SSAC's Martin Eli Weir Essay Prize. See also Dani Sharir-Smith's blog, "From the Archives: residential School Architecture," Society for the Study of Architecture in Canada, https://canada-architecture.org/from-the-archives-residential-school-architecture/, last accessed 25 July 2022.

Afterword

12
AFTERWORD

Nancy Stieber

The stories told about architectural history have changed considerably over the past fifty years. There are any number of reasons for this shift including the spatial turn in cultural history, the establishment and growth of doctoral programs in architecture schools, and the changing foci of art history as it engaged in issues of post-colonialism, gender, and race. New purviews have opened; interdisciplinarity has been embraced. As the questions asked about the built environment have changed, narrative patterns and rhetorical devices have necessarily and inexorably altered. This volume is a testament to the multifarious methods with which women in architectural history have been shaped by and have shaped the changing landscape of the discipline. I would like to draw attention more particularly to the ways in which storytelling has been shifted and manipulated to produce narratives counter to the canonic forms that predominated in the past and still predominate today.

First, let's consider the inherited forms that narratives about architecture have taken. Architectural history is a relatively recent field of scholarship, as is history itself if defined as an area of academic endeavor. Antiquarian obsession with identifying, categorizing, and periodizing styles was eventually joined with an interest in recounting the careers of selected architects and in recording the design history of monumental buildings. These became the primary topics of monographs written by art historians. As architects themselves became involved in writing the history of their own profession, they followed similar patterns of narrative structure: explaining stylistic development, elucidating the career of an architect, demonstrating what led to the construction of a particular building.

Each of these three types of story followed a psychologically satisfying narrative arc. In the case of style, the story usually followed a bell-curved pattern, roughly speaking, that began with antecedents and influences, identified the earliest occurrences of the forms, pinpointed the dissemination of the ideas, emphasized the key monuments, demonstrated the efflorescence of the style, and followed its decline. Paired with the ideas of *zeitgeist* or nationalism, the story might also argue teleologically for the inevitable emergence of the style as reflection of an underlying impetus, in which case some historical contextualization would be incorporated. The climax of the story would be the achievement of a fully expressed representation of the style. Reaching

DOI: 10.4324/9781003224662-18

this point in the story would provide a satisfying reward, a sense of shared pride, a fulfillment of promise, and a congratulatory tone, subliminal or explicit.

Biographies of architects similarly tracked an inevitable path toward satisfying fulfillment. While they might begin with the background and training of the architect and the early minor work, emphasis would eventually be placed on crowning achievements and resulting career success, in some cases following the twist and turns of that career, but always looking for the thread that linked them. Like stylistic inquiries, there would be a linear flow to the narrative, a continuous unfolding of development – or occasionally stagnation.

Stories about buildings were similarly constructed. They might start with the circumstances of the commission, but lead inevitably toward the happy ending when the building was completed. Like a detective story that ends with the solving of a mystery, or a romance that ends with the couple united, the reader would know from the start that the narrative was heading toward a pleasing resolution. With completion of the building, everyone lived happily ever after.

Both the myth of the hero or the triumph of style are seductive and powerful story lines that parallel structures common in other narrative forms such as the epic poem or the romantic novel. They emphasize individual creativity on the one hand, perception of architecture as formal aestheticism on the other. They are the product of two communities: first, the inheritors of German *Kunstgeschichte* invested in the history of architecture as formal development; and second, architects for whom a genealogy of "*Lieber Meisters*" provides disciplinary identity. Both construct historical narratives asking the questions, "how did this building come to take this form?" or "What was the development and influence of this architect?" Both inquiries exploit a temporal conception of development internal to the architectural discipline.

The romantic narrative offers plot that seems "natural." That is because we can follow a straight story line from conception to completion. There appears to be an inevitable sequence that unfolds in a readily comprehensible line. These kinds of stories are also attractive because they configure heroes and models, both the designer and the building itself. And for both architects and students aspiring to become architects, such stories are quite flattering. It's no surprise that architectural history has tended to privilege narratives so constructed. They emerge directly out of professional and pedagogical practice where the study of past and current architecture as model and foil has been a useful means of conveying architectural ideas – even though we all know full well that architecture is a collaborative process inadequately reflected by studying creative geniuses or paradigmatic buildings.

While stories about styles, architects, and buildings may be told with objectively gathered evidence in service to rational arguments and may provide useful foundations for further research, they are also, as mentioned, constructed in such a way as to result in a sense of culmination and satisfaction on the part of the reader. I do not mean to suggest that this rhetorical effect necessarily distracts from the validity of the scholarship that was applied to produce the narrative. I only want to focus our attention on an aspect of history writing that remains largely unconscious, namely, the nature of its narrativity or plot line. These standard patterns of writing architectural history have in common the linear narrative structure of origin, development, and climax. That structure has been so embedded, so anchored in our cognitive map of historicity that it has long been taken for granted and rarely questioned as a model for writing history.

Have these narrative structures served a useful purpose? Do they still do so? In many respects, the answer must be in the affirmative. While operating under such narrativity, art history produced methods that are still central to any responsible approach to the history of architecture: careful formal analysis, development of a rich descriptive vocabulary; practices of archival research, acknowledgment of the work of other scholars and the careful notation of sources. As a way to organize information and provide opportunities for the critique and judgment that must be at the core of any rational discipline, these approaches have proved perfectly amenable to critical inquiry. Have they also embodied a number of assumptions that have been and need to be challenged? Yes, very much so. We have seen those challenges repeatedly over the past half century and in the contributions to this volume.

It has long become evident to many of us that we need other kinds of stories to convey the agency of the built environment. I will mention a few obvious examples here without belaboring the point, since these revisions to the historic record are already well known. Architectural history, as has been the case with other forms of historical research, began to incorporate the voices of those previously unheard, erased, or neglected. The influence of social history became particularly important in cultivating the inclusion of designers formerly overlooked and the undervalued experiences of the people who occupied the buildings. Stories no longer necessarily ended with the completion of the building; for some, the story only began there as uses changed over time and a building's meaning became re-interpreted. Indeed, the life of the building, in which the building is no longer seen as finished when constructed but is viewed as being dynamically produced through its usage may end up narrating an episodic story, with no specific directionality, but one that reveals the way that buildings work. The *zeitgeist* theory was challenged; the notion of an all-encompassing monolithic spirit of the times was shattered by historical insight into the tensions and contradictions within any given time period and its many simultaneous and imbricated story lines. Stories of alternative modernisms have enriched and complicated our sense of any "correct" line of historical development, with the concomitant rejection of any narrative line that privileges the assumption of improvement, progress, development, evolution, those products of nineteenth century historicism. History that was intended to promote a particular style or disciplinary position was exposed for its polemical tendencies. The architect as hero was supplanted by awareness of the intrinsically collaborative nature of design practice. Focus on monuments was displaced by an interest in everyday environments. Questions arose about the nature of daily and domestic life as expressed through and influenced by the built environment. The experiential, the building as a space lived in and occupied by people, became of interest and incorporated the concept of embodied sensation and subjectivities including the study of the senses, in particular the aural, as well as consideration of the feelings evoked by space. This list is perforce partial; there are a myriad of ways the history of architecture is being engaged and the opening of new research trajectories is far from exhausted. To the extent that the built environment is connected to all aspects of life, we can expect the discovery and pursuit of new queries and new investigations in the coming years.

We can observe here the shift from asking "how did this form come to exist" to asking instead "what work in society does this form perform?" or to asking what roles architecture plays in social processes and how those social processes inform architecture? What can the evidence of architecture tell us about modernization, global exchange, colonialization, nation building, and civil society and vice versa? What do those processes tell us about architecture? How can architecture, design, and landscape be used to enlighten us about the nature of everyday life in the past, domestic life, gender relations, sexual identity, racism, and class distinctions? What can it tell us about how our mentalities have formed, who we have become, and what we might become? The focus is on design as an active verb: as something that shapes, informs, constrains and enables human experience.

Questions such as these do not easily conform to old narrative structures; they demand new ones. As the issues under consideration proliferate and the questions we ask about the history of the built environment take new forms, so too must the forms of storytelling. This volume presents examples of various forms of narrativity. They represent histories whose temporal shapes diverge from straight linearity, that spiral, branch, flow, or eschew the line altogether to create other images of time. They are episodic; they stretch and collapse time. They follow simultaneous, parallel threads. They speak in multiple voices. As a result, they allow us to understand the agency of designed spaces in the making of lives and to shed light on social processes including inequalities and power relations. They invite us to think empathetically. They reject formal analysis of the static, completed building in favor of studying human interaction with the built environment over time, encompassing the life of a building and the way people have responded to it. This involves several shifts from standard architectural history: a privileging of the user's perceptions and actions; awareness of spaces operating as ongoing processes.

These kinds of narrative tend not to place the architect at their center. Indeed, the architect as protagonist may disappear altogether from the story in favor of the client, the builder, the taste-maker, and others who have not fit easily into the progressive story line of stylistic development. Instead, the focus may be on social processes, allowing exploration of questions that can demonstrate the operations of architecture in society and culture that may not appear in a history that privileges individual achievement or the genesis of form. It is evident that stories about the hero architect and the development of style have obscured the even more compelling case for architecture's social centrality in history.

We learn from the stories in this volume to consider architecture and design as woven into daily life, as centrally experienced. As we sit around the fire and tell more inclusive, less teleological stories, some without clear endings, some with multiple threads, some structured with back flashes, many breaking the conventions of place and time, we launch explorations into the nature of the built environment that the old narrative structures could not reveal. Rather than serving the interests of art history or the design professions, such stories study how architecture performs in society, what aspects of the human condition it constrains or enables, what modes of being it represses and creates. Instead of a single model of linear development, these alternative narrative strategies liberate many different historicities, many ways to construe and construct the past.

This essay itself follows the old narrative pattern by telling a story culminating in the happy emergence of an autonomous architectural history, a cultural history of the built environment asking probing questions about the meaning and use of the world we build for ourselves and others. Such a history might even foster storytelling for a broader audience, inviting the public and those in other fields to listen to what architectural historians have to tell.

Acknowledgements

This essay is based in part on the lecture "Architectural Stories: Time, Representation, and Narrative," delivered at FAU USP, Sao Paulo, 14 May 2018.

INDEX

Note: *Italic* page numbers refer to figures and page numbers followed by "n" denote endnotes.

For Product Safety Concerns and Information please contact our EU representative GPSR@taylorandfrancis.com Taylor & Francis Verlag GmbH, Kaufingerstraße 24, 80331 München, Germany

* 9 7 8 1 0 3 2 1 2 4 5 8 2 *

T - #0172 - 210725 - C0 - 246/174/11 - PB - 9781032124582 - Matt Lamination

THE EVOLVING CULTURE OF

KUWAIT

Hello Anne.

Very good to meet again - kindred spirits must keep in touch.

All the best

Jennifer

Edinburgh 10 August 2005

Royal Scottish Museum
Edinburgh
Her Majesty's Stationery Office

First Published 1985

ISBN 0 11 492436 8

Cover illustration
Kuwaiti Sunset courtesy of the Middle East Photographic Archive.

CONTENTS

PREFACE

Kuwait has recently passed through a period of rapid change and development which has transformed it from a traditional seafaring nation to a modern state. Despite the inevitable progress of modernisation, much traditional life has survived, which is strikingly evident in the costumes and textiles of both the urban and Bedu population. Kuwaitis are keenly aware of the value of their traditions and aim to combine the best of both old and new. I and my associates are delighted to have been able to support the Royal Scottish Museum in recording some aspects of Kuwaiti life and customs as illustrated in the exhibition *Costumes and textiles from Kuwait* and this associated publication.

Hussa Sabah al-Salem al-Sabah
Director
Dar Al-Athar Al-Islamiya
(Museum of Islamic Art)
Kuwait National Museum

ACKNOWLEDGEMENTS

This publication, which accompanies and supplements the exhibition *Costumes and textiles from Kuwait,* is the result of a long-standing professional and personal interest in the Arabian Gulf. My first visit to Kuwait, at the invitation of Sheikh Nasser Sabah al-Ahmad al-Sabah and his wife Sheikha Hussa Sabah al-Salem al-Sabah, to the opening of the Museum of Islamic Art in the Kuwait National Museum in February 1983 convinced me that a study of surviving aspects of traditional life and customs would be a rewarding project. The Royal Scottish Museum has a policy of collecting and exhibiting material from the contemporary Islamic world. During my visit to Kuwait I had noticed the striking costumes worn by men and women in both urban and Bedu environments. I was able to return to Kuwait in 1984 to acquire and document costumes and textiles. This field work and research has been greatly aided by the following people.

In Kuwait I am deeply indebted to Sheikha Hussa Sabah al-Salem al-Sabah, Director of the Museum of Islamic Art, for her constant enthusiasm and support at all stages of the project. Members of her staff, Ghada Qaddoumi, Fatima ben Touq and Hana Farid, also helped me. His Excellency Sheikh Nasser Mohammad al-Ahmad al-Sabah, Minister of Information, and the Ministry of Information generously sponsored my visit and this publication. Mariam Rashid and Bazza al-Battini of the Centre for the Preservation of Popular Arts and Folklore unceasingly and generously shared their knowledge of Kuwaiti traditions and family life. George Gibb and Barbara Hayward, English Department, Faculty of Medicine, Kuwait University, aranged interviews with their students. I am also grateful to Dr Ibrahim al-Baghly, Director of the Kuwait National Museum, Nejat Hamid Sultan, General Secretary of the al-Sadu Foundation for the Preservatin of Bedu Handicrafts, Aisha ben Touq, Head of the Dress Department, Kuwaiti Television, T. C. White, British Council Representative in Kuwait, and Anne and Henry Hill of the Kuwait Oil Company.

In Britain I was much helped by Mr H al-Saidan, First Secretary, and Mr Mohammad Ragab of the Press Office, of the Embassy of the State of Kuwait, and Katie Marsh and Elizabeth Richardson. I am also grateful for the advice and help I received from Dr Keith McLachlan, Department of Geography, School of Oriental and African Studies of London University, Zeinab al-Harbi, Heriot Watt University Edinburgh, Gillian Grant, Middle East Centre Oxford, Philippa Angrave, Royal Geographical Society London, and Zoreh and Suzy Bailey.

Thanks are due to the Middle East Centre Oxford and the Royal Geographical Society London for the inclusion of photographs in this publication (plates 45-49), and to Allen and Unwin for the use of quotations from Violet Dickson, **Forty Years in Kuwait** (1971) and Zahra Freeth, **A new look at Kuwait** (1972).

Jennifer M. Scarce
Royal Scottish Museum, Edinburgh

DIAGRAMS AND MAPS

KUWAIT
THE LAND AND ITS RESOURCES

Until the discovery of oil reserves in the 1930s and their subsequent exploitation after World War II, Kuwait's most valuable natural resource was its bay, one of the only two good harbours along the Arabian Gulf, the other being Bahrain. Situated at the north-west tip of the long narrow waters of the Gulf the bay of Kuwait was not only an excellent starting point for Kuwait merchants and sailors but also provided access to trade entering and leaving the hinterland of north-east Arabia and Iraq. Visual evidence of the bay's traditional and continuing economic importance may be seen today in the tangle of small wooden vessels, battered motorboats (Plate 1) and the wire balloons of fishing nets (Plate 2) still used by coastal fishermen and the harbour at Doha where skilled carpenters fashion the distinctive trading craft of *dhow* and *boom* (Plate 3), dramatically contrasted with the modern port areas of Shuwaikh and Shuaiba and their associated industrial complexes. As the area around Kuwait bay had a fresh water source which in the 18th century was sufficient to provide water for a fleet of 800 *dhows* and which could always be supplemented by water imported from Iran and Iraq, it was natural that a permanent settled population should concentrate here. This community always maintained contact with the nomadic Bedu tribes whose migration routes traced a complex network across Arabia. This pattern continues today, though Kuwait City has extended into suburbs and many of the Bedu are now settled in government housing schemes.

Fanning out from the bay the territory of the present day Emirate of Kuwait forms a compact area of about 6960 square miles bounded on the north and west by Iraq and on the south by the Neutral Zone[1] and Saudi Arabia, Nine offshore islands, of which Bubiyan and Failaka are the most important in

1 Kuwait City, Arabian Gulf Street. Dhows and motorboats moored on shore.

2 Kuwait City, Arabian Gulf Street. Fishing nets on the shore.

3 Dhowyard at Doha. Dhow under construction.

4 Kuwait City. Ministry of Information.

terms of oil reserves and archaeological sites, are close to Kuwait's eastern coastal boundary and form part of her territory. Physically the terrain of Kuwait is harsh sandy desert, of four main zones—an area of coastal dunes, salt marshes and saline depressions around Kuwait bay, desert plateau in the west and a desert plain which covers most of the country. Certain hills notably the Zor ridge along the northern shore of Kuwait bay, help to relieve the flatness which still dominates the Kuwait horizon despite the proliferation of varyingly proportioned building projects (Plate 4). The climate is typical of desert regions with hot summers and cool winters.[2] In Kuwait, however, it is modified by directional winds—hot and dry from the north and warm and humid from the south and by the presence of an extensive coastline. The warm days and cool nights of the short autumn are followed by increasingly cold sharp days and nights and interrupted by abrupt rain showers and even storms. A short cool spring often accompanied by dust storms precedes a long hot summer which peaks in July and August at temperatures of c. 45-50°C. and extreme humidity.

Within such austere conditions of terrain and climate resources are limited, erratic and precious. Water supply has always been a problem dependent on the annual rainfall. The presence of a permanent water source in Kuwait bay together with its natural harbour ensured that it would be a centre of permanent human settlement. Vegetation again is a variable resource. Usually the desert plain is scattered with patches of coarse grass but a good rainfall can produce a surprisingly abundant growth of lush grass and many species of wild flower. Within easy range of Kuwait City the coastal strip was once cultivated with vegetable gardens while the oasis of Jahra was a source of date palms and fruit trees. Animals in the desert of value to man are sheep and goats[3] and to a lesser extent the camel whose traditional role has been increasingly eroded through the development of a modern economy, which rests on Kuwait's most recently discovered and negotiable resource—the deposits of oil. Following the first drillings at the oil field of Burgan in 1938, further deposits have been located and exploited at Rawdatain and Sabriya in north Kuwait, Ahmadi, Maqwa, Minagish, Wafra in the Neutral Zone, and at various offshore concessions.

KUWAIT IN THE PAST

1 Development from Arabian Gulf Port to Independent Emirate

While many centuries were to elapse before the full potential of Kuwait's resources could be realised she managed gradually and steadily to evolve into a major port. She developed profitable sidelines in trading voyages and pearl fishing without losing any independence either to neighbouring Arab kingdoms or powerful outsiders such as the Ottoman Turks, and Persians, or European forces such as the Portuguese, Dutch and British, who competed for control of the Arabian Gulf's trade routes. Kuwait's history should properly be understood against the varying perspective of the Arabian peninsula and more specifically of the Gulf.

Traditionally Arabia presented a pattern of contrast between two ways of life. The nomad tribes wandered constantly in search of grazing for their flocks across the great deserts of Najd located in the heart of the peninsula and extending as far east as the river Euphrates. The settled communities inhabited the more fertile coastal regions of Hejaz on the west with its trading centres of Mecca, Medina and Jedda and of the highlands of Yemen and Oman curving along the south. Despite problems of access and terrain Arabia was never totally isolated. Desert nomads of necessity had to come into contact with city dwellers for products which they could not produce themselves and there were in turn steady commercial relations with the empires of Persia and Byzantium which controlled most of the Middle East and Mediterranean worlds. In this context Mecca by the late 5th century A.D. had eclipsed all rivals to become the most important and thriving commercial city in the Hejaz During the 6th and 7th centuries it assumed a more universal significance as the centre of the dynamic new religious and political creed of Islam. The Prophet Muhammad, son of Abdullah of the Hashim clan of the Quraysh tribe was born in Mecca in 571. During a successful career as a merchant he began to preach the revelations which Allah had made to him, presenting them as an all-embracing way of life based on a omnipotent monotheism combined with practical rules of ethics and social behaviour. Initial opposition to Muhammad's preaching was such that in 622 he was forced to emigrate from Mecca to Medina where the transformation of Islam from purely a religion to a politically organised community began.

From Medina Muhammad and his supporters launched a series of military campaigns culminating in the capture of Mecca in 630. During the last two years of his life Muhammad functioned as a head of state as Arab tribes increasingly became converted to Islam and recognised his authority. After his death at Medina on 8th June 632, the Islamic community underwent various changes. For a short period until 661 four successors—Abu Bakr, Muhammad's father-in-law, Omar, one of his companions, Othman of the Ummayad Family of Mecca, and finally Ali, husband of his daughter Fatima, ruled as caliphs based on Mecca and Medina. They all experienced considerable difficulties in keeping the Arab tribes united, but their reigns saw the rapid expansion of both Islam and Arab domination with the conquests of Syria, Egypt, Iraq and Persia between 634 and 651. By the 8th century Arab armies had reached North Africa, Spain, Central Asia and the Punjab.

The significant point here is that Islam had extended well beyond the boundaries of the Arabian peninsula a process which was completed by the establishment of the capitals of the Ummayad (661-750) and Abbasid (750-1258) dynasties at Damascus and Baghdad respectively, which flourished as brilliant centres of culture and learning. Apart from the importance of Mecca and Medina as the holy places of Islam Arabia reverted to its traditional pattern of disparate nomadic tribal groups and coastal communities whose only unifying factor was religion. It is in this background especially of the desert of Najd that Kuwait's origins are to be sought as members of the Beni Khalid and Anaiza tribes migrated in the 17th and 18th centuries towards the coast of the Arabian Gulf in search of better water supplies and grazing.

The Gulf shared in the traditional division of Arabia's terrain in which the coastal regions had always assumed a more significant role in the peninsula's economy than the bleak desert. While less fertile than the west and south coasts it was of great strategic importance because of its ports and location as a vital line of communication between West and East both from a military point of view and as a trade route. Consequently there is a venerable historical record in the Gulf, which has resulted in the accumulation of considerable—if at times uneven—information about its geography, resources, settlements, population and occupations. From contrasting points of the Oriental world, for example, the Sumerians of Iraq and the Chinese were both well acquainted with the Gulf. Classical geographers such as Ptolemy (127-148 A.D.), Pliny (23-79 A.D.), Strabo (64 B.C.-21 A.D.), and Polybius (c.200-118 B.C.) industriously collected facts about the region.

In the context of Kuwait the most significant references are to be found in the Greek historian Arrian's account of the adventurous voyage of Alexander the Great's admiral Nearchos who sailed up the Gulf in 325-326 B.C. to the Euphrates, and stopped at the island of Ikaros before proceeding on to the Indus.[1] This has been identified with Kuwait's offshore island of Failaka where recent excavations have revealed evidence of a Greek trading colony which flourished from the 3rd to the 1st century B.C. The extensive remains include a temple to the goddess Artemis (Plate 5), fortifications and well-planned dwellings and workshops. Among the more significant finds are a stone tablet engraved with the name Ikaros, and a hoard of silver coins dated to the reign of the Seleucid Antiochos III (242-187 B.C.), who as one of a line of Alexander the Great's Hellenistic successors ruled a vast area extending from Turkey through Syria and Iran down to the Gulf. Late Bronze Age (c.3000-2100 B.C.) finds at Failaka, such as stone seals, indicate a human presence well before the arrival of the Greeks. Contemporary with the Greek settlement at Failaka was the leading trading community of Gerrha situated on the mainland just opposite Bahrain and inhabited by Arabs. They are discussed by the geographer Strabo who records that they made great profits by trading in goods imported from India, notably spices. The pattern of Gulf trade had

Failaka Island. Temple of Artemis.

therefore, become established early and was to develop as merchants made more ambitious sea voyages in search of new markets.

In pre-Islamic times merchandise consisting of both the indigenous products of Arabia, especially the myrrh and frankincense of Yemen, dates and pearls, and goods from India—practical items such as spices necessary to preserve and flavour food, and the luxuries of precious stones and fabrics were shipped via the Euphrates up to Iraq and through Gerrha to Syria, Palestine and Egypt. The harbours at the tip of the Gulf—those of Kuwait and Bahrain—were therefore of vital importance to this trade. During Islamic times the establishment of capitals at Damascus and later Baghdad heightened the demand especially for luxury goods and Gulf merchants catered to this by combining methods of barter and direct payment. The trade in spices, gems and fabrics of India continued unabated, while silks and porcelains from China, and ivory and slaves from Africa were exchanged for pearls and rugs, cotton cloth and metalware.

From the 15th century onwards the conflicting interests of outside powers gradually intruded upon the trading communities of the Gulf and affected their long-established equilibrium. Close neighbours such as the Persians and Ottoman Turks were basically concerned to maintain mutually convenient relations. The Persians confined their interests to ports on their own side of the Gulf, traded with the Arabs and became involved in hostilities such as disputes over the islands of Bahrain in the 17th century sparked off by the presence of Europeans. The interests of the Ottoman Turks arose out of their military conquests of the 16th century. Sultan Selim I conquered Syria and Egypt in 1517 and brought the territories of the Hejaz with the holy cities of Mecca and Medina,[2] and of Iraq under his control. Sultan Süleyman the Magnificent completed the conquest of Iraq by taking Baghdad in 1534 and Basra in 1546. The total area was then divided, following Ottoman practice, into administrative units staffed with Turkish bureaucrats and garrisons. The Pasha of Baghdad's authority extended as far as Basra, which in its turn was governed by a Mutasallim who had to maintain good relations with neighbouring Arab tribes on whom he depended for both defence and co-operation in the transport of goods inland. Three main tribes were involved who had all migrated from Najd, the Muntafiq west of Basra and the al-Zafir who were loyal to the Mutasallim, and the Bani Ka'b east and south-east of the city whose allegiance alternated between Persians and Ottoman Turks. Ottoman influence finally extended down the Arabian side of the Gulf by the conquest in 1555 of the oasis of al-Hasa located in the hinterland between Qatar and Najd.

The entry of three European powers into the Gulf resulted in a new alignment of its political and economic affairs. The Portuguese, Dutch and English, all active trading and seafaring peoples, used the Gulf as a stage in the extension of their merchant ventures to the mainland of India. Their activities and rivalries had far-reaching consequences, culminating in the supremacy of the English who dominated the Gulf until the mid-20th century. The earliest arrivals were the Portuguese who, between 1481 and 1487, sent exploratory expeditions to India to sound out the trade prospects and returned via Hormuz In 1948 Vasco da Gama navigated the first direct sea journey to India via the Cape of Good Hope which made east-west trade more accessible and greatly weakened Egyptian, Venetian and Turkish trade by avoiding the traditional Red Sea and Gulf routes. Control of the Gulf, however, was still of great importance to the Portuguese as a means of providing bases for storage of goods in transit, having access to local products such as pearls, and of intercepting their commercial rivals. Portuguese activities in the 16th century concentrated on establishing factories in India and dominating the Gulf. To this latter end they took Bahrain and in 1506 conquered Muscat and Hormuz But Portuguese settlement was shortlived as the Persians, much encouraged by the English, objected to their presence on Persian territory. They expelled the Portuguese from Bahrain in 1602 while the English beseiged them in Hormuz in 1622 and handed it back to the Persians. The Portuguese were left only with Muscat which they strengthened with the forts of Mirali and Jalali which still dominate the harbour today, only to lose it to the Arabs of Oman in 1651. This event marked the end of real Portuguese influence in the Gulf although Portuguese shipping survived in the 18th century on a much reduced scale.

The 17th and 18th centuries witnessed the arrival and active competition of both the Dutch and English East India Companies in the Gulf. The Dutch sponsored a series of exploratory expeditions beginning with the voyage and long stay in India of Jan Huyghen van Linschoten from 1583 to 1592. His thorough survey of the resources and markets of India[3] convinced the Dutch that it was worthwhile to open up trade relations so that from 1597 to 1601 they explored the feasibility of the route around the Cape of Good Hope before formally establishing the Dutch East India Company in 1602, which brought them into rivalry with the English. Like the Portuguese, the Dutch also wanted to secure bases in the Gulf and they founded a factory at Bandar Abbas which the Persian ruler Shah Abbas Safavi (1588-1629) intended to develop as a major port.

Meanwhile the English had been consolidating their position. They conducted two expeditions to India, the first from 1580 to 1582 under John Newberie who stopped at Hormuz, and a second longer voyage from 1583 to 1591 led again by John Newberie accompanied by Ralph Fitch, William Deedes and James Story which took a route from Syria to Baghdad, then down the Tigris to Basra from where the party took the Gulf route to Hormuz before embarking for the Indian continent. The enthusiastic reports of these voyages[4] confirmed the view that India was worthy of serious commercial interest and on 31st December 1600 the English East India Company was established by Royal Charter. Between 1600 and 1612 the Company sent twelve trading expeditions to India and eventually formalised relations by appointing Thomas Roe in 1615 as ambassador to the Mughal court.

During this time, relations with the communities on either side of the Gulf were not neglected. At first these were concentrated on the Persian side following the first English embassy to the court of Shah Abbas Safavi in 1598. The East India Company established factories in 1617 at Shiraz and Isfahan, in 1619 at Jask and in 1623 at Bandar Abbas thus ensuring bases for both coastal and overland trade with Persia. Contacts were extended to the Arab side by the establishment of a factory at Basra between 1643 and 1645 as the English were being constantly harrassed by the intrigues of the Dutch at Bandar Abbas. It was, however good commercial sense to diversify between Persian and Ottoman Turkish territory for several reasons. English goods could be traded on both Persian and Arab sides, and Basra was an excellent centre for access to both the Red Sea and overland routes via Aleppo to Europe for trade; dispatches could also be sent between Company bases at Bombay and Surat and the Court of Directors in London. Slowly the English managed to overshadow the Dutch by energetically encouraging Persian hostility to their overbearing methods and intrigues. The English also began the process of transforming the Company from a purely commercial enterprise to a more overt political presence by establishing a factory at Bombay in 1688 which maintained a civil administration and a contingent of troops. During the 18th century the English political role in the Gulf was consolidated further by the creation of a Consulate at Basra in 1764 and a Residency at Bushire in 1778 which was to become their main centre. During this period Persian influence in the Gulf declined because after the death in 1779 of Karim Khan Zand who had controlled the south from his capital at Shiraz Persia was in a state of civil war and internal chaos. The consequent neglect of the Gulf was epitomised by the loss of Bahrain in 1783 to the Utub tribe of Arabs.

During these centuries Kuwait doubtless had continued as a small community, overshadowed by the affairs of her Persian and Turkish neighbours. However source materials have not as yet been discovered to illustrate her history and economy at this period. It is not until the late 17th and early 18th centuries that admittedly modest records concerning Kuwait come to light from which it is clear that the long established tradition of tribal migration from Najd to both the towns and shores of the Arabian Gulf in search of better opportunities persisted.

The great tribal federation of the Adnani dominated areas in north west and east Arabia and it is amongst Adnani subgroups that the origins of present-day Kuwaitis must be sought. The first tribes to migrate to Kuwait and its hinterland were the Bani Khalid who traditionally migrated between Basra and Qatar, and arrived in the late 17th century. Under their energetic ruler Sheikh Barrak (1669-1682) they successfully contested Ottoman Turkish control of al-Hasa by besieging the Ottoman governor Omar Pasha in 1670 causing him to retreat. They consolidated their position thereafter in valuable territory with access to pearl fishing and good ports on the trade route between India and Najd, Iraq and Syria, extending from Qatar in the south to Kuwait in the north. The Bani Khalid maintained a situation of prosperity and stability which encouraged further tribal migrations to the shores of the Gulf. They clearly continued in this position through the 18th century as they are mentioned by the Dane Niebuhr, one of the first Europeans to explore Arabia between 1761 and 1764. He says of the Beni Khalid: "The province of Lachsa belongs in sovereignty at present to the Schiech of the Arabian tribe of *Beni Khaled.* The reigning Schiech, in 1765 was *Arar*. The tribe of *Beni Khaled* is one of the most powerful in Arabia. They are so far spread through the desert, as often to harras the caravans passing between Bagdad and Kaleb. The greater part of Lachsa is inhabited by Bedouins, and other petty tribes; but these all acknowledge the dominion of the Schiech of *Beni Khaled*.

"I could learn nothing concerning the cities in the interior parts of this province. Lachsa, the seat of the reigning Schiech is probably a large city, containing considerable buildings."[5]

It was during the domination of the Bani Khalid that clear evidence of Kuwait's existence appears in European sources. Kuwait was known by two names, which apparently were used at random by European travellers—Grane and Kuwait—both based on diminutives of the Arabic words "qarn" high hill and "kut" castle or fortress respectively. The term Grane is used on a chart of the Dutch East India Company dated to c.1660, while it is believed that Sheikh Barrak constructed the small fort "Kuwait" in 1680. Both names are featured for the first time on the map constructed in 1765 by the Dane Niebuhr to accompany his description of Kuwait:—

"*Koueit* or *Graen*, as it is called by the Persians and Europeans, is a sea-port town, three days journey from *Zobejer* or old Basra. The inhabitants live by the fishery of pearls and of fishes. They are said to employ in this series of naval industry more than eight hundred boats. In the favourable season of the year, this town is left almost desolate, every body going out either to the fishing, or upon some trading adventure. Graen is governed by a particular Schiech, of the tribe of *Othema*, who is a vassal to the Schiech of Lachsa, but sometimes aspires at independence. In such cases, when the Schiech of Lachsa advances with his army, the citizens of Graen retreat with their effects into the little island of *Feludsje.*

"Near Graen are the remains of another Portuguese fortress.

"Between the territories of the Schiech of Lachsa and the dominions of the Sovereign of Oman, are a numerous tribe denominated *Al Musallim*, and possessing several considerable towns, the names of which are unknown to me."[6]

Niebuhr both vividly summarises the activities which were essential to Kuwait's economy until the mid-20th century and mentions the presence of the *Othema*—who are to be identified with the Utub Arabs, under whose rule the wealth and stability of the community were maintained.

The Bani Utub of pure Arabian Bedu origin, who were of the Jumayla group of the Anaiza division of the great Adnani tribal federation and were based in Haddar in Al-Aflaj of Najd, included the families of al-Sabah and al-Khalifa, rulers today of Kuwait and Bahrain respectively, among their members. According to local tradition they were forced to migrate in the late 17th and early 18th centuries to the region of Qatar, then under the control of the Bani Khalid, because of a long and severe drought in Najd. Sometime between 1710 and 1716 the al-Sabah left Qatar and moved north to Kuwait. Little is known of their early years here and it is supposed that they were tributary to the Bani Khalid. Eventually their leader Sabah bin Jaber was elected Sheikh of Kuwait in about 1756, thus beginning an unbroken line of al-Sabah rule over an independent community. The few years of his rule until 1762 were concentrated on encouraging pearl fishing and profiting from Kuwait's position as a transit stage on the overland desert route in the transport of passengers and merchandise to Aleppo. Kuwait's boundaries encompassed offshore islands such as Failaka and extended inland to Jahra whose wells were vital to the water supply, while the settlement boasted a mud brick enclosure wall constructed in 1760 as a defense against Bedu raids. Sheikh Sabah also established a basic civil and religious administration.

By the late 18th century there was an even distribution of Utub influence around the upper reaches of the Arabian Gulf as related families controlled Kuwait, Qatar from the settlement of Zubara, and Bahrain. This situation, however, had not been achieved without harassment from Arab tribes of both Najd and the Gulf and the resulting need to establish good relations with the English East India Company. In Najd the rise and development of the fundamentalist Islamic doctrines of Wahhabism emphasising strict interpretation of the Qur'an, became a serious threat to the Gulf communities when their founder Muhammad bin Abd al-Wahhab allied himself in 1745 with Muhammad ibn Su'ud, a powerful chief based at al-Dir'iyya. Following a now familiar pattern of raids from the arid deserts of central Arabia, the Wahhabis repeatedly attacked Kuwait and Iraq, and clashed with the Bani Khalid their immediate eastern neighbours and rivals in the comparatively fertile region of al-Hasa. Between 1745 and 1765 Wahhabi raids against the Bani Khalid were mainly defensive but in 1795 the Bani Khalid were finally defeated thus altering the balance of power in eastern Arabia. Harassment from hostile Arab tribes of the Gulf was more localised than the Wahhabi threat and ultimately was contained. The main groups involved here, all concentrated on the Persian side of the Gulf, were the Bani Ka'b who had migrated from Najd and had joined the migrations of the 17th century settling at Dawraq, the Arabs of Bandar Abbas, and the al-Matarish of Bushire. Disputes, especially with the Bani Ka'b, caused members of the al-Khalifa family to emigrate from Kuwait in 1766 to Zubara as they preferred to branch out independently at a site nearer the pearl fishing beds rather than come to terms. Eventually the raids and intrigues of the Bani Ka'b forced Kuwait to make overtures to both the Ottoman Turks at Basra and to the English East India Company which were to her lasting advantage.

The English had established a trading station or factory at Basra between 1643 and 1645 where they had been chiefly concerned to maintain friendly relations with the Ottoman authorities and to stay aloof from the internal affairs of the Gulf unless commercial priorities required otherwise. Two serious events proved advantageous to Kuwait—the outbreak of bubonic plague at Basra in 1773 which diverted trade to Kuwait, Zubara and Bushire, and the Persian siege and occupation of Basra which lasted from 1775 to 1779 and was supported by the Bani Ka'b and the Arabs of Bushire and Bandar Riq. The Persian occupation of Basra resulted in the establishment of direct relations between Kuwait and the East India Company, as during its four years duration all goods from India en route for Aleppo were diverted and unloaded at Kuwait and Zubara. Kuwait also replaced Basra as the centre for dispatching mail between India and England and two East India Company civil officers were stationed there to supervise the work involved. In 1783 the al-Khalifa or Zubara took Bahrain which was now to remain in the control of a family on good terms with Kuwait. Relations with the English continued to progress. Because of problems with the Ottoman officials at Basra the East India Company's factory was transferred to Kuwait on 30th April 1793 where it remained until 27th August 1795. The reasons for this choice are easily understood; Kuwait had been an effective centre for the Company's mail and an alternative trading base between 1775 and 1779, Sheikh Abdullah I (1762-1812) had shrewdly kept on good terms with the English, and its location was near enough to Basra for the move to be accomplished with minimum inconvenience. Wahhabi attacks on Kuwait during these two years eventually forced the English back to Basra, but Kuwait had profited greatly from trade and postal revenues.

Kuwait's progress in the 19th century indicates how effective her rulers of the 18th century had been for despite increasing problems with the Wahhabis of Najd and threats from Gulf pirates, she managed to maintain her independence, by adroitly keeping on good terms with opposing factions, and steadily to pursue her mercantile interest. Information concerning Kuwait's development at this period is more plentiful as there are more accounts both in the records of the East India Company and of the various Residencies situated around the Gulf, and in the accounts of naval and military personnel and independent European travellers. One of the most interesting is that of James Silk Buckingham who visited Kuwait in 1816 and summed up the results of the East India Company's problems with Basra. "The next port above El Kateef of any note on this coast is that of Graine, as it is called in our English charts, though known among the Arabs by the name of Koete only. This is a port of some importance, seated in a fine bay; and the town is large and populous, though the sandy desert presses close upon its walls, and no vegetation is to be seen around it, within the range of human view. It seems always to have preserved its independence too, even at the time when Ormuz, Muscat, Bahrein, Lahsa, and even Kateef and Bussorah, which two last were garrisoned by Turks, were assailed by the Portuguese arms, and they still bear the reputation of being the freest and bravest people throughout the Gulf.

"The town and bay of Graine is in lat. 29°15′ north and about long 48°0′ east, or nearly south-south-west from the bar of the Euphrates, at the distance of about fifty miles. The town itself is chiefly inhabited by mercantile and trading people, who engage in all the branches of commerce carried on throughout the Gulf. The port sends out, at least, a hundred sail of vessels, large and small; and the people who navigate them, as well as those for whom they sail, have the highest character for probity, skill, firmness and courage. The bay admits of excellent anchorage, in convenient depths, from ten to five fathoms water; and it was for some time used as the station of the East India Company's cruisers, to land and wait for dispatches transmitting between India and Europe, during the temporary residence there of the Company's Agent, who had quitted Bussorah, on account of some differences with the Turkish Government."[7]

Despite these considerable advantages Kuwait was to be long troubled by the Wahhabis and pirates which drew her into yet closer relations with the Ottoman Turks and the East India Company. By the early 19th century the Wahhabis had made considerable advances from their base of al-Dir'iyya in Najd. They had defeated the Bani Khalid of al-Hasa in 1795, they had repeatedly attacked the important cities of Basra, Kerbela, Najaf, and Baghdad in Ottoman Iraq between 1801 and 1810. This expansion naturally provoked a quick reaction from the Ottoman Turks who in co-operation with their nominal subject and powerful ally, Muhammad Ali of Egypt (ruled 1805-1848) mounted two expeditions to re-capture their provinces in Arabia. During the first expedition they re-occupied the Hejaz in 1811 and pressed on to Najd destroying the Wahhabi capital of al-Dir'iyya in 1818. The second expedition of 1836-1839 penetrated eastern Arabia to the Gulf when the Egyptians took al-Hasa and Bahrain and it became clear to the Ottoman Turks that Muhammad Ali entertained ambitions of taking Iraq. The Egyptian presence in the Gulf threatened both Kuwait and Britain—Kuwait feared being invaded and occupied; both the British presence and interests in the Red Sea trade route would be undermined. Sheikh Jaber I (1812-1859) had little option but to allow the Egyptians to use Kuwait as a base for shipping, supplies and intelligence gathering while maintaining neutrality by also receiving Wahhabi refugees and keeping on good terms with the Ottoman Mutasallim of Basra. The Wahhabi problem re-emerged in 1865 provoked by a power struggle between two brothers of the Al-Saud family, Abdullah bin Faisal and Saud bin Faisal. The settled Arab tribes of Najd supported Abdullah. The Ottoman Turks gave him the title of Qa'immaqam of Najd implying that he was to rule both Najd and al-Hasa in their name as they wished to reclaim these territories. Accordingly in 1869 Midhat Pasha, the Ottoman governor of Baghdad, began preparations for a campaign, and in 1871 the Turkish troops supported by horsemen of the Muntafiq tribe and naval transports from Kuwait left Basra to proceed to al-Hasa which came under Ottoman control until 1874. Kuwait's policy again was to keep on good terms with all sides in order to preserve her independence and prosperity.

The problem of piracy was both local and more widespread. Certain Arab tribes, notably the Qawasim of Ras al-Khaima constantly attacked shipping in the Gulf and were also prepared to support the Wahhabis at sea. The British concerned by the threat to the security of their interests in the Gulf and India caused by Napoleon's invasion of Egypt in 1798 began to negotiate treaties with the rulers of the Gulf states thus making their presence more overtly political. The first such treaty was signed with Muscat in 1798, by which the Sultan agreed to take the side of the British Government in any international dispute. Later treaties dealt more specifically with piracy. One of the most flamboyant characters who terrorised shipping in the Gulf was a certain Kuwaiti Rahmah bin Jaber well described by James Silk Buckingham in 1816:—

"This (anchorage at Bushire) was at present occupied by the fleet of a certain Arab, named Rahmah-ben-Jaber, who has been for more than twenty years the terror of the Gulf, and who is the most successful and the most generally tolerated pirate perhaps that ever infested any sea. This man is by birth a native of Graine, on the opposite coast, and nephew of the present governor, or Sheikh, of that place. His fellow-citizens have all the honesty, however, to declare him an outlaw, from abhorrence of his profession, and he has found that shelter and protection at Bushire, which his own townsmen very properly denied to him. With five or six vessels, most of which are very large, and manned by crews of from two to three hundred each, he sallies forth, and captures whatever he may think himself strong enough to carry off as his prize, the vessels of Graine, of Bussorah, of Bahrein, of Muscat, and even of Bushire, where he resides, falling equally a prey to him. His followers, to the number perhaps of two thousand are maintained by the plunder of his prizes and as these are most of them his own bought African slaves and the remainder equally subject to his authority, he is sometimes as prodigal of their lives in a fit of anger as he is of those of his enemies. . . . This butcher chief, like the celebrated Djezzar of Acre, affects great simplicity of dress, manners and living, and whenever he goes out, he is not to be distinguished by a stranger from the crowd of his attendants. He carries this simplicity to a degree of filthiness which is disgusting, as his usual dress is a shirt, which is never taken off to be washed from the time it is worn out, no drawers or coverings for the legs of any kind, and a large goat's hair cloak, wrapped over all with a greasy and dirty handkerchief, called the keffea, thrown loosely over his head. Infamous as was this man's life and character, he was not only cherished and courted by the people of Bushire, who dread him, but was courteously received and respectfully entertained whenever he visited the British factory!

"Rahmah-ben-Jaber's figure presented a meagre trunk, with four lank members, all of them cut and hacked, and pierced with wounds of sabres, spears and bullets, in every part, to the number perhaps of more than twenty different wounds. He had, besides, a face naturaly ferocious and ugly, and now rendered still more so by several scars there, and by the loss of one eye. . . ."[8]

From this description it is clear that Rahmah bin Jaber commanded considerable resources of ships and men and as he was not the only pirate sailing the Gulf waters British concern to establish peace was understandable. They gradually accomplished this by a series of treaties beginning with the General Treaty of Peace of 1820 and concluding with the Treaty of Peace in Perpetuity signed in 1853 by which any disputes at sea were to be referred to the British authorities for settlement. During this period the British had again favoured Kuwait by temporarily moving the East India Company's factory from Basra in 1821 to the island of Failaka owing to a dispute with the Ottoman governor of Baghdad. Their stay on this occasion was short as the factory moved back to Basra in 1822.

By the late 19th century, when Sheikh Mubarak bin Sabah (1896-1915) came to power the contemporary political situation had changed. In eastern Arabia independent states lined the shores of the Gulf and many had treaty relations with Britain which was now the dominant power as the Ottoman Empire declined. Other European colonial powers were in competition with Britain—France, Germany and Russia who had long coveted access to both the Mediterranean and the warm water ports of the Gulf. Sheikh Mubarak was extremely concerned at the Ottoman decline, as Kuwait's proximity to Iraq although valuable strategically and commercially was also vulnerable to any change which might take place there. In preference to being at the mercy of uncertain events he therefore turned to the British to negotiate a mutually advantageous treaty. The moment was right as the British in turn had closed the Arabian Gulf to the French and Russians and were apprehensive of Ottoman activity concerning railway concessions. In 1898 for example the Ottoman government had granted a concession to the Russian Count Kapnist for a railway which would run from Syrian Tripoli via Homs and Baghdad to Kuwait and in 1900 were to undertake negotiations for a railway from Berlin to Baghdad with their new allies the Germans. The British hastened therefore to include Kuwait in a treaty relationship as it was the only state uncommitted on the Gulf of great strategic importance.

In 1899, a treaty—the Exclusive Agreement—was signed between Sheikh Mubarak and the British. The main clauses stipulated that Sheikh Mubarak would not lease or dispose of any part of his domains without British permission and that in turn Britain would ensure Kuwait's defence in the case of any foreign threat. This treaty therefore guaranteed the integrity of Kuwait's domains. Later agreements with the British dealt with such subjects as limiting arms traffic with Afghanistan in 1900, allowing the establishment of both a British postal service and a British Political Residency in 1904[9] whose tasks were to include curtailing Sheikh Mubarak's activities outside Kuwait and the easing of tensions along Kuwait's northern border. Agreements also forbade foreigners to fish for pearls or dive for sponges without the British Resident's permission in 1911, and permitted an extension of the Gulf telegraph cable to Kuwait in 1912. Probably the most significant agreement between Sheikh Mubarak and Sir Percy Cox, the Political Resident at Bushire in 1913, stipulated that the operations involved in exploration for and production of oil should be a British monopoly. The result of World War I justified Sheikh Mubarak's decisions to co-operate with the British. The Germans and their Ottoman allies were defeated and in the ensuing dismemberment of Ottoman possessions the British established their mandate in Palestine, Jordan and Iraq and therefore were able to guarantee and protect Kuwait's borders. During these complex manoeuvres of foreign policy Kuwait had been able to continue to prosper through trade which the improved communications resulting from the establishment of the postal service and telegraph line encouraged. Also social services had been introduced; in 1904 the British Assistant Political Agent began to practice in medicine and two Arabian American Mission hospitals for men and women respectively were opened in 1911; and in education with the building of the Mubarakiyya School also in 1911.

The years between World Wars I and II were difficult for Kuwait for both political and economic reasons. During World War I Kuwait had managed to stay loyal to the British according to the terms of the Exclusive Agreement and profit from trade going by the overland route to Syria even though she was so close to Ottoman territory. External problems, however, arose through hostilities with Abdul Aziz, the Saudi ruler of Najd (1902-1953) and boundary disputes. Initially relations with Abdul Aziz had been amiable as Sheikh Mubarak had in 1902 helped him capture Riyadh using Kuwait as his base. By 1915, however, the situation had changed. Abdul Aziz with the help of Mubarak's successor, Sheikh Salim bin Mubarak (1917-1921), consolidated his authority in al-Hasa by defeating the Ajman tribes who were based there. Sheikh Salim, instead of pursuing and destroying the Ajman as Abdul Aziz wished, allowed them to take refuge in Kuwait's territory. Abdul Aziz did not forget this and initiated a campaign in 1920. Here the Ikhwan (Brotherhood) movement which preached an ascetic revivalism of strict adherence to Qur'anic doctrine that had spread rapidly between 1912 and 1914 among the tribes of Najd was useful to him. Initially the Ikhwan opposed his authority but he managed to make them accept him as both religious and political leader and directed them against Kuwait. Salim realised that Abdul Aziz was behind the Ikhwan's campaign and sent a tribal contingent to camp near Manifa mountain at Kuwait's southern border. On 4th April 1920 the Ikhwan under their leader Faisal al-Duwaish attacked and massacred the Kuwaitis. Salim responded by ordering all inhabitants of Kuwait to build an enclosure wall as protection around the city and hearing that the Ikhwan were marching north he went to Jahra with troops. On 10th October 1920 the Kuwaitis were defeated in a battle outside Jahra suffering great loss of life. Salim and the survivors retreated to the Red Fort (Plate 6) at Jahra hoping to delay the Ikhwan advance to Kuwait by forcing a siege. This strategy succeeded and also put the clause of the Exclusive Agreement by which the British would come to Kuwait's defence in case of foreign attack to the test. The arrival of British warships in Kuwait Bay eventually caused the Ikhwan to raise the siege of the Red Fort and withdraw. The Ikhwan threat did not disappear immediately, however, as they continued to raid Kuwait sporadically until 1930 when Abdul Aziz discovered that they were also defying his authority. He attacked and defeated them and imprisoned their leaders.

Negotiations over boundary disputes lingered on and were never satisfactorily resolved. They took place against a continuing background of hostility between Abdul Aziz and Kuwait, and were further complicated by the collapse of the Ottoman Empire and the partition of her territories in the Middle East between British and French mandates. Additionally with the discovery of oil reserves near Mosul it became a matter of urgency to define

6 Jahra. Red Fort.

Iraq's boundaries so that contracts for exploration and drilling operations could be signed. The troubled saga of boundary problems can be traced through a series of agreements and conferences, beginning in 1913 when the British and Ottomans in discussion about the frontiers of Iraq, Kuwait and Najd positioned Kuwait's southern border at Jabal Munifa about 160 miles south of her present border with Saudi Arabia. At another conference held in1922 at Muhammarah on the Persian side an agreement was signed regulating the Iraq/Najd border and accepting the southern frontier of Kuwait as defined in 1913. Abdul Aziz's rejection of this agreement led to another conference in 1922 held at al-Uqair in al-Hasa. Here the representatives were Sir Percy Cox, British High Commissioner in Iraq, Major More, British Political Resident at Kuwait, and Abdul Aziz representing Najd. Sir Percy Cox's aims were to settle Iraq's borders in order to guarantee its independent status, to organise Najd's frontiers so that tribal raids into Kuwait, Iraq and Jordan would cease, and to maintain Kuwait as a buffer state between Iraq and Najd. The main results of the conference were that Kuwait lost to Najd the southern territory which had been granted in 1913 and that two neutral zones were defined—between Kuwait and al-Hasa to the south and between Najd and Iraq in the north to allow free access to nomad tribes who had traditionally used these lands for grazing.

Kuwait's economic problems in the 1920s and 1930s arose from both local and world affairs. Abdul Aziz conducted an economic boycott against Kuwait from 1923 to 1937. He had requested that Sheikh Ahmad al-Jabar al-Sabah (1921-1950) collect taxes on his behalf from the Najdi Bedu tribes who purchased food and clothing in Kuwait's markets paying for them in sheep and camels. Sheikh Ahmad refused to do this and also forbade the presence of a Najdi tax collector in Kuwait. The tribes therefore had to shop elsewhere which resulted in heavy losses for Kuwait's merchants. These local problems were compounded by the world recession of the 1930s, the slump in the Gulf's pearl trade caused by the development of the cultured pearl industry in Japan, and the start of World War II which delayed the exploitation of Kuwait's oil resources discovered in 1938. The situation, however, improved dramatically after the war with the drilling of Kuwait's first oil wells in 1946. The escalating revenues of the oil industry were to underwrite swift development of an infrastructure and social services and to lead to Kuwait's formal independence from Britain in June 1961.

2 The settlement, population and government

Kuwait's emergence from an unpretentious sprawling sea port, whose hinterland extended haphazardly beyond its walls into the desert, to a modern state within carefully defined boundaries focused on a busy city full of tall buildings was sudden, beginning in the 1950s on the basis of proliferating oil revenues. Throughout the 19th century Kuwait's appearance much resembled that of the settlement described by Niebuhr in 1765 and Buckingham in 1816. Various European travellers and officials give interesting accounts of its gradual development building up a picture of a modest place determined to make the most of such resources as were available. J. Stocqueler, who visited Kuwait in 1831, says that "Koete, or Grane as it is called in the maps, is in extent about a mile long, and a quarter of a mile broad, it consists of houses built of mud and stone, occasionally faced with a coarse chunam, and may contain about four thousand inhabitants. The houses being for the most part square in form, with a courtyard in the centre, (having windows looking into the yard), present but a very bare and uniform exterior, like indeed, all the houses in the Persian Gulph. . . . The streets of Kuwait are wider than those of Muscat or Bushire, with a gutter running down the centre."[1]

He notes also that Kuwait's wall was more decorative than functional "as it is not a foot thick".

Captain S. Hennell, British Resident in the Gulf in 1841 expands upon this rather terse description, by concentrating upon Kuwait's major resource:— "The principal point in favour of Grane, is its Harbour, which is certainly an exceedingly fine one, capable of holding the navy of Great Britain, but so far as my observation goes, it possesses no other advantage. The country around is a salt and sandy desert, of the most barren and inhospitable description, with not a tree or shrub visible, as far as the eye can reach, excepting a few bushes which mark the wells. From the taste and quality of the water, I feel amost certain that it would not agree with the constitutions of either Europeans, or Indians, and that the latter especially, would from drinking it, be liable to the attack of a dangerous disease called the Bereherse.

"This Town presents a singluar instance of commercial prosperity, although wanting in almost every advantage, excepting its magnificent harbour. It's population is large, as it can produce about six thousand men capable of bearing arms, which at a moderate average would make the total number of inhabitants nearly twenty five thousand individuals. They possess thirty-one Buglas and Bateels, from one hundred and fifty Tons burthen, which trade constantly with India. Fifty smaller vessels are employed in the coasting commerce of the Gulf, and about three hundred and fifty boats engaged in fishing and on the Pearl Banks. The energy and courage of the people, who are closely united, and free from feuds and factions, render them respected and feared by all the other Maritime tribes, and as in fact, they are as prompt to resent insult or aggression toward themselves as they are cautious in refraining from injury or arrogance towards their peaceful neighbours, piracy upon a Grane boat is of rare occurence. The government of Shaikh Jabir is of a truly mild and paternal character. Both himself and his sons are perhaps among the worst dressed and most ill lodged residents in the place. Excepting a small duty levied upon the sales and purchases of the Bedouins who resort to his Town, the Sheik collects no taxes or customs, the port being entirely a free one, nearly all the small revenue realized by him, not perhaps exceeding 3000 Dollars yearly, together with the profits derived from his trading vessels are expended in keeping up a sort of public label of a plentiful but coarse description to which everyone appears to be welcome. This liberality together with the utter absence of all pretensionof outward superiority, renders Shaikh Jabir and his Son Soobah (to whom the management of affairs has been made over by his father) most popular among his subjects, who are consequently devoted to them in an unusual degree, and ready to place at their disposal, both person and property, when called upon to do so."[2]

While Stocqueler's account captures the appearance of the city with its spare functional houses made of local stone and mud, materials which were still in use up to the 1950s, there are wide discrepancies between his and Hennell's calculations of the population. It is likely that Stocqueler's four thousand inhabitants corresponded most closely to Hennell's "six thousand men capable of bearing arms". The shortness of his visit compared with Hennell's residency would have enabled him to gain little more than an estimate of the male and most visible section of Kuwait's citizens.

Kuwait's continuing prosperity through trade and pearl fishing enabled the settlement to expand both along the coast and inland. This was noticed by Lorimer, the British Political Resident at Bushire, whose excellent and detailed survey of Kuwait is based both on personal research and information gathered from other colleagues in the Gulf between 1904 and 1907.[3] Kuwait was of great strategic and commercial importance to Britain at that time hence the thoroughness of Lorimer's work. His comments on boundaries are revealing of the close relationship between settled townsmen and Bedu tribe. He notes that "The boundaries of the Kuwait principality are for the most part fluctuating and undefined; they are, at any given time, the limits of the tribes which then, either voluntarily or under compulsion, own allegiance to the Shaikh of Kuwait."[4] The means at that time did not exist for absorbing the Bedu into employment and encouraging permanent settlement. Some boundaries were more vague than others; on the east the sea coast imposed obvious limits, on the north and south they were reasonably fixed at the Turkish outposts of Umm Qasr and Saftwan, and at Jabal Manifa respectively. The western boundary stretching towards the desert was extremely vague depending on how the current rulers of Kuwait and Najd interpreted it. Despite the importance of Kuwait's geographical position it was not particularly easy to journey out of it because of the difficulty of ensuring a supply of provisions outside a 20-25 mile radius of the town, and the conditions of the roads which made up the two main routes to Basra and the four routes into Najd.

Within its somewhat controversial boundries the settlement of Kuwait had doubled in size. Lorimer noted that "The town now measures about 2 miles along the shore, and is rapidly extending towards Ras Ajuzah; its depth inland is from one-fourth to three-fourths of a mile. Free sites granted by the Shaikh on all sides of the town are, on account of the increasing prosperity of the place, being rapidly taken up and built upon by enterprising individuals as a commercial speculation."[5] It is hardly surprising therefore that the old town walls had disappeared and only one of its seven gates, the Darwazat Jana'at on the east was still standing. In general the city presented an open haphazard appearance conforming to no systematic plan with the fortified house of Sheikh Mubarak's eldest son on the west and the black tents of Bedu encampments on the south forming landmarks.

Apart from the main bazaar which ran from the centre of the town to the sea and another main route to the north-east the streets were irregular and winding enclosing residential quarters of which "Most of the houses have only a ground floor, but appear higher owing to a parapet-wall enclosing the roof; they are generally built surrounding a courtyard. The better sort are of stone plastered with Juss and have high arched gateways, sometimes with a wicket-door in the middle of the gate; a few arches appear also in upper storeys."[6] Numerous buildings catered to the religious needs of the community—"There are between 20 and 30 mosques, of which 4 are Jami's, or Friday congregational mosques; these are the chief mosque, which stands on the west side of the main bazaar, the Shaikh's mosque on the sea front near his residence, the mosque of Haddad, and the mosque of the Jana'at; none of these have any architectural pretensions."[7]

While the general alignment of the town's main residential and service quarters remained the same various developments had taken place by the 1950s as noted by Harold Dickson, who had served as the British Political Agent in Kuwait from 1929 to 1936 and continued to live there after his retirement. Kuwait town had increased in size now extending three and a half miles along the coast towards Ras Ajuza where Sheikh Jaber II (1915-1917) had built the Dasman Palace, and inland about a mile and a quarter. A new wall had been built in 1920 as a defence against the Ikhwan who were then besieging the Red Fort at Jahra. Dickson has carefully described this wall:—"The wall is a little over four miles in length. From Ras al Ajuzah it runs approximately south-west for two and a half miles, then west by south for a little over a mile, then west by north to the sea, which it joins a quarter of a mile beyond the headquarters of the American Mission.

"Today there are four gates; the Darwazat Dasman; the Darwazat al Burai'isi (now named Darwazat al Sha'ab), leading to Hawali, Dimnah etc.; the Darwazat Naif, on the main road to Riyadh; and the Darwazat al Jahra, leading to Jahra. In addition to the four gates, which are protected by towers, there is a round-shaped bastion—or *qala'ah*, as it is called—about every two hundred yards throughout the length of the wall."[8] The areas outside the Darwazat Naif and the Darwazat al Jahra were favourite spots for Bedu encampments. The town's two main streets remained as noted by Lorimer at the beginning of the century[9] while others were gradually being modernised. Among the residential quarters where houses were still built along traditional lines new buildings were gradually intruding such as hospitals and schools and: ". . . the magnificent new building, situated near the Darwazat naif, that houses the public security department and offices; to the million-pound college for boys, the new technical college, and the tuberculosis hospital that are going up three miles west of the town; to the modern quarantine station, the Cable & Wireless station, and the score of new boys and girls schools recenty completed inside the town. . . ."[10]

Mosques continued to flourish—"There are over forty mosques, of which nine are *jami'*, or Friday congregational mosques. These all have minarets and include the Masjid as Suq, the chief mosque, which stands on the west side of the main bazaar; the Masjid al Adsani, a little to the west of it; the Masjid Hilal and the Masjid Saleh Fudhalah in the Murqab quarter; the Masjid an Nusf, a little to the east of the old Political Agency; the Shaikh's mosque, Masjid al Khalifah, with its fine new minaret, on the sea front near his town palace; the Masjid as Seyid Yasin, the Masjid al Badar and the Masjid as Saiyir in the western portion of the town. A tenth, the Masjid Mulla Saleh on the road from the Safat to the Darwazat al Jahra, is likely to be converted shortly into a *jami'*."[11]

Dickson also gives an interesting account of the environs of Kuwait town which were then full of small isolated villages now mainly absorbed into densely populated suburbs.[12] The most important was Jahra, a large village and oasis dominated by the Red Fort, about twenty miles west of the town, and the main local source of agricultural produce due to the presence of nineteen deep wells which ensured irrigation for cereal and vegetable crops and dates. It was naturally enough a permanent location for Bedu encampments during the summer months. South of Kuwait were the settlements of Hawalli, a large village of five hundred houses, two mosques, a school and market gardens, and Fintas, Fahaheel and Shuaiba of more modest size and cultivation. East of the town was the village of Dimna inhabited by Arabs of the Awazim tribe and a favoured country retreat of Kuwaitis, which was renamed Salmiya in 1953.

Despite the extensive construction programmes which have taken place in Kuwait since the 1950s certain of the old buildings have survived, and it is possible to supplement observation of them with information recorded by officials and travellers to gain a more intimate impression of the traditional environment in which its inhabitants lived and worked. Building materials were both local and imported, and employed in practical and sensible methods of construction. Local volcanic pebble stones were used for foundations on which walls were erected using a mixture of coral blocks and mud brick; surfaces were then smoothed and coated with lime plaster. Wood was an essential material used in roofing and doors and apart from a few local sources of date palm, teak and other hardwoods from India and Africa, and mangrove poles from Africa were imported. Yellow clay floor tiles and glass which was only used for windows in affluent establishments both came from Iraq and Persia.

The city wall of 1920 was built of mud brick punctuated by the four gates (Plate 7) which were massive rectangular but low structures each pierced by a single entrance. Within the city the dominant impression was of angular buildings of modest height which presented blank outer walls to maintain the privacy of their inhabitants. Facing the sea along the east coast stood the Shaikh's Seif Palace (Plate 8) and the Majlis where public business was conducted and guests received. Zahra Freeth, the daughter of Harold Dickson, has given a well-observed account of the Majlis in 1970 which had survived with much of its decoration intact:—"The old Majlis was built in 1904 by Kuwait's great Shaikh Mubarak, at the time when he was influenced by the new houses of his bosom friend Shaikh Khazaal. Together they planned this new palace which was to be the finest building in Kuwait. It was constructed of yellow Amarah bricks imported from Iraq, and Persian workmen were brought over to make the latticed windows and interior wooden panelling in the Persian style. As a building it was far ahead of the standards of its time in Kuwait, and even in the 1930s it remained an outstanding piece of architecture by comparison with the mud and mortar houses which surrounded it. . . . The Majlis is so placed that there is a private courtyard between the L-shaped old building and the sea-front, with the new Sief Palace today making the third side. . . . We went up an outside staircase

7 Kuwait City. Jahra Gate.

8 Kuwait City, Arabian Gulf Street. Seif Palace.

on the western wing to reach the offices on the first floor, and paused at the top to look back at the main south section. From here we had a good view of one large bay window, made in wood with latticed apertures, which projects in a medieval manner at first-floor level. It was situated at one end of the inner facade, whose rounded arches on this side were filled in with Persian woodwork and glass to form more windows. . . . Opening off the upstairs gallery are three large reception rooms which are the focal point of interest for visitors to the palace. In these three rooms Sheikh Mubarak had the ceilings made entirely of brightly-coloured framed oleographs most of them depicting Edwardian society beauties. . . . In the other two rooms with similar ceilings the subjects of the prints were slightly more varied; children at play, skating parties, Dickensian coaching scenes and the like. "The Majlis is today being modernised and renovated, essential repairs are being made to the structure, and central air-conditioning is being installed. It is to be used for yet more government offices, but the authorities have recognised the historic interest of the interior adornments; the old woodwork, the coloured glass, and the ladies on the ceilings are to be preserved for future generations."[13]

Extending westwards along the sea shore from the Palace and Majlis area were the large houses of the merchant families. Only a few now remain along what is today known as Arabian Gulf Street, spaced between modern buildings but they are sufficiently preserved to give a clear picture of the town's traditional appearance and architecture. One of the most explicit here is the large house known as Bayt al-Badr thought to have been built between c.1837 and 1847. It is constructed according to an L-shaped plan[14] which enables the public quarters to be kept separate from the women's quarters which were private and reserved for family members. As in all traditional Kuwait houses the exterior is sharply angled, uninviting and secretive (Plate 9)—a blank plastered surface inset with long seats along the wall facing the sea, and interrupted by two handsome wooden doors each leading into a separate courtyard. Such doors made of imported teak studded with bosses and elaborately carved posts and lintels were a traditional feature of houses all along the Gulf (Plate 10), whose decoration varied regionally: Kuwaiti doors, for example, generally have quatrefoil clusters of bosses at the edges and rosette motifs. The reasons for

Kuwait City, Arabian Gulf Street. Bayt al-Badr, exterior.

0 Kuwait City, Arabian Gulf Street. Bayt Sadu, wooden door.

concentrating all interest on the interior of a house are both practical and social. In a harsh climate with especially fierce hot summers it is more comfortable to live in thick walled rooms shaded beneath columned arcades around an open courtyard rather than in enclosed spaces or in quarters facing on to the street. The concealed courtyard also ensures the privacy and seclusion traditionally required for the women of a family.

In Bayt al-Badr, therefore, the two doors lead into public courtyards. On the right the larger courtyard functions as a reception area with a long elaborately decorated room beneath a deep loggia which serves as the *majlis* or *diwaniya* for male guests. Close to the *diwaniya* is a small room where coffee was prepared. The remaining three sides of the courtyard are lined with rooms which could be used as accommodation for male guests and guards, and as storage areas. The door on the left leads into a parallel but smaller courtyard which functioned as a business area. Here the rooms lining the court were used as offices for the owner of the household, workrooms depending on the nature of his business and store rooms. Thus spare parts and tackle of boats were kept here and also merchandise which could include both permanent stock, and goods in transit. If workmen or sailors associated with the owner's business required sleeping quarters they would be lodged in this courtyard. Leading from the back of the business court was the entrance to the kitchen court which served to link both public and private quarters of the household. The kitchen court in turn was open with a well as its focal point (Plate 11). The cooking area was enclosed on one side of the court and contained bread ovens and a series of hearths necessary for the cooking required for an extended family and its dependents. A masonry wood channelled the fumes and smoke to a chimney immediately adjacent to the kitchen was a small yard which provided stabling for the family's sheep and goats who were taken out to graze on the outskirts of the town during the day.

At right angles to the public area and entered from the kitchen is the family's living quarters, the courtyard where the women spent their time (Plate 12). Here the rooms beneath the columned arcade functioned as more spacious and elaborate sleeping quarters with individual washing facilities. Each bedroom had either a sleeping gallery or ample space for a mattress or four-poster bed which could be screened with curtains. The women's court

11 Kuwait City, Arabian Gulf Street. Bayt al-Badr, well in kitchen court.

12 Kuwait City, Arabian Gulf Street. Bayt al-Badr, family courtyard.

13 Kuwait City, Arabian Gulf Street. Former Political Residency.

also had a separate entrance on the north so that the ladies and their guests could come and go unobserved. As in the men's area the women's court also had richly decorated reception and coffee making rooms near the entrance. Additionally a staircase led to the roof which functioned as a family sleeping area in hot weather. Despite the differences of functions between the four courtyard units they all had certain features in common. The rooms were roofed with mangrove beams, covered with bamboo strips and reed mats over which a thick layer of straw and mud was stamped which could be repaired after rain by another application. This method of roof construction, however, conditioned the size of the rooms which depended on the length of the mangrove beams. The courtyards were paved with flat bricks imported from Iraq and Persia.

Other surviving houses along the sea front show interesting variations on this plan and also the outside influences that Kuwait as a seafaring town received. The former residence of the British Political Agents demonstrates these points well (Plate 13). It was described by Violet Dickson, remembering her arrival there in 1929:—

"It was a two-storey structure, shaded along the upper floor by wide verandahs overlooking the harbour. It had been adapted from a traditional Arab-style house, built like most others in Kuwait—with walls of sun-dried mud bricks and coated with a plaster of white gypsum. Heavy rain would soak through the plaster and soften the mud of such walls, and these houses needed constant repair after every wet season.

"The ground floor consisted of Agency offices, Post Office, and kitchen, and the living quarters were upstairs. A tall arched passageway made a cool dark corridor straight through the lower storey from the main gate on the road to the inner courtyard, and the walls here were permeated with damp. . . . The guest-room of the Agency was on the upper floor of a separate block which stood a few yards from the main house. A little wooden bridge ran across from the house to the verandah of the spare room, but when we arrived this verandah was lying in a heap on the ground, and access was impossible.

"We found a clever Persian builder, Usta Ahmad, who came to our rescue. Using coral rocks from the sea, he strengthened the foundations and built four buttresses in the front of the house.

"In the old days it had two curving stairways leading down to the road from the entrance to the upstairs living quarters, and these, with its green-painted woodwork, gave it a distinctive look, but in general style it blended in with the houses flanking it on either side along the sea-front.

"The house was built of traditional Arab materials, and the rooms, were narrow, as the width was limited by the standard length of the mangrove poles (imported from the Rufiji River in East Africa). It was Captain Shakespear's idea to make a drawing-room and a second bedroom upstairs, between the two existing rooms, but the area was too wide to roof over in their usual way. He consulted the Rev. and Mrs (Dr.) Calverley and Dr. C. S. G. Mylrea of the American Mission, who advised him to order an iron girder from England. If this were supported in the middle of the space to be roofed in, shorter beams would reach from it to the walls of the existing upstairs rooms on either side. But since mangrove poles were liable to be attacked by termites, which were plentiful in Kuwait in those days, they suggested using beams of teak, a timber which was imported for boat-building, and was available in Kuwait. So with the help of this advice and that of Kuwaiti and Persian builders the present central drawing room was completed. One strong wood pillar supported the girder on the south wall. Over the teak beams the roof was finished in the customary way, first with split bamboos laid criss-cross, and then with reed mats from Iraq. Over the reed matting was placed a layer of clay mixed with cut straw eighteen inches thick. The view from the underside is of teak beams supporting the diagonal pattern of red-stained bamboo against faded yellow matting. In other rooms I still have mangrove poles supporting the ceiling, an old Arab feature which gives me pleasure and causes much comment among visitors.

"The cold winters in Kuwait made a fireplace a necessity, and though such a thing was not normally found in Arab houses, the builders contrived to make a chimney against the east wall of the drawing room, with an open fireplace. . . .[15]

" Close parallels with the form and proportions of this house may be found in the former headquarters of British Political Residencies elsewhere in the Gulf which in turn were ultimately derived from the colonial verandah house of India. The fine details of construction, however, were carried out by local craftsmen who were well able to adapt their skills.

Extending inland from this concentration of large establishments were homes built on a more modest scale but observing the same principles; rooms planned around courtyards concealed within blank outer walls and public and private quarter, divided. In such homes, however, there were usually only one courtyard so that the women had to retreat into their rooms and close the doors when male guests were entertained, instead of circulating freely. The plan of rooms grouped around an open square or rectangular courtyard was adaptable and a well-preserved example of one of its many uses is seen in the famous Red Fort at Jahra. Of uncertain date this fort is a large rectangular structure[16] whose thick mud brick walls are flanked by a square tower at each corner (Plate 14), and are pierced by three gates—two large projecting ones on the north-west and north-east sides which lead into the military area and a small one on the north-west giving entry to the private courtyard of the Sheikh's residence (Plate 15). Within the main courtyard are grouped in orderly fashion the soldiers' barracks, officers' quarters, and stabling for horse and sheep. There is also a mosque

14 Jahra. Red Fort, entrance.

15 Jahra. Red Fort, interior, Sheikh's quarters.

which is both adjacent to the Sheikh's residence in the north-west corner and accessible to the main courtyard so that all the inhabitants could use it.

Mosques within the town were many as noted by European travellers and residents ranging from the congregational to the small local mosque. They were simple buildings where considerations of function took precedence over ornament (Plate 16). They were made of the same materials as used in houses and were planned with a columned prayer hall aligned in the direction of Mecca and opening on to an open court. Minarets were of modest dimensions either square or circular in shape rising above the outer wall which could be pierced by low windows, at one corner. Other public buildings were of a much more transient nature. The *suq* or market, for example, was a rambling arrangement of an open square with rows of shops and stalls roofed with at most matting or sacking supported on timber poles. Among them were coffee houses often consisting only of a row of benches in a lane between shops.

16 Kuwait City. Traditional mosque building.

17 Kuwait City. Safat Square *suq*.

18 Kuwait City. Small cafe in *suq*.

Precise figures for the population who occupied and used the buildings of Kuwait town and inhabited its hinterland of villages and desert are difficult to find, but enough information has been recorded from the late 19th to mid-20th centuries to reveal both a steady increase before the large immigration from the 1950s onwards, and a fascinating pattern of relationships between settled and nomad Arab. From an estimate of some 20,000 in 1863[17] the population had more than doubled to about 50,000 by 1904 according to Lorimer[18] who analysed his total into 35,000 permanent residents in Kuwait town, c.2000 in the neighbouring villages, and c.13,000 nomadic Bedu. This latter figure was naturally variable. Dickson writing of 1952[19] gives a steep increase to c.160,000 inhabitants of Kuwait town which again had almost doubled by 1953 to 250,000 as immigrants begin to arrive to supply the labour force required for construction projects. During this period the basic composition and proportion of the different groups forming the population changed very little. The majority were Arabs who were Sunni Muslims though a few were Wahhabis from Najd. They ranged in lifestyle from permanent inhabitants of the town and villages of Kuwait, through semi-nomadic communities who chose to camp near or live in the settlements in summer and migrate to the desert in winter and were a specific feature of the Kuwait region, to nomadic Bedu tent dwellers.

Considerable information is available about Kuwait's tribal groupings, revealing origins in Najd or north-east Arabia.[20] Prominent among the town's residents were the Utub and Anaiza who had migrated from Najd during the late 17th and early 18th centuries and included the ruling al-Sabah and other important merchant families among their members. Others who came at times into the town were the Ajman, a powerful tribe of north-east Arabia who owed allegiance to the al-Saud of Najd but married their daughters to the al-Sabah of Kuwait and the al-Khalifah of Bahrain thus contributing to the complex pattern of tribal alliances, the Duwasir from an area south of Riyadh in Najd, and the Bani Khalid who had traditionally dominated al-Hasa south of Kuwait. Yet other groups observed a more clearly defined migratory way of life, only coming into or near Kuwait at certain seasons, such as the Awazim from north-east Arabia and the Dhafir from Najd who camped outside Kuwait town. Important among them were the Mutair who ranged between Kuwait and Najd. They bred camels and horses and camped at grazing grounds near Jahra. A subgroup of the Mutair, the Rashaidah both maintained their traditional pastoral way of life and also served as retainers of the Sheikh of Kuwait. Arabs who did not graze animals were the Jana'at, a small colony of merchants and sailors who lived permanently in Kuwait town, and the Sulubba, best described as tinkers, as they dwelt in large sprawling settlements outside the town walls and mended pots and pans.

Intermingled with all these Sunni Arabs were communities of other religions and races.[21] There were Arabs of the Shi'a sect of Islam from Bahrain who were mainly involved in the boat-building trade, and from al-Hasa to the south. The most prominent Shi'a community, however, was of Persian origin which had grown from c.1000 in Lorimer's time to c.30,000 by the early 1950s. These Persians were town dwellers, scattered among their Arab neighbours and not grouped together in any specific quarter, who worked as merchants, shopkeepers in the *suq* and labourers. In the early 20th century there was a small Jewish community of merchants, cloth-sellers, and goldsmiths, and about 4000 negroes of slave origin of whom a considerable number had been emancipated.

Authority over all Kuwait's inhabitants, whether permanent resident or transient Bedu, was the responsibility of the Sheikh who followed a long-established system of direct personal rule.[22] He settled all civil and criminal disputes applying the principles of Islamic law, and gave audience for one or two hours each morning in Kuwait town's market place where individuals could present petitions. He was supported by a modest personal retinue of armed retainers, from which the town's watchmen were also recruited, and could draw on levies from the Bedu tribes. Little information is available about the revenue of either state or ruler but it would seem that he maintained his household and entourage by levying taxes on shops and the produce brought into Kuwait, and by investing in pearl fishing and trading enterprises.

3 The Economy

Kuwait's population took part in a remarkable diversity of economic activity which included food production although local resources were limited and had to be supplemented by imports. Agriculture, for example, was practised on a very modest scale, and here the oasis of Jahra with its dependable water supplies was vital.[1] A diversity of crops was cultivated of which the staple were cereals—wheat, barley and alfafa—which was either reaped in early spring and sent to Kuwait town after local needs had been satisfied, or cut when still "green" and used for animal fodder. Vegetables and fruit produce included pumpkins, beans, onions, leeks, radishes, aubergines, okra, tomatoes and melons, while clover and cress were grown for seasoning. Jahra also supported a vigorous growth of date palms. The villages of Fahaheel, Fintas, Shuaiba and Hawalli also cultivated cereals, onions, radishes, melons and dates.[2] All these agricultural products could be bartered with the Bedu for meat, butter and milk products. The other obvious local source of food was the sea, which was extensively fished. Nets were cast after sunset and hauled in three times during the night. A characteristic sight along Kuwait bay was the lines of reed stakes extending into the sea into which fish would swim at high tide only to be stranded and trapped at low tide. Many species of fish including the *naqrur* and *nawaibi* usually one to two feet in length were caught during a short spring season of March to April, and the large succulent prawn for which all the Gulf coast was famous.

The sea and the excellent natural harbour were Kuwait's most important and reliable economic resources and gave rise to three major activities—boat-building, pearl fishing and trade. Kuwait's boats were indeed famous throughout the Gulf and in much demand for the quality of their workmanship and the range of types built (Plate 20). The yards were located on beaches near deep water so that the finished boats could be easily launched. They were built of teak wood imported from India by teams of skilled carpenters who were mainly Shi'a Arab immigrants from Bahrain, which also had long been established as a centre of boat-building. The vessels were of long graceful streamlined shape and constructed according to well-tried methods. The hull had a foundation of curved vertically placed

19 Kuwait City, Arabian Gulf Street. Reed stakes for catching fish.

20 Kuwait City, Arabian Gulf Street. Al-Muhalab, *boom* erected in the courtyard of the National Museum of Kuwait.

21 Dhowyard at Doha. Drilling holes in planks.

ribs to which horizontally aligned planks were nailed (Plate 21). They were fitted with decks, hatchways, ports and two masts. Coats of sharks' oil were applied to both exterior and interior surfaces to prevent the timbers from splitting and warping. Sails were of a high-peaked triangular shape and made locally from lengths of thick cotton canvas pegged out on the ground and cut and sewn to shape.

Dhow is the term most commonly used to describe the type of ship traditionally plying the Gulf but it does not account for the many types which were built for specific purposes. In the Kuwait yards alone, for example, ten types of ship were still being built at the beginning of the 20th century. There was the *baghla*—a large vessel suitable for deep-sea trading voyages able to carry from 80 to 300 tons of cargo and manned by a crew of 20 to 50 sailors. It had three hatchways and also carried life-boats. The *ghuncha* was a smaller version of the *baghla* with only two hatchways, a cargo capacity of 20 to 80 tons and a crew of 15 to 20 men. The *batil* again was a small vessel with a long overhanging bow and steered by a rudder. It was used for both trading and pearl fishing carrying 15 to 60 tons of cargo and a crew of 10 to 30. Yet another small cargo boat was the *sanbuk* very similar to the *ghuncha* but to be distinguished by its plain undecorated stem head. Probably the most familiar and frequently used craft was the *boom* which could vary in length from 40 to 80 feet, had a pointed stern and long bow, and was steered with a rudder and wheel. It was chiefly used for cargo carrying 20 to 200 tons with a crew of 15 to 40 men but could also be used for pearl fishing. Unique to Kuwait was the *dangi*, a cargo boat like the *boom* but with a beaked stem-head. The remaining four vessels were of smaller size. The *shu'ai* was a small *sanbuk* of about 4.5 to 6 metres in length propelled by oars and sails with a crew of 6 to 10 men and was mainly used in fishing. The *mushuwa* ranging from 6 to 12 metres had a square stern and plenty of deck space, and was steered with a rudder and wheel. It carried a crew of 6 to 12 men and was used either for cargo or fishing. The *badan* was 3 to 6 metres long with only one mast and was propelled by oars or sails. It had only a small crew of 4 to 8 men and was used for cargo and fishing. The last type of vessel, the *jali*, was a small square-sterned craft of 6 to 9 metres often with a half-deck, manned by a crew of 4 to 6 and used for passenger transport.

The pearl fishing industry involved a large number of Kuwait's urban population at various levels as it was labour intensive; in 1904 for example the fleet of 461 boats supplied work for 9200 men. It was also extremely profitable and in many cases a family's only source of income, so despite the dangers and harshness of a pearl diver's life there was never any shortage of recruits. The industry was collectively known locally as *ghaus*, which simply means "diving", and was seasonal. There were two seasons—*ghaus al-kabir*—the "great diving" from mid-May to mid-September, and the *radda*—or "return" lasting only from late September to October. The winter season—*mujanna*—was reserved for shore operations and wading in shallow waters which, only yielded small pearls of low quality. From 1889 onwards, therefore, this winter season was filled with long voyages to the pearl banks of Ceylon. Pearl fishing was organised in independent units in which a captain either financed and controlled the expedition using his own ship or sailed on behalf of merchants who had invested capital. The ships used for pearling were the *batil, sanbuk, boom* and *shu'ai*. A pearling expedition was organised along the following lines. The ship's captain (*nakhuda*), would put together the required capital from his own resources if he were the owner, often supplemented by a loan from a financier—a *musaqqam*—who specialised in investments in the pearl industry. The captain then recruited his crew in number depending on the size of his ship and his financial investment. Crew members consisted of *ghais* (divers)—a mixed collection of poorer Arabs, Persians, Baluchis and negroes, who divided and searched for oysters, *siyub* (haulers) who as their name implied were responsible for letting divers up and down from the sea bed and who were themselves often retired divers, *radhafa* (labourers) who assisted the haulers, and occasionally a *walad* (apprentice) whose duties included cooking and coffee making.

The daily routine on a pearling ship was arduous beginning in fine weather an hour after sunrise and ending an hour before sunset, breaking only at about 1.30 to 2.00pm for the noon prayers and a rest. Rations were frugal—coffee and dates in the morning, coffee only at noon, and fish, rice and dates in the evening. The diver prepared himself for work by stripping off his clothes, placing a pair of small horn pincers (*fatam*) over his nostrils, plugging his ears with cotton wool or bees' wax, covering his fingers with protective leather finger-stalls (*khabat*), and hanging a small matting bag (*diyin*) around his neck to contain his catch. Two ropes were attached to him (*zaibal*) one with a stone weight above a loop through which he slipped a foot, the other (*ida*) fixed at his waist. On diving he released his foot from the *zaibal*, which one of the haulers would then pull up, and would grope along the bottom of the pearl bank collecting oysters. When he could no longer continue he would jerk the *ida* to signal that he was to be pulled up to the surface. A diver could remain below the water for 40 to 75 seconds, during which he might collect from 3 to 20 oysters. In good weather he made up to 50 dives a day, but only 10 to 20 if it was cold. The day's catch was opened up the following day before diving started again under the supervision of the captain who would weigh and register the pearls. A diver did not receive a salary for his labour but only a share of the money raised from the sale of the pearls. As he had already mortgaged a percentage of this by borrowing money from the captain to support his family during the pearling season he was under pressure to dive as many times as his strength would permit.

Kuwait, together with Bahrain and Qatar, was a major centre of Gulf trade, engaging not only in its own merchant voyages but also acting as transit point for goods en route for Najd, Basra and Aleppo. Kuwait, apart from the enterprise and initiative of her merchant fleet, had one outstanding advantage—an excellent harbour which not only allowed participation in sea trade of the Gulf and places further afield, but was so located that it was an important stage on the caravan desert route inland. The sea trade involved stopping at Basra, Bahrain and Muscat to pick up goods which in turn may have been imported, and also to offload merchandise, which resulted in quite a complicated system of exchange. From the 18th century onwards with the development of large vessels such as the *baghla* and *boom* which had the cargo and crew capacities to make long deep-sea voyages worthwhile, Kuwaiti merchants ventured direct to the coasts of India and Africa where they could acquire their goods without the need of middlemen. Parallel with these highly profitable sea trading enterprises Kuwait organised inland caravan voyages to Basra, Baghdad and Aleppo via the desert route. The assembling of a caravan involved considerable organisation and the participation of skilled personnel. Camels, mules and donkeys had to be hired to transport both merchants and their goods. Negotiations with local sheikhs had to be conducted to arrange for the hire of the animals, guards and payment of duties to Bedu tribal leaders en route for safe conduct. The journey from Kuwait or Basra to Aleppo could take from about 30 to 70 days depending on whether a stop was made at Baghdad and on the size of the caravan. This varied according to the nature of the business and whether other caravans joined en route: a large caravan could include from 2000 to 5000 camels.

The Gulf sea trade was of great importance during the late 18th and 19th century and even after the opening of the Suez canal in 1868 both for local commerce and for the British in the transport of mail, personnel and goods to and from India. There is consequently a considerable amount of information recorded in 19th century British sources from which it is clear that Kuwait in particular enjoyed a lively diverse trade. Captain George Barnes Brucks records in 1829 that Kuwait traded with Najd in wheat, coffee and goods brought from India.[3] Kuwait's imports both supplied this market and supplemented her own limited food resources as they included cloth, rice, sugar, wood, spices and coffee from Yemen, tobacco and dried fruit from Persia, wheat and dates from Basra, and cloth, dates and fish from Bahrain. As exports Kuwait traded pearls to local markets and also horses which had been obtained from neighbouring Bedu tribes.

Lieutenant Felix Jones who visited Kuwait's harbour in 1839 supplied further details on imports especially foodstuffs. Dates, citrus fruits, pomegranates, watermelons and lentils were imported from Basra and Bushire, while wheat, barley and rice came from India. Bedu neighbours continued to supply livestock—cattle and poultry. He also records that teak for shipbuilding was brought from Bombay. Colonel John Pelly, British Resident in the Gulf, wrote between 1863 and 1865 three detailed reports which apart from cataloguing goods, give interesting information on the organisation of the trade stressing the shift in Kuwait's interests from local to Indian commerce. Small boats would bring produce from northern Gulf ports to Kuwait's harbour to be loaded on to the larger ships voyaging to Bombay which on their return journey would bring Indian goods to be distributed around the Gulf. The principal imports from India were teak wood, cloth, rice and spices. By the early 20th century according to Lorimer's notes and figures for 1905 to 1906 it was clear that modern steamers had been added to Kuwait's traditional sailing fleet and that a complicated network of import and redistribution of goods existed. Certain transactions seemed relatively simple; rice for example was simply imported from Iraq and India, barley from Iraq and Persia, and sugar mainly from Germany and also from India. Dates, however, were imported from Iraq and re-exported to Persia and other parts of the Arabian Gulf, wheat came from Persia and much was sent to Iraq and the Gulf coast, while coffee was brought from India to be consumed in Kuwait and Najd. Lorimer's analysis of the ratios of Kuwait's sea trade reveals that approximately a third each was with India and Iraq, leaving a little less than a third to be divided between Persia and Britain. A general view of Kuwait's commerce as monitored during the 18th to 20th centuries reveals as its basic characteristics a steady consistency in the nature of its merchandise and a readiness to investigate new sources which could both supply home markets and be exploited in the intricacies of the transit trade.

4 Traditional social and cultural patterns in Kuwait's town and desert

a) Everyday life in urban society

Economic activity also included a lively service industry which was well-developed by the beginning of the 20th century as related in Lorimer's fascinating account:—

"The other occupations and industries of the town are directed to the satisfaction of local requirements: an enumeration of them as they were in 1904 will help to elucidate the character of Kuwait. There were then 36 dealers in piece goods, 21 goldsmiths, 11 blacksmiths, 12 tinsmiths, 7 gunsmiths, 11 lamp makers, 132 dealers in Bedouin requisites (such as carpets, cheap 'Abas or cloaks, nails, horse shoes, lead and shot), 13 leather workers, 17 quilt makers, 23 haberdashers, 21 tailors, 37 cloak embroiderers, 7 gold and silver braid workers, 12 makers of Aqals or Arab head fillets, 13 barbers, 11 confectioners, 8 bakers, 3 professional cooks, 11 fishmongers, 36 butchers, 14 tobacconists, 9 ghi sellers, 32 date merchants, 16 druggists, 28 fruiterers, 24 rice merchants, 15 wheat dealers, 2 oil pressers, 147 grocers and druggists, 9 grass sellers and, lastly, 35 male and 32 female brokers of private goods on commission who had fixed places of business. There were at the same time 12 tea shops, 7 cafes, 70 business offices, 250 warehouses for the storage of grain, and 6 stores for the materials used in pressing oil."[1]

Apart from its statistics, the real interest of Lorimer's list is that it is a summary of a complex structured way of life in which both town Kuwaiti and Bedu shared. This way of life can be interpreted from contemporary written and oral sources, and certain traditions which have survived today. Together they reveal how Kuwait's population spent its time when not engaged in public business, how the products of its trade were used, and that it is impractical and misleading to separate town dweller from nomad as they were mutually dependent and in many cases shared and were conscious of a common family background.

Common to all sectors of Kuwait's society in the broadest sense was a routine of life established within the framework of the Moslem religion and its year based on a lunar calendar whose major festivals therefore rotated through the climatic seasons. The basic tenets were the five traditional pillars of Islam—belief in Allah and Muhammad as his prophet, prayer, fasting during the month of Ramadhan, charity which may be interpreted as ranging from kindness and hospitality to neighbours and guests to large scale donations of funds for the building of mosques, and pilgrimage to the holy cities of Mecca and Medina. The majority of people, apart from the small communities of Persians and Arabs from Bahrain and al-Hasa who were of the Shi'a persuasion, were Sunni Moslems influenced in varying degrees by the puritanical Wahhabi doctrines of Najd which emphasised strict adherence to the teachings of the Qur'an and frowned upon excess of outward display and emotion. Places of worship in Kuwait town were mosques of simple and modest plan, while in the Bedu encampments a line with a semicircular indentation to indicate the direction of Mecca was scored in the ground to indicate the location of a communal prayer area. Five prayers divided the day into manageable units at times which were practical and sensible in a climate where extremes of heat could be intolerable, and also in the days before electricity where people had to rise and retire according to the duration of natural light. The prayers were *al-fajr*—the dawn prayer just before or at sunrise, *al-zuhr*—the noon prayer at about 12pm before the midday meal, *al-'asr*—the afternoon prayer between 3 and 4pm, *al-maghrib*—the sunset prayer, just before or at sunset, and *al-'asha*—the evening prayer, before going to bed. While all these prayers could be said anywhere it was generally the practice for men to go to the mosque for the noon and sunset prayers, especialy for the noon prayer on Friday, the weekly religious holiday. Women normally prayed at home, rarely going to the mosque, except on special occasions such as Ramadhan where they sat in a part reserved for them.

Within a day urban and Bedu communities led broadly comparable lives divided between business and domestic activities. In Kuwait town there were graduated degrees of affluence ranging from the wealthy households of the merchant families located along the sea front to the small homes further inland whose occupants could be semi-nomadic, moving to the desert as they wished. In all households, however, the fundamental social unit was the extended family with its strong web of obligations and responsibilities which could encompass the owner, his wife and children, grandparents, various associated womenfolk including divorced or widowed relatives, visiting relatives, and about six or seven male and female servants who were often black Africans. Households were planned to accommodate the traditional division of men and women into separate quarters which were furnished and equipped according to the owner's taste and means and the stock available in the Kuwait *suq*, which could also be supplemented by items brought directly from abroad if the family had merchant trading interests.

The men's courtyard—*diwaniya*—functioned as the public area where business colleagues and male guests were received and entertained. Here the main doors were left open to the sea front during the day and early evening indicating that callers were welcome, and led to a corridor lined with benches where they could wait. The main reception room—*diwan*—opened on to the courtyard and was comfortably furnished with cushions which could be grouped around the walls as seats and arm-rests. The floor was covered with knotted wool pile carpets and flat-woven kilims imported from Persia, of which a wide and plentiful selection was and still is available in the *suq*. Essential furnishing for the *diwan* included equipment for the preparation of the cardamon-flavoured coffee which was served to guests. This was brewed on a low rectangular brazier at the far end of the *diwan* or in a small adjacent room either by the host himself or by a specially appointed servant. A coffee set consisted of four gleaming brass pots (*dallal*) with lids and long beaked spouts (Plate 22), in graduated sizes, and a large selection of utensils. As coffee was freshly ground for every serving, there was a spoon-like long-handled metal pan—*mahmasa*—for roasting the beans, which were turned over and stirred with a narrow spatula (*yed al-mahmasa*) and then put into a shallow slipper-shaped wooden container (*mubarrad*) for cooling. The roasted beans were then pulverised in a cylindrical brass pestle and mortar (*hawan*), and infused with water in one of the pots, from which it was poured into small cups (*finajil*) which were often of imported Chinese or European porcelain.

At the back of the *diwaniya* there was an entrance to the women's courtyard (*harim*) as it functioned as the private living quarters for all the family. The *harim* also had a separate entrance so that the women and their friends

22 Kuwait City, Arabian Gulf Street. Bayt al-Badr, brass coffee pots on display.

23 Kuwait City, Arabian Gulf Street. Bayt al-Badr, wooden storage chest—*sanduq*.

could come and go discreetly. Several of the rooms which opened on to the courtyard primarily served as bedrooms often with separate washing facilities. In the grandest homes the focal point was the large curtained Indian four-poster bed, otherwise the furnishings were simple and flexible enabling the room to be turned into a sitting and reception area. Woven mats of straw and palmleaves covered the floors, while mattresses and quilts could be arranged and folded in the day to provided floor-level seating, supplemented with hard cushions for arm-rests as in the men's *diwan*. Traditionally another prized item of furnither was the large rectangular wooden chest (*sanduq*) (Plate 23) which had elaborate brass fittings and was imported from India. Such chests were given to a woman at marriage for storage of the clothes and textiles of her dowry. They were beginning to go out of local use by the 1930s as Violet Dickson records their apearance in the Kuwait *suq*:—

"Amongst other treasures we bought there were four fine examples of the India-made brass-bound dowry chests, now known as 'Kuwaiti chests' because they were originally made only for the Kuwait market. We paid about rupees 75 each for the larger ones. As the years passed and all available examples were bought up by the English and Americans it became harder to find one for sale and prices rose accordingly."[2]

Large baskets and tin trunks provided additional storage. While the women normally entertained friends in the courtyard or their own apartments, there were also a reception room which was more luxuriously furnished with coffee making equipment as in the men's *diwan*, and wall niches to contain imported glass lamps, rose water sprinklers—*marash*, and personal ornaments. The roof was also used in the *harim* courtyard, as in the hot weather bedding was taken up and the family slept screened from public view by a concealing parapet. The kitchen yard was located between the *diwaniya* and *harim* courtyards so that both sections could be easily supplied with food.

A family's day began early with the dawn prayer after which the husband would take breakfast with his wife and children in the *harim.* After this their ways diverged, the husband departing for the day's business, returning to the *harim* after the noon prayer for family lunch and siesta and then leaving again during the late afternoon. The women meanwhile spent their time supervising or carrying out domestic tasks according to their means and the number of servants available. The first task was to organise the sweeping of the courtyards and rooms, and shaking of mats and airing of bedding. Then the day's food was planned and in rich households a servant dispatched to the *suq* for shopping. Cooking occupied the rest of the morning, taking a long time in the absence of labour-saving devices; rice for example had to be picked over and cleaned several times, bread had to be baked fresh for every meal. All these processes were treated as sociable activities which the women did in groups, interrupted by breaks for drinking glasses of sweet tea which they shared with neighbours who dropped in for a visit. At this time a household's drinking water would be delivered either by boys bringing goatskins loaded on to donkeys or by men with tin cans suspended from yokes balanced across their shoulders. Water was a constant problem in Kuwait town as local supplies and the wells of Jahra were not sufficient for everybody's needs. Wealthy households had a well in the kitchen yard which was used for ablutions and dish-washing, but had to rely for drinking water on the supplies brought in by ship from Iraq. Women from poorer houses had a more varied domestic routine as they spent less time indoors. They did their own shopping in the *suq*, washed their laundry on the beach, and collected the family's drinking water direct from the supply ships carrying it home in large tins balanced on their heads. Parallel with all these activities a family's young children, both boys and girls, played freely together in the *harim* courtyard or in the street. Boys from the age of about six or seven attended a local school where they studied and memorised the Qur'an, but girls when they reached the age of puberty at about twelve to thirteen were segregated in the *harim* with the older women. After lunch and siesta men and women again separated until the eveninig meal, which the men often took in the *diwaniya* with their friends. Shortly after the last prayer of the day the family retired to bed.

This survey of daily life reveals that there was little time available for organised entertainment, but as a clear demarcation between work and leisure was not identified as such, it is arguable that there was little place for it. Normal social life was interwoven with homebased activities both in the *diwaniya* and *harim*; for example men would be offered coffee and refreshments while discussing business affairs, and women would assemble to share domestic tasks, tea and gossip. As much of this life revolved around the preparation and serving of food and drink it is both interesting and possible fromthe sources available to analyse the eating habits and menus of a range of families. Local sources of food were meagre—cereals, dates, vegetables and fruit such as pumpkins, beans, onions, leeks, radishes, aubergines, okra, tomatoes and melons mainly from the oasis of Jahra—and had to be supplemented by imports such as rice, cereals and pulses and tea from India, dates and fruits from Basra and Bushire, coffee from Yemen and later from Brazil. While some households had their own goats to provide milk, dairy products and proteins—milk, butter, cooking oil, lamb and camel meat, and poultry—were usually obtained from Bedu communities. Kuwait's waters could not guarantee consistently reliable supplies of fish which had to be supplemented by imports from Bahrain. A glance at Lorimer's figures for the number of food retailers in Kuwait in 1904 produces some ratios which can be directly related to the population's eating habits.[3] There were, for example, 15 wheat dealers and 250 warehouses for grain storage clearly showing the dependence on imports, but only 8 bakers which suggests that most bread was baked at home. The 32 date merchants, 28 greengrocers, and 24 rice merchants confirm the other stable foods, while the proportion of 36 butchers to only 11 fishmongers perhaps means that many families obtained their fish direct from the fishermen at the sea front or were themselves engaged in fishing.

Within this fairly restricted range of ingredients, menus tended to be somewhat repetitive, and in poor families limited to bread, rice and dates with some vegetables and occasional servings of fish. Breakfast at all levels was simple, consisting of bread and dates with coffee for those who could afford it. Bread was prepared in fresh batches daily by kneading and rolling unleavened dough into rounds which were shaped around the sides of a circular clay oven to produce crispy tasty flat loaves. The midday meal was the principal one of the day based on a communal dish of rice and meat served on a circular palmleaf mat around which the family sat and helped themselves. It was at this meal that the poorer families would have fish.

In wealthy households the midday meal could be extremely elaborate when guests were entertained. Here the dishes showed the influence of the sophisticated cuisines of Kuwait's neighbours—Persia on the opposite side of the Gulf and Iraq to the north, where Ottoman Turkish food traditions had penetrated—whose recipes made ingenious use of available ingredients. The main rice dish, for example, could be flavoured with raisins, finely shredded strips of fried onion, spices and sometimes pomegranate seeds, inspired by the sweet rice *pilaus* of Persian cooking. If lamb was the accompanying meat, it was rendered more succulent and tempting by slow roasting in an oven or by sauteing in clarified butter after long simmering. A selection of tasty side dishes was also served such as *maraq*, a stew of meat, aubergines and okra in a tomato sauce a basic recipe popular throughout the Middle East, and skewered *kababs* of grilled minced meat mixed with rice and seasoning. Stuffed vegetable dishes showed the influence of Ottoman Turkey—such as *dolma*—the classic preparation of vine leaves enfolding a mixture of minced meat, rice and onion, and courgettes filled with minced meat, nuts and rice. A smooth-textured Turkish pudding, *muhallabi*, of ground rice cooked with sugar and milk flavoured with cardamom, chopped nuts and sometimes coloured yellow with saffron was also served. The meal was completed with dishes of dates, bowls of *leben* (diluted yoghurt), fruit and bread. Adaptations of such lavish meals could also be prepared for the men of the family to serve to their male guests at evening meals in the *diwaniya*, and for special occasions such as circumcisions and weddings. Coffee was always served at the beginning and end of such meals, and was also the main refreshment provided as normal hospitality in both *diwaniya* and *harim*. Here after several cups of coffee had been drunk and conversation finished, the visit was brought to an end by an agreeable ritual of sprinkling the guests' hands with rosewater, and passing an incense burner (*mabkhar*) containing *bokhur* (frankincense) among them so that they could perfume their clothes and depart refreshed. In poorer households where the men had no separate *diwaniya* they had to sit with their friends in the street outside or in the town's coffeeshops.

Apart from home-centred entertainment, social diversions were few. Neighbourhoods were from time to time enlivened by the attractive custom of parading a boy dressed in his best clothes through the streets when he had completed his study of the Qur'an. Both men and women also enjoyed excursions. "It used to be the custom in Kuwait for well-to-do men to own secluded walled gardens (hauta) on the outskirts of town, where they would go of an evening to meet their men friends, enjoying the open air away from the dust and noise of the built-up area. A few sidr trees had been coaxed to grow in such places, since vegetation with its association of coolness and shade has always been attractive to the Arab, and even a scattering of stunted shrubs was enough to enhance such evening retreats."[4] Women, however, had fewer opportunities for excursions for if they were rich they rarely left their homes but they did enjoy infrequent visits to female relatives, and during the springtime went on day picnics to the desert.

b) Everyday life in Bedu society

Such excursions are revealing of the close relationship which persisted between settled town dweller and Bedu nomad, and the resulting points of contact in their lives. Many town Kuwaitis were conscious of their Bedu tribal origins and would express this by going with their families to camp in the desert during springtime. Occupants of the more modest homes at the outskirts of the town were often semi-nomadic and would depart for long periods of migration. On a day to day economic level both types of community were mutually dependent. The town relied on the herds of the Bedu for supplies of meat and dairy products (Plate 24), while the Bedu needed the town for food and equipment which they could not produce for themselves. This mutual dependence was so important that the Bedu devoted a period of their year to the *musabila*, or movement to the town for marketing, and Kuwait town according to Lorimer catered to their needs by providing "132 dealers in Bedouin requisites (such as carpets, cheap 'Abas or cloaks, nails, horse shoes, lead and shot)."[1] Each Bedu tribe had its own special town for its *musabila* chosen for convenience of location along its migration route and for a plentiful selection of goods. Kuwait town was patronised by the Mutair, Awazim, Northern Ajman, Harb and Shammar tribes, who would camp outside around Jahra and Fahaheel.

24 Kuwait. Friday market, sheep for sale.

Bedu tribal life was of necessity highly specialised and organised around the annual cycle of migration in search of grazing and water for their livestock of camels, sheep and goats. They were on the move throughout autumn, winter and spring from the arrival of the first rains in October until about May when they began to converge on their summer camping grounds near wells and for the *musabila.* Migration was certainly not improvised and haphazard, as each tribal group had its *dira* or territory where it had rights to the grazing and wells. The *dira* of the Mutair tribe, for example, was roughly 22,000 square miles in area and ran parallel with Kuwait's southern boundary on the north before looping south and west over territory which included the Dahana sands. A tribe, however, could not always stay in its own *dira.* If rains had failed, it was often necessary to migrate further afield, crossing into the *dira* of neighbouring tribes which therefore involved the establishment of alliances. Such negotiations often fell within the responsibilities of the tribal sheikhs who were chosen from the members of their family not necessarily according to patrilineal succession but for their qualities of leadership, courage and standards of hospitality. Their authority was not absolute as they were expected to discuss important matters with the older men of the tribe before a decision was reached, especially concerning intertribal relationships, the right time for migration etc. They and their wives were also expected to provide social services for poorer members of the tribe by feeding them lavish feasts held to celebrate the arrival of important guests, weddings, religious festivals, and by sending them presents of clothing.

At times of migration the tribe would move in extensive groups made up of individual families living in the distinctive black tents (Plate 25). As in urban life the extended family was the most important social unit and mutual respect and honour among its members were scrupulously valued. While the tent could not accommodate the range of generations that might occupy the courtyard of a spacious town house it could include besides the owner, his wife and children, certain unmarried female relatives and dependents. The family lived in a long low tent (*bayt al-sha'ar*) made of lengths of coarse black or dark brown cloth known as *filjan* supported on wooden poles (*amdan*), and kept taut by suspension ropes (*atnab*). The size of a tent

25 Kuwait. Example of a traditional Bedu tent—*bayt al-sha'ar*.

naturally varied according to both function and the means of the owner. Wealthy tribal sheikhs and the rulers of Kuwait, Bahrain and Qatar would once have used enormous tents as base camps for spring hunting expeditions. Tents used as permanent living quarters were of more practical sizes ranging between lengths of 21 and 7 metres and supported respectively on 3-4 and 2 sets of poles. The *filjan* were woven of goat's hair or sheep's wool. Black goat's hair produced the best quality fabric but a mixture of goat's hair and sheep's wool was also satisfactory. Much of this fabric was woven in towns and villages such as Kuwait town and Jahra and was bought by women who could afford it. Poorer women, both wove and repaired their own *filjan*. Four to six strips were sewn together depending on the volume of the tent and were strengthened by stitching bands of webbing (*tara'ij*) at the points which would support the poles. Wooden loops (*artab*) to take the ropes (*atnab*) were then attached. Two long curtains known as *ruag* were then anchored to the *filjan* by wooden bodkins (*khilla*) suspended vertically to form the back and sides of the tent and pegged to the ground at their lower end. They were again made of 4 woven strips sewn together horizontally—alternating bands of black and white being a favourite combination—and joined vertically at the centre back. Surplus cloth was rolled back at the sides of the tent's entrance during the day and was pulled close at night. During hot weather the *ruag* could be rolled up to increase ventilation. The most decorative part of the tent's structure is the *qata*, another handwoven curtain made of four lengths patterned with bold colourful designs sewn together. It is attached to the roof of the tent and divides the interior from back to front separating the men's and women's quarters. During the migration seasons a camp moved on about once every ten days for short distances thus progressing slowly through the grazing. Through long practice the tent could be rapidly dismantled and erected. Women did this under the supervision of the men who set the pace. The erection of a tent was a streamlined process in which the poles, *filjan*, and ropes were laid out in order on the ground. The ropes were tied to the *filjan* which was then pushed up on the poles. Again the ropes were stretched and secured to pegs in the ground,while the *ruag* and *qata* were pinned into place. For additional warmth and security during winter a barrier of brushwoodd could be built around the front of the tent.

Within the tent the division between the men's section (*raba'a*) and the women's section (*muharram*) was as carefully maintained in principle as that between the *diwaniya* and *harim* of the town house. Women were expected to behave modestly and segregate themselves from men who were not relatives. They were usually aware of what was going on, however, as they were only separated from the men's section by the *qata*. The *raba'a* which was located on the left side of the tent as approached from the open front was furnished and arranged as a public area for the reception of guests. The ground was carpeted with home-woven strips (*busat*) or Persian carpets if the owner was affluent. Mattresses (*dawashak*) were set in an L-shape against the *ruag* and *qata* and furnished with cushions (*masanad*). The owner's camel saddle (*shadad*) was put into use as extra seating by stacking cushions on each side of it. Once the furnishings had been arranged the owner then dug a hearth for the preparation of coffee near the entrance, and set up an array of coffee pots and utensils, comparable to those used in the town. An additional item, however, was a *shat finajil*, a cylindrical brass container for carrying coffee cups. His personal possessions—camel stick, rifle, clothing—were hung on hooks driven into the tent poles.

The *muharram* on the right of the tent was equally compactly and efficiently arranged. Heavy sacks (*'adul*) containing stores of rice, flour, sugar and dates were stacked up against the *qata* and covered with red cotton quilts (*lahaf*) which functioned both as bedding and seating. Saddle bags (*mizawal*) filled with clothes, spindles and supplies of wool were suspended fromthe tent poles. Each woman also had a box containing coffee, and spices which she kept locked. The cooking hearth with its array of pots and pans was located at the extreme left of the *muharram.* Other essential furnishings included children's hammocks (*hababa*) and cradles (*mizba*) which were placed between storage and cooking areas, and the horizontal loom (*nattu*). Grouped at the back of the tent were the distinctive litters (*maksar*) in which the women sat as they travelled on camelback from one camp to another. Shapes and decoration varied throughout Arabia but the Mutair of the Kuwait hinterland, for example, used a *maksar* constructed of a high looped wooden frame supporting woven hangings which concealed the woman from view. Outside the *muharram* were placed leather water skins and buckets, and also the tripod—*mirjaha*—on which the skin containing *leben* is slung and shaken.

As in the town a Bedu family's day began early with the dawn prayer after which men and women pursued separate tasks. The women immediately began work on food preparation by rocking milk in the skin suspended from the *mirjaha* to make the days' supply of *leben.* They also made coffee and tea for the shepherds and camelherds and gave them enough dates for breakfast and midday rations. The men wre busy taking lambs from the tent where they were kept at night to their mothers for feeding and then returning them. They then checked the sheep and camels and set off to graze them. Sheep were usually grazed at a distance of about two miles from the tents while camels had to be taken about five to eight miles further afield. After the men had departed the women had their own breakfast of tea and dates before continuing domestic chores. Bedding had to be shaken and aired and the cooking pots used in the previous day's evening meal cleaned. The children who played about in the area of the tent did not escape their share of work, as girls were sent off equipped with small chopping axes and hanks of goathair rope to gather brushwood for fuel. They usually returned after about two hours balancing bundles of brushwood on their heads. If there was a spare shepherd available he would be sent off with some camels loaded with skin containers in search of water. The midday meal, which was only taken if the family was reasonably prosperous, was frugal consisting o rice lubricated with clarified sheep's butter. After the lunch dishes were cleaned, the women settled to an afternoon of weaving. Here there was always work—a new *qata* to be woven, worn patches in the tent to be re-woven. Weaving was also a source of family income as a woman could sell any of the attractively patterned *qata* and *masanad* in the town during the *musabila*. Following a short late afternoon break of strolling and playing with the children the women filled a large leather trough (*haudh*) with wate for the returning sheep to drink; camels, who did not require water daily, were watered at wells along the migration routes. By sunset the men had returned and settled the animals for the night. An evening meal was prepared of boiled rice, bread, *leben* and coffee which was served to the men separately and shortly after the family slept.

This austere routine was repetitive and offered little opportunity for leisure and entertainment other than that provided by the company of tent neighbours during the day's activities. Occasionally Bedu from other tribes would pass by and would be given coffee and food in the men's quarters. More lavish hospitality was available when a sheikh offered a celebratory midday or evening meal, but as food resources were so limited this was based on a large communal tray of a whole boiled lamb or sheep served on a bed of oily rice, and bowls of *leben* and dates. Hunting for gazelle and *hubara*—bustard—occupied the men seasonally, but for women social activity concentrated on visits to each other especially during the afternoons of weaving. These were not idle occasions as weaving was very rightly considered to be work and not a leisurely hobby, and visitors would bring spinning with them or assist their hostess in her weaving. The craft of weaving (*sadu*) has had a long history in the Middle East where it was valued for the versatility, practicality and visual attractiveness of its products. In Bedu tribal society weaving was the speciality of the women who made comfortable furnishings for tents, storage bags, and animal trappings, all portable colourful objects which suited their nomadic way of life and enlivened their desert surroundings. Weaving also provided a source of income as pieces surplus to the family's requirements could be sold in market towns along the migration routes (Plate 26).

26 Kuwait. Friday market, Bedu weaving for sale.

Bedu women learnt the craft early as young girls watching their mothers at work and helping with the more simple tasks such as winding wool. They also absorbed the repertoire of design motifs characteristic of their tribe, which did not remain static as new patterns were learnt from neighbouring groups. All the materials and equipment were local. Goat and camel hair and sheep's wool was spun into yarn. Colours ranged through natural black, browns, greys, creams and white to reds, oranges and sometimes a dark blue and green which traditionally were produced by using plant and root dyes, though from the early 20th century onwards artificial dyes purchased in the market towns increasingly began to be used. Spinning and weaving tools were simple and portable so that work could be quickly set in motion (Plate 27). In spinning the raw wool was wrapped around a distaff stick (*taghzala*) which the woman held under her right arm. She then teased a strand of wool out and fastened the end to the head of the spindle (*maghzal*). By continuously twirling she produced a twisted thread which was wrapped around the spindle (Plate 28). Woman and girls were always busy at this work, in spare moments in the camp between cooking and cleaning, and on camel back during the migration.

27 Bedu spinning equipment. Carding combs, distaff and spindle (Royal Scottish Museum Edinburgh 1958.151 & A; 152; 153).

28 Kuwait City, Arabian Gulf Street. Bayt Sadu, Bedu woman spinning.

The loom (*nattu*) was an equally simple and portable device consisting of four sticks (Plate 29) which when threaded up with a piece of work in progress could be quickly staked out on the ground beside a tent and folded up again when the time came to move. When a new piece of work was begun the parts of the loom and materials were assembled in a certain order. Two short narrow sticks, *ras* and *ga'ah*, were first placed on pegs in the ground parallel to each other and at a distance apart which depended on the required length of the finished article. These functioned as warp beams around which the coarsely plied wool was wrapped to produce a double thickness of parallel warps. Another device was then inserted into the loom fabric which functioned as a shed, enabling alternate warps to be raised and depressed in sequence as the rows of horizontal weft thread were pushed forward and back. The shed was made of a wooden rod (*minyar*) supported at each end on a wooden block or stone (*marakib*), to which alternate warps were tied with short wool loops. Another wooden rod had to be inserted behind it to raise the other set of warps for every second row of weaving. The shed was moved down the loom as work progressed. The wool selected for the weft was then wrapped around a long wooden shuttle (*misha*), which was pushed through the warps creating a fabric lattice. After each row of weaving a flat wooden stick (*mishizza*) was inserted to tighten up the fabric by pushing the wefts closer together. Another small tool, traditionally a gazelle horn, (*middra*) was used to pluck and neaten the threads.

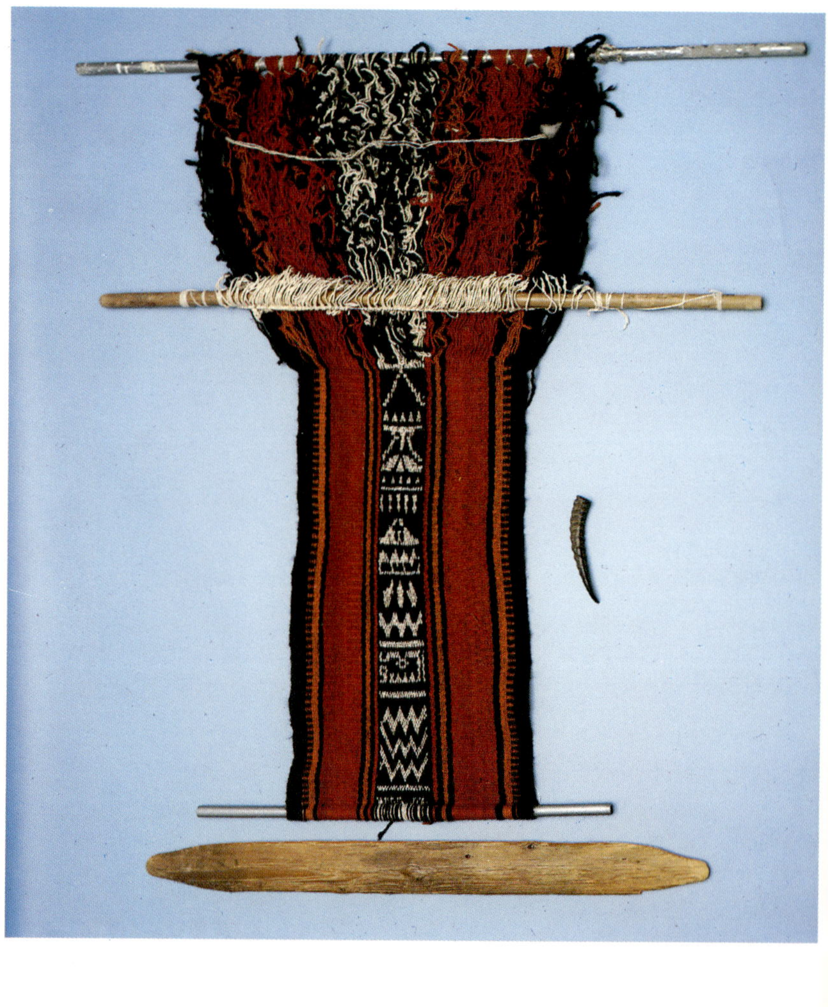

29 Bedu weaving equipment. Loom with warp beams, shed, stick and horn (Royal Scottish Museum Edinburgh) 1985.154 & A; 155).

30 Bedu weaving. Detail of a tent hanging—*qata*, to show warp-faced weave (Royal Scottish Museum Edinburgh 1983.982).

31 Bedu weaving. Detail of a tent hanging—*qata*, to show weft-faced weave and warp fringes (Royal Scottish Museum Edinburgh 1983.982).

Various weaving and finishing techniques were used which were well suited to the coarse thick textures of the wools. The most commonly used weaving technique was warp-faced weave (Plate 30), which was especially suited to vertically striped designs. Here the weft threads are stretched taut and pushed close together so that the vertical warps dominate the surface of the fabric. Horizontal weft tapestry weave was also used taking the weft threads over pairs of warps (Plate 31). This weave suited designs composed of triangular or lozenge motifs, which were used as overall repeating patterns or as borders. Vertical edges of the woven fabric were treated as simple selvages formed by the reversal of the weft, while horizontal edges were usually finished with twisted warp fringes (Plate 31). Lengths of wool were also plaited, braided and knotted in a wide range of colour combinations to make decorative fringes and tassels.

32 Bedu weaving. Tent hanging—*qata.* (Royal Scottish Museum Edinburgh 1983.982).

33 Bedu weaving. Floor covering—*busat* (Royal Scottish Museum Edinburgh 1983.131).

Weaving was done in narrow strips depending on the maximum width of the loom. Strips were then sewn together sufficient for the size and shape of the required article. The tent curtains of *ruag* and *qata (gharara* in Kuwaiti dialect) were each made of four strips sewn together with wool in a flat insertion stitch (Plate 32). The floor coverings—*busat*—were normally of two lengths (Plate 33), while the cushions—*masanid*—were of one strip joined together at the sides with overlocking fishtail stitch. Depending on their width storage bags were of one or two strips. The large storage (*'adul*) (Plate 34) and camel bags (*mazawida*) were of two strips width while one strip was enough for the smaller saddlebag (*khuruj*) (Plate 35) which was often decorated with long plaited cords. The narrow strips, however, which were made as bands to decorate the saddles, necks and knees of camels (*safayif*) (Plate 36), and the sides of the women's transport litters, offered the most scope for lavish arrangements of cord and tassel decoration.

The designs used in Bedu weaving while broadly based on tribal repertoires, cannot always be identified precisely unless accompanied by exact documentation, for example, concerning provenance, family details of the weaver and her range of patterns. Pieces which were sold in the *suq* of the town which served as the market centre of a tribe's *musabila* all too often were not accompanied by this information. Bearing this reservation in mind, it is however, possible within broad limits to allocate certain designs to tribal groups. The tribes who camped in the vicinity of Kuwait were the Mutair, Awazim, Northern Ajman, Harb and Shammar who broadly shared a repertoire of geometrical motifs. Common to all was the use of vertical

34 Bedu weaving. Storage bag — *'adul* (Royal Scottish Museum Edinburgh 1985.134).

35 Bedu weaving. Saddlebag — *khuruj* (Royal Scottish Museum Edinburgh 1985.142).

36 Bedu weaving. Camel trapping — *safayif* (Royal Scottish Museum Edinburgh 1985.146).

stripes of various widths and colour combinations made by grouping the warp threads together in the required sequence. Broad alternating stripes of natural light brown and white were used in large storage and camel bags. The sequences of plain stripes could be varied by the inclusion of patterned stripes. These could consist of small granular or checked motifs. *Hubab*, for example, was made up of narrow alternating bars of black and white, and was used to break up the broad plain stripes of the storage bags (Plate 34). *'Llwairajan*, a band of reciprocal checked triangles was another distinctive design (Plate 37). A design worked in weft tapestry weave was *janah hanbaliyya*, based on intersecting triangles in a wide range of colours—green, orange, red, sometimes violet—which could be used as a background pattern or picked out as a horizontal border (Plate 31).

The most striking designs, were reserved for the *qata*, where broad stripes of white with geometrical motifs picked out in black outline were reserved against the background which was usually black and white but in turn could consist of a secondary sequence of plain boldly coloured stripes in dark red and orange, or worked in granular *hubab* and *'Ilwairajan* (Plate 30). The four bands of the *qata*, followed a strict sequence from top to bottom. The first band (*shaffa*) was approximately 30 cm wide with a bold pattern stripe in the centre of repeated geometrical motifs of triangles, lozenges, zigzag lines, saltire crossed devices in black against white which were typical of the Mutair and Ajman tribes (Plate 30). The second and third bands (*matabba* and *afra*) were approximately 46 cm wide and were decorated with narrower variations of the black and white stripe of the first band. The last band—*sawda*—was also about 46 cm wide and consisted of two plain stripes in white and brown.

37 Bedu weaving. Storage bag—*'adul* (Royal Scottish Museum Edinburgh 1983.984).

c) *Festivals and rituals*

In both town and Bedu society the everyday routine was, however, enlivened and interrupted by the festivities concerned with the major events of the Moslem religious year and the rituals of celebration or lament which marked the significant stages of an individual's life. The religious festivals celebrated publicly in Kuwait were two, *Eid al-Fitr*, at the end of the fast of the 9th month Ramadhan, and *Eid al-Adha*, the 10th day of the 12th month Dhu'l Hijja, when the pilgrims entered the Great Mosque at Mecca. In the town the end of Ramadhan was traditionally announced by the Sheikh when the new moon of the next month had been seen. Families spent that night feasting and preparing themselves for the following days of celebration. The women in particular would spend much time in preparation at the bath—washing their hair, hennaeing hands and feet—ready to put on the new dresses which they had made themselves or which their husbands had given them. *Eid al-Fitr* officially was a three-day holiday, but in practice lasted for seven days. On the first day a gun salute announced that the Sheikh and male members of his family had finished their prayers at the al-Khalifa mosque and were ready to receive guests in the *diwaniya* of the Seif Palace. Similar receptions were taking place in the homes where the men would receive a constant steam of visitors who would be offered the normal hospitality ritual of coffee, rosewater and incense, while presenting their greetings and best wishes before moving on. The women in their separate quarters would also be exchanging calls on each other. They also entertained each other with dances. The children received special attention as in each section of the town a small fair—with swings and roundabouts—had been set up for them where they happily spent the day. During the afternoon other amusements were available for the adults, as both men and women went down to the main square (*safat*), to watch and encourage the *ardha* dance. This was a men's traditional war dance, in which the participants carrying swords or rifles moved to and fro in two slow moving lines, to the accompaniment of drums and tambourines. At *Eid al-Fitr* it was performed by teams recruited from the Rashaidah Bedu retainers of the Sheikh and the sailors of the trading and pearling fleets.

Eid al-Adha, which also lasted seven days in Kuwait town, was celebrated in much the same way as *Eid al-Fitr.* In the Bedu encampments both festivals were celebrated with horse and camel races. Additional to the exchange of hospitality, unmarried girls would dance in the women's part of the tents swirling their long hair loose around their heads. In the town, another festival, which was not religious but characteristic of Kuwait and indeed of all the pearling areas of the Arabian Gulf, was held to rejoice at the safe return of the crews. Here the women would parade along the sea front in a lively procession singing and clapping with their most colourful dresses hung on poles like banners, to welcome their menfolk home.

The events of a person's life which were emphasised by ritual were birth, circumcision initiating a boy into manhood, marriage witnessing a change in adult responsibilities, pilgrimage to Mecca fulfilling religious obligations, and death. Birth required no elaborate preparations and rituals, as in both town *harim* and Bedu tent female relatives and neighbours assisted. Immediately after birth the baby was washed and swaddled. Here the Bedu observed certain customs of rubbing the baby's eyes with antimony to make them strong, and using black cloth for the wrappings. As Bedu women resumed their work quickly after childbirth, the baby was put into a portable leather cradle (*mizba*) which could be slung over the mother's back or into a saddlebag. The child spent most of its early life as a conveniently swaddled bundle which was unwrapped for a few hours at night. Common to both town and Bedu women was a waiting period of forty days after the birth when they were regarded as unclean. In the town the birth of a son was celebrated by the father entertaining his male relatives and friends in the *diwaniya* to coffee and refreshments while receiving their congratulations.

A boy continued to receive attention as the next important ritual was his circumcision which was generally performed between the ages of three and seven, and accompanied by lavish entertainment which the women especially enjoyed. For a week before the operation women friends and neighbours of the family would be entertained every evening to coffee and sweets in the town *harims* where they would also dance to the drumming and singing of black musicians. Comparable celebrations would take place in the Bedu tent, where guests would be invited to eat and the women dance among themselves. The operation of circumcision would be performed by a specialist (*hindi*) in the presence of the family only, to be followed by more entertainment in the men's and women's quarters. In the town the father offered his friends supper in the *diwaniya*, while the women continued their singing and dancing. Bedu families who welcomed an opportunity for feasting and enjoying themselves would continue the entertainment for as many days after the operation as their means permitted.

In an environment where the family was the most important social unit its extension and continuation by marriage was treated with great care. Marriage in a Moslem society was a civil contract with clearly established principles. In the choice of a marriage partner certain categories of relationship were strictly forbidden. The Qur'an is very explicit here:—"You are forbidden to take in marriage your mothers, your daughters, your sisters, your paternal and maternal aunts, the daughters of your brothers and sisters, your foster-mothers, your foster sisters, the mothers of your wives, your step-daughters who are in your charge, born of the wives with whom you have lain (it is no offence for you to marry your step-daughters if you have not consumated your marriage with their mothers), and the wives of your own begotten sons. Henceforth you are also forbidden to take in marriage two sisters at one and the same time. Allah is forgiving and merciful. You are also forbidden to take in marriage married women, except captives whom you own as slaves."[1]

Marriages between first cousins, were not prohibited and this traditionally was the preferred choice in both town and Bedu families especially between the *walad 'um* and *bint 'um*—male and female first cousins on the bridegroom's father's side. This specific linkage in Bedu society was regarded as so binding that it could not be evaded unless the man first waived his right. There were practical reasons for first cousin marriages—property would remain in the family, both groups of parents would already have considerable information about the qualities of the couple who themselves in a segregated society would have had some chance to know each other. Normally in a first marriage the age of the couple was young—fifteen to sixteen for the bride and eighteen to twenty for the groom.

Traditionally there were three main stages to a marriage before the couple lived together. First the prospective bridegroom asked for the girls's hand from her father in front of the *imam* (religious leader) and other witnesses. If the father agreed the couple were then considered married. Then the two families discussed and negotiated the provisions of the contract which included the all-important *mahr*—the marriage portion, a sum of money which the groom gave to the bride. This was her permanent property which she could also retain after divorce. The bridegroom also contributed towards a *jehaz* (trousseau) with presents of clothes, jewellery, household furnishings etc. In the town the signing of the contract was followed by a short period, approximately equivalent to an engagement, during which parties were held for several nights in the bride's home, as related by Violet Dickson: "It was on the third night that we were invited to take part in the rejoicing. It was about seven o'clock in the evening on a day in January 1939 when we went to Hamda's house. Her little courtyard was crowded with women, some veiled, some unveiled, and the whole lit up by an incandescent lamp hanging from a pole jutting out of the wall. We were ushered into Hamda's room, where we were given coffee, and then we both sat in her doorway, my husband somewhat in the shadows, while the chorus of *'aidaus*, who consisted mostly of old negresses, played their drums and sang songs befitting the occasion. . . . From time to time one of the many Arab girls present, more smartly dressed than the others perhaps, would shyly undo her plaits, come forward into the small space behind the door and do her dance. If she was an 'Azmi girl from a neighbouring garden she danced the dance peculiar to the Badawin Awazim women; if a town lass, dressed in short frock and cotton stockings, she dance the dance of the town women, which is a more sedate affair, but includes the wriggling of the hips and neck amid much ululation and applause. This is the achievement of a first-class dancer. Some girls danced well, while others were too shy, insisting that they did not know how."[2]

About a week later the final celebration took place when the groom was taken to the bride. Here the women were busy preparing a room in the bride's home, decorating it with glass lamps, candles and colourful furnishings:—"Blue silk mattresses and cushions were next placed on the floor around the wall of the room, and on Hamda's large bed were hung new curtains of pink georgette tied with bows of blue ribbon. On the bed was placed a new mattress and over that a new red cotton quilt—supplied by the bridegroom, following Arab custom—and a hard stuffed pillow of blue silk with a white frilled cotton covering round the centre."[3]

During this period the bride was attended by a special woman—*hawafa*—who instructed and groomed her, preparing her skin, hair, hennaeing her hands and feet, and finally dressing her. In contrast the groom had much less attention as on the day of the wedding he dressed in new clothes, prayed at the mosque, and during the evening arrived at the bride's house accompanied by a procession of friends and musicians. At large weddings this procession took some time as frequent stops were made en route to greet neighbours and well-wishers. At the bride's house where singing and dancing had been taking place, the groom was taken directly to the bridal chamber. Later the bride was brought to him cloaked and veiled. After the wedding night—"The bride's mother and friends went in to her, washed her, which included the pouring of water over her head, changed all her clothes and prepared her once more for her husband who would return to her later in the morning."[4] During the evening of the third day the bride arrayed in her jewellery received congratulatory calls from her friends, who were offered coffee and refreshments after which "The bride was next brought in and presented. She knelt before us in turn to be congratulated on her marriage. She looked really beautiful, a very different person from the one I had seen weeping in a corner on the night of the wedding."[5] Seven days after the wedding festivities ended and the bride went to live in her husband's home. Marriage ceremonies naturally varied in the lavishness and quality of their entertainment and in the length of the intervals between each stage, but common to all town dweller and Bedu alike was the wish to do the best possible within their means.

During a life of family responsibility there were spiritual and religious duties culminating in the pilgrimage to Mecca (*haj*) which was obligatory for all Moslems who could afford to do so. Preparations were lengthy and expensive, involving for a town person the purchasing of camels for travelling, food, tents, litters so that women could ride in privacy, and hiring of guides, which further illustrated the dependence on the Bedu. The pilgrims would collect together in the market square and set out on the long journey under the supervision of an *amir al-haj.* The journey took forty to forty-five days each way and followed an unvarying routine of dawn starts, marches of three to four hours interrupted by coffee breaks and a long rest at midday before arriving at the night's camping place. After completion of the pilgrimage rites at Mecca and the arduous return journey, the arrival of the pilgrims caravan in Kuwait was joyfully welcomed by relatives and friends. Death was quickly followed by modest burial rites, since Islam discouraged a display of excessive grief. The body was washed always by a member of the same sex, wrapped in a shroud, and taken on a wooden bier by male relatives to the cemetery in the town, or simply carried to an open space in the desert. The body was then laid in the grave facing towards Mecca and covered with stones and bricks or brushwood. After the grave was filled in with earth there was nothing to identify a Bedu burial, while in a town cemetery only rough stones at head and foot marked the place. Relatives never visited the grave again. During a short mourning of three days the men of a family would receive visitors in the *diwaniya* who called to offer condolences, while the women wept and grieved in the *harim.* Widows were expected to seclude themselves for a period of four months and ten days after a husband's death.

d) Clothing traditions

In all societies, costume plays an essential role not only in satisfying such practical and cultural requirements as warmth, protection and modesty, but also in functioning as a readily identifiable symbol of status, occupation, and ceremony. These criteria may be applied to Kuwaiti society, where costume played a prominent role at the festivals of *Eid al-Fitr* and *Eid al-Adha* and at marriage celebrations, which were all opportunities for acquiring new clothes. Kuwaiti costume evolved steadily along rather eclectic lines as it included versions of basic garment types which were worn over a wide area of the Arabian peninsula as far north as Syria. New influences in cut, fabric and decoration imported through Kuwait's extensive trading contacts, came directly to the town dweller through the goods available in the *suq* and filtered more slowly into the Bedu tribes. While there is not a great range of surviving costumes available it is possible to reconstruct the broad historical development of Kuwaiti costume through the descriptions of travellers combined with a study of modern garments worn in more conservative sections of today's society which faithfully preserve traditional shapes and tailoring methods.

James Silk Buckingham's racy description of the pirate Rahmah bin Jaber in 1816 should not be regarded as a typical account of Kuwaiti men, who wore cleaner and smarter versions of his shirt, cloak and headdress. The Kuwaiti merchants stationed in Basra in 1816 thus presented a completely different image.

"The Arabs are mostly persons born in the town, or in its immediate neighbourhood with occasional settlers from Bagdad, Kourna, and the villages along the banks of the Tigris and Euphrates, as well as some few Desert Arabs from the country of Nedjed, and trading people from Coete or Graine, the great sea-port of that part of Arabia. The occupations of the Arab population are chiefly commercial among the higher order, and labour and cultivation among the lower. . . .

"The dress of the merchants, who are originally of Bussorah, as well as those who come from Moosul and Bagdad, differs but little from that of the same class of people in Syria, except that it is here gayer and more costly in the same rank of life. Indian muslins and Angora shalloons are worn in the summer, but fine broad cloths of the brightest colours, Indian stuffs, and Cashmere shawls, form the winter apparel; and these are displayed in such variety, as to make the wardrobe of a well dressed man exceedingly expensive. The Arabs from Nedjed, and those from Coete or Graine, wear invariably the Bedouin handkerchief, called Maharama and Keffeea; the poorer people bind them round their heads with bands of camel's hair threads made into a sort of rope; but the wealthier class, although they are clad in the most costly robes, still retain this mark of their Desert origin, and sometimes even wear a rich Indian shawl as a turban over it, while the long ends of the coarse Bedouin keffeea hang over their shoulders, forming a singular mixture of the costumes of the Desert and the town. The light Bagdad cloak, in alternate stripes of reddish brown and white, is worn by all in the summer; and thicker abbas, of a similar form and pattern, by the poor in the winter; but the rich at this season wear fine thick cloaks of a black colour, with a broad and deep three-forked stripe of gold, woven into the cloth, and descending from the top of the right shoulder down the back."[1]

The costume as worn by Kuwaitis in Basra may be summarised as a blend of their local traditional garments, particularly the distinctive headdress worn by town dweller and Bedu nomad alike, with clothes made of luxurious imported Indian and Kashmiri fabrics. Forms of dress associated with the Bedu may further be traced back to the 18th century when Niebuhr during his travels of 1762 to 1764 noted that:—

"The common class of Arabs wear only two caps, with the *Safch* carelessly bound on the head. Some have drawers and a shirt, but the greater number have only a piece of linen about their loins, a large girdle, and a piece of cloth upon the shoulders; in other respects they are naked, having neither shoes nor stockings. In the highlands, where the climate is colder, the people wear sheep skins. The scanty clothes which they wear through the day, are also their covering by night; the cloth swaddled about the waist serves for a mattress; and the linen garment worn about the loins is a sheet to cover the Arab when he sleeps.

"The ordinary dress of the Arab is indeed simple enough, but they have also a sort of great coat, without sleeves, called *Abba* which is simpler still. I was acquainted with a blind tailor at Basra, who earned his bread by making *Abbas*."[2]

Allowing for a certain awkwardness of phrase, doubtless due to unfamiliarity with the garments which he was trying to describe, Niebuhr's account does give an impression of basic loose garments which had to be practical and versatile.

Such principles continued to govern the composition and style of Kuwait male dress whose variations at different levels of society depended more on number of garments and quality of fabric rather than shape and cut. This basically democratic costume evolved for comfort and protection in a harsh climate was therefore made up of a combination of garments (Plate 38) which were of simple cut and construction based on square or rectangular main pattern units to which triangular pieces were added at sides and underarms to give the required shape. Garments were traditionally handsewn until the introduction of the sewing machine in the early 20th century either by the women at home or in certain cases by specialists such as the "21 tailors, 37 cloak embroiderers, 7 gold and silk braid workers, 12 makers of 'Aqals or Arab head fillets"[3] who were recorded by Lorimer as working in Kuwait town in 1904. Among the Bedu tailoring and dressmaking resources were extremely limited—"Women in the desert make most of their own clothes; they possess no scissors or thread, but tear up the cloth (using teeth) and sew with thread taking out of the cloth;. Their usual scale of measurement is from thumb to first finger extended and from eye corner to eye corner (outer edge)."[4]

The first item of men's costume was the *sirwal*—a pair of loose ankle-length trousers which were worn by townsmen and all Bedu who could afford them (Plate 39 & diagram 1). They were made of white cotton cloth, increasingly of imported European manufacture which was on sale in the *suq*. They were of simple construction two straight pieces folded in half at

38 Kuwait. Friday market, carpet merchant in traditional dress.

39 Man's trousers—*sirwal* (Royal Scottish Museum Edinburgh 1985.31).

Man's robe with pointed sleeves—*thob shillahat* (Royal Scottish Museum Edinburgh 1985.10).

Man's robe—*dishdasha* (Royal Scottish Museum Edinburgh 1983.976).

the outer leg and either joined to a triangular centre piece or curved at the inner leg and sewn together at centre front and back. A garment which was always worn, however, was the long loose robe which came in two styles, *thob shillahat* and *dishdasha*, which were again made of white cotton. They were both of the same basic shape with close-fitting round necks and centre front openings down to chest level, and shaped from underarm to hem by the insertion of triangular side sections, but differed in certain details. The most distinctive feature of the *thob shillahat* (Plate 40 & diagram 2) was its long sleeves with wide pointed cuffs which were either worn loose and flowing or were wound around the wrists. This type of sleeve construction was not unique to the Arabian Gulf region as it occurs in a wide area extending from Syria-Palestine down to Iraq. The *dishdasha* (Plate 41 & diagram 3) which was made in a wider range of colours had long close-fitting sleeves and was to be increasingly influenced, certainly in the town, by details introduced from European-style shirt tailoring such as pointed collars, front fastenings with buttonholes, and buttoned cuffs. From the early 20th century these influences were introduced from both Iraq and by Indian tailors who came in increasing numbers to Kuwait and had been long accustomed to making shirts and suits for the British.

The basic garments were sober in both shape and colour. Layers of coats and cloaks could be built up over them for additional warmth, decoration and expression of individual taste. Affluent townsmen and Bedu could wear a coat called a *zebun*. like the *dishdasha* it was an anklelength garment with a close-fitting neck and long tight sleeves, but open at the centre front. The front sections were wide, however, and with the addition of triangular shaping pieces, formed a deep wrapover. The *zebun* was a luxurious garment generally made of Indian or Persian silk brocade patterned with small repeating floral motifs. In cut and shape it had parallels with garments which had been worn in Syria, Turkish Iraq and Persia in the mid-19th century, and local Kuwaiti versions may well have been copied from originals. A short jacket with sleeves embroidered in gold thread—*damir*—or a sleeveless waistcoat made of imported Kashmir or Persian Kerman wool twill woven with a floral sprig pattern could also be worn over the *dishdasha*.

While the *zebun* and *damir* were optional a voluminous mantle, *'abba* or *bisht* (Plate 42 & diagram 4) as it is known in Kuwait was regularly worn especially in winter. This again was simple in cut and construction consisting of two lengths of fabric joined together horizontally to make a rectangle of the required size. The ends were then folded over to the centre front, shoulder seams joined, and two slits cut for the wearer's wrists. The *bisht* was made of finely woven sheep or camel wool in colours ranging from black through browns, greys to beige in various weights and textures, according to use. It was a versatile garment which could be seen in many forms from the plain cloak worn by poor Bedu as the only warm and protective covering over their shabby *dishdashas* to the elegant and dignified black mantle with gold embroidered borders and shoulder seams worn by rich citizens and sheikhs. *Bishts* came into Kuwait from various sources, from Basra and Baghdad in Iraq and from Damascus and Aleppo in Syria. There was also a local industry in the Kuwait *suq* which still continues:—

"A little farther on we came to the quarter where *abbas*—men's brown cloaks—are made and sold. Here we found men sitting on the ground at the side of the street sewing by hand the gold embroidery which adorns the necks of the best quality cloaks. While we watched they would from time to time complete a section and then hammer it with a mallet on a wood block

42 Man's cloak—*bisht* (Royal Scottish Museum Edinburgh 1985.5).

Man's coat—*farwah* (Royal Scottish Museum Edinburgh 1985.1).

Since they use pure gold thread this beating fuses the separate threads, giving the embroidery a smooth embossed look.

"Aware of our curiosity, the *abba* merchant was anxious to tell us about his trade. He explained that each embroiderer is a specialist in only one section of the traditional ornamentation, and that the garment must pass through five hands before the neck pattern, the piping down the sleeves, and the two tassels at the front edges are all completed. The *abba* is made from two pieces of straight cloth, joined horizontally around the middle, and the last step in the making is to join the lower half of the garment to the upper. The gold in one good *abba* costs about £7, and we were shown the boxes of gold thread imported from France and Germany. Not only the gold is costly, for the *abba* cloth as well can be very expensive. We looked at a normal-quality machine-made brown cloth which would make an *abba* priced at £40. A cloak of the finest hand-woven camel-wool can sell for as much as £70. Because of the high prices, badawin who formerly loved their *abbas* can hardly afford to wear them now."[5]

A particularly striking and boldly shaped garment was the *farwah*—a bulky warm coat (Plate 43 & diagram 5) which could be worn instead of the *bisht* in the coldest weather, usually by Bedu who did, however, have to come into the town to buy it as it was made and sold in the *suq*. The *farwah* was made of closely woven wool broadcloth, often of English manufacture, in many colours—beige, light and dark brown, maroon, dark blue—and lined with black or white lamb skin. Made of a single piece of fabric which was folded in at each side to form the centre front opening, it was slashed from shoulder to armpit for the insertion of straight edged long sleeves and then the shoulder seams were joined. Bands of flat braid either self-coloured or contrasting were sewn over seams, borders, and over the body and sleeves in angular patterns. The *farwah* was usually draped over the wearer's shoulders, with the sleeves hanging empty behind him.

Probably the most distinctive item of male dress, which had certainly always been noted by travellers, was the headdress which consisted of up to three pieces—a close-fitting skull cap (*keffiya*) a square cloth folded to form a triangle (*gatra*) and a cord circlet (*'agal*) (Plate 44). It had survived because it was so admirably functional; it provided shade during the heat of summer, it could be pulled across the face and wrapped round the head during winds and sandstorms, its ends could be twisted up into a turban if the wearer was busy with some manual task. It was also a flattering and handsome accessory. Of its parts the *keffiya*, which was not invariably worn, served to prevent the *gatra* and *'agal* from slipping off the wearer's head. The *gatra* when folded was carefully centred so that a neat fold covered the forehead and the ends hung down equally over the shoulders. Finally the *'agal* was firmly placed over the *gatra*. There were several variations possible with this headdress dependent on the materials used and the wearer's taste. At its simplest it consisted of a plain *gatra* of coarse plain cloth held in place by a twisted rag which served as an *'agal* (Plate 45). There was a choice of several materials for the *gatra*; a red and white checked cloth called a *shemagh* (Plate 46), which was normally reserved for winter wear in town and desert, a square of fine white Kashmiri twill weave wool patterned with floral cones at the corners and along the borders, commonly known as *shal*, which was an expensive variant worn by town merchants and wealthy sheikhs, and a lighter weight white cotton or muslin worn in summer. The *'agal* traditionally was a skein of thick threads of black or brown sheep and camel wool bound together at intervals with brightly coloured wools and twisted

44 Man's headdress and accessories. Crotchet cap—*shemagh*, two types of head cord—*'agal*, prayer beads—*mesbaha* (Royal Scottish Museum Edinburgh 1985.19,23,30,149,172).

45 Ikhwan (Brotherhood) members at Kuwait, 1926. (Lt. Col. Sir Arnold T. Wilson Collection, Royal Geographical Society, London).

46 Sheikh Fahad at Kuwait 1919 (Dorothy Van Ess Collection, Middle East Centre, Oxford).

47 Group of al-Sabah and al-Saud at Kuwait, March 1910 (Captain Shakespear Collection, Royal Geographical Society, London).

around the wearer's head like a stylised garland (Plate 46). Gradually this was replaced by a double circlet of twisted black cord which was usually imported from Syria (Plate 44). A more refined style, traditionally exclusive to sheikhs, was made of fine black wool or silk tightly bound with gold thread which formed stiff bars.

The *gatra* and *'agal* could be worn in various styles each with their own subtle modification (Plate 47). In the simplest style the *gatra* was firmly centred on the head and pulled down well over the forehead so that its three pointed ends were arranged on each side of the face and at the back. The *'agal* was usually set straight on the head and tilted a little back from the forehead. This was a sedate and dignified style always worn by sheikhs and older men. Variations included the positioning of the *'agal*, which could be tilted further backward or forward, slanted at an oblique angle, or pulled rakishly down over one eye. The *gatra* was equally versatile as both ends could be flipped back over the wearer's shoulders, folded up and over the *'agal*, crossed under the chin and thrown back. Asymetrical variants included tossing one end behind the shoulder or under the chin and up to be tucked into the *'agal*. By the early 20th century an interesting divergence had arisen in the treatment of hair between town Kuwaiti and Bedu. Adult men in both

48 Saud ibn Abdur Rahman al-Saud, April 1911 (Captain Shakespear Collection, Royal Geographical Society, London).

49 Sheikh Ahmad al-Jabar al-Sabah, ruler of Kuwait 1926 (Lt. Col. Sir Arnold T. Wilson Collection, Royal Geographical Society, London).

environments wore full moustaches and usually short pointed beards. While men in the town, however, generally wore their hair cut quite short, Bedu men were more constructive and kept their hair long in twisted locks or plaits (Plate 48). This style had been noted by Niebuhr in 1762, and described by Charles Doughty in 1880 as "... long hair shed in the midst, and hanging down at either side in braided horns. . . ."[6]

Once a man was dressed in his choice of flowing garments, had arranged his headdress to his liking, and was suitably shod in leather sandals or boots depending on the season, he needed certain accessories. If he was a Bedu of sufficient means he would enwrap himself with leather belt and crossed bandoliers through which he would thrust a large and small dagger (*khusa* and *huardhi*). He also had a rifle in a finely worked leather holster (*jiffar al-tufaq*), a camel stick (*mish'ab*) and a wool or leather money bag (*mizuda*). A townsman would perhaps carry a wooden staff and wear a single bandolier. An indispensible accessory in both environments was the *mesbaha*, a string usually of thirty three beads used for counting prayers, which was made in a range of materials such as sandalwood, coral, glass and precious gems and metals.

The gradual intrusion of European details of tailoring into the *dishdasha* in the early 20th century has already been noted. This influence also extended to the substitution of European style garments for traditional items of clothing. Tailored jackets with buttons and lapels often holding watch chains replaced the embroidered *damir* (Plate 49), leather shoes with laced uppers worn with socks replaced boots. Eventually by the 1940s tailors were making suits of English imported cloth often in sober pinstripe consisting of *dishdasha* with shirt collar and cuffs, a fitted waistcoat with buttons, and a single or double breasted jacket. Despite these innovations in everyday dress, certain garments always retained their traditional form notably those associated with religious practice such as the *ihram*, a long white loin cloth and shoulder wrap worn by pilgrims in Mecca.

Women's costume was as receptive to imported influences both in fabric and style as that of their menfolk, but as they customarily lived in seclusion and were heavily cloaked and veiled in black when they ventured out of their homes exact contemporary detail of their clothing is elusive. The women of Kuwait's territory shared face-veiling habits with their neighbours in other parts of Arabia which had been noted by Niebuhr in the 18th century:— "The women of Hedsjas veil their faces like those of Egypt, with a narrow piece of linen, which leaves both eyes uncovered. In Yemen they wear a larger veil which covers the face so entirely, that the eyes can hardly be discerned. At Sana and Mokha, they cover the face with a gauze veil which is oftened embroidered with gold."[7]

Yet the outward seemingly restrained appearance could be misleading, as Charles Doughty discovered:—

"This simple blue smock of calico dipped in indigo, the woman's garment in all the Arab countries, they wear here with a large-made and flowing grace of their own; the sleeves are embroidered with needlework of red worsted, and lozenges sewn upon them of red cotton. The most have bracelets, *hadyd*, of beautiful great beads of unwrought amber, brought as they tell me anciently from Hayil . . .Tamar's garment of patches and party-colours was perchance of such sort as are these Arabian women's worked gowns. . . ."[8]

In Kuwait also women's discreet black cloaks often concealed garments in which brilliant colour and texture were strikingly combined. Both town and Bedu women enjoyed wearing as much finery as their means permitted. In the town women had access to a wide choice of imported fabrics from Syria, Iraq, Persia and especially India whose many and varied textile enterprises catered to a foreign market, which were all on sale in the main *suq*. Women of the wealthy merchant class also had access to a more exclusive range of goods, as groups of them would sell privately among themselves luxurious fabrics, perfumes and cosmetics which their menfolk brought directly to them from India. Bedu women of the tribes who migrated to Kuwait's territory were also dependent on ready made fabrics as their own weaving concentrated on heavy wool textiles for tent furnishings. They would buy lengths of material direct from the *suq* on their visits to town or possibly through female acquaintances among the semi-nomadic population which lived on the outskirts. Town women usually had their clothes made by tailors or neighbourhood dressmakers. These women were versatile in their skills, making both wedding and everyday clothes, and specialising in certain types of embroidery in gold and silver thread. They also had supplies of cosmetics and were often called to a household on special occasions such as weddings to help adorn the bride. The introduction of the sewing machine, at first of the type with a wheel turned by hand, broadened their scope considerably as they were able to make clothes more quickly and also to do machine embroidery. Bedu women either sewed their own clothing using very simple patterns and techniques or if they were fortunate could have garments made for them in the town.

As in men's costume certain garments common to both town and Bedu women differ mainly in the quality and richness of their material and decoration. Shapes were loose and comfortable with cut and construction traditionally based on square and rectangular pattern pieces. Anklelength trousers (*sirwal*) (Plate 50 & diagram 6) were worn known specifically as *imkessr* and *abu mahruma* depending on the degree of embroidered decoration. They were voluminous but tapered to close-fitting ankles which could be decorated with bands of gold embroidery usually worked in geometrical motifs in broad stitches. Materials were generally brightly coloured—green, red, blue—cotton or silk. The construction was similar to that of men's trousers, but the two leg pieces tapered towards the ankle.

50 Woman's trousers—*sirwal* (Royal Scottish Museum Edinburgh 1985.95).

51 Woman's costume. Dress—*dara'a*, worn with gauze overdress—*thob al-tour bilteil* (Royal Scottish Museum Edinburgh 1985.49,64).

52 Woman's dress—*fustan* (Royal Scottish Museum Edinburgh 1985.44).

53 Woman's costume. Wrapover coat—*zebun*, worn with a head covering—*milfa* (Royal Scottish Museum Edinburgh 1985.68,79).

Over the trousers an anklelength dress with long sleeves was worn known as a *dishdasha* or *fustan*. It was traditionally of simple construction with front and back formed either of one long rectangular piece folded over at the shoulders or of two pieces joined at the shoulders. Long tight sleeves were set in at armhole level and then the sides were seamed together. The fabrics varied from plain and patterned cotton to fine Indian silks embroidered with tambour work motifs of flowers and tendrils in gold thread (Plate 51 & diagram 7). Gradually European influences such as fitted bodices, gathered skirts and curved sleeves (Plate 52 & diagram 8) altered the traditional straight and flowing line. Wealthy townswomen sometimes wore a *zebun* over the dress which was of the same cut and shape as the type worn by men and made in luxurious brocaded silks (Plate 53 & diagram 9).

Common to both town and Bedu women, was a voluminous graceful overdress known as a *thob*. It was basically a long straight-sided garment with wide sleeves of exaggerated proportions, either a low deep-pointed or close-fitting round neck. The pattern consisted of a central rectangular length folded double at the shoulders to which a deep rectangular sleeve section and a narrower skirt piece were added at each side. A triangular insertion between sleeve and side skirt formed a curious underarm detail. Many variations were possible depending on the colour, texture and decoration of fabric, and scale of pattern pieces. Many Bedu women wore a simple plain *thob* of black cotton. A handsome variant worn in the town was the *thob jez* (Plate 54 & diagram 10) which was a winter garment which could be made of a heavy coarse black silk, but was also made of wool and cotton. Here the proportions were very large and voluminous. The garment's plain black colour was relieved and lightened by the use of gold thread to boldly outline every seam and to embroider floral motifs on the underarm section, thus using the construction to striking decorative effect. Black gauze and net in varying thicknesses were also used in the town to make *thobs* (Plate 55 & diagram 11). The most brilliant versions, were reserved for festivals and wedding parties, made of transparent silks and gauzes in vivid colours—scarlet, green, violet, blue—and lavishly embroidered in gold and silver. The long wide sleeves could be folded back over the shoulders or pulled over the face to form a becoming veil when dancing (Plate 51).

Both town and Bedu women modestly covered their heads in sober black. In the town a length of black gauze—*milfa* (Plate 53) was wrapped and twisted around the head like a wimple, framing the face tightly to conceal the hair. A Bedu woman could also wear the *milfa* but usually preferred a *sheileh* (Plate 56), a close-fitting hood made of four pieces of black cloth joined to form a triangular shape and seamed under the chin. Her head covering was completed by a *burqa*—a rectangular face mask which hangs from the forehead to just below the neck (Plate 56). The *burqa* consisted of two pieces of black cloth—a narrow band, which was lined, and a rectangular veil attachment which was folded double at eye level (Plate 57). Both pieces were sewn together at the outer edges and centre to form two long narrow eye slits. Three pairs of cords secured the *burqa* tightly at the back of the wearer's head. Bedu women never removed the *burqa* so that they could move freely around the areas of their tent and beyond. When a townswoman left her home, she maintained her seclusion by covering her face completely with a black veil (*bushiya*) (Plate 58). Both town and Bedu women wore an all-enveloping black cloak (*'abbaya*) when out of doors which was suspended from head to foot effectively concealing any brightly coloured clothes. The *'abbaya* was made of two lengths of cloth joined

54 Woman's traditional overdress—*thob jez* (Royal Scottish Museum Edinburgh 1985.67).

55 Woman's overdress—*thob* al-*messarah* (Royal Scottish Museum Edinburgh 1983.969).

56 Bedu woman's costume. Trousers—*sirwal*, dress—*fustan*, overdress—*thob*, head covering—*milfa*, face mask—*burqa*, and sandals (Royal Scottish Museum Edinburgh 1985.41,61,76,92,93 & A,1983.974).

57 Bedu woman's face mask—*burqa* (Royal Scottish Museum Edinburgh 1985.974).

58 Woman's costume. Cloak—*'abbaya* worn over a *thob jez* and a face veil—*bushiya* (Royal Scottish Museum Edinburgh 1985.67,69,76).

59 Woman's cloak—*'abbaya* (Royal Scottish Museum Edinburgh 1985.73).

60 Woman's bath accessories and cosmetics. Wooden pattens, pumice stone, crotchet loofah, comb, henna, *maswak* bark (Royal Scottish Museum Edinburgh 1985.113 & A, 174,179,180,183,184).

horizontally (Plate 59 & diagram 12) and was of the same construction as the men's *bisht.* As the shape was simple basic variation was possible only in the texture and quality of the fabric and certain discreet details of decoration. Examples made of heavy smoothly woven black wool or silk could have narrow borders of gold thread along the shoulder seams and all edges.

Considerable attention, especially in the town was paid to personal grooming, hair-dressing, application of cosmetics, and perfume (Plate 60), and the acquisition of a good collection of jewellery. Niebuhr in the 18th century had noted the striking appearance of Arab women in Yemen:— "They wear all rings on their fingers, arms, nose and ears. They stain their nails red, and their hands and feet of a brownish yellow colour with the juice of the plant *Elhenne.* The circle of the eyes and even the eyelashes they paint black with a preparation of lead ore called *Kochhel*."[9]

In the town the process of beautification began with the bath (*hammam*). As Kuwait did not have the custom of the public bath so well established in the Ottoman Turkish Empire, Persia and North Africa washing was done at home where among the wealthy there were bathing facilities adjacent to bedrooms in the *harim* courtyard. Essential items were a pair of wooden patterns—to protect the feet from the cold stone floor, and a range of fibre and thread loofahs—(*lifa*) and pumice stone (*sakhra*) to soap and clean the skin. Hair was washed and dressed with oil, (*dehen*), which was also used among the Bedu. At this stage henna (*hinna*) was applied to decorate the hands, feet and hair. A powder obtained from the leaves and berries of plants, *hinna* was valued both as a beauty aid and as a medicinal product as it hardened and protected the skin and acted as a disinfectant for cuts and scratches. The *hinna* traditionally used in Kuwait came from Mecca and Basra. Its application was a slow process as the powder first had to be mixed with water to form a paste of the right consistency. This was then thickly painted on to the skin using a wooden spatula and packed over the hair and left to dry, after which it was picked off.

Varying depths of colour were achieved by repeated applications. The use of *hinna* was comparatively restrained among Bedu women who stained their hands, finger and toe nails red. In the town red *hinna* was applied to the finger and toe nails only. A black *hinna* known as *saumar* was painted on the hands in a range of patterns which included bold oblique stripes across the palms and rows of triangles extending up the fingers, and coated over the soles and sides of the feet in a slipper shape. The dark colour was produced by applying a strong paste of powdered lime and ammonia crystals over a red *hinna* base. The *hinna* patterns lasted about a month slowly fading to a soft orange red. In 1935 a black hair dye imported from Germany began to be used as an easy less time-consuming substitute for *saumar* but proved less satisfactory as its effects lasted for about a week only.

The application of *hinna* to thick black hair gave it both a glossy healthy appearance and rich burnished colour tints. Women wore their hair long and braided into several plaits, which could be worn in various ways. The Bedu women of the tribes around Kuwait, for example, wore nine plaits—two on each side of the face, six around the back of the head, and one at the nape of the neck.

61 Woman's accessories. Mirror, khol pot, rosewater sprinkler, perfume bottle (Royal Scottish Museum Edinburgh 1985.159,160 & A, 162,165 & A).

Wealthy women entwined strings of gold pendants into their plaited hair. After hairdressing there only remained a selection of cosmetics to be applied (Plate 61). A fine black powder—*kuhl* or *kuhr* ground from antimony and malachite was applied using a small fine stick to elongate and outline the eyes. Like *hinna* it was also regarded as a medicinal and amuletic product giving protection against eye-diseases and the glare of the sun, and promoting strong vision. It was kept in small containers (*makhlah*) which were often of metal imported from India with elaborately wrought stoppers. The use of lip and cheek colour was usual among townswomen. They used flat strips of bark—*maswak* to clean their teeth, which also stained their lips a deep orange red. *Zerkoun*, a fine red powder prepared from safflower was dusted over the cheeks as rouge. Perfume (*dihin'ud*) was much admired and in the form of rosewater was always sprinkled on the hands of guests. Fragrances such as musk, amber and jasmine were also imported from India and used as personal enhancement.

Jewellery was important among both town and Bedu women both as decoration and investment. There were rings for every finger, either plain gold or silver bands, or set with large turquoise stones, bracelets of large amber beads of pieces of coral, nose-rings, anklets, necklaces of beads and coins, and an elaborate array of head ornaments especialy those worn by brides. Bedu women generally wore silver jewellery while townswomen preferred gold. A woman's jewellery was acquired gradually and many valuable pieces were passed on to daughters:—

". . . she poured them from her hands till a pile of glittering gold lay before us. All the pieces were large and spectacular, necklaces of gold Turkish coins, solid plaques of gold set with turquoise, such as brides wear upon their heads, and belts of pure gold made of a number of hinged plates. This was the old-fashioned jewellery, made by the local Arab craftsmen, but besides this there were more modern pieces brought from India, elaborate necklaces of filigree butterflies set with rubies, and wide gold bracelets with rubies and pearls. Though the custom of investing in gold is of great antiquity, the rich Arab did not formerly buy pearls and precious stones for his women. Only within the last fifteen years have the sheikhs and merchants bought gem-set jewellery from India,and a few have presented pearl necklaces to their wives.

"I asked our hostess when she wore these lovely ornaments, and she answered that she was now an old woman, and had no longer any occasion to adorn herself with gold. So the hoard of treasures remained locked in her tin trunk, year after year, to be passed on in due course to the younger generation, as some of it had been passed to our hostess herself."[10]

The garments and accessories of Kuwaiti women's costume were versatile, as by adapting the fabric and decoration they could be worn for both everyday life and special occasions. Entertainment of guests and weddings provided good opportunities for the display of finery. Certain combinations of colour and texture were seen to advantage when women and girls danced for their guests.

"Six women first stood in two rows facing each other, and began their song to the clapping of hands. Three improvised a verse as they went along, and the others repeated it. Haiya emerged from behind the curtain divide, her *goba* now removed and her long wavy hair unplaited and flying. A short cane in her hand, her eyes downcast, and a very serious expression on her face, she began tossing her head this way and that, in time with the clapping and singing of the women, and doing the jumping step of the Awazim tribal dance, until the song came to an end. After a few minutes, Wadha's eldest daughter, Muttra, wearing a pink silk dress with a black gold-embroidered *thaub* over it, did a similar dance. Then came Bebe, who is Wadha's unmarried sister, wearing a flower-patterned silk dress surmounted by a green and gold embroidered *thaub*, and a golden necklace round her throat."[11]

The provision of a woman's trousseau (*jehaz*) gave opportunities for acquiring a wardrobe of clothes which were suitable for visiting and entertaining guests and attending wedding parties. By the 1930s in Kuwait town such costume could present an interesting combination of European and traditional influences. Some garments surviving from 1934 which were specially made for a *jehaz* show such features. Silk, woven in smooth satin weave and transparent tulle and georgette, was imported from India for these garments which were sewn and embroidered in Kuwait. Three examples of dresses machine-stitched in cream and turquoise silks were of contemporary European shape with gathered skirts of mid-calf length fitted on to a high waistband. Bodices were tight with long narrow sleeves set into curved armholes. The dresses were decorated, however, in traditional style with floral motifs embroidered in couched gold and silver thread. The three *thobs* which could be worn over the dresses in combinations according to the wearer's choice were handsewn of black and red georgette and blue tulle following traditional methods of cut and construction, and embroidered also in gold and silver thread.

During the sequence of celebrations which marked the stages of a wedding the bride would wear different costumes for the engagement, the wedding night and for receiving her guests during the days after. Wedding costumes were again more elaborate versions of everyday dress with the addition of special jewellery:—

At a wedding night for example:—

"She was rather quietly dressed in a simple silk under-dress and a black *thaub* with a little gold embroidery round the neck. Her hair was nicely braided and oiled, the palms of her hands and her feet being coloured black with a preparation of lime put on over the orange henna."[12]

Later after her wedding:—

"The bride was next brought in and presented. She knelt before us in turn to be congratulated on her marriage. She looked really beautiful, a very different person from the one I had seen weeping in a corner on the night of the wedding. She had on a peach-coloured under-dress of silk and over it a blue georgette *thaub* beautifully embroidered in gold thread. On her head was a golden covering, studded with turquoise and with a fringe of golden Dutch guilder (Plate 62), which lay on her forehead. She wore golden earrings and a nose-ring of pearls and turquoise. A necklace of golden chains hung down on the front of her dress. Down her back hung long black pieces of cloth on which were sewn solid golden ornaments in the shape of tiny inverted basins. Her wrists were adorned with many golden bracelets, her ankles with two large, heavy golden anklets."[13]

63 Kuwait. Children in traditional dress at the Gulf Co-operation Council exhibition 1984.

62 Woman's costume. Multicoloured silk trousers – *sirwal*, and dress – *dara'a al-mufahah*, worn with reconstructed bridal jewellery (Royal Scottish Museum Edinburgh 1985.40 & A-B).

All finery was put aside, however, when the time came for pilgrimage to Mecca. Here traditional and accepted dress consisted of green *sirwal*, *fustan* and *thob* modestly covered with a black *'abbaya* and *milfa*.

Children also had their clothing traditions which closely followed those of their parents. Boys wore the *thob shillahat*, *dishdasha* and *bisht* and if they were Bedu wrapped the *gatra* and *'agal* around their heads. In the towns this headdress tended not to be worn until the boy was considered to be adult. Exceptions were made at the religious festivals when boys were dressed in miniature versions of adult dress (Plate 63). Girls again wore the *sirwal* and *fustan* like their mothers and also a special shawl-like hood *bukhnug* or *goba* which fitted closely round their faces and hung like a cloak down their backs. These hoods were usually of black fabric which for special occasions could be of fine transparent gauze embroidered in gold. The exchange of *bukhnug* for *'abbaya*, *milfa* and face veil symbolised the girl's transition to adulthood at about 15 years old.

KUWAIT IN THE PRESENT

1 The establishment of a constitution, and development of the economy and infrastructure.

When Kuwait emerged as a fully independent Emirate in 1961 the process of transformation from a traditional Arabian Gulf maritime community to an evolving modern state had already begun. The oil industry, which was to eclipse pearl fishing, boat building and sea trade to become the foundation of Kuwait's economic prosperity, had been steadily developed since the first commercially viable wells had been drilled at Burgan in 1938 until by the early 1960s the Kuwait Oil Company had over four hundred wells in operation whose products were exported worldwide. The results were becoming apparent at all levels of society. There were the construction projects which were to transform the appearance of Kuwait (Plate 64), and the immigration of an international expatriate work force. A comprehensive welfare infrastructure was established especially in education and medical facilities where the modest schools and missionary hospitals of the early 20th century were gradually replaced by a state system of primary and secondary education and a range of clinics and hospitals.

Kuwait City. Office blocks under construction.

This rapid economic and social development has been accompanied by changes in the government which indeed had to be broadened from its traditional base of personal rule by the Sheikh and his advisers into a more comprehensive system able to cope with the increasing complexity of modern Kuwait. Certain experiments aiming at a more broadly based system had already been attempted, before World War II resulting in the formation in 1938 of a short-lived Legislative Council followed in 1939 by a Consultative Council of four sheikhs of the al-Sabah family and nine advisers. After independence Sheikh Abdullah al-Salem al-Sabah (1950-1965) appointed a constituent assembly to draft a constitution and to act as a chamber of deputies. On 29th January 1963 the constitution became law and the first National Assembly of Kuwait was convened. The Constitution consists of 183 articles which define fundamental provisions—that Kuwait is an Arab state and an hereditary Emirate whose ruler must be a descendant of Sheikh Mubarak al-Sabah (1896-1915), that Islam is the state religion and Islamic law the major source of legislation, that personal liberty and freedom of conscience and the press is guaranteed—and practical recommendations concerning legislative executive and judicial powers, financial and military affairs.

As head of state the Emir has ultimate authority to make legislative decisions in consultation with the Crown Prince, who is also Prime Minister, and the Council of Ministers. The Crown Prince chooses the fourteen members of the Council of Ministers, from candidates which include National Assembly deputies who serve a four year legislative term. Between them they are responsible for the ministries handling education, housing, foreign affairs, defence, the interior oil, finance, transport and communications, public health, social affairs and labour, public works, justice, religious endowments (*awqaf*) and Islamic affairs, commerce and industry, electricity and water, and information. The National Assembly consists of fifty deputies, two each for Kuwait's twenty-five constituencies, elected by a secret ballot of Kuwaiti male adults. Only Kuwaiti citizens are eligible for candidature. Normally the National Assembly serves a term of four years, during which the deputies work by debate and in committee on the affairs handled by the various ministries. Laws have to be approved by the National Assembly and ratified by the Emir. The revised and extended system of government required a professional administration with the result that a civil service was established, whose classification and conditions of service, patterned mainly on Egyptian models, were codified in the Civil Service Regulations of 1960. Kuwaiti citizens are therefore eligible for graded permanent appointments, with a commensurate salary structure, annual leave allowance, promotion prospects and pension rights. A corresponding local authority administration has developed as Kuwait and its suburbs now include the municipalities of Kuwait City, Hawalli, Ahmadi and Jahra.

Kuwait's remarkable economic expansion has primarily depended on abundant reserves of crude oil and associated natural gas, totalling about 11% of current world resources. These depending on variable factors such as fluctuations in demand, discovery of new deposits, advances in recovery technology, and the continued application of a conservation policy which controls production levels,[1] are estimated to be likely to last for about another seventy to eighty years. Early explorations for oil were concentrated in the operations of the Kuwait Oil Company (KOC) which, formed jointly by the Anglo-Persian Oil Company (now British Petroleum) and Gulf Oil, had been granted a licence in 1934. Between1938 and 1942 numerous wells had been drilled in the huge oil field at Burgan but production declined during the last years of World War II and was not resumed until 1945. Progress was rapid and in 1946 Kuwait's first exports of crude oil were made. KOC then set about creating an infrastructure for the developing oil industry and between 1946 and 1949 built its headquarters, which included both offices, homes and social facilities for its employees, and a refinery and terminal at Ahmadi with the aid of expatriate construction teams. Refineries were also built later at Shuaiba and Mina Abdullah. During the 1950s and 1960s KOC flourished as new wells were drilled and world demand for Kuwait's oil escalated. In 1974 and 1975 negotiations with British Petroleum and Gulf Oil resulted in first 60% and then the remaining 40% of their shares in KOC being bought out by the Kuwait Government. Kuwait, which is a member of OPEC (Organisation of Petroleum Exporting Countries), now controls its oil industry through the Kuwait Petroleum Corporation (KPC) which was established in 1980. KPC co-ordinates the activities of KOC in exploration, drilling and production, Kuwait National Petroleum Company (KNPC founded in 1961) in refining, local marketing and gas liquefaction, and Kuwait Oil Tankers Company (KOTC founded in 1957) in transporting crude oil, gas and downsteam products abroad through the terminals at Ahmadi, Shuaiba, Mina Abdullah and most recently Mina al-Zour in the Neutral Zone. Bearing in mind that export figures vary according to market demand, the main customers for Kuwait's crude oil and refined products are currently in Europe, and the Far East especially Japan.

As oil is a finite resource, and Kuwait's domestic absorptive capacity is limited, the economy has been diversified by investing revenues in different enterprises. In the oil industry itself this has been achieved by promoting the associated downstream industries of refining—yielding motor spirit, gas oil, diesel, kerosene, light and heavy fuel oils; petrochemicals, fertilisers and aromatic products; and marine transport. An area of growth which has rapidly developed as a necessary adjunct to the oil industry and which also draws on traditional assets of mercantile skills and Kuwait's strategic position on important trade and transit routes is finance. Here a system of both national and commercial banks, insurance companies, and overseas investment notably of surplus oil capital, has been established. Efforts have also been made to stimulate an industrial base, but here there are difficulties concerning availability of cheap raw materials, a relatively small local market, and a steady supply of labour at costs which would make the products competitive. Manufacturing enterprises are located around the port of Shuweikh and in the Shuaiba and recently established Sabhan industrial complexes. They concentrate on a range of products such as materials—cement, bricks, asbestos for the construction industry, chemicals, electrical goods, and increasingly foodstuffs—bread, biscuits, and ready-made clothing. At the other end of the scale are small labour intensive workshops of variable usually short lifespan.

A division of the economy where profits could be made through diversification was trade which was especially attractive to the private sector. Here the prosperity brought by the oil revenues had led to a greatly improved standard of living which in turn created a demand for consumer goods which trading enterprises hastened to satisfy by acting as retail outlets for agencies and products of foreign companies thus updating a traditional pattern of mixed commerce. Imports ranged from cars and air conditioning units from America, through food products from Europe and the Middle East, textiles from the Far East, and luxury items of household furnishing and decoration, smart clothing and electronic equipment from numerous sources. Kuwait also functioned as a transit trade centre as many of these goods were re-exported to neighbouring Gulf states. Other traditionally based supplies into the economy such as agriculture and fishing have not been neglected. It has already been seen that in the past Kuwait's production of cereals, vegetables and fruit grown in the oasis of Jahra and scattered smallholdings had not then been sufficient for the population's needs, due to limitations of water supply, fertile soil, climate and manpower. These problems still exist and much foodstuff needs to be imported, but government investment and the work of the Kuwait Experimental Farm have led to improvements whereby existing resources are more efficiently utilised. Experiments, for example, have concentrated on finding species of crops that would cope better with local conditions and that would grow in brackish water, with the result that locally raised supplies of tomatoes, cucumbers, cabbage, watermelons, citrus fruits and dates are now found in the markets. Water distilled from the sea has greatly increased traditional water supplies and lessened reliance on imports from the Shatt al-Arab. Meat and dairy product needs had been customarily met by the herds of the Bedu. This has declined for several reasons. Many of the Bedu are now settled and no longer pursue a nomadic way of life grazing flocks and herds. Farms in Kuwait yield cattle, sheep, goats and poultry, while any shortfall is supplemented by imports. Fishing continues along mixed lines. Small *dhows* and motorboats concentrated along the bay still meet local market needs, while the factory ships of the United Fisheries of Kuwait range the Gulf,

Atlantic and Indian Oceans. Scientific research has concentrated on improving fish stocks as the increased population of the Gulf has led to serious overfishing.

A massive income of the oil revenues has been channelled into the development of social services with priority given to education and medicin where all facilities are freely available to Kuwaiti citizens. An active interes in expanding education was a natural consequence of the transformation o the system of government and the economy which required the services of adequately trained personnel. The educational system is predominantly public and government sponsored and can now take a child through from kindergarten to university. Schooling is based on a four part progression of kindergarten followed by primary, intermediate and secondary stages each of four years. A balanced curriculum includes both art and science subjects with Islamic religion and Arab history. Schools are modern and lavishly equipped with libraries, audio-visual aids, sport and recreation facilities. From secondary school students continue with higher education at technica vocational or university level. A technical college was established in 1954, followed by teacher training colleges for men and women in 1962. Until 1966 when Kuwait University was founded, students had to go to other Arab countries, notably Lebanon and Egypt, or to Britain and America, fo university education. Kuwait University now offers courses in arts, sciences, economics, law, engineering and medicine. Great importance is attached t adult or continuing education where students attend evening classes in languages, commercial and technical subjects to improve their existing skill Special institutions such as a centre for Islamic religious studies and school for the handicapped exist. Selected attendance figures demonstrate how these educational facilities have been used; the number of students in publi schools, for example, increased from 4,665 in 1948/49 to 334,942 in 1982/83 while 3,276 students were registered at Kuwait University durin the first term of 1982/83. Parallel with the public sector are the private schools catering to the needs of the international expatriate community.

Impressive advances have been made in creating a comprehensive health care system from the modest beginnings of one hospital and four doctors i government service in 1949 to fifteen hospitals and 2,487 doctors in 1982. Ministry of Health priorities have concentrated on establishing well-equipped hospitals with specialist units and a network of community healt care. In 1950 the Amiri hospital was extended to include X-ray, ophthalmology and dentistry departments, while later foundations such as the al-Sabah hospital and the Mubarak al-Kabir hospital completed in 196 and the late 1970s respectively had all-embracing facilities. Community health care, which includes preventive medicine and dental treatment, is provided by suburban and school clinics. A blood bank and fully equipped medical stores centre support the medical services. Recruitment of staff at a levels occurs through specialist and vocational training both in Kuwait and abroad and through employing qualified expatriates on contract.

Various factors have shaped government housing policy apart from a need to upgrade and extend house ownership. Demolition of traditional residenti areas in Kuwait town during the reconstruction programmes from the 1950 onwards created a need for new homes for displaced tenants. Purchase of land for housing development schemes also offered a means of distributing portion of the oil revenues among the Kuwaiti population. The most urge priority was given to supplying accommodation to low income groups and settled Bedu who had traditionally lived in poor quality temporary homes on the outskirts of the town. A Rural Housing Programme by which modest houses are rented out for nominal amounts caters initially for the Bedu until they are considered eligible for Kuwaiti nationality. Then along with other low income groups they can qualify for housing stock built by the National Housing Authority. Here the family pays rent which can count towards the purchase of the house if over a minimum of ten years it has covered the estimated cost of construction. The National Housing Authority currently operates a scheme for families of average income comparable to a mortgage, whereby the head of a household applies to the Credit and Savings Bank for a loan to purchase one of the Authority's houses. Projects for blocks of apartments are also being developed.

The development of Kuwait's internal resources and infrastructure has been accompanied by increased activity in foreign policy which broadly aims to maintain a balance between international and more Islamic-orientated affairs, epitomised by membership of both the United Nations and the Islamic Conference Organisation. A reciprocal network of diplomatic missions between Kuwait and states in the Middle East, Europe, Africa and Asia has been established to encourage international relations. Foreign affairs also absorbs a share of the oil revenues in the Kuwait fund for Arab Economic Development which has been created to finance infrastructure projects in for example, power supplies, agriculture, industry, transport and communication. Its funds have also been extended to non-Arab countries such as Malaysia, India and Pakistan. Nearer home steps have been taken to formalise relations with Arab neighbours by the creation in 1981 of the Gulf Co-operation Council, consisting of Kuwait, Saudi Arabia, Bahrain, Qatar, the United Arab Emirates and Oman, which aims to co-operate in the broad areas of security, economic, social and cultural affairs.

2 The settlement

The accelerated development of Kuwait's economy and infrastructure inevitably had repercussions on both its physical environment and demographic patterns. Indeed if Niebuhr and Buckingham who described Kuwait in 1765 and 1816 were to see it today, apart from the tangle of small ships clustered along the bay, they would have severe identification problems, so completely have the city and its environs been transformed through a concentrated programme of demolition and reconstruction. Until the 1950s Kuwait had managed to balance tradition with encroaching modernity as the old town continued to function within its mud brick walls. Further south the employees of the Kuwait Oil Company pursued their drilling operations and gradually moved from camps into permanent quarters at Ahmadi whose bungalows, gardens and clubs were intended to create a European-style home environment. It soon became clear, however, that Kuwait could not continue indefinitely in this way as its facilities were not adequate for the integration of new public buildings, for housing and support services for an expanding population, or for traffic circulation for the increasingly heavy use of cars and trucks. The problem required urgent solution and today Kuwait's appearance is the result of an accumulated series of master plans designed by European planning consultants.

Three master plans have contributed to Kuwait's renovation. The first, submitted in 1952 by the British firm of Miniprio and Spenceley, was based on the then contemporary principles of planning whereby a town was zoned into distinct areas. Administrative and office accommodation occupied the town centre, around which self-contained residential suburbs complete with shopping and recreational facilities were grouped in regular units all linked by a network of radial and ring roads and motorways. This plan was rapidly implemented in Kuwait by demolishing most of the old town including the city wall, of which by 1954 only the gates were left standing as a memorial to the past (Plate 7). The line of the city wall was, however, treated as a "green belt" planted with trees and plots of grass, and encircled by the first ring road. Within the resulting enclosure at the tip of the bay Kuwait City, focused on the old port area and the Seif Palace as the administrative centre, proliferated with the chequerboard facades of office and commercial blocks (Plate 65). Radiating from the old gates was the road system sliced into concentric segments of residential suburbs by three more ring roads.

65 Kuwait City. Kuwait Airways Corporation buildings.

During the 1960s the character of the building programme began to change and certain areas of the town, notably the traditional houses along the sea front and the old *suq*, were preserved. A second master plan prepared in 1968 by the British consultants Buchanan and McCulloch to supplement the Minoprio and Spenceley plan, recommended schemes at various levels for the development of the city centre, the extension of the city as far as Ahmadi, and the creation of another city across the bay from Kuwait City at al-Subiya. Following the recommendations of Buchanan and McCulloch an advisory panel was established to invite architects to submit plans for the continued development of Kuwait City and suburbs. Certain principles had to be observed; the "green belt" of the 1952 plan had to be kept as a boundary to the city centre; new government buildings were to be located near the Seif Palace; the waterfront buildings and the old *suq* were to be preserved and restored; if possible residential areas were to be integrated into the city centre. The third master plan of Shankland and Cox in 1976 was intended to develop and update the recommendations of the 1968 plan rather than initiate new projects, other than a proposal for a third city near the border between Kuwait and Saudi Arabia. The basic recommendations of both plans were adopted and serious work began on the revision of Kuwait City and its neighbourhood.

One obvious result of all the planning and construction is that the area of urban settlement has greatly expanded, though along the traditional alignments of south, and east, both inland and down the coast. Inland, areas which were once isolated villages have been absorbed into a continuous development which extends to a sixth ring road. The consequent transformation of Adailiya, Hawalli and Salmiya was thus noted by Zahra Freeth in 1970.

Of Adailiya she says "Now it is a built-up area indistinguishable from the rest of the endless new urban development, but in my childhood the name had denoted a pleasant hollow in the undulating desert. The subsoil here retained water, and fairly shallow wells yielded an abundant supply. This had made it a place where wheat could be grown, the only such place in the countryside outside Kuwait town. We had always enjoyed walking by the fresh green of the springing crops after the rainy season.

"Hawalli was another name which had meant something to me in old Kuwait. It had been a desert village eight miles out of town, characterised by its small vegetable gardens surrounded by low mud walls. Where is Hawalli now? It is one of the neighbourhood units of the suburbs, with its own high street, shopping centre and cinema.

"In the open country near the Ras in the old days there stood a small village consisting of a few mud huts clustered around a single tamarisk tree. The name of the place was Dimna . . . when the new suburb was built the name had to be changed. It was called Salamiyah after Sheikh Abdullah as Salim. Today it is hard to know exactly where the village stood; it has been completely obliterated.

"Our road ran through the Salmiyah shopping centre, with its supermarkets, drug-stores, furniture shops . . . and window displays of European women's fashions."[1]

Similarly the road to Jahra is now lined with government housing schemes starkly outlined against the desert (Plate 66). Extending south from Salmiya

66 Kuwait City-Jahra road. Government housing scheme.

67 Fahaheel. Main road and *suq*.

68 Kuwait City, Safat Square. Modern office buildings and mosque.

69 Kuwait City, Arabian Gulf Street. Bayt Sadu, exterior.

70 Dhowyard at Doha. Demonstration of a dhow drill.

is a ribbon development bounded by a major coastal highway passing through Fintas, Fahaheel to Mina Abdullah. The suburb of Fahaheel in particular is densely built with houses, apartment blocks and a shopping precinct (Plate 67).

Enclosed within the confines of the first ring road, the "green belt" and the coast road, three main streets cut horizontally through Kuwait City's assortment of buildings where modern multi-storey office blocks, hotels of the major international chains, recently completed government buildings such as the Ministry of Foreign Affairs, the Ministry of Information and the National Museum, and new shopping complexes, mingle and contrast with the sprawl of the old *suq* and traditional houses and mosques of modest size (Plate 68). West of the city are public buildings, faculties of Kuwait University and the Shuweikh Industrial Area. Beyond the first ring road old quarters of tenement blocks merge into new residential suburbs which in turn give way to more industrial areas, the buildings of Kuwait International Airport and on to Ahmadi. This recently urbanised landscape which is still interrupted by stretches of desert is also punctuated by certain distinctive landmarks such as the three sharp-pointed spheres of the Kuwait Towers located at the eastern tip of Kuwait bay the Dasman headland, and the five groups of graceful mushroom-shaped water reservoirs.

The remains of traditional Kuwait, with the exception of the Red Fort at Jahra, are naturally grouped within the limits of the old town, and have been preserved either as historical monuments or functioning buildings. The old gates which once would have seemed solid impenetrable constructions are now dwarfed by the height of the buildings surrounding them, and have been integrated into the "green belt" as roundabouts landscaped with palm trees and grass around which the traffic whirls on the main roads in and out of the city. Along the seafront concentrated within a relatively compact strecth of Arabian Gulf Street are the most important surviving examples of traditional houses. Bayt al-Badr is now part of the National Museum complex, while its neighbour functions as the headquarters of the al-Sadu Foundation for the preservation of Bedu weaving crafts (Plate 69). Further along the coast near the Seif Palace the former Political Agency is now a residence. Within the same area are most of the city's old mosques which are still functional. The boat-building yards which played such a major role in Kuwait's traditional economy are now confined to Doha on the north side of the bay, where there is always a ship in various stages of construction and craftsmen glad to explain their work and demonstrate the simple drills used (Plate 70). At Jahra, the Red Fort has been restored and is now open as a museum.

Recently commissioned public buildings demonstrate sympathetic and imaginative solutions to the problems of functional requirements. The need to ensure shade and coolness in a hot climate and the integration of principles of Islamic architecture and decoration, while employing modern materials and construction techniques are recognised. Kuwait's main administration is still centred at the Seif Palace located on the coast along Arabian Gulf Street approximately halfway between the western and eastern limits of Kuwait City. The original late 19th century building, with its series of articulated brick arcades and courtyards overhung with wooden latticed loggias, is still in use. This was extended along the same principles in the 1960s when a clock tower was also built (Plate 8). Later two Finnish architects, Reima and Raili Pietila, were commissioned to design a further extension to house the Prime Minister's Office, the Council of Ministers and Ministry of Foreign Affairs, which was completed in 1983. Here they have built along the coastline skilfully deploying its natural formation and making the water front an integral feature of their design. Tradition has been continued and interpreted by facing both sea and road sides of the complex with arched beige brick colonnades. Within are courtyards with overhanging faceted eaves to give maximum shade, whose austere proportions are enlivened by bands and borders of ceramic tile glazed in blue, green and deep yellow.

The new headquarters of the Ministry of Information designed by Jacques Satour incorporates features of traditional Islamic architecture. The main building is a dramatic white tower whose sides ascend in ribbed arches to a geometrical interpretation of a stalactite *muqarnas* cornice with facets and pinnacles.This building looks down a rectangular colonnaded courtyard enclosing a large pool. Along the coast west of the Seif Palace the National Assembly building designed by the Danish architect Jorn Utzon is under construction. Here a tent-like roof ascends in a bold curve to an entrance of massively proportioned columns (Plate 71), to ultimately cover an internal network of conference hall and courts with members rooms. Modern public building programmes also include mosques which must be designed according to Islamic ritual specifications. Many striking and innovative

71 Kuwait City, Arabian Gulf Street. National Assembly building under construction.

72 Kuwait, Abdullah Salem suburb. Mosque.

73 Kuwait City, Arabian Gulf Street. State mosque.

decorative features such as tiled domes (Plate 72), intricate minarets, are found in the many new mosques of Kuwait which have been built by both state and private charity. Apart from local mosques which service areas of Kuwait City and the suburbs there is a State Mosque under construction opposite the Seif Palace (Plate 73). Designed by the Iraqi firm of Muhammad Makiya, its light grey stone structures include a domed chamber approached by a spacious open entrance court.

Outside the boundaries of Kuwait City and extending well beyond the first ring road the modern residential buildings commence, which in both their external appearance and internal structure present varied architectural styles. The old type of house based on a series of open courtyards lined with cool thick-walled rooms is no longer built, though some of its principles are beginning to be re-introduced. Zahra Freeth had noted in 1970:—

"The coming of air-conditioners caused many Kuwaitis to feel that the old principles of keeping the sun off the outer walls, and retaining coolness within the thickness of masonry were outdated. They abandoned the wide veranda, running the length of the house, since it was assumed that modern householders would stay indoors, not needing to sit in the evening breeze.

But when they lost the veranda the houses also lost the graceful pillared facade which had been a charming feature of Arab architecture, and without the shade of a veranda the sun beats mercilessly on every side of a house heating it like an oven, so that air-conditioning becomes essential even at the beginning of the hot season, while older houses can be comfortable without it for the early weeks of summer.

"By now, those who have lived several years in some of the less well-designed houses have discovered their disadvantages, and this is one of the reasons why even modern buildings are regularly demolished and rebuilt. There now appears to be a gradual return to more traditional forms of building, and we saw three or four new houses which were good to look at, making use of arches and arcaded verandas."[2]

Blocks of flats which line the coast road and dominate certain of the suburbs near to Kuwait City have been constructed with outward facing balconies and windows which give the impression of a chequerboard lattice (Plate 74). In some areas individual homes are remarkable for the personal eclectic taste reflected in their architecture which ranges from interpretations of tents (Plate 75), to stately classical porticos, and the stark cuboid shapes familiar from the Mediterranean coast, but generally houses are of square or rectangular form with flat roofs. It is interesting however, to observe that despite the effective abandonment of the form of the traditional courtyard house, a social continuity may be traced in the alignment and function of space within a modern villa. As in the past, houses present a blank anonymous view to the outside world, as they are enclosed within a high wall with nowadays a huge metal gate, which leads into a paved yard or carefully landscaped garden whose proportions and furnishings depend on the family's means. Within the yard some houses have a spacious room on one side with bathroom and small kitchen en suite, entirely separate from the main part, which continues the traditional function of a *diwaniya* where the men of the family can entertain their friends. In general, houses have two to three fully air-conditioned storeys with living and kitchen areas on the ground floor and bedrooms and bathrooms on the upper levels. From the yard the main door of the house may lead directly into a sitting room or into a spacious hall which can also function sometimes as a family sitting or dining room. The downstairs area usually has two to three sitting rooms which can be sealed off into quite separate units by doors or corridors, depending on a family's social customs. In some houses, for example, an indoor sitting room can function as a *diwaniya*.

74 Kuwait City. Office blocks and apartments.

75 Kuwait, Abdullah Salem suburb. "Tent" house.

Variations are to be found in the grouping of the rooms on the ground floor. One house had sitting rooms on each side of the hall which in turn led to combined kitchen and dining area which in turn opened on to a small yard with an outhouse for doing rough work such as gutting and cleaning fish. Yet another house had three adjacent sitting rooms with a separate entrance from the yard to one of them recalling the old tradition of a separate entrance to the women's courtyard. Sometimes the separation of family from public reception area was achieved by using different floors; a comfortable sitting room with a small kitchen attached for the preparation of tea and coffee where ladies were entertained could be reached by stairs from the ground floor. There can also be two dining rooms—one for informal family meals and one for guests.

The upper storeys contain both master and children's bedrooms and bathrooms and also sitting rooms especially if several generations of a family share one house. Government-sponsored low-income housing schemes such as those built at Jahra, while on a more modest scale than privately owned villas, incorporate similar principles of planning. A high wall encloses a yard which may contain a separate *diwaniya.* Otherwise the front door opens directly into a main sitting room from which doors open into two or three adjacent rooms. A stair leads up to the second storey where the bedrooms are located. At the back of the house is a narrow yard which leads to a separate kitchen and also functions as an alley to and from neighbouring houses. In this way women can move among their friends and neighbours without having to go into the street.

The new settlement patterns which have resulted from the development of Kuwait's housing infrastructure have correspondingly affected the facilities which service them. This is especially noticeable in the shopping districts. Formerly Kuwait town was small enough for the centrally located *suq* to supply most needs from the range of goods and services which it offered to both the resident population and the Bedu who visited it seasonally. Changes in styles of living have been created by the extension of employment opportunities made possible through the development of the economy and demands for a wider range of consumer goods. Modern methods of manufacturing and processing such as refrigeration which means that food does not have to be purchased daily, are also factors which have contributed to the establishment of new retail enterprises, beside which, however, the traditional *suq* still survives. The evolution of Kuwait's commercial quarters may therefore be traced from *suq* and associated markets, through urban shopping complexes residential suburban facilities, and to a lesser extent the department store.

Within Kuwait City the *suq* though considerably altered and reduced in area still sprawls around Safat Square, but its covered passages and open stalls have to be tracked down among banks and office blocks. The *suq*'s area is still divided according to product and presents a colourful bustling appearance throughout opening hours. There are the vegetable (Plate 76) and fish markets (Plate 77) with stalls plentifully heaped with the day's produce and streets of small shops selling dried fruits, olives, herbs, spices, nuts (Plate 78), and also imported brands of European confectionery such as chocolate bars and toffees. Other areas again specialise in more durable goods, metalwork for household uses, braziers, cooking pots, serving dishes and crockery (Plates 79-81). One distinctive section is reserved for the making and selling of traditional clothing: men's *bisht*, *farwah* and

76 Kuwait City, *suq*. Vegetable market.

77 Kuwait City, *suq*. Fish market.

78 Kuwait City, *suq*. Dried fruit stall.

79 Kuwait City, *suq*. Crockery merchant.

80 Kuwait City, *suq*. Brassware merchant.

81 Kuwait City, *suq*. Rope merchants.

82 Kuwait City, *suq*. Trader in men's and women's cloaks—*bisht* and *'abbaya*.

83 Kuwait City, *suq al-harim*.

accessories (Plate 82), women's *'abbaya*, and also carpets imported from Persia, Turkey and Pakistan. The *suq* is also crowded with shops selling jewellery, bales of fabrics for furnishing and clothes, ready-made clothes and also tailors' workshops where men's *dishdasha* are quickly machine sewn either for a customer's order or to be hung up for sale. A special *suq* which still retains its traditional character even though the nature of some of its goods has changed is the *suq al-harim*, the women's *suq* (Plate 83). This is still a long high covered way located near the headquarters of the National Bank. Traditionally it was active in spring doing a brisk trade with the Bedu in foodstuffs such as rice, sugar, tea and coffee in exchange for their products. Now its most distinctive section consists of a central row of stalls run by women traders of mixed Kuwaiti, Iraqi, Egyptian and Bedu origin, who market an assortment of traditional style goods. These include ready-made men's, women's and children's clothes—*dishdasha*, *sirwal*, sequin trimmed dresses and *thob*, *'abbaya* and also the veils and face masks—*burqa*, still worn by Bedu women. An interesting range of cosmetic and toilet articles are also sold—packets of henna and its fixative, twists of *maswak* bark for cleaning the teeth and staining the lips, small bottles of kohl and elaborate gilt metal containers, a traditional shampoo imported from Iraq which looks like large blocks of rough soap, and all manner of crotchet and knitted bath loofahs. The shops on each side of the *suq* sell traditional items of men's clothing especially the components of the headdress, and also a wide selection of sandals and European-style shoes and slippers. Passages lead off the suq *al-harim* to other busy streets full of tailors and small shops selling men's clothes.

Kuwait also has other *suqs* outside the city centre where traditional goods are still sold. At Abbassiya beyond the sixth ring road is situated what is perhaps the most conservative of these suburban *suqs* in that most of its produce is sold to Bedu. The shops therefore specialise in traditional clothing—*bisht* and *farwah*, and basic household utensils. The *suq* at Fahaheel is divided by a main road into two sections; one is newly built on a grid plan and full of brightly lit shops selling all manner of modern clothes and gadgets; the other retains a more casual traditional character (Plate 84). Jahra's *suq* is mixed. In addition to the shops selling Bedu goods and clothes, and also distinctive gold jewellery, there are also new establishments selling

84 Fahaheel. Modern *suq*.

85 Kuwait. Friday market. Bedu weaving for sale.

86 Kuwait. Friday market. Canvas tents for sale.

87 Kuwait. Friday market. Secondhand furniture for sale.

88 Jahra. Camel market.

89 Jahra. Camel market, herdsmen.

lengths of fabric, perfumes and cosmetics, and a government sponsored vegetable market.

Traditional markets of a more semi-permanent nature have also survived in Kuwait. One of the most important and well-known is the so-called Friday or Bedu market located near the fourth ring road. As its names imply this is operational on Fridays only from early morning until lunchtime and also serves Bedu customers. It occupies a huge area of open land only lightly enclosed by a wire fence. The goods sold there illustrate both traditional Bedu and modern tastes. In one section sheep and goats are sold (Plate 24), while nearby are covered sheds spread out with Bedu weavings—rugs, storage bags, animal trappings from the Kuwait region, Iraq. Syria and Jordan (Plate 85). Today they are brought to market in trucks rather than on camel back. Rows of square and rectangular white canvas tents (Plate 86) with bright block-printed linings imported from Pakistan extend along one side of the market enclosure. These are popular with Kuwaitis for desert picnics, or as spacious garden furnishings. A large area of the market is devoted to a lively trade in secondhand furniture—chests, wardrobes, children's cots, clothing and a few antiques—coffee pots, grinders, braziers, weapons (Plate 87). A more specialist traditional market is held seasonally at Jahra, the camel market attractively described by Zahra Freeth in 1970 and little changed since then.

"On the eastern fringe of the oasis the usual new three-storey concrete houses have risen, colour-washed pink, green, blue or cream. Originally the dwellings which clustered round the palm-groves presented a view of low mud-built walls. Some still survive, but hidden now behind more modern buildings. We had come to look at the camel market. My son and daughter, new to Arabia, had dreamed of camels against a desert landscape, but alas when we came to Kuwait we found that camels were no longer a common element in the desert scene. However we heard that there were usually camels in Jahra, for badu from the wastes of northern Najd would bring animals to sell in the market there. Such men were true nomads who still led the ancient life of poverty and hardship, making contact with the affluent society of Kuwait only when they came to buy or sell. But the camel-sellers would have been lost in the business-centre of Kuwait, for they were not men who needed banks and modern shopping facilities. Indeed in central Kuwait there is today no place where a man may take a camel to sell. So they came to Jahra, where the surroundings still have a friendly informal air in which they can feel at home, and wait with their camels in an open space at the corner of the village.

"When we came to the market we found about a dozen camels gathered there. I have always found camels attractive. They are creatures tough enough to survive great privation, yet the best of them are biddable and obedient in the hands of their masters. For me they symbolised the very essence of desert life. Among this group of beasts we enjoyed the pretty sight of a female with a young calf. The camels were shedding their coats with the onset of the hot season, and felted lumps of wool were hanging loose on their flanks."[3]

Today the camel market has an atmosphere of isolated impermanence. The camels are kept in large open enclosures (Plate 88) where they are tended by herdsmen (Plate 89) who live in small corrugated iron shacks. The owners who may live at some distance away, in Fahaheel for example, drive out at intervals to inspect or sell their animals. Camel herding in the Kuwait region is apparently developing as a business enterprise rather than continuing as an integral part of life.

Prominent among the goods in the *suq* is a rich selection of modern electrical items. On sale are radios, tape recorders, television and video sets, photographic equipment, household gadgets such as blenders and food processors, which are indicative of the changes in traditional shopping patterns. This process was already in hand in a modest way in the 1930s as Zahra Freeth notes:—

"In about 1934 an Indian trader named Jashanmal received permission from my father, then Political Agent, to open a shop in Kuwait. He stocked modern necessities of a practical kind which had not previously been available in the town—stationery, patent medicine, toilet goods, and so on. Because he was a pioneer he prospered. I can remember old Mr Jashanmal, wearing his astrakhan cap and Indian-style shirt outside his white trousers, selling me an electric torch when I was about ten years old. After my absence from Kuwait in the war years I found that Jashanmal's had moved into new premises in the Safat, where in a bigger modern shop he was still setting the pace in providing newer and bigger goods for the changing tastes of Kuwait."[4]

The pace of change steadily accelerated until by the 1970s:—

"It is only twenty years since the first really modern shops began to appear in Kuwait, and now the main streets are lined with stores which in equipment and stock are totally European. To me, the interest of such shops lay in the way they reflected the changing consumer tastes in Kuwait. Fifteen years before I had not seen European-type restaurants, dry cleaners and laundries, hairdressing salons, shops full of prams and modern infants' clothes, and women's dress shops."[5]

The modernisation of shopping facilities has developed in various ways. Originally shops and services were concentrated in long streets, notably in Fahad al-Salem Street in Kuwait City which supplied clothing, electrical goods, travel agencies, restaurants and cafes, and in the older suburbs of Salmiya, Hawalli and Nuzha which specialised respectively in smart boutiques, furnishing stores and general clothing and fabric shops. Recently, however, shopping has moved from the streets into multi-storeyed indoor complexes allowing plenty of space for the public to circulate and window shop, and often equipped with fountains, seats and cafes. These schemes, which are modern developments in Europe, much appealed to the Kuwaiti public, as in basic concept and plan they are comparable to the traditional *suq*. They have developed, therefore, all over Kuwait City either as extensions behind main streets or as independently planned centres. Two notable examples are the large Awqaf Complex newly built on Mubarak al-Kabir Street (Plate 90), whose spacious premises include smart dress shops, furniture and china shops, confectioners, jewellers, newsagents, and the two-storeyed Salhia Complex near the Jahra gate roundabout (Plate 91), whose select establishments sell designer fashions, Italian handbags and shoes, exclusive brands of cosmetics and perfumes, glass and porcelain, high quality patisserie and delicatessen foods.

90 Kuwait. Awqaf shopping complex, main concourse.

91 Kuwait City. Salhia shopping complex, clothes boutique.

92 Kuwait. Display of Chinese goods in a department store.

The multi-storey department store, familiar in western Europe and America, may be considered as a vertically aligned variation of the *suq* or shopping complex, except that its wide selection of branded goods are allocated to floor areas and marketed by one enterprise rather than by independent retailers. As yet this shopping concept has not been much developed in Kuwait. There is one recently built department store just outside Kuwait City whose stock of household wares and linens, cosmetics, perfumes and jewellery, and smart clothes for men and women, is divided between three floors all connected by escalators. Many European lines are stocked and the store also organises special promotions and displays for example of products from China—porcelain, lacquer, jade, embroidered textiles—aimed at an export market (Plate 92). It is clear, however, that the modern shopping complexes and department store concentrate on consumer durables and luxuries rather than the staples of everyday life. In this sector there have been drastic changes as needs which were once supplied by the *suq* and small neighbourhood units such as bakeries are now met by large supermarkets exhaustively stocked with basic meat, fish, greengroceries, bread and dairy products, tinned, packaged and frozen foods, condiments, detergents etc. where families can shop in weekly sessions rather than daily visits. The supermarkets have developed as a result of the original master plan imposed on Kuwait, whereby suburban residential units enclosed within the grid of arterial and ring roads had their own self-contained service centres (Plate 93) which included supermarket, garage, bank, library and often a children's nursery and some additional shops.

The rapid expansion of Kuwait's economy and infrastructure has been matched by a population increase which amounts to an explosion when compared with the modest 50,000 recorded by Lorimer in 1904. Today it is possible to calibrate the pace of this increase by examining the returns of the six censuses taken in 1957, 1961, 1965, 1970, 1975 and 1980.[6] A total of 206,473 was recorded for 1957, which then rose by approximately 100,000 between each of the next two censuses, then by 300,000 by 1970, levelling out at a 200,000 increase by 1975, and then suddenly escalating by 400,000 to 1,357,952 in 1980. Intercensus estimates have predicted a further increase by 1985 ti 1m910,856. Certain qualifying factors, however, must be taken into account as these figures include totals for both Kuwaiti and non-Kuwaiti groups, and therefore do not necessarily record a permanent growth. While the native Kuwaiti population has increased steadily through a drop in infant mortality rates, a longer adult life expectancy due to improved medical services, and the decline of high-risk occupations such as pearl-diving, there has been large scale immigration to supply the labour needed to maintain the expanded economy. As many of these immigrants are employed on contracts of variable length their periods of residence fluctuate and correspondingly affect the population figures. The 1980 census records the following percentage analysis; Kuwaitis 41.7%, other Arabs 42.3%, Asians 15%, Africans 1%, Europeans .8% and Americans .1%.[7]

These groups may be further defined according to area of employment. Kuwaiti citizens tend to occupy permanent government and administrative posts, professions such as medicine, university and specialised teaching, and management of commercial enterprises. As the traditional Bedu nomadic way of life is changing, many Bedu have increasingly taken employment in Kuwait's army and police services and in time become eligible to be considered for Kuwaiti citizenship. Other Arabs, numbering Palestinians, Jordanians, Egyptians, Lebanese, Syrians, Iraqis, are found at various levels in the public and private sectors as administrators, accountants, managers, and in the professions of teaching, medicine and social work. Europeans and Americans have tended to stay on relatively short term contracts where their professional skills in, for example, engineering, computing, banking, medicine and dentistry, and certain sections of university teaching notably in language faculties are useful. The Asian section is the most varied in both race and occupation. Traditionally Indians and Pakistanis have been the longest established Asian immigrants especially in view of the traditional Kuwaiti trade with the subcontinent. They have filled a range of office and service activities especially in retailing and tailoring, and skilled technical posts. Immigrants from Bangladesh, the Filipines, Srilanka and Thailand now dominate some service areas—as servants in both private homes and hotels, restaurant staff, construction projects—and have also entered the tailoring and dressmaking trades, formerly the monopoly of the Indians and Pakistanis. The most recent immigrants are Koreans and Chinese employed in building schemes on fixed-term contracts.

93 Kuwait. Abdullah Salem suburb, service complex.

3 Present-day social and cultural patterns

a) *Everyday life in urban society*

While it was inevitable that the recent economic and social changes would have affected Kuwaiti life, especially in the presentation of new choices and perspectives, it would be incorrect to assume an abrupt departure from traditional ways. It is much more interesting and rewarding to study Kuwait's contemporary life in the context of a traditional background and to therefore realise that seemingly conflicting customs and modern influences in fact subtly intermingle and complement each other.

The Moslem religion and its five basic obligations of faith, prayer, fasting, charity and piligrimage, are still fundamental to Kuwaiti society. Indeed this is categorically stated in Article 2 of the Constitution:—"The religion of the State is Islam, and Islamic Law shall be a main source of legislation."[1]

In support of this a Ministry of Awqaf and Religious Affairs was established. Among its wide-ranging responsibilities are the care and maintenance of mosques and their staff, the administration of religious endowments—*awqaf*, the organisation of seminars and Qur'an classes, and a publication programme which includes both magazines with articles of a religious nature and editions of texts. Religious instruction, which was once mainly confined to memorising the Qur'an under the supervision of a local teacher, now forms part of the curriculum of state schools, and there is also a religious college whose courses form a foundation for further study. Modern communications media play an important role in encouraging religion as the radio and both channels of Kuwait television have daily Qur'an readings and also discussion programmes which can take form of question and answer sessions between members of the religious establishment and laymen. At the weekends local newspapers publish the Thursday and Friday prayer times.[2] In the past five prayers divided the day into units which both suited the climate and the duration of natural light. Today it is still possible for conscientious Moslems to observe them as Kuwait's official working day begins early at 7.30am and is interrupted by a long midday break. While it is desirable for men to go to themosque for the noon and sunset prayers, and many indeed manage to do so, during the working week, it is acceptable for them to be said elsewhere. Women continue to follow traditional practice and pray at home. They do this in a most natural traditional practice and pray at home. They do this in a most natural and unaffected way and when guests are present simply move to another part of the room taking a small prayer mat (*sejada*), and a white hooded prayer shawl (*khedra*) with them. Mosques have both increased in number and grandeur of architecture and ornament to accommodate the increased population and to express charity by wealthy donors. While Kuwait is a Moslem country there are however Roman Catholic and Protestant churches for the religious needs of Christians among the expatriate communities.

While the choice of occupation and activity is today more extensive the family is still the basic social unit at all levels of Kuwaiti life. Its mutual obligations and responsibilities continue to bind the family closely together even though all its members no longer inhabit one household. Increased affluence and modern standards of living have spaced out the generations and led to more varied living patterns. The normal unit is centred on man and wife together with their children whose number may vary from about three to five in younger families and from about seven to twelve in older more traditional families. Children of both sexes live with their parents until they marry and in some cases may continue to do so after marriage with their own children, thereby resulting in three generations in a single household. It is still customary for unmarried sisters of either husband or wife to live with them if both parents are dead. Elderly people normally do not stay alone as it is still regarded as a family duty to take care of them, so often a widowed mother will live with a married son and his family if there are no unmarried children still at home. Servants, who are now recruited from Indian, Srilankan, Thai and Filipino immigrants, vary in number and function according to a family's means, but they are normally employed in the domestic tasks of cooking and cleaning and caring for small children.

Customs have gradually changed so that the division of a house into totally separate men's and women's quarters is no longer strictly maintained, yet the interiors of modern homes can accommodate segregated social lives when required. While all houses now have a common courtyard within their walls some are equipped with a separate suite of rooms which function as a *diwaniya* for the menfolk and are usually furnished in a modern variation of the traditional style. The reception room (*diwan*) has a fitted pile carpet and floor level seating with cushioned back and arm rests around the wall on three sides. These furnishings have usually been chosen from the wide range of imported manufactured carpets and fabrics which are now available in Kuwait's shops. Additionally the *diwan* is equipped with television and video sets, and a private telephone whose number is independent from that of the main house. Where there is a kitchen and bathroom these rooms are equipped with refrigerator and modern ceramic fittings.

If the household does not have a separate *diwaniya*, an internal sitting room may be adapted as required. Within the house which is equipped as a comfortable family environment, rooms are less flexible than in the past as the adoption of certain pieces of European-style furniture in place of mattresses, quilts and cushions, means that they cannot be converted easily from sitting room to dining room and finally to bedroom by a quick rearrangement of the soft furnishings. Now interior decorating schemes are eclectic, elaborate and colourful or restrained according to the family's means and taste. Reception and sitting rooms retain the closest links with former custom. Here the seating consists of low sofas and cushions placed around the walls. Floors now all have fitted carpets. Coffee tables, small occasional tables, television and video sets, potted plants, painting and wall ornaments complete the furnishings. Sometimes an ornately patterened Persian carpet is used as a wall hanging.

In some cases, especially where sitting rooms are used by older women of the family, a small day bed is fitted in with the sofas thus recalling the versatile function of the rooms grouped around the old *harim* courtyard. One sitting room is usually set aside as a more formal reception room for the entertainment of guests. Here the furniture is more elaborately upholstered, often in patterned velvet, and in some households armchairs replace the continuous sofas. Often in this room a set of gilt and glass shelves hold ornaments including imported Indian and Chinese trinkets, which may be compared to the niches with their glass lamps found in the reception rooms of the traditional *harim.* Sets of brass coffee pots in a brazier may be positioned as an ornamental centre piece. Dining rooms show the influence of European furnishing styles as they are equipped with a large table and matching chairs. Sideboard units and cabinets contain glass and china, while trolleys may be used for the serving of food and drink. Bedrooms are now furnished with large beds, dressing tables and fitted wardrobes and have lavishly equipped bathrooms en suite. In autumn and spring a house can be temporarily extended by erecting a canvas tent in the courtyard which when furnished with cushions, rugs, brazier and coffee table provides a comfortable and airy retreat.

Although more diverse activities are now included in a modern family's life the day still begins early as much because of the pattern of employment hours as of the time of the first prayer. Generally all members of a family take breakfast together, though this meal may be spaced according to personal choice or timetable. Older people, for example, to whom the dawn prayer and the arrival of daylight were synonymous, will get up and then take a very early breakfast. The family members then go their separate ways. As in the past, men depart for the day's business though to a greater choice of employment. Here through the demands of climate and the survival of custom, the working day is still divided into a long morning session on average from 7am to noon, an extended lunch interval, and an afternoon session from about 4pm to 7pm. Government departments and banks work a six day week of mornings only from 7.30am to 1.30pm; in summertime this routine begins and ends half an hour earlier. Some private enterprises, however, prefer a continuous daily programme from 7am to 4pm or 8.30am to 5pm with only a short lunch break. The use of air conditioning in modern offices makes such a day feasible.

The most significant change in daily routine is, however, in the lives of women who now have a choice between staying at home or going out to work. If they prefer the former, continuing the traditional female tasks of supervising the housework and cooking, and taking care of young children, their lives are made easier by the availability of both servants and labour saving gadgets such as washing machines, vacuum cleaners, food processors etc. Shopping for food also need no longer be a daily task as women can drive to the local supermarket and purchase at least a week's supplies which can be kept in refrigerators and deep-freezers. While employment levels remain high among Kuwaiti men, there is still a survival of traditional attitudes for if they can afford to provide for their wives and unmarried daughters and sisters men feel that there is no need for the women to go out to work and they should therefore devote themselves to home life. Women have, however, been steadily entering the labour force from the 1950s onwards and here it is interesting to observe that Kuwait was in advance of its Arabian peninsula and Gulf neighbours in this respect.

Several reasons account for this comparatively rapid development. Kuwait has always been a seafaring mercantile community with outside contacts both with their trading areas and later with the British, and therefore always had more opportunity to observe and receive new influences than an inland rural country. Kuwait's recent pattern of economic and social growth has accentuated this trend, with the creation of jobs which were often filled by women from Arab countries with a well-established tradition of female participation in outside employment, whose example undoubtedly influenced Kuwaiti women. It has also been official Government policy to sponsor broader educational and employment opportunities for women as the need for qualified labour is too important to permit a significant percentage of Kuwait's population to remain excluded from it. The survival, even in its present comparatively diminished form, of the extended family has made it possible for married as well as unmarried women to go out to work. There are usually older female relatives and servants available to take care of small children of pre-nursery age and children returning early from school or during vacation time. Women's employment has as yet tended to follow certain patterns. Women occupy positions in the areas of education, health and social welfare and certain types of office work, which may be regarded as a natural and less abrupt transition from their traditional domestic role. They work as civil servants, as school and university teachers, as specialist teachers of handicapped and disabled children, as doctors, nurses, physiotherapists, speech therapists and social workers. There is increasing female participation in the media as announcers on radio and television and as journalists. Women are now also entering the more technical fields of computer programming and engineering. Some women have business interests in commercial and residential property which may be regarded as a continuation of traditional economic activity as Islam has always legislated for female property owning rights. Children's activities which previously had been confined to playing with neighbourhood friends or attending Qur'an school are equally varied. Depending on their age they attend the various levels of state school, or university or vocational training institute whose teaching programmes are concentrated into mornings. Lunch therefore is normally the main family meal followed by a long break for a siesta, or television viewing. By about 5pm the family again resumes different activities—the afternoon work session, shopping, visiting and receiving friends. The use of electricity now prolongs the day beyond the last hours of natural light which results in a new flexibility in the times of evening meals and going to bed.

The broadening of the daily routine is matched in the increased scope of recreation and entertainment facilities now available. The introduction of a more structured pattern of working life with weekend breaks and annual leave allowances has led to a clearer identification between work and leisure. Yet the regular basis of social life is still centred on the family and the offering of hospitality in the home to relatives and friends which naturally revolves around the provision of food and drink. To a certain extent this is found in business life which, although now conducted in ministries, offices, banks and shops in place of the old *diwaniya* courtyard and *suq*, still observes the polite custom of offering cups of cardamom-flavoured coffee and sweet tea to clients and customers.

At home men continue to entertain their friends in either the separate *diwaniya* apartment or in one of the many sitting rooms; the atmosphere is that of a social club where the members take refreshments, watch television and video programmes, play cards, discuss business and neighbourhood affairs, or sit in companionable silence. *Diwaniya* sessions usually begin in the early evening after work and may continue late into the night, when a meal based on a large dish of rice and meat with varying accompaniments will be served either freshly prepared or kept from the family's evening meal depending on the formality of the occasion. Patterns of *diwaniya* visiting are variable as Kuwaiti men do not necessarily spend every evening there. In one family, for example, the father will entertain his friends on Saturday and Sunday, while his son will do the same on Thursday and Friday. Again in some families the men will only visit a *diwaniya* once a week.

The women of a family maintain regular social contact by telephone calls and visits. Older more conservative women, who remember a time when they rarely left their homes, find the telephone a convenient means of combining traditional seclusion with sociability. Visiting patterns vary depending on whether women are at home all day or out at work. Housewives visit each other at intervals throughout the day but otherwise women see their relatives and friends in the late afternoon between about 5pm and 8pm. As the car now affords greater mobility several visits may be made in an evening and combined with shopping expeditions. Refreshments are offered at each visit. Coffee and tea are now often kept hot in elaborately fashioned vacuum containers instead of being freshly prepared for each occasion. A selection of cakes, sweets and nuts are offered, such as the traditional *baklava* and *konafa*—confections of layers of flaky and shredded pastry and nuts soaked in a sugar and lemon syrup, *ma'moul*—slices of sweet pastry with a date stuffing, European-style sponge and fruit cakes, gateaux, biscuits, and sugared almonds. Depending on the occasion all these refreshments will be presented on elaborate glass and porcelain dishes. At the end of a visit guests' hands may be sprinkled with perfume, now usually an imported French brand rather than the traditional rosewater. Such entertainment may be provided at children's parties, especially those held to when a child first attends at school which has now replaced the traditional celebration of the completion of the study of the Qur'an.

As hospitality also involves invitations to meals, whether to share in a family lunch or some more formal occasion, it is revealing to analyse eating habits and menus in comparison with those of the past. The most immediately observable difference is in the range of food now available. Whereas in the past Kuwaitis managed with limited and season local produce of fish, cereals, vegetables such as beans, onions, leeks, aubergines, okra, pumpkin and tomatoes, and fruits of dates and melons, supplemented by meat and dairy products from the Bedu, and imported fruits, pulses, rice, tea and coffee, the selection of fresh and packaged food now stocked on market stall and in supermarket and specialist delicatessen is comprehensive. Regular fresh supplies of fish, meat and poultry are abundant. Greengroceries are provided through improved local agriculture and imports and include vegetables such as lettuce, cucumber, cauliflower and asparagus, and fruits such as avocado pears, bananas, mangos and lychees. The staples of rice and bread are various. Popular types of rice are basmati, imported from Pakistan, and branded packages from America. Bread ranges from flat unleavened rounds and strips which are either made daily in traditional bakeries attached to supermarkets or sold in plastic packages, and European-style block and plaited white and brown loaves and rolls. French, Italian, and Swiss natural and processed cheeses are available. Accompanying all these products is a rich selection of tinned, packaged, and frozen foods, ready made dishes, preserves, sauces, soft drinks etc. The recent arrival of fast food chains and takeaway restaurants has added further choices to the Kuwaiti diet. They supply, for example, minced meat preparations and fried potatoes, pizzas, Indian curries, and Levantine foods such as *hummous*—a purée of chick peas and sesame paste, grilled meats, and *dolma*—stuffed vine leaves. At a more formal level the outside catering services of the large hotels supply mixed Arab and European menus for functions.

As in all societies faced with such an abundance of food it is sometimes difficult to make a choice. Various modern aids to the imagination exist in television advertisements, magazine articles, and cookery books featuring Kuwaiti and other Arab dishes and also collections of recipes from foreign cuisines. The average pattern of meals which emerges from all these choices is eclectic involving both past customs and a mixture of home cooked and convenience foods. Breakfast still continues to be a simple meal of bread and jam sometimes with eggs and cheese, and accompanied by tea and coffee. The family lunch is usually a plentiful array of dishes all presented together so that everyone can help themselves. Here the basic foods are generous servings of rice and meat, usually baked and stewed lamb or chicken, and plenty of bread. Side dishes can include vegetables such as *fasulya*, a preparation of green beans simmered in a tomato and onion sauce, salads of cucumber, tomato, lettuce, radish, and food brought in from restaurants, such as prawn and meat curries, prawn in mayonnaise, pizzas with tomato, cheese and olive topping, and *samosa*, Indian-style fried savoury pastries. Desserts consist of a choice of fruits and sometimes cakes and sweets. Water, diluted yoghurt or *leben* and soft drinks are taken continuously through the meal. Coffee and tea, served in one of the sitting rooms, completes the meal. Evening meals are a simplified version of lunch.

Elaborate and lavishly presented lunch parties continue to be a preferred way of entertaining guests. In the past the menus of such meals reflected Kuwait's receptiveness to the influence of other cuisines notably Persian and Ottoman Turkish. This has continued, stimulated both by the availability of a wide range of ingredients and by the influence of the cooking habits of the other nationalities at present living in Kuwait, especially those from other Arab countries. A menu will therefore mingle Kuwaiti dishes, such as the long-established rice and lamb and often a casserole of meat cooked with lentils and tomatoes, with those of Egyptian and Levantine inspiration. These may be Egyptian dishes of macaroni or carrots and courgettes baked with a cheese sauce. Succulent portions of roast chicken are piled on to layers of carrots and potatoes coated in tomato sauce. The classic *dolma* of vine leaves or long narrow green peppers stuffed with spiced minced meat and rice continue to be popular. Supporting dishes include *sanbusak*-fried pastries with cheese and spinach fillings, assorted salads, and Levantine appetisers of *hummous*, and *tabbouleh*—chopped parsley, tomato, onion and burghul wheat grains mixed in an olive oil and lemon juice dressing. Throughout the meal *leben* and fruit juices are drunk. Desserts in addition to fruits and sweet confections may also include creme caramel pudding. For evening parties celebrating engagements and weddings, a family may prefer to use the services of a hotel caterer, who will arrange a buffet usually of grilled lamb kebabs, prawns, chicken dishes, rice, and a choice of gateaux, ice cream and fruit dessert.

Domestic leisure activities are not confined only to entertaining guests. There is a wide range of television and video programmes available to broaden the viewers' horizons. Popular viewing choices include comedy films, news programmes, science documentaries and football matches. Reading and study habits are served by many Arabic newspapers and magazines published both in Kuwait and abroad. There is also the wide selection of English language material stocked by local bookshops and displayed anually at the international book fair, held at the Mishrif Exhibition Centre on the Sixth Ring Road, which is always well attended. Exposure to such choices is reflected in the bookshelves of Kuwaiti families which, depending on individual interests, may contain works in classical Arabic such as the Qur'an and religious commentaries, selections of English,

French and German literature, together with practical handbooks on cookery, gardening and handicrafts.

In addition to home-centred recreation there is increased scope for outside activities. Family groups and friends may choose to meet in the coffee lounges and restaurants of the large hotels instead of entertaining at home. Hotels also function as social centres by organising exhibitions of paintings and jewellery and special food promotions. Cultural programmes in Kuwait City include museum exhibitions and lecture series, meetings of professional associations special interest societies, and occasional performances by theatre and folklore groups. Kuwait is well supplied with cinemas which compete with television and video programmes for the public's attention.

Sports are always popular in surviving traditional forms such as falconry and hunting, which contrast with the recent introduction of soccer football, water skiing and ice skating, where the spacious rink provides a cool retreat in summer. All the major companies, ministries and enterprises have well-equipped social and sports clubs for their employees, often including private beaches. The Government has played an active role in developing leisure facilities through the Touristic Enterprises Company which manages the Kuwait Towers complex, a number of beach clubs extending down the coast and a new tourist complex on Failaka island which offers a ferry service, chalet and hotel accommodation, restaurants, supermarket, and a swimming pool as an alternative to the sea. Kuwaitis, however, participate selectively in the newly developed leisure sector. Many have access to beach chalets where they will spend weekends. Vacations combine traditional and new activities, as Kuwaitis will camp in the desert during the spring holiday but go abroad to Europe and America in the summer.

b) Everyday life in Bedu society

The lives of many Bedu have long been involved with Kuwait have been profoundly modified by economic and social development. Their tribal organisation and social structure has been subject to political pressure from the modern states whose boundaries overlap with the territories through which they traditionally migrated, so that it has become increasingly expedient to adapt and penetrate settled society. While certain tribes continue to migrate around Saudi Arabia, Iraq, Jordan and Syria, Bedu whose routes included Kuwait's territory have settled in large numbers, especially as the Government has allocated special housing schemes to them. This process of settlement has in fact been so marked, that Kuwaiti townspeople now generally identify Bedu as the nomads of Iraq, Syria and Jordan who periodically come into Kuwait, and maintain that there is no such species as a Kuwaiti Bedu. Assimilation may well have been helped by the close relationships gradually formed between Bedu and settled population demonstrated in the marriage alliances between the al-Sabah family and daughters of tribal sheikhs. Such mixed marriages penetrated society at various levels as Kuwaitis today will often speak of fathers of Bedu origin or of sisters now married to Bedu.

The organisation of modern Arab states does provide opportunities for the absorption of Bedu into urban society as they are recruited as national guards in the entourage of a ruler and into the security and police forces. The oil companies have had success in training them as guards, drivers and mechanics from the 1950s onwards. This was well observed by Violet Dickson: —

"My second companion is Nasser Rashid of the Al Murra tribe. I have only known Nasser since 1961. He came to drive for me then while Ali was in Ahmadi, taking a three months course in driving heavy vehicles, in order to get promotion to a higher grade in the Company. Nasser had been trained by the Oil Company as a driver, and had been employed by them for about five years at that time, and was then driving cars for their VIP visitors.

"I was delighted to have him drive for me, for not only did he know well the tracks and roads of the northern part of Saudi Arabia and al Hasa, but he was also instinctively a desert guide and tracker, being of the Al Murra, the famous trackers of South Arabia, although if you asked him about this, he would tell you that he could not track. His tribe had migrated from the south towards Kuwait some years ago, and he and his cousin Muhammad had found employment with the Kuwait Oil Company."[1]

From this description of Nasser's qualities and resourcefulness it is clear why certain types of work initially appealed to Bedu accustomed to an active outdoor life. As a family settles, however, and is granted nationality rights, the children will move into the state school system and then eventually will be eligible for employment in the bureaucracy and professions.

The most immediately noticeable result of the gradual transformation of Bedu life in Kuwait is the absence of the distinctive black tents which were once pitched within distance of the town. As most of Kuwait's Bedu now live in housing schemes in the outlying suburbs of Jahra (Plate 66), Farwaniya and Ahmadi, it is necessary to go increasingly further afield to Raudathain in the north or down to the Saudi border to see communities who still live in tents. In Kuwait the only tents are those of a Bedu group which occasionally camps near Fahaheel, or those which appear in the Bedu housing schemes at election times where they function as mobile offices and meeting places for candidates.

Bedu have lived in Government houses in Farwaniyeh and Ahmadi for about twenty-five years, but still retain close links with their nomadic origins. Middle-aged women, for example, can remember spending their childhood in tents camped either just outside Kuwait or as far distant as Saudi Arabia. They still have relatives in their homelands who often graze sheep and goats for them who are regularly visited by male members of the settled branch of the family. The houses in Kuwait are spacious with courtyards at the back and front. There are usually two or three storeys of rooms as generally several generations of a family live together. These rooms in contrast to those of long-established Kuwaiti townspeople are sparsely furnished recalling the conditions of desert life where immovable possessions were merely a cumbersome nuisance. Therefore apart from fixed kitchen and bathroom units, the only furnishings are carpets, mattresses and cushions which enable rooms to be easily adapted for sitting, eating and sleeping. In addition to their city home a Bedu family may still possess a tent which they will take off into the desert for a few days camping.

The changes in living conditions have made the daily routine of the Bedu certainly much easier, especially for the women who no longer have to cook and clean in a difficult environment with restricted supplies of food, water and fuel, as they now have access to Kuwait's shopping and service facilities. They do, however, continue their traditional craft of weaving although this has been modified by altered circumstances. Both middle-aged women, their daughters and daughters-in-law, continue to weave so it seems that the craft is not in danger of extinction through lack of young recruits. The women learnt all stages of the craft from their mothers beginning at the age of about five or six by spinning. They then progressed to weaving at about the age of nine. Today they obtain their raw materials of sheep's wool, goat and camel hair, from various sources, sometimes from their family's animals, but more often from markets at Jahra, Fahaheel and Wafra. The traditional range of colours are still used—natural black, browns, greys, cream and white, and dyed red (Plate 94), orange, dark blue and green, though a deep pink and bright blue have now intruded. Some women still use natural dyes derived from plants, but many use only chemical dyes of Indian manufacture which they buy in the *suq*.

The simple horizontal loom is still used but now stretched out as a permanent fixture in the back yard (Plate 95). Traditional weaving techniques and forms continue, resulting in narrow strips worked in both warp-faced and horizontal weft tapestry weaves which can be sewn together to make the required article. Designs are still based on combinations of plain and patterned vertical stripes or continuous bands of interlocking triangles. It is interesting to note how faithfully traditional shapes and designs are still produced (Plates 30-37). Large storage bags are made of pieces with broad white and brown stripes, while more elaborate motifs and weaves are reserved for saddle bags and long rugs (Plate 96). The women have a repertoire of designs learnt along with the technical skills from their mothers, but are capable of adapting them and inventing new ones, such as motifs based on Arabic calligraphy, scissors and aeroplanes.

Bedu women weave today for both home use and for sale, adapting their products to both their changed way of life and to the demands of their retail markets. Some can still remember spending eight months weaving all the fittings and pieces of a tent, but as demand has declined they concentrate now on carpets, cushions (Plate 97), storage and saddle bags which can all be used as attractive items of interior decoration. They also weave decorative pieces inspired by animal trappings which can be used as wall hangings (Plate 98). Bedu weaving is displayed and sold in a mixed range of outlets—the traditional Friday market (Plate 85), the carpet and soft

94 Farwaniya. Selection of wools used by Bedu weaver.

95 Farwaniya. Loom in the backyard of a Bedu house.

96 Farwaniya. Bedu weaving, floor covering—*busat* (Royal Scottish Museum Edinburgh 1985.128)

97 Bedu weaving. Cushion—*masanad* (Royal Scottish Museum Edinburgh. 1983.989).

98 Bedu weaving. Wall hanging (Royal Scottish Museum Edinburgh 1985.139).

99 Kuwait City, Arabian Gulf Street. Bayt Sadu. Bedu cover draped over balcony.

furnishings sections of certain shops, and the al-Sadu foundation (Plate 99), a charitable organisation established for the preservation and encouragement of Bedu handicrafts.

c) Festivals and rituals

Interwoven with the everyday lives of both long-established Kuwaiti town dweller and recently settled Bedu are the religious festivals and the occasions which celebrate or lament the important stages of an individual life. In the past they also played a major social role as they provided entertainment and diversion in a society where such opportunities were limited. Today while their importance has not diminished they are emphasised differently, as they now take their place beside the many alternatives which compete for attention in Kuwaiti society. Naturally the main religious festivals of *Eid al-Fitr*, at the end of the fast of Ramadhan, and *Eid al-Adha*, on the tenth day of the pilgrimage month of Dhu'l Hijja, retain their traditional significance and are observed with respect. They are of three and four days duration respectively and comparable in their manner of celebration.

During the month of Ramadhan, however, it seems that mosque visiting patterns now vary. The men who have always followed a regular schedule of prayer continue to do so though they may visit the mosque more frequently. Women, who normally pray at home, will go to the mosque in Ramadhan, for example, on Fridays. On the fifteenth day of Ramadhan children will visit the mosque in a group. During the religious holidays all offices and business enterprises are closed while families and friends visit each other to offer their salutations and greetings and to enjoy the refreshments offered. As in the past the last night of Ramadhan is an occasion for lavish entertainment. In addition to these traditional festivals Kuwait also observes a one day holiday each for the Prophet Muhammad's birthday, Isra and Miraj, the ascensions to heaven of the prophets Jesus and Muhammad, and the Islamic New Year. These are modest quiet occasions, centred mainly on services in the mosque. Secular public holidays with dates fixed according to the western Gregorian calendar which is used in business life, are New Year's Day on the 1st january and National Day on 25th February commemorating Kuwait's achievement of independence in 1961.

The stages of a person's life which are commemorated by ritual remain unaltered—birth, circumcision, marriage, pilgrimage to Mecca, and death. Birth normally takes place in a hospital among professional medical and nursing staff instead of the female relatives and neighbours of former times. Certain traditions do however continue. The baby may still be swaddled and in religious families is given its name seven days after birth. Sometimes a family will give a small party for relatives and close friends who will bring gifts for the baby such as clothing and additionally a blanket for a boy and jewellery—earrings, brooch, necklace and bracelets—for a girl. Nowadays a boy's circumcision may also take place in hospital and at a much earlier age than formerly. A family party may be given to celebrate the occasion.

Marriage continues to be an occasion which is treated with great care and as much expense as the family can afford. Changing social customs have to a certain extent influenced the choice of a marriage partner. Generally a first cousin is still considered desirable for the traditional reasons that he or she is already known to the family, that property would stay in the family, and that the couple's children would continue the family name, as in Islamic marriage a woman does not take her husband's name. The supply, however, of eligible cousins cannot be guaranteed, and young people have to search outside the close family circle. The relaxation of the customs of segregation and seclusion at least provides a chance for young men and women to meet through social gatherings, university, places of work, clubs etc. This has resulted in mixed marriages, as Kuwaiti girls may become engaged to young men from other Gulf states who come to Kuwait for higher education, and Kuwaiti men who study abroad often bring back foreign wives. The opportunities for further education and more varied types of employment have delayed the usual age of marriage to at least twenty three or twenty four for both sexes.

Once a partner has been chosen and the family's approval and consent gained, the marriage formalities proceed, blending traditional and modern customs to a degree which depends on the position and habits of the family. As in the past the bridegroom formally requests permission to marry the girl from her father, or if he is dead, the oldest male member of the family. Then the financial and material provisions of the marriage contract or *mahr*, which are the bridegroom's responsibility, are discussed and concluded. This stage is celebrated by the equivalent of an engagement party held at the bride's home, where the refreshments may be provided by an outside catering service, or at a hotel. The engaged couple will now both be present to receive their guests, the girl usually in an attractive European-style dress, while her fiance wears traditional costume. The bridegroom still contributes towards the trousseau (*jehaz* or *dezza*), with gifts of jewellery and clothes, but these are not necessarily given at the time of signing the contract. If the bridegroom is not of Kuwaiti origin, he may bring family jewellery on a separate occasion and formally adorn the girl with it.

The interval between the contract and the final wedding ceremony is variable but usually lasts about a month. Nowadays the wedding party is usually held in a large public hall or hotel to accommodate the guests without crowding. The family may, for example, hire the hall of a local community centre or youth club for the night. It will be prepared for the occasion by clearing away the furniture covering the floor with carpets and putting a few rows of chairs around the walls. Only female guests will be present, the relatives, neighbours and friends of the bridal couple and their families all dressed in their smartest clothes. Refreshments of tea, soft drinks and sweets are served to the accompaniment of music and songs of about six to eight negress musicians, who still perform at the weddings of traditionally minded families. Eventually the bride is brought in and seated on a platform at one end of the hall. Her hair and face have been carefully adorned for the occasion and nowadays she always wears an elaborate white European-style wedding dress with accessories of diadem, veil and gloves.

Meanwhile the bridegroom, who has been attending a party of his male relatives and guests, enters wearing traditional costume and sits beside the bride. Both parents of the couple stand beside them as the groom receives the congratulations of his men friends who have entered the hall with him. After approximately an hour the bridal couple depart leaving the women alone to continue the entertainment. For many hours now they will dance gracefully and provocatively with scarves tied around their undulating hips and pulling the wide sleeves of transparent black net or tulle *thobs* over their faces. Occasionally a girl will move over the floor in crouching slow movements swinging her long black hair around her head until she reaches a stage of dizzy trance. In the past, wedding parties could continue for several days but now one night is usually considered sufficient. After the wedding the couple may go away on a honeymoon trip before going to their new home. Both engagement and wedding parties will have been fully recorded in photograph and video film which afford the families many hours of enjoyment.

These customs are generally observed among town Kuwaitis. The weddings of settled Bedu present a more conservative appearance.

"It was now Thursday, January 26th, and would soon be the eve of Friday. I set off at half past five with Ali and Salim, to go to the house at Asherij, and although it was getting dark I easily found where the wedding was to take place. I was escorted by Ali Hindal to the back of the women's quarters, where I met Naufa. She ushered me into the bride's new room, which was thronged with women and babies. The floor was covered in thick handwoven rugs in bright colours, and at one end of the room under a white muslin canopy, made like a mosquito net and suspended from the ceiling, the bride was reclining on a new mattress and cushion. Unless one lifted up the curtain, the bride was invisible. She was a pretty girl and appeared to be composed. She was not wearing the gold belt, I noticed.

"Outside in the mat-enclosed yard, there was also much activity. Several fires were burning, over which were enormous cooking-pots, propped up on stones. Large trays were being washed and got ready, and Ali kept coming in and urging the women to hurry up with the preparation of dinner. At intervals I came out from the hut to watch, and then returned to the new room to sit with the women guests, all of whom seemed to have babies, which were being fed in the hope that they would soon sleep quietly.

"At last, seven great trays were piled up with rice and a large piece of meat placed on the top of each one. The men then carried them outside and deposited them on mats to one side of the big tent. 'Dinner is ready; come and eat', they called out to the assembled company, the male members of which displayed a polite reluctance to appear hungry or to hurry forward.

"When everyone had finished eating, Ali came into the hut and brought a special dish of rice and pieces of meat for me, while Naufa served the other women guests. As soon as we had finished, one of the prettiest young girls began to unbraid her long hair in readiness for dancing. Drumming on several old tin cans started up, and the girl with one companion began to dance, swinging her long hair this way and that, while the other women clapped their hands and sang in time with the drumming. Each line of the song was first sung by Naufa, and after a few short words of approval from the others, it was repeated seven or eight times. Each line eulogised the young Mariam and her groom.

"The drumming seemed to be the signal for the bridegroom to be escorted into the bridal chamber by his grandfather and a small party of men friends, who left him at the threshold. Now the drumming waxed louder than ever; the dancing of the girls and the singing went on for at least three-quarters of an hour. I left them at it, and went over to the men's tent, where I sat beside Haji Fiza and watched a youth dancing and listened to more singing and drums.

"I stayed on a little longer before returning to Kuwait. The family begged me to come to the large lunch party next day, when fifteen sheep were to be killed, but this I could not manage."[1]

After marriage and the raising of a family two events remain. The pilgrimage to Mecca is no longer the arduous ordeal which needed such careful preparation in the past as with modern technical advances in communication and transport it is possible to fly there. The pilgrimage is also now within the financial means of more people, and is better organised. Today it is possible for groups of families and professional colleagues to engage a travel agent to arrange a package inclusive of transport and accommodation in Mecca. Modern customs, however, have not changed the essential nature of the pilgrimage as an obligation for all practising Moslems and those who make the journey are regarded with considerable respect. Death, the last event in life, is treated with the same rapid and modest rites as in the past. A bereaved family may stay at home for three days to receive condolences.

100 Kuwait City, Arabian Gulf Street. Opening of the Museum of Islamic Art (Dar al-Athar al-Islamiya) 25th February 1983.

d) Clothing traditions

The costumes worn in Kuwait today are clear examples of recent change. In contrast to the past where everyone wore the local version of Arab dress, which had steadily evolved to suit climatic and cultural conditions, present practices are more varied. European-style suits and dresses are worn not only by Europeans working in Kuwait, but also by other Arabs in professional and service jobs, and many Kuwaiti women. Working clothes of jeans and T-shirts are favoured by the various nationalities involved in technical and construction work. These costumes mingle with the traditional Arab dress still dominant among Kuwaiti men and some other Arabs, the saris of Indian, Bangladeshi and Srilankan women, and the full trousers and robes of Punjabis. Among both male and female Kuwaitis there is an awareness, whether consciously or intuitively expressed, of the significance of the continuity of traditional costume as a symbol of national identity. This is certainly acknowledged officially in various ways. State occasions and celebrations are attended by Kuwaiti men immaculately dressed in the dignified headdress and flowing robes of traditional costume. Depending on the formality of the occasion groups of musicians may be present, and young women gaily dressed in long robes covered by graceful transparent *thobs* glittering with designs embroidered in gold or silver (Plate 100). The media also contribute to a knowledge and awareness of costume traditions. The press includes articles on clothing,[1] and Kuwaiti television features documentary programmes on music, dance, folklore and historical drama series which all need extensive wardrobes. These are supplied by Kuwaiti television's dress department which has a specialist staff of designers, seamstresses, and embroiderers.

The traditional style costumes still favoured by Kuwaiti men are comparable in appearance to those of the smart merchants stationed in Basra so admiringly described by James Silk Buckingham in 1816. This smart well-groomed appearance is today easier to maintain through the availability of modern uncrushable fabrics, detergents and laundering processes. Kuwaiti men, when questioned, generally admit that they prefer to wear traditional dress in Kuwait, as its garments are cooler and more comfortable than the trousers and jackets of European tailoring. It also suits them very well. Many, however, are equally at ease in European dress which they would normally wear when studying or travelling in Europe or America.

101 Kuwait City, *suq*. Shop selling ready-made clothing.

A wide choice of services exists to supply the male Kuwait's clothing requirements. There are plenty of shops in both *suq* and the new commercial complex well-stocked with bales of fabrics imported from many sources—light weight wools both plain and pin-striped in black, navy blue, grey and beige suitable for winter clothes, and cottons and synthetic mixtures from India, China and Japan, in white, pale blue and grey, and beige used for summer wear. The customer simply purchases the length required, for example for a *dishdasha*, and takes it to an Indian or Punjabi tailor who will make it up within two to three days. Alternatively he may prefer ready made garments which are also available. Shops and tailoring establishments in the *suqs* of Kuwait and Fahaheel have rails loaded with ready-made *dishdashas* (Plate 101) which they have either made up themselves or imported direct from China and Thailand which caters to this profitable export market. The overgarments of *bisht* and *farwah* may be bought in special areas of the Kuwait *suq* and the suburban *suqs* of Abbassiya and Jahra. There is a wide choice of headgear and footwear available especially in the shops and stalls of the *suq al-harim*.

The Kuwaiti men circulating among the streets, offices and shops of the city and its suburbs today wear what may seem a remarkably uniform and indeed conservative costume to the uninitiated eye, consisting at its most basic of a long robe—*dishdasha*, and the shawl-like headdress. This is a misleading impression, however, as there are numerous variations and combinations of fabric and tailored detail according to season, the current fashion and personal taste. First of all, such a practical and seemingly timeless garment as the *sirwal* (Plate 39), the long white trousers worn as underwear, has changed. Today the leg pieces are cut and shaped to fall straight to the ankle, which gives a neater and smarter appearance beneath the hem of the *dishdasha.* This is the most popular and widely worn style, but there is also the *nuss sirwal*, a pair of kneelength shorts whose cut and shape recall those of traditional British military uniform for hot climates.

The long *dishdasha*, usually worn over a short-sleeved white T-shirt, offers plenty of scope for subtleties of style and fashion. Naturally the smartest *dishdashas* are those which have been tailor-made to the wearer's measurements. The shape now most generally favoured in Kuwait is severe, (Plate 41) falling in a loose straight line from shoulder to ankle, though here a streamlined appearance can be achieved through the cutting skills of the tailor and the relative proportion of the centre pattern piece and the triangular side inset. Some *dishdashas* still have a centre back with two pleats sewn to a shoulder yoke as in a European shirt but this is being replaced by a version in which the back is straight. The treatment of neck, front opening, and sleeves also responds to fashion. The pointed shirt collar was widely worn until about three years ago. Now a neat mandarin collar is preferred which is fastened with one to four small buttons. Centre front openings as in a European shirt may have a single or double overlap to reveal or conceal the row of buttons. The long sleeves which used to be gathered into cuffs which took button or link fastenings, now fall straight to

102 Kuwait City, *suq*. Man in cafe wearing summer *dishdasha* and headdress.

the wrist. Pockets are interesting details. All *dishdashas* have two large pockets, one on each side at hip level. These are made by leaving a slit-like opening in the side seam and sewing behind it a large bag pocket which can easily contain most of the wearer's personal possessions—cash, cheque book, car keys etc. Often there will also be a patch pocket at the top left front useful for holding pens and pencils.

Colour and weight of materials for winter and summer *dishdashas* are important. Smooth finely woven woollen fabrics are suitable for winter *dishdashas.* Here black, navy blue, beige and gray are the most popular colours in plain textures among young men while older men still prefer pin stripes. Repeated questions concerning the light weight cottons used for summer *dishdashas* revealed a firm preference for white (Plate 102) with occasional changes of very pale blue and gray. Clearly among these straight garments, the old *thob shillahat* with its flaring pointed sleeves (Plate 40), has no place and it is not seen today, though a few elderly dressmakers who recall the old styles, can still be persuaded to make them. They have basically passed into the realm of historical and pageant costume as seen in occasional television and theatrical programmes and at special exhibitions.

Similarly the *zebun*, a long coat with a wrapover front, and the *damir*, a short jacket, which were always made of luxurious fabrics and were an optional means of adding colour and textural contrast to the sober *dishdasha*, are now no longer in fashion. Occasionally the *damir*, made in velvet and richly embroidered in gold or silver thread is seen, worn over a toning *dishdasha* as part of the costume of folklore groups.

The arrival of cool weather during winter requires the wearing of extra clothes as the winter-weight *dishdasha* alone does not provide sufficient warmth. Here the traditional *bisht* cloak (Plate 42) and *farwah* coat (Plate 43) are the most popular and appropriate garments. A significant feature of the modern examples is that changes have occurred in type of fabric and method of manufacture rather than in shape and decoration. Indeed it would be difficult to improve on the simple cut and construction of the traditional *bisht* based on two straight lengths of fabric, which produces so practical and elegant a garment. The *bisht* is still made of two types of fabric—a thick closely woven wool in natural colours of soft browns, gray, beige (Plate 38), and a fine sometimes almost transparent wool or synthetic mixture in black, brown, beige and gray. The former is reserved for the practical plain winter *bisht* and here the most expensive are always made of camel wool. The light weight material is used for the *bisht* worn in spring and summer and on special occasions. It has a narrow plaited gold cord sewn along the shoulder seams and around the wrist openings, and a broad band of gold thread embroidered in a geometrical pattern around the neck and front edges (Plate 103).

As in the past, *bishts* are sold in the Kuwait *suq* either as ready made imports from Syria or stitched by tailors seated in their small crowded shops. Here it is possible to see all stages of the craft from stitching the shoulder seams, embroidering the gold neck border to finishing the centre back seam and hems (Plates 104-106). A recent development, however, is the application of factory processes of manufacture to this traditional Arab garment using immigrant workers on a continuous shift system. Here the wool, already spun, dyed and wound on to large drums, is imported from England and West Germany. In the factory this wool is would on to bobbins (Plate 107) which are then inserted into power looms. In one factory, for example, a

103 Kuwait City, *suq*. Man trying on a *bisht*.

104 Kuwait City, *suq*. Tailor stitching the shoulder seam of a *bisht*.

105 Kuwait City, suq. Craftsman hammering the gold neck border of a *bisht*.

106 Kuwait City, *suq*. Tailor completing a *bisht*.

107 Kuwait. *Bisht* factory. Winding the wool on to bobbins.

dozen power looms of Indian manufacture busily weave great lengths of cloth in four weights. The cloth is then washed, pressed, dried and cut into the seven metre lengths required for a *bisht*. These may be packed into plastic bags to be sold to retail tailors, or taken to another section of the factory where they are sewn and embroidered using imported German gold thread, into complete garments. Such a system produces about 2000 *bisht* lengths per month for both local and neighbouring Arab markets.

Like the *bisht* the *farwah*, the angular tent-like coat traditionally worn by Bedu in winter, is conservative in its cut, construction and decoration of bands of flat plaited braid. The shops of the *suqs* of Kuwait City, Jahra and Abbassiya are lined with stacks of neatly folded *farwah* mainly imported ready made from Syria. The fabrics are generally in subdued colours— beige, light and dark brown, rust, black, maroon, and dark blue, and of close firm weave but of both wool and synthetic mixtures from various sources including Italy and Thailand. The lining which was once of lamb skin is now made of nylon fur fabric usually in white or brown, but also in colours matching those of the *farwah*. This in itself is revealing of the change in lifestyle of the Bedu who formerly grazed enough sheep to supply meat,

108 Kuwait City, *suq*. Man wearing a *farwah*.

109 Kuwait City, *suq*. Man wearing white *dishdasha*, black *bisht*, and thick black wool *'agal*.

wool and fleeces sufficient for local food and clothing needs. Now it is easier to import synthetic fur than sheepskins. The *farwah* is still worn by Bedu who in other respects will now dress like the long established town Kuwaiti, but they may also substitute a European style overcoat, or even an army surplus khaki greatcoat.

The costume would be incomplete without the characteristic headdress, which is both practical and pleasing in appearance and is rarely put aside except in private. It still consists of three pieces—the *keffiya*, a closefitting cap, the *gatra*, a large square coth, and the *'agal*. These have changed in form so that they are clearly distinguishable from those worn in the past. The *keffiya* is made of fine white cotton thread crotcheted in a range of openwork lace patterns such as radiating stripes, repeated diamonds, linked stars and circles. Traditionally these were worked by hand, but are now imported machine-made from China. A full range of designs can be purchased from the stalls and shops of the *suq al-harim*. Here it is also possible to find some women traders who are still able to crotchet the caps.

The *gatra* may be chosen from a varied selection of fabric weight and design. The red and white evenly checked cloth known as the *shemagh* is still worn in winter (Plates 103 & 108), but may now be woven in a relatively lightweight synthetic fabric imported from Japan as well as the traditional thick cotton. The white wool *shal* which used to have corners and borders embroidered with floral cone motifs now comes in a modern version of a light plain weave of blended cotton and synthetic thread with the design printed in green, red, yellow and black. White is still the colour favoured for the summer *gatra* which is made of fine white cotton voile which may be either plain or machine—embroidered all over with flower sprays in lustrous white thread (Plate 102). These are usually imported from Syria. The style of *'agal* most widely worn is the *'agal thabit*, a double circlet of twisted black wool or nylon cord which has to be bought in the correct size. It is rare now to see the thick wool *'agal* bound with coloured threads, except occasionally on a few old men (Plate 109).

There have always been many ways of wearing the headdress, which gave an appearance of severe dignity or rakish panache depending on the character of the wearer and his skill in manipulating its three component parts. Its versatility continues to be seen today where the old styles and new fashions are equally worn. The use of the *keffiya* is optional, especially if the wearer has had his hair cut and styled. It is, however, essential for expert headdress construction as it provides a firm foundation upon which to drape the *gatra*. A modern stylistic development is the careful puckering of the edge of the *gatra* which falls over the forehead into either a regular or an inverted "V" (Plate 102), whereas formerly it hung in random folds. To achieve this effect the *gatra* is folded twice diagonally and each fold carefully pressed. It is then opened out once, resulting in a triangular shape with a distinct centre crease extending direct from the point to the long edge. This triangle is carefully centred over the *keffiya*, which itself should be put on straight, and aligned so that the three points are equally distributed—two over the shoulders and one hanging down the back. The crease should then be centred over the forehead. Depending on whether the fold of the crease faces inwards or outwards a normal or an inverted "V" will be formed. The *'agal* is then put on over the *gatra* and the "V" shaped fold pulled into final shape before any more stylistic adjustments are made.

Much care and attention is devoted to the draping of the *gatra*. The simplest style, still favoured by older men, is created by letting the two ends fall equally on each side of the face (Plate 108). This may be varied by draping an end under the chin and over one shoulder or tucking it up into the *'agal*. Both ends may also be crossed under the chin and thrown over the shoulders. In a modern variation, the ends are flipped back, crossed behind the neck and then brought to the front again over the shoulders. A very popular style consists of folding the two ends up to the crown of the head and crossing them over the *'agal* (Plate 104 & 108). This has given rise to many versions in which the ends are coiled and twisted, caught up in loose folds and set at different angles over the *'agal*. This revealing style is not only smart and attractive, but enables a well-cut head of hair to be seen to advantage. Both city Kuwaiti and Bedu men now have short hair. The long curly hair and plaits of the Bedu went out of fashion by the early 1950s. They are now only remembered by older Kuwaitis, or Europeans who worked at Ahmadi on the post-war construction projects of the Kuwait Oil Company.

The accessories with which a man completes his outfit have also changed. He now wears smart leather moccasin-style shoes of Italian or Spanish origin. While older men are conservative and prefer brown and black shoes, younger men will carefully choose colours to tone with their *dishdashas*. In

110 Kuwait City, *suq*. Craftsman making strings of prayer beads—*mesbaha*.

111 Kuwait City, Arabian Gulf Street. Bayt Sadu, musician in winter clothes.

summer, therefore, they will usually wear white shoes, and in autumn and winter gray and black shoes depending on the choice of *dishdasha.* Fine textured matching wool socks will also be worn. In summer the traditional flat open leather sandals, usually of Indian manufacture, are still popular. The array of belts and weapon holsters with which a Bedu embellished his costume are still be be bought in the Kuwait and Abbassiya *suqs* but are rarely seen except at parades and folklore performances. Entwined around the fingers, however, is the *mesbaha* or string of prayer beads (Plate 110).

It would be a mistake to think that Kuwaiti men keep rigidly to the division between winter and summer clothing as both garments and accessories can be mixed according to personal taste. A few selected images will demonstrate this point. Probably the most familiar image, which is both dignified and attractive, is that given by a winter costume of grey wool *dishdasha* worn with a beige or brown plain camel hair *bisht* and headdress with a red and white checked *shemagh* (Plate 111). This is indeed worn by many Kuwaitis particularly of an older generation. A tall slim man, however, wearing a well-cut navy blue winter *dishdasha* may prefer the contrast given by a plain white *gatra.* For a special occasion on a winter evening an elegant costume of toning grey *dishdasha*, fine grey wool *bisht* with gold edging, grey shoes, and headdress of white *gatra* and rakishly slanted black *'agal* may be seen. The *bisht* can be folded and slung casually over the shoulder. Young stylish men may have as many as fifteen *dishdashas* in their wardrobes, but white still remains the favourite colour for summer worn with a white *gatra.* Some young men also do not wear the headdress all the time, but carry it with the *gatra* slotted through the loop of the *'agal* in their hand or over their shoulder ready to be worn when needed. For his wedding, however, a man will still follow conservative tradition and appear well and appropriately dressed in white *dishdasha*, light brown *bisht* with gold trimming, and a white *gatra* worn framing his face. However innovative a man's clothes are in everyday life, if he decides to go on pilgrimage to Mecca, he will, as in the past, wear the *ihram*, the long white loin cloth and shoulder wrap.

In the past the brightness of women's costume was shrouded from public view by the black *'abbaya* and veils which they wore when moving about outside their homes (Plate 58). A glimpse beneath this discreet outdoor wear would, however, have revealed robes of fabrics imported from Syria, Iraq, Persia and India, whose richness and quality was only limited by the wearer's means. Today women's clothes are more easily observed, as the cloak and veil are no longer universally worn, and women present a more colourful and varied appearance than those of Kuwaiti men. Women in currently fashionable European outfits mingle with those who still observe traditional customs by wearing long dresses and headscarves which may also be covered by the black *'abbaya*, and with the veiled figures of Bedu women. Dress distinctions are not absolute as there are subtle gradations depending on such factors as a woman's personal taste, conservatism and family attitudes. A woman, for example, who wears European clothes to work, may change on arriving home into a long dress which she will drape with an *'abbaya* when going out to pay informal afternoon visits to neighbours and relatives. In some cases a woman may revert to more traditional costume as she grows older.

As with men's clothing plenty of services are available to furnish the Kuwaiti woman's wardrobe. Dress fabrics are stocked in both the traditional *suqs* of Kuwait City and the suburbs, and in the shops of the modern

112 Kuwait City, *suq*. Shop selling dress fabrics.

113 Kuwait City, *suq*. Shop selling fabric for party dresses.

commercial complexes. Certain areas specialise in fabrics for specific markets. Deep within the Kuwait *suq*, for example, there are streets of open-fronted shops run by Indian, Pakistani and Persian traders, which stock brightly coloured cottons, velvets, Lurex decorated materials and tulle—imported from China, Korea, Japan and India, which are bought by Bedu women (Plate 112). In contrast the glass-fronted shops managed by Syrians in a small arcade near a main road of banks and offices, are full of neat rolls of French and Italian lightweight flowered wools suitable for winter dresses and lavishly embroidered and sequin-trimmed satins and organzas of Korean manufacture used for evening dresses (Plate 113). Once the fabric has been selected and purchased it may be taken to a choice of dressmakers and tailors. Women who prefer traditional garments will, if they are unable to sew themselves, go to one of the dressmakers who make the old styles of *sirwal*, *fustan* and *thob* both for private customers and for sale in the *suq al-harim* where they may also have a stall. Garments which require elaborate decoration will still be made by Indian and Pakistani tailors. Their establishments include embroiderers who may be seen busily stitching gold and silver thread or hooking pearls and sequins through material stretched taut over tambour and rectangular frames (Plate 114). Modern European style clothes can be made by Filipino dressmakers, Syrian, Indian and Pakistani tailors.

There are also plenty of ready-made alternatives to the work of dressmakers and tailors. Here the choice of garment varies according to the location of the shopping area. The *suq al-harim* is an excellent source of traditional dresses, *thobs* in various styles, *'abbayas*—and the various forms of headdress such as the *milfa* and *burqa. 'Abbayas* of different fabrics and decoration are also made and sold in the section of the Kuwait *suq* which specialises in men's *bisht* and *farwah.* The new shopping centres, such as the Awqaf Complex on Mubarak al-Kabir street, feature smart boutiques selling evening dresses inspired by European fashions, and also attractive housedresses—*dara'a*, which may be either of Kuwaiti manufacture or imported from Dubai, Bahrain and India. The small arcade in the city where smart dress materials are available, also has shops selling ready-made clothes and accessories such as elaborate white wedding dresses made up in Kuwait, and day dresses and suits, often with long maxi skirts imported from Turkey. Costume in a more definite European style ranges from locally made garments through inexpensive imports from Taiwan and Thailand to high quality designer clothes on sale in the exclusive boutiques of the Salhia Complex and in certain department stores (Plate 115). Such clothes are also purchased on visits abroad.

The closest links with traditional costume survive today in the clothing of older townswomen and Bedu women of all age groups. Although the clothes are now made up in modern synthetic fabrics which give a great range of colour and pattern, the basic principles of cut and construction are little altered. The shape of women's *sirwal*, for example, has not changed. It is still a voluminous comfortable garment tapering into close-fitting ankles. *Sirwal* (Plate 50) are made of plain brightly coloured cottons and striped and sprigged fabrics. Modern details are ankle trimmings of Lurex braid and the occasional use of metal zip fasteners extending from mid-calf to ankle.

114 Kuwait. Awqaf shopping complex, embroiderer hooking pearls through tulle.

115 Kuwait. Department store, display of wedding dresses.

16 Woman's costume. Dress—*dara'a*, headscarf and cloak—*'abbaya* (Royal Scottish Museum Edinburgh 1985.50,73,106).

17 Kuwait City, *suq*. Woman wearing the *'abbaya* and *bushiya*.

Over the *sirwal* a long-sleeved dress—*fustan* also known today as a *dara'a* is worn. This may be of simple shape, falling in a long straight line from shoulder to ankle (Plate 116) or have a full skirt gathered into a fitted bodice. Necklines are round and closefitting and sleeves which may be set into straight or curved armholes are long and tapering to the wrist. Sometimes a neat pointed collar is added. Texture and colour of fabric vary according to the wearer's age and taste. The older women generally prefer plain dark colours of black and blue with occasionally a discreet striped or spotted pattern. Bedu women of all ages, however, take advantage of the boldly patterned glittering synthetic fabrics now in plentiful supply which they will wear for both everyday use and for special occasions. They either make the dresses themselves or take the fabric to a tailor. Favoured designs include strong contrasts of colour and texture such as white nylon patterned with flowers in red flocked pile (Plate 52) or black gauze with gold motifs (Plate 56).

Certain adaptions have been made in the garments worn over the *sirwal* and *fustan* all tending towards greater simplicity. The long coat, *zebun* (Plate 53), traditionally made in luxurious fabrics, is now not worn. The heavy black *thob jez* made of black, silk, cotton or wool, and embroidered in gold thread, is also out of fashion (Plate 54). The light graceful *thob* is still worn as an overdress which has retained the traditional shape of a long straight-sided garment with extremely wide sleeves (Plate 55). Basic pattern details are also unaltered and depend on a central rectangular length folded in half at the shoulders to which a rectangular sleeve and skirt section are added at each side. These are joined by a triangular insertion which may be embroidered or made in a contrasting colour. A modern *thob* for everyday wear is usually made of a fine black gauze or net often imported from Japan.

Discreet black headdresses continue to be worn by older townswomen and all Bedu women. Lengths of black, gauze, net, organza or *milfa* are folded and twisted around the head to frame the face and conceal the hair. Many Bedu women still prefer the *sheileh*, a closefitting black hood stitched from four pieces of black cloth. Veiling customs have, however, changed. A townswoman on leaving her home, may still envelope herself from head to foot in the folds of the *'abbaya* which is made of two straight lengths of black silk or crepe joined horizontally, but the *bushiya*, which completely screens the face, is rarely now worn (Plate 117). Bedu women are more conservative and continue to tie the *burqa*, a black rectangular face veil with long narrow eye slits, over their head coverings (Plate 56). In pattern and stitching the *burqa* is unchanged. As most of Kuwait's Bedu are now living in permanent housing schemes behind high retaining walls, the women are more free to throw back or remove the *burqa* when at home among family and women friends than formerly in the more open environment of the tented encampments. They also wear the *'abbaya* when out of doors.

Although Kuwaiti women's dress was always receptive to external influences in fabric or detail of cut, the wearing of European styles did not become widespread until the late 1950s-early 1960s. Its adoption coincided with the increasing involvement of women in work outside the home and it spread more rapidly among young women who were participating in the opportunities available for education and a wider choice of activity, than among their mothers and grandmothers. At first girls would compromise with family concern for reputation and modesty and would cover their new clothes with the *'abbaya* when out of doors. Family photographs of the 1960s, however, show groups of girls cheerfully posing in the then current European fashions of short skirts, stiletto-heeled shoes and bouffant hairstyles.

Now that Kuwaiti women are both accepted as part of the work force and are familiar with European-style clothing, it is no longer regarded as either a symbol of emancipation or a novelty with the interesting result that there is not necessarily now a clear demarcation between it and traditional costume. This is especially seen in the manner of wearing the *dara'a*, a contemporary version of the long dress or *fustan*. The *dara'a* is a versatile and attractive garment, receptive to new influences in fabric and decoration, which may be worn in varying degrees of formality ranging from a house dress to a party gown. It is of basically simple shape and cut, falling in a loose easy-fitting line from shoulder to ankle. The long sleeves which may be tight or bell-shaped fit into a curved armhole. It is not usually worn with either the *sirwal* or *thob*. There is a large choice of ready-made *dara'a* available, which are stocked by all shops, whether in *suq* or sophisticated shopping complex, which sell women's clothes. The *dara'a* is frequently worn as an everyday house dress by women who do not go out to work. Here it is usually of cotton, synthetic fabric or wool, depending on the season, usually plain or patterned with striped and checked designs in a wide range of generally dark shades of blue, red, green and black. Sometimes a European-style buttoned housecoat with long sleeves in chenille or velvet may be substituted for this informal and comfortable *dara'a*.

118 Woman's costume. Detail of embroidered motif on a *dara'a*.

Women also have a wardrobe of more brightly coloured and ornamented *dara'a*, which can be worn for receiving guests. These *dara'a* may be of fine wool, cotton, silk and smooth synthetic fabrics, in such colours as black, turquoise, yellow, scarlet, bright pink and orange (Plate 116). Embroidered decoration is worked as broad panels on front and back yokes, as borders along cuffs and hems, and often as independent motifs scattered all over the *dara'a* in coloured, gold and silver threads. The designs are now machine-embroidered in traditional geometric schemes of bands of lozenges and triangles, and in a lively assortment of motifs (Plate 118). Beads and sequins may be added for final embellishment. A shop's collection of *dara'a* is from various sources—Kuwait, Bahrain, Dubai, India and Thailand. When questioned some women said that they particularly admired the garments brought from Bahrain both for the quality of the fabric and the imaginative and skilfully embroidered decoration. A *dara'a* may also be made to a customer's requirements by a dressmaker or tailor. It is possible to buy lengths of fabric which have the embroidered yoke, cuffs and hem already worked, so that it is necessary only to cut out the front, back and sleeve pieces and stitch them together. Otherwise a woman takes her chosen fabric to the tailor where she also discusses the decoration. This will be embroidered from a choice of designs, such as samples in the craftsman's repertoire, copies of favourite motifs on existing garments, and most recently, patterns in the women's magazines of the Arabic language press.

The *dara'a* is the garment which a Kuwaiti woman, who would wear European clothes at work, will normally adopt on returning home as it is both practical and attractive. If she wishes to entertain guests to lunch, she will wear a correspondingly formal *dara'a*, perhaps of scarlet or white adorned with gold embroidery. On leaving the house for shopping or paying visits, all women who wear the *dara'a* invariably drape an *'abbaya* over it. This garment is also susceptible to changes of fashion. It is made in a range of black fabrics, natural and synthetic silks of plain or satin weave, and fine crepe. Individual taste is expressed in the manner of treating the shoulder seams, wrist openings and front borders. They may be left severe and unadorned, or sewn with gold thread. If a fabric is used which has a machine-embroidered border worked in openwork flowers and scallops, the *'abbaya* is cut so that this forms the front edges. A currently popular fashion consists of stitching a row of silver diamante beading along seams and borders which pleasingly contrasts with the black fabric (Plate 59).

A more eclectic version of women's costume is the wearing of long-skirted garments (Plate 119) which also include certain European stylistic features. A long-sleeved blouse with a bow at the neck and pleated yoke, for example, can be worn with an anklelength flared skirt and covered with a tailored blazer jacket or loose coat. A long dress may have batwing sleeves and a blouson top softly gathered into a dropped waistline. These clothes, which are always modest and discreet, are often smartly accessorised with toning handbags and neat high-heeled court shoes. It is customary also for a covering to be worn. This may take the form of a loosely draped *milfa* or a scarf which is pulled well down over the forehead, drawn tightly round the face, and tied firmly under the chin, thus concealing all the hair. This type of scarf, which is usually black, white or beige in colour, can be triangular in shape with a pair of ribbon-like ties which when knotted at the nape of the neck ensure that the front section is kept in place over the forehead (Plate 116). Collectively the wearing of such a scarf with a long dress is known as *hejab*, which means that it fulfils the specifications for a Moslem woman's dress. According to strict interpretation of the recommendation in both the Qur'an and Hadith a woman is required to conceal everything except her face and hands in loose opaque garments. Some women, therefore, wear a severe loose robe of sober colour instead of a smart maxi

119 Kuwait. Women wearing long dresses and headscarves at the Gulf Co-operation Council exhibition 1984.

120 Kuwait. Woman in maxi dress and headscarf modelling wedding jewellery.

dress. While principles of modest and decent dress have always been understood in Kuwaiti society, the adoption of this readily identifiable form of *hejab* at the expense of European dress among younger women, has been noticeable since about the middle of the 1970s. The *'abbaya* can be worn out of doors with *hejab* especially if a woman is going shopping.

As in the past careful attention is paid to personal grooming and hairdressing. The traditional cosmetic and toilet preparations, for example of henna, kohl, *maswak* bark for cleaning the teeth, are still readily available in the *suq al-harim* but their use is declining (Plates 60 & 61). The application of henna to hands, feet and hair is now mainly seen among older townswomen and Bedu women. Here again it is no longer painted in a range of patterns, but simply applied as a uniform wash over palms and soles. Hairstyles have also changed along with costume, but show a certain continuity with the past in a preference for long hair. Thus women who wear a *milfa* or headscarf will plait their hair in a single braid or comb it back from the forehead to the nape of the neck. There are many hairdressers who create modern European hairstyles using techniques of blow-drying and setting. The traditional black powdered kohl is still used to outline and elongate the eyes and in many cases is the only cosmetic used (Plate 120). Full ranges of imported European and American brands of skin care items and cosmetics are available. Their use naturally enough reflects the influence of past custom; eyes are outlined in black eyeliner, and clear red lipsticks, glosses and nail enamels are used to colour lips, cheeks and nails (Plate 121). An application of French perfume completes the appearance.

The clothes worn at parties, especially those connected with the stages of a wedding, are interesting because they provide opportunities for the display of traditional garments made in lavishly decorated fabrics, together with gowns of European style and cut. As it is now fashionable to wear traditional dress for formal occasions, many shops and boutiques now stock well-made modern versions. There are, for example, *dara'a* made in heavy black silk embroidered with stylised floral and foliate motifs in gold thread (Plate 51). Another striking example consists of a set of matching *sirwal*, *fustan* and belt, all worked in silk in brilliant shades of green, red and purple. The dress is stitched together from pattern pieces of the different colours creating a

121 Kuwait. Detail of woman's hands showing jewellery and the use of nail enamel.

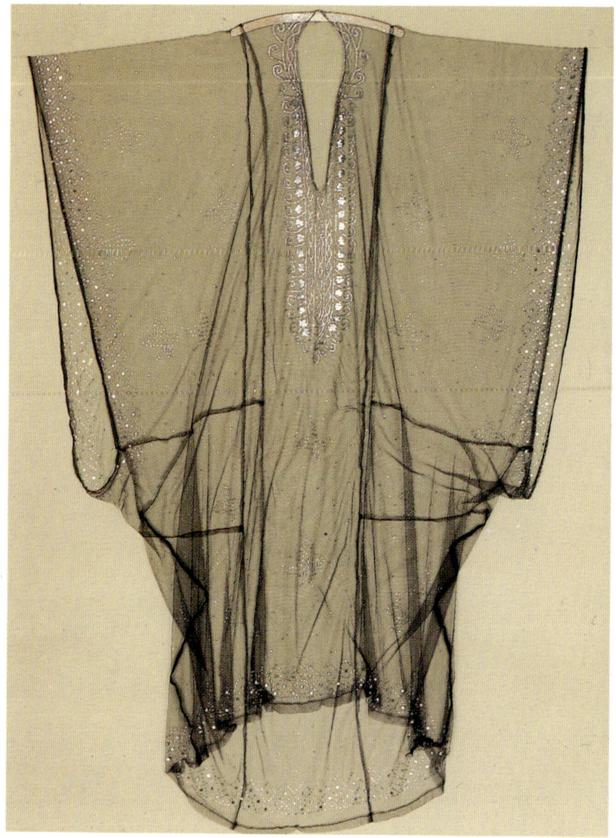

122 Woman's costume. Multicoloured silk trousers—*sirwal*, and dress—*dara'a al-mufahah* worn with reconstructed bridal jewellery (Royal Scottish Museum Edinburgh 1985.40 & A-B).

123 Woman's gauze overdress—*thob al-tour bilteil* (Royal Scottish Museum Edinburgh 1985.64).

patchwork effect and is thus known as a *dara'a al-mufahah.* (Plate 122) Gold embroidered bands of geometrical motifs decorate the *sirwal*, and the cuffs, bodice and seams of the *dara'a.*

The versatile overdress, the *thob*, is also worn at parties. Many types of *thob* may be bought from the *suq al-harim* or specially made to the customer's requirements. A becoming version of lightweight black net, embroidered with delicate geometrical and floral motifs in flat silver thread, is known as a *thob al-tour bilteil* (Plate 123 & diagram 13) and is usually worn as a graceful accessory when dancing (Plate 51). The *thob al-messarah* shows the most elaborate and innovative use of embroidery (Plate 55). Made of transparent silk and gauze in black and a range of bright colours—red, green, violet and blue—it can be decorated at front and back, and along sleeves and hems with foliage scroll, floral sprays, and large palmette motifs, worked in gold thread embellished with sequins and beads. The continued use of traditional dress also enables family jewellery to be worn (Plate 120), which would be out of place with modern clothes.

Evening gowns in European styles are equally colourful, employing all manner of natural and synthetic silk, satin and lace fabrics, trimmed with embroidery, elaborate appliqué flowers, beads and sequins. Dazzling effects are created such as that given by an anklelength full skirted gown in deep fuchsia pink whose closefitting bodice and long gathered sleeves are decorated with petal shapes stitched at neck and shoulders.

While a woman's trousseau or *jehaz* will include a mixture of traditional and modern party clothes, her wedding dress is now invariably white and influenced by European styles. Such a dress may range from expensive imported designer models (Plate 115), through locally produced ready-to-wear garments, to copies of fashion magazine illustrations made by a dressmaker. In all cases, it will be the best that can be afforded. The bride will wear such a dress during the final marriage ceremony, when she is escorted to the wedding hall and seated on a chair on a raised platform so that the guests can see and admire her. Her white dress will be elaborately decorated with a tight bodice and full sleeves. The very full skirt will be carefully spread out and displayed over the sides of her chair. Headdresses vary but a charming compromise between tradition and modernity may be seen in the combination of a white scarf framing the face and surmounted by a pearl or silver tiara from which the folds of a white tulle veil fan out behind her. White lace or embroidered gloves and white satin court shoes complete the picture. White wedding dresses have also been accepted in Bedu society as Violet Dickson records in 1967: – "That evening the bride's father dined us, and Dhafia helped her mother with the cooking wearing her white satin long-sleeved dress, the latest fashion in bridal clothing."[2]

As in the past, all this varied costume is put aside when a woman decides to make the pilgrimage to Mecca. Here again the prescribed costume has been modified and she wears a long green dress covered by a hooded waistlength cape resembling the *khedra* or prayer shawl.

An examination of Kuwait's costumes, reveals a continually evolving situation in which fashions both develop naturally from traditional forms of garment and easily absorb new stylistic influences. The clothing of children and teenagers is a striking example of the mingling of past and present. Small boys and girls now wear modern European clothes, and teenagers are keenly aware of current fashion trends. The traditional garments, however, are made in all sizes and it is possible to see boys of various ages wearing either the *dishdasha* role informally at home or the complete masculine costume for special occasions. Girls in turn will dress in the attractive long *fustan* dress and the embroidered hood or *bukhnug*. The existence of varied forms of costume ensures the vitality of the Kuwaiti sartorial tradition.

REFERENCES

KUWAIT—THE LAND AND ITS RESOURCES

1 Jointly administered by Kuwait and Saudi Arabia.
2 The official dates of the four seasons are:—spring 15 February-21 May; summer 22 May-4 November; autumn 5 November-6 December; winter 7 December-15 February.
3 Kuwait's animal life has been exhaustively studied by the Ahmadi Natural History Group which is affiliated to the Kuwait Oil Company. See *The Kuwaiti Digest* (quarterly magazine of KOC). April/June 1984, pp. 15-20, for an account of the Group's activities and publications.

KUWAIT IN THE PAST

Development from Arabian Gulf port to independent Emirate

1 Anabasis of Alexander and Indica. Translated and edited by Edward James Chinnock, Loeb Classical Library, London 1893.
2 The Mamluk sultans of Egypt and Syria (1250-1517) had inherited the rights of the Caliphate which included protection of the holy cities of Mecca and Medina.
3 His journey is recorded in the *Voyage of John Huyghen van Linschoten to the East Indies*, London 1598.
4 Both voyages are recorded in *Samuel Purchas, His Pilgrimes*, 5 volumes, London 1625.
5 Niebuhr, C., *Travels in Arabia and other countries in the East*, 2 volumes, Edinburgh 1792, Vol. 2, pp. 126-127.
6 Niebuhr, Travels. Vol. 2, pp. 127-128.
7 Buckingham, James Silk, *Travels in Assyria, Media and Persia, including a journey from Bagdad by Mount Zagros to Hamadan, the ancient Ecbatana, researches in Ispahan and the ruins of Persepolis and journey from thence by Shiraz and Shapoor to the sea-shore, description of Bussorah, Bushire, Bahrein, Ormuz and Muscat*, 2 volumes, London 1830, Vol. 2, pp. 314-317.
8 Buckingham, *Travels*, Vol. 2, pp. 121-124.
9 The British Political Residents in Kuwait were:—see enclosed photocopy.

The settlement, population and government

1 Stocqueler, J. H., *Fifteen months pilgrimage through untrodden tracts of Khuzistan and Persia in a journey from India to England through parts of Turkish Arabia, Armenia, Russia, and Germany, performed in the years 1831 and 1832*, 2 volumes, London 1832, Vol. 1, p. 18.
2 Captain S. Hennell, British Resident Persian Gulf. Letter written to the Honourable the Secret Committee of the Honourable Court of Directors of the East India Company, 24th April 1841.
3 Collated and published in Lorimer, J. G., *Gazetteer of the Persian Gulf*, 2 volumes, Calcutta 1908 and 1915.
4 Lorimer, *Gazetteer*, Vol. 2 B, p. 1059.
5 Lorimer, *Gazetteer*, Vol. 2 B, pp. 1049-1050.
6 Lorimer, *Gazetteer*, Vol. 2 B, p. 1050.
7 Lorimer, *Gazetteer*, Vol. 2 B, p. 1050.

8 Dickson, Harold, R. P., *Kuwait and her neighbours*, London 1956, pp. 35-36.
9 Lorimer, *Gazetteer*, Vol. 2 B, p. 1050.
10 Dickson, *Kuwait*, p. 36.
11 Dickson, *Kuwait*, p. 35.
12 Dickson, *Kuwait*, pp. 50-52, 61-64, 69.
13 Freeth, Zahra, *A new look at Kuwait*, London 1972. pp. 27-29.
14 See Lewcock, Ronald and Freeth, Zahra, *Traditional architecture in Kuwait and the northern Gulf*, London 1978, p. 116 for the plan of Bayt al-Badr.
15 Dickson, Violet, *Forty years in Kuwait*, London 1971, pp. 76-78.
16 See Lewcock, *Traditional architecture*, p. 118, for the plan of the Red Fort.
17 Pelly, L., *Recent tour around the northern portions of Persian Gulf*, Transactions of the Bombay Geographical Society XVII (1863-64), pp. 118-121.
18 Lorimer, *Gazetteer*, Vol. 2 B, p. 1074.
19 Dickson, *Kuwait*, p. 40.
20 Lorimer, *Gazetteer*, Vol. 2 B, p. 1051 and p. 1074, and Dickson, *Kuwait*, pp. 82-107.
21 Lorimer, *Gazetteer*, Vol. 2 B, p. 1051.
22 Lorimer, *Gazetteer*, Vol. 2 B, pp. 1074-1075.

The economy

1 Dickson, *Kuwait*, pp. 64-64.
2 Dickson, *Kuwait*, pp. 50-52, 69.
3 Brucks, George Barnes, *Memoir descriptive of the navigation of the Gulf of Persia*, Bombay Selections, Vol. XXIV, pp. 532-576.

Traditional social and cultural patterns in Kuwait's town and desert

a) Everyday life in urban society

1 Lorimer, *Gazetteer*, Vol. 2 B, p. 1054.
2 Dickson, *Forty years*, p. 90.
3 Lorimer, *Gazetteer*, Vol. 2 B, p. 1054.
4 Freeth, *A new look*, p. 60.

b) Everyday life in Bedu society

1 Lorimer, *Gazetteer*, Vol. 2 B, p. 1054.

c) Festivals and rituals

1 The *Qur'an*, translated by N. J. Dawood, Penguin Classics edition, London 1956, p. 357.
2 In Dickson, *Kuwait*, p. 417.
3 In Dickson, *Kuwait*, p. 418.
4 In Dickson, *Kuwait*, pp. 420-421.
5 In Dickson, *Kuwait*, pp. 421.

d) Clothing traditions

1 Buckingham, *Travels*, Vol. 2, pp. 146-147.
2 Niebuhr, *Travels*, Vol. 2, pp. 233-235.
3 Lorimer, *Gazetteer*, Vol. 2 B, p. 1054.
4 Dickson, Harold R. P., *The Arab of the desert*, London 1949, p. 156.

5 Freeth, *A new look*, pp. 105-107.
6 Doughty, Charles, *Travels in Arabia Deserts*, 2 vols., Cambridge 1888, Vol. 1, p. 237.
7 Niebuhr, *Travels*, Vol. 2, p. 235.
8 Doughty, *Travels*, Vol. 1, p. 292.
9 Niebuhr, *Travels*, Vol. 2, pp. 235-236
10 Freeth, Zahra, *Kuwait was my home*, London 1956, p. 86.
11 Dickson, *Forty years*, p. 236.
12 In Dickson, *Kuwait*, p. 419.
13 In Dickson, *Kuwait*, p. 421.

KUWAIT IN THE PRESENT

The establishment of a constitution and development of the economy and infrastructure

1 For example 1,002,465 million barrels of crude oil were produced in 1973 as against 300,221 million barrels in 1982. *Annual Statistical Abstract 1983*, Edition XX, Ministry of Planning, Central Statistical Office, p. 163.
2 *Annual Statistical Abstract 1983*, p. 314.

The settlement

1 Freeth, *A new look*, pp. 54-56.
2 Freeth, *A new look*, p. 53.
3 Freeth, *A new look*, pp. 141-142.
4 Freeth, *A new look*, p. 109.
5 Freeth, *A new look*, p. 102.
6 *Annual Statistical Abstract 1983*, p. 25.
7 *Annual Statistical Abstract 1983*, p. 27.

Present day social and cultural patterns

a) Everyday life in urban society

1 *Kuwait Today—a welfare state.* Ministry of Guidance and Information of Kuwait 1964, p. 55.
2 For example in the *Arab Times* of November 22-23, 1984 the weekend prayer times are given:—

Thursday			Friday		
	Fajr	4.55		Fajr	4.56
	Zuhr	11.34		Zuhr	11.35
	'Asr	2.31		'Asr	2.31
	Maghreb	4.50		Maghreb	4.50
	Isha	6.11		Isha	6.12

b) Everyday life in Bedu society

1 Dickson, *Forty years*, p. 221.

c) Festivals and rituals

1 Dickson, *Forty years*, pp. 211-214.

d) Clothing traditions

1 For example Musaab Meinke, *A guide to Arab Gulf dress*; Part 1, Mmen, Arab Times Supplement 12 May, 1983, pp. 14-19; part 2, Women, 19 May, 1983, pp. 34-37.
2 Dickson, *Forty years*. p. 303.

The Rulers of Kuwait of the Al-Subah Family

1756-1762	Sheikh Sabah Bin Jaber
1762-1812	Sheikh Abdullah I
1812-1859	Sheikh Jaber I
1859-1866	Sheikh Sabah II
1866-1892	Sheikh Abdullah II
1892-1896	Sheikh Muhammad I
1896-1915	Sheikh Mubarak Al-Sabah
1915-1917	Sheikh Jaber II
1917-1921	Sheikh Salim Al-Mubarak
1921-1950	Sheikh Ahmad Al-Jabar Al-Sabah
1950-1965	Sheikh Abdullah Al-Salem Al-Sabah
1965-1977	Sheikh Sabah Al-Salem Al-Sabah
1978-	Sheikh Jaber Al-Ahmed Al-Sabah

GENERAL VIEW OF KUWAIT

KUWAIT CITY AND SUBURBS

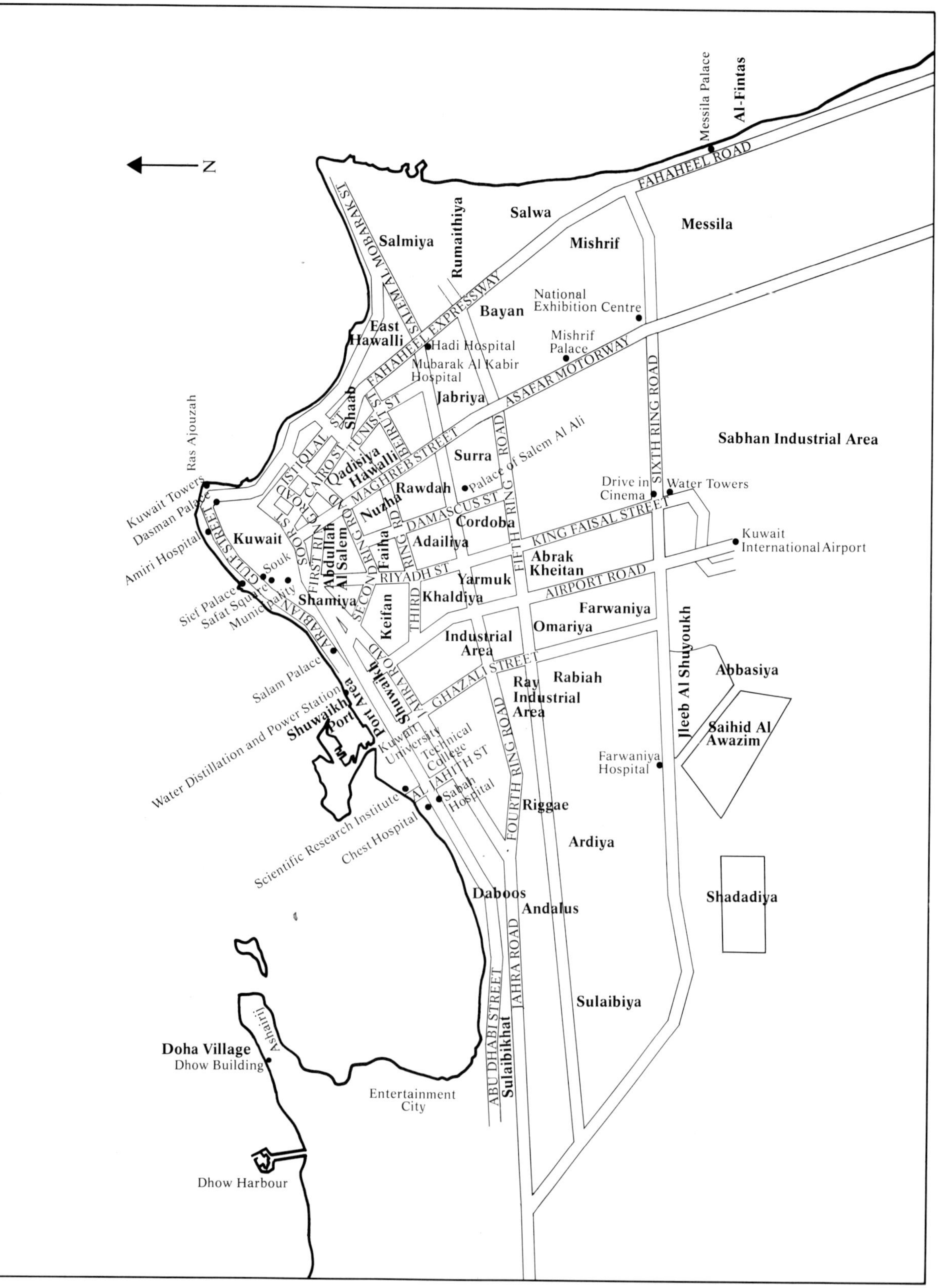

CATALOGUE

CATALOGUE OF COSTUMES AND TEXTILES EXHIBITED IN THE ROYAL SCOTTISH MUSEUM EDINBURGH

The Royal Scottish Museum holds an extensive collection of costumes and textiles from both the urban and Bedu environments of Kuwait. The selection catalogued here is on display in the exhibition **Costumes and Textiles from Kuwait.**

1. Men's Costumes

MAN'S WINTER COSTUME

KUWAIT 1984

Here the choice of weight and colour of fabric are important. Over long white trousers (*sirwal*) a long robe (*dishdasha*) of a thick sober-coloured fabric is worn. For extra warmth a flowing cloak (*bisht*) may be added. The headdress consists of a crotchet cap (*keffiya*), a winter scarf (*gatra*) and a retaining cord circlet (*'agal*). A string of prayer beads (*mesbaha*) completes the outfit.
1985.4,14,20,24,29,31,170.
Plate 39; diagram 1.

TROUSERS—SIRWAL

A loose garment with legs falling straight to the ankle. Made of a white mixed cotton and polyester fabric.
1985.31; length 109 cm.
Plate 39; diagram 1.

ROBE—DISHDASHA

Garment falling in a loose straight line from shoulder to ankle. Long staright sleeves. Neat high collar fastened with two buttons. A bag-shaped pocket at each side at hip level and a patch pocket on left side of chest. Made of gray and white pin-striped mixed wool and synthetic fabric.
1985.14; length 148 cm.

CLOAK—BISHT

A loose flowing garment draped over the shoulders. Here made of a heavy black wool and decorated with gold braid along the shoulder seams, front borders and narrow wrist openings. A *bisht* decorated in this manner is usually worn on special occasions.
1958.4; length 140 cm.

CAP—KEFFIYA

A close-fitting skull cap crotchetted in white mercerised thread in pattern of stars against an openwork background. Machine-made in China.
1985.20; diameter 25 cm.

HEAD CLOTH—GATRA

A square of white synthetic fabric printed in red, green and black with a floral border and as a floral cone motif at each corner. Made in Japan. A modern version of an accessory once made in wool and embroidered in coloured silks.
1985.29; 113 x 116.5 cm.

HEAD CIRCLET—'AGAL

A double circlet of twisted black nylon cord.
1985.24; diameter 22 cm.

PRAYER BEADS—MESBAHA

A string of thirty three amber-coloured beads linked to a brown silk fringed tassel.
1985.170; length 17 cm.

MAN'S SUMMER COSTUME

KUWAIT 1984

The garments here are light both in weight and colour. Over long white trousers (*sirwal*) is worn a long white robe (*dishdasha*). A cloak (*bisht*) is optional depending on the formality of the occasion and sudden changes in termperature. The headdress consists of a crotchet cap (*keffiya*), a white scarf (*gatra*) and a retaining cord circlet (*'agal*). A string of prayer beads completes the costume.
1985.5,11,21,23,28,171.
Plate 42, diagram 4.

TROUSERS—SIRWAL

A loose garment with legs falling straight to the ankle. Made of a white mixed cotton and polyester fabric.
1985.32; length 110 cm.

ROBE—DISHDASHA

Garment falling in a loose straight line from shoulder to ankle. Long straight sleeves.

Neat high collar fastened with two buttons. A bag-shaped pocket on each side at hip level and a patch pocket on left side of the chest. Made of a light weight white mixed cotton and synthetic fabric.
1985.11; length 146 cm.

CLOAK—BISHT

A loose flowing garment draped over the shoulders. Here made of a light beige wool and decorated with gold braid along the shoulder seams, front borders and narrow wrist openings. Made in Syria.
1985.5; length 136 cm.
Plate 42; diagram 4.

CAP—KEFFIYA

A close-fitting skull cap crotchetted in white mercerised thread in a pattern of stars and circles against an openwork background. Machine-made in China.
1985.21; diameter 23 cm.

HEAD CLOTH—GATRA

A square of white synthetic fabric. machine-embroidered with rows of white floral sprigs. Made in China.
1985.28; 122 x 122 cm.

HEAD CIRCLET—'AGAL

A double circlet of twisted black silk-textured cord. Made in Syria.
1985.23; diameter 22 cm.

PRAYER BEADS—MESBAHA

A string of thirty three brown beads linked to a brown silk fringed tassel.
1985.171; length 17 cm.

BEDU MAN'S WINTER COSTUME

KUWAIT 1984

In general a modern Bedu's clothing closely resembles that of the town Kuwaiti. Here, for example, he wears a long beige robe (*dishdasha*). His headdress consists of a crotchet cap (*keffiya*), a red and white checked head cloth (*shemagh*) which is usually worn in winter, and a retaining cord circlet (*'agal*). He may still wear a very traditional garment, a bulky warm coat (*farwah*) draped over the shoulders.
1985.1,13,18,25,30.

ROBE—DISHDASHA

Garment falling in a straight loose line from shoulder to ankle. Long straight sleeves. neat high collar fastened with two buttons. A bag-shaped pocket at each side at hip level and a patch pocket on the left side of the chest. Made of beige mixed cotton and synthetic fabric.
1985.13; length 148 cm.

COAT—FARWAH

An anklelength bulky coat of straight square proportions. Short straight projecting sleeves. Made of a dark brown suede-textured fabric and lined with dark brown synthetic fur. Decorated with applied bands of light brown plainted braid. Made in Italy.
1985.1; length 130 cm.

CAP—KEFFIYA

A close-fitting skull cap crotchetted in white cotton in a design of radial and vertical shell-patterned bands. Machine-made in Shanghai, China.
1985.18; diameter 24 cm.

HEAD CLOTH—SHEMAGH

A square of white synthetic fabric. Central zigzag checked pattern and chevron stripe border woven in red in supplementary satin weave.
1985.30; 133 x 131 cm.

HEAD CIRCLET—'AGAL

A double circlet of black twisted wool. Made in Damascus, Syria.
1985.25; diameter 22 cm.

BEDU MAN'S COSTUME

KUWAIT 1984

Although the costume is modern certain garments are made in styles that had gone out of fashion by the early 1950s. Instead of a smart *dishdasha* a robe with long pointed sleeves (*thob shillahat*) is worn, while the crotchet cap (*keffiya*) and scarf (*gatra*) of the headdress are kept in place by a head circlet made of a thick skein of dark brown wool bound by coloured threads. The hair is dressed in long coiled plaits, a style which had disappeared. A wool cloak (*bisht*) is still worn today.
1985.3,10,17,27,149.
Plate 40; diagram 2.

ROBE—THOB SHILLAHAT

Garment falling in a loose straight line from shoulder to ankle, flaring slightly towards the hem of the skirt. Long full sleeves with wide pointed cuffs. Neat round neck and centre front opening. A bag-shaped pocket on each side at hip level. Made of a white mixed cotton and synthetic fabric.
1985.10; length 115 cm.
Plate 40; diagram 2.

CLOAK—BISHT

A loose flowing garment draped over the shoulders. Here a practical beige wool plain winter garment with shoulder seams, front borders and wrist openings decorated with beige thread worked in fishtail overcast stitch.
1985.3; length 136 cm.

CAP—KEFFIYA

A close-fitting skull cap crotchetted in white cotton in a pattern of star and diamond-shaped motifs. Machine-made in China.
1985.17; diameter 24 cm.

HEAD CLOTH—GATRA

A square of plain white synthetic fabric. Made in Shanghai, China.
1985.27; 118 cm.

HEAD CIRCLET—'AGAL

A skein of thick strands of dark brown wool bound together at intervals with bands of cream, emerald green, scarlet and yellow wools.
1985.149; length 138 cm.

2. Men's Accessories

CAP—KEFFIYA

KUWAIT 1984

A close-fitting skull cap crotchetted in white mercerised thread in a pattern of star motifs and zigzag borders. Made in Shanghai, China.
1985.19; diameter 25 cm.
Plate 44.

HEAD CLOTH—SHEMAGH

KUWAIT 1982

A square of white synthetic fabric. Diagonally checked centre pattern and zigzag border woven in red in supplementary satin weave. For winter wear.
1983.981; 118 x 122 cm.

HEAD CIRCLET—'AGAL

KUWAIT 1984

A double circlet of black twisted synthetic cord. Made in Syria.
1985.26; diameter 22 cm.

HEAD CIRCLET—'AGAL

KUWAIT 1984

A skein of thick strands of brown wool bound together at intervals with bands of emerald green, orange and blue wools.
1985.150; length 140 cm.

PRAYER BEADS—MESBAHA

KUWAIT 1984

A string of ninety three black beads spaced at intervals by red beads.
1985.172; length 38 cm.
Plate 44.

3. Women's Costumes

WOMAN'S OUTDOOR COSTUME

KUWAIT c.1940-1984

The garments of this costume are interesting because although they are modern in date, they illustrate styles and uses which could be observed in the streets and markets of Kuwait town from the beginning of the 20th century to the early 1950s. The heavy overdress (*thob jez*) is no longer worn, while it is rare to see a woman now totally concealed in the face veil (*bushiya*) and cloak (*'abbaya*).
1985.67,69,76.
Plates 54,58; diagram 10.

OVERDRESS—THOB JEZ

A voluminous anklelength garment with a deep pointed neck and flowing sleeves made of a heavy black cotton. The embroidery in gold thread makes the construction details of the garment into decorative features. Seams are joined with gold insertion stitch and underarm gussets are embroidered with floral sprays in chain stitch.
1985.67; length 160 cm.
Plate 54; diagram 10.

CLOAK—'ABBAYA

A loose flowing garment which can be draped around the shoulders or pulled up to cover the head. Here made of a black wool and synthetic fabric. Gold thread is sewn as a plaited border along shoulder seams, front borders and narrow wrist openings.
1985.69; length 160.

HEAD COVERING—MILFA

A black gauze scarf which is usually draped around the head to frame the face is here used as a veil (*bushiya*) which completely obscures the features.
1985.76; 230 x 90 cm.

WOMAN'S COSTUME

KUWAIT 1984

Although modern European dress is worn in Kuwait, women still like traditional styles and alternate between the two fashions with ease. Here a long dress (*dara'a*) is combined with a cloak (*'abbaya*) for outdoor wear. The use of a head covering is optional.
1985.50,73,106.
Plates 59,116; diagram 12.

DRESS—DARA'A

An anklelength loose-fitting dress with long sleeves made of a Japanese polyester fabric in vivid fuchsia pink. Sprays of roses are machine-embroidered on the front yoke.
1985.50; length 150 cm.

CLOAK—'ABBAYA

A graceful light version of a traditional garment made in black silk and decorated with diamanté bead edging along the shoulder seams, front borders and wrist openings.
1985.73; length 130 cm.
Plate 59; diagram 12.

HEAD COVERING

A scarf which is pulled tightly round the face modestly concealing the hair may be worn instead of the more loosely draped *milfa.* This example, made of white polyester, is of triangular shape with two long ties which fasten at the nape of the neck.
1985.106; 152.5 x 74 cm.

WOMAN'S COSTUME

KUWAIT 1984

The main feature of this costume is the long coat (*zebun*) with a wrapover front which is made of a brightly coloured and patterned fabric. This is a traditional garment which was worn by wealthy townswomen over a dress (*fustan*) and trousers (*sirwal*).
1985.68,79,91.
Plate 53; diagram 9.

TROUSERS—SIRWAL

A loose garment gathered at the waist and tapering to close-fitting ankles. Made of a bright blue synthetic silk. Ankles and lower part of legs machine-embroidered with leaf palmette motifs and scrolls in gold thread in chain stitch.
1985.91; length 110 cm.

COAT—ZEBUN

The use of a modern polyester fabric striped in glittering turquoise, mauve, silver and gold for this coat is appropriate because it was a garment usually made in luxurious brocaded silks. It is anklelength with a fitted bodice and bell-shaped skirt and deep wrapover front. Traditional features of cut and construction have been faithfully reproduced.
1985.68; length 137 cm.
Diagram 9.

HEAD COVERING—MILFA

A length of black georgette embroidered in chain stitch with gold thread. Within a sprigged border are four coffee pot motifs, one at each corner. The *milfa* is loosely draped over the head. One end passes under the chin and over the shoulder.
1985.79; 181 x 81 cm.

WOMAN'S COSTUME

KUWAIT 1984

This costume is a modern interpretation for party wear of garments which could have been worn as bridal dress, since the fashion for white wedding gowns is recent. The most striking feature is the use of a patchwork of different coloured silks for the dress, a technique known as *al-mufahah.* The costume was made in Bahrain. (The bridal jewellery is a reconstruction folowing traditional models.)
1985.40 & A-B.
Plates 62,122.

DRESS—DARA'A AL-MUFAHAH

An anklelength slim dress slit at the side of the skirt from knee to ankle. Tapered long sleeves. Silk in vibrant shades of emerald green, fuchsia pink, purple and orange is used for separate pattern pieces which are stitched together to create a striking decorative effect. Machine-embroidered chain stitch designs in orange, purple and gold embellish the front yoke, and cuffs and seams.
1985.40; length 145 cm.

TROUSERS—SIRWAL

A loose garment of emerald green silk tapering to neat close-fitting ankles which are lavishly embroidered with borders of stripes, spirals and sunflower motifs.
1985.40A; length 106 cm.

BELT—HAZAM

A long narrow band consisting of a double thickness of emerald green silk embroidered with rows of scrolling motifs. Ties of twisted gold cord.
1985.40B; length 205 cm.

WOMAN'S COSTUME

KUWAIT 1984

The garments of this costume, a long dress (*dara'a*) and a loose overdress (*thob al-tour bilteil*) are worn on special occasions such as wedding parties. They are comparable in shape and construction to everyday clothes but are more luxurious in fabric and decoration.
1985.49, 64.
Plates 51,123; diagrams 7,13.

DRESS—DARA'A

An anklelength loose-fitting dress made of a lustrous black synthetic satin fabric. Long sleeves are inserted into curved armholes. Designs of a large floral spray and sunray border motifs are embroidered in gold sequins. Made in India.
1985.49; length 147 cm.
Plate 51; diagram 7.

OVERDRESS—THOB AL-TOUR BILTEIL

A transparent graceful garment whose wide sleeves can be used to provocatively veil the face during dancing. Constructed from rectangular pieces of a fine black synthetic silk net. Trefoil motifs scattered over the back and front and floral scroll and lozenge borders are delicately embroidered in silver thread. Made in Bombay, India.
1985.64; length 161 cm.
Plate 123; diagram 13.

GIRL'S COSTUME

KUWAIT 1984

This costume is frequently worn by young girls on special occasions such as wedding parties, school and state functions. While the dress and overdress (*thob al-messarah*) are small versions of adult female clothing, a close-fitting hood (*bukhnug*) was traditionally worn by girls until they were old enough to wear the *'abbaya* and *milfa*. (The dress is a reconstruction.)
1983.972; 1985.117.

OVERDRESS—THOB AL-MESSARAH

This version of the *thob* is reserved for festivals and parties. It is made of black silk gauze lavishly embroidered in gold thread with a central panel of repeated lozenge motifs and delicate scrolling borders along the edges of sleeves and skirt. Made in India.
1985.117; length 110 cm.

HOOD-BUKHNUG

A shawl-like accessory which closely frames the face and hangs down the back like a cloak. This example is made of black silk gauze with a gold embroidered border.
1983.972; length 76 cm.

BEDU WOMAN'S COSTUME

KUWAIT 1984

Bedu women still prefer the traditional styles of garment but take advantage of the boldly patterned synthetic fabrics available to indulge their taste for colourful finery which they use for both everyday and party wear. They continue to shroud their heads in black hoods (*sheileh*) and face masks (*burqa*).
1985.44,83,87,95.
Plates 50,52; diagrams 6,8.

TROUSERS—SIRWAL

Voluminous garment tapering to close-fitting ankles. Made of scarlet cotton fabric imported from China. Decorated with bands of bright blue and gold braid at the ankles.
1985.95; length 99 cm.
Plate 50; diagram 6.

DRESS-FUSTAN

Anklelength garment with fitted bodice, full gathered skirt and long sleeves. Made of white nylon boldly patterned with swirling rose motifs in flocked red pile and gold Lurex thread.
1985.44; length 132 cm.
Plate 52; diagram 8.

HOOD-SHEILEH

A close-fitting accessory framing the face and falling in points at the back and over the shoulders. Made of black gauze.
1985.83; length 90 cm.

FACE MASK—BURQA

A simple rectangle with narrow slits for the eyes. It extends from the forehead to just below the chin. Tied at the back of the head over the *sheileh*. Made of black cotton.
1985.87; 37 x 35 cm.

BEDU WOMAN'S COSTUME

KUWAIT 1984

This costume is relatively subdued in colour scheme. It also demonstrates the use of an overdress (*thob*) and of a swathed headscarf (*milfa*) instead of the hood (*sheileh*).
1983.974; 1985.41,61,77,92.
Plate 56.

TROUSERS—SIRWAL

Voluminous garment tapering to close-fitting ankles. Made of emerald green synthetic silk. Decorated with a deep band of quatrefoil motifs and palmettes machine-embroidered in gold and silver thread at the ankles.
1985.92; length 104 cm.

DRESS—FUSTAN

A loose anklelength garment with long sleeves. Made of black synthetic gauze embossed with pairs of gold leaves.
1985.41; length 132 cm.

OVERDRESS—THOB

A practical version of the voluminous overdress for everyday wear. Made of spotted black net.
1985.61; length 165 cm.

HEAD COVERING—MILFA

A scarf of coarse black net is here draped and swathed tightly around the head.
1985.77; 200 x 90 cm.

FACE MASK—BURQA

A simple rectangle with narrow slits for the eyes. It extends from the forehead to just below the chin. Tied at the back of the head over the *sheileh*. Made of black cotton.
1983.974; 42 x 32.5 cm.

BEDU WOMAN'S COSTUME

KUWAIT 1984

Gaily coloured trousers (*sirwal*) and dress (*fustan*) are worn with the traditional black hood (*sheileh*) and face mask (*burqa*).
1985.43,84,88,90.

TROUSERS—SIRWAL

A loose garment tapering slightly towards the ankles. Made of light blue cotton. Machine-embroidered around the ankles with leaf motif bands in yellow, scarlet and gold threads.
1985.90; length 92.5 cm.

DRESS—FUSTAN

Anklelength garment with fitted bodice, full skirt and long sleeves. A collar and cuffs are also added. Made of mauve nylon fabric printed with chrysanthemum sprays. Vertical stripes in coloured Lurex—pink, green, orange, blue and gold—are superimposed.
1985.43; length 130 cm.

HOOD—SHEILEH

A close-fitting accessory framing the face and falling in points at the back and over the shoulders. Made of black gauze.
1985.84; length 70 cm.

FACE MASK—BURQA

A simple rectangle with narrow slits for the eyes. It extends from the forehead to just below the chin. Tied at the back of the head over the *sheileh*. Made of black cotton.
1985.88; 34 x 36 cm.

4. Woman's Accessories

HEAD COVERING—MILFA

KUWAIT 1984

A length of black georgette crouched in silver and blue Lurex thread. Within a floral scroll border are four crescent and flower motifs, one at each corner.
1985.50; 170 x 81 cm.

HOOD—SHEILEH

KUWAIT 1984

A close-fitting accessory framing the face and falling in points at the back and over the shoulders. Made of black gauze.
1985.86; length 90 cm.

FACE MASK—BURQA

KUWAIT 1983

A simple rectangle with narrow slits for the eyes. It extends from the forehead to just below the chin. Tied at the back of the head over the *sheileh*. Made of black cotton.
1983.973; 45 x 33 cm.

BATH PATTENS–

KUWAIT 1984

Made of wood with a raised narrow stilt at heel and toe. A peg projects up between the first and second toe to keep the patten in place
1985.113 & A; length 25.6 cm.
Plate 60.

PUMICE STONE–SAKHRA

KUWAIT 1984

A shaped piece of black coarse granular stone used to remove rough hard skin.
1985.184; 8 cm.
Plate 60.

BATH MITTEN–LIFA

KUWAIT 1984

A circular mitten with a long cuff crotchetted in cream cotton thread. Used to scrub and clean the skin.
1985.179; length 30 cm.
Plate 60.

HENNA–HINNA

KUWAIT 1984

A finely ground green powder used in colouring the hair and palms of the hands red. Imported from Saudi Arabia.
1985.174.
Plate 60.

HENNA FIXATIVE

KUWAIT 1984

A bottle of amber-coloured oil which is mixed with henna.
1985.175.

COSMETIC BARK–MASWAK

KUWAIT 1984

Strips of light brown fibrous bark which are traditionally used for cleaning the teeth and staining the lips red.
1985.180.
Plate 60.

KOHL POT AND APPLICATOR–MAKHLAH

KUWAIT 1984

A fine black powder ground from antimony and malachite (*kuhl*) was and is still used to elongate and outline the eyes. It is kept in small pots whose stoppers have sticks for application. This example of brass has an elaborately wrought stopper. Made in India.
1985.165 & A; height 12.5 cm.
Plate 61.

KOHL POT AND APPLICATOR–MAKHLAH

KUWAIT 1984

A facetted container with an elaborate fan-shaped stopper made of silver-gilt metal. Made in India
1985.163 & A; height 14 cm.

MIRROR

KUWAIT 1984

A rectangular silvered glass set within a wooden frame painted in red and green. Made in China.
1985.162; 21 x 16 cm.
Plate 61.

COMB

KUWAIT 1984

A flat piece of wood with teeth on both sides, fine and coarse.
1985.183; 10 x 8.5 cm.
Plate 61.

PERFUME BOTTLE AND STOPPER

KUWAIT 1984

Rich emerald green glass with splashes and swirls in deep red and blue. Made in a traditional shape with a globular base and a long neck fitted with an elaborate fan-shaped gilded stopper. Made in Cologne, West Germany.
1985.160 & A; height 17 cm.
Plate 61.

ROSEWATER SPRINKLER–MARASH

KUWAIT 1984

Brass with a pear-shaped body and a long narrow neck. Made in India.
1985.159; 30 cm.
Plate 61.

5. Household Furnishings

CHEST–SANDUQ

KUWAIT, early 20th century

Large wooden chests with brass fittings were imported from India and given to a woman at marriage for storage of clothes and textiles of her dowry. This example is made of smoothly worked dark mahogany wood with elaborate brass hinges and lock. The front and lid are studded with flat-headed brass nails in star panel and rosette designs. It is supported on four wooden feet painted in bright scarlet, yellow and green.
1985.123 & A-D; 88 x 39.5 x 40 cm.

INCENSE BURNER–MABKHAR

KUWAIT 1984

Incense burners containing frankincense (*bokhur*) are traditionally used to perfume the clothes before a party or special occasion. They are also passed among guests for the same purpose. This example of brass in a beaker shape was made in India.
1985.156; 23 cm.

INCENSE BURNER–MABKHAR

KUWAIT 1984

An incense burner of brass with a spherical bowl and lid on a circular pedestal. Made in Taiwan.
1985.157 & A; 24 cm.

ROSEWATER SPRINKLER–MARASH

Rosewater was traditionally sprinkled on guests' hands after the serving of coffee or a meal. This example of brass has a pear-shaped base and long narrow neck. Made in India.
1985.158; 35.5 cm.

6. Bedu Weaving

A. Equipment

PAIR OF CARDING COMBS

KUWAIT 1984

Two rectangular pieces of wood studded with fine nails which are used to tease and fluff wool in preparation for spinning.
1985.151 & A; 29 x 21 cm.
Plate 27.

DISTAFF–TAGHZALA

KUWAIT 1984

A long wooden stick with a notched end to which the wool to be spun is attached.
1985.152; 91 cm.
Plate 27.

SPINDLE—MAGHZAL

KUWAIT 1984

A drop spindle made of a length of wood with a cross-shaped and piece. The spun wool is attached to a hook and wound around the spindle.
1985.153; 36 cm.
Plate 27.

LOOM—NATTU

KUWAIT 1984

A simple horizontal easily portable loom. Two metal rods (*ras* and *ga'ah*) are set apart to function as beams around which the warp threads are wrapped. A wooden rod (*minyar*) with a raised support (*marakib*) at each end is inserted into the loom fabric and tied with short loops to alternate warps. The weft wool is wound around a long wooden shuttle (*misha*). A flat wooden stick (*mishizza*) is used to tighten the fabric by pushing the woven weft threads close together. A gazelle horn (*middra*) is used to pluck and neaten the threads of the warp-faced weave.
1985.154 & A; 1.19 x 1.22 m; 1985.155; 70 cm.
Plate 29.

B. Examples

TENT CURTAIN—QATA

KUWAIT 1982

Black, crimson, scarlet wools and cream cotton woven in compound warp-faced double weave and tapestry weave. Design of vertical stripes worked in cream on black with geometrical motifs of triangles, lozenges, zigzag bands and saltire crosses. Border of interlocked triangles.
1983.982; 5.98 x 1.37 m.
Plate 32.

STRIP FOR A TENT DIVIDING CURTAIN—MATABBAH

KUWAIT 1982

Normally a Bedu tent curtain is made of four strips sewn together. The second strip (*matabbah*) is light coloured and elaborately patterned.
Black, crimson, orange, green, dark blue wools and cream cotton woven in compound warp-faced double weave and tapestry weave. Design of vertical stripes reserved against a cream ground. Main stripe woven in cream on black with bold lozenge and zigzag motifs. The stripes are crossed at intervals by horizontal bands with triangular patterns woven in crimson, orange, green and blue.
1983.998; 9.1 m x 38 cm.

TENT FLOOR COVERING—BUSAT

KUWAIT 1982

Dark and light brown, brick red wools and cream cotton woven in compound warp-faced double weave and tapestry weave. Design of plain vertical stripes in dark and light brown and cream separated by narrow bands of brick red and checked brown and white bars. Border of diamond shaped motifs. Fringed ends.
1983.983; 4.70 x 1.10 m.

TENT FLOOR COVERING—BUSAT

KUWAIT 1984

Cream, dark blue wools and cream, gray, black, scarlet, turquoise, brown and orange cotton woven in compound warp-faced double weave. Design of red, cream and blue diamond and zigzag patterned stripes and plain gray and brown stripes against a cream background.
1985.128; 3.54 x .81 m.

TENT FLOOR COVERING—BUSAT

KUWAIT 1984

Black, orange, red wools and cream, yellow, blue cotton woven in compound warp-faced double weave. Design of vertical stripes in red and black worked with checked and geometrical motifs in cream, all against a cream background.
1985.129; 3.77 x .91 m.
Plate 96.

TENT FLOOR COVERING—BUSAT

KUWAIT 1984

Cream, brown, crimson, dark purple wools woven in compound warp-faced double weave. Design of vertical crimson and purple stripes patterned with checked, zigzag, hexagonal and chevron motifs against a cream background.
1985.131; 2.4 x .92 m.
Plate 33.

STORAGE BAG—'ADUL

KUWAIT 1982

Dark and light brown, brick red, green wools and cream cotton woven in compound warp-faced double weave. Design of narrow stripes with granular zigzag and checked motifs against a plain red background.
1983.984; 55 x 83 cm.
Plate 37.

STORAGE BAG—'ADUL

KUWAIT 1982

Dark blue, light brown, beige wools and cream cotton woven in comound warp-faced double weave. Design of broad plain stripes.
1983.986; 98 x 93 cm.

STORAGE BAG—'ADUL

KUWAIT 1984

Black, light brown, cream, orange, brick red and green wools woven in compound warp-faced double weave. Designs of black and cream checked vertical bands against plain black, light brown and cream stripes.
1985.134; 85 x 90 cm.
Plate 34.

STORAGE BAG—'ADUL

KUWAIT 1984

Dark blue, crimson, brick red, orange, brown, green wools and cream cotton woven in compound warp-faced double weave and tapestry weave. Design of narrow blue and white speckled bands against broad vertical cream and brown stripes.
1985.135; 1.18 m x 68 cm.

CUSHION—MASANAD

KUWAIT 1983

Dark brown, beige and cream wools woven in compound warp-faced weave. Design of broad vertical stripes. Sides and ends brightly overcast in scarlet and orange wools. Tassel at each corner.
1983.987; 64 x 36.5 cm.

CUSHION—MASANAD

KUWAIT 1982

Dark and light brown and cream wools woven in compound warp-faced double weave. Design of vertical stripes. Tassel at each corner.
1983.989; 67 x 38.5 cm.
Plate 97.

CUSHION—MASANAD

KUWAIT 1982

Dark brown, crimson, orange, green, blue wools and cream cotton woven in compound warp-faced double weave. Design of vertical stripes patterned with spotted zigzags and geometrical motifs of checks, diamonds in black and cream on a crimson background.
1983.991; 68 x 46 cm.

WALL HANGING

KUWAIT 1984

Dark brown, beige and cream wools woven in tapestry weave and long shaggy knotted pile. Design of horizontal stripes of triangular motifs. Plaited cord fringes.
1985.139; 1.6 m x 33 cm.
Plate 98.

SADDLE BAG—KHURUJ

KUWAIT 1984

Dark brown, cream, crimson, orange, blue and green wools woven in compound warp-faced double weave and tapestry weave. Design of horizontal bands of bold diamond motifs reserved against vertically striped ground of brown and cream. Adorned with rows of long plaited cords and fringed tassels.
1985.142; 2.91 m x 52 cm.
Plate 35.

CAMEL TRAPPING—SAYAYIF

KUWAIT 1984

Black, brick red, crimson, orange, dark blue, green wools and cream cotton woven in compound warp-faced double weave and tapestry weave. A long strip of black and white geometrical motifs—lozenges, spotted diamonds, bars. Ends woven with brightly coloured diamond motifs.
1985.140; 3.2 m x 15 cm.

CAMEL TRAPPING—SAYAYIF

KUWAIT 1984

Dark brown, crimson, orange, ochre yellow, green, blue wools and cream cotton woven in warp-faced plaited weave and tapestry weave. Long strip of black plaited weave with ends brightly patterned in lozenge and triangle motifs. Plaited cords with heavy tassels.
1985.146; 1.56 m x 23 cm.

CAMEL TRAPPING—SAYAYIF

KUWAIT 1984

Dark brown, red, orange, blue wools and cream cotton woven in warp-faced plaited weave and tapestry weave. Long strip of dark brown plaited weave with ends decorated in diamond patterns. Plaited cords with heavy tassels.
1985.145; 3.80 m x 15 cm.

FLOOR COVERING—BUSAT

IRAQ 1984

Brown, ochre yellow, orange, red, purple wools and cream cotton woven in tapestry weave. Design of a central vertical band of diamond motifs composed of triangular units.
1985.130; 5.35 x 1.03 m.

FLOOR COVERING—BUSAT

IRAQ 1984

Crimson wool woven in twill weave. Embroidered in cream, crimson, brick red, orange, green, blue wools in chain stitch. Elaborate design of panels of checked, diamond and quatrefoil motifs repeated all over the cover.
1985.136; 3.74 x 1.52 m.

CUSHION—MASANAD

IRAQ 1984

Dark blue, green, brick red, orange wools and cream cotton woven in tapestry weave. Design of stepped diamond motifs.
1985.137; 80.5 x 40.5 cm.

CUSHION—MASANAD

IRAQ 1984

Dark blue, green, crimson, orange wools and cream cotton woven in tapestry weave. Design of repeated intersecting diamond motifs.
1985.138; 80.5 x 43 cm.

STORAGE BAG—'ADUL

SYRIA 1982

Dark blue, crimson, scarlet, green wools and cream cotton woven in compound warp-faced double weave. Design of vertical bands in white and blue patterned in zigzag and diamond motifs against a ground of plain blue and crimson stripes.
1983.985; 1.12 x .95 m.

STORAGE BAG—'ADUL

SYRIA 1982

Dark blue, brick red wools and cream cotton woven in compound warp-faced double weave. Design of blue and white, red and blue vertical stripes patterned with checked, hooked, zigzag, chevron, saltire cross motifs against a blue ground.
1983.997; 1.19 x 1.13 m.

STORAGE BAG—'ADUL

SYRIA 1984

Dark blue, crimson and cream wools woven in compound warp-faced double weave. Design of finely worked zigzag, lozenge, saltire cross and stylised human figure motifs in white on blue stripes all against a blue background.
1985.127; 1.60 x 1.10 m.

CAMEL TRAPPING—SAYAYIF

SYRIA c. 1975-80

Dark brown, brick red, scarlet, orange, blue, green and cream wools woven in compound warp-faced double weave, weft-wrapped brocaded weave and warp-faced plaited weave. A long broad strip with ends decorated with bold diamond motifs and hung with thick plaited cords and tassels.
1985.143; 3.36 m x 27 cm.

CAMEL TRAPPING—SAYAYIF

SYRIA 1982

Dark blue, navy blue, maroon, crimson, red, green and cream wools woven in tapestry weave. A long broad strip with a design of hooked diamond motifs and adorned with plaited cord strung with tassels.
1985.144; 1.77 m x 18 cm.

DIAGRAM 1. MAN'S TROUSERS – SIRWAL. KUWAIT 1984 [RSM 1985.31] PATTERN AND CONSTRUCTION

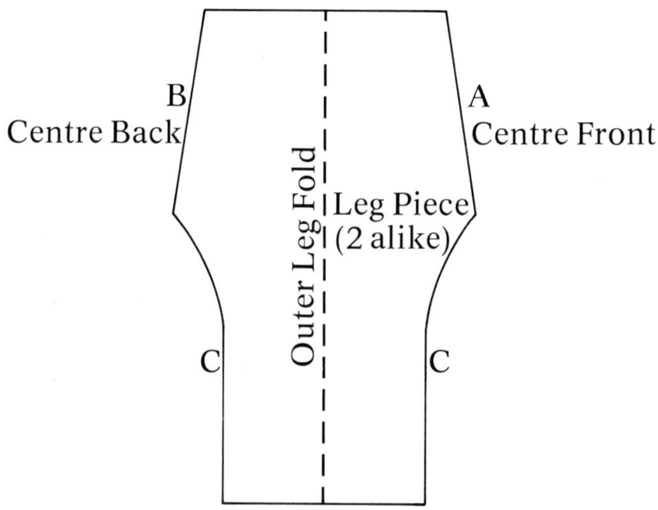

Leg pieces folded in half at
Outer Leg joined at A-A, B-B
for Centre Back and Front.
Inner Leg joined at C-C.
1.5cm Seam Allowance.
Waist – 3.5cm Hem turned in
and sewn down over elastic.
Ankles – 7cm Hem turned in.
Scale ⅛″ = 2⅜″; .3cm = 5.8cm.

DIAGRAM 2. MAN'S ROBE – THOB SHILLAHAT. KUWAIT 1984 [RSM 1985.10] PATTERN AND CONSTRUCTION

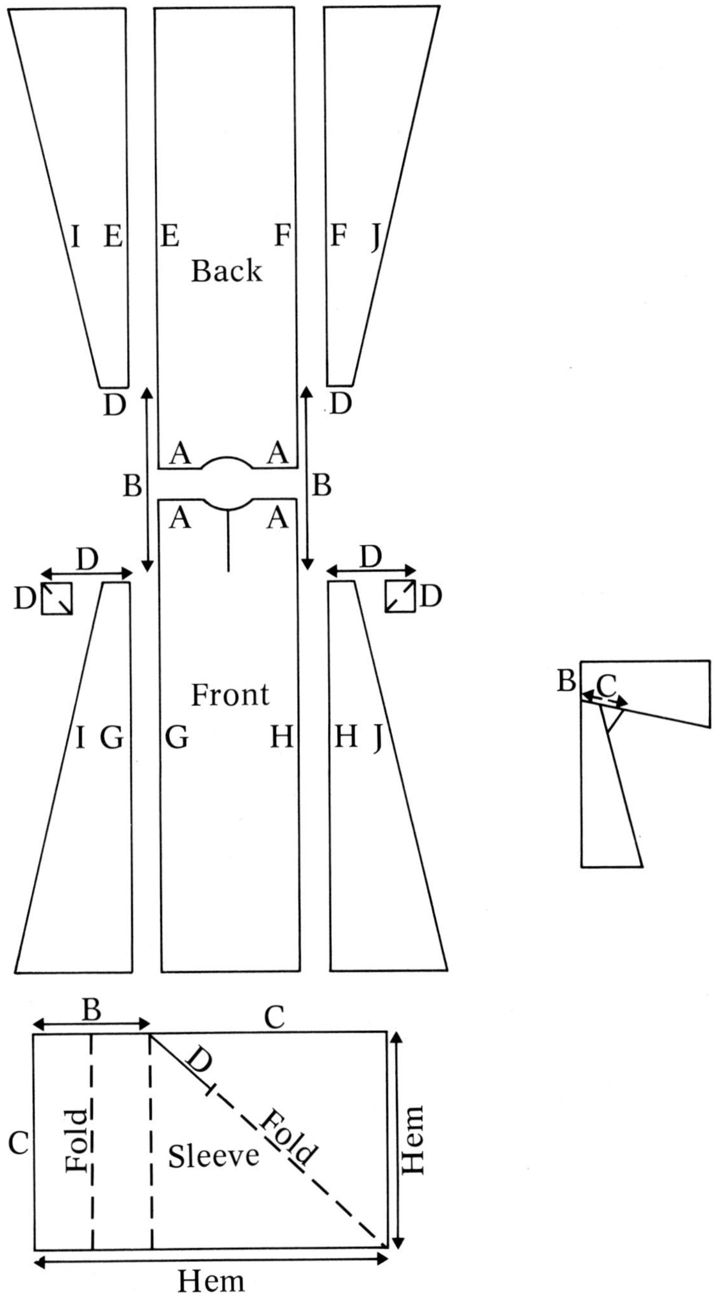

All pieces joined, matching edges from A-A to J-J.
1cm Seam and Hem Allowance.
Scale ⅛″ = 2⅜″; .3cm = 5.8cm.

DIAGRAM 3. MAN'S ROBE – DISHDASHA. KUWAIT 1983 [RSM 1983.976] PATTERN AND CONSTRUCTION

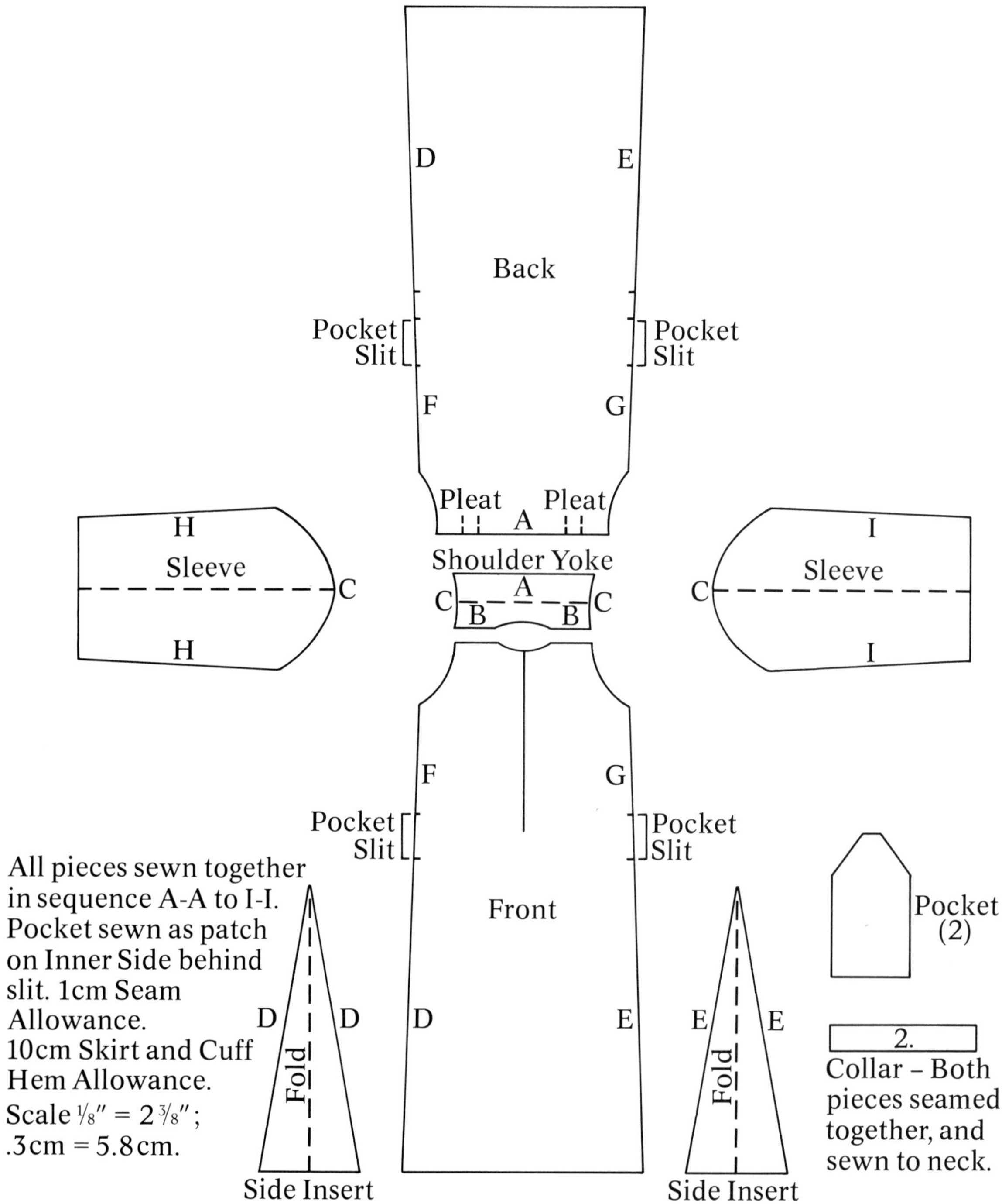

DIAGRAM 4. MAN'S CLOAK – BISHT. KUWAIT 1984 [RSM 1985.5] PATTERN AND CONSTRUCTION

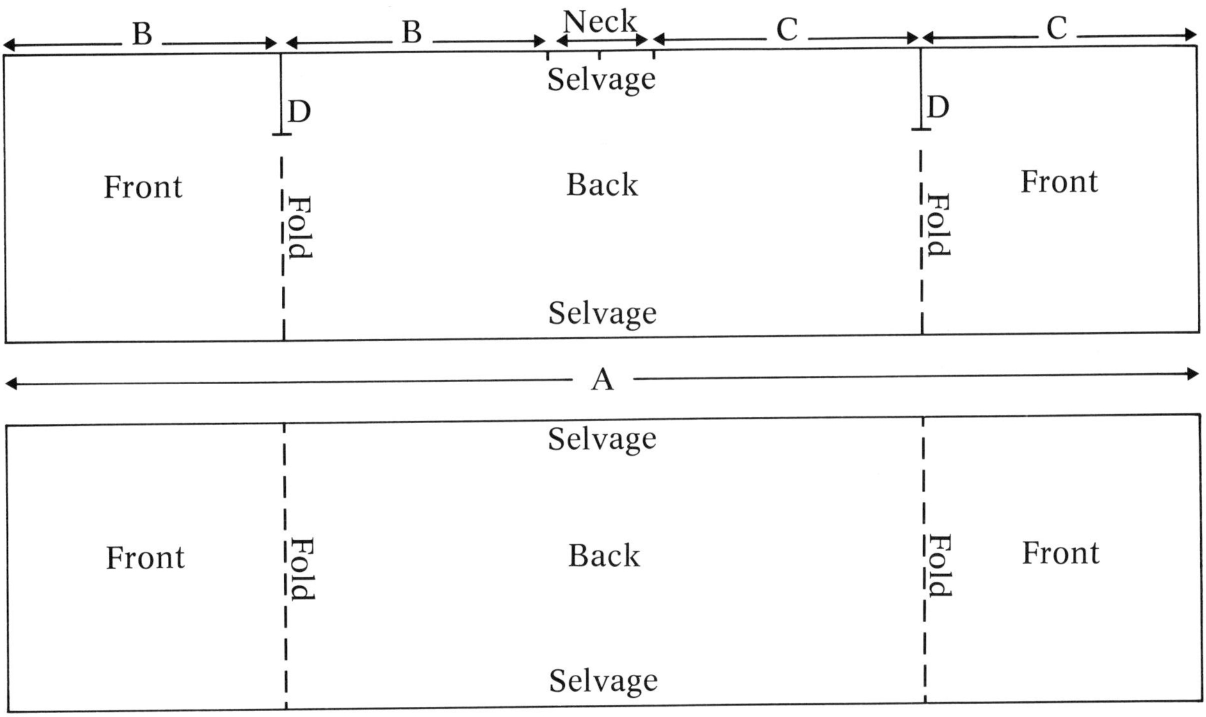

Cloak made of two loomwidths of fabric joined together at A. Fronts folded in and seamed to form Shoulders at B-B, C-C. Slashed along fold on each side for Wrist Openings at D. 2.5 cm turned in at front edges for Hem; Wrist Openings turned in and Hemmed.

Scale 1/8″ = 2 3/8″; .3 cm = 5.8 cm.

DIAGRAM 5. MAN'S COAT – FARWAH. KUWAIT 1984 [RSM 1985.2] PATTERN AND CONSTRUCTION

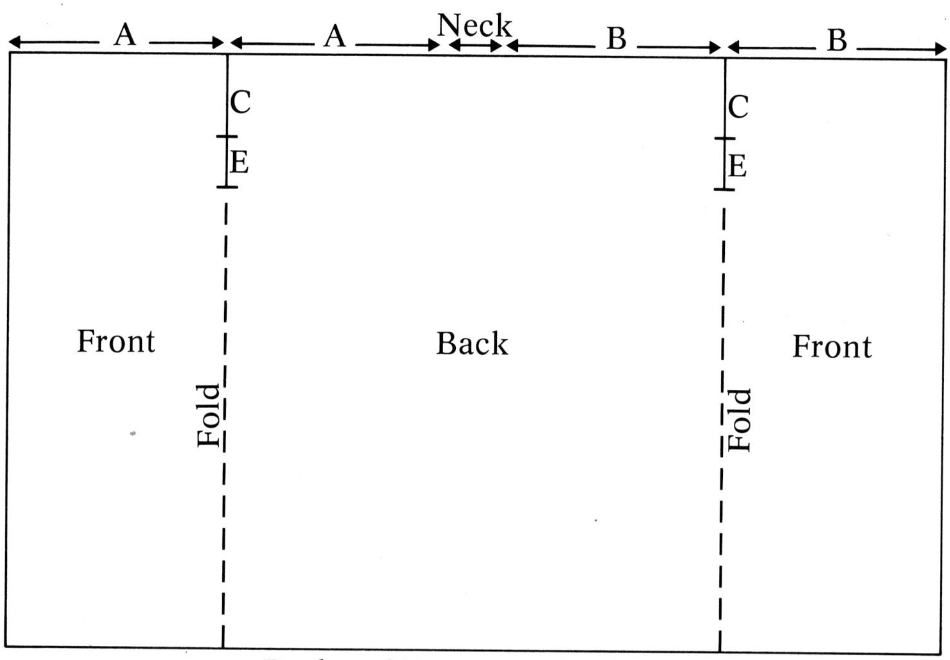

Back and Fronts made of one long piece folded at sides and joined at A-A, B-B for Shoulders.
Slashed along fold at C-E on each side for Armholes.

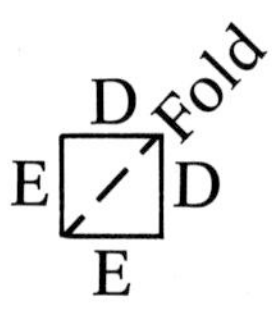

Underarm Shaping (both alike).
Folded diagonally
D-D joined to sleeve
E-E joined to main piece.

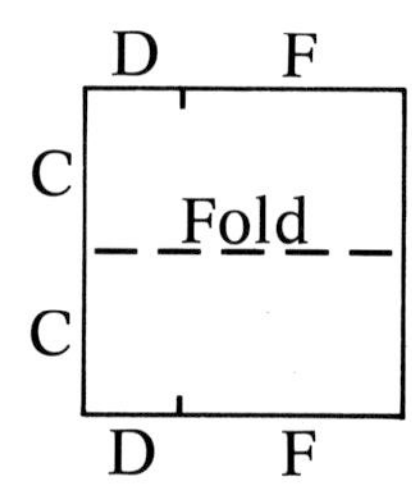

Sleeves (both alike).
Folded and inserted at C to main piece.
D-D joined to underarm shaping.
F-F seamed together.

Scale ⅛″ = 2⅜″; .3cm = 5.8cm.

DIAGRAM 6. WOMAN'S TROUSERS – SIRWAL. KUWAIT 1984 [RSM 1985.95] PATTERN AND CONSTRUCTION

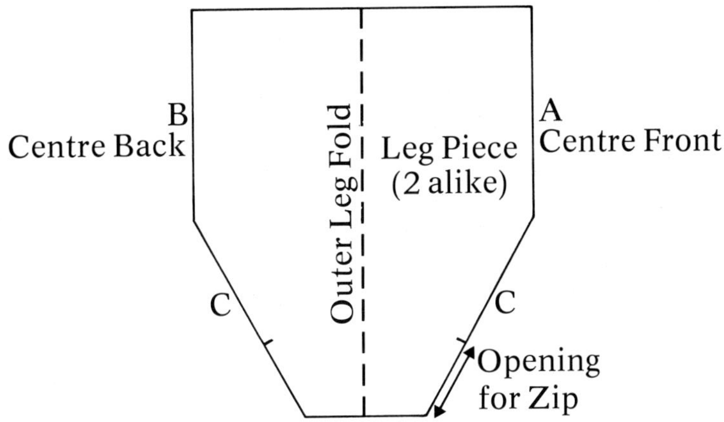

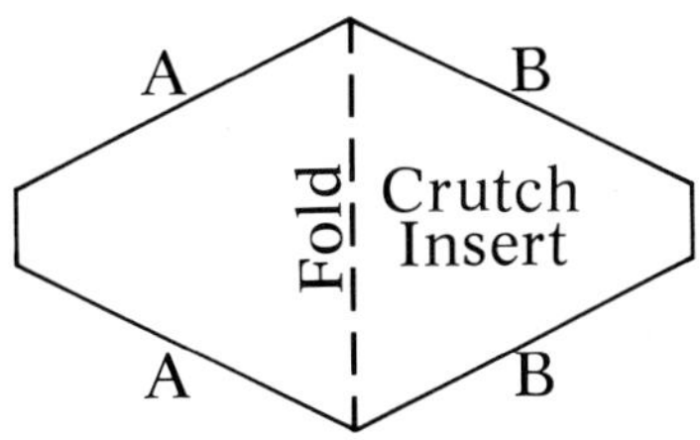

Leg pieces folded in half at Outer Leg, joined to Crutch Insert at A-A, B-B. Inner Leg joined at C-C leaving opening for zip.
.5cm Seam Allowance; 2.5cm Hem Allowance turned in at waist.
Scale ⅛″ = 2⅜″; .3cm = 5.8cm.

DIAGRAM 7. WOMAN'S DRESS – DARA'A. KUWAIT 1984 [RSM 1985.49] PATTERN AND CONSTRUCTION

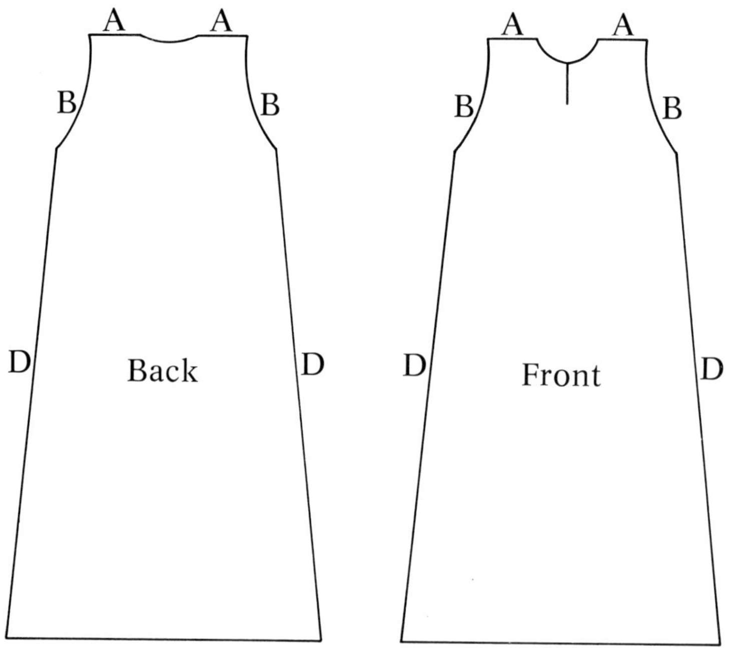

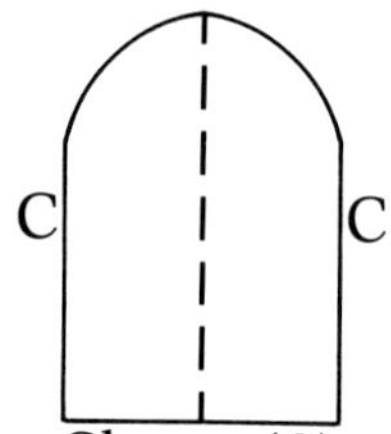

Sleeve (2)

Pieces joined in sequence A-A to D-D.
.5cm Seam Allowance.
2cm Hem Allowance.
Scale ⅛″ = 2⅜″; .3cm = 5.8cm.

DIAGRAM 8. WOMAN'S DRESS – FUSTAN. KUWAIT 1984 [RSM 1985.44] PATTERN AND CONSTRUCTION

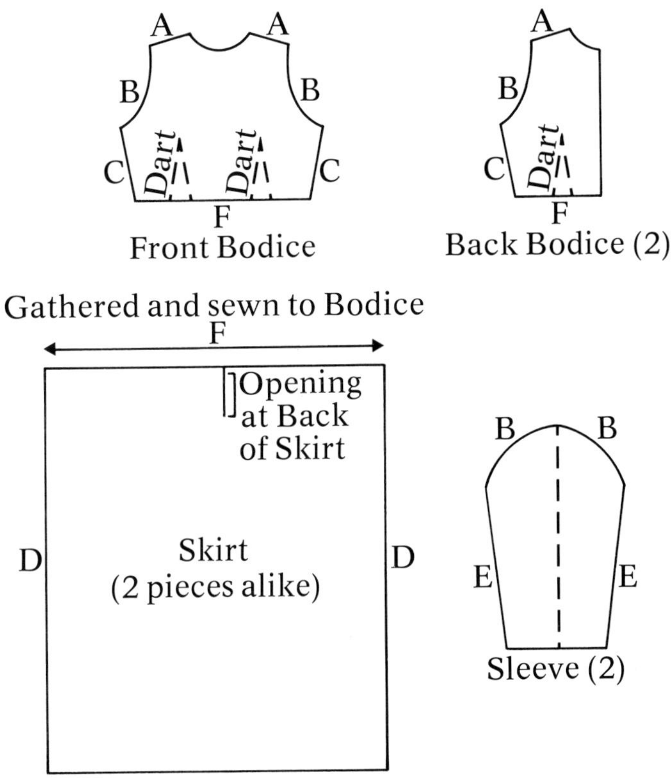

All pieces joined in sequence
A-A to F-F.
2.5cm Seam Allowance.
7.5cm Hem Allowance.
Scale ⅛″ = 2⅜″; .3cm = 5.8cm.

DIAGRAM 9. WOMAN'S COAT – ZEBUN. KUWAIT 1984 [RSM 1985.68] PATTERN AND CONSTRUCTION

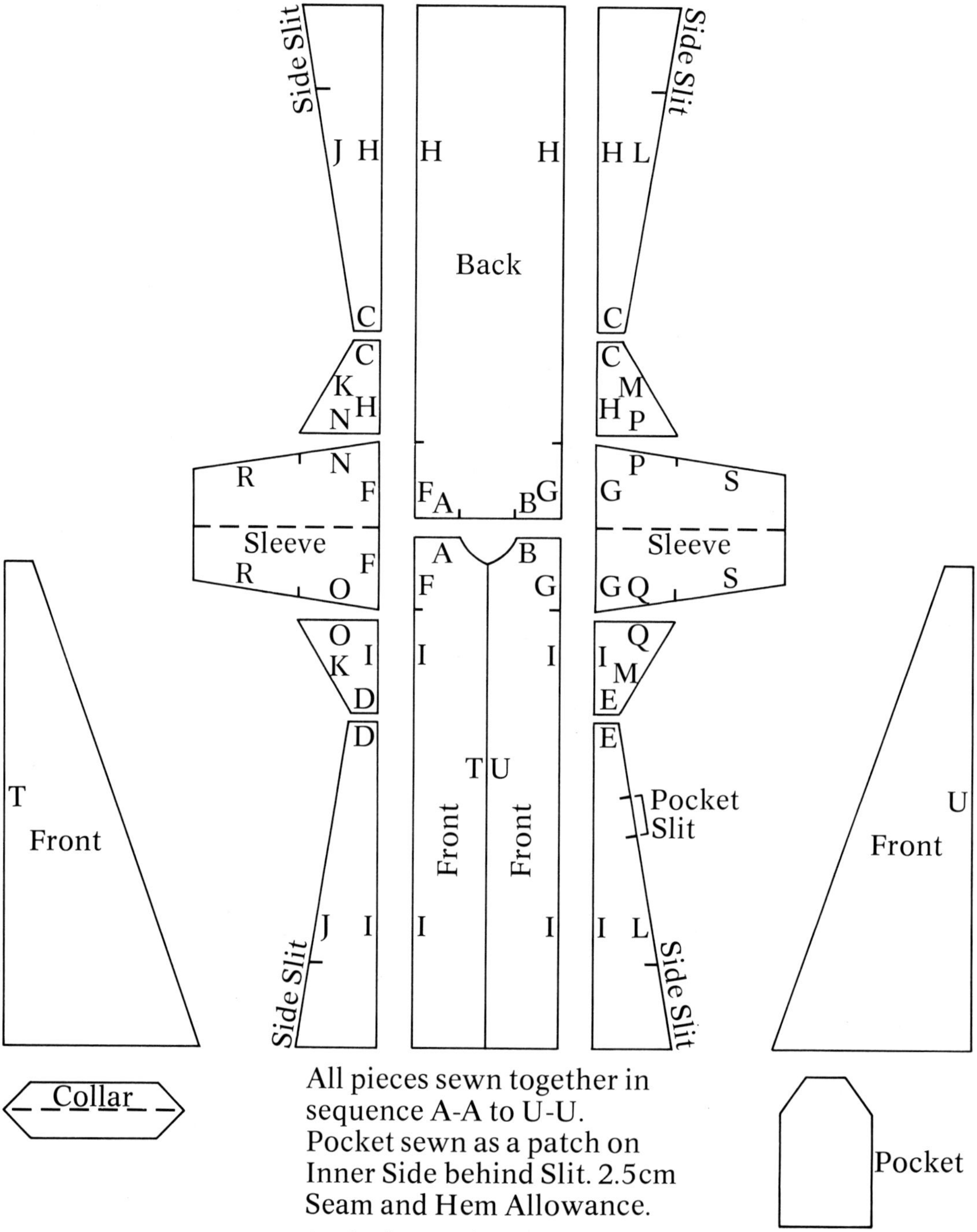

All pieces sewn together in sequence A-A to U-U. Pocket sewn as a patch on Inner Side behind Slit. 2.5cm Seam and Hem Allowance.

Scale ⅛″ = 2⅜″; .3cm = 5.8cm.

DIAGRAM 10. WOMAN'S OVERDRESS – THOB JEZ. KUWAIT c. 1940 [RSM 1985.67] PATTERN AND CONSTRUCTION

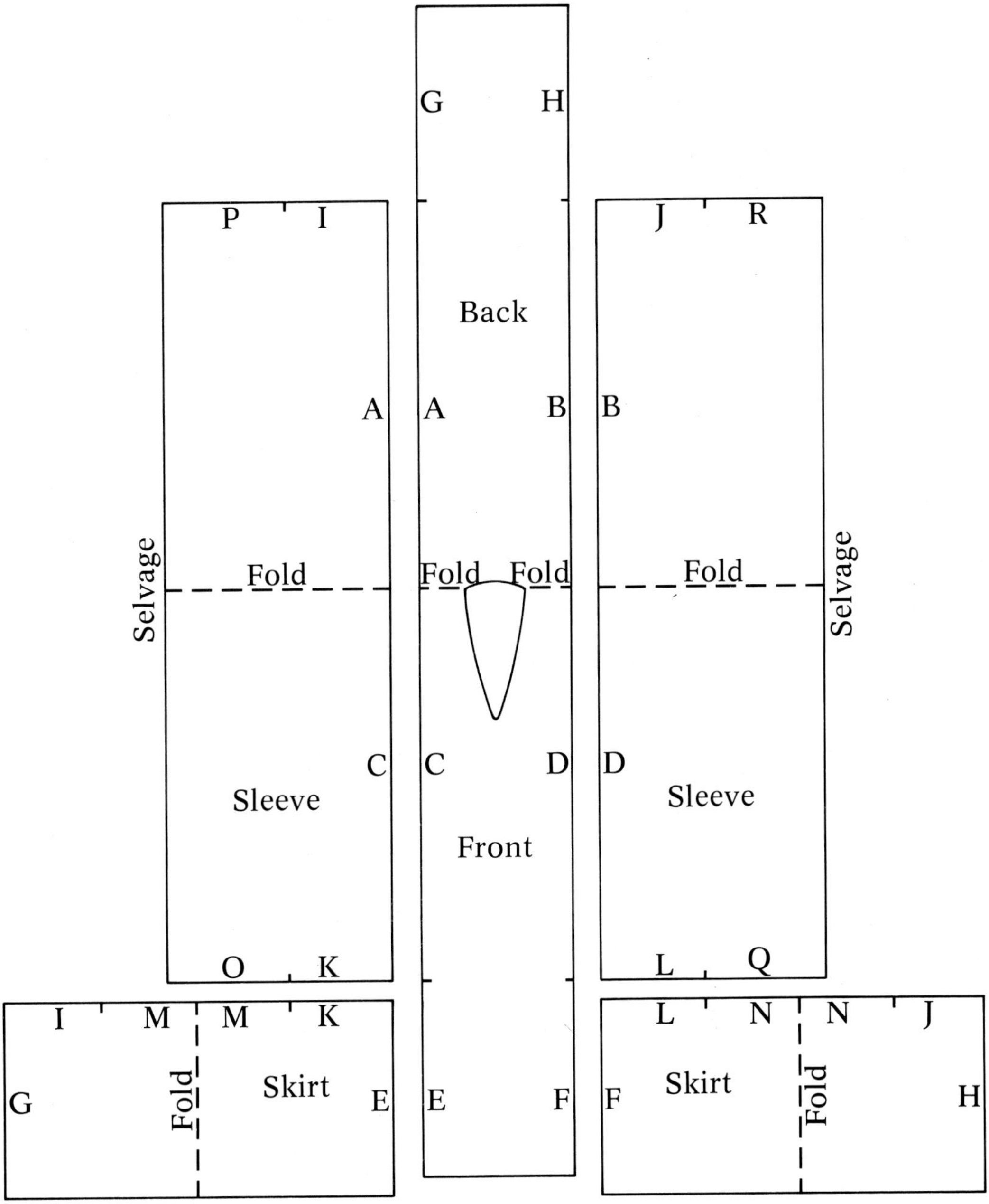

All pieces joined together in sequence A-A to R-R.
1cm Seam and Hem Allowance.
Scale ⅛″ = 2⅜″; .3cm = 5.8cm.

DIAGRAM 11. WOMAN'S PARTY OVERDRESS – THOB-AL-MESSARAH. KUWAIT 1983 [RSM 1983.969] PATTERN AND CONSTRUCTION

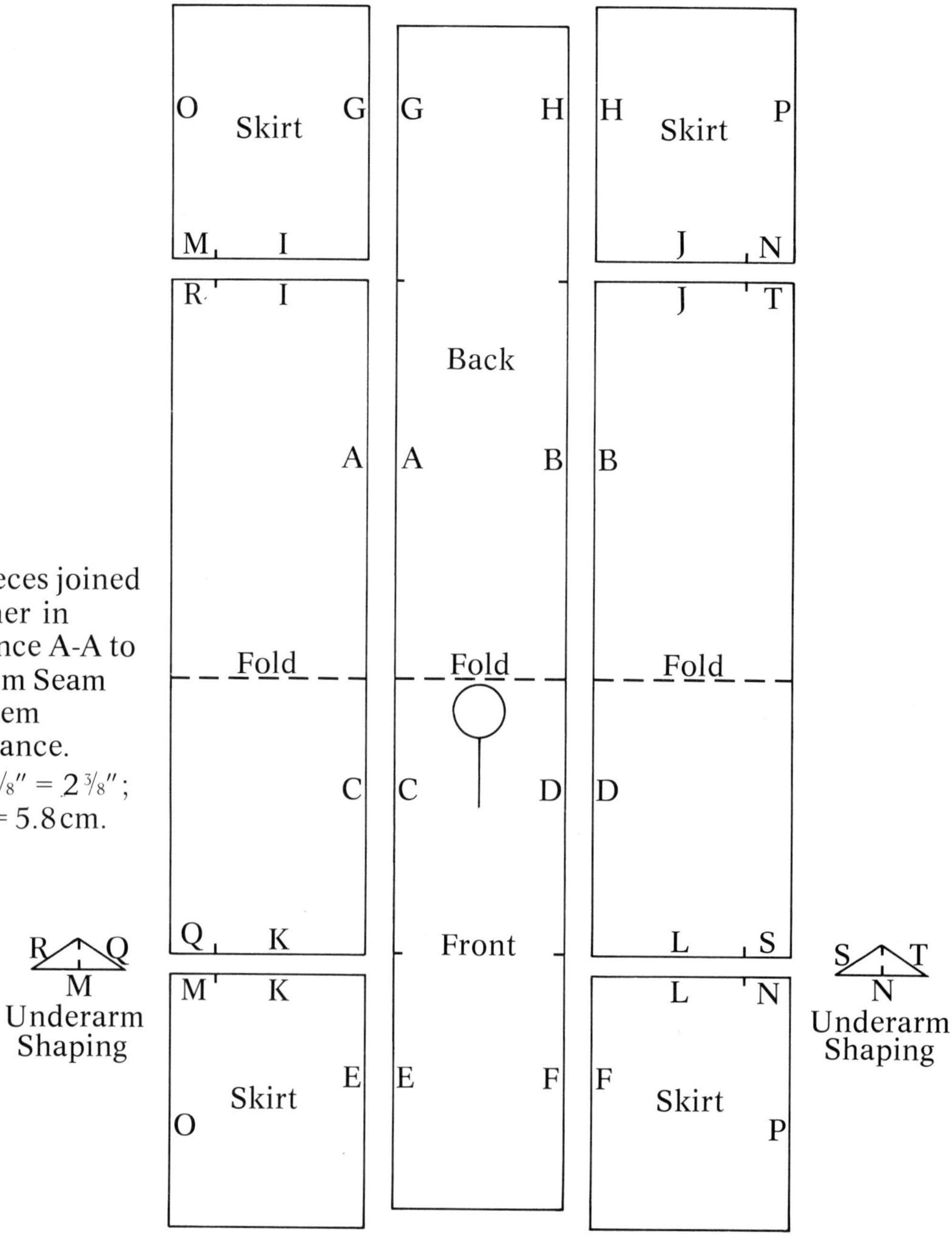

All pieces joined together in sequence A-A to T-T. 1cm Seam and Hem Allowance.

Scale ⅛″ = 2⅜″; .3cm = 5.8cm.

DIAGRAM 12. WOMAN'S CLOAK – 'ABBAYA. KUWAIT 1984 [RSM 1985.73] PATTERN AND CONSTRUCTION

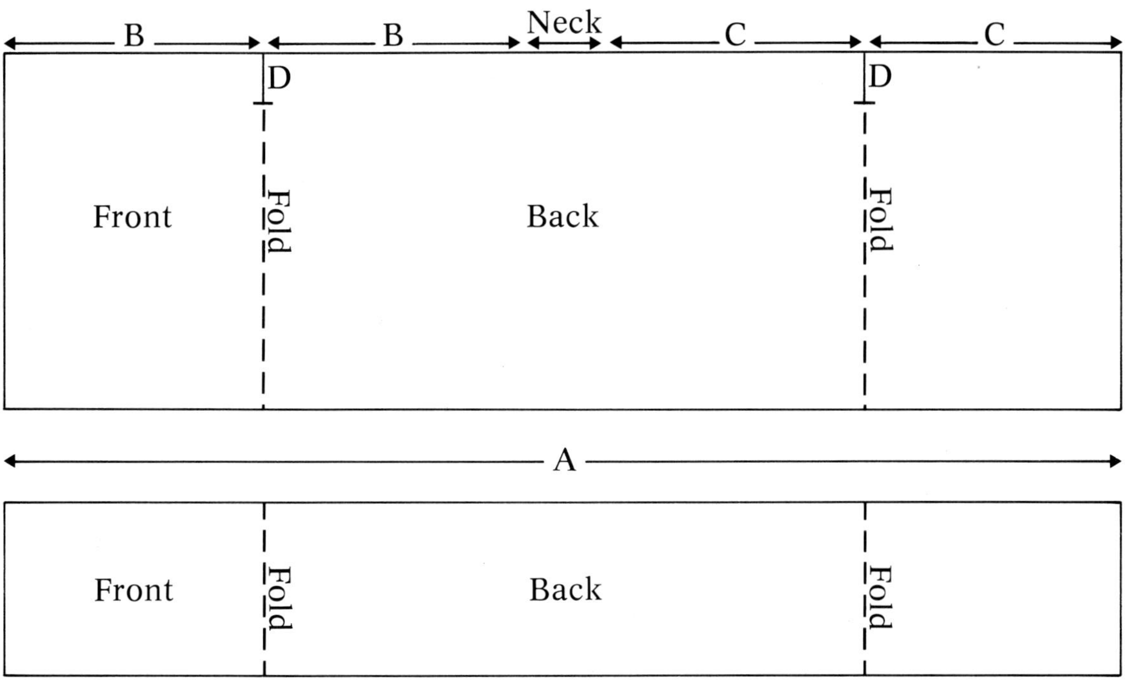

Cloak made of two lengths of fabric joined together at A.
Fronts folded in and seamed to form Shoulders at B-B, C-C.
Slashed along fold on each side for Wrist Openings at D.
Seam Allowance .5cm; Hem Allowance 1cm.
Scale 1/8″ = 2 3/8″; .3cm = 5.8cm.

DIAGRAM 13. WOMAN'S OVERDRESS – THOB AL-TOUR BILTEIL. KUWAIT 1984 [RSM 1985.64] PATTERN AND CONSTRUCTION

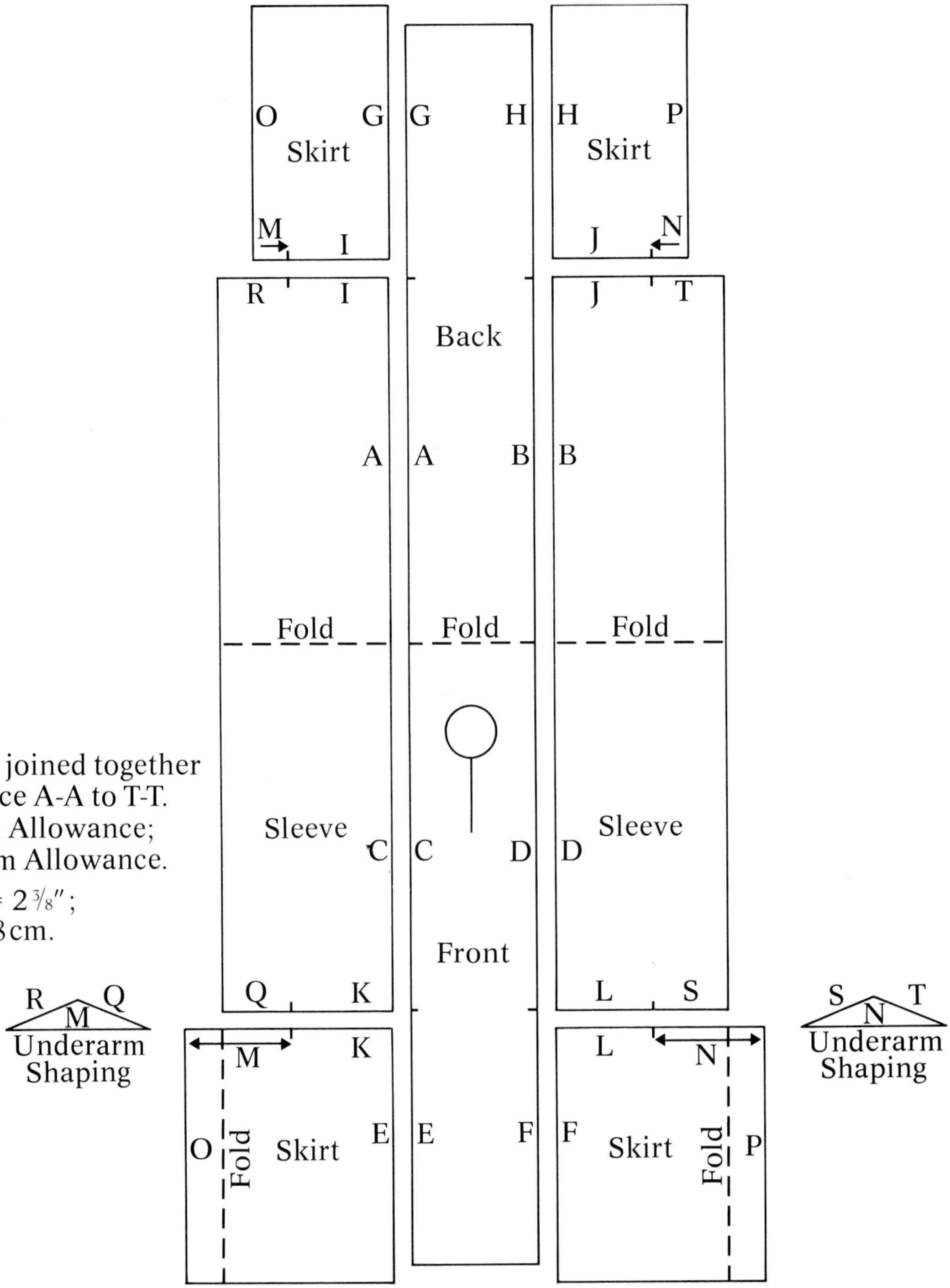

All pieces joined together in sequence A-A to T-T.
1cm Seam Allowance;
1.5cm Hem Allowance.

Scale ⅛″ = 2⅜″;
.3cm = 5.8cm.

SELECT BIBLIOGRAPHY

Kuwait has an extensive bibliography which mainly concentrates on the country's affairs since the exploitation of the oil reserves from the 1940s onwards and includes both general surveys and specialised studies of such topics as the economy, infrastructure, labour resources etc. The works listed here aim to offer the reader a balanced picture of Kuwait and an encouragement to further study. Certain accounts such as the writings of the Dickson family which describe the changes in Kuwaiti life over a span of fifty years and the detailed entry in Lorimer's Gazetteer are essential reading. Where comparison is enlightening on subjects such as the Bedu tribes, who by the very nature of their lifestyle are difficult to confine within exact limits, works more strictly pertaining to Kuwait's neighbours have been included.

ABDUL-WAHAB, M.
Kuwait's petroleum, its role in its economic development and social structure.
Iraqi Geographical Journal, Vol. 4, 1967, pp. 35-45.

ABU-HAKIMA, H.M.
History of eastern Arabia 1750-1800, the rise and development of Bahrain and Kuwait.
Beirut 1965.

ABU-HAKIMA, Ahmad Mustafa.
The Modern history of Kuwait 1750-1965.
London, 1983.

AL-ABDUL-RAZZAK, Fatimah H.Y.
Marine resources of Kuwait, their role in the development of non-oil resources.
London, 1984.

AL EBRAHEEM, Hassan A.
Kuwait; a political study.
Kuwait University 1975.

AL-HIJJI, Yacoub Y.
The story of Al-Muhalab
Kuwait 1983
A study of the history and restoration of Al-Muhalab one of the large trading vessels now preserved in the National Museum Kuwait.

AL-MOOSA, Abdulrasool & McLACHLAN, Keith.
Immigrant labour in Kuwait.
London 1985.

AL-SABAH, Dr S.M.
Development planning in an oil economy and the role of the woman: the case of kuwait.
London 1983.

AL-SADU, Foundation for the preservation of Bedu handicrafts.
Portfolio of Bedu weaving.
Kuwait 1979; 2nd edition 1982.

ALESSA, Shamlan Y.
The manpower problems in Kuwait.
London 1981.

Annual Statistical Abstract
1983 Edition XX.
Ministry of Planning, Central Statistical Office, State of Kuwait.

ANTHONY, J.D.
Arab. states of the Lower Gulf; people, politics and petroleum.
Washington 1975.

ARRIAN (Flavius Arrianus)
Anabasis of Alexander and Indica.
Loeb Classical Library edition, London 1893.

ASHKENAZI, T.
The Anazah tribes.
Southwestern Journal of Anthropology, New Mexico 1948, pp. 222-239.

BIBBY, Geoffrey.
Looking for Dilmun.
London 1972.

BIDWELL, R.
The affairs of Kuwait 1896-1905.
2 vols. London 1971.

BLUNT, Lady Anne.
Bedouin tribes of the Euphrates.
2 vols. London 1879.

BLUNT, Lady Anne.
A pilgrimage to Nejd.
London 1881.

BOWEN, R.
The pearl fisheries of the Persian Gulf.
The Middle East Journal, vol. 5, no. 2, 1951, pp. 161-180.

BROWN, E.
The Saudi Arabia Kuwait Neutral Zone.
Middle East Oil Monographs No. 4, Middle East Research and Publishing Centre Beirut 1963.

BRUCKS, George Barnes.
Memoir descriptive of the navigation of the Gulf of Persia.
Bombay Selections, Vol. XXIV. pp. 532-576, Bombay 1856.

BUCHANAN, COLIN & PARTNERS
Studies for National Physical Plan and Master Plan for urban areas; first estimates of population and employment growth for Kuwait. 1969-1990.
Technical paper 3, London 1969.

BUCHANAN, COLIN & PARTNERS.
Studies for National Physical Plan and Master Plan for urban areas, Kuwait second report.
London 1971.

BUCKINGHAM, James Silk.
Travels in Assyria, Media and Persia, including a journey from Bagdad by Mount Zargos to Hamadan, the ancient Ecbatana, researches in Ispahan and the ruins of Persepolis and journey from Hence by Shiraz and Shapoor to the sea-shore, description of Bussorah, Bushire, Bahrein, Ormuz and Muscat.
2 Vols. London 1830.

BULLOCH, John.
The Gulf—a portrait of Kuwait, Qatar, Bahrain and the U.A.E.
London 1984.

BURCKHARDT, J.L.
Travels in Arabia.
London 1829.

BURCKHARDT, John L.
Notes on the Bedouins and Wahabys.
London 1830.

BUSCH, B.C.
Britain and the Persian Gulf.
1894-1914.
Los Angeles 1967.

BUSCH, B.C.
Britain, India and the Arabs.
1914-1921.
Los Angeles 1971.

CALVERLEY, Dr Eleanor T.
My Arabian days and nights.
New York 1958.

CHISHOLM, A.H.T.
The first Kuwait oil concession, a record of the negotiations for the 1934 Agreement.
London 1975.

COLE, Donald P.
Nomads of the nomads, the Al Murrah Bedouin of the empty Quarter.
Chicago 1975.

COOK, D.
Kuwait, miracle on the desert.
New York 1970.

DANIELS, J.
Kuwait journey.
White Crescent Press 1971.

DEMIR, S.
The Kuwait Fund and the political economy of Arab regional developoment.
New York 1976.

DICKSON, Harold R.P.
The Arab of the desert.
London 1949 first edition: 1951 second edition.

DICKSON, HAROLD R.P.
Kuwait and her neighbours.
London 1956.

DICKSON, Violet
Forty years in Kuwait.
London 1971.

DOUGHTY, Charles M.
Travels in Arabia Deserts.
2 Vols. Cambridge 1888, also London 1921.

DOZY, R.P.A.

Dictionnaire detaillé des noms des vêtements chez les Arabes.
Amsterdam 1845.

ECONOMIST INTELLIGENCE UNIT.
Quarterly economic review of Kuwait.
1st quarter 1978-ongoing.
London, Economic Intelligence Unit, 1978-ongoing.

EDWARDS, F.M.
George Forster Sadleir (1789-1859) of the 47th Regiment, the first European to cross Arabia.
Journal of the Royal Central Asian Society 44, 1957. pp. 38-49.

EL MALLAKH, R.
Economic development and regional co-operation: Kuwait.
Chicago 1969.

EL MALLAKH, Ragaei & ATTA, Jacob K.
The absorptive capacity of Kuwait.
Domestic and international perspectives.
Lexington 1981.

FEILBERG, C.G.
La tente noire.
Copenhagen 1944.

FRASER, Lovat.
The problem in the Persian Gulf.
National Review 1907, Sept-Feb.

FRASER, Lovat.
Some problems of the Persian Gulf.
Proc. Cent. Asian. Soc. 1908, Jan.

FREETH, Zahra.
Kuwait was my home.
London 1956.

FREETH, Zahra and WINSTONE, V.
Kuwait, prospect and reality.
London 1972.

FREETH, Zahra.
A new look at Kuwait.
London 1972.

FRENCH, G.E. & HILL, Allan.
Kuwait; urban and medical ecology.
Berlin 1971.

FURBER, Holden.
John Company at work, a study of European expansion in India in the late eighteenth century.
Cambridge (Mass.) 1948.

GARDINER, Stephen.
Kuwait, the making of a city.
Longman 1983.

GRAHAM, Helga.
Arabian time machine, self-portrait of an oil state.
London 1978.

GRIFFITHS, J.
Travels in Europe, Asia Minor and Arabia.
London 1805.

HEWINS, R.
A golden dream, the miracle of Kuwait.
London 1963.

HOPWOOD, Derek (ed).
The Arabian Peninsula, society and Politics.
London 1972.

HURGRONJE, C. Snouck.
Mekka in the latter part of the 19th century.
Leiden 1931.

JONES, Lieutenant J. Felix.
Extracts from a report on the harbour of Grane (or Kuwait) and the island of Pheleechi, in the Persian Gulf.
Prepared in November 1839, Bombay Selections, Vol. XXIV, Bombay 1856.

KATAKURA, Motoko.
Bedouin village.
A study of a Saudi Arabian People in transition.
University of Tokyo Press 1977.

KELLY, J.B.
Britain and the Persian Gulf 1795-1880.
London 1968.

KEMBALL, Lieutenant A.B.
Historical sketch of the Uttoobee tribe of Arabs.
Bombay Selections XXIV, 1856.

KEMBALL, Lieutenant A.B.
Memoranda on the resources, localities and relations of the tribes inhabiting the Arabian shores of the Persian Gulf.
Bombay Selections, Vol. XXIV, Bombay 1856.

KHAWAJKIE, M.
Kuwait and the economic integration of Arabian Gulf countries.
Journal of the Gulf and Arabian Peninsula Studies, Vol. 3, No. 9, Kuwait 1977, pp. 9-30

Kuwait today—a welfare state.
Ministry of Guidance and Information Kuwait 1964.

Kuwait facts and figures 1984.
Ministry of Information Kuwait 1984.

Kuwaiti Fashion.
Ministry of Information Kuwait (n.d.).

LANCASTER, William.
The Rwala Bedouin today.
Cambridge 1978.

LEVY, Reuben.
The social structure of Islam.
Cambridge 1971.

LEWCOCK, Ronald and FREETH, Zahra.
Traditional architecture in Kuwait and the northern Gulf.
London 1978.

LORIMER, J.G.
Gazetteer of the Persian Gulf, Oman and Central Arabia.
2 Vols. Calcutta, 1908 & 1915.

MEDIARMID, O.J. (and others).
The economic development of Kuwait.
The International Bank for Reconstruction and Development.
Baltimore 1965.

MANSFIELD, Peter.
The New Arabians.
New York 1981.

MANSFIELD, Peter.
The Arabs. Revised edition.
London 1980.

MARLOWE, J.
The Persian Gulf in the Twentieth Century.
London 1962.

MEINKE, Musaab.
A guide to Arab Gulf dress. Part 1, men.
Arab Times Supplement, May 12, 1983, pp. 14-19.

MEINKE, Musaab.
A guide to Arab Gulf dress. Part 2, women.
Arab Times Supplement, May 19, 1983, pp. 34-37.

MERNISSI, Fatima.
Beyond the veil male-female dynamics in modern Muslim society.
New York 1975.

MILES, S.B.
Countries and tribes of the Persian Gulf.
London 1919.

MONROE, Elizabeth.
The shaikhdom of Kuwait.
International Affairs, Vol. 30, No. 3, July 1954, pp. 271-284.

MUSIL, Alois.
The northern Hegaz.
New York 1926.

MUSIL, Alois.
The manners and customs of the Rwala Bedouins.
New York 1926.

MUSIL, Alois.
Arabia Deserta, a topographical itinerary.
New York 1927.

MUSIL, Alois.
Northern Negd, a topographical itinerary.
New York 1928.

NEIBUHR, Carsten.
Travels in Arabia and other countries in the east.
2 Vols. Edinburgh 1792.

PALGRAVE, W.G.
Narrative of a year's journey through central and eastern Arabia (1862-1863).
2 Vols., London 1865.

PELLY, L.
Accounts of a recent tour around the northern portion of the Persian Gulf.
Transactions Bombay Geographical Society 1863, XVII.

PELLY, L.
The Persian Gulf as an area of trade.
Proceedings of the Royal Geographical Society, 1863-4, VIII.

PELLY, L.
Remarks on the pearl oyster beds in the Persian Gulf.
Transactions Bombay Geographical Society 1867, XVIII.

PELLY, L.
Remarks on the tribes, trade and resources around the shore line of the Persian Gulf.
Transactions Bombay Geographical Society 1863, XVIII.

RASWAN, C.R.
The black tents of Arabia (My life among the Bedouins).
London 1935.

RAUNKAIER, B.
Through Wahabiland on camel-back.
Cairo Government Press 1916.

ROSS, Heather Colyer.
The art of Arabian costume—a Saudi Arabian profile.
Fribourg 1981.

ROSS, Heather Colyer.
The art of Bedouin jewellery—a Saudi Arabian profile.
Fribourg 1981.

SADLIER, Captain G. Foster.
Diary of a journey across Arabia from el-Khatif in the Persian Gulf, to Yambo in the Red Sea, during the year 1819.
Bombay 1866.

SAPSTED, David.
Modern Kuwait.
Ministry of Information, Kuwait 1980.
London 1980.

SHIBER, Suba George.
The Kuwait organization — being an urbanistic case — study of a developing country.
Kuwait 1964.

SMITH, W. Robertson.
Kinship and marriage in early Arabia.
London 1885.

STOCQUELER, J.H.
Fifteen months pilgrimage through Khuzistan and Persia.
2 Vols. London 1832.

THESIGER, Wilfrid.
Arabian sands.
London 1959.

THESIGER, Wilfrid.
The marsh Arabs.
London 1964.

TOPHAM, John (and others).
Traditional crafts of Saudi Arabia.
London 1981.

TUSON, Penelope.
The records of the British Residency and Agencies in the Persian Gulf.
London 1979.

VILLIERS, Alan.
Some aspects of the Arab dhow trade.
Middle East Journal Vol. 2, October 1948, pp. 399-416.

WARDEN, Francis.
Extracts from brief notes relative to the rise and progress of the Arab tribes of the Persian Gulf. Prepared in August 1819.
Bombay Selections XXIV, Bombay 1856.

WARDEN, Francis.
Historical sketch of the Uttoobee tribe of Arabs (Bahrein) from the year 1716 to the year 1817.
Bombay Selections XXIV, Bombay 1856.

WEIR, Shelagh.
The Bedouin, aspects of the material culture of the bedouin of Jordan.
World of Islam Festival, London 1976.

WELSTED, J.R.
Travels in Arabia.
2 Vols. London 1838.

WELSTED, J.R.
Travels to the city of the Caliphs, along the shores of the Persian Gulf and the Mediterranean, including a voyage to the coast of Arabia, and a tour on the island of Socotia.
2 Vols. London 1840.

WILSON, Lt. Col. Sir Arnold
The Persian Gulf. An Historical sketch from the earliest times to the beginning of the 20th century.
Oxford 1928.

WILSON, D.
Memorandum respect in the pearl fisheries in the Persian Gulf.
Journal of the Royal Geographical Society, Vol. 3, 1833, pp. 283-286.

YAJIMA, H.
The Arab dhow trade in the Indian Ocean, preliminary report.
Institute for the study of languages and culture of Asia and Africa.
Tokyo 1976.

YASIN, M.
Manpower resource requirements and problems of Kuwait.
Planning Board Kuwait 1974.

Printed in Scotland for HMSO by Alna Press 7/85. Dd. 762111